AC 43.13-1A
—CHANGE THREE—
Acceptable Methods, Techniques And Practices

AC 43.13-2A
Aircraft Alterations

REVISED JUNE 1988

International Standard Book Number 0-89100-306-1
For Sale by: IAP, Inc.
P.O. Box 10000, Casper, Wyoming 82602-1000
7383 6WN Road, Casper, Wyoming 82604-1835
(800) 443-9250 • (307) 266-3838 • FAX: (307) 472-5106

U.S. Department
of Transportation

**Federal Aviation
Administration**

Advisory
Circular

Subject: Acceptable Methods, Techniques, and
Practices—Aircraft Inspection And Repair

Date: 1988
Initiated by: AVN-113

AC No: 43.13-1A
Change: 3

---

*1. **PURPOSE.** This advisory circular contains methods, techniques, and practices acceptable to the Administrator for inspection and repair to civil aircraft, only when there is no manufacturer repair or maintenance instructions. This data generally pertains to minor repairs. It may be used as a basis for FAA data approval for major repairs. This data may be used as approved data when: (1) The user has determined that it is appropriate to the product being repaired; (2) directly applicable to the repair being made; and (3) not contrary to manufacturer's data. *

2. **CANCELLATION.** The Advisory Circular 43.13-1 dated 1965 is canceled.

3. **REFERENCE.** FAR Part 43 requires that methods, techniques, and practices acceptable to the Administrator must be used for inspection and repair to civil aircraft. Techniques, practices, and methods other than those prescribed in this advisory circular may be used providing they are acceptable to the Administrator. FAA Inspectors are prepared to answer questions that may arise in this regard. Persons engaged in inspection and repair of civil aircraft should be familiar with FAR Part 43, Maintenance, Preventive Maintenance, Rebuilding, and Alteration, and Subparts A, D, and E of FAR Part 65, Certification: Airmen Other Than Flight Crewmembers, and the applicable airworthiness requirements under which the aircraft was type certificated.

4. **HOW TO GET THE HANDBOOK.** Order additional copies of this publication from the Superintendent of Documents, U.S. Government Printing Office, Washington, D.C. 20402. Identify the publication in your order as:

FAA AC No. 43.13-1A
Acceptable Methods, Techniques, and Practices—Aircraft Inspection and Repair, 1972.

William T. Brennan
Acting Director of Flight Standards

TABLE OF CONTENTS

Chapter 1.   AIRCRAFT WOOD STRUCTURES

Section 1.   MATERIALS AND PRACTICES

Section 2.   FINISHING WOOD STRUCTURES

Chapter 2.   AIRCRAFT METAL STRUCTURES

Section 1.   REFERENCES AND PRECAUTIONARY MEASURES

TABLE OF CONTENTS (Continued)

TABLE OF CONTENTS (Continued)

TABLE OF CONTENTS (Continued)

TABLE OF CONTENTS (Continued)

TABLE OF CONTENTS (Continued)

TABLE OF CONTENTS (Continued)

TABLE OF CONTENTS (Continued)

TABLE OF CONTENTS (Continued)

TABLE OF CONTENTS (Continued)

TABLE OF CONTENTS (Continued)

LIST OF ILLUSTRATIONS

LIST OF ILLUSTRATIONS (Continued)

LIST OF ILLUSTRATIONS (Continued)

LIST OF ILLUSTRATIONS (Continued)

LIST OF ILLUSTRATIONS (Continued)

Chapter 1. AIRCRAFT WOOD STRUCTURES

Section 1. MATERIALS AND PRACTICES

1. MATERIALS. Three forms of wood are commonly used in aircraft: solid wood, plywood, and laminated wood. Although several kinds of modified wood are sometimes used for special purposes, these three forms constitute the bulk of all wood aircraft construction materials.

a. *Quality of Wood*. All wood and plywood used in the repair of aircraft structures should be of aircraft quality. Figure 1.2 lists the permissible variations in characteristics and properties of aircraft wood.

b. *Species Substitution*. The species used to repair a part should be the same as that of the original whenever possible; however, permissible substitutes are given in figure 1.2.

c. *Effects of Shrinkage*. When the moisture content of wood is lowered, its dimensions decrease. The dimensional change is greatest in a tangential direction (across the fibers and parallel to the growth rings), somewhat less in a radial direction (across the fibers and perpendicular to the growth rings), and is negligible in a longitudinal direction (parallel to the fibers). These dimensional changes can have several detrimental effects upon a wood structure, such as loosening of fittings and wire

bracing and checking or splitting of wood members.

A few suggestions for minimizing these shrinkage effects are:

(1) Use bushings that are slightly short so that when the wood member shrinks the bushings do not protrude and the fittings may be tightened firmly against the member.

(2) Gradually drop off plywood face plates either by feathering or by shaping as shown in figure 1.1.

2. REPLACEMENT OF DRAINHOLES AND SKIN STIFFENERS. Whenever repairs are made that require replacing a portion that includes drainholes, skin stiffeners, or any other items, the repaired portion must be provided with similar drainholes, skin stiffeners, or items of the same dimensions in the same location. Reinforcing, under skin repairs, that interferes with the flow of water from some source, such as inspection holes, is to be provided with drainholes at the lowest points.

3. CONTROL SURFACE FLUTTER PRECAUTIONS. When repairing control surfaces, especially on high-performance airplanes, care must be exer-

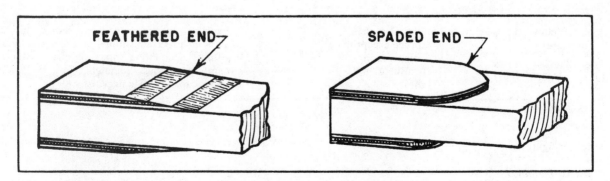

FIGURE 1.1.—Tapering of face plates.

FIGURE 1.2.--Selection and properties of aircraft wood.

Species of wood	Strength properties as compared to spruce	Maximum permissible grain deviation (slope of grain)	Remarks
1	2	3	4
Spruce (Picea) Sitka (P. Sitchensis) Red (P. Rubra) White (P. Glauca).	100%	1:15	Excellent for all uses. Considered as standard for this table.
Douglas Fir (Pseudotsuga Taxifolia).	Exceeds spruce.	1:15	May be used as substitute for spruce in same sizes or in slightly reduced sizes providing reductions are substantiated. Difficult to work with hand tools. Some tendency to split and splinter during fabrication and considerable more care in manufacture is necessary. Large solid pieces should be avoided due to inspection difficulties. Gluing satisfactory.
Nobe Fir (Abies Nobiles).	Slightly exceeds spruce except 8 percent deficient in shear.	1:15	Satisfactory characteristics with respect to workability, warping, and splitting. May be used as direct substitute for spruce in same sizes providing shear does not become critical. Hardness somewhat less than spruce. Gluing satisfactory.
Western Hemlock (Tsuga Heterophylla).	Slightly exceeds spruce.	1:15	Less uniform in texture than spruce. May be used as direct substitute for spruce. Upland growth superior to lowland growth. Gluing satisfactory.
Pine, Northern White (Pinus Strobus).	Properties between 85 percent and 96 percent those of spruce.	1:15	Excellent working qualities and uniform in properties but somewhat low in hardness and shock-resisting capacity. Cannot be used as substitute for spruce without increase in sizes to compensate for lesser strength. Gluing satisfactory.
White Cedar, Port Orford (Charaecyparis Lawsoniana).	Exceeds spruce.	1:15	May be used as substitute for spruce in same sizes or in slightly reduced sizes providing reductions are substantiated. Easy to work with hand tools. Gluing difficult but satisfactory joints can be obtained if suitable precautions are taken.
Poplar, Yellow (Liriodendrow Tulipifera).	Slightly less than spruce except in compression (crushing) and shear.	1:15	Excellent working qualities. Should not be used as a direct substitute for spruce without carefully accounting for slightly reduced strength properties. Somewhat low in shock-resisting capacity. Gluing satisfactory.

(See notes following table.)

Notes for figure 1.2.

1. *Defects Permitted.*
   a.*Cross grain.* Spiral grain, diagonal grain, or a combination of the two is acceptable providing the grain does

not diverge from the longitudinal axis of the material more than specified in column 3. A check of all four faces of the board is necessary to determine the amount of divergence. The direction of free-flowing ink will frequently assist in determining grain direction.

b. *Wavy, curly, and interlocked grain.* Acceptable, if local irregularities do not exceed limitations specified for spiral and diagonal grain.

c. *Hard knots.* Sound hard knots up to ⅜-inch in maximum diameter are acceptable providing: (1) they are not in projecting portions of I-beams, along the edges of rectangular or beveled unrouted beams, or along the edges of flanges of box beams (except in lowly stressed portions); (2) they do not cause grain divergence at the edges of the board or in the flanges of a beam more than specified in column 3; and (3) they are in the center third of the beam and are not closer than 20 inches to another knot or other defect (pertains to ⅜-inch knots—smaller knots may be proportionately closer). Knots greater than ¼-inch must be used with caution.

d. *Pin knot clusters.* Small clusters are acceptable providing they produce only a small effect on grain direction.

e. *Pitch pockets.* Acceptable, in center portion of a beam providing they are at least 14 inches apart when they lie in the same growth ring and do not exceed 1½ inch length by ⅛-inch width by ⅛-inch depth and providing they are not along the projecting portions of I-beams, along the edges of rectangular or beveled unrouted beams, or along the edges of the flanges of box beams.

f. *Mineral streaks.* Acceptable, providing careful inspection fails to reveal any decay.

2. *Defects Not Permitted.*

a. *Cross grain.* Not acceptable, unless within limitations noted in 1a.

b. *Wavy, curly, and interlocked grain.* Not acceptable, unless within limitations noted in 1b.

c. *Hard knots.* Not acceptable, unless within limitations noted in 1c.

d. *Pin knot clusters.* Not acceptable, if they produce large effect on grain direction.

e. *Spike knots.* These are knots running completely through the depth of a beam perpendicular to the annual rings and appear most frequently in quartersawed lumber. Reject wood containing this defect.

f. *Pitch pockets.* Not acceptable, unless within limitations noted in 1e.

g. *Mineral streaks.* Not acceptable, if accompanied by decay (see 1f).

h. *Checks, shakes, and splits.* Checks are longitudinal cracks extending, in general, across the annual rings. Shakes are longitudinal cracks usually between two annual rings. Splits are longitudinal cracks induced by artificially induced stress. Reject wood containing these defects.

i. *Compression wood.* This defect is very detrimental to strength and is difficult to recognize readily. It is characterized by high specific gravity; has the appearance of an excessive growth of summer wood; and in most species shows but little contrast in color between spring wood and summer wood. In doubtful cases reject the material, or subject samples to a toughness machine test to establish the quality of the wood. Reject all material containing compression wood.

j. *Compression failures.* This defect is caused from the wood being overstressed in compression due to natural forces during the growth of the tree, felling trees on rough or irregular ground, or rough handling of logs or lumber. Compression failures are characterized by a buckling of the fibers that appear as streaks on the surface of the piece substantially at right angles to the grain, and vary from pronounced failures to very fine hairlines that require close inspection to detect. Reject wood containing obvious failures. In doubtful cases reject the wood, or make a further inspection in the form of microscopic examination or toughness test, the latter means being the more reliable.

k. *Decay.* Examine all stains and discolorations carefully to determine whether or not they are harmless, or in a stage of preliminary or advanced decay. All pieces must be free from rot, dote, red heart, purple heart, and all other forms of decay.

cised that the repairs do not involve the addition of weight aft of the hinge line. Such a procedure may adversely disturb the dynamic and static balance of the surface to a degree which would induce flutter. As a general rule, it will be necessary to repair control surfaces in such a manner that the structure is identical to the original so that the weight distribution and resulting mass balance are not affected in any way.

4. GLUING PRECAUTIONS. Satisfactory glue joints in aircraft will develop the full strength of wood under all conditions of stress. To produce this result, the gluing operation must be carefully controlled so as to obtain a continuous, thin, uniform film of solid glue in the joint with adequate adhesion to both surfaces of the wood. Some of the more important conditions involve:

a. Properly prepared wood surfaces.

b. Glue of good quality, properly prepared.

c. Good gluing technique.

5. PREPARATION OF WOOD SURFACES FOR GLUING.

It is recommended that no more than 8 hours be permitted to elapse between final surfacing and gluing. The gluing surfaces should be machined smooth and true with planers, jointers, or special miter saws. Planer marks, chipped or loosened grain, and other surface irregularities will not be permitted. Sandpaper must never be used to smooth softwood surfaces that are to be glued. Sawed surfaces must approach well-planed surfaces in uniformity, smoothness, and freedom from crushed fibers.

a. *Tooth-planing,* or other means of roughening smooth well-planed surfaces of normal wood before gluing, is not recommended. Such treatment of well-planed wood surfaces may result in local irregularities and objectionable rounding of edges. While sanding of planed surfaces is not recommended for softwoods, sanding is a valuable aid in improving the gluing characteristics of some hard plywood surfaces, wood that has been compressed through exposure to high pressure and temperatures, resin-impregnated wood (impreg and compreg), and laminated paper plastic (papreg).

b. *Wood surfaces for gluing* should be free from oil, wax, varnish, shellac, lacquer, enamel, dope, sealers, paint, dust, dirt, oil, glue, crayon marks, and other extraneous materials.

c. *Wetting tests* are useful as a means of detecting the presence of wax. Drops of water placed on the surface of wax-coated wood do not spread or wet the wood. At present, preliminary gluing tests appear to be the only positive means of actually determining the gluing characteristics of plywood surfaces.

6. GLUES.

Glues used in aircraft repair fall into two general groups: casein glues and resin glues. Any glue that meets the performance requirements of applicable United States military specifications or has previously been accepted by the Federal Aviation Administration (FAA) is satisfactory for use in certified civil aircraft. In all cases, glues are to be used strictly in accordance with the glue manufacturer's recommendations.

a. *Casein Glues.* Casein glues have been widely used in wood aircraft repair work. The forms, characteristics, and properties of water-resistant casein glues have remained substantially the same for many years, except for the addition of preservatives. Casein glues for use in aircraft should contain suitable preservatives such as the chlorinated phenols and their sodium salts to increase their resistance to organic deterioration under high-humidity exposures. Most casein glues are sold in powder form ready to be mixed with water at ordinary room temperatures.

Caution

Casein glue deteriorates over the years after exposure to moisture in the air and temperature variations. Many of the modern glues are incompatible with casein glue. If a joint that has been glued with casein is to be reglued with resin glue, all traces of the casein must be scraped off before the new glue is applied. If any alkalinity of any casein glue is left, it may cause the new glue to fail to cure properly.

b. *Plastic resin glue.* Plastic resin glue, a powdered glue that is mixed with water, is perhaps the most popular glue used today for aircraft woodwork. It must be mixed in the exact proportions specified by the manufacturer.

Typically this glue is prepared by mixing five parts by volume of the powdered glue with two parts, by volume, of cold water. This is the same as 10 parts of powder and 6 parts of water by weight. Pour a small amount of water into the powder and stir into a heavy paste and then add the remainder of the water. Continue to stir until the mixture is about as thick as heavy cream. The glue is ready for use as soon as it is mixed. Figure 1.2a shows the working timetable for plastic resin glues.

c. *Resorcinol glue.* This is a two-part synthetic resin glue consisting of resin and a hardener and is the most water resistant of the glues used. The appropriate amount (per manufacturer's instruction) of hardener is added to the resin, and it is stirred until it is consistently mixed; the glue is now ready for immediate use.

Caution

Read and observe material safety data.

"7. [Deleted] — Change 3"

*

FIGURE 1.2a.—Plastic resin glue working timetable.

Condition	Temperature		
	70° F (21° C)	80° F (27° C)	90° F (32° C)
Mixture pot life (hours)	4 - 5	2 1/2 - 3 1/2	1 - 2
Maximum assembly time	15	10	5
Open (minutes)	15	10	5
Closed (minutes)	25	15	8
Pressure period (hours)	14	8	5

Note: Assembly must be maintained at a temperature of 70° F. or above to assure a satisfactory cure of the glue line. *

This page intentionally left blank.

8. SPREADING OF GLUE. To make a satisfactory glue joint, spread the glue evenly on both surfaces to be joined. It is recommended that a clean brush be used and care taken to see that all surfaces are covered. The spreading of glue on but one of the two surfaces is not recommended.

9. ASSEMBLY TIME IN GLUING. Where pieces of wood are coated and exposed freely to the air, a much more rapid change in consistency of the glue occurs than where the pieces are laid together as soon as the spreading has been done. The condition of free exposure is conveniently referred to as "open assembly" and the other as "closed assembly."

When cold-setting glues are coated on wood parts and left exposed to the atmosphere (open assembly), the time for complete assembly is appreciably reduced compared with closed assembly periods. Use assembly time and gluing pressures recommended by the glue manufacturer.

The pressing time for casein and resin glue joints should, in general, be 7 hours or more. Other types of glue require various times and temperatures for curing. Glue joints increase in strength mainly as a result of drying; hence, where it is convenient to do so, it is better to maintain pressure from one day to the next. The longer pressing periods are desirable, as this enables the joints to reach a higher proportion of their final strength before being disturbed.

10. GLUING PRESSURE. Pressure is used to squeeze the glue out into a thin continuous film between the wood layers, to force air from the joint, to bring the wood surfaces into intimate contact with the glue, and to hold them in this position during the setting of the glue.

Pressure should be applied to the joint before the glue becomes too thick to flow and is accomplished by means of clamps, presses, or other mechanical devices.

Nonuniform gluing pressure commonly results in weak and strong areas in the same joint. The amount of pressure required to produce strong joints in aircraft assembly operations may vary from 125 to 150 pounds per square

inch for softwoods and 150 to 200 pounds per square inch for hardwoods. Insufficient pressure or poorly machined wood surfaces usually result in thick gluelines which indicate a weak joint, and should be carefully guarded against.

a. Method of Applying Pressure. The methods employed in applying pressure to joints in aircraft gluing operations range from the use of brads, nails, screws, and clamps to the use of hydraulic and electrical power presses. Hand-nailing is used rather extensively in the gluing of ribs and in the application of plywood skins to the wing, control surfaces, and fuselage frames.

On small joints, such as found in wood ribs, the pressure is usually applied only by nailing the joint gussets in place after spreading the glue. Since small nails must be used to avoid splitting, the gussets should be comparatively large in area to compensate for the relative lack of pressure. At least 4 nails per square inch are to be used, and in no event must nails be more than 3/4-inch apart. Small brass screws may also be used advantageously when the particular parts to be glued are relatively small, and do not allow application of pressure by means of clamps.

Clamp spar splices by means of cabinet makers, parallel clamps or similar types. Use handspring clamps in conjunction with softwood only. Due to their limited pressure area, they should be applied with a pressure distributing strip or block at least twice as thick as the member to be pressed.

11. SCARF JOINTS. The scarf joint is the most satisfactory method of making a joint in the grain direction between two solid wood members. Cut both parts accurately because the strength of the joints depend upon maximum contact between the surfaces being glued.

a. Grain Direction. Make the scarfcut in the general direction of the grain slope as shown in figure 1.3. (See figure 1.3 for note concerning allowable deviation from grain direction.)

12. SPLICING OF SPARS. A spar may be spliced at any point except under wing attachment fit-

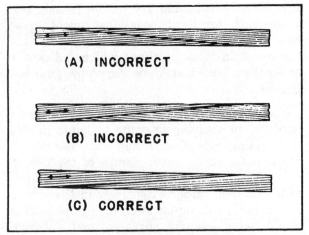

(A) INCORRECT

(B) INCORRECT

(C) CORRECT

FIGURE 1.3.—Consideration of grain direction when making scarf joints.

No grain deviation steeper than 1 in 15 should be present in an outer eighth of the depth of the spar. In adjacent eighths, deviations involving steeper slopes, such as a wave in a few growth layers, are unlikely to be harmful. Local grain slope deviations in excess of those specified may be permitted in spar flanges only in the inner one-fourth of the flange depth.

tings, landing-gear fittings, engine-mount fittings, or lift-and-interplane strut fittings. Do not permit these fittings to overlap any part of the splice. Splicing under minor fittings such as drag wire, antidrag wire, or compression strut fittings is acceptable under the following conditions:

a. *The reinforcement plates* of the splice should not interfere with the proper attachment or alinement of the fittings. Do not alter the locations of pulley support brackets, bellcrank support brackets, or control surface support brackets.

b. *The reinforcement plate* may overlap drag or antidrag wire or compression strut fittings, if the reinforcement plates are on the front-face of the front spar or on the rear-face of the rear spar. In such cases it will be necessary to install slightly longer bolts. The inside reinforcement plate should not overlap drag strut fittings, unless such overlapping does not require sufficient shortening of compression struts, or changes in drag-truss geometry to prevent adjustment for proper rigging. Even

though takeup is sufficient, it may be necessary to change the angles on the fittings. Space splices so that they do not overlap. (Acceptable methods of splicing the various types of spars are shown in figures 1.4 through 1.7.) Reinforcement plates must be used as indicated on all scarf repairs to spars and the slopes of scarfs shown are minimum slopes.

13. SPLICING OF BOX SPAR WEBS. Always splice and reinforce plywood webs with the same type of plywood. Do not use solid wood to replace plywood webs, as plywood is stronger in shear than solid wood of the same thickness due to the variation in grain direction of the individual plies. The face-grain of plywood replacement webs and reinforcement plates must be in the same direction as the original member to insure that the new web will have the required strength. (The method of splicing plywood webs is shown in figure 1.8.)

14. REPLACING SOLID-TYPE SPARS WITH LAMINATED TYPE. Solid spruce spars may be replaced with laminated ones or vice versa, provided the material is of the same high quality. External plywood reinforcement must always be replaced with plywood as in the original structure.

15. SPAR LONGITUDINAL CRACKS AND LOCAL DAMAGE. Cracked spars (except box spars) may be repaired by gluing plates of spruce or plywood of sufficient thickness to develop the longitudinal shear strength to both sides of the spar. Extend the plates well beyond the termination of the cracks as shown in figure 1.9. A method of repairing small local damage to either the top or bottom side of a spar is also shown in this figure.

a. *Longitudinal Cracking of Wood Wing Spars in Airplanes Operating in Arid Regions.* Airplanes having wood spars and being operated in arid regions may develop longitudinal spar cracks in the vicinity of the plywood reinforcement plates. These cracks result from the tendency of the spar to shrink when drying takes place. Plywood resists this tendency and causes a cross-grain tensile failure in the basic spar. Cracks start under the plywood plates, usually,

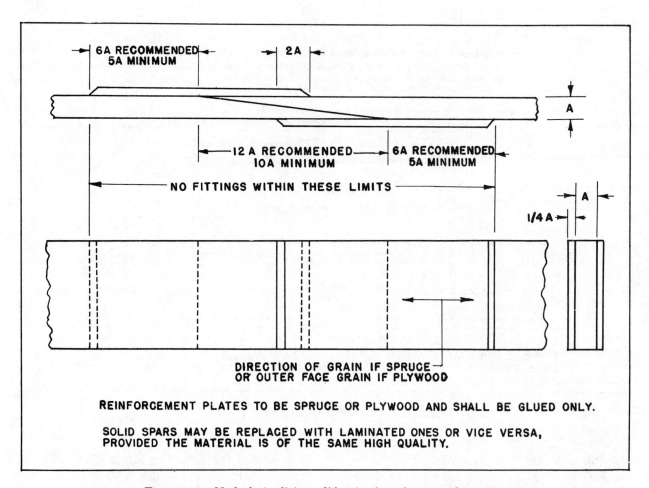

6A RECOMMENDED
5A MINIMUM

2A

A

12 A RECOMMENDED
10A MINIMUM

6A RECOMMENDED
5A MINIMUM

NO FITTINGS WITHIN THESE LIMITS

A

1/4 A

DIRECTION OF GRAIN IF SPRUCE
OR OUTER FACE GRAIN IF PLYWOOD

REINFORCEMENT PLATES TO BE SPRUCE OR PLYWOOD AND SHALL BE GLUED ONLY.

SOLID SPARS MAY BE REPLACED WITH LAMINATED ONES OR VICE VERSA,
PROVIDED THE MATERIAL IS OF THE SAME HIGH QUALITY.

FIGURE 1.4.—Method of splicing solid or laminated rectangular spars.

but not necessarily, at a bolthole or cutout and spread in each direction until, in most cases, they extend a short distance beyond the ends of the plates where the resistance to spar shrinkage disappears. Other factors which have been found conducive to the formation of cracks, due to spar shrinkage in the region of plywood plates, are poor protective finishes, large cutouts, and metal fittings which utilize two lines of large diameter bolts.

The presence of cracks does not necessarily mean that the spar must be discarded. If the crack is not too long or too close to either edge and can be reinforced properly, it will probably be more economical and satisfactory to effect a repair than to install a new spar or section. However, a generally acceptable procedure suitable for all airplane models cannot be

described here. It is recommended the manufacturer or the Federal Aviation Administration be contacted for specific instructions before making repairs not in accordance with the manufacturer's approved instructions or the recommendations of this advisory circular, because of the possibility of strength deficiencies.

16. ELONGATED HOLES IN SPARS. In cases of elongated boltholes in a spar or cracks in the vicinity of boltholes, splice in a new section of spar, or replace the spar entirely, unless the method of repair is specifically approved by a representative of the FAA. In many cases, it has been found advantageous to laminate the new section of the spar (using aircraft plywood for the outer faces), particularly if the spar roots are being replaced.

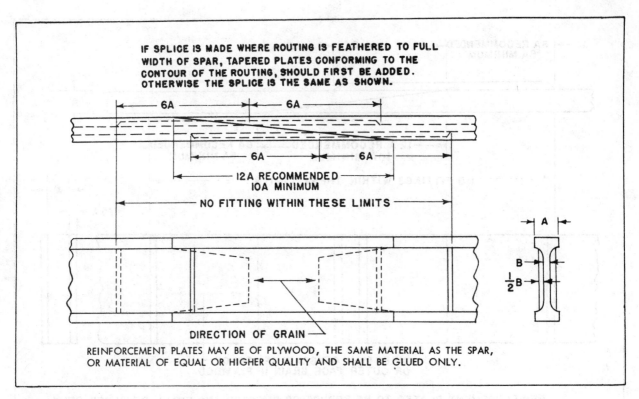

IF SPLICE IS MADE WHERE ROUTING IS FEATHERED TO FULL
WIDTH OF SPAR, TAPERED PLATES CONFORMING TO THE
CONTOUR OF THE ROUTING, SHOULD FIRST BE ADDED.
OTHERWISE THE SPLICE IS THE SAME AS SHOWN.

REINFORCEMENT PLATES MAY BE OF PLYWOOD, THE SAME MATERIAL AS THE SPAR,
OR MATERIAL OF EQUAL OR HIGHER QUALITY AND SHALL BE GLUED ONLY.

FIGURE 1.5.—Method of splicing solid "I" spars.

17. RIB REPAIRS. Make replacement ribs from a manufacturer's approved drawing, or from a drawing made by the repair agency, and certified by the manufacturer as correct. The original rib may be used as a pattern in making the new rib if it is not too seriously damaged to permit comparison. Wood ribs should not be attached to wood spars by nails driven through the rib capstrips, as this weakens the rib materially. The attachment should be by means of glue with cement-coated, barbed, or spiraled nails driven through the vertical rib members on each side of the spar. The drawing or pattern should be retained by the repair agency for use by the FAA inspector when making his inspection. (Acceptable methods of repairing damaged ribs are shown in figure 1.10.)

a. Compression Ribs. Acceptable methods of repairing damaged compression ribs are shown in figure 1.11. (A) illustrates the repair of a compression rib of the "I" section type; i.e., wide, shallow capstrips, a center plywood web with a rectangular compression member on

each side of the web. The rib is assumed to be cracked through capstrips, web member, and compression member. Cut the compression member as shown in (D), remove and replace the shortest section, adding the reinforcement blocks as also shown in figure 1.11(D). Cut and replace the aft portion of the capstrips, and reinforce as shown in figure 1.10 except that the reinforcement blocks are split in the vertical direction to straddle the center web. The plywood sideplates, as indicated in figure 1.11(A), are glued on. These plates are added to reinforce the damaged web. (B) illustrates a compression rib of the type that is basically a standard rib with rectangular compression members added to one side and plywood web to the other side. The method used in this repair is essentially the same as in (A) except that the plywood reinforcement plate shown in solid black in section B–B is continued the full distance between spars. (C) illustrates a compression rib of the "I" type with a rectangular vertical member each side of the web. The

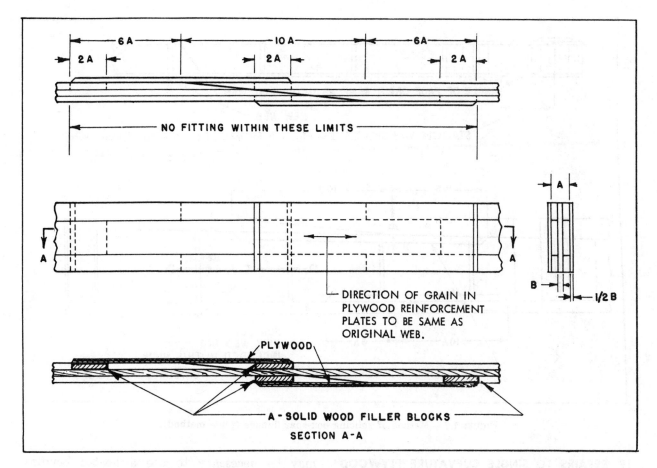

FIGURE 1.6.—Repairs to built-up "I" spar.

method of repair is essentially the same as in (A) except the plywood reinforcement plates on each side shown in solid black in section C–C are continued, as in (C), the full distance between spars.

18. PLYWOOD SKIN REPAIR. Make extensive repairs to damaged stressed skin plywood structures in accordance with specific recommendations from the manufacturer. It is recommended that repairs be made by replacing the entire panel from one structural member to the next, if damage is very extensive. When damaged plywood skin is repaired, carefully inspect the adjacent internal structure for possible hidden damage. Repair any defective frame members prior to making skin repairs.

   a. Types of Patches. Four types of patches—the surface or overlay patch, the splayed patch, the plug patch, and the scarf patch—are acceptable for repairing plywood skins. Surface patches should not be used on skins over 1/8 inch thick. Splayed patches should not be used on skins over 1/10 inch thick. There are no skin thickness limitations for the use of scarf patches and plug patches.

   b. Determination of Single or Double Curvature. Much of the outside surface of plywood aircraft is curved. On such areas, plywood used for repairs to the skin must be similarly curved. Curved skins are either of single curvature or of double (compound) curvature. A simple test to determine which type of curvature exists may be made by laying a sheet of heavy paper on the surface in question. If the sheet can be made to fit the surface without wrinkling, the surface is either flat or has single curvature. If, however, the sheet cannot be made to fit the surface without wrinkling, the surface is of double curvature.

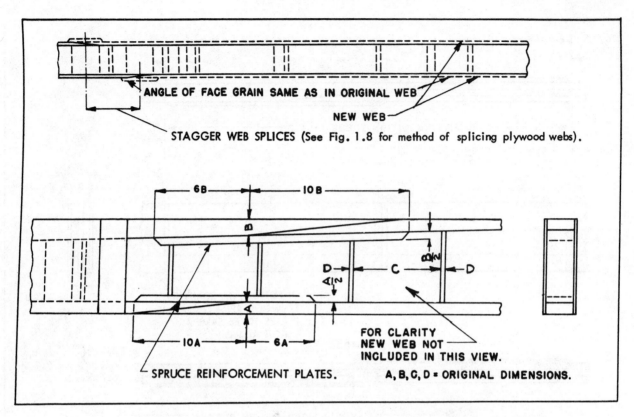

ANGLE OF FACE GRAIN SAME AS IN ORIGINAL WEB

NEW WEB

STAGGER WEB SPLICES (See Fig. 1.8 for method of splicing plywood webs).

6B — 10B

10A — 6A

D — C — D

FOR CLARITY
NEW WEB NOT
INCLUDED IN THIS VIEW.

SPRUCE REINFORCEMENT PLATES.

A, B, C, D = ORIGINAL DIMENSIONS.

FIGURE 1.7.—Method of splicing box-spar flanges (plate method).

19. REPAIRS TO SINGLE CURVATURE PLYWOOD SKIN. Repairs to skins of single curvature may usually be formed from flat plywood, either by bending it dry or after soaking it in hot water. The degree of curvature to which a piece of plywood can be bent will depend upon the direction of the grain and the thickness. Figure 1.12 is presented as a guide in determining which process of bending should be used for the curvature being considered. Plywood, after softening, may be bent on a cold ventilated form, or it may be bent over the leading edge near the part being patched if space permits. In either method it should be allowed to dry completely on the form. When bending plywood over a leading edge, drying may be hastened by laying a piece of coarse burlap over the leading edge before using it as a bending form.

A fan to circulate the air over the bent piece will speed the drying. In bending pieces of small radii, or to speed up the bending of a large number of parts of the same curvature, it may be necessary to use a heated bending form. The surface temperature of this form may be as high as 149° C. (300° F.), if necessary, without danger of damage to the plywood. The plywood should be left on the form, however, only long enough to dry to room conditions.

20. REPAIRS TO DOUBLE CURVATURE PLYWOOD SKIN. The molded plywood necessary for a repair to a damaged plywood skin of double curvature cannot be made from flat plywood unless the area to be repaired is very small, or is of exceedingly slight double curvature; therefore, molded plywood of the proper curvature must be on hand before the repair can be made. If molded plywood of the proper curvature is available, the repair may be made following the recommended procedures.

21. SPLAYED PATCH. Small holes with largest dimensions not over 15 times the skin thickness, in skins not more than 1/10 inch in thickness,

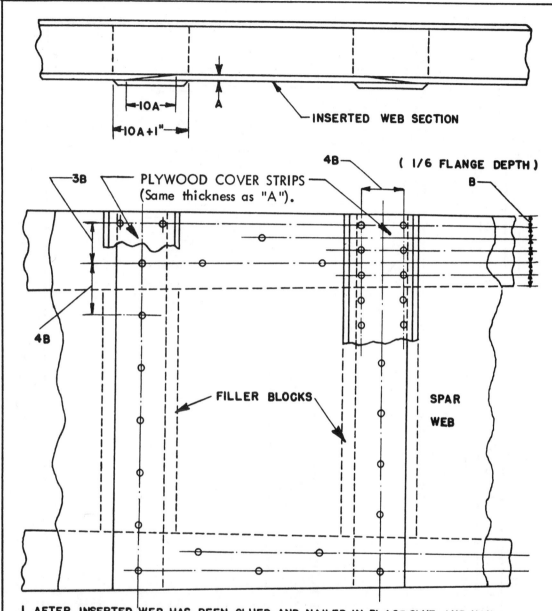

FIGURE 1.8.—Method of splicing box-spar webs.

1. AFTER INSERTED WEB HAS BEEN GLUED AND NAILED IN PLACE, GLUE AND NAIL COVER STRIP OVER ENTIRE LENGTH OF SPLICE JOINTS.

2. SECTIONAL SHAPE OF FILLER BLOCKS MUST CONFORM EXACTLY TO TAPER OF SPAR. THEY MUST NOT BE TOO TIGHTLY FITTED OR WEDGING ACTION WILL LOOSEN EXISTING GLUE JOINTS OF WEBS TO FLANGES. IF TOO LOOSELY FITTED, CRUSHING OF WEB WILL OCCUR WHEN CLAMPING.

3. DIRECTION OF FACE GRAIN OF NEW PLYWOOD WEB AND COVER STRIPS TO BE SAME AS ORIGINAL WEB.

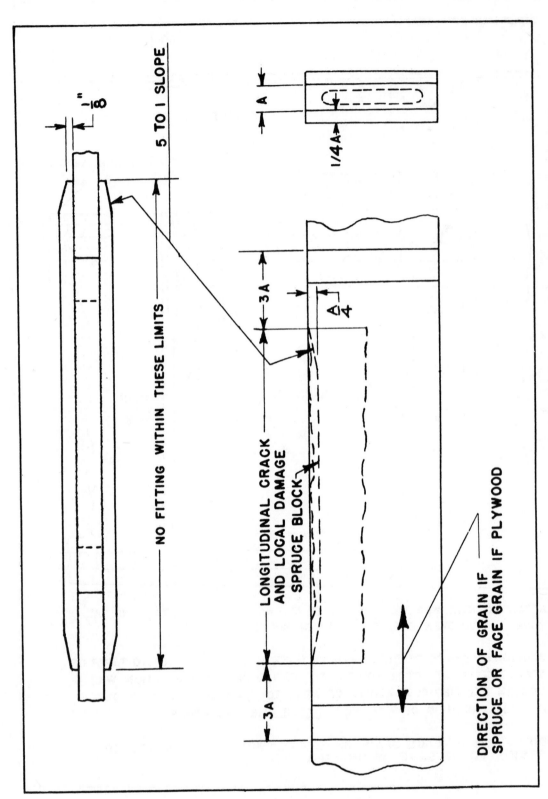

FIGURE 1.9.—Method of reinforcing a longitudinal crack and/or local damage in a solid or internally routed spar.

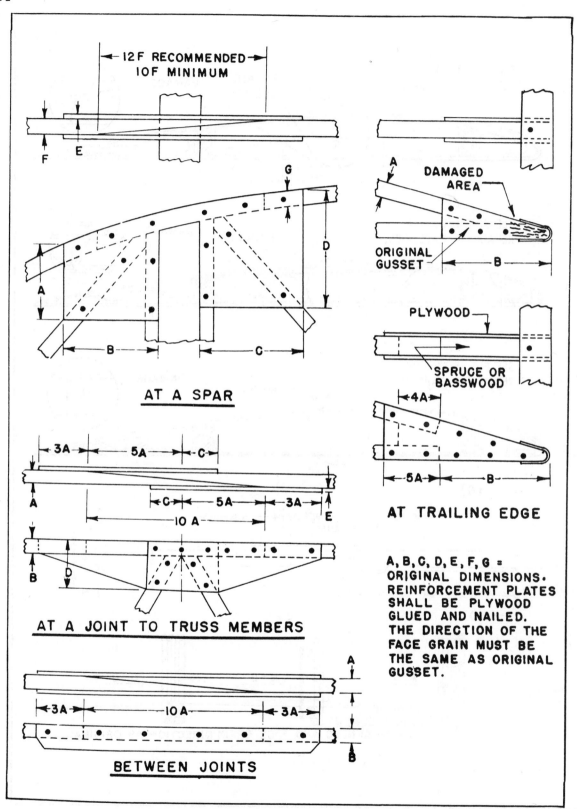

FIGURE 1.10.—Repair of wood ribs.

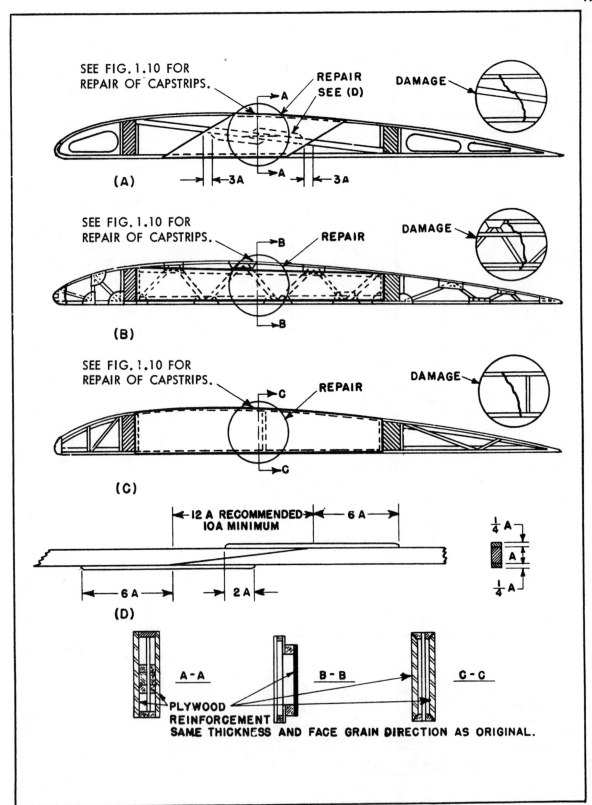

SEE FIG. 1.10 FOR
REPAIR OF CAPSTRIPS.

REPAIR
SEE (D)

DAMAGE

(A)

3A   A   3A

SEE FIG. 1.10 FOR
REPAIR OF CAPSTRIPS.

B

REPAIR

DAMAGE

(B)

B

SEE FIG. 1.10 FOR
REPAIR OF CAPSTRIPS.

C

REPAIR

DAMAGE

(C)

C

12 A RECOMMENDED
10A MINIMUM   6 A

¼ A
A
¼ A

6 A   2 A

(D)

A - A   B - B   C - C

PLYWOOD
REINFORCEMENT
SAME THICKNESS AND FACE GRAIN DIRECTION AS ORIGINAL.

FIGURE 1.11.—Typical wing compression rib repairs.

(1) Plywood thickness	(2) No. plies	10 Percent moisture content, bent on cold mandrels		Thoroughly soaked in hot water and bent on cold mandrels	
		(3) At 90° to face grain 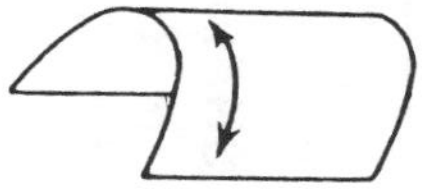	(4) At 0° or 45° to face grain 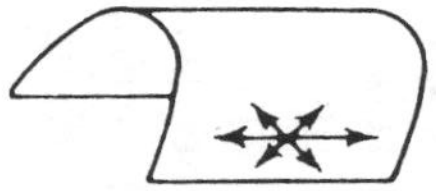	(5) At 90° to face grain 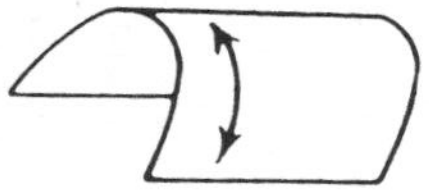	(6) At 0° or 45° to face grain 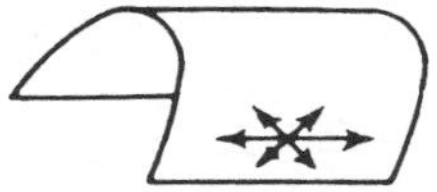
Inch		Inches	Inches	Inches	Inches
0.035	3	2.0	1.1	0.5	0.1
.070	3	5.2	3.2	1.5	.4
.100	3	8.6	5.2	2.6	.8
.125	3	12	7.1	3.8	1.2
.155	3	16	10	5.3	1.8
.185	3	20	13	7.1	2.6
.160	5	17	11	6	2
.190	5	21	14	7	3
.225	5	27	17	10	4
.250	5	31	20	12	5
.315	5	43	28	16	7
.375	5	54	36	21	10

FIGURE 1.12.—Minimum recommended bend radii for aircraft plywood.

Columns (1) and (3) may also be used for determining the maximum thickness of single laminations for curved members.

may be repaired by using a circular splayed patch as illustrated in figure 1.13. The term "splayed" is used to denote that the edges of the patch are tapered, but the slope is steeper than is allowed in scarfing operations. The steps shown in figure 1.13 should be taken in making a splayed patch.

a. *Lay out the patch* according to figure 1.13. Tack a small piece of plywood over the hole for a center point, and draw two circles, the inner one to be the size of the hole, and the outer one marking the limits of the taper. The difference between the radii is 5T (5 times the thickness of the skin). If one leg of the dividers has been sharpened to a chisel edge, the dividers may be used to cut the inner circle completely through.

b. *Taper the hole* evenly to the outer mark with a chisel, knife, or rasp.

c. *Prepare a circular tapered patch* to fit the prepared hole and glue the patch into place with face-grain direction matching that of the original surface.

d. *Use waxed paper* between the patch and a plywood pressure plate cut to the exact size of the patch. This prevents extruded glue from binding patch and plate together. Center the plate carefully over the patch.

e. *Apply pressure.* As there is no reinforcement behind this patch, care must be used so that pressure is not great enough to crack the skin. On horizontal surfaces, weights or sandbags will be sufficient. On patches too far in for the use of standard hand clamps, jaws of greater length may be improvised.

f. *Fill, sand,* and refinish the patch.

22. **SURFACE PATCH.** Plywood skins that are damaged between or along framing members may be repaired by surface or overlay patches as shown in figure 1.14. Trim the damaged skin to a rectangular or triangular shape and round the corners. The radius of rounded corners should be at least 5 times the skin thickness. Cover surface patches with fabric before finishing. Fabric should overlap the original skin at least 2 inches. Surface patches located

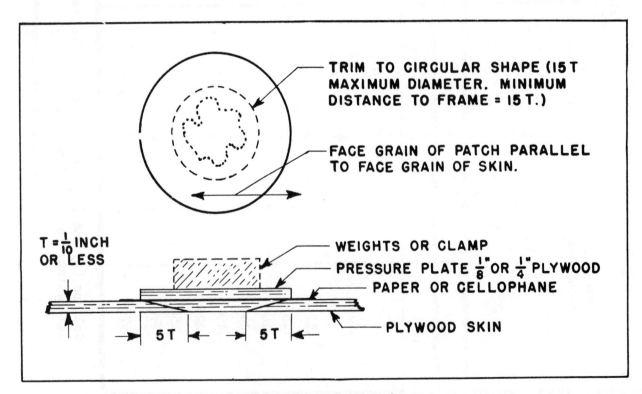

TRIM TO CIRCULAR SHAPE (15 T MAXIMUM DIAMETER. MINIMUM DISTANCE TO FRAME = 15 T.)

FACE GRAIN OF PATCH PARALLEL TO FACE GRAIN OF SKIN.

$T = \frac{1}{10}$ INCH OR LESS

WEIGHTS OR CLAMP
PRESSURE PLATE $\frac{1}{8}$" OR $\frac{1}{4}$" PLYWOOD
PAPER OR CELLOPHANE
PLYWOOD SKIN

5T   5T

FIGURE 1.13.—Splayed patch.

entirely aft of the 10 percent chordline, or which wrap around the leading edge and terminate aft of the 10 percent chordline are permissible. Bevel forward edges of patches located entirely aft of the 10 percent chordline to 4 times the skin thickness. Surface patches may have as much as a 50-inch perimeter and may cover as much as 1 frame (or rib) space. The face-grain direction must be the same as the original skin.

23. SCARF PATCH. A properly prepared and inserted scarf patch is the best repair for damaged plywood skins and is preferred for most skin repairs. Figure 1.15 shows the details and dimensions to be used when installing typical scarf skin patches when the back of the skin is accessible. Follow figure 1.16 when the back of the skin is not accessible. The scarf slope of 1 in 12 shown in both figures is the steepest slope permitted for all species of plywood. If the radius of curvature of the skin at all points on the trimmed opening is greater than 100 times the skin thickness, a scarf patch may be installed.

Scarf cuts in plywood may be made by hand plane, spoke shave, scraper, or accurate sandpaper block. Rasped surfaces, except at the corners of scarf patches and sawed surfaces, are not recommended as they are likely to be rough or inaccurate.

Nail-strip gluing is often the only method available for gluing scarf joints in plywood when used in repair work; therefore, it is essential that all scarf joints in plywood be backed with plywood or solid wood to provide adequate nailholding capacity. The face grain direction of the plywood patch should be the same as that of the original skin.

a. Scarf Patches (Back of Skin Accessible). When the back of a damaged plywood skin is accessible (such as a fuselage skin), it should be repaired with scarf patches following the details shown in figure 1.15. Whenever possible, the edge of the patch should be supported as shown in section C–C. When the damage follows or extends to a framing member, the scarf may be supported as shown in section B–B.

Damages that do not exceed 25 times the skin thickness in diameter after being trimmed to a circular shape, and if the trimmed opening is not nearer than 15 times the skin thickness to a framing member, may be repaired as shown in figure 1.15, section D–D. The backing block is carefully shaped from solid wood and fitted to the inside surface of the skin, and is temporarily held in place with nails. A hole, the exact size of the inside circle of the scarf patch, is made in the block, and is centered over the trimmed area of damage. The block is removed, after the glue on the patch has set, and leaves a flush surface to the repaired skin.

b. Steps in Making Scarf Patch (Back of Skin Not Accessible).

(1) After removing damaged sections, install backing strips, as shown in figure 1.16, along all edges that are not fully backed by a rib or a spar. To prevent warping of the skin, backing strips should be made of a soft-textured plywood, such as yellow poplar or spruce rather than solid wood. All junctions between backing strips and ribs or spars should have the end of the backing strip supported by a saddle gusset of plywood.

(2) If needed, nail and glue the new gusset plate to rib. It may be necessary to remove and replace the old gusset plate by a new saddle gusset; or, it may be necessary to nail a saddle gusset over the original.

(3) Attach nailing strips to hold backing strips in place while the glue sets. Use bucking bar where necessary to provide support for nailing. Unlike the smaller patches made in a continuous process, work on the airplane must wait while the glue, holding the backing strips, sets. After setting, complete finishing in usual manner.

24. PLUG PATCHES. Two types of plug patches, oval and round, may be used on plywood skins provided the damage can be covered by the patches whose dimensions are given in figures 1.17 and 1.18. As the plug patch is strictly a skin repair, it should be used only for damage that does not involve the supporting structure under the skin. Oval patches must be prepared

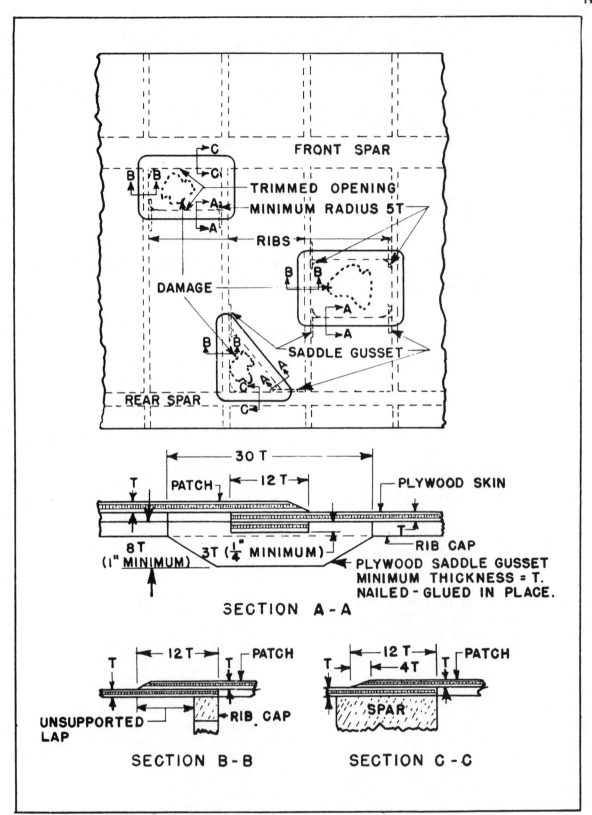

FIGURE 1.14.—Surface patches.

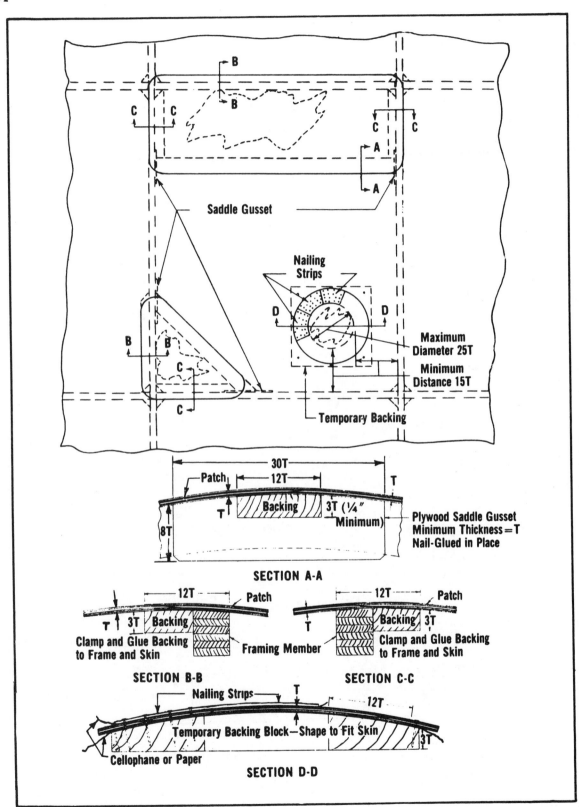

FIGURE 1.15.—Scarf patches—back of skin accessible.

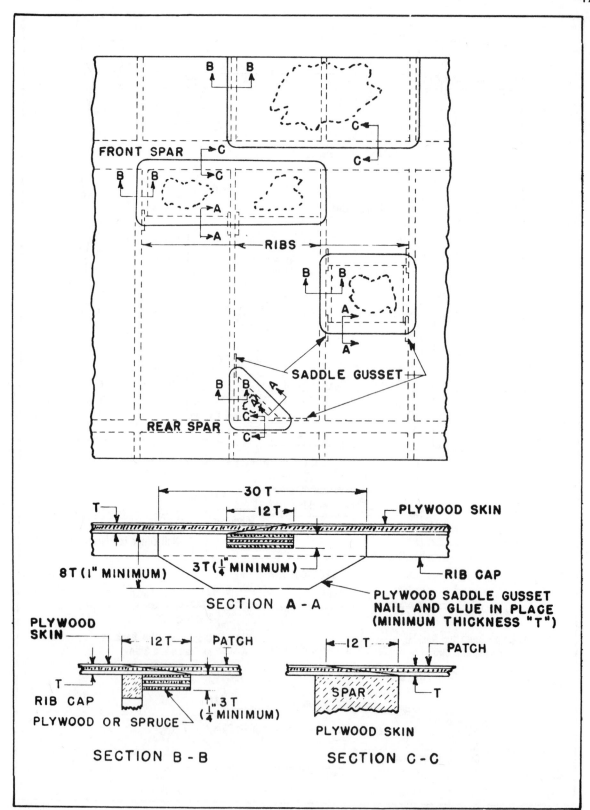

FIGURE 1.16.—Scarf patches—back of skin not accessible.

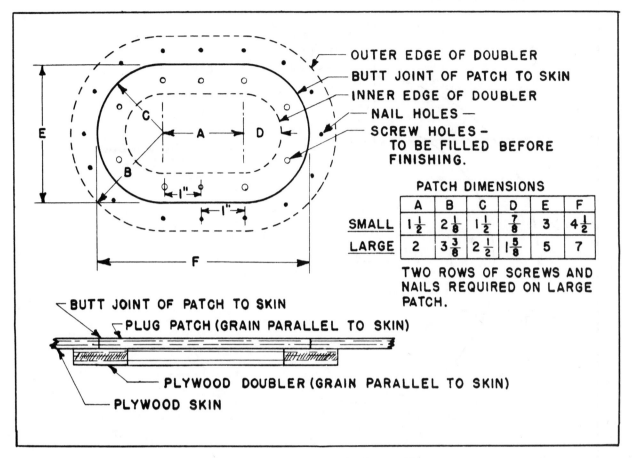

FIGURE 1.17.—Oval plug patch assembly.

Labels in figure:
- OUTER EDGE OF DOUBLER
- BUTT JOINT OF PATCH TO SKIN
- INNER EDGE OF DOUBLER
- NAIL HOLES —
- SCREW HOLES -
  TO BE FILLED BEFORE
  FINISHING.
- BUTT JOINT OF PATCH TO SKIN
- PLUG PATCH (GRAIN PARALLEL TO SKIN)
- PLYWOOD DOUBLER (GRAIN PARALLEL TO SKIN)
- PLYWOOD SKIN

PATCH DIMENSIONS

	A	B	C	D	E	F
SMALL	$1\frac{1}{2}$	$2\frac{1}{8}$	$1\frac{1}{2}$	$\frac{7}{8}$	3	$4\frac{1}{2}$
LARGE	2	$3\frac{3}{8}$	$2\frac{1}{2}$	$1\frac{5}{8}$	5	7

TWO ROWS OF SCREWS AND
NAILS REQUIRED ON LARGE
PATCH.

with the face grain carefully oriented to the same direction as the original skin. Orientation of the face grain direction of the round plug patch to that of the skin surface is no problem, as the round patch may be rotated until grain directions match.

a. Steps in Making Oval Plug Patch.

(1) Explore the area about the hole to be sure it lies at least the width of the oval doubler from a rib or a spar. Refer to figure 1.17 for repair details.

(2) Lay a previously prepared oval plug patch over the damage and trace the patch. Saw to the line and trim the hole edges with a knife and sandpaper.

(3) Mark the exact size of the patch on one surface of the oval doubler and apply glue to the area outside the line. The oval doubler should be made of some soft-textured plywood,

such as yellow poplar or spruce. Insert doubler through the hole and bring it, glue side up, to the underside of the skin with its pencil outline of the patch matching the edges of the hole. If the curvature of the surface to be repaired is greater than a rise of 1/8 inch in 6 inches, the doubler should be preformed by hot water or steam bending to the approximate curvature.

(4) Apply nailing strips outlining the hole to apply glue pressure between doubler and skin. Use bucking bar to provide support for nailing. When two rows of nails are used, stagger nail spacing.

(5) Apply glue to remaining surface and to an equivalent surface on the patch.

(6) Lay the patch in position over the doubler, and screw the pressure plate to the patch assembly using a small nail to line up the holes

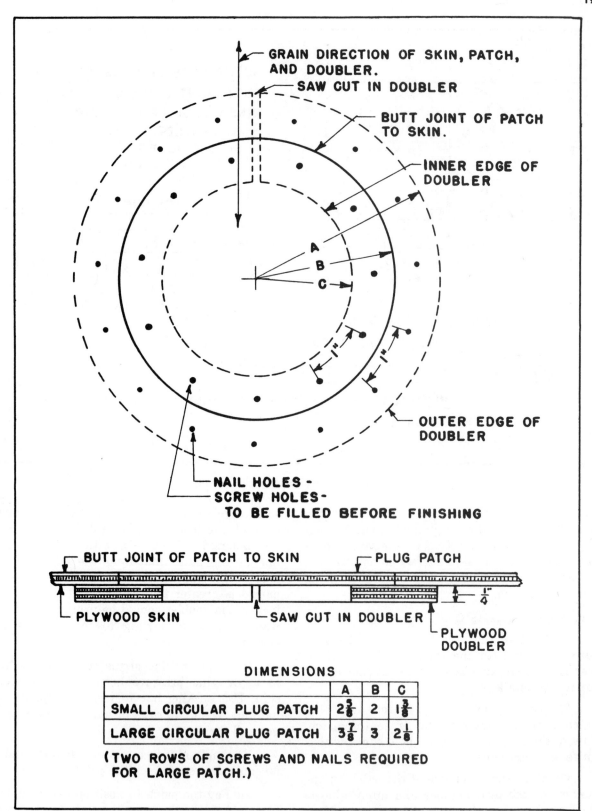

FIGURE 1.18.—Round plug patch assembly.

that have been previously made with patch and plate matching. No. 4 roundhead screws are used. Lead holes in the plywood doubler are not necessary. Waxed paper or cellophane between the plate and patch prevents glue from sealing the plate to the patch. No clamps or further pressure need be applied as the nailing strips and screws exert ample pressure. Hot sandbags, however, may be laid over the patch to speed the setting of the glue. Finish in the usual manner.

b. *Round Plug Patch.* The steps in making a round plug patch shown in figure 1.18 are identical with those for making the oval patch except the insertion of the doubler. In using the round patch, where access if from only one side, the round doubler cannot be inserted unless it has been split.

25. FABRIC PATCH. Small holes not exceeding 1 inch in diameter, after being trimmed to a smooth outline, may be repaired by doping a fabric patch on the outside of the plywood skin. The edges of the trimmed hole should first be sealed and the fabric patch should overlap the plywood skin by at least 1 inch. Holes nearer than 1 inch to any frame member, or in the leading edge or frontal area of the fuselage, should not be repaired with fabric patches.

26.–36. RESERVED.

Section 2. FINISHING WOOD STRUCTURES

37. GENERAL. Any repair to spars, ribs, skin surfaces, or other structural parts of the airframe involves finishing as the final step of the job. The time and effort spent during the preparatory phase of the refinishing process will be reflected in the appearance of the finished surface. Adherence to the instructions issued by the finish manufacturer is necessary to obtain the appearance desired and protective characteristics for the product used.

38. PRECAUTIONS TO BE OBSERVED. When making repairs, avoid excessive contamination of surfaces with glue squeezeout at joints and on all surfaces. Excess glue should always be removed before applying finish. Because paints and glues are incompatible, even a slight amount of glue underneath the finish may cause premature deterioration.

 a. *Soiling substances,* such as oil and grease, should be removed as completely as possible. Naphtha may be used to sponge off oil and grease. Markings that are made by grease pencils or lumber crayons containing wax are harmful and should be removed, but marks made by ordinary soft graphite pencils and nonblotting stamp pad inks may be safely finished over. All dust, dirt, and other solid particles should be cleaned off.

 b. *Sawdust, shavings,* and chips must be removed from enclosed spaces before they are sealed off by replacement of skin. A vacuum cleaner is useful for such cleaning.

 c. *Since no satisfactory gluable sealer* has yet been developed, it is necessary to avoid applying sealer over the areas where glue will be applied. Mark off areas to receive glue, allowing an additional 1/4 inch on each side of the glue area to provide for misalinement when mating the parts. It is preferable to leave some unsealed areas rather than risk weakening the glue joint by accidental overlap of the sealer into the glued areas.

 d. *Finish is likely to crack* when applied over flush-driven nails and screws. To avoid this, a strip of tape may be applied over the heads after application of sealer and before the final finish is applied.

 e. *Fill all holes* left from nail-strip gluing or countersunk nails and screws with a wood filler before finishing the surface. It may be necessary to cover with a patching putty the slight depressions left after applying filler, if a completely smooth surface is desired; but, as a rule, patching putty may be dispensed with safety.

 f. *Treat surfaces* which are likely to come in contact with fabric during the doping process with a dope-proof paint, cellophane tape, etc., to protect them against the action of the solvents in the dope.

39. FINISHING OF INTERIOR SURFACES. Finish repaired ribs, spars, interior of plywood skin, and other internal members, including areas of contact between metal and wood, by applying at least two coats of spar varnish. Protect built-up box spars and similar closed structures on the interior by at least one heavy coat of spar varnish or lionoil. Where better protection is required, as on the surfaces of wheel wells and the bottoms of hulls below the floor boards, an additional coat of aluminized sealer consisting of 12 to 16 ounces of aluminum paste per gallon of sealer may be applied.

40. FINISHING OF EXTERIOR SURFACES. Exterior surfaces should first be sealed with at least two coats of sealer or spar varnish. The surface finish should then be completed by the application of enamel, aluminized varnish, or other special finish as required to duplicate the original finish. If dope or lacquer is used to complete the finish, the sealer coats should be dope-proof. Spar varnish or sealer conforming to Specification MIL–V–6894 is satisfactory.

41. FINISHING OF END GRAIN SURFACES. End grain surfaces, such as edges of plywood skins and holes in spars and other primary structural members, require careful protection. Sand these surfaces smooth. Apply two coats of a highly pigmented sealer, or one coat of wood filler, and one coat of clear sealer to end grain interior surfaces and cut holes. Exterior end grain surfaces (except those covered with doped fabric) require an additional (third) coat of clear sealer. A final coat of aluminized varnish may be applied to end grain surfaces. If the surfaces are to be finished with dope or lacquer, a dope-proof sealer similar to Specification MIL–V–6894 should be used.

Exposed end grain includes such surfaces as those around ventholes, inspection holes, fittings, and exposed scarfed or tapered surfaces such as those of tapered blocking.

42. FINISHING WITH FABRIC OR TAPE. To refinish with fabric or tape, it is first necessary to insure that paint has been removed from an area greater than that to be covered by the fabric.

   a. *Apply two brush coats* of a dope-proof sealer similar to Specification MIL–V–6894, allowing the first coat to dry 2 hours and the second coat as least 6 hours. Follow with one coat of clear dope, and allow it to dry 45 minutes. Apply a second coat of clear dope and lay into the wet film a piece of pinked-edge airplane cloth. All air bubbles should be worked out by brushing to insure maximum adherence. Allow this to dry 45 minutes. Apply one brush coat to insure proper penetration, and at least one spray coat of clear dope, allowing each to dry 45 minutes. The dried spray coat may be sanded with fine sandpaper to obtain a smoother finish. Complete the refinishing of the surface by application of lacquer, enamel, or aluminized varnish as required to match the adjacent area.

   b. *The size of the fabric patch* should be such as to extend at least 1/2 inch on each side of any

crack or group of cracks, at least 1 inch on each side of a scarfed joint glue line, and at least 2 inches beyond any edge of a skin patch to insure proper adhesion.

* 43. INSPECTION OF WOOD IN AIRCRAFT STRUCTURES.

   a. *Inspect for evidence of mildew.* This is evidence of excessive humidity and heat. Extensive mildew will attack the cellulose in the wood which will develop into dry rot.

   b. *Inspect glue joints* for indication of loss of adhesion, i.e.;

   (1) Opening up of joint — in joint cracks.

   (2) Discoloration of glue joint — adverse chemical reaction in glue joint.

   c. *Inspect for loosening of nails* in a scarf patch — this could be evidence of adverse movement developing in the spar.

   d. *Inspect for evidence of wood shrinkage* at installation of fittings — loose bolts or screws.

   e. *Inspect for evidence of wood being excessively wet* — immersed or water flow over structure or entrapped water. Fittings will be embedded in wood instead of flush.

   f. *Inspect for evidence of cracking* — could be caused by excessive stress, excessively tight fittings or impact, or many other causes.

   g. *Inspect for loss of finish* — could be from abrasion or deterioration of chemical stability. Loss of finish will permit attack by mildew, fungus, or oxidation.

   h. *Inspect for fungus* — usually caused by "hot house" conditions; moisture, heat, and exposure to spores released by fungus in the storage areas.

   i. *Inspect for dry rot* — loss of finish, mildew, fungus, excessive shrinkage, discoloration, and cracks. Wood crumbles under pressure.

   j. *Inspect for excessive wood defects* — use figure 1-2 and notes to determine the correct standards.   *

44.-53. RESERVED.

Chapter 2. AIRCRAFT METAL STRUCTURES

Section 1. REFERENCES AND PRECAUTIONARY MEASURES

54. REFERENCES. The following chapters of this AC should be referred to when accomplishing repairs to aircraft metal structures:

a. *Identification and Inspection of Materials*. Identification and inspection of materials should be conducted in accordance with Chapter 7.

b. *Corrosion Protection*. Corrosion protection treatment, cleaners, and paint removing should be accomplished in accordance with Chapter 6.

c. *Aircraft Hardware*. Acceptable means of attachment are listed in Chapter 5.

55. FLUTTER AND VIBRATION PRECAUTIONS. To prevent the occurrence of severe vibration or flutter of flight control surfaces during flight, precautions must be taken to stay within the design balance limitations when performing maintenance or repair.

a. *Balance Changes*. The importance of retaining the proper balance and rigidity of aircraft control surfaces cannot be underestimated. As a general rule, repair the control surface in such a manner that the structure is identical to the original so that the weight distribution is not affected in any way. In order to preclude the occurrence of flutter of the control surface in flight, a degree of static and/or dynamic balance is established for each model of aircraft. Under certain conditions, counter-balance weight is added forward of the hinge line to maintain balance. Remove or add balance weight only when necessary in accordance with the manufacturer's instructions, or obtain FAA approval. Flight testing may be required. Failure to check and retain control surface balance within the original or maximum allowable value could result in a serious flight hazard.

b. *Materials and Construction Techniques*. The development of new materials and techniques has made possible the use of control surfaces of less mass weight for a given area than some aircraft of older design. The effect of repair or weight change on the balance and center of gravity is proportionately greater on lighter surfaces than on the older designs. Since control surfaces on some models are balanced for flutter-free operation up to maximum speed for which the aircraft was originally designed, special attention, therefore, must be given to such surfaces relative to the effects of structural repairs and rework on their balance condition.

c. *Painting and Refinishing*. Special emphasis is directed to the effect indiscriminate application of extra coats of dope or paint has on the balance of control surfaces. Proper maintenance of control surface balance may require removal of dope or paint, down to the base coat, prior to application of finish coats. Consult the aircraft manufacturer's instructions relative to finishing and balance of control surfaces.

d. *Trapped Water or Ice*. Instances of flutter have occurred from unbalanced conditions caused by the collection of water or ice within the surface. Therefore, ventilation and drainage provisions must be checked and retained when maintenance is being done. Certain construction designs do not provide for ventilation and may collect moisture through condensation which will affect balance. In the event this condition is found, refer to the manufacturer's instructions for moisture removal.

e. *Trim Tab Maintenance*. In addition to unbalanced control surface, loose or vibrating trim tabs will increase wear of actuating mechanisms and hinge points which may develop serious flutter conditions. Most trim tabs are not balanced separately from the control surface. Minimum tab flutter is maintained through rigid actuating mechanisms. Trim tabs and their actuating mechanism are constructed as lightly as possible to keep the weight aft of the hinge line of the control surface as low as possible. Actuating mechanisms are highly susceptible to wear, deformation, and fatigue failures because of the buffeting nature of airflow over the tab mechanism. Trailing-edge play of the tab may increase, through wear of the mechanism, to an unsafe condition. Careful inspection of the tab and its mechanism should be conducted during overhaul and inspection periods. Compared to other systems on the aircraft, only a minor amount of tab-mechanism wear can be tolerated.

* The total free play at the tab trailing edge should be less than the following. If the tab span does not exceed 35 percent of the span of the supporting control surface, the total free play shall not exceed 2 percent of the distance from the tab hinge line to the trailing edge of the tab perpendicular to the tab hinge line. If the tab span equals or exceeds 35 percent of the span of the supporting control surface, the total free play is not to exceed 1 percent of the distance from the tab hinge line to the trailing edge of the tab perpendicular to the tab hinge line. For example, a tab that has a chord of 4 inches would have a maximum permissible free play of 4 inches x .020 or .080 inches (total motion up and down) measured at the trailing edge. Correct any free * play in excess of this amount. Care must also be exercised during repair or rework to prevent stress

concentration points or areas which could increase the fatigue susceptibility of the trim tab system.

56. BRAZING. Brazing may be used for repairs to primary aircraft structures only if brazing was originally approved for the particular application. Brazing is not suitable for repair of welds in steel structures due to lower strength values of the brazed joint as compared to welded joints. Brazing may be used in the repair of secondary structures.

Due to the large number of brazing alloys used, it is difficult to be certain that the material selected for repairing a brazed joint will result in a joint having the same strength characteristics as the original. In cases where it is necessary to apply copper alloy brazing material more than once on a steel surface, and particularly if temperatures over 2,000° F. are reached, there is a possibility that brazing metal may penetrate between the grains in the steel to an extent that may cause cracking. Copper brazing of steel is normally accomplished in a special furnace having a controlled atmosphere, and at a temperature so high that field repairs are seldom feasible. If copper brazing is attempted without a controlled atmosphere, the copper will probably not completely flow and fill the joint. Therefore, copper brazing in any other than appropriately controlled conditions is not recommended.

57.-67. RESERVED.

Section 2. WELDING

68. GENERAL. This section covers weld repairs to aircraft and component parts thereof with the exception of welding on powerplants and propellers which is provided in chapters 12 and 14 respectively. Observe the following when using such equipment as tungsten inert gas (TIG), metal inert gas (MIG), plasma arc, shield carbon arc, and oxygen-acetylene gas.

a. Equipment Selection. Use the welding equipment manufacturers' information to determine if the equipment will satsify the requirements for the type of welding operation being undertaken. Disregarding such detailed operating instructions may cause substandard welds. For example, when using TIG equipment, a weld can be contaminated with tungsten if the proper size electrode is not used when welding with direct current reverse polarity. Another exam-

ple, the depletion of the inert gas supply below the critical level causes a reduction in the gas flow and will increase the danger of atmospheric contamination.

(1) Electric welding equipment versatility requires careful selection of the type current and polarity to be used. Since the composition and thickness of metals are deciding factors, the selection may vary with each specific application. Metals having refractory surface oxide films, i.e., magnesium alloys and aluminum and its alloys, are generally welded with A.C., while D.C. is used for carbon, low alloy, noncorrodible, and heat-resisting steels, copper, etc. General recommendations covering current and polarity are shown in figure 2.1.

(2) Oxygen-acetylene gas equipment is suitable for welding most metals. It is not, how-

FIGURE 2.1.—Current and polarity selection for inert gas welding.

MATERIAL	ALTERNATING CURRENT* With High-Frequency Stabilization	DIRECT CURRENT STRAIGHT Polarity	REVERSE Polarity
Magnesium up to 1/8 in. thick	1	N.R.	2
Magnesium above 3/16 in. thick	1	N.R.	N.R.
Magnesium Castings	1	N.R.	2
Aluminum up to 3/32 in. thick	1	N.R.	2
Aluminum over 3/32 in. thick	1	N.R.	N.R.
Aluminum Castings	1	N.R.	N.R.
Stainless Steel	2 *	1	N.R.
Brass Alloys	2 *	1	N.R.
Silicon Copper	N.R.	1	N.R.
Silver	2	1	N.R.
Silver Cladding	1	N.R.	N.R.
Hard-facing	1	1	N.R.
Cast Iron	2 *	1	N.R.
Low Carbon Steel, 0.015 to 0.030 in.	2**	1	N.R.
Low Carbon Steel, 0.030 to 0.125 in.	N.R.	1	N.R.
High Carbon Steel, 0.015 to 0.030 in.	2 *	1	N.R.
High Carbon Steel, 0.030 in. and up	2 *	1	N.R.

1. Recommended   2. Acceptable   N.R. Not Recommended

*Where A.C. is recommended as second choice, use approximately 25% higher current than is recommended for DCSP.

**Do not use A.C. on tightly jigged part.

ever, the best method to use on such materials as stainless steels, magnesium, and aluminum alloys because of base metal oxidization, distortion, and loss of ductility.

NOTE: When oxyacetylene is used, all flux must be removed, as it may cause corrosion.

b. Accurately Identify the Type of Material to be Repaired. Reference to chapter 7 may provide this information. If positive identification is not possible, contact the aircraft manufacturer or subject the item to a metallurgical laboratory analysis. Before any welding is attempted, carefully consider the weldability of the alloy since all alloys are not readily weldable. The following steels are readily weldable: plain carbon of the 1000 series, nickel steel of the SAE 2300 series, chrome-nickel alloys of the SAE 3100 series, chrome-molybdenum steels of the SAE 4100 series, and low nickel-chrome-molybdenum steel of the SAE 8600 series.

c. Preparation for Welding. Hold elements to be welded in a welding jig or fixture which is sufficiently rigid to prevent misalinement due to expansion and contraction of the heated material and which positively and accurately position the pieces to be welded.

d. Cleaning Prior to Welding. Clean parts to be welded with a wire brush or other suitable methods. When cleaning with a wire brush, do not use a brush of dissimilar metal; for example, brass or bronze on steel. The small deposit left by a brass or bronze brush will materially weaken the weld and may cause cracking or subsequent failure of the weld. In case members were metallized, the surface metal may be removed by careful sandblasting followed by a light buffing with emery cloth.

e. Condition of Complete Weld. Make sure that:

(1) The finished weld has a smooth seam and is uniform in thickness;

(2) The weld metal is tapered smoothly into the base metal;

(3) No oxide has formed on the base metal at a distance of more than 1/2 inch from the weld;

(4) The weld shows no signs of blowholes, porosity, or projecting globules;

(5) The base metal shows no signs of pitting, burning, cracking, or distortion;

(6) The depth of penetration insures fusion of base metal and filler rod; and

(7) Welding scale is removed by wire brushing or sandblasting.

f. Practices to Guard Against. Do not file welds in an effort to make a smooth-appearing job, as such treatment causes a loss of strength. Do not fill welds with solder, brazing metal, or any other filler. When it is necessary to reweld a joint which was previously welded, remove all old weld material before rewelding. Avoid welding over a weld because reheating may cause the material to lose its strength and become brittle. Never weld a joint which has been previously brazed.

g. Torch Size (Oxyacetylene Welding). The size of the torch tip depends upon the thickness of the material to be welded. Commonly used sizes proved satisfactory by experience are:

Thickness of steel (in inches)	Diameter of hole in tip	Drill size
0.015 to 0.031	0.026	71
0.031 to 0.065	.031	68
0.065 to 0.125	.037	63
0.125 to 0.188	.042	58
0.188 to 0.250	.055	54
0.250 to 0.375	.067	51

h. Welding Rods and Electrodes. Use welding rods and electrodes that are compatible with the materials to be welded. Welding rods and electrodes for various applications have special properties suitable for the application intended. Figure 2.3 shows the allowable strength for the weld metal. Figure 2.2 lists specifications for corresponding metals, and the applicable specification will identify the use of A.C. or D.C., straight or reverse polarity.

i. Rosette Welds. Rosette welds are generally employed to fuse an inner reinforcing tube (liner) with the outer member. Where a rosette weld is used, drill the hole, in the outside tube only, of a sufficient size to insure fusion of

FIGURE 2.2.—Specifications guide for welding metals.

Material To Be Welded	Electric Welding	Tungsten Inert Gas (TIG)	Metal Inert Gas (MIG)	Shield Carbon—ARC	Oxygen Acetylene
Medium & High Tensile Steel. Stress Relieved	MIL–E–22200/1 MIL–9018	MIL–E–23765/1B Class MIL–E–705–2	MIL–E–23765/1B Class MIL–E–705–4	NONE	MIL–R–908A Class 1
High Carbon Steel	MIL–E–7018 MIL–E–22200	MIL–E–23765/1B Class MIL–E–705–2	MIL–E–23765/1B Class MIL–E–705–6	MIL–R–CUS1–A	MIL–R–908A Class 1
Low and Medium Carbon Steel	MIL–E–15599–C [1]	MIL–E–23765/1B Class MIL–E–705–2	MIL–E–23765/1B Class MIL–E–705–6	MIL–R–CUS1–A	MIL–R–5632 Class 1
Aluminum and Aluminum Alloy	MIL–E–15997A	QQR–566 MIL–E–16053–K [2]	QQR–566 MIL–E–16053–K [2]	QQR–566 [2]	QQR–566 [2]
Stainless Alloys	MIL–E–6844 M–L–E–22200 [3]	MIL–R–5031B [3]	MIL–R–5031B [3]	MIL–R–5031B [3]	MIL–R–5031B [3]
Copper and Nickel Alloys	NONE	QQR–571A [4]	MIL–E–21659 [4]	QQR–571A [4]	QQR–571A [4]
Magnesium Alloys	NONE	MIL–R–6944 Specify Alloy	MIL–W–18326 Specify Alloy	NONE	MIL–R–6944 Specify Alloy
Hard Surface Filler	MIL–E–19141 (Refer to A.W.S A5.13 or ASTM–A399)	MIL–E–19141 (Refer to A.W.S A5.13 or ASTM–A399)	MIL–E–19141 (Refer to A.W.S. A5.13 or ASTM–A399)	MIL–E–19141 (Refer to A.W.S. A5.13 or ASTM–A399)	MIL–19141 (Refer to A.W.S. A5.13 or ASTM–A399)

[1] Specify MIL Type 6010, 6011, 6012, 6013, 6020, 6024, 6027—Same as A.W.S. Number for type.
[2] Specify Aluminum Alloy by Aluminum Assoc. Number e.g.: Type 1100, 5083, etc.
[3] Specify Alloy by A.I.S.I. Number e.g.: 304, 316, 342, etc.
[4] Specify type per A.W.S. A5.6–66 or ASTM B–225–66.

A.W.S.   American Welding Society
ASTM   American Society for Testing Materials
A.I.S.I.   American Iron and Steel Institute (SAE).

FIGURE 2.3.—Strengths of welded joints.

Material	Heat treatment subsequent to welding	Welding rod or electrode	Ultimate stress in shear × 1000	Ultimate tensile stress × 1000
Carbon and Alloy steels	None	MIL–R–5632, Class I MIL–E–15599, Classes E–6010 & E–6013	32 32	51 51
Alloy steels	None	MIL–R–5632, Class 2	43	72
Alloy steels	Stress relieved	MIL–E–6843, Class 10013 MIL–E–18038, Class E–10015 & E–10016	50	85
Alloy steels	Stress relieved	MIL–E–18038, Class E–12015 & E–12016	60	100

the inner tube. A hole diameter of approximately one-fourth the tube diameter of the outer tube serves adequately for this purpose. In cases of tight-fitting sleeves or inner liners, the rosettes may be omitted.

j. Heat-Treated Members. Certain structural parts may be heat-treated and therefore could require special handling. In general, the more responsive an alloy steel is to heat treatment, the less suitable it is for welding because of its tendency to become brittle and lose its ductility in the welded area. Weld the members which depend on heat treatment for their original physical properties, using a welding rod suitable for producing heat-treated values comparable to those of the original members (see paragraph 68h). After welding, reheat-treat such members to the manufacturer's specifications.

69. STEEL PARTS NOT TO BE WELDED.

a. Brace Wires and Cables. Do not weld airplane parts whose proper function depends upon strength properties developed by cold-working. Among parts in this classification are streamlined wires and cables.

b. Brazed and Soldered Parts. Do not weld brazed or soldered parts as the brazing mixture or solder will penetrate the hot steel and weaken it.

c. Alloy Steel Parts. Do not weld alloy steel parts such as aircraft bolts, turnbuckle ends, etc., which have been heat-treated to improve their mechanical properties.

70. REPAIR OF TUBULAR MEMBERS.

a. Inspection. Prior to repairing tubular members, carefully examine the structure surrounding any visible damage to insure that no secondary damage remains undetected. Secondary damage may be produced in some structure remote from the location of the primary damage by the transmission of the damaging load along the tube. Damage of this nature usually occurs where the most abrupt change in direction of load travel is experienced. If this damage remains undetected, subsequent normal loads may cause failure of the part.

b. Location and Alinement of Welds. Unless otherwise noted, welded steel tubing may be spliced or repaired at any joint along the length of the tube. Pay particular attention to the proper fit and alinement to avoid distortion.

c. Members Dented at a Cluster. Repair dents at a steel-tube cluster-joint by welding a specially formed steel patch plate over the dented area and surrounding tubes, as shown in figure 2.4. To prepare the patch plate, cut a section of steel sheet of the same material and thickness as the heaviest tube damaged. Trim the reinforcement plate so that the fingers extend over the tubes a minimum of 1.5 times the respective tube diameter as shown in the figure. Remove all the existing finish on the damaged cluster-joint area to be covered by the reinforcement plate. The reinforcement plate may be formed before any welding is attempted, or it may be cut and tack-welded to one or more of the tubes in the cluster-joint, then heated and

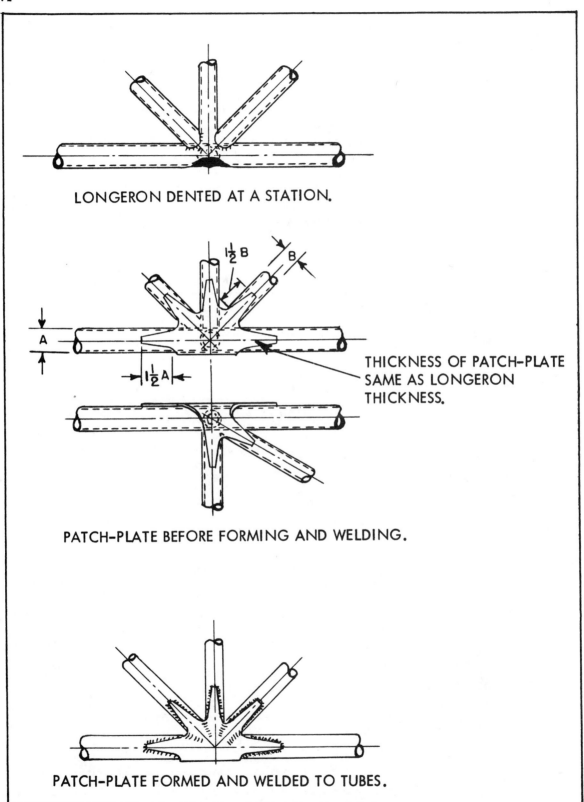

LONGERON DENTED AT A STATION.

$1\frac{1}{2}$ B

B

A

$1\frac{1}{2}$ A

THICKNESS OF PATCH-PLATE
SAME AS LONGERON
THICKNESS.

PATCH-PLATE BEFORE FORMING AND WELDING.

PATCH-PLATE FORMED AND WELDED TO TUBES.

FIGURE 2.4.—Members dented at a cluster.

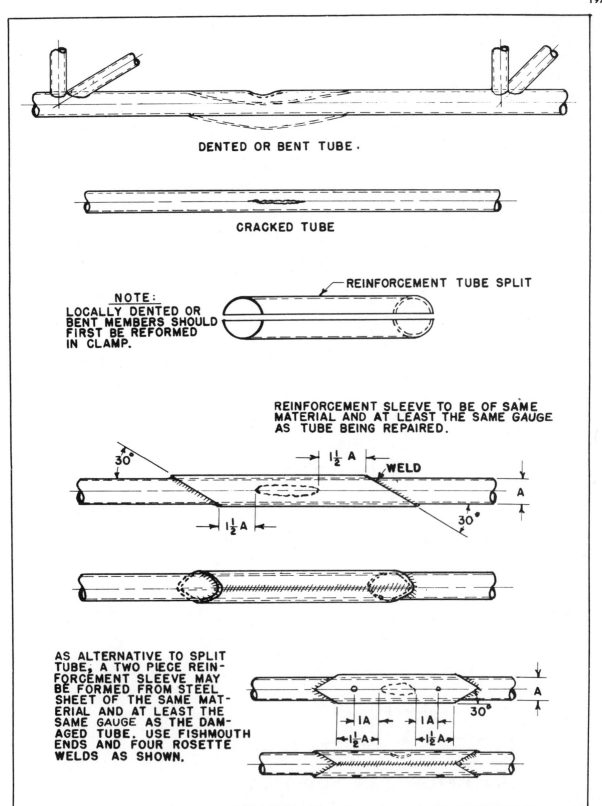

FIGURE 2.5.—Members dented in a bay—repairs by welded sleeve.

formed around the joint to produce a smooth contour. Apply sufficient heat to the plate while forming so that there is generally a gap of no more than 1/16 inch from the contour of the joint to the plate. In this operation avoid unnecessary heating, and exercise care to prevent damage at the point of the angle formed by any two adjacent fingers of the plate. After the plate is formed and tack-welded to the cluster-joint, weld all the plate edges to the cluster-joint.

d. *Members Dented in a Bay*. Repair dented, bent, cracked, or otherwise damaged tubular members by using a split-sleeve reinforcement; carefully straighten the damaged member; and in the case of cracks, drill No. 40 (0.098) stop-holes at the ends of the crack.

71. REPAIR BY WELDED SLEEVE. This repair is outlined in figure 2.5. Select a length of steel tube sleeve having an inside diameter approximately equal to the outside diameter of the damaged tube and of the same material, and at least the same wall thickness. Diagonally cut the sleeve reinforcement at a 30° angle on both ends so that the minimum distance of the sleeve from the edge of the crack or dent is not less than 1 1/2 times the diameter of the damaged tube. Cut through the entire length of the reinforcement sleeve, and separate the half-sections of the sleeve. Clamp the two sleeve sections to the proper positions on the affected areas of the original tube. Weld the reinforce-

ment sleeve along the length of the two sides, and weld both ends of the sleeve to the damaged tube as shown in the figure. The filling of dents or cracks with welding rod in lieu of reinforcing the member is not acceptable.

72. REPAIR BY BOLTED SLEEVE. Do not use bolted sleeve repairs on welded steel tube structure unless specifically authorized by the manufacturer or the FAA. The tube area removed by the boltholes in this types of repair may prove critical.

73. WELDED-PATCH REPAIR. Dents or holes in tubing may be repaired by a welded patch of the same material and one gauge thicker, as shown in figure 2.6 provided:

a. *Dented Tubing*.

(1) Dents are not deeper than 1/10 of tube diameter, do not involve more than 1/4 of the tube circumference, and are not longer than tube diameter.

(2) Dents are free from cracks, abrasions, and sharp corners.

(3) The dented tubing can be substantially reformed without cracking before application of the patch.

b. *Punctured Tubing*. Holes are not longer than tube diameter and involve not more than 1/4 of tube circumference.

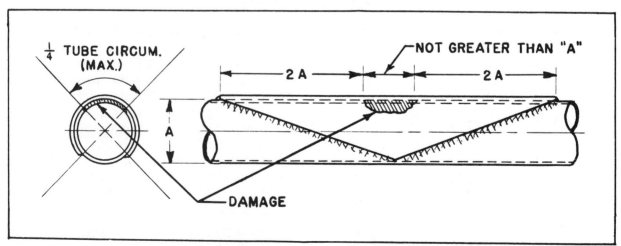

FIGURE 2.6.—Welded patch repair.

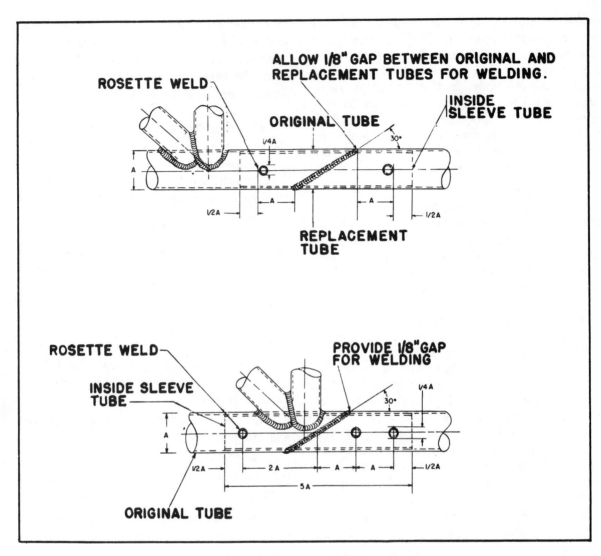

FIGURE 2.7.—Splicing by inner sleeve method.

74. SPLICING TUBING BY INNER SLEEVE METHOD. If the damage to a structural tube is such that a partial replacement of the tube is necessary, the inner sleeve splice shown in figure 2.7 is recommended, especially where a smooth tube surface is desired. Make a diagonal cut when removing the damaged portion of the tube and remove the burr from the edges of the cut by filing or similar means. Diagonally cut a replacement steel tube of the same material and diameter, and at least the same wall thickness, to match the length of the removed portion of the damaged tube. At each end of the replacement tube allow a 1/8-inch gap from the diago-

nal cuts to the stubs of the original tube. Select a length of steel tubing of the same material, and at least the same wall thickness, and of an outside diameter, equal to the inside diameter of the damaged tube. Fit this innersleeve tube material snugly within the original tube, with a maximum diameter difference of 1/16 inch. From this inner-sleeve tube material cut 2 sections of tubing, each of such a length that the ends of the inner sleeve will be a minimum distance of 1 1/2-tube diameters from the nearest end of the diagonal cut.

If the inner sleeve fits very tightly in the replacement tube, chill the sleeve with dry ice or

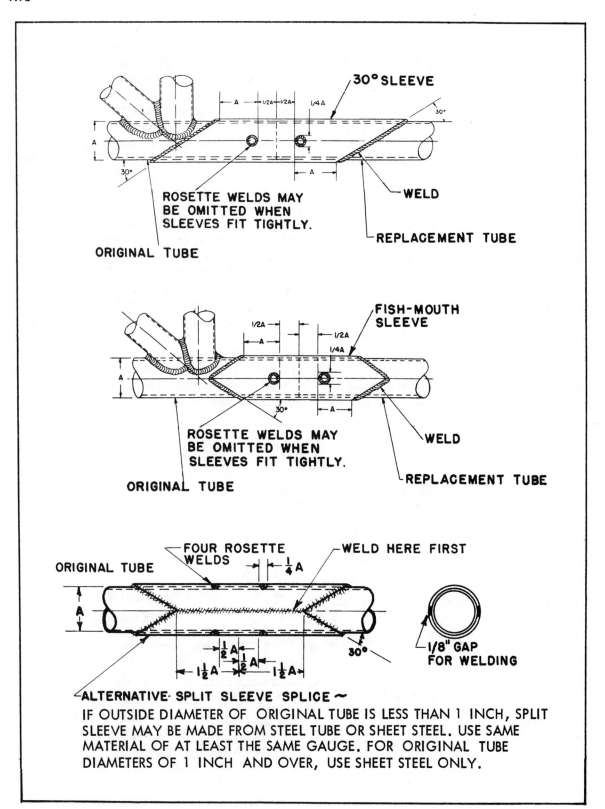

FIGURE 2.8.—Splicing by outer sleeve method—replacement by welded outside sleeve.

in cold water. If this is insufficient, polish down the diameter of the sleeve with emery cloth. Weld the inner sleeve to the tube stubs through the 1/8-inch gap, forming a weld bead over the gap.

75. SPLICING TUBING BY OUTER SLEEVE METHOD.

If partial replacement of a tube is necessary, make the outer sleeve splice using a replacement tube of the same diameter. Since the outer sleeve splice requires the greatest amount of welding, it should be used only when the other splicing methods are not suitable. Information on the replacement by use of the welded outside sleeve method is given in figures 2.8 and 2.9.

Remove the damaged section of a tube utilizing a 90° cut. Cut a replacement steel tube of the same material, diameter, and at least the same wall thickness to match the length of the removed portion of the damaged tube. This replacement tube must bear against the stubs of the original tube with a total tolerance not to exceed 1/32 inch. The outer sleeve tube material selected must be of the same material and at least the same wall thickness as the original tube. The clearance between inside diameter of the sleeve and the outside diameter of the original tube may not exceed 1/16 inch. From this outer sleeve tube material, cut diagonally (or fishmouth) 2 sections of tubing, each of such length that the nearest end of the outer sleeve is a minimum distance of 1 1/2-tube diameters from the end of the cut on the original tube. Use a fishmouth sleeve wherever possible. Remove the burr from the edges of the sleeves, replacement tube, and the original tube stubs. Slip the two sleeves over the replacement tube, aline the replacement tube with the original tube stubs, and slip the sleeves out over the center of each joint. Adjust the sleeves to suit the area and to provide maximum reinforcement. Tackweld the two sleeves to the replacement tube in two places before welding. Apply a uniform weld around both ends of one of the reinforcement sleeves and allow the weld to cool; then, weld around both ends of the re-

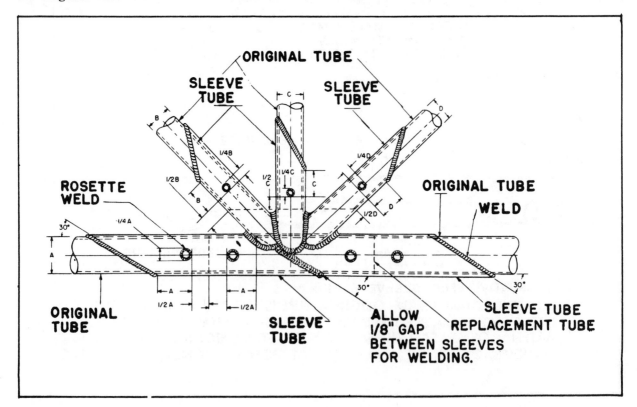

FIGURE 2.9.—Tube replacement at a station by welded outer sleeves.

maining reinforcement tube. Allow one sleeve weld to cool before welding the remaining tube to prevent undue warping.

76. SPLICING USING LARGER DIAMETER REPLACEMENT TUBES.

The method of splicing structural tubes, as shown in figure 2.10, requires the least amount of cutting and welding. However, this splicing method cannot be used where the damaged tube is cut too near the adjacent cluster-joints, or where bracket-mounting provisions make it necessary to maintain the same replacement tube diameter as the original. As an aid in installing the replacement tube, squarely cut the original damaged tube leaving a minimum short stub equal to 2 1/2-tube diameters on one end and a minimum long stub equal to 4 1/2-tube diameters on the other end. Select a length of steel tube of the same material and at least the same wall thickness, having an inside diameter approximately equal to the outside diameter of the damaged tube. Fit this replacement tube material snugly about the original tube with a maximum diameter difference of 1/16 inch. From this replacement tube material, cut a section of tubing diagonally (or fishmouth) of such a length that each end of the tube is a minimum distance of 1 1/2-tube diameters from the end of the cut on the original tube. Use a fishmouth cut replacement tube wherever possible. Remove the burr from the edges of the replacement tube and original tube stubs. If a fishmouth cut is used, file out the sharp radius of the cut with a small round file. Spring the long stub of the original tube from the normal position, slip the replacement tube over the long stub, then back over the short stub. Center the replacement tube between the stubs of the original tube. In several places tack-weld one end of the replacement tube, then weld completely around the end. In order to prevent distortion, allow the weld to cool completely, then weld the remaining end of the replacement tube to the original tube.

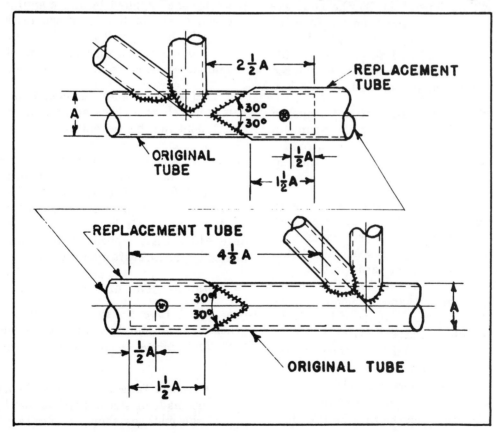

FIGURE 2.10.—Splicing using larger diameter replacement tube.

77. REPAIRS AT BUILT-IN FUSELAGE FITTINGS. Make splices in accordance with the methods described in paragraphs 70 through 75. Repair built-in fuselage fittings in the manner shown in figure 2.11. The following paragraphs outline the different methods as shown in the figure:

a. *Tube of Larger Diameter Than Original.* A tube (sleeve) of larger diameter than original is used in the method shown in figure 2.11(A). This necessitates reaming the fitting holes (at longeron) to a large diameter. The forward splice is to be a 30° scarf splice. Cut the rear longeron (right) approximately 4 inches from the centerline of the joint and a spacer 1 inch long fitted over the longeron. Edge-weld this spacer and longeron; make a tapered "V" cut approximately 2 inches long in the aft end of the outer sleeve and swage the end of the outer sleeve to fit the longeron and weld.

b. *Tube of Same Diameter as Original.* In the method shown in figure 2.11(B) the new section is the same size as the longeron forward (left) of the fitting. The rear end (right) of the tube is cut at 30° and forms the outside sleeve of the scarf splice. A sleeve is centered over the forward joint as indicated.

c. *Simple Sleeve.* It is assumed the longeron is the same size on each side of the fitting in this case, figure 2.11(C), and it is repaired by a simple sleeve of larger diameter than the longeron.

d. *Large Difference in Longeron Diameter Each Side of Fitting.* Figure 2.11(D) assumes that there is 1/4 inch difference in the diameter of the longeron on the two sides of the fitting. The section of longeron forward (left) of the fitting is cut at 30°, and a section of tubing of the same size as the tube and of such length as to extend well to the rear (right) of the fitting is slipped through it. One end is cut at 30° to fit the 30° scarf at left and the other end fishmouthed as shown. This makes it possible to insert a tube of such diameter as to form an inside sleeve for the tube on the left of the fitting and an outside sleeve for the tube on the right of the fitting.

78. ENGINE MOUNT REPAIRS. All welding on an engine mount should be of the highest quality, since vibration tends to accentuate any minor defect. Engine-mount members should preferably be repaired by using a larger diameter replacement tube telescoped over the stub of the original member and using fishmouth and rosette welds. However, 30° scarf welds in place of the fishmouth welds will be considered acceptable for engine-mount repair work.

a. *Check of Alignment.* Repaired engine mounts must be checked for accurate alignment. When tubes are used to replace bent or damaged ones, the original alignment of the structure must be maintained. This can be done by measuring the distance between points of corresponding members that have not been distorted, and by reference to the manufacturer's drawings.

b. *Cause for Rejection.* If all members are out of alinement, reject the engine mount and replace by one supplied by the manufacturer or one which was built to conform to the manufacturer's drawings. The method of checking the alignment of the fuselage or nacelle points should be requested from the manufacturer.

c. *Engine Mount Ring Damage.* Repair minor damage, such as a crack adjacent to an engine attachment lug, by rewelding the ring and extending a gusset or a mounting lug past the damaged area. Engine mount rings which are extensively damaged must not be repaired, unless the method of repair is specifically approved by an authorized representative of the FAA, or the repair is accomplished in accordance with FAA approved instructions furnished by the aircraft manufacturer.

79. LANDING GEAR REPAIR.

a. *Round Tube Construction.* Repair landing gears made of round tubing using standard repairs and splices as shown in figures 2.5 and 2.11.

b. *Streamline Tube Construction.* Repair landing gears made of streamlined tubing by either one of the methods shown in figures 2.12 and 2.15.

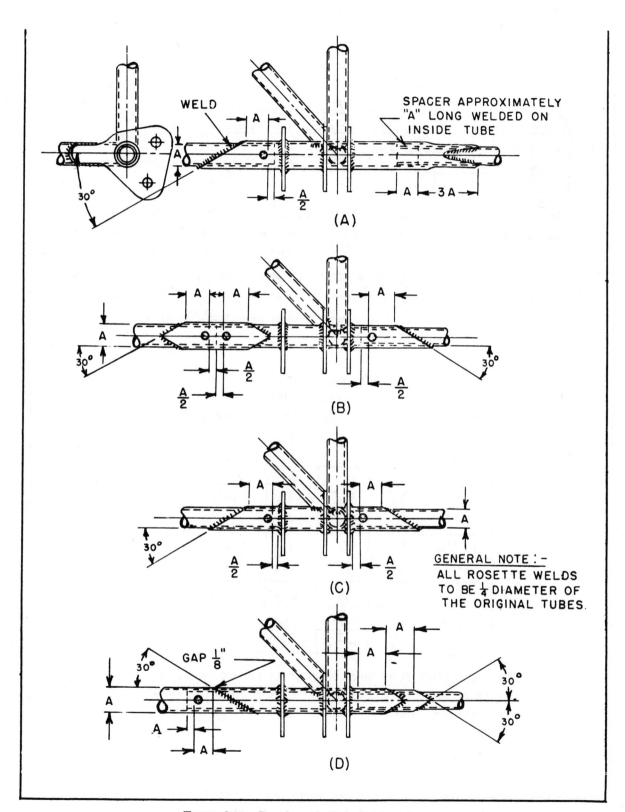

FIGURE 2.11.—Repairs at built-in fuselage fittings.

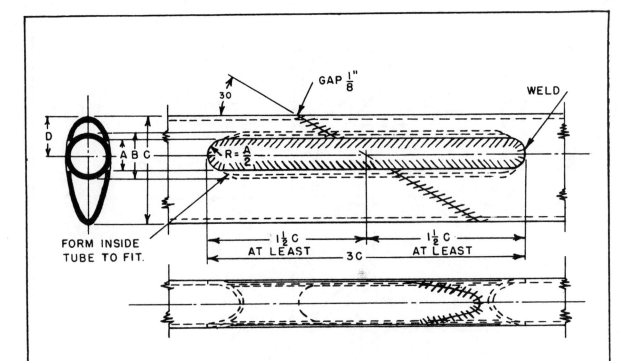

A – SLOT WIDTH (ORIGINAL TUBE)
B – OUTSIDE DIAMETER (INSERT TUBE)
C – STREAMLINE TUBE LENGTH OF MAJOR AXIS

S.L. SIZE	A	B	C	D
1"	3/8"	9/16"	1.340"	.496"
1-1/4	3/8	11/16	1.670	.619
1-1/2	1/2	7/8	2.005	.743
1-3/4	1/2	1	2.339	.867
2	1/2	1-1/8	2.670	.991
2-1/4	1/2	1-1/4	3.008	1.115
2-1/2	1/2	1-3/8	3.342	1.239

ROUND INSERT TUBE (B) SHOULD BE AT LEAST OF SAME
MATERIAL AND ONE GAUGE THICKER THAN ORIGINAL
STREAMLINE TUBE (C).

FIGURE 2.12.—Streamline tube splice using round tube (applicable to landing gears).

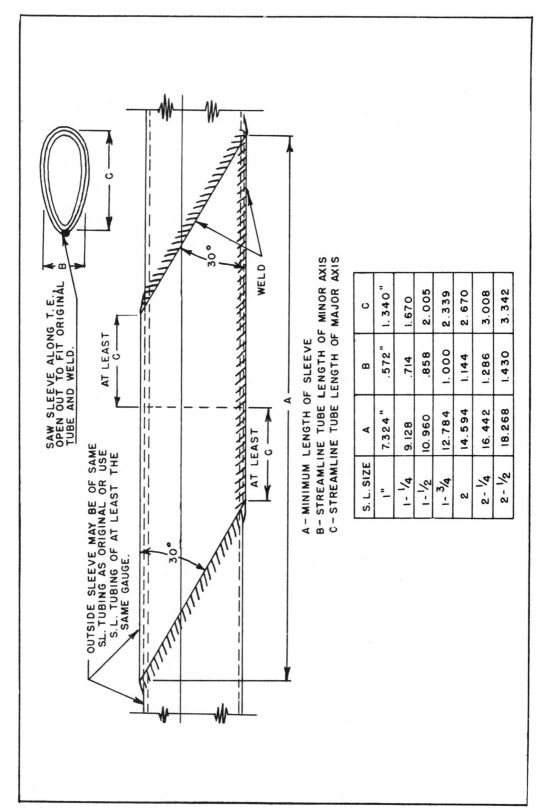

SAW SLEEVE ALONG T.E.
OPEN OUT TO FIT ORIGINAL
TUBE AND WELD.

OUTSIDE SLEEVE MAY BE OF SAME
SL. TUBING AS ORIGINAL OR USE
S.L. TUBING OF AT LEAST THE
SAME GAUGE.

A – MINIMUM LENGTH OF SLEEVE
B – STREAMLINE TUBE LENGTH OF MINOR AXIS
C – STREAMLINE TUBE LENGTH OF MAJOR AXIS

S. L. SIZE	A	B	C
1"	7.324"	.572"	1.340"
1-¼	9.128	.714	1.670
1-½	10.960	.858	2.005
1-¾	12.784	1.000	2.339
2	14.594	1.144	2.670
2-¼	16.442	1.286	3.008
2-½	18.268	1.430	3.342

FIGURE 2.13.—Streamline tube splice using split sleeve (applicable to wing and tail surface brace struts and other members).

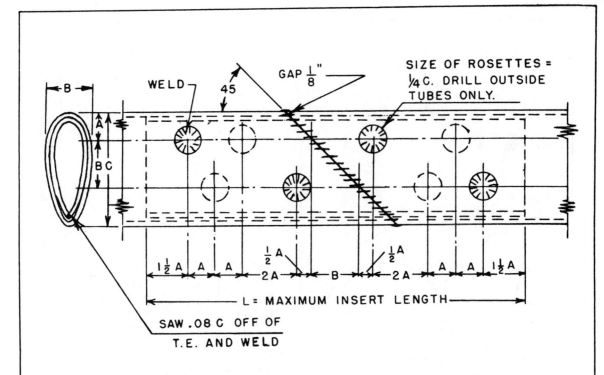

INSERT TUBE IS OF SAME STREAMLINE TUBING AS ORIGINAL.

A IS $\frac{2}{3}$ B

B IS MINOR AXIS LENGTH OF ORIGINAL STREAMLINE TUBE
C IS MAJOR AXIS LENGTH OF ORIGINAL STREAMLINE TUBE

S. L. SIZE	A	B	C	L
1"	.382	.572	1.340	5.16
1 1/4	.476	.714	1.670	6.43
1 1/2	.572	.858	2.005	7.72
1 3/4	.667	1.000	2.339	9.00
2	.763	1.144	2.670	10.30
2 1/4	.858	1.286	3.008	11.58
2 1/2	.954	1.430	3.342	12.88

FIGURE 2.14.—Streamline tube splice using split insert (applicable to landing gears).

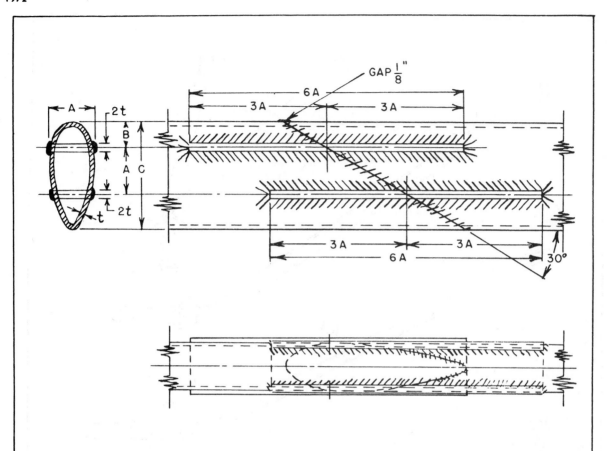

A- STREAMLINE TUBE LENGTH OF MINOR AXIS, PLATE WIDTHS.
B- DISTANCE OF FIRST PLATE FROM LEADING EDGE, $\frac{2}{3}$ A.
C- STREAMLINE TUBE LENGTH OF MAJOR AXIS.

S.L. SIZE	A	B	C	6 A
1"	.572	.382	1.340	3.43
1-$\frac{1}{4}$	.714	.476	1.670	4.28
1-$\frac{1}{2}$	.858	.572	2.005	5.15
1-$\frac{3}{4}$	1.000	.667	2.339	6.00
.2	1.144	.762	2.670	6.86
2-$\frac{1}{4}$	1.286	.858	3.008	7.72
2-$\frac{1}{2}$	1.430	.954	3.342	8.58

FIGURE 2.15.—Streamline tube splice using plates (applicable to landing gears).

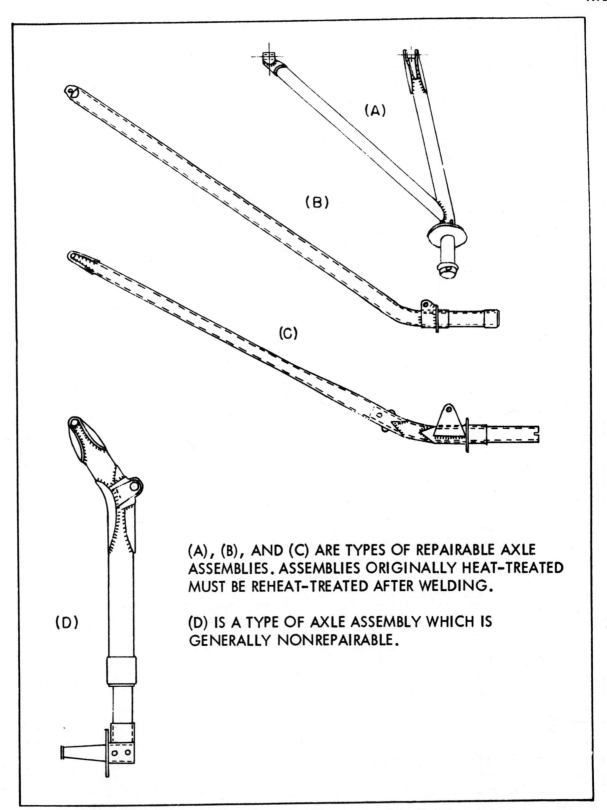

(A), (B), AND (C) ARE TYPES OF REPAIRABLE AXLE
ASSEMBLIES. ASSEMBLIES ORIGINALLY HEAT-TREATED
MUST BE REHEAT-TREATED AFTER WELDING.

(D) IS A TYPE OF AXLE ASSEMBLY WHICH IS
GENERALLY NONREPAIRABLE.

FIGURE 2.16.—Representative types of repairable and nonrepairable axle assemblies.

c. *Axle Assemblies.* Representative types of repairable and nonrepairable landing gear axle assemblies are shown in figure 2.16. The types as shown in A, B, and C of this figure are formed from steel tubing and may be repaired by the applicable method shown in figures 2.5 thru 2.15 in this Advisory Circular. However, it will always be necessary to ascertain whether or not the members are heat treated.

The axle assembly as shown in figure 2.16(D) is, in general, of a nonrepairable type for the following reasons:

(1) The axle stub is usually made from a highly heat-treated nickel alloy steel and carefully machined to close tolerances. These stubs are usually replaceable and should be replaced if damaged.

(2) The oleo portion of the structure is generally heat-treated after welding and is perfectly machined to assure proper functioning of the shock absorber. These parts would be distorted by welding after machining.

80. BUILT-UP TUBULAR WING OR TAIL SURFACE SPARS.
Repair built-up tubular wing or tail surface spars by using any of the applicable splices and methods of repair shown in figures 2.5 through 2.15 provided the spars are not heat-treated. In the case of heat-treated spars, the entire spar assembly would have to be re-heat-treated to the manufacturer's specifications after completion of the repair. In general, this will be found less practicable than replacing the spar with one furnished by the manufacturer.

81. WING AND TAIL BRACE STRUTS.
In general, it will be found advantageous to replace damaged wing-brace struts made either from rounded or streamlined tubing with new members purchased from the original manufacturer. However, there is no objection from an airworthiness point of view to repairing such members in a proper manner. An acceptable method, in case streamlined tubing is used, will be found in figure 2.13. Repair similar members made of round tubes using a standard splice, as shown in figures 2.5, 2.7, or 2.8.

a. *Location of Splices.* Steel brace struts may be spliced at any point along the length of the strut, provided the splice does not overlap part of an end fitting. The jury strut attachment is not considered an end fitting; therefore, a splice may be made at this point. The repair procedure and workmanship should be such as to minimize distortion due to welding and the necessity for subsequent straightening operations. Observe every repaired strut carefully during initial flights to ascertain that the vibration characteristics of the strut and attaching components are not adversely affected by the repair. A wide range of speed and engine-power combination must be covered during this check.

(1) *Fit and Alignment.* When making repairs to wing and tail surface brace members, pay particular attention to proper fit and alinement to avoid distortion.

82. REPAIRS TO WELDED PARTS.
Repairs to welded assemblies may be made by:

a. *Replacing welded joints*—cutting out the welded joint and replacing it with one properly gusseted, or

b. *Replacing weld deposit*—chipping out the metal deposited by the weld process and rewelding after properly reinforcing the joint by means of inserts or external gussets.

83. STAINLESS STEEL STRUCTURE.
Repair structural components made from stainless steel, particularly the "18–8" variety (18 percent chromium, 8 percent nickel), joined by spot welding in accordance with the instructions furnished by the manufacturer. Substitution of bolted or riveted connections for spot-welded joints are to be specifically approved by an authorized representative of the FAA.

a. *Secondary Structural and Nonstructural Elements.* Repair such elements as tip-bows or leading and trailing edge tip-strips of wing-and-control surfaces by soldering with a 50–50 lead-tin solder or a 60–40 alloy of these metals. For best results use a flux of phosphoric acid (syrup). Since the purpose of flux is to attack the metal so that the soldering will be effective, remove excess flux by washing the joint. Due to the high-heat conductivity of the stainless steel, use a soldering iron large enough to do the work properly. Repair leaky spot-welded seams in boat hulls, fuel tanks, etc., in a similar manner.

84.–94. RESERVED.

Section 3. METAL REPAIR PROCEDURES

95. RIVETED OR BOLTED STEEL TRUSS-TYPE STRUC-TURES. Repairs to riveted or bolted steel truss-type structures should be made, employing the general principles outlined in the following paragraphs on aluminum alloy structures. Methods for repair of vital members should be specifically approved by a representative of the Federal Aviation Administration.

96. ALUMINUM ALLOY STRUCTURES. Extensive repairs to damaged stressed skin on monocoque types of aluminum alloy structures should preferably be made in accordance with specific recommendations of the manufacturer of the aircraft. In many cases, repair parts, joints, or reinforcements can be designed, and proof of adequate strength shown, without the calculation of the design loads and stresses, by properly considering the material and dimensions of the original parts and the riveted attachments. Examples illustrating the principles of this method as applied to typical repairs are given in this handbook, or may be found in textbooks on metal structures. An important point to bear in mind in making repairs on monocoque structures is that a repaired part must be as strong as the original with respect to all types of loads and general rigidity.

a. Use of Annealed Alloys for Structural Parts. The use of annealed 2017 or 2024 for any structural repair of an aircraft is not considered satisfactory because of its poor corrosion-resisting properties.

b. Hygroscopic Materials Improperly Moisture-Proofed. The use of hygroscopic materials improperly moisture-proofed, such as impregnated fabrics, or leather, and the like, to effect water-tight joints and seams is not an acceptable practice.

c. Drilling Oversized Holes. Avoid drilling oversized holes or otherwise decreasing the ef-fective tensile areas of wing-spar capstrips, wing, fuselage, or fin longitudinal stringers, or other highly stressed tensile members. Make all repairs or reinforcements to such members in accordance with factory recommendations or with the specific approval or a representative of the Federal Aviation Administration.

d. Disassembly Prior to Repairing. If the parts to be removed are essential to the rigidity of the complete structure, support the remaining structure prior to disassembly in such a manner as to prevent distortion and permanent damage to the remainder of the structure. When rivets are to be removed, weaken the rivet head by drilling. Use a drill of the same size as the rivet. Drilling must be exact center and to the base of the head only. After drilling, break off the head with a pin punch and carefully drive out the shank. Removal of rivet heads with a cold chisel and hammer is not recommended because skin damage and distorted rivet holes will probably result. Care must also be taken whenever screws must be removed for disassembly or removal of stress plates, access plates, fillets, etc., to avoid damage to adjoining structure. When properly used, impact wrenches can be effective tools for removal of screws; however, damage to adjoining structure may result from excessive vertical loads being applied through the screw axis. Excessive loads are usually related to improperly adjusted impact tools or attempting to remove screws that have seized from corrosion. Remove seized screw by drilling and use of a screw extractor. Structural cracks may appear in the doubler or tang that runs parallel to the line of anchor or plate nuts installed for securing access doors or plates. Inspect rivet joints adjacent to damaged structure for partial failure (slippage) by removing one or more rivets to see if holes are elongated or the rivets have started to shear.

97. SELECTION OF ALUMINUM FOR REPLACEMENT PARTS. In selecting the alloy, it is usually satisfactory to use 2024 in place of 2017 since the former is stronger. Hence, it will not be permissible to replace 2024 by 2017 unless the deficiency in strength of the latter material is compensated by an increase in material thickness, or the structural strength is substantiated by tests or analysis. Information on the comparative strength properties of these alloys, as well as 2014, 6061, 7075, etc., is contained in MIL–HDBK–5, *Metallic Materials and Elements for Flight Vehicle Structure*. The choice of temper depends upon the severity of the subsequent forming operations. Parts having single curvature and straight bend lines with a large bend radius may be advantageously formed from heat-treated material, while a part, such as a fuselage frame, would have to be formed from soft, annealed sheet, and heat-treated after forming. Make sure sheet metal parts which are to be left unpainted are made of clad (aluminum coated) material. Make sure all sheet material and finished parts are free from cracks, scratches, kinks, tool marks, corrosion pits, and other defects which may be factors in subsequent failure.

a. Forming Sheet Metal Parts. Bend lines should preferably be made to lie at an angle to the grain of the metal (preferably 90°). Before bending, smooth all rough edges, remove burrs, and drill relief holes at the ends of bend lines and at corners, to prevent cracks from starting. For material in the heat-treated condition, the bend radius should be large. (See figure 2.17 for recommended bend radii.)

FIGURE 2.17.—Recommended radii for 90° bends in aluminum alloys.

Alloy and temper	Approximate sheet thickness (t) (inch)					
	0.016	0.032	0.064	0.128	0.182	0.258
2024–0 [1]	0	0–1t	0–1t	0–1t	0–1t	0–1t
2024–T3 [1][2]	1½t–3t	2t–4t	3t–5t	4t–6t	4t–6t	5t–7t
2024–T6 [1]	2t–4t	3t–5t	3t–5t	4t–6t	5t–7t	6t–10t
5052–0	0	0	0–1t	0–1t	0–1t	0–1t
5052–H32	0	0	½t–1t	½t–1½t	½t–1½t	½t–1½t
5052–H34	0	0	½t–1½t	1½t–2½t	1½t–2½t	2t–3t
5052–H36	0–1t	½t–1½t	1t–2t	1½t–3t	2t–4t	2t–4t
5052–H38	½t–1½t	1t–2t	1½t–3t	2t–4t	3t–5t	4t–6t
6061–0	0	0–1t	0–1t	0–1t	0–1t	0–1t
6061–T4	0–1t	0–1t	½t–1½t	1t–2t	1½t–3t	2½t–4t
6061–T6	0–1t	½t–1½t	1t–2t	1½t–3t	2t–4t	3t–4t
7075–0	0	0–1t	0–1t	½t–1½t	1t–2t	1½t–3t
7075–T6 [1]	2t–4t	3t–5t	4t–6t	5t–7t	5t–7t	6t–10t

[1] Alclad sheet may be bent over slight smaller radii than the corresponding tempers of uncoated alloy.
[2] Immediately after quenching, this alloy may be formed over appreciably smaller radii.

98. HEAT TREATMENT OF ALUMINUM ALLOY PARTS. All structural aluminum alloy parts are to be heat-treated in accordance with the heat-treatment instructions issued by the manufacturers of the materials. If the heat-treatment produces warping, straighten the parts immediately after quenching. Heat-treat riveted parts before riveting, to preclude warping and corrosion. When riveted assemblies are heated in a salt bath, the salt cannot be entirely washed out of the crevices, thus causing corrosion.

a. Quenching in Hot Water or Air. Quench material from the solution heat-treating temperature as rapidly as possible, with a minimum delay after removal from the furnace. Quenching in cold water is preferred, although less drastic chilling (hot or boiling water, air blast) is sometimes employed for bulk sections, such as forgings, to minimize quenching stresses.

b. Transferring Too Slowly From Heat-Treatment Medium to Quench Tank. Transfer of 2017 alloys from the heat-treatment medium to the quenchtank should be accomplished as quickly as possible. An elapsed time of 10 to 15 seconds will, in many cases, result in noticeably impaired corrosion resistance.

c. Reheating at Temperatures Above Boiling Water. Reheating of 2017 and 2024 alloys at temperatures above that of boiling water after heat treatment, and the baking of primers at temperatures above that of boiling water, will not be considered acceptable without subsequent complete and correct heat treatment, as such practice tends to impair the original heat treatment.

99. RIVETING.

a. Identification of Rivet Material. Identification of rivet material is contained in Chapter 5.

b. Replacement of Aluminum Alloy Rivets. All protruding head rivets (roundhead, flathead, and brazier head) may be replaced by rivets of the same type or by AN–470 Universal head rivets. Use flushhead rivets to replace flushhead rivets.

c. Replacement Rivet Size and Strength. Replace rivets with those of the same size and strength whenever possible. If the rivet hole becomes enlarged, deformed, or otherwise damaged, drill or ream the hole for the next large size rivet; however, make sure that the edge distance and spacings are not less than minimums listed in the next paragraph. Rivets may not be replaced by a type having lower strength properties, unless the lower strength is adequately compensated by an increase in size or a greater number of rivets.

d. Replacement Rivet-Edge Distances and Spacings for Sheet Joints. Rivet-edge distance is defined as the distance from the center of the rivet hole to the nearest edge of the sheet. Rivet spacing is the distance from the center of the rivet hole to the center of the adjacent rivet hole. The following prescribes the minimum edge distance and spacing:

(1) **Single row**—edge distance not less than 2 times the diameter of the rivet and spacing not less than 3 times the diameter of the rivet.

(2) **Double row**—edge distance and spacing not less than the minimums shown in figure 2.18.

(3) **Triple or multiple rows**—edge distance and spacing not less than the minimums shown in figure 2.18.

e. Use of 2117–T3 Aluminum Alloy Replacement Rivets. It is acceptable to replace 2017–T3 rivets of 3/16-inch diameter or less, and 2024–T4 rivets of 5/32-inch diameter or less with 2117–T3 rivets for general repairs, provided the replacement rivets are 1/32 inch greater in diameter than the rivets they replace and the edge distances and spacing are not less than the minimums listed in the preceding paragraph.

f. Driving of Rivets. The 2117 rivets may be driven in the condition received, but 2017 rivets above 3/16 inch in diameter and all 2024 rivets are to be kept either refrigerated in the "quenched" condition until driven, or be reheat-treated just prior to driving, as they would otherwise be too hard for satisfactory riveting. Dimensions for formed flat rivet heads are shown in figure 2.19, together with commonly found rivet imperfections.

g. Blind-Type and Hollow Rivets. Do not substitute hollow rivets for solid rivets in load-carrying members without specific approval of the application by a representative of the Federal Aviation Administration.

Blind rivets may be used in blind locations in accordance with the conditions listed in Chapter 5, provided the edge distances and spacings are not less than the minimum listed in paragraph 99d.

h. New and Revised Rivet Patterns. Design a new or revised rivet pattern for the strength required in accordance with the specific instructions in paragraphs 100e and 100j.

A general rule for the diameter of rivets used to join dural sheets is to use a diameter ap-

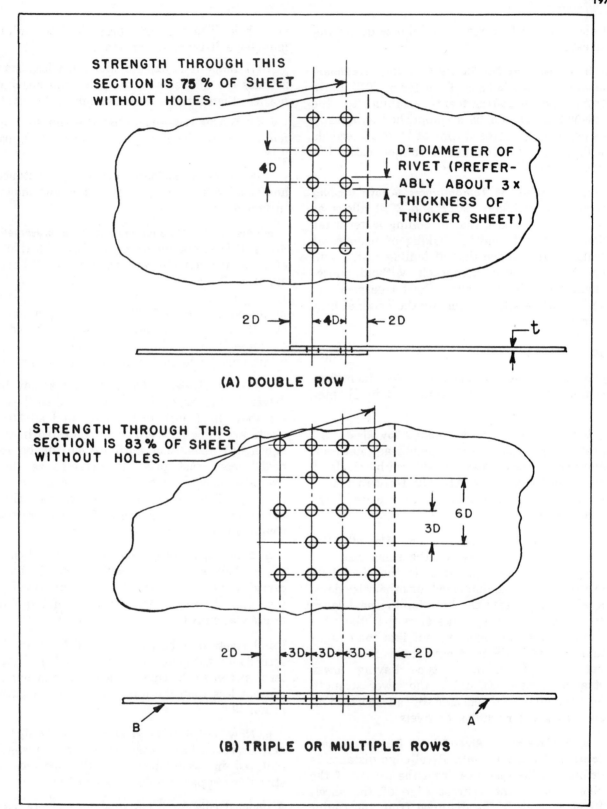

FIGURE 2.18.—Rivet hole spacing and edge distance for single-lap sheet splices.

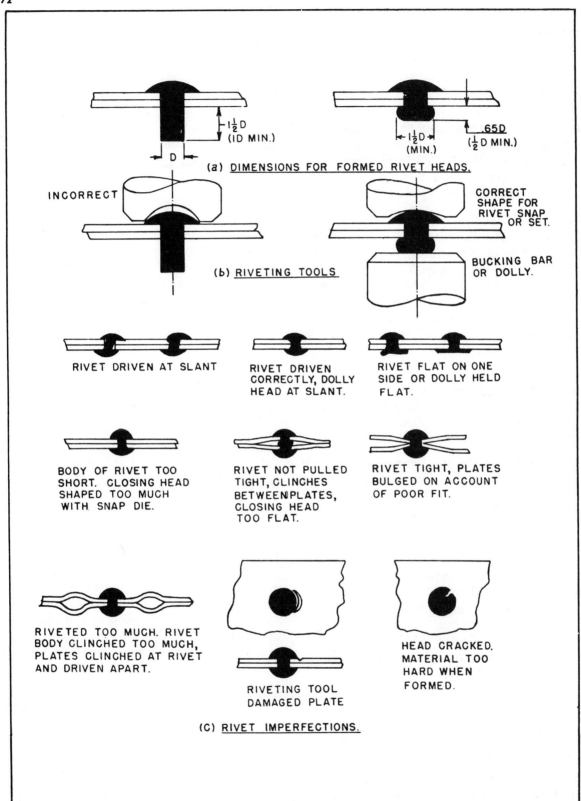

FIGURE 2.19.—Riveting practice and rivet imperfections.

proximately 3 times the thickness of the thicker sheet. Do not use rivets where they would be placed in tension tending to pull the heads off. Back up a lap joint of thin sheets by a stiffening section.

100. REPAIR METHODS AND PRECAUTIONS FOR ALUMINUM STRUCTURE. Carefully examine all adjacent rivets after the repair or alteration is finished to ascertain that they have not been harmed by operations in adjacent areas.

Drill rivet holes round, straight, and free from cracks. The rivet-set used in driving the rivets must be cupped slightly flatter than the rivethead as shown in figure 2.19. Rivets are to be driven straight and tight, but not over-driven or driven while too hard, since the finished rivet must be free from cracks. Information on special methods of riveting, such as flush riveting, usually may be obtained from manufacturer's service manuals.

a. Splicing of Tubes. Round or streamline tubular members may be repaired by splicing as shown in figure 2.20. Splices in struts that overlap fittings are not acceptable.

When solid rivets go completely through hollow tubes, their diameter must be at least one-eighth of the outside diameter of the outer tube. Rivets which are loaded in shear should be hammered only enough to form a small head, and no attempt made to form the standard roundhead. The amount of hammering required to form the standard roundhead often causes the rivet to buckle inside the tube. Satisfactory rivetheads may be produced in such installations by spinning, if the proper equipment is available. (Correct and incorrect examples of this type of rivet applications are incorporated in figure 2.20.)

b. Repairs to Aluminum Alloy Members. Make repairs to aluminum alloy members with the same material or with suitable material of higher strength. The 7075 alloy has greater tensile strength than other commonly used aluminum alloys such as 2014 and 2024, but is subject to somewhat greater notch sensitivity. In order to take advantage of its strength characteristics, pay particular attention to de-

sign of parts to avoid notches, small radii, large or rapid changes in cross sectional areas. In fabrication, exercise caution to avoid processing and handling defects, such as machine marks, nicks, dents, burrs, scratches, and forming cracks. Cold straightening or forming of 7075–T6 can cause cracking; hence, it may be advisable to limit this processing to minor cold straightening.

c. Wing and Tail Surface Ribs. Damaged aluminum alloy ribs either of the stamped sheetmetal type or the built-up type employing special sections, square or round tubing, may be repaired by the addition of suitable reinforcement. (Acceptable methods of repair are shown in figures 2.21 and 2.22.) These examples deal with types of ribs commonly found in small and medium aircraft. Repair schemes developed by the aircraft manufacturer are acceptable, and any other methods of reinforcement will be specifically approved by a representative of the FAA.

(1) Trailing and Leading Edges and Tip Strips. Repairs to wing and control surface trailing and leading edges and tip strips should be made by properly executed and reinforced splices. Acceptable methods of trailing edge repairs are shown in figure 2.23.

d. Repair of Damaged Skin. In case metal skin is damaged extensively, make repairs replacing an entire sheet panel from one structural member to the next. The repair seams are to lie along stiffening members, bulkheads, etc., and each seam must be made exactly the same in regard to rivet size, splicing, and rivet pattern as the manufactured seams at the edges of the original sheet. If the two manufactured seams are different, the stronger one will be copied. (See figure 2.24 for typical acceptable methods of repairs.)

(1) Patching of Small Holes. Small holes in skin panels which do not involve damage to the stiffening members may be patched by covering the hole with a patch plate in the manner shown in figure 2.24.

Flush patches also may be installed in stressed skin-type construction. An acceptable and easy flush patch may be made by trimming

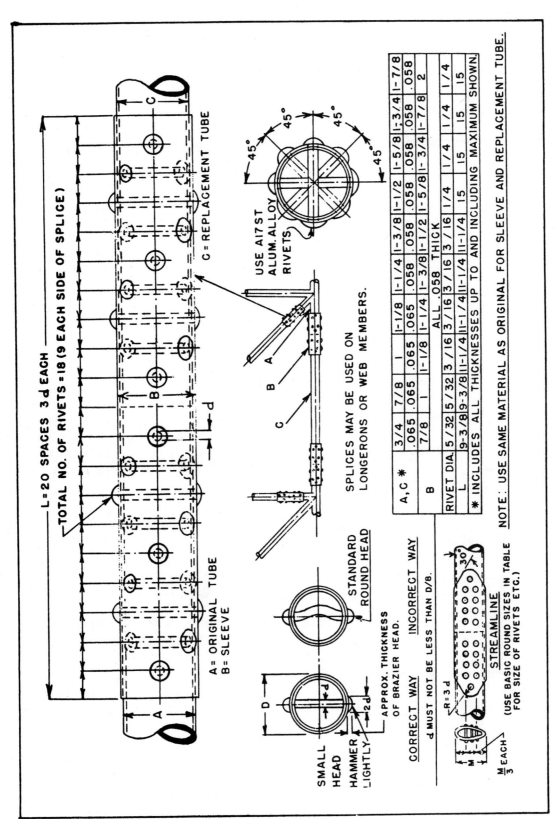

FIGURE 2.20.—Typical repair method for tubular members of aluminum alloy.

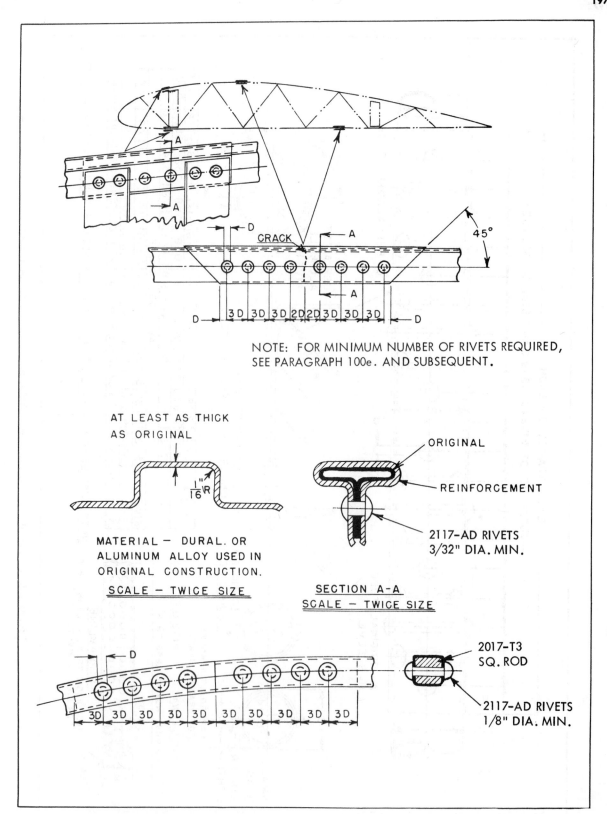

NOTE: FOR MINIMUM NUMBER OF RIVETS REQUIRED,
SEE PARAGRAPH 100e. AND SUBSEQUENT.

AT LEAST AS THICK
AS ORIGINAL

$\frac{1}{16}$"R

MATERIAL – DURAL. OR
ALUMINUM ALLOY USED IN
ORIGINAL CONSTRUCTION.

SCALE – TWICE SIZE

ORIGINAL

REINFORCEMENT

2117–AD RIVETS
3/32" DIA. MIN.

SECTION A-A
SCALE – TWICE SIZE

2017–T3
SQ. ROD

2117–AD RIVETS
1/8" DIA. MIN.

FIGURE 2.21.—Typical repair for buckled or cracked formed metal wing rib capstrips.

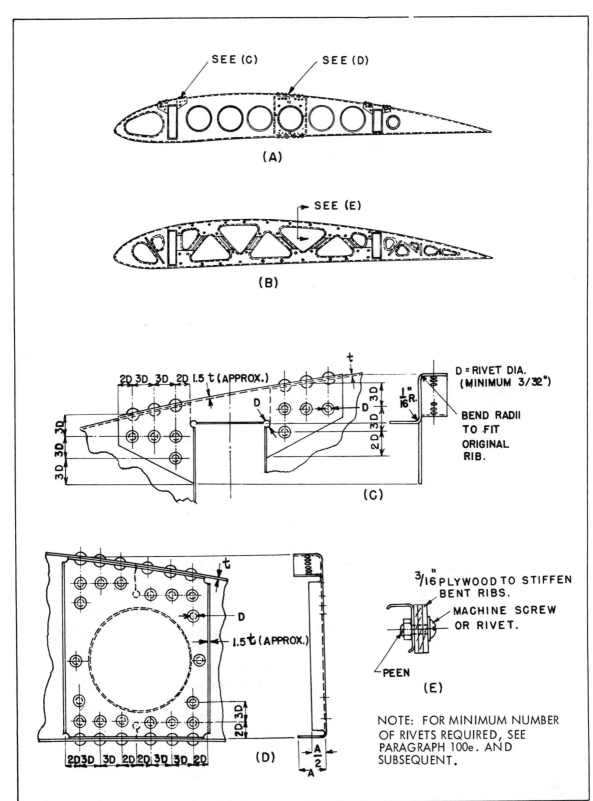

FIGURE 2.22.—Typical metal rib repairs (usually found on small and medium-size aircraft).

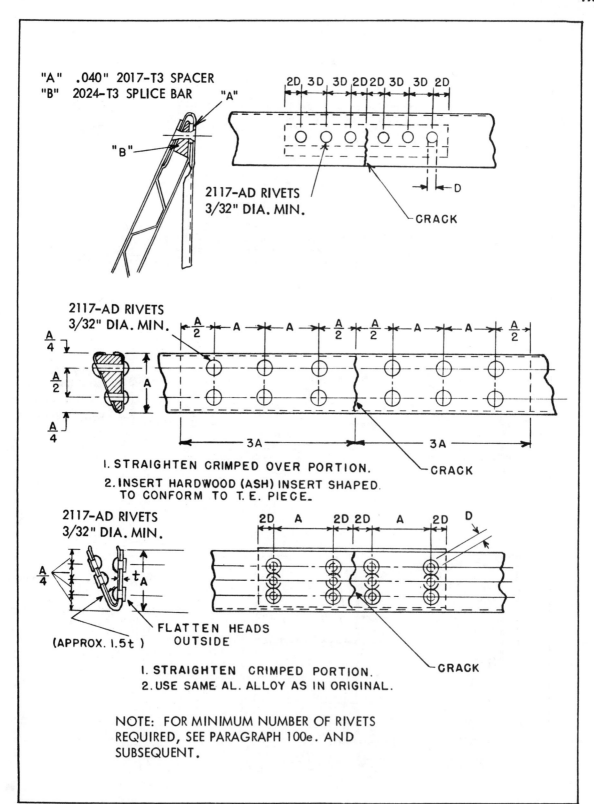

FIGURE 2.23.—Typical repairs of trailing edges.

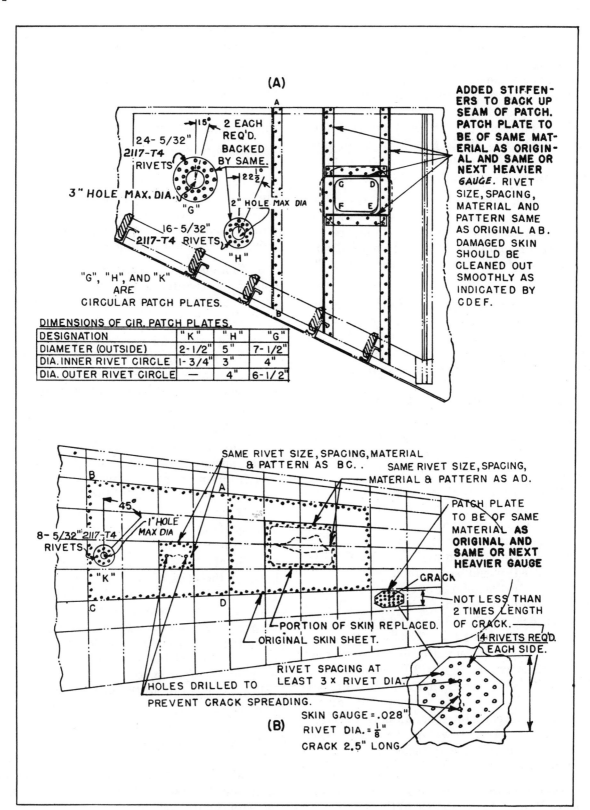

FIGURE 2.24—Typical repairs of stressed sheet metal covering.

out the damaged area and then installing a conventional patch on the underneath side or back of the sheet being repaired. A plug patch plate of the same size as the opening may then be inserted and riveted to the patch plate. Other types of flush patches similar to those used for patching plywood may be used (ref. Chapter 1). The riveting pattern used, however, must follow standard practice to maintain satisfactory strength in the sheet.

In general, patches in metal skin are not restricted as to size or shape; however, those of rectangular, circular, square, oval, and rectangular with round ends usually are more desirable because of appearance and ease of installation.

e. **Splicing of Sheets.** The method of copying the seams at the edges of a sheet may not always be satisfactory; for example, when the sheet has cutouts, or doubler-plates at an edge-seam, or when other members transmit loads into the sheet, the splice must be designed as illustrated in the following examples:

(1) Material: Clad 2024 sheet, 0.032-inch thickness. Width of sheet (i.e., length at splice) = "W" = 10 inches.

(2) Determine rivet size and pattern for a single-lap joint similar to figure 2.18.

(a) Use rivet diameter of approximately three times the sheet thickness, $3 \times 0.032 = 0.096$-inch. Use 1/8-inch 2117 AD rivets (5/32-inch 2117–AD would be satisfactory).

(b) Use the number of rivets required per inch of width "W" from figure 2.29. (Number per inch $4.9 \times .75 = 3.7$ or the total number of rivets required = 10×3.7 or 37 rivets.)

(c) Lay out rivet pattern with spacing not less than shown in figure 2.18. Referring to figure 2.18(A), it seems that a double row pattern with the minimum spacing will give a total of 40 rivets. However, as only 37 rivets are required, two rows of 19 rivets each equally spaced over the 10 inches will result in a satisfactory splice.

f. **Straightening of Stringers or Intermediate Frames.** Members which are slightly bent may be straightened cold and examined with a mag-

nifying glass for injury to the material. Reinforce the straightened parts to an extent, depending upon the condition of the material and the magnitude of any remaining kinks or buckles. If any strain cracks are apparent, make complete reinforcement in sound metal beyond the damaged portion.

(1) **Local Heating.** Do not apply local heating to facilitate bending, swaging, flattening, or expanding operations of heat-treated aluminum alloy members, as it is difficult to control the temperatures closely enough to prevent possible damage to the metal, and it may impair its corrosion resistance.

g. **Splicing of Stringers and Flanges.** Make splices in accordance with the manufacturer's recommendations, which are usually contained in a repair manual.

Typical splices for various shapes of sections are shown in figures 2.25 and 2.26. Design splices to carry both tension and compression, and use the splice shown in figure 2.26 as an example illustrating the following principles:

(1) **Statement of Principles:**

(a) To avoid eccentric loading and consequent buckling in compression, place splicing or reinforcing parts as symmetrically as possible about the centerline of the member, and attach to as many elements as necessary to prevent bending in any direction;

(b) To avoid reducing the strength in tension of the original bulb angle the rivet holes at the ends of the splice are made small (no larger than the original skin attaching rivets), and the second row of holes (those through the bulbed leg) are staggered back from the ends. In general arrange the rivets in the splice so that the design tensile load for the member and spliceplate can be carried into the splice without failing the member at the outermost rivet holes;

(c) To avoid concentration of load on the end rivet and consequent tendency toward progressive rivet failure, the splice is tapered at the ends, in this case, by tapering the backing angle and by making it shorter than the splice bar (ref. figure 2.26) ; and

(d) The preceding principles are espe-

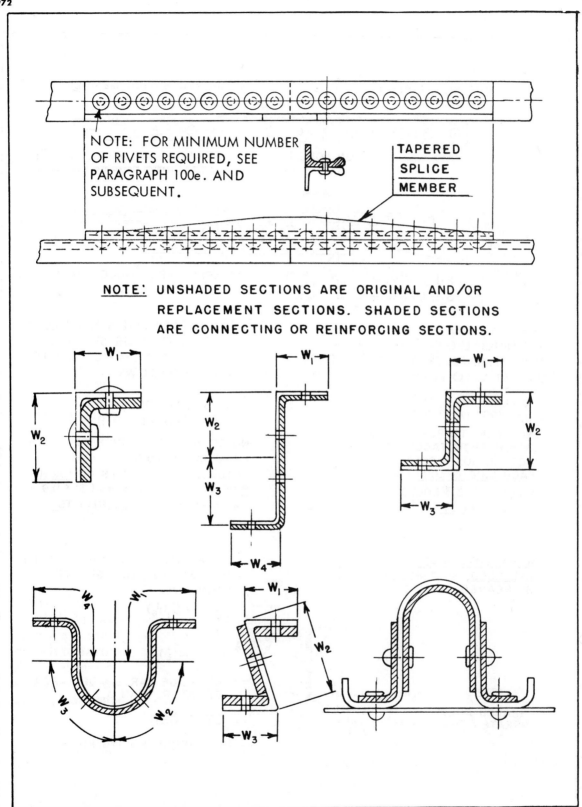

NOTE: FOR MINIMUM NUMBER OF RIVETS REQUIRED, SEE PARAGRAPH 100e. AND SUBSEQUENT.

TAPERED
SPLICE
MEMBER

NOTE: UNSHADED SECTIONS ARE ORIGINAL AND/OR REPLACEMENT SECTIONS. SHADED SECTIONS ARE CONNECTING OR REINFORCING SECTIONS.

FIGURE 2.25.—Typical stringer and flange splices.

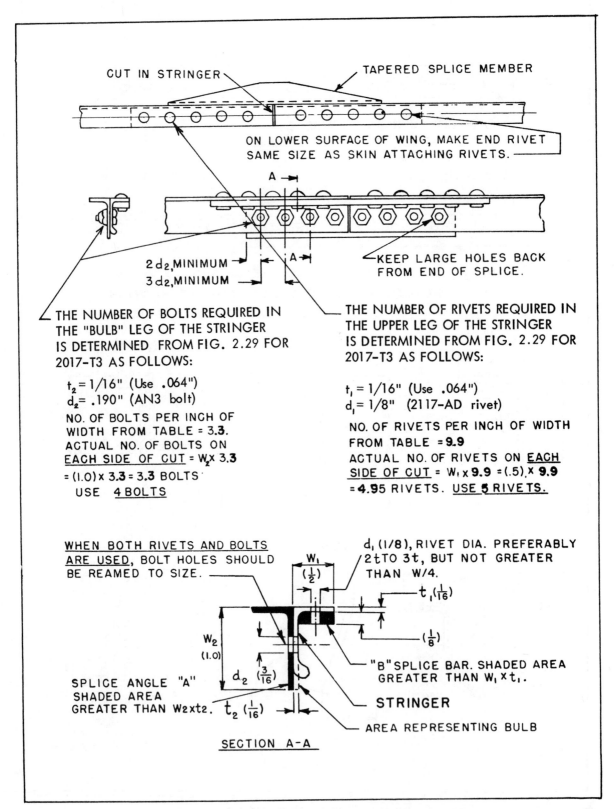

CUT IN STRINGER

TAPERED SPLICE MEMBER

ON LOWER SURFACE OF WING, MAKE END RIVET
SAME SIZE AS SKIN ATTACHING RIVETS.

A →

← A

$2d_2$, MINIMUM →

$3d_2$, MINIMUM →

KEEP LARGE HOLES BACK
FROM END OF SPLICE.

THE NUMBER OF BOLTS REQUIRED IN
THE "BULB" LEG OF THE STRINGER
IS DETERMINED FROM FIG. 2.29 FOR
2017–T3 AS FOLLOWS:

t_2 = 1/16" (Use .064")
d_2 = .190" (AN3 bolt)

NO. OF BOLTS PER INCH OF
WIDTH FROM TABLE = 3.3.
ACTUAL NO. OF BOLTS ON
<u>EACH SIDE OF CUT</u> = W_2 x 3.3

= (1.0) x 3.3 = 3.3 BOLTS
    USE 4 BOLTS

THE NUMBER OF RIVETS REQUIRED IN
THE UPPER LEG OF THE STRINGER
IS DETERMINED FROM FIG. 2.29 FOR
2017–T3 AS FOLLOWS:

t_1 = 1/16" (Use .064")
d_1 = 1/8" (2117-AD rivet)

NO. OF RIVETS PER INCH OF WIDTH
FROM TABLE = 9.9
ACTUAL NO. OF RIVETS ON <u>EACH</u>
<u>SIDE OF CUT</u> = W_1 x 9.9 = (.5) x 9.9
= 4.95 RIVETS. <u>USE 5 RIVETS.</u>

<u>WHEN BOTH RIVETS AND BOLTS
ARE USED,</u> BOLT HOLES SHOULD
BE REAMED TO SIZE.

d_1 (1/8), RIVET DIA. PREFERABLY
2t TO 3t, BUT NOT GREATER
THAN W/4.

W_1
$(\frac{1}{2})$

$t_1 (\frac{1}{16})$

$(\frac{1}{8})$

W_2
(1.0)

d_2 $(\frac{3}{16})$

"B" SPLICE BAR. SHADED AREA
GREATER THAN W_1 x t_1.

SPLICE ANGLE "A"
SHADED AREA
GREATER THAN W_2 x t_2.

$t_2 (\frac{1}{16})$

STRINGER

AREA REPRESENTING BULB

SECTION A-A

FIGURE 2.26.—Example of stringer splice (material—2017 alloy).

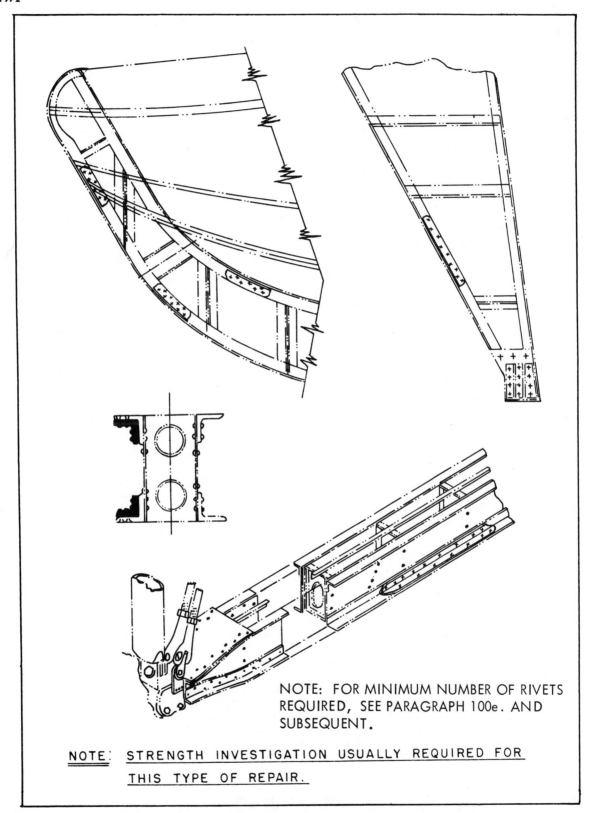

NOTE: FOR MINIMUM NUMBER OF RIVETS
REQUIRED, SEE PARAGRAPH 100e. AND
SUBSEQUENT.

NOTE: STRENGTH INVESTIGATION USUALLY REQUIRED FOR
THIS TYPE OF REPAIR.

FIGURE 2.27.—Application of typical flange splices and reinforcement.

cially important in splicing stringers on the lower surface of stressed skin wings, where high tension stresses may exist. When several adjacent stringers are spliced, stagger the splices if possible.

h. *Size of Splicing Members.* When the same material is used for the splicing members as for the original member, the next cross-section area (i.e., the shaded areas in figure 2.25) of the splicing member will be greater than the area of the section element which it splices. The area of a section element (e.g., each leg of an angle or channel) is equal to the width multiplied by the thickness. For example, the bar "B" in figure 2.26 is assumed to splice the upper leg of the stringer, and the angle "A" to splice the bulbed leg of the stringer. Since the

splice bar "B" is not as wide as the adjacent leg, and since the rivet diameter is also subtracted from the width, the bar is made twice as thick in order to obtain sufficient net area.

i. *The Diameter of Rivets in Stringers.* The diameter of rivets in stringers might preferably be between 2 and 3 times the thickness "t" of the leg, but must not be more than 1/4 the width "W" of the leg. Thus, 1/8-inch rivets are chosen in the example, figure 2.26. If the splices were in the lower surface of a wing, the end rivets would be made the same size as the skin-attaching rivets or 3/32 inch.

j. *The Number of Rivets.* The number of rivets required on each side of the cut in a stringer or flange may be determined from standard text-

FIGURE 2.28.—Number of rivets required for splices (single-lap joint) in bare 2014–T6, 2024–T3, 2024–T36, and 7075–T6 sheet, clad 2014–T6, 2024–T3, 2024–T36, and 7075–T6 sheet, 2024–T4, and 7075–T6 plate, bar, rod, tube, and extrusions, 2014–T6 extrusions.

Thickness "t" in inches	No. of 2117–AD protruding head rivets required per inch of width "W"					No. of bolts
	3/32	1/8	5/32	3/16	1/4	AN–3
0.016	6.5	4.9				
.020	6.9	4.9	3.9			
.025	8.6	4.9	3.9			
.032	11.1	6.2	3.9	3.3		
.036	12.5	7.0	4.5	3.3	2.4	
.040	13.8	7.7	5.0	3.5	2.4	3.3
.051		9.8	6.4	4.5	2.5	3.3
.064		12.3	8.1	5.6	3.1	3.3
.081			10.2	7.1	3.9	3.3
.091			11.4	7.9	4.4	3.3
.102			12.8	8.9	4.9	3.4
.128				11.2	6.2	3.2

NOTES:

a. For stringers in the upper surface of a wing, or in a fuselage, 80 percent of the number of rivets shown in the table may be used.

b. For intermediate frames, 60 percent of the number shown may be used.

c. For single lap sheet joints, 75 percent of the number shown may be used.

ENGINEERING NOTES: *The above table was computed as follows:*

1. The load per inch of width of material was calculated by assuming a strip one inch wide in tension.

2. Number of rivets required was calculated for 2117–AD rivets, based on a rivet allowable shear stress equal to 40 percent of the sheet allowable tensile stress, and a sheet allowable bearing stress equal to 160 percent of the sheet allowable tensile stress, using nominal hole diameters for rivets.

3. Combinations of sheet thickness and rivet size above the heavy line are critical in (i. e., will fail by) bearing on the sheet; those below are critical in shearing of the rivets.

4. The number of AN–3 bolts required below the heavy line was calculated based on a sheet allowable tensile stress of 70,000 p.s.i. and a bolt allowable single shear load of 2,126 pounds.

books on aircraft structures, or may be found in figures 2.28, 2.29, and 2.30. In determining the number of rivets required in the example, figure 2.26, for attaching the splice bar "B" to the upper leg, the thickness "t" of the element of area being spliced is 1/16 inch (use 0.064), the rivet size is 1/8 inch, and figure 2.29 shows that 9.9 rivets are required per inch of width. Since the width "W" is 1/2 inch, the actual number of rivets required to attach the splice-bar to the upper leg on each side of the cut is 9.9 (rivets per inch) × 0.5 (inch width) = 4.95 (use 5 rivets).

For the bulbed leg of the stringer "t" = 1/16 inch (use 0.064); AN–3 bolts are chosen and the number of bolts required per inch of width = 3.3. The width "W" for this leg, however, is 1 inch and the actual number of bolts required on each side of the cut is 1 × 3.3 = 3.3 (use 4 bolts). When both rivets and bolts are used in

the same splice, the boltholes must be accurately reamed to size. It is preferable to use only one type of attachment, but in the above example, the dimensions of the legs of the bulb angle indicated rivets for the upper leg and bolts for the bulb leg.

(1) Splicing of Intermediate Frames. The same principles used for stringer-splicing may be applied to intermediate frames, when the following point is considered:

(a) *Conventional frames of channel or Z section* are relatively deep and thin compared to stringers, and usually fail by twisting or by buckling of the free flange. Reinforce the splice-joint against this type of failure by using a splice plate heavier than the frame and by splicing the free flange of the frame with a flange of the spliceplate, as illustrated in figure 2.31. Since a frame is likely to be subjected to bending loads, make the length of spliceplate

FIGURE 2.29.—Number of rivets required for splices (single-lap joint) in 2017, 2017 ALCLAD, 2024–T36 and 2024–T36 ALCLAD sheet, plate, bar, rod, tube, and extrusions.

Thickness "t" in inches	No. of 2117—AD protruding head rivets required per inch of width "W"					No. of bolts
	³⁄₃₂	⅛	⁵⁄₃₂	³⁄₁₆	¼	AN–3
0. 016	6. 5	4. 9				
. 020	6. 5	4. 9	3. 9			
. 025	6. 9	4. 9	3. 9			
. 032	8. 9	4. 9	3. 9	3. 3		
. 036	10. 0	5. 6	3. 9	3. 3	2. 4	
. 040	11. 1	6. 2	4. 0	3. 3	2. 4	
. 051		7. 9	5. 1	3. 6	2. 4	3. 3
. 064		9. 9	6. 5	4. 5	2. 5	3. 3
. 081		12. 5	8. 1	5. 7	3. 1	3. 3
. 091			9. 1	6. 3	3. 5	3. 3
. 102			10. 3	7. 1	3. 9	3. 3
. 128			12. 9	8. 9	4. 9	3. 3

NOTES:

a. For stringers in the upper surface of a wing, or in a fuselage, 80 percent of the number of rivets shown in the table may be used.

b. For intermediate frames, 60 percent of the number shown may be used.

c. For single lap sheet joints, 75 percent of the number shown may be used.

ENGINEERING NOTES: *The above table was computed as follows:*

1. The load per inch of width of material was calculated by assuming a strip one inch wide in tension.

2. Number of rivets required was calculated for 2117–AD rivets, based on a rivet allowable shear stress equal to 50 percent of the sheet allowable tensile stress, and a sheet allowable bearing stress equal to 160 percent of the sheet allowable tensile stress, using nominal hole diameters for rivets.

3. Combinations of sheet thickness and rivet size above the heavy line are critical in (i.e., will fail by) bearing on the sheet; those below are critical in shearing of the rivets.

4. The number of AN–3 bolts required below the heavy line was calculated based on a sheet allowable tensile stress of 55,000 p.s.i. and a bolt allowable single shear load of 2,126 pounds.

"L" more than twice the width "W₂" and the rivets spread out to cover the plate.

101. REPAIRING CRACKED MEMBERS. Acceptable methods of repairing various types of cracks in structural elements are shown in figures 2.32 to 2.35. The following general procedures apply in repairing such defects:

a. *Drill small holes* 3/32 inch (or 1/8 inch) at the extreme ends of the cracks to minimize the possibility of their spreading further.

b. *Add reinforcement* to carry the stresses across the damaged portion and to stiffen the joints (as shown in figures 2.32 to 2.35).

The condition causing cracks to develop at a particular point is stress concentration at that point in conjunction with repetition of stress, such as produced by vibration of the structure.

The stress concentration may be due to the design or to defects such as nicks, scratches, tool marks, and initial stresses or cracks from forming or heat-treating operations. It should be noted, that an increase in sheet thickness alone is usually beneficial, but does not necessarily remedy the conditions leading to cracking.

102. STEEL AND ALUMINUM FITTINGS.

a. *Steel Fittings—Inspection for Defects.*

(1) Fittings are to be free from scratches, vise and nibbler marks, and sharp bends or edges. A careful examination of the fitting with a medium power (at least 10 power) magnifying glass is acceptable as an inspection.

(2) When repairing aircraft after an accident or in the course of a major overhaul, inspect

FIGURE 2.30.—Number of rivets required for splices (single-lap joint) in 5052 (all hardnesses) sheet.

Thickness "t" in inches	No. of 2117—AD protruding head rivets required per inch of width "W"					No. of bolts
	³⁄₃₂	⅛	⁵⁄₃₂	³⁄₁₆	¼	AN–3
0.016	6. 3	4. 7				
.020	6. 3	4. 7	3. 8			
.025	6. 3	4. 7	3. 8			
.032	6. 3	4. 7	3. 8	3. 2		
.036	7. 1	4. 7	3. 8	3. 2	2. 4	
.040	7. 9	4. 7	3. 8	3. 2	2. 4	
.051	10. 1	5. 6	3. 8	3. 2	2. 4	
.064	12. 7	7. 0	4. 6	3. 2	2. 4	
.081		8. 9	5. 8	4. 0	2. 4	3. 2
.091		10. 0	6. 5	4. 5	2. 5	3. 2
.102		11. 2	7. 3	5. 1	2. 8	3. 2
.128			9. 2	6. 4	3. 5	3. 2

NOTES:
    a. For stringers in the upper surface of a wing, or in a fuselage, 80 percent of the number of rivets shown in the table may be used.
    b. For intermediate frames, 60 percent of the number shown may be used.
    c. For single lap sheet joints, 75 percent of the number shown may be used.
ENGINEERING NOTES: *The above table was computed as follows:*
    1. The load per inch of width of material was calculated by assuming a strip one inch wide in tension.
    2. Number of rivets required was calculated for 2117–AD rivets, based on a rivet allowable shear stress equal to 70 percent of the sheet allowable tensile stress, and a sheet allowable bearing stress equal to 165 percent of the sheet allowable tensile stress, using nominal hole diameters for rivets.
    3. Combinations of sheet thickness and rivet size above the heavy line are critical in (i.e., will fail by) bearing on the sheet; those below are critical in shearing of the rivets.

THE NUMBER OF RIVETS REQUIRED IN EACH LEG ON EACH SIDE OF THE CUT IS DETERMINED BY THE WIDTH "W", THE THICKNESS OF THE FRAME "t", AND THE RIVET DIAMETER "d" USING FIG. 2.29 IN A MANNER SIMILAR TO THAT FOR STRINGERS IN FIG. 2.26.

NOTE b. IN FIG. 2.29 INDICATES THAT ONLY 60% OF THE NUMBER OF RIVETS SO CALCULATED NEED BE USED IN SPLICES IN INTERMEDIATE FRAMES

EXAMPLE (For 2017–T3 aluminum alloy frame)

FLANGE LEG

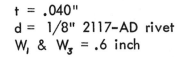

$t = .040"$
$d = 1/8"$ 2117–AD rivet
W_1 & $W_3 = .6$ inch

NO. OF RIVETS PER INCH OF WIDTH FROM FIG. 2.29 = 6.2

No. of rivets required = W x 6.2 = .6 x 6.2 = 3.72 or 4 rivets.
60% of 4 rivets = 2.4 rivets.
USE 3 RIVETS ON EACH SIDE OF THE CUT IN EACH FLANGE LEG.

WEB OF ZEE (OR CHANNEL)

$t = .040"$
$d = 1/8"$ 2117–AD rivet
$W = 2.0$ inches

NO. OF RIVETS PER INCH OF WIDTH FROM FIG. 2.29 = 6.2

No. of rivets required = W x 6.2 = 2.0 x 6.2 = 12.4 or 13 rivets.
60% of 13 rivets = 7.8 rivets.
USE 8 RIVETS ON EACH SIDE OF CUT IN THE WEB OF ZEE (OR CHANNEL).

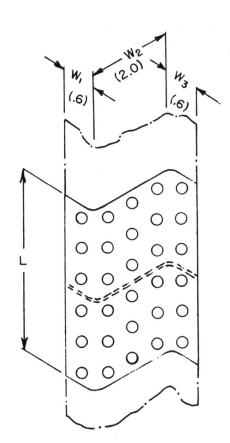

"L" SHOULD BE MORE THAN TWICE W_2
Thickness of splice plate to be greater than that of the frame to be spliced.

FIGURE 2.31.—Example of splice of intermediate frame (material 2017 AL alloy).

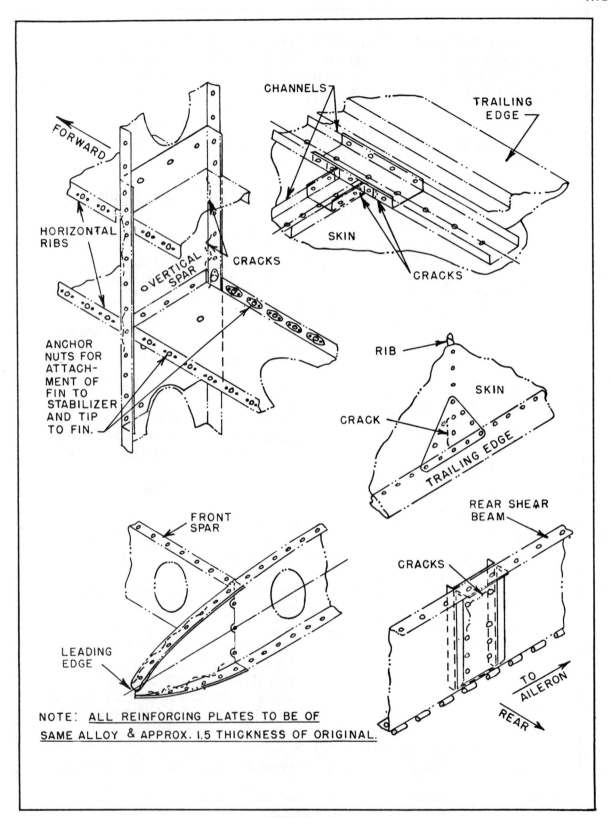

FIGURE 2.32.—Typical methods of repairing cracked leading and trailing edges and rib intersections.

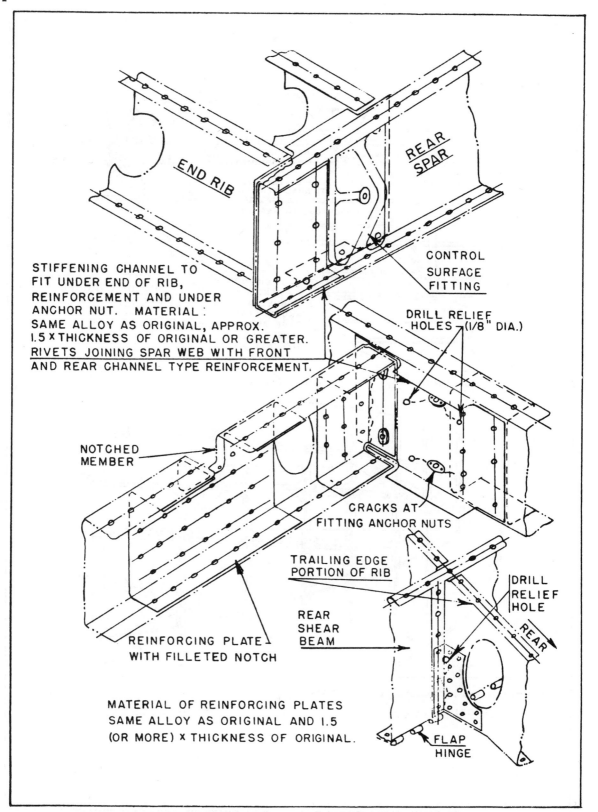

STIFFENING CHANNEL TO
FIT UNDER END OF RIB,
REINFORCEMENT AND UNDER
ANCHOR NUT. MATERIAL:
SAME ALLOY AS ORIGINAL, APPROX.
1.5 × THICKNESS OF ORIGINAL OR GREATER.
RIVETS JOINING SPAR WEB WITH FRONT
AND REAR CHANNEL TYPE REINFORCEMENT.

END RIB

REAR SPAR

CONTROL SURFACE FITTING

DRILL RELIEF HOLES (1/8" DIA.)

NOTCHED MEMBER

CRACKS AT FITTING ANCHOR NUTS

TRAILING EDGE PORTION OF RIB

DRILL RELIEF HOLE

REAR

REINFORCING PLATE WITH FILLETED NOTCH

REAR SHEAR BEAM

FLAP HINGE

MATERIAL OF REINFORCING PLATES
SAME ALLOY AS ORIGINAL AND 1.5
(OR MORE) × THICKNESS OF ORIGINAL.

FIGURE 2.33.—Typical methods of replacing cracked members at fittings.

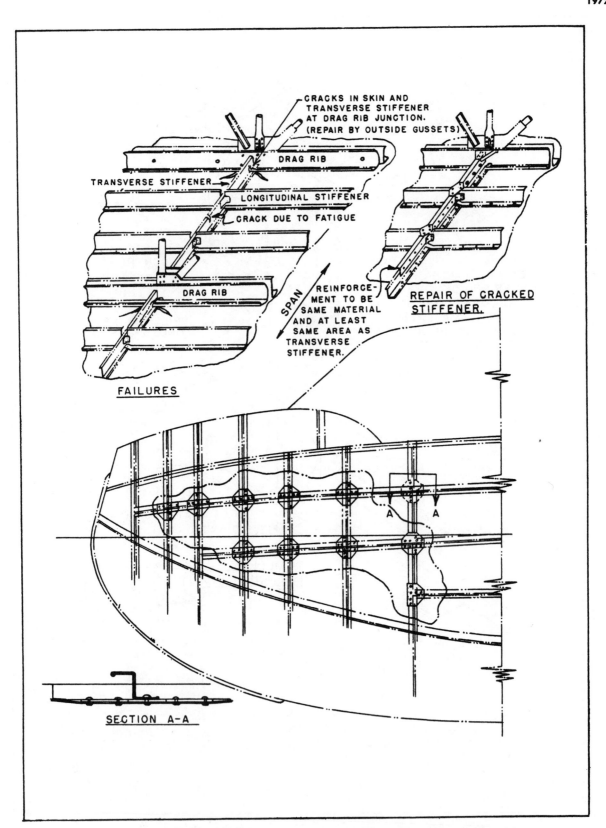

FIGURE 2.34.—Typical methods of repairing cracked frame and stiffener combinations.

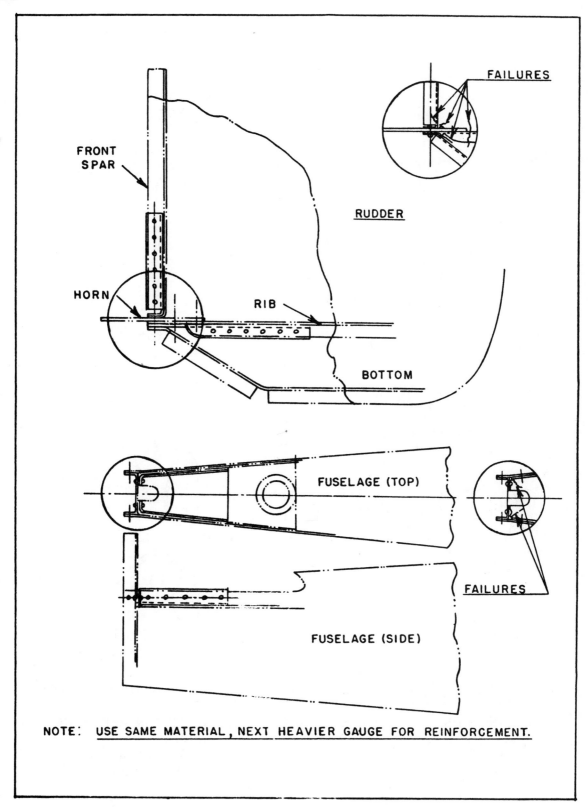

FIGURE 2.35.—Typical repairs to rudder and to fuselage at tail post.

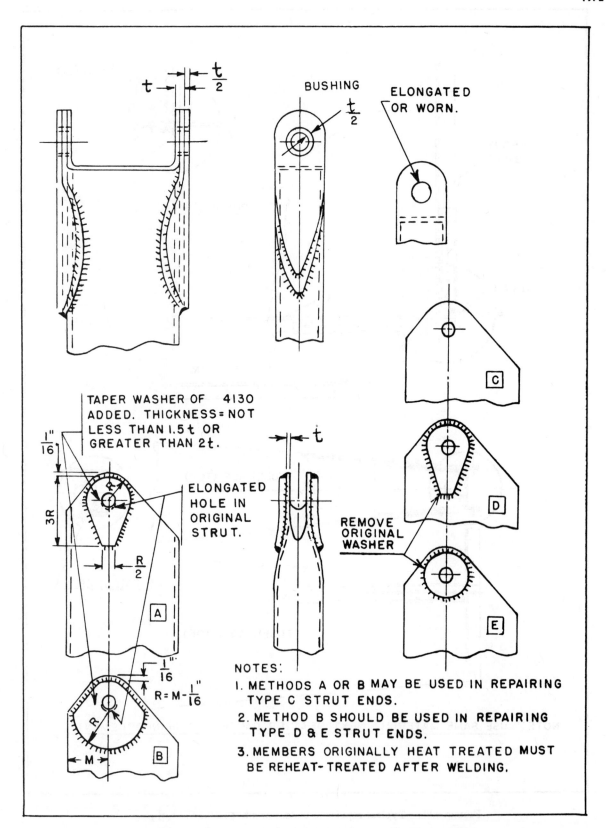

FIGURE 2.36.—Typical methods of repairing elongated or worn boltholes.

all highly stressed main fittings, as set forth in Chapter 7, and if necessary, take corrosion prevention measures as recommended in Chapter 6.

(3) Replace torn, kinked, or cracked fittings.

(4) Elongated or worn boltholes in fittings which were designed without bushings are not to be reamed oversize. Replace such fittings, unless the method of repair is approved by a representative of the FAA. Do not fill holes with welding rod. Acceptable methods of repairing elongated or worn boltholes in landing gear, stabilizer, interplane, or cabane-strut ends only, not originally equipped with pin plates, are shown in fiigure 2.36. (Also see figure 2.11 on longeron repair at fitting.)

b. Aluminum and Aluminum Alloy Fittings.

(1) Replace damaged fittings with new parts, having the same material specifications.

(2) Repairs may be made in accordance with data furnished by the aircraft manufacturer or data substantiating the method of repair may be submitted to the FAA for review.

103. CASTINGS. Damaged castings are to be replaced and not repaired unless the method of repair is specifically approved by the aircraft manufacturer or substantiating data for the repair has been reviewed by the FAA.

*104. SELECTIVE PLATING IN AIRCRAFT MAINTENANCE. Selective plating is a method of depositing metal from an electrolyte to the selected area. The electrolyte is held in an absorbent material attached to an inert anode. Plating contact is made by brushing or swabbing the part (cathode) with the electrolyte-bearing anode.

a. Selective Plating Uses. This process can be utilized for any of the following reasons:

(1) To prevent or minimize disassembly, reassembly, or masking costs.

(2) Resizing worn components (plate to size).

(3) Filling in damaged or corroded areas.

(4) To plate small areas of extremely large parts.

(5) To plate electrical contacts.

(6) To plate parts too large for existing baths.

(7) To supplement conventional plating.

(8) To plate components which become contaminated if immersed in a plating bath.

(9) To cadmium-plate ultra high strength steels without hydrogen embrittlement.

(10) On-site plating.

(11) Reverse current applications (e.g., stain removal, deburring, etching, dynamic balancing).

b. Specifications. Selective plating (electrodeposition), when properly applied, will meet the following specifications and standards:

QQ–C–320	Chromium Plating
QQ–N–290	Nickel Plating
QQ–P–416	Plating, Cadmium
QQ–S–365	Silver Plating
QQ–Z–325	Zinc Plating
MIL–T–10727	Tin Plating
MIL–C–14550	Copper Plating
MIL–G–45204	Gold Plating

c. General Requirements.

(1) Areas to be repaired by this process should be limited to reasonably small areas of large parts, although it may be desirable to plate small parts, particularly electrical or electronic parts, in their entirety.

(2) All solutions should be kept clean and free from contamination. Care should be taken to insure that the solutions are not contaminated by used anodes or other plating solutions. Brush plating solutions are not designed to remove large amounts of scale, oil, or grease. Mechanical or chemical methods should be used to remove large amounts of scale or oxide. Use solvents to remove grease or oil.

(3) Brush plating solutions are five to fifty times as concentrated as tank solutions. The current densities used range from 500 to 4,000 amps/feet^2. The voltages listed on the solution bottles have been precalculated to give proper current densities. Too high a current density burns the plating, while too low a current density produces stressed deposits and low efficiencies. Agitation is provided by anode/cathode motion. Too fast a motion results in low efficiencies and stressed deposits; too slow a motion causes burning. A dry tool results in burnt plate, coarse grain structure, and unsound deposits. The tool *

*cannot be too wet. Solution temperatures of 110° to 120° F. are reached during operation.

(4) Materials such as stainless steel, aluminum, chromium, and nickel, which have a passive surface, will require an activating operation to remove the passive surface. During the activating process, do not use solutions that have been previously used with reverse current because of solution contamination.

d. Equipment. The power source should operate on either 110 or 220 volt alternating current (AC), 60 Hertz, single phase input. It should have a capability to produce direct current having smooth characteristics with controlled ripple and be able to output a current of at least 25 amperes at 0 to 25 volts. Minimum instrumentation of the power source should include a voltmeter, ammeter, and ampere-hour meter.

(1) The ammeter should provide a full scale reading equal to the maximum capacity of the power source with an accuracy of ±5 percent of the current being measured.

(2) The voltmeter should have sufficient capacity to provide a full scale reading equal to the maximum capacity of the power source and an accuracy of ±1.0 volt.

(3) An ampere-hour meter should be readable to 0.001 ampere-hour and have an accuracy of ±0.01 ampere-hour.

(4) The stylus should be designed for rapid cooling and to hold anodes of various sizes and configurations. For safety, the anode holder should be insulated.

(5) The containers for holding and catching runoff solutions should be designed to the proper configuration and be inert to the specific solution.

(6) The mechanical cleaning equipment and materials should be designed and selected to prevent contamination of the parts to be cleaned.

e. Materials. The anodes should be of high-purity dense graphite or platinum-iridium alloys. Do not mix solutions from different suppliers. This could result in contamination.

f. Detail Requirements. On large parts, no area greater than approximately 10 percent of the total area of the part should be plated by this process. Small parts may be partially or completely plated. Special cases exceeding these

limitations should be coordinated with the manufacturer of the plating equipment being used and his recommendations should be followed.

g. Anode Selection. As a general guide, the contact area of the anode should be approximately one-third the size of the area to be plated. When selecting the anode, the configuration of the part will dictate the shape of the anode.

h. Required Ampere-Hour Calculation. The selected plating solution has a factor which is equal to the ampere-hours required to deposit 0.0001 inch on one square inch of surface. Determine the thickness of plating desired on a certain area and multiply the solution factor times the plating thickness times the area in square inches to determine the ampere-hours required. This factor may vary because of temperature, current density, etc.

i. Cleaning. Remove corrosion, scale, oxide, and unacceptable plating prior to processing. Use a suitable solvent or cleaner to remove grease or oil.

j. Plating on Aluminum and Aluminum Base Alloys.

(1) Electroclean the area using forward (direct) current until water does not break on the surface. This electroclean process should be accomplished at 10 to 15 volts, using the appropriate electroclean solution.

(2) Rinse the area in cold clean tap water.

(3) Activate the area with reverse current, 7 to 10 volts, in conjunction with the proper activating solution until a uniform gray to black surface is obtained.

(4) Rinse thoroughly in cold, clean tap water.

(5) Immediately electroplate to color while the area is still wet, using the appropriate nickel solution.

(6) Rinse thoroughly.

(7) Immediately continue plating with any other solution to desired thickness.

(8) Rinse and dry.

k. Plating on Copper and Copper Base Alloys.

(1) Electroclean the area using forward (direct) current until water does not break on the surface. The electroclean process should be accomplished at 8 to 12 volts using the appropriate electroclean solution.

*

* **(2)** Rinse the area in cold, clean tap water.

(3) Immediately electroplate the area with any of the plating solutions except silver. Silver requires an undercoat.

(4) Rinse and dry.

l. *Plating on 300 and 400 Series Stainless Steels, Nickel Base Alloys, Chrome Base Alloys, High Nickel Ferrous Alloys, Cobalt Base Alloys, Nickel Plate, and Chrome Plate.*

(1) Electroclean the area using forward (direct) current until water does not break on the surface. This electroclean process should be accomplished at 12 to 20 volts using the appropriate electrocleaning solution.

(2) Rinse the area in cold, clean tap water.

(3) Activate the surface using forward (direct) current for 1 to 2 minutes using the activating solution and accomplish at 6 to 20 volts.

(4) Do not rinse.

(5) Immediately nickel flash the surface to a thickness of 0.00005 to 0.0001 inch using the appropriate nickel solution.

(6) Rinse thoroughly.

(7) Immediately continue plating with any other solution to desired thickness.

(8) Rinse and dry.

m. *Plating on Low-Carbon Steels (Heat Treated to 180,000 psi).*

(1) Electroclean the area using forward (direct) current until water does not break on the surface. This electroclean process should be accomplished at 12 to 20 volts using the appropriate electrocleaning solution.

(2) Rinse the area in cold, clean tap water.

(3) Reverse current etch at 8 to 10 volts, using the appropriate activating solution, until a uniform gray surface is obtained.

(4) Rinse thoroughly.

(5) Immediately electroplate the part using any solutions except copper acid or silver. Both these require undercoats.

(6) Rinse and dry.

n. *Plating on Cast Iron and High-Carbon Steels (Steels Heat Treated to 180,000 psi).*

(1) Electroclean the area using forward (direct) current until water does not break on

the surface. This electroclean process should be accomplished at 12 to 20 volts using the appropriate electrocleaning solution.

(2) Rinse the area thoroughly in cold, clean tap water.

(3) Reverse current etch at 8 to 10 volts, using the appropriate etching solution, until a uniform gray is obtained.

(4) Rinse thoroughly.

(5) Remove surface smut with 15 to 25 volts using the appropriate activating solution.

(6) Rinse thoroughly.

(7) Electroplate immediately using any of the solutions except copper or silver (both these require undercoats).

(8) Rinse and dry.

o. *Plating on Ultra High Strength Steels (Heat Treated Above 180,000 psi).*

(1) Electroclean the area using REVERSE current until water does not break on the surface. This electroclean process should be accomplished at 8 to 12 volts using the appropriate electroclean solution.

(2) Rinse the area thoroughly in cold, clean tap water.

(3) Immediately electroplate the part, using either nickel, chromium, gold, or cadmium. Other metals require an undercoat of one of the above. Plate initially at the highest voltage recommended for the solution so as to develop an initial barrier layer. Then reduce to standard voltage.

(4) Rinse and dry.

(5) Bake the part for 4 hours at 375° ±25° F.

Note 1: Where the solution vendor provides substantiating data that hydrogen embbrittlement will not result from plating with a particular solution, then a post bake is not required. This substantiating data can be in the form of aircraft industry manufacturers' process specifications, military specifications, or other suitable data.

Note 2: Acid etching should be avoided, if possible. Where etching is absolutely necessary, it should always be done with reverse current. Use alkaline solutions for initial deposits.

p. *Dissimilar Metals and Changing Base.* As a general rule, when plating two dissimilar metals, follow the plating procedure for the one with the most steps or activation. If activating * *steps have to be mixed, use reverse current activation steps prior to forward (direct) current activation steps.

q. Plating Solution Selection.

(1) Alkaline and neutral solutions are to be used on porous base metals, white metals, high-strength steel, and for improved coating ability. Acid solutions are to be used for rapid buildup and as a laminating structure material in conjunction with alkaline type solutions.

(2) Chrome brush plating solutions do not yield as hard a deposit as bath plating solutions. The hardness is about 600 Brinell as compared to 1,000 Brinell for hard chrome deposited from a tank.

(3) Silver immersion deposits will form with no current flowing on most base metals from the silver brush plating solutions; such deposits have poor adhesion to the base metal. Consequently, a flash or a more noble metal should be deposited prior to silver plating to develop a good bond.

(4) In general, brush plating gives less hydrogen embrittlement and a lower fatigue strength loss than does equivalent tank deposits. However, all brush-plated, ultra high strength steel parts (heat treated above 180,000 psi)

should be baked as mentioned in paragraph 104.o.(5), unless it is specifically known that embrittlement is not a factor.

r. Qualification Tests.
All brush plated surfaces shall be tested for adhesion of the electrodeposit. Apply a 1-inch wide strip of Minnesota Mining and Manufacturing tape code 250, or an approved equal, with the adhesive side to the freshly plated surface. Apply the tape with heavy hand pressure and remove it with one quick motion perpendicular to the plated surface. Any plating adhering to the tape shall be cause for rejection.

s. Personnel Training for Quality Control.
Manufacturers of selective plating equipment provide training in application techniques at their facilities. Personnel performing selective plating must have adequate knowledge of the methods, techniques, and practices involved. These personnel should be products of those training programs and certified as qualified operators by the manufacturers of the products used, as well as by local quality control departments. *

105.–114. RESERVED.

INTENTIONALLY LEFT BLANK

Section 4.   REPAIR OF LAMINATE STRUCTURES

115. GENERAL. There is a wide variation in the composition and structural application of laminates, and it is essential that these factors be given major consideration when any restoration activities are undertaken. To a similar extent, there also exist many types of laminate structure repairs that may or may not be suitable for a given condition. For this reason, it is important that the aircraft or component manufacturer's repair data be reviewed when determining what specific type of repair is permissible and appropriate for the damage at hand.

The materials used in the repair of laminate structures must preserve the strength, weight, aerodynamic characteristics, or electrical properties of the original part or assembly. This can best be accomplished by replacing damaged material with material of identical chemical composition or a substitute approved by the manufacturer.

In order to eliminate dangerous stress concentrations, avoid abrupt changes in cross-sectional areas. Whenever possible, for scarf joints and facings, make small patches round or oval-shaped, and round the corners of large repairs. Smooth and properly contour aerodynamic surfaces.

It is recommended that test specimens be prepared at the same time that the actual repair is accomplished. These can then be subjected to a destructive test to establish the quality of the adhesive bond in the repaired part. To make this determination valid, the specimens must be assembled with the same adhesive batch mixture and subjected to curing pressure, temperature, and time identical with those in the actual repair.

a. *Fiberglass Laminate Repairs.* The following repairs are applicable to fiberglass laminate used for fairings, covers, cowlings, honeycomb panel facings, etc. Prior to undertaking the repair, clean the repair area thoroughly with a castile soap and warm water. Remove any paint by wet or dry sanding methods. Bead blasting may be used but

caution must be exercised to not abrade the surfaces excessively.

Superficial scars, scratches, surface abrasion, or rain erosion can generally be repaired by applying one or more coats of a suitable resin, catalyzed to cure at room temperature, to the abraded surface. The number of coats required will depend upon the type of resin and severity of the damage.

Damage not exceeding the first layer or ply of fiberglass laminate can be repaired by filling with a putty consisting of a compatible room-temperature-setting resin and clean short glass fibers. Before the resin sets, apply a sheet of cellophane over the repair area and work out any bubbles and excess resin. After the resin has cured, sand off any excess and prepare the area for refinishing.

Damage deep enough to seriously affect the strength of the laminate (usually more than the first ply or layer of fabric) may be repaired as illustrated in figure 2.37 below. Coat the

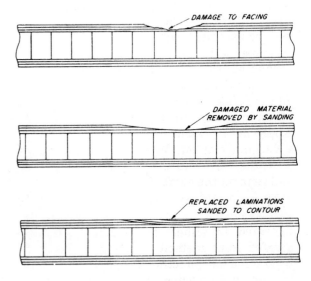

FIGURE 2.37.—Typical laminate (facing) repair.

sanded area with room-temperature-setting resin and apply contoured pieces of glass fabric soaked in resin. Apply a cellophane sheet over the repair and work out any bubbles and excess resin. After the resin has cured, scrape off the excess resin and sand the surface of the repair to the original contour.

Damage that extends completely through one facing and into the core requires the replacement of the damaged core and facing. A method for accomplishing this type of repair is shown in figure 2.38. An alternate method for repairing the facing is shown in figure 2.39. The damaged portion is carefully trimmed out to a circular or oval shape and the core material removed completely to the opposite facing. Exercise caution so as not to damage the opposite facing or to start delamination between the facings and the core around the damage.

CAUTION

Sanding fiberglass laminates gives off a fine dust that may cause skin and/or respiratory irritation unless suitable skin and respiration protection is used.

Use replacement core stock of the same material and density as the original (or an acceptable substitute) and cut it to fit snugly in the trimmed hole. When all pieces of replacement facing laminations are cut and soaked in resin, coat all surfaces of the hole and the scarfed area with resin. Then coat all surfaces of the core replacement with resin and insert it into the hole. After all of the pieces of resin-impregnated glass-fabric facing are in place, cover the entire area with a piece of cellophane and carefully work down the layers of fabric to remove any air bubbles and excess resin. Apply light pressure by means of sand bags or a vacuum blanket. When the resin has cured, sand the repair to match the original contour and refinish the surface.

Damage that is completely through a laminate sandwich structure may be repaired as illustrated in either figure 2.39 or 2.40. The scarfed joint method, figure 2.40, is normally used on small punctures up to 3 or 4 inches in maximum dimension and in facings which are made of thin fabric that is difficult to peel. The stepped joint, figure 2.39, is most often used on

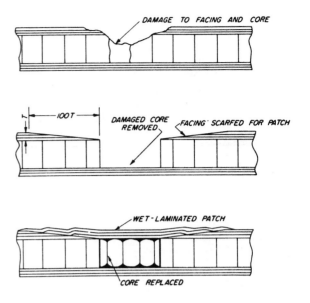

FIGURE 2.38.—Typical core and facing repair.

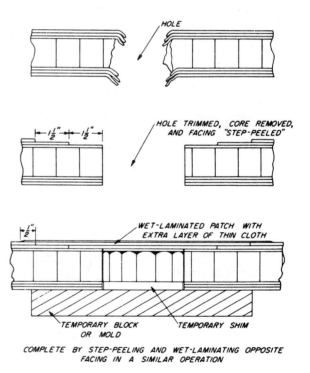

FIGURE 2.39.—Typical stepped joint repair.

larger repairs to facings composed of thick fabrics.

When access for repair is possible from only one side, blind repair procedures are employed.

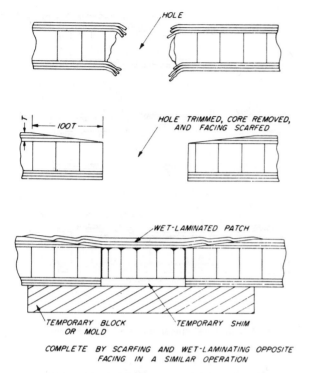

FIGURE 2.40.—Typical scarfed joint repair.

Repairs of this type have been made by using a glass-fiber-reinforced plastic backing plate approximately 0.060-inch thick. The backing plate can be fabricated from layers of glass fabric and room-temperature-curing resin by sandwiching the resin-impregnated layers between two sheets of cellophane. Work the excess resin out and allow the plate to cure on a flat surface or a cellophane-covered surface of the proper curvature near the damaged area, or at the same location on a comparable undamaged part. The technique for bonding the backing plate in place is similar to that illustrated in figure 2.41 for metal-faced laminate repairs. After the backing plate is bonded in place with resin, complete the repair as shown in figure 2.38.

b. Metal-Faced Laminate Repairs. Repairs to laminate with magnesium, titanium, or stainless steel facings require procedures which are specially devised and not included in the following methods of repair. Aluminum alloys such as 7075–T6, 2024–T3, and 2014–T6 are

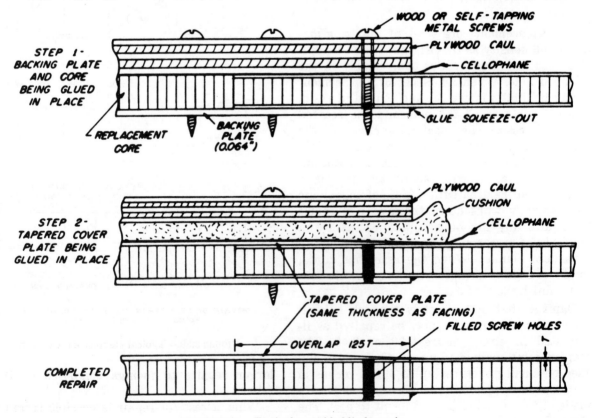

FIGURE 2.41.—Typical one side blind repair.

commonly used for the repair of facings for laminated structural parts having aluminum facings. For maximum corrosion resistance, use only clad aluminum for repairs to clad aluminum alloy facings.

Dents, scratches, or fractures, not exceeding one-fourth inch in largest dimension, in aluminum facings may be repaired with a suitable filler such as viscous epoxy resin. Thoroughly clean the repair area with fine sandpaper and acetone before applying the filler. After the resin has partially cured, remove any excess resin with a sharp scraper or chisel. When completely cured, sand to original contour. If the damage included a fracture, reclean the area around the filled hole and apply a surface patch, as shown in figure 2.42, by means of epoxy resin and a similar curing cycle.

Fractures or punctures in one facing and partial damage to the core of an aluminum-faced laminate may be repaired by several different methods. The technique used will depend upon the size of the damage and the strength, aerodynamic, and sonic fatigue resistance requirements of the area involved. If the repair requires aerodynamic smoothness, the facing surrounding the repair core cavity

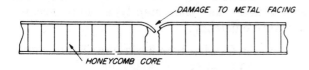

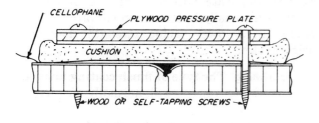

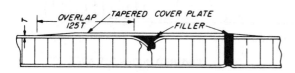

FIGURE 2.42.—Typical metal facing patch.

may have to be step cut to one-half its thickness. This can be done by using a router with an end mill bit and a template.

Damage that extends completely through the core and both facings may be repaired using the same general techniques as those used for repairing fiberglass laminates when both facings are accessible (see figures 2.39 and 2.40). When the inner facing is not accessible, a procedure such as that shown in figure 2.41 may be used. The outer surface patch could then be installed in a manner similar to the repair shown in figure 2.42.

After locating the extent of the total damaged area by tapping or other nondestructive test methods, remove the damaged facing and that portion of the core material which is also affected. The depth to which the core must be removed will depend upon the type of core material and method of repair. If the replacement core material is the same as the original, fabricate it to shape keeping the same core ribbon or grain direction. When a substitution is permissible, wood or glass-fabric honeycomb cores are sometimes used in the repair of aluminum honeycomb cores as they are generally easier to shape. Typical types of core replacements are shown in figure 2.43. Resin fills can be used to replace the core and facing where smaller core damage exists. Phenolic microballoons, low-density insulating materials and/or other ingredients, are added to lower the density and give greater flexibility, thus lowering stress concentrations in the repair area.

For the repair of larger holes in which it is inconvenient to use a face patch because of aerodynamic smoothness requirements in that area, both the core and facing are sometimes replaced with glass-fiber fabric discs and resin. Undercut the core, as shown in figure 2.44, in order to obtain a better bonding of the fill with the facing. Fill the core cavity with accurately shaped resin-saturated glass cloth discs, and press each ply down to remove any air bubbles. Special care should be taken that the final plies fit well against the underside of the top facing. When the core cavity is filled, close the cutout in the facing with resin-impregnated glass-fiber fabric discs that have been precut to size.

There are five general types of facing

A. REPLACEMENT WITH CORE PLUG OF SAME
OR OTHER TYPES OF CORE MATERIAL

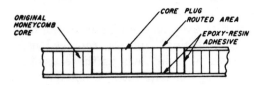

B. RESIN FILL

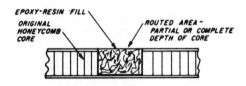

C. RESIN FILL, UNDERCUT CORE

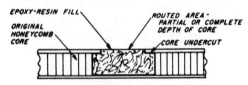

D. GLASS-CLOTH-RESIN LAMINATE, UNDERCUT CORE

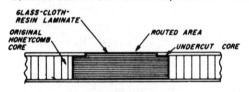

E. REPLACEMENT WITH CORE PLUG OF SAME
TYPE OF SANDWICH CONSTRUCTION

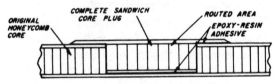

FIGURE 2.43.—Typical types of core replacement.

patches used after replacement of the core has been completed and they are described below. Each of these patches meet certain service requirements that must be considered before a decision can be reached as to which is appropriate for a specific application.

(1) A Small, Flush Plug-type. A plug of the same material and thickness as the facing is bonded in place after the core has been replaced. This type of patch gives aerodynamic smoothness but does not replace any of the strength initially lost in the damaged facing.

(2) An Overlap Type Metal Facing Patch. The overlap surface patch is bonded in place over the facing and replaced core. With this type of patch, and good bonding techniques, practically full strength of the facing is regained. Overlaps of less than 125 times the thickness of the facing can be used in repairs where the skins are not highly stressed.

(3) A Step-type Facing Patch. The step-type facing patch retains aerodynamic smoothness but has only a maximum of 50 percent of the original facing tensile strength.

(4) A Scarf-type Facing Patch. This is a combination of the overlap and the step-type which results in the same aerodynamic smoothness as the step-type but greater strength efficiency.

(5) An Overlap Type Resin-glass Facing Patch. An overlap patch of glass-fiber fabric and resin has fair aerodynamic smoothness and is easy to fabricate with a minimum of equipment. It fits easily in transition curvatures, but results in a lower facing strength than the original skin.

c. Finishing. The type of finish coating applied to a laminate repair will normally be deter-

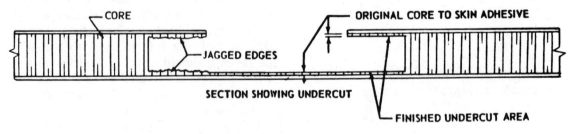

FIGURE 2.44.—Typical undercut core material cavity.

mined by the facing material and the application of the part or assembly. Rain erosion of plastic parts, the need for electrical or dielectric properties and/or the necessity for anticorrosion coatings must be considered when the choice of finish is made. Plastic-faced parts such as radomes are finished primarily for rain erosion while aluminum- or other metal-faced laminates are finished for corrosion protection. For coatings to perform their function properly, it is essential that they be applied to surfaces that are clean, free of voids, and exceedingly smooth.

The edges of all parts not protected by a bonding of aluminum or glass-fabric laminate must be sealed to reduce the rate of moisture absorption. The wood-bonded edges of plywood, mahogany, spruce, or balsa may be given two coats of aluminized spar varnish.

116.–126. RESERVED.

Chapter 3.   FABRIC COVERING

Section 1.   PRACTICES AND PRECAUTIONS

127. TEXTILE MATERIALS. All fabric, surface tape, reinforcing tape, machine thread, lacing cord, etc., used for re-covering or repairing an aircraft structure must be high-grade aircraft textile material of at least as good quality and equivalent strength as those described in subparagraphs a through g.

a. *Aircraft Fabric.* Acceptable fabrics such as cotton and linen for covering wings, control surfaces, and fuselages are listed in figure 3.1. Fabrics conforming to the Aeronautical Material Specifications (AMS) incorporate a continuous marking showing the specification number to permit identification of the fabric in the field.

b. *Re-covering Aircraft.* Re-cover or repair aircraft with fabric of at least as good quality and equivalent strength as that originally used on the aircraft. However, in re-covering aircraft which were originally covered with low strength or so-called "glider cloth," it is considered more desirable to use Grade A or "intermediate" fabric conforming to AMS 3806 or 3804, as amended, respectively. Certain synthetic and fiberglass fabrics have been developed that are acceptable alternates to AMS 3806 or AMS 3804 fabric, providing the Supplemental Type Certificate (STC) installation instructions furnished with the material are followed. Specification MIL-C-9084, MIL-Y-1140C, and MIL-G-1140 materials in the untreated condition have equivalent strength characteristics to Technical Standard Order TSO-C15 material specifications.

c. *Reinforcing Tape.* Acceptable reinforcing
* tape is listed in figure 3.2. Use reinforcing tape which meets specification MIL-T-5661. Reinforcing tape for lightweight fabric should be made from combed cotton yarn, should be unbleached, and should contain no more than 3.5 percent sizing, finishing, and other nonfibrous materials. Breaking strength should be not less than one half of that prescribed in figure 3.2.

d. *Surface Tape.* Use surface tape (also finishing tape) having approximately the same properties as the fabric used. See figure 3.2.

e. *Lacing Cord.* Use lacing cord having a strength of at least 80 pounds double or 40 pounds single strand. See figure 3.2.

f. *Machine Thread.* Use machine thread having a strength of at least 5 pounds single strand. See figure 3.2.

g. *Hand-Sewing Thread.* Use hand-sewing thread having a strength of at least 14 pounds single strand. See figure 3.2.

128. COVERING PRACTICES. The method of fabric attachment should be identical, as far as strength and reliability are concerned, to the method used by the manufacturer of the airplane to be re-covered or repaired. Fabric may be applied so that either the warp or fill-threads are parallel to the line of flight. Either the envelope method or blanket method of covering is acceptable.

a. *Flutter Precautions.* When re-covering or repairing control surfaces, especially on high performance airplanes, make sure that dynamic and static balances are not adversely affected. Weight distribution and mass balance must be considered to preclude the possibility of induced flutter.

129. PREPARATION OF THE STRUCTURE FOR COVERING. One of the most important items in covering aircraft is proper preparation of the structure. Dopeproofing, covering edges which are likely to wear the fabric, preparation of plywood surfaces, and similar operations, if properly done, will do much toward insuring an attractive and long-lasting job.

a. *Dopeproofing.* Treat all parts of the structure which come in contact with doped fabric with a protective coating such as aluminum foil, dope-proof paint, or cellulose tape. Clad aluminum and
* stainless steel parts need not be dopeproofed.

b. *Chafe Points.* Cover all points of the structure, such as sharp edges, boltheads, etc., which are likely to chafe or wear the covering with doped-on fabric strips or cover with an adhesive tape. After the cover has been installed, reinforce the chafe points of the fabric by doping on fabric patches. Where a stronger reinforcement is required, apply a cotton duck or leather patch sewed to a fabric patch and then dope in place. Reinforce all portions of the fabric pierced by wires, bolts, or other projections.

c. *Inter-Rib Bracing.* Conventional wing ribs, which do not have permanent inter-rib bracing, should be bound in position by means of cotton tape running parallel to the beams. Apply the tape diagonally between the top and bottom capstrips of each successive rib approximately halfway between the front and rear beams. Apply the tape continuously from the butt rib to the tip rib with one turn of tape around each intermediate rib capstrip.

d. *Preparation of Plywood Surfaces for Covering.* Prior to covering plywood surfaces with fabric, prepare the surface by cleaning and applying sealer and dope.

(1) Cleaning. Sand all surface areas which have been smeared with glue in order to expose a clean wood surface. Remove loose deposits such as woodchips and sawdust. Remove oil or grease spots by carefully washing with naphtha.

(2) Applying of Sealer and Dope. Apply one brush coat or two dip coats (wiped) of a dopeproof sealer such as that conforming to Specification MIL-V-6894 thinned to 30 percent nonvolatile content and allow to dry 2 to 4 hours. Finally, before covering, apply two brush coats of clear dope allowing the first coat of dope to dry approximately 45 minutes before applying the second coat.

130. FABRIC SEAMS. Seams parallel to the line of flight are preferable; however, spanwise seams are acceptable.

a. *Sewed Seams.*

(1) Machine-sewn seams (parts D, E, and F of figure 3.3) should be of the folded fell or French fell types. Where salvage edges or pinked edges are joined, a plain lap seam is satisfactory.

(2) Begin hand sewing or tacking at the point where machine sewing or uncut fabric is again reached. Lock hand sewing at intervals of 6 inches, and finish the seam with a lock stitch and a knot (figure 3.4). At the point where the hand sewing or permanent tacking is necessary, cut the fabric so that it can be doubled under before sewing or permanent tacking is performed (figure 3.3 (C)). After hand sewing has been completed, remove the temporary tacks. In hand sewing, use a minimum of four stitches per inch.

(3) Cover a sewed spanwise seam on a metal- or wood-covered leading edge with pinked-edge surface tape at least 4 inches wide.

(4) Cover a sewed spanwise seam at the trailing edge with pinked-edge surface tape at least 3 inches wide. For aircraft with never-exceed speeds in excess of 200 m.p.h., cut notches at least 1 inch in depth and 1 inch in width in both edges of the surface tape when used to cover spanwise seams on trailing edges, especially the trailing edges of control surfaces. Space notches at intervals not exceeding 18 inches. On tape less than 3 inches wide, the notches should be 1/3 the tape width. In the event that the surface tape begins to separate because of poor adhesion or other causes, the tape will tear at a notched section, thus preventing progressive loosening of the entire length of the tape which could seriously affect the controlling of the aircraft.

(5) Cover a double-stitched lap joint with pinked-edge surface tape at least 4 inches wide.

(6) Make sewed spanwise seams on the upper or lower surface in a manner that the amount of protuberance is minimum. Cover the seam with pinked-edge tape at least 3 inches wide.

(7) Sewed seams parallel to the line of flight (chordwise) may be located over ribs; however, place the seam on the rib so that the lacing will not penetrate through the seam.

FIGURE 3.1.—Textile fabric used in aircraft covering.

Materials	Specification	Minimum tensile strength new (undoped)	Minimum tearing strength new (undoped)	Minimum tensile strength deteriorated (undoped)	Thread count per inch	Use and remarks
Airplane cloth mercerized cotton (Grade "A").	Society Automotive Engineers AMS 3806 (TSO-C15 references this spec.).	80 pounds per inch warp and fill.	5 pounds warp and fill.	56 pounds per inch.	80 min., 84 max. warp and fill.	For use on all aircraft. Required on aircraft with wing loadings greater than 9 p.s.f. Required on aircraft with placarded never-exceed speed greater than 160 m.p.h.
"	MIL–C–5646	"	"	"	"	Alternate to AMS 3806.
*Airplane cloth cellulose nitrate predoped.	....	"	"	"	"	Alternate to MIL–C–5646 * or AMS 3806 (undoped). Finish with cellulose nitrate dope.
*Airplane cloth cellulose acetate butyrate, predoped.	....	"	"	"	"	Alternate to MIL–C–5646 * or AMS 3806 (undoped). Finish with cellulose acetate butyrate dope.
Airplane cloth mercerized cotton.	Society Automotive Engineers AMS 3804 (TSO–C14 references this spec.).	65 pounds per inch warp and fill.	4 pounds warp and fill.	46 pounds per inch.	80 min., 94 max. warp and fill.	For use on aircraft with wing loadings of 9 p.s.f. or less, provided never-exceed speed is 160 m.p.h. or less.
Airplane cloth mercerized cotton.	Society Automotive Engineers AMS 3802.	50 pounds per inch warp and fill.	3 pounds warp and fill.	35 pounds per inch..	110 max. warp and fill.	For use on gliders with wing loading of 8 p.s.f. or less, provided the placarded never-exceed speed is 135 m.p.h. or less.
Glider fabric cotton.	A.A.F. No. 16128. AMS 3802	55 pounds per inch warp and fill.	4 pounds warp and fill.	39 pounds per inch.	80 mini. warp and fill.	Alternate to AMS 3802–A.
Aircraft linen	British 7F1	....	....	....	....	This material meets the minimum strength requirements of TSO–C15.

Materials	Specification	Yarn size	Minimum tensile strength	Yards per pound	Use and remarks
Reinforcing tape, cotton.	MIL–T–5661	------------	150 pounds per one-half-inch width.	------------	Used as reinforcing tape on fabric and under rib lacing cord. Strength of other widths approx. in proportion.
Lacing cord, pre-waxed braided cotton.	MIL–C–5649	------------	80 pounds double.	310 minimum.	Lacing fabric to structures. Unless already waxed, must be lightly waxed before using.
Lacing cord, special cotton.	U.S. Army No. 6–27.	20/3/3/3	85 pounds double.	------------	"
Lacing cord, braided cotton.	MIL–C–5648	------------	80 pounds single.	170 minimum.	"
Lacing cord thread; linen and linen-hemp.	MIL–T–6779	9 ply / 11 ply	59 pounds single. / 70 pounds single.	620 minimum. / 510 minimum.	"
Lacing cord thread; high-tenacity cotton.	MIL–T–5660	Ticket No. 10.	62 pounds single.	480 minimum.	"
Machine thread cotton.	Federal V–T–276b.	20/4 ply	5 pounds single.	5,000 normal.	Use for all machine sewing.
Hand sewing thread cotton.	V–T–276b. Type III B.	8/4 ply	14 pounds single.	1,650 normal.	Use for all hand sewing. Use fully waxed thread.
Surface tape cotton (made from AN–C–121).	MIL–T–5083	------------	80 lbs/in.	------------	Use over seams, leading edges, trailing edges, outer edges and ribs, pinked, scalloped or straight edges.
Surface tape cotton.	Same as fabric used.	------------	Same as fabric used.	------------	Alternate to MIL–T–5083.

FIGURE 3.2.—Miscellaneous textile materials.

b. *Doped Seams.*

(1) For a lapped and doped spanwise seam on a metal- or wood-covered leading edge, lap the fabric at least 4 inches and cover with pinked-edge surface tape at least 4 inches wide.

(2) For a lapped and doped spanwise seam at the trailing edge, lap the fabric at least 4 inches and cover with pinked-edge surface tape at least 3 inches wide.

131. COVERING METHODS.

a. *The Envelope Method.* The envelope method of covering is accomplished by sewing together widths of fabric cut to specified dimensions and machine sewn to form an envelope which

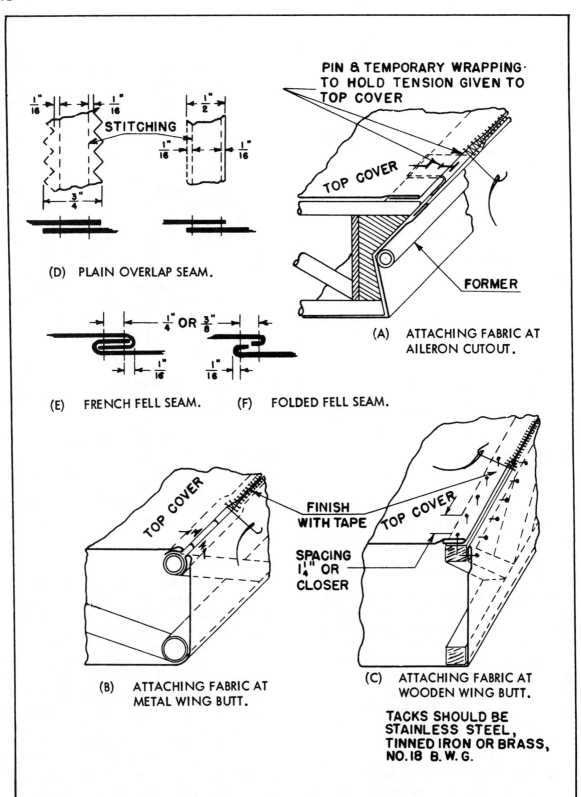

FIGURE 3.3.—Typical methods of attaching fabric.

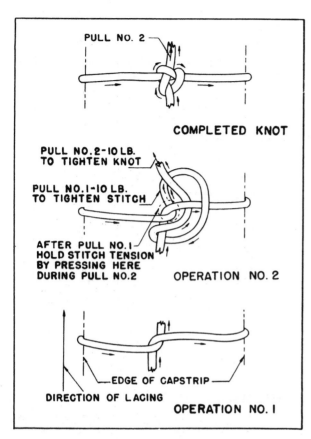

FIGURE 3.4.—Standard knot for rib lacing and terminating a sewed seam (modified seine knot).

can be drawn over the frame. The trailing and outer edges of the covering should be machine sewn unless the component is not favorably shaped for sewing, in which case, the fabric should be joined by hand sewing.

b. The Blanket Method. The blanket method of covering is accomplished by sewing together widths of fabric of sufficient lengths to form a blanket over the surfaces of the frame. Join the trailing and outer edges of the covering by a plain overthrow or baseball stitch. For airplanes with placard never-exceed speed of 150 miles per hour or less, the blanket may be lapped at least 1 inch and doped to the frame or the blanket, lapped at least 4 inches at the nose of metal- or wood-covered leading edges, doped, and finished with pinked-edge surface tape at least 4 inches wide. When fabricating both the envelope and blanket coverings, cut the fabric in lengths sufficient to pass com-

pletely around the frame, starting at the trailing edge and returning to the trailing edge.

132. REINFORCING TAPE. Place reinforcing tape of at least the width of the capstrips under all lacing. In the case of wings with plywood or metal leading edge covering, the reinforcing tape need be brought only to the front spar on the upper and lower surfaces.

a. Use of Antitear Strips. On aircraft with never-exceed speed in excess of 250 miles per hour, antitear strips are recommended under the reinforcing tape on the upper surface of wings, and the bottom surface of that part of the wing in the slipstream. Where the antitear strip is used on both the top and bottom surfaces, pass it continuously up to and around the leading edges and back to the trailing edge. Where the strip is used only on the top surface, carry it up to and around the leading edge and back on the lower surface as far aft as the front beam. For this purpose the slipstream should be considered as being equal to the propeller diameter plus one extra rib space on each side.

Cut antitear strips from the same material as used for covering and wide enough to extend beyond the reinforcing tape on each side so as to engage the lacing cord. Attach the strips by applying dope to that part of the fabric to be covered by the strip, and apply dope freely over the strip.

133. LACING.

a. Securely fasten both surfaces of fabric covering on wings and control surfaces to the ribs by lacing cord or any other method originally approved for the aircraft. Care should be taken to insure that all sharp edges against which the lacing cord may bear are protected by tape in order to prevent abrasion of the cord. Join separate lengths of lacing cord by the splice knot shown in figure 3.5. Do not use the common square knot for this purpose. Exercise the utmost care to assure uniform tension and security of all stitches. For the first or starting stitch use a double loop as illustrated in figure 3.6. Make all subsequent stitches using a single loop tied off with the standard knot for rib lacing (modified seine type shown in figure 3.4). The spacing between the starting stitch and the next stitch should be one-half the normal stitch spacing. Final location of the knot depends upon the original location selected by the manufacturer. If such information is not available, consider positioning the knot where it will have the least effect on the aerodynamics of the airfoil. The seine knot admits a possibility of improper tightening, resulting in a false (slip) form with greatly reduced efficiency and must not be used for stitch tie-offs. Lock the tie-off knot for the last stitch by an additional half-hitch. Where stitching ends, as at the rear beam and at the trailing edge, space the last two stitches at one-half normal spacing. Under no circumstances pull tie-off knots back through the lacing holes.

b. *The double-loop lacing* illustrated in figure 3.7 represents a method for obtaining higher strengths than possible with the standard single lacing. When using the double-loop lacing, use the tie-off knot shown in figure 3.8.

c. *Fuselage Lacing.* Fabric lacing is also necessary in the case of deep fuselages, and on fuselages where former strips and ribs shape the fabric to a curvature. In the latter case, lace the fabric at intervals to the formers. Attachment of the fabric to fuselages must be so accomplished as to be at least the equivalent in strength and reliability to that used by the manufacturer of the airplane.

* **d.** *Blind Stitch Lacing.* Thick airfoil sections, and those places on an aircraft where a conventional stitch cannot be used to secure fabric, require blind stitch lacing.

A 4- to 6-inch curved needle and standard rib lacing card are used. Lay out stitch pattern according to manufacturer's instructions. Follow the step-by-step instructions given in figure 3.9. *

134. STITCH SPACING. The stitch spacing should not exceed the spacing approved on the original
* aircraft. In case the spacing cannot be ascertained due to destruction of the covering, acceptable rib-stitch spacing is specified in figure 3.10. Place the* lacing holes as near to the capstrip as possible in order to minimize the tendency of the cord to tear the fabric. Lightly wax all lacing cords with

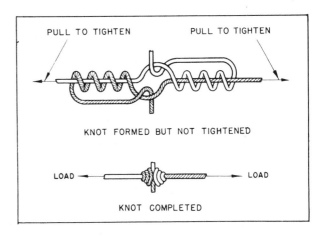

FIGURE 3.5.—Splice knot.

beeswax for protection. In case waxed-braided cord is used, this procedure is unnecessary. (See figure 3.2 for acceptable lacing cords.)

135. SURFACE TAPE (FINISHING TAPE). Cover all lacing with tape of at least the quality and width used on the original airplane. This tape should not be applied until the first coat of dope has dried. Replace all inspection openings in the covering, and reinforce the fabric around them and along leading edges with tape. Wear or friction, induced by moving parts or fittings, can be repaired by sewing a leather patch on a fabric patch and doping in place. Pinked surface tape is sometimes applied over the trailing edges of control surfaces
* and airfoils. For such applications, the tape should be at least 3 inches in width and should be notched along both edges at intervals not exceeding 6 inches. If separation of the tape from the trailing* edge begins, it will tear at a notched section and thereby prevent loosening of the entire strip which could seriously affect the controllability of the aircraft.

136. SPECIAL FASTENERS. When repairs are made to fabric surfaces attached by special mechanical methods, duplicate the original type of fastener. When self-tapping screws are used for the attachment of fabric to the rib structure, observe the following procedure:

a. *Redrill the holes where necessary* due to wear, distortion, etc., and in such cases, use a screw one size larger as a replacement.

*   **b. *Extend the length of the screw*** beyond the rib capstrip at least two threads of the grip (threaded part).

  c. *Install a thin washer,* preferably celluloid, under the heads of screws and dope pinked-edge tape over each screw head.   *

This page intentionally left blank.

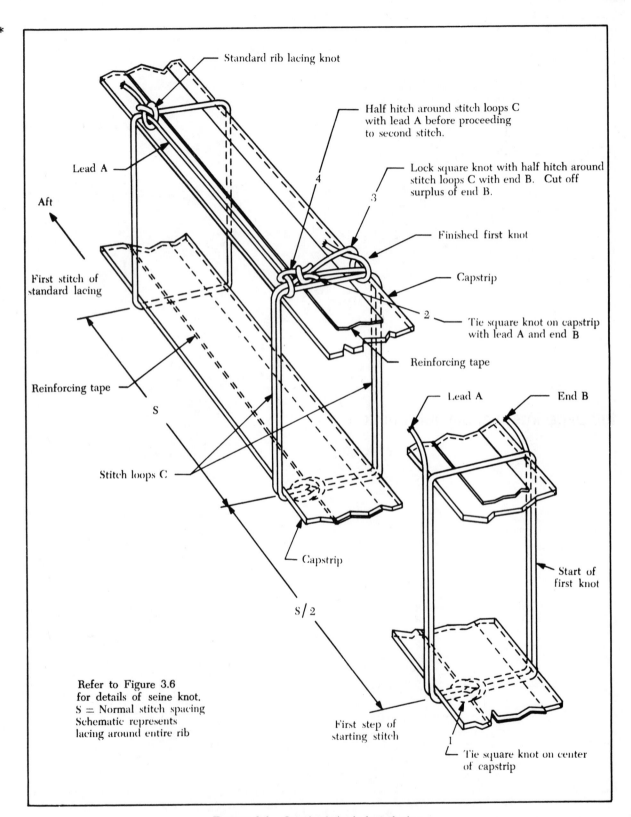

FIGURE 3.6.—Standard single loop lacing.

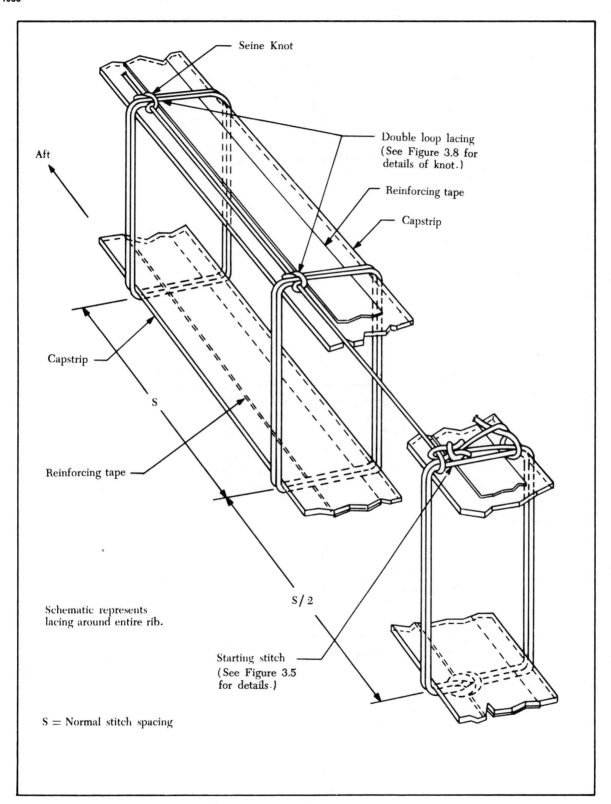

Seine Knot

Double loop lacing
(See Figure 3.8 for
details of knot.)

Reinforcing tape

Capstrip

Aft

Capstrip

S

Reinforcing tape

S/2

Schematic represents
lacing around entire rib.

Starting stitch
(See Figure 3.5
for details.)

S = Normal stitch spacing

FIGURE 3.7.—Standard double loop lacing.

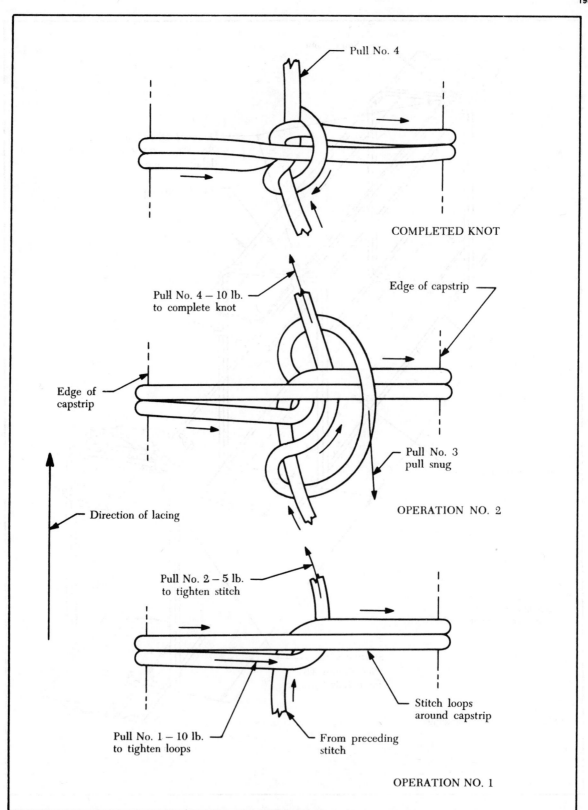

Pull No. 4

COMPLETED KNOT

Pull No. 4 – 10 lb.
to complete knot

Edge of capstrip

Edge of
capstrip

Pull No. 3
pull snug

OPERATION NO. 2

Direction of lacing

Pull No. 2 – 5 lb.
to tighten stitch

Stitch loops
around capstrip

Pull No. 1 – 10 lb.
to tighten loops

From preceding
stitch

OPERATION NO. 1

FIGURE 3.8.—Standard knot for double loop lacing.

*

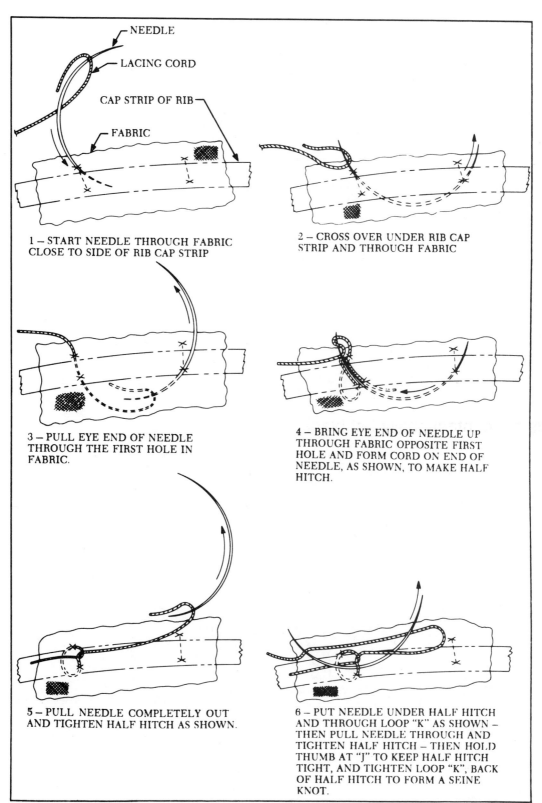

1 – START NEEDLE THROUGH FABRIC CLOSE TO SIDE OF RIB CAP STRIP

2 – CROSS OVER UNDER RIB CAP STRIP AND THROUGH FABRIC

3 – PULL EYE END OF NEEDLE THROUGH THE FIRST HOLE IN FABRIC.

4 – BRING EYE END OF NEEDLE UP THROUGH FABRIC OPPOSITE FIRST HOLE AND FORM CORD ON END OF NEEDLE, AS SHOWN, TO MAKE HALF HITCH.

5 – PULL NEEDLE COMPLETELY OUT AND TIGHTEN HALF HITCH AS SHOWN.

6 – PUT NEEDLE UNDER HALF HITCH AND THROUGH LOOP "K" AS SHOWN – THEN PULL NEEDLE THROUGH AND TIGHTEN HALF HITCH – THEN HOLD THUMB AT "J" TO KEEP HALF HITCH TIGHT, AND TIGHTEN LOOP "K", BACK OF HALF HITCH TO FORM A SEINE KNOT.

FIGURE 3.9.—Blind stitch lacing.

*

This page intentionally left blank.

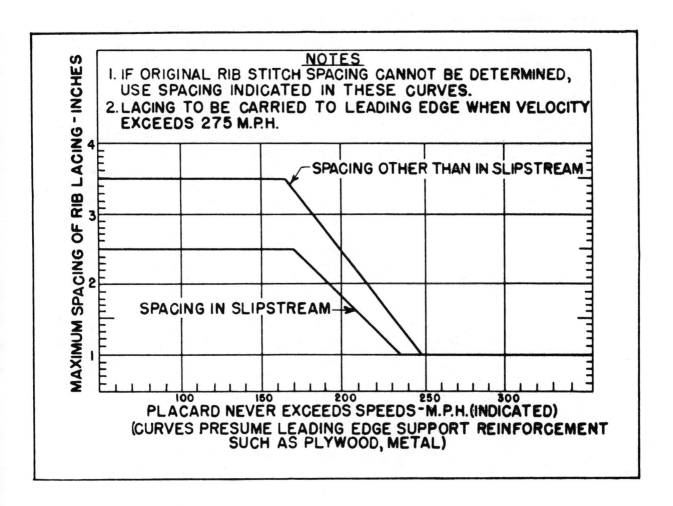

FIGURE 3.10.—Fabric attachment spacing.

*

*

137.-147. RESERVED.

Section 2. DOPING

148. APPLICATION OF AIRCRAFT DOPE, EPOXY, AND RESINS. Determine that dope and fabric materials are compatible by consulting the product manufacturer's instructions before applying finish to aircraft surfaces. Compatibility of products may also be determined by wetting samples of the fabric with the impregnating materials and thorough examination of the material after it has dried. The following military specifications, or later revisions thereof, apply to aircraft dope, epoxy, and polyester resins:

* FIGURE 3.11.—Military specifications for aircraft fabric finishes. *

MIL–D–5549A–1	Clear dope, cellulose-acetate butyrate.
MIL–D–7850	Fungicidal dope, first coat, cellulose-acetate, butyrate.
MIL–D–5550A–1 :......	Pigmented dope, cellulose-acetate, butyrate.
MIL–D–5551A–2	Pigmented dope, gloss, cellulose-acetate butyrate.
MIL–D–5553A–2	Clear dope, nitrate.
MIL–D–5552A–1	Clear dope, gloss, cellulose nitrate.
MIL–D–5554A–1	Clear dope, cellulose nitrate.
MIL–D–5555–1...........	Pigmented dope, cellulose nitrate.
MIL–R–9300A............	Resin, epoxy, low pressure laminating.
MIL–R–25042A..........	Resin, polyester, low pressure laminating.
MIL–R–7575B	Resin, polyester, low pressure laminating.

a. *Thinning*. Finishing materials are generally supplied at a consistency ready for brush application. For spraying operations, practically all aircraft dope, epoxy, or resin requires thinning. Thinning instructions are usually listed on the container label. Avoid use of thinning agents other than those specified by the product manufacturer. To do so may result in adverse chemical action. The amount of thinner to be used will depend on the material, atmospheric conditions, spraying equipment, the spraying technique of the operator, and the type of thinning agent employed. Thinning influences the drying time and the tautening properties of the finish, and it is necessary that it be done properly. Since local atmospheric conditions affect the doping process, determine the amount of the thinner necessary at the time the finishing material is to be applied by first using it on experimental panels.

149. BLUSHING AND USE OF BLUSH-RETARDING THINNER. Blushing of dopes is very common when doping is accomplished under humid conditions. The condition is caused by the rapid evaporation of thinners and solvents, which lowers the temperature on the surface, causing condensation of moisture and producing the white appearance known as "blush." Blushing tendencies are also increased, if strong currents of air flow over the surface when applying dope or immediately thereafter.

A blushed finish has very little protective or tautening value. When the relative humidity is such that only a small amount of blushing is encountered, the condition may be eliminated by thinning the dope with a blush-retarding thinner and slightly increasing the room temperature. If it is not possible to correct humidity conditions in the dope room, suspend doping operations until more favorable atmospheric conditions prevail. The use of large amounts of blush-retarding thinner is not advisable because of the undesirable drying properties accompanying the use of this material.

150. NUMBER OF COATS. Apply as many coats of dope as are necessary to result in a taut and well-filled finish job. A guide for finishing fabric-covered aircraft follows:

a. *Two coats of clear dope*, brushed on and sanded after the second coat.

b. *One coat of clear dope*, either brushed or sprayed, and sanded.

c. *Two coats of aluminum pigmented dope*, sanded after each coat.

d. *Three coats of pigmented dope* (the color desired), sanded and rubbed to give a smooth glossy finish when completed.

e. *Care should be taken* not to sand heavily over the center portion of pinked tape and over spars in order not to damage the rib-stitching cord and fabric.

151. TECHNIQUE. Use a brush to spread the first two coats of dope uniformly on the surface. Work the dope into the fabric thoroughly, exercising care not to form an excessive film on the reverse side. The first coat should produce a thorough and uniform wetting of the fabric. To do so, work the dope with the warp and the filler threads for three or four brush strokes and stroke away any excess material to avoid piling up or dripping. Apply succeeding brush or spray coats with only sufficient brushing to spread the dope smoothly and evenly.

When doping fabric over plywood or metal-covered leading edges, make sure that an adequate bond is obtained between the fabric and the leading edge. Also, when using pre-doped fabric, use a thinned dope in order to obtain a good bond between the fabric and the leading edge.

a. *Surface Tape and Reinforcement Patches.* Apply surface tape and reinforcement patches with the second coat of dope. Apply surface tape over all rib lacing and over all sewed seams as well as all other points of the structure where tape reinforcements are indicated.

b. *Installation of Drain Grommets.* With the second coat of dope, install drain grommets on the underside of airfoils, at the center of the underside in each fuselage bay, located so that the best possible drainage is obtained. On seaplanes, installation of special shielded or marine grommets is recommended to prevent the entry of spray. Also, use this type of grommet on landplanes in that part of the structure which is subject to splash from the landing gear when operating from wet and muddy fields. Dope plastic-type grommets directly to the covering. When brass grommets are used, mount them on fabric patches and then dope them to the covering. After the dope scheme is completed, open the drainholes by cutting out the fabric with a small-bladed knife. Do not open drain-grommets by punching.

c. *Use of Fungicidal Dope.* Fungicidal dope is normally used as the first coat for fabrics to prevent rotting. While it may be more advisable to purchase dope in which the fungicide has already been incorporated, it is feasible to mix the fungicide with the dope.

Specification MIL-D-7850 specifies that the requirements for cellulose acetate butyrate dope incorporate a fungicide for first coat use on aircraft. The fungicide specified in this specification is zinc dimethyldithiocarbonate which forms a suspension with the dope. This material is a fine powder, and if it is mixed with the dope, it should be made into a paste-using dope, and then diluted to the proper consistency according to the manufacturer's instructions. It is not practicable to mix the powder with a large quantity of dope.

Copper napthonate is also used as a fungicide and forms a solution with dope. However this substance has a tendency to "bleed out," especially on light-colored fabric. It is considered satisfactory from a fungicidal standpoint.

Apply the first coat of fungicidal dope extremely thin so that the dope can thoroughly saturate both sides of the fabric. Once the fabric is thoroughly saturated, subsequent coats can be applied at any satisfactory working consistency.

152. REJUVENATION OF FABRIC. Before using fabric rejuvenator products to improve the appearance or condition of doped surfaces, care should be exercised to establish that the fabric strength has not deteriorated beyond safe limits. Experience has indicated that rejuvenation may at times cause fabric-sag rather than tautening. When the surface to be rejuvenated has been thoroughly cleaned and the rejuvenator applied according to the manufacturer's directions, the old dope should soften through to the fabric. Cracks may then be sealed and the surface allowed to set. Finishing coats of clear and pigmented dopes can then be applied in the normal manner.

153. COMMON DOPE TROUBLES.

a. In cold weather, dopes become quite viscous. Cold dopes pull and rope under the brush, and if thinned sufficiently to spray, lack body when dry. Prior to use, allow dopes to come to a temperature approximately that of the dope room, 24° C. (75° F.).

b. Orange peel and pebble effect result from insufficiently thinned dope or when the spray gun is held too far from the surface being sprayed.

c. Runs, sags, laps, streaks, high and low spots are caused by improperly adjusted spraying equipment or improper spraying technique.

d. Blisters may be caused by water or oil entering the spray gun. Drain air compressors, air regulators, and air lines daily.

e. Pinholes may be caused by not allowing sufficient time for drying between coats or after water sanding, or they may be due to insufficiently reduced dope.

f. Wet areas on a doped surface indicate that oil, grease, soap, etc., had not been properly removed before doping.

154.–164. RESERVED.

Section 3.   REPAIRS TO FABRIC COVERING

165. GENERAL. Make repairs to fabric-covered surfaces in a manner that will return the original strength and tautness to the fabric. Sewed repairs and unsewed (doped-on patches or panels) may be made. Do not dope fabric or tape onto a surface which contains aluminum or other color coats. Whenever it is necessary to add fabric reinforcement, remove the old dope either by softening and scraping, or by sanding down to the point where the base coat or clear coat is. exposed. Use clear dope in doping the fabric to the surface. After reinforcement is made, normal finishing procedures may be followed.

* **166. REPAIR OF TEARS IN FABRIC.** Repair tears as shown in figure 3.12 by sewing the torn edges together using a baseball stitch and doping a piece of pinked-edge fabric over the tear. If the * tear is a straight rip, the sewing is started at one end so that, as the seam is made, the edges will be drawn tightly together throughout its entire length. If the openings are cut in wings to inspect the internal structure, start the sewing at the corner or point so that the edges of the cover will be held in place while the seams are being made. The sewing is done with a curved needle and well-waxed thread. Clean the surface to be covered by the patch by rubbing the surface with a rag dipped in dope, wiping dry with a clean rag, or by scraping the surface with a putty knife after it has been softened with fresh dope. Dope solvent or acetone may be used for the same pur-

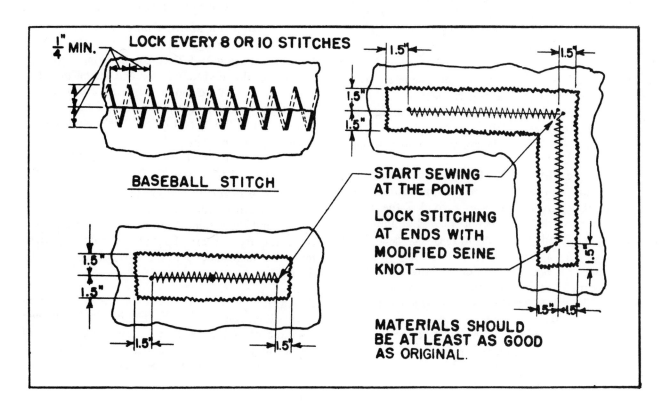

FIGURE 3.12.—Repair of tears in fabric.

pose, but care should be taken that it does not drop through on the inside of the opposite surface, causing the dope to blister. Cut a patch of sufficient size from airplane cloth to cover the tear and extend at least 1 1/2 inches beyond the tear in all directions. The edges of the patch should either be pinked similar to surface tape or frayed out about 1/4 inch on all edges.

167. SEWED PATCH REPAIR. When the damage is such that it will not permit sewing the edges together, a sewed-in repair patch may be used if the damage is not longer than 16 inches in any one direction (see figure 3.12). Cut out the damaged sec- tion, making a round or oval-shaped opening trimmed to a smooth contour. Clean the area of the old fabric to be doped as indicated in paragraph 166. Turn the edges of the patch 1/2 inch and sew to the edges of the opening. Before sewing, fasten the patch at several points with a few temporary stitches to facilitate sewing the seams. After the sewing is completed, clean the area of the old fabric to be doped as indicated for small repairs and then dope the patch in the regular manner. Apply surface tape over the seam with the second coat of dope. If the opening extends over or closer than 1 inch to a rib or other laced member, extend the patch 3 inches beyond the member. After sewing has been completed, rib lace the patch to the rib over a new section of reinforcing tape, using the method explained in paragraph 133. Do not remove the old rib lacing and reinforcing tape.

168. UNSEWED (DOPED-ON) REPAIRS. Unsewed (doped-on) repairs may be made on all aircraft fabric-covered surfaces provided the never-exceed speed is not greater than 150 miles per hour. A doped patch repair may be used if the damage does not exceed 16 inches in any direction. Cut out the damaged section making a round or oval shaped opening, trimmed to a smooth contour. Clean the edges of the opening which are to be covered by the patch with a grease solvent. Sand or wash off the dope from the area around the patch with dope thinner. Support the fabric from underneath while sanding.

For holes up to 8 inches in size, make the fabric patch of sufficient size to provide a lap of at least 2 inches around the hole. On holes over 8 inches in size, make the overlap of the fabric around the hole at least 1/4 the hole diameter with a maximum limit of lap of 4 inches. If the hole extends over a rib or closer than the required overlap to a rib or other laced member, extend the patch at least 3 inches beyond the rib. In this case, after the edges of the patch have been doped in place and the dope has dried, lace the patch to the rib over a new section of reinforcing tape in the usual manner. Do not remove the old rib lacing and reinforcing tape. All patches should have pinked edges or, if smooth, should be finished with pinked-edge surface tape.

169. REPAIR BY A DOPED-IN PANEL. When the damage exceeds 16 inches in any direction, make the repair by doping in a new panel. This type of repair may be extended to cover both the upper and lower surfaces and to cover several rib bays if necessary. Lace the panel to all the ribs covered, and dope or sew as in the blanket method.

a. *Remove the surface tape* from the ribs adjacent to the damaged area and from the trailing and leading edges of the section being repaired. Leave the old reinforcing tape and lacing in place. Next, cut the fabric along a line approximately 1 inch from the ribs on the sides nearest the injury and continue the cuts to completely remove the damaged section. Do not remove the old fabric from the leading and trailing edges, unless both upper and lower surfaces are being re-covered.

b. *Cut a patch* to run around the trailing edge 1 inch and to extend from the trailing edge up to and around the leading edge and back approximately to the front beam. Extend the patch approximately 3 inches beyond the ribs adjacent to the damage.

As an alternative attachment on metal- or wood-covered leading edges, the patch may be lapped over the old fabric at least 4 inches at the nose of the leading edge, doped, and finished with at least 4 inches of pinked-edge surface tape.

c. *Clean the area of the old fabric* that is to be covered by the patch and apply a generous coat of dope to this area. Put the new panel in place, pull as taut as possible, and apply a coat of dope to that portion of the panel which overlaps the old fabric. After this coat has dried, apply a second coat of dope to the overlapped area and let dry.

d. *Place reinforcing tape over the ribs* under moderate tension and lace down in the approved manner.

e. *Give the panel a coat of clear dope* and allow to dry. Install surface tape with the second coat of dope over the reinforcing tape and over the edges of the panel. Finish the dope scheme, using the regular doping procedure.

170.–180. RESERVED.

Section 4. FABRIC TESTING

181. TESTING OF FABRIC COVERING. Field test instruments that are commonly used to test the tensile strength of aircraft fabric covering give only approximate indications of the fabric condition. Since the accuracy of field test instruments is affected by climatic and environmental conditions, a laboratory test is recommended when aircraft fabric covering is found to be marginal by field test methods. Laboratory test procedures are set forth in Federal Specification CCC–T–191B, methods 5122, 5132, 5134, or 5136; American Society of Testing Materials (ASTM) Method D39–61 or D39–49, and others. In all cases, test fabric specimens in the undoped condition. Use acetone, dope thinner, or other appropriate thinning agents for the removal of finishing materials.

a. *Strength Criteria for Aircraft Fabric.*

(1) Present minimum strength values for new aircraft fabric covering are contained in figure 3.1.

(2) The maximum permissible deterioration for used aircraft fabric based on a large number of tests is 30 percent. Fabric which has less than 70 percent of the original required tensile strength would not be considered airworthy. Figure 3.1 contains the minimum tensile strength values for deteriorated fabric as tested in the undoped condition.

(3) Grade A fabric may be used where only intermediate fabric is required. When testing for deteriorated condition, 46 pounds (70 percent of original requirements for intermediate fabric) is considered airworthy.

(4) Failures may occur in fiberglass covering where rib stitching has worn through the reinforcing tape and covering material without being detected through visual inspection. Such failures can be located by using a suitable suction cup and lifting the fabric in the rib stitched area. If the fabric pulls away from the ribs, new stitching will need to be applied using additional reinforcing tape and doubling the number of stitches throughout the affected area. Give particular attention to the areas within the propeller slipstream area.

182.-192. RESERVED.

Chapter 4. CONTROL CABLES AND TERMINALS

Section 1. INSPECTION AND REPAIR

193. GENERAL. Aircraft control cables are generally fabricated from carbon steel or corrosion-resistant steel wire and may consist of either flexible or nonflexible type construction.

Contents of this section may be used for control cable installations pertaining to both primary and secondary system applications.

a. Cable Definitions. Construction features of various cables are shown in figure 4.1. The following terms define components used in aircraft control cables.

(1) Wire—Each individual cylindrical steel rod or thread.

(2) Strand—Each group of wires helically twisted or laid.

(3) Core Strand—The central strand about which the remaining strands of the cable are helically laid.

(4) Cable—A group of strands helically twisted or laid about a central core.

(5) Preformed Cable—Cable in which the wires and strands are shaped prior to fabrication of the cable.

(6) Diameter—The diameter of cable is the diameter of the circumscribed circle.

(7) Lay or Twist—The helical form taken by the wires and strands in a cable. A cable is said to have a right-hand lay if the wires and strands twist in the same direction as the thread on a right-hand screw.

(8) Pitch—The distance in which a strand or wire makes one complete revolution about the axis of the cable or strand respectively.

194. CABLE SPECIFICATIONS. Cable size and strength data are given in figure 4.2. These values are acceptable for repair and modification of civil aircraft.

a. Cable Proof Loads. Cable terminals and

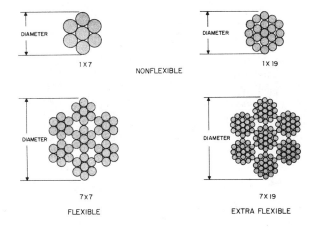

FIGURE 4.1.—Cable cross section.

splices should be tested for proper strength prior to installation. Gradually apply a test load equal to 60 percent of the cable breaking strengths given in figure 4.2 for a period of 3 minutes. Place a suitable guard over the cable during the test to prevent injury to personnel in the event of cable failure.

195. REPLACEMENT OF CABLES. Replace control cables when they become worn, distorted, corroded, or otherwise injured. If spare cables are not available, prepare exact duplicates of the damaged cable. Use materials of the same size and quality as the original. Standard swaged cable terminals develop the full cable strength and may be substituted for the original terminals wherever practical. However, if facilities and supplies are limited and immediate corrective action is necessary, repairs may be made by using cable bushings, eye splices, and the proper combination of turnbuckles in place of the original installation. (See figure 4.6c.)

a. Location of Splices. Locate splices so that no portion of the splice comes closer than two

FIGURE 4.2.—Strength of steel cable.

Diameter (inch)	1 x 7 and 1 x 19				7 x 7, 7 x 19, and 6 x 19 (1WRC)			
	Nonflexible, carbon		Corrosion resisting		Flexible, carbon		Flexible, corrosion resisting	
	MIL-W-6940		MIL-W-5693		MIL-W-1511		MIL-C-5424	
	Weight, pounds per 100 feet	Breaking strength, pounds	Weight, pounds per 100 feet	Breaking strength, pounds	Weight, pounds per 100 feet	Breaking strength, pounds	Weight, pounds per 100 feet	Breaking strength, pounds
1/32	0.25	185	0.25	150				
3/64	.55	375	.55	375				
1/16	.85	500	.85	500	0.75	480	0.75	480
5/64	1.40	800	1.40	800				
3/32	2.00	1,200	2.00	1,200	1.60	920	1.60	920
7/64	2.70	1,600	2.70	1,600				
1/8	3.50	2,100	3.50	2,100	2.90	2,000	2.90	1,760
5/32	5.50	3,300	5.50	3,300	4.50	2,800	4.50	2,400
3/16	7.70	4,700	7.70	4,700	6.50	4,200	6.50	3,700
7/32	10.20	6,300	10.20	6,300	8.60	5,600	8.60	5,000
1/4	13.50	8,200	13.50	8,200	11.00	7,000	11.00	6,400
9/32					13.90	8,000	13.90	7,800
5/16	21.00	12,500	21.00	12,500	17.30	9,800	17.30	9,000
11/32					20.70	12,500		
3/8					24.30	14,400	24.30	12,000
7/16					35.60	17,600	35.60	16,300
1/2					45.80	22,800	45.80	22,800

*The strength values listed were obtained from straight tension tests and do not include the effects of wrapped ends.

inches to any fair-lead or pulley. Locate connections at points where jamming cannot occur during any portion of the travel of either the loaded cable or the slack cable in the deflected position.

b. Cutting and Heating. Cut cables to length by mechanical means. The use of a torch in any manner is not permitted. Do not subject wires and cables to excessive temperature. Soldering bonding braid to control cable will not be considered satisfactory.

c. Ball-and-Socket Type Terminals. Do not use ball-and-socket type terminals or other types for general replacement that do not positively prevent cable untwisting, except where they were utilized on the original installation by the aircraft manufacturer.

d. Substitution of Cable. Substitution of cable for hard or streamlined wires will not be acceptable unless specifically approved by a representative of the Federal Aviation Administration.

196. MECHANICALLY FABRICATED CABLE ASSEMBLIES.

a. Swage Type Terminals. Swage type terminals, manufactured in accordance with Air Force-Navy Aeronautical Standard Specifications, are suitable for use in civil aircraft up to and including maximum cable loads. When swaging tools are used, it is important that all the manufacturers' instructions, including "go and no-go" dimensions, be followed in detail to avoid defective and inferior swaging. Observance of all instructions should result in a terminal developing the full rated strength of the cable. Critical dimensions, both before and after swaging, are shown in figure 4.3.

(1) Terminals. When swaging terminals onto cable ends, observe the following procedure:

(a) Cut the cable to the proper length, allowing for growth during swaging. Apply a preservative compound to the cable ends before insertion into the terminal barrel.

* FIGURE 4.3.—Straight-shank terminal dimensions (cross reference AN to MS: AN–666 to MS 21259, AN–667 to MS 20667, AN–668 to MS 20668, AN–669 to MS 21260) *

Cable size (inches)	Wire strands	Before swaging				After swaging	
		Outside diameter	Bore diameter	Bore length	Swaging length	Minimum breaking strength (pounds)	Shank diameter*
1/16............................	7 x 7	0.160	0.078	1.042	0.969	480	0.138
3/32............................	7 x 7	.218	.109	1.261	1.188	920	.190
1/8	7 x 19	.250	.141	1.511	1.438	2,000	.219
5/32............................	7 x 19	.297	.172	1.761	1.688	2,800	.250
3/16............................	7 x 19	.359	.203	2.011	1.938	4,200	.313
7/32............................	7 x 19	.427	.234	2.261	2.188	5,600	.375
1/4	7 x 19	.494	.265	2.511	2.438	7,000	.438
9/32............................	7 x 19	.563	.297	2.761	2.688	8,000	.500
5/16............................	7 x 19	.635	.328	3.011	2.938	9,800	.563
3/8	7 x 19	.703	.390	3.510	3.438	14,400	.625

*Use gauges in kit for checking diameters.

NOTE: Never solder cable ends to prevent fraying since the presence of the solder will greatly increase the tendency of the cable to pull out of the terminal.

(b) Insert the cable into the terminal approximately 1 inch, and bend toward the terminal; straighten the cable back to normal position and then push the cable end entirely into the terminal barrel. The bending action puts a kink or bend in the cable end and provides enough friction to hold the terminal in place until the swaging operation can be performed. Bending also tends to separate the strands inside the barrel, thereby reducing the strain on them.

NOTE: If the terminal is drilled completely through, push the cable into the terminal until it reaches the approximate position shown in figure 4.4. If the hole is not drilled through, insert the cable until the end rests against the bottom of the hole.

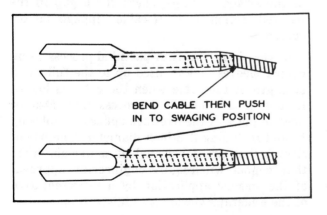

FIGURE 4.5.—Gauging terminal shank after swaging.

(c) Accomplish the swaging operation in accordance with the instructions furnished by the manufacturer of the swaging equipment.

(d) Inspect the terminal after swaging to determine that it is free from die marks and splits, and is not out-of-round. Check for cable slippage in the terminal and for cut or broken wire strands.

(e) Using a "go no-go" gauge or a mi-

BEND CABLE THEN PUSH IN TO SWAGING POSITION

FIGURE 4.4.—Insertion of cable into terminal.

crometer, check the terminal barrel diameter as shown in figure 4.5.

(f) Test the cable by proof-loading it to 60 percent of its rated breaking strength.

(2) Splicing. Completely severed cables, or those badly damaged in a localized area, may be repaired by the use of an eye terminal bolted to a clevis terminal. (See figure 4.6a.) However, this type of splice can only be used in free lengths of cable which do not pass over pulleys or through fair-leads.

(3) Swaged Ball Terminals. On some aircraft cables, swaged ball terminals are used for attaching cables to quadrants and special connections where space is limited. Single shank terminals are generally used at the cable ends, and double shank fittings may be used at either the end or in the center of the cable. Dies are supplied with the swaging machines for attaching these terminals to cables in the following manner:

(a) The steel balls and shanks have a hole through the center, and are slipped over the cable and positioned in the desired location.

(b) Perform the swaging operation in accordance with the instructions furnished by the manufacturer of the swaging equipment.

(c) Check the swaged fitting with a "go no-go" gauge to see that the fitting is properly

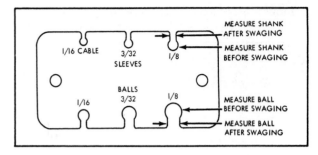

FIGURE 4.7.—Typical terminal gauge.

compressed. (See figure 4.7.) Also inspect the physical condition of the finished terminal.

(4) Cable Slippage in Terminal. Ensure that the cable is properly inserted in the terminal after the swaging operation is completed. Instances have been noted wherein only 1/4 inch of the cable was swaged in the terminal. Observance of the following precautions should minimize this possibility:

(a) Measure the length of the terminal end of the fitting to determine the proper length of cable to be inserted into the barrel of the fitting.

(b) Lay off this length at the end of the cable and mark with masking tape. Since the tape will not slip, it will provide a positive marking during the swaging process.

(c) After swaging, check the tape marker to make certain that the cable did not slip during the swaging operation.

(d) Remove the tape and, using red paint, paint the junction of the swaged fitting and cable.

(e) At all subsequent service inspections of the swaged fittings, check for a gap in the painted section to see if cable slippage has occurred.

b. Nicopress Process. A patented process using copper sleeves may be used up to the full rated strength of the cable when the cable is looped around a thimble. This process may also be used in place of the five-tuck splice on cables up to and including 3/8-inch diameter. The use of sleeves that are fabricated of materials other than copper will require engineering approval of the specific application by a representative of the Federal Aviation Administration.

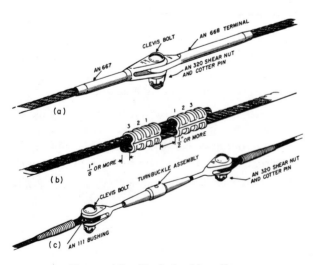

FIGURE 4.6.—Typical cable splices.

FIGURE 4.8.—Copper oval sleeve data.

Cable size	Copper oval sleeve stock No.		Manual tool No.	Sleeve length before compression (approx.) (inches)	Sleeve length after compression (approx.) (inches)	Number of presses	Tested strength (pounds)
	Plain	Plated*					
$\frac{3}{34}$....................	18-11-B4	28-11-B4	51-B4-887	$\frac{3}{8}$	$\frac{7}{16}$	1	340
$\frac{1}{16}$....................	18-1-C	28-1-C	51-C-887	$\frac{3}{8}$	$\frac{7}{16}$	1	550
$\frac{3}{32}$....................	18-2-G	28-2-G	51-G-887	$\frac{7}{16}$	$\frac{1}{2}$	1	1,180
$\frac{1}{8}$....................	18-3-M	28-3-M	51-M-850	$\frac{9}{16}$	$\frac{3}{4}$	3	2,300
$\frac{5}{32}$....................	18-4-P	28-4-P	51-P-850	$\frac{5}{8}$	$\frac{7}{8}$	3	3,050
$\frac{3}{16}$....................	18-6-X	28-6-X	51-X-850	1	$1\frac{1}{4}$	4	4,350
$\frac{7}{32}$....................	18-8-F2	28-8-F2	51-F2-850	$\frac{7}{8}$	$1\frac{1}{16}$	4	5,790
$\frac{1}{4}$....................	18-10-F6	28-10-F6	3-F6-950	$1\frac{1}{8}$	$1\frac{1}{2}$	3	7,180
$\frac{5}{16}$....................	18-13-G9	28-13-G9	3-G9-950	$1\frac{1}{4}$	$1\frac{5}{8}$	3	11,130
			No. 635 Hy-draulic tool dies				
$\frac{3}{8}$....................	18-23-H5	28-23-H5	Oval H5	$1\frac{1}{2}$	$1\frac{7}{8}$	1	16,800
$\frac{7}{16}$....................	18-24-J8	28-24-J8	Oval J8	$1\frac{3}{4}$	$2\frac{1}{8}$	2	19,700
$\frac{1}{2}$....................	18-25-K8	28-25-K8	Oval K8	$1\frac{7}{8}$	$2\frac{1}{2}$	2	25,200
$\frac{9}{16}$....................	18-27-M1	28-27-M1	Oval M1	2	$2\frac{5}{8}$	3	31,025
$\frac{5}{8}$....................	18-28-N5	28-28-N5	Oval N5	$2\frac{3}{8}$	$3\frac{1}{8}$	3	39,200

* *Required on stainless cables due to electrolysis caused by different types of metals. *

Before undertaking a nicopress splice, determine the proper tool and sleeve for the cable to be used. Refer to figures 4.8 and 4.10 for details on sleeves, tools, and the number of presses required for the various sizes of aircraft cable. The tool must be in good working condition and properly adjusted to assure a satisfactory splice.

To compress a sleeve, have it well centered in the tool groove with the major axis of the sleeve at right angles to the tool. If the sleeve appears to be out of line after the press is started, open the tool, re-center the sleeve, and complete the press.

(1) Thimble-Eye Splice. Initially position the cable so that the end will extend slightly beyond the sleeve, as the sleeve will elongate somewhat when it is compressed. If the cable end is inside the sleeve, the splice may not hold the full strength of the cable. It is desirable that the oval sleeve be placed in close proximity to the thimble points, so that when compressed the sleeve will contact the thimble as shown in figure 4.9. The sharp ends of the thimble may be cut off before being used; how-

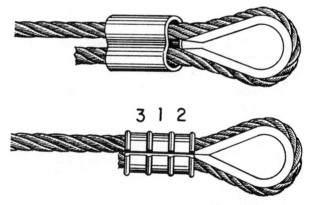

FIGURE 4.9.—Typical thimble-eye splice.

ever, make certain the thimble is firmly secured in the cable loop after the splice has been completed. When using a sleeve requiring three compressions, make the center compression first, the compression next to the thimble second, and the one farthest from the thimble last.

(2) Lap Splice. Lap or running splices may also be made with copper oval sleeves. When making such splices, it is usually necessary to use two sleeves to develop the full strength of the cable. The sleeves should be positioned as shown in figure 4.6b, and the compressions made in the order shown. As in the case of eye splices, it is desirable to have the cable ends extend beyond the sleeves sufficiently to allow for the increased length of the compressed sleeves.

(3) Stop Sleeves. Stop sleeves may be used for special cable end and intermediate fittings and they are installed in the same manner as Nicopress oval sleeves.

NOTE: All stop sleeves are plain copper—certain sizes are colored for identification.

(4) Terminal Gauge. To make a satisfactory copper sleeve installation, it is important that the amount of sleeve pressure be kept uniform. The completed sleeves should be checked periodically with the proper gauge. Hold the gauge so that it contacts the major axis of the sleeve. The compressed portion at the center of the sleeve should enter the gauge opening with very little clearance, as shown in figure 4.11. If it does not, the tool must be adjusted accordingly.

(5) Other Applications. The preceding information regarding copper oval sleeves and stop sleeves is based on tests made with flexible aircraft cable. The sleeves may also be used on

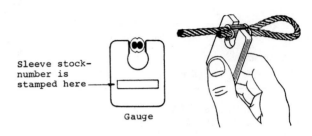

FIGURE 4.11.—Typical terminal gauge.

wire ropes of other constructon if each specific type of cable is proof tested initially. Because of variation in rope strengths, grades, construction, and actual diameters, the test is necessary to insure proper selection of materials, the correct pressing procedure, and an adequate margin of safety for the intended use.

197. HAND FABRICATED CABLE ASSEMBLIES.

a. Woven Splice Terminal. The 5-tuck woven splice may be utilized on 7×7 flexible and 7×19 extra-flexible cables of 3/32 inch diameter or greater; however, this type of terminal will only develop 75 percent of the cable strength. It should not be used to replace high efficiency terminals unless it is definitely determined the design load for the cable is not greater than 75 percent of the cable minimum breaking strength.

In some cases it will be necessary to splice one end of the cable on assembly. For this reason, investigate the original installation for pulleys and fair-leads that might restrict the passage of the splice. The procedure for the fabrication of a woven splice is as follows. (Refer to figure 4.12 for the designation of numbers and letters referred to in this sequence of operations.)

(1) Secure the cables around a bushing or thimble, by means of a splicing clamp in a vise, with the free end to the left of the standing wire and away from the operator. If a thimble is used as the end fitting, turn to point outward approximately 45°.

(2) Select the free strand (1) nearest the standing length at the end of the fitting, and free this strand from the rest of the free ends. Next, insert a marlinspike under the first three

Cable size (inch)	Sleeve No.	Tool No.	Sleeve length (inch)	Sleeve O.D. (inch)	Tested strength (pounds
3/64	871-12-B4	51-B4-887	7/32	11/64	280
1/16	871-1-C	51-C-887	7/32	13/64	525
3/32	871-17-J (Yellow)	51-MJ	5/16	21/64	600
1/8	871-18-J (Red)	51-MJ	5/16	21/64	800
5/32	871-19-M	51-MJ	5/16	27/64	1, 200
3/16	871-20-M (Black)	51-MJ	5/16	27/64	1, 600
7/32	871-22-M	51-MJ	5/8	7/16	2, 300
1/4	871-23-F6	3-F6-950	11/16	21/32	3, 500
5/16	871-26-F6	3-F6-950	11/16	21/32	3, 800

NOTE: All stop sleeves are plain copper—certain sizes are colored for identification.

FIGURE 4.10.—Copper stop sleeve data.

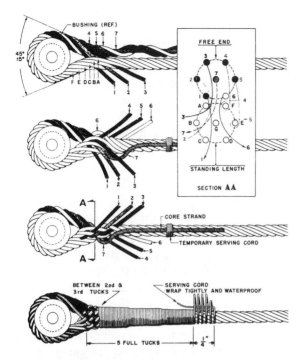

FIGURE 4.12.—Preparation of a woven cable splice.

toward the end fitting with the pliers. This completes the first tuck.

(5) Begin with the first free strand (1) and work in a counterclockwise direction, tucking free strands under every other strand. After the completion of every tuck, pull the strands tight with pliers toward the end fitting. After the completion of the third complete tuck, cut in half the number of wires in each free strand. Make another complete tuck with the wires remaining. At the completion of the fourth tuck, again halve the number of wires in the free strands and make one final tuck with the wires remaining. Cut off all protruding strands and pound the splice with a wooden or rawhide mallet to relieve the strands in the wires.

(6) Serve the splice with waxed linen cord. Start 1/4 inch from the end of the splice and carry the wrapping over the loose end of the cord and along the tapered splice to a point between the second and third tucks. Insert the end of the cord back through the last five wrappings and pull snug. Cut off the end, and if a thimble is used as an end fitting, bend down the points. Apply two coats of waterproofing to the cord, allowing two hours between coats. Carefully inspect the cable strands and splices for local failure. Weakness in a woven splice is made evident by a separation of the strand of serving cord.

b. *Wrap-Soldered Terminal.* The wrap-soldered splice terminal shown in figure 4.13 may be utilized on flexible cables less than 3/32 inch in diameter and on nonflexible single strand (19 wire) cable. This type of terminal will develop only 90 percent of the cable strength and should not be used to replace high efficiency terminals, unless it is definitely known that the design load for the cable is not greater than 90 percent of the cable minimum breaking strength. The method of making the wrapped and soldered splice is as follows.

(1) Use serving or wrapping wire made of commercial soft-annealed steel wire or commercial soft iron wire, thoroughly and smoothly tinned or galvanized.

(2) Use half tin and half lead solder conforming to Federal Specification QQ–S–571.

strands (A, B, and C) of the standing length nearest the separated strand of the free end and separate them momentarily by twisting the marlinspike. Insert the free strand (1) under the three separated strands, through the opening created by the marlinspike. Pull the free end taut by means of pliers.

(3) Unlay a second strand (2), located to the left of the first strand tucked, and insert this second strand under the first two standing strands (A, B). Loosen the third free length (3), located to the left of the first two, and insert it under the first standing strand (A) of the original three (section AA).

(4) Remove the center or core strand (7) from the free end and insert it under the same standing strands (A, B). Temporarily secure the core strand to the body of the standing cable. Loosen the last free strand (6) located just to the right of the first (1) and tuck it under the last two strands (E, F) of the standing cable. Tuck the free strand (5) around standing strand (E). Tuck the free end (4) around the sixth standing strand (F) (see figure 4.12 section AA). Pull all strands snug

The melting point of this solder varies from 320 to 390° F., and the tensile strength is approximately 5,700 pounds per square inch.

(3) Use solder flux consisting of stearic acid (there should be no mineral acid present) and resin, with a composition of 25 to 50 percent resin. A warming gluepot to keep the flux in fluid state is desirable.

(4) Before the cable is cut, solder the wires to prevent slipping. The preferred process is to tin and solder the cable thoroughly 2 to 3 inches by placing in a solder trough, finishing smooth with a soldering tool. The cable may be cut diagonally to conform to the required taper finish.

(5) After being soldered and cut, the cable is securely bent around the proper size thimble, and clamped so that the cables lie close and flat and the taper end for finish lies on the outside. If it is necessary to trim the taper at this point in the process, it is preferable that it be done by nipping. Grinding is permissible, provided a steel guard at least 3 inches long and 1/32 inch thick is placed between

the taper end and the main cable during the operation; and that the heat generated from the grinding does not melt the solder and loosen the wires.

(6) Serving may be done by hand or machine, but in either case each serving convolution must touch the adjoining one and be pulled tightly against the cable, with spaces for permitting a free flow of solder and inspection. (See figure 4.13a.)

(7) Prevent drawing of the temper of any cable resulting from excessive temperature or duration of applied heat. Use a soldering flux consisting of stearic acid and resin. The use, as a flux, of sal-ammoniac or any other compound having a corrosive effect is not acceptable.

(8) Soldering is accomplished by immersing the terminal alternately in the flux and in the solder bath, repeating the operation until thorough tinning and filling with solder under the serving wire and thimble is obtained. The temperature of the solder bath and place where terminal is withdrawn should not be above 450° F. A soldering iron may be used in the final operation to give a secure and good-appearing terminal. Assure that the solder completely fills the space under the serving wire and thimble. A slightly hollowed cast-iron block to support the splice during soldering may help in securing the best results. The use of abrasive wheels or files for removing excess solder is not recommended.

(9) As an alternative process for making terminals for nonflexible cable, the oxyacetylene cutting method and the presoldering method (soldering before wrapping) are acceptable, but only under the following conditions:

(a) That the process of cutting securely welds are all wires together;

(b) that the annealing of the cable does not extend more than one cable diameter from the end;

(c) that no filing is done either before or after soldering;

(d) that for protection during the operation of grinding the tapered end of the cable, a steel guard at least three inches in length and 1/32 inch thick should be placed between the taper and the main cable;

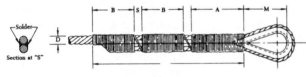

(a) Soldered & wrapped cable terminal with thimble

(b) Soldered & wrapped cable terminal with bushing

D	L	A	B	M	S	Wrapping wire No. 48-19		Specification No.	
		Plus or minus 1/32"				Dia. inch	Approx. length	Thimble (A)	Bushing (B)
3/32	2-1/4	3/4	5/8	3/4	1/8	.020	37"	AN-100-3	AN-111-3
1/8	2-3/4	1	3/4	3/4	1/8	.025	58"	AN-100-4	AN-111-4
5/32	3-3/8	1-1/8	1	7/8	1/8	.025	82"	AN-100-5	AN-111-5
3/16	3-5/8	1-1/4	1	1-1/8	3/16	.035	109"	AN-100-6	AN-111-6
7/32	4	1-3/8	1-1/8	1-1/4	3/16	.035	––	AN-100-7	AN-111-7
1/4	4-1/2	1-1/2	1-1/4	1-1/2	1/4	.035	159"	AN-100-8	AN-111-8
5/16	5-1/4	1-3/4	1-1/2	1-7/8	1/4	.050	195"	AN-100-10	AN-111-10
3/8	6-1/4	2-1/4	1-3/4	2-1/8	1/4	.050	––	AN-100-12	AN-111-12
7/16	7	2-1/2	2	2-1/2	1/4	.050	––	AN-100-14	––––––
1/2	8	2-3/4	2-1/4	2-7/8	3/8	.050	––	AN-100 16	––––––

* FIGURE 4.13.—Preparation of a wrapped soldered terminal. Under Specification No. Bushing (B) column should be used for reference only. Obsolete for procurement.

(e) that heat from grinding does not draw the temper of the cable.

(10) Do not use wrap-soldered splice terminals ahead of the firewall, or in other fire zones, or in other locations where they might be subjected to high temperature.

198. CABLE SYSTEM INSPECTION. Aircraft cable systems are subject to a variety of environmental conditions and forms of deterioration that ultimately may be easy to recognize as wire/strand breakage or the not-so-readily visible types of wear, corrosion, and/or distortion. The following data will aid in detecting the presence of these conditions:

a. *Cable Damage.* Critical areas for wire breakage are those sections of the cable which pass * through fairleads and around pulleys. To properly inspect each section which passes over a pulley or through a fairlead, remove the cable from the aircraft to the extent necessary to expose that particular section. Examine cables for broken wires by * passing a cloth along the length of the cable. This will clean the cable for a visual inspection, and detect broken wires if the cloth snags on the cable. When snags are found, closely examine the cable to determine the full extent of the damage.

The absence of snags is not positive evidence that broken wires do not exist. Figure 4.14 (see (a)) shows a cable with broken wires that were not detected by wiping, but were found during a visual inspection. The damage became readily apparent (figure 4.14b) when the cable was removed and bent using the techniques depicted in figure 4.14c.

NOTE: Tests by various aeronautical agencies have indicated that a few broken wires spread over the length of a cable will not result in a critical loss of strength. Obtain specific information regarding acceptable wire breakage limits from the manufacturer of the aircraft involved.

*Control cables should be removed periodically for a more detailed inspection. Consult the manufacturer's maintenance manual, engineering department, or the FAA for guidance on frequency and procedures. *

(1) External Wear Patterns. Wear will normally extend along the cable equal to the distance the cable moves at that location and may occur on one side of the cable only or on its entire circumference. Replace flexible and non-flexible cables when the individual wires in each strand appear to blend together (outer

*

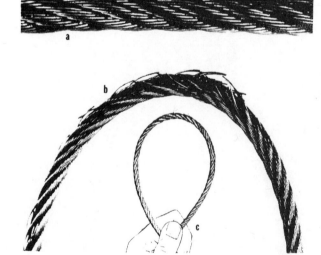

FIGURE 4.14.—Cable inspection technique.

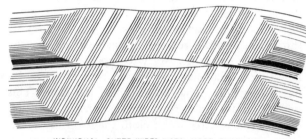

INDIVIDUAL OUTER WIRES WORN MORE THAN 50%

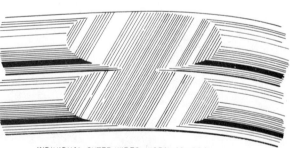

INDIVIDUAL OUTER WIRES WORN 40-50%
(NOTE BLENDING OF WORN AREAS)

INDIVIDUAL OUTER WIRES WORN LESS THAN 40%
(WORN AREAS INDIVIDUALLY DISTINGUISHABLE)

FIGURE 4.15.—Cable wear patterns.

*

This page intentionally left blank.

FIGURE 4.16.—Worn cable (replacement necessary).

wires worn 40–50 percent) as depicted in figure 4.15. Actual instances of cable wear beyond the recommended replacement point are shown in figures 4.16 and 4.17.

(2) Internal Cable Wear. As wear is taking place on the exterior surface of a cable, the same condition is taking place internally, particularly in the sections of the cable which pass over pulleys and quadrants. This condition (shown in figure 4.18) is not easily detected unless the strands of the cable are separated. Wear of this type is a result of the relative motion between inner wire surfaces. Under certain conditions the rate of this type wear can be greater than that occurring on the surface.

(3) Corrosion. Carefully examine any cable

FIGURE 4.17.—Worn cable (replacement recommended).

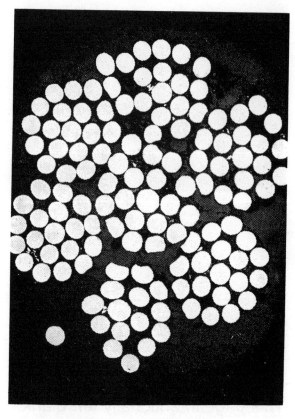

FIGURE 4.18.—Internal cable wear.

for corrosion that has a broken wire in a section not in contact with wear producing airframe components such as pulleys, fairleads, etc. It may be necessary to remove and bend the cable to properly inspect it for internal strand corrosion as this condition is usually not evident on the outer surface of the cable. Replace cable segments if internal strand rust or corrosion is found.

Areas especially conducive to cable corrosion are battery compartments, lavatories, wheel wells, etc., where concentrations of corrosive fumes, vapors, and liquids can accumulate.

NOTE: Check all exposed sections of cable for corrosion after a cleaning and/or metal-brightening operation has been accomplished in that area.

An example of cable corrosion, attributable to battery acid, is shown in figure 4.19.

b. Wire Splices. Standard manufacturing splices have been mistaken for defects in the cable because individual wire end splices were

FIGURE 4.19.—Corrosion.

FIGURE 4.20.—Manufacturer's wire splice.

visible after assembly of a finished cable length. In some instances, the process of twisting outer strands around the core strand may also slightly flatten individual outer wires, particularly in the area of a wire splice. This flattening is the result of die sizing the cable and does not affect the strength of the cable. These conditions, as shown in figure 4.20, are normal and are not a cause for cable rejection.

c. **Cable Maintenance.** Frequent inspections and preservation measures such as rust prevention treatments for bare cable areas will help to extend cable service life. Where cables pass through fairleads, pressure seals, or over pulleys, remove accumulated heavy coatings of corrosion prevention compound. Provide corrosion protection for these cable sections by lubricating with a light coat of graphite grease or general purpose, low-temperature oil.

CAUTION

Avoid the use of vapor degreasing, steam cleaning, methylethylketone (MEK) or other solvents to remove corrosion-preventative compounds, as these methods will also remove the cable internal lubricant.

d. *Routing.* Examine cable runs for incorrect routing, fraying, twisting, or wear at fairleads, pulleys, anti-abrasion strips, and guards. Look for interference with adjacent structure, equipment, wiring, plumbing, and other controls. Inspect cable systems for binding, full travel, and security of attaching hardware. Check for slack in the cable system by attempting to move the control column and/or pedals while the gust locks are installed on the control surfaces. With the gust locks removed, actuate the controls and check for friction or hard movement. These are indications that excessive cable tension exists.

NOTE: If the control movement is stiff after maintenance operations are performed on control surfaces, check for parallel cables twisted around each other or cables connected in reverse.

e. *Cable Fittings.* Check swaged treminal reference marks for an indication of cable slippage within the fitting. Inspect the fitting assembly for distortion and/or broken strands at the terminal. Assure that all bearings and swivel fittings (bolted or pinned) pivot freely to prevent binding and subsequent failure. Check turnbuckles for proper thread exposure and broken or missing safety wires/clips.

f. *Pulleys.* Inspect pulleys for roughness, sharp edges, and presence of foreign material embedded in the grooves. Examine pulley bearings to assure proper lubrication, smooth rotation, freedom from flat spots, dirt, and paint spray. Periodically rotate pulleys, which turn through a small arc, to provide a new bearing surface for the cable. Maintain pulley alignment to prevent the cable from riding on the flanges and chafing against guards, covers, or adjacent structure. Check all pulley brackets and guards for damage, alignment, and security.

(1) **Pulley Wear Patterns.** Various cable system malfunctions may be detected by analyzing pulley conditions. These include such discrepan-

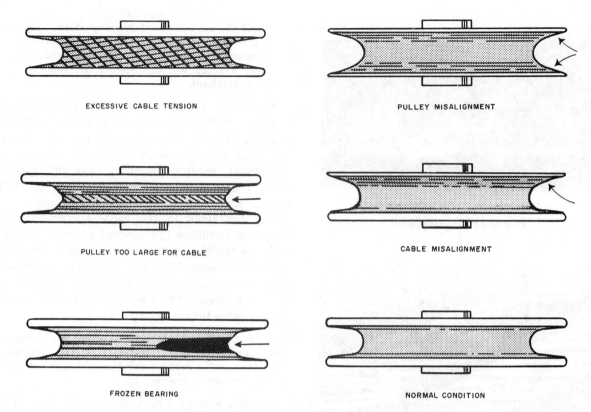

FIGURE 4.21.—Pulley wear patterns.

cies as too much tension, misalignment, pulley bearing problems, and size mismatches between cables and pulleys. Examples of these conditions are shown in figure 4.21.

g. Fairleads, Guides, Anti-Abrasion Strips. Inspect fairleads for wear, breakage, alignment, cleanness, and security. Examine cable routing at fairleads to assure that deflection angles are no greater than 3° maximum. Determine that all guides and anti-abrasion strips are secure and in good condition.

h. Pressure Seals and Seal Guards. Examine pressure seals for wear and/or material deterioration. Determine that the seal guards are positioned to prevent jamming of a pulley if a pressure seal fails and pieces slide along the cable.

199. CABLE TENSION ADJUSTMENT. Carefully adjust control cable tension in accordance with the airframe manufacturer's recommendations.

On large aircraft, take the temperature of the immediate area into consideration when using a tensiometer. For long cable sections, use the average of two or three temperature readings to obtain accurate tension values. If necessary, compensate for extreme surface temperature variations that may be encountered if the aircraft is operated primarily in unusual geographic or climatic conditions such as arctic, arid, or tropic locations.

Use rigging pins and gust locks as necessary to assure satsifactory results. At the completion of rigging operations, check turnbuckle adjustment and safetying in accordance with Section 2 of this chapter.

200. CORROSION AND RUST PREVENTION. To insure a satisfactory service life for aircraft control cables, use a cable lubricant to reduce internal friction and prevent corrosion. Loose rust and surface corrosion may be removed with a stainless steel brush, being careful not to damage the cable. Care should be taken to remove all residue from the cable strands prior to rust prevention treatment. If the cable is made from tinned steel, coat the cable with rust preventive oil and wipe off any excess. It should be noted that corrosion-resistant steel cable does not require this treatment for rust prevention.

201.–211. RESERVED.

Section 2.   SAFETY METHODS FOR TURNBUCKLES

212. GENERAL. Safety all turnbuckles with safety wire using either the double or single wrap method, or with any appropriately approved special safetying device complying with the requirements of FAA Technical Standard Order TSO–C21. The swaged and unswaged turnbuckle assemblies are covered by AN Standard Drawings. For safety wire sizes and materials, refer to figure 4.22. Do not reuse safety wire. Adjust the turnbuckle to the correct cable tension so that no more than three threads are exposed on either side of the turnbuckle barrel. Do not lubricate turnbuckles.

213. DOUBLE WRAP METHOD. Of the methods using safety wire for safetying turnbuckles, the method described here is preferred, although either of the other methods described is satisfactory. The method of double wrap safetying is shown in figure 4.23(A). Use two separate lengths of the proper wire (see figure 4.22). Run one end of the wire through the hole in the barrel of the turnbuckle and bend the end of the wire towards opposite ends of the turnbuckle. Then pass the second length of the wire into the hole in the barrel and bend the ends along the barrel on the side opposite the first. Spiral the two wires in opposite directions around the barrel to cross each other twice between the center hole and the ends. Then pass the wires at the end of the turnbuckle in opposite directions through the holes in the turnbuckle eyes or between the jaws of the turnbuckle fork, as applicable, laying one wire along the barrel and wrapping the other at least four times around the shank of the turnbuckle and binding the laid wires in place before cutting the wrapped wire off. Wrap the remaining length of safety wire at least four turns around the shank and cut it off. Repeat the procedure at the opposite end of the turnbuckle.

When a swaged terminal is being safetied, pass the ends of both wires, if possible, through the hole provided in the terminal for this purpose and wrap both ends around the shank as described above. When the hole in the terminal is not large enough to accommodate the ends of both wires, the hole may be enlarged in accordance with note 2 of figure 4.22 and the safetying completed as described above. If the hole is not large enough to allow passage of both wires, pass the wire through the hole and loop it over the free end of the other wire, and then wrap both ends around the shank as described.

a. Another satisfactory double wrap method is similar to the above, except that the spiraling of the wires is omitted as shown in figure 4.23(B).

b. The wrapping procedures described and shown on MS 33591 may be used in lieu of the safetying method shown herein.

Cable size	Type of wrap	Diameter of safety wire	Material (annealed condition)
$\frac{1}{16}$	Single	0.040	Copper, brass.[1]
$\frac{3}{32}$	Single	0.040	Copper, brass.[1]
$\frac{1}{8}$	Single	0.040	Stainless steel, Monel and "K" Monel.
$\frac{1}{8}$	Double	0.040	Copper, brass.[1]
$\frac{1}{8}$	Single	0.057 min.	Copper, brass.[1]
$\frac{5}{32}$ and greater.	Double	0.040	Stainless steel, Monel and "K" Monel.[1]
$\frac{5}{32}$ and greater.	Single	0.057 min.	Stainless steel, Monel or "K" Monel.[1]
$\frac{5}{32}$ and greater.	Double	0.051 [2]	Copper, brass.

[1] Galvanized or tinned steel, or soft iron wires are also acceptable.
[2] The safety wire holes in $\frac{5}{32}$-inch diameter and larger turnbuckle terminals for swaging may be drilled sufficiently to accommodate the double 0.051-inch diameter copper or brass wires when used.

FIGURE 4.22—Turnbuckle safetying guide.

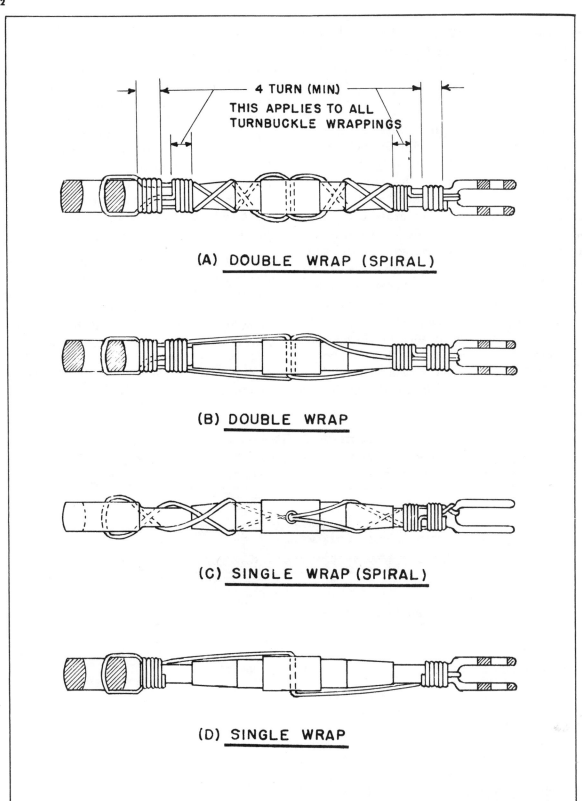

4 TURN (MIN)
THIS APPLIES TO ALL
TURNBUCKLE WRAPPINGS

(A) DOUBLE WRAP (SPIRAL)

(B) DOUBLE WRAP

(C) SINGLE WRAP (SPIRAL)

(D) SINGLE WRAP

FIGURE 4.23.—Safetying turnbuckles.

214. SINGLE WRAP METHOD. The single wrap methods described in the following paragraphs and as illustrated in figures 4.23 (C) and (D) are acceptable but are not the equal of the double wrap methods.

a. Pass a single length of wire through the cable eye or fork, or through the hole in the swaged terminal at either end of the turnbuckle assembly. Spiral each of the wire ends in opposite directions around the first half of the turnbuckle barrel so as to cross each other twice. Thread both wire ends through the hole in the middle of the barrel so that the third crossing of the wire ends is in the hole. Again, spiral the two wire ends in opposite directions around the remaining half of the turnbuckle, crossing them twice. Then, pass one wire end through the cable eye or fork or through the hole in the swaged terminals, in the manner described above, wrap both wire ends around the shank for at least four turns each, cutting off excess wire. This method is shown in figure 4.23(C).

b. Pass one length of wire through the center hole of the turnbuckle and bend the wire ends toward opposite ends of the turnbuckle. Then pass each wire end through the cable eye or fork, or through the hole in the swaged terminal and wrap each wire end around the shank for at least four turns, cutting off excess wire. This method is shown in figure 4.23(D). After safetying, no more than three threads of the turnbuckle threaded terminal should be exposed.

215. SPECIAL LOCKING DEVICES. Several turnbuckle locking devices are available for securing turnbuckle barrels. Persons intending to use a special device must assure the turnbuckle assembly has been designed to accommodate such device. A typical unit is shown in figure 4.24. When special locking devices are not readily available, the use of safety wire is acceptable.

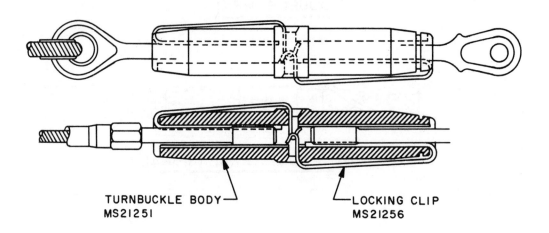

TURNBUCKLE BODY—
MS21251

—LOCKING CLIP
MS21256

CLIP TYPE LOCKING DEVICE

FIGURE 4.24.—Clip type locking device.

216.–226. RESERVED.

Chapter 5. AIRCRAFT HARDWARE

Section 1. IDENTIFICATION AND USE OF AIRCRAFT HARDWARE

227. BOLTS. Most bolts used in aircraft structures are either general purpose Army-Navy (AN) bolts, or National Aircraft Standard (NAS) internal wrenching or close-tolerance bolts. In certain cases, aircraft manufacturers make up special bolts for a particular application and it is necessary to use them or their equivalent in replacement.

a. Identification. The AN-type aircraft bolts can be identified by the code markings on the bolt heads. The markings generally denote the bolt manufacturer, the material of which the bolt is made, and whether the bolt is a standard AN-type *or a special purpose bolt. The AN standard steel bolts are marked with either a raised cross or asterisk, corrosion-resistant steel is indicated by a single raised dash, and AN aluminum alloy bolts are marked with two raised dashes. The strength and* dimensional details of AN bolts are specified on the Army/Navy Aeronautical Standard Drawings.

Special purpose bolts include the high-strength type, low-strength type, and close-tolerance type. Such bolts are normally inspected by magnetic, fluorescent, or equivalent inspection methods. Typical markings include "SPEC" (usually highly heat treated), an aircraft manufacturer's part number stamped on the head, or plain heads (low strength). Close-tolerance NAS bolts are marked with either a raised or recessed triangle. The material markings for NAS bolts are the same as for AN bolts, except *that they may be either raised or recessed. Bolts inspected magnetically or by fluorescent means are identified by means of colored lacquer, or a head marking of a distinctive type. Figure 5.1 shows the* typical coding used on aircraft boltheads.

b. Grip length. In general, bolt-grip lengths should equal the material thickness. However, bolts of slightly greater grip length may be used provided washers are placed under the nut or the bolt- *head. In the case of plate nuts, if proper bolt-grip length is not available, add shims under the plate. * For proper washers, refer to paragraph 231.

c. Locking or Safetying of Bolts. Lock or safety all bolts and/or nuts, except self-locking nuts. Do not reuse cotter pins and safety wire.

d. Bolt Fit. Many boltholes, particularly those in primary connecting elements, have close tolerances. Generally, it is permissible to use the first lettered drill size larger than the normal bolt diameter, except where the AN hexagon bolts are used in light-drive fit (reamed) applications and where NAS close-tolerance bolts or AN clevis bolts are used. Boltholes are to be normal to the surface involved to provide full bearing surface for the bolthead and nut, and not be oversized or elongat- *ed. In case of oversized or elongated holes in critical members, consult the manufacturers' structural repair manual, the manufacturers' engineering department, or the Federal Aviation Administration (FAA) before drilling or reaming the hole to take the next larger bolt. Items such as edge distance, * clearance, etc., must be considered.

e. Torques. The importance of correct application cannot be overemphasized. Undertorque can result in unnecessary wear of nuts and bolts as well as the parts they are holding together. When insufficient pressures are applied, uneven loads will be transmitted throughout the assembly which may result in excessive wear or premature failure due to fatigue. Overtorque can be equally damaging because of failure of a bolt or nut from overstressing the threaded areas. There are a few simple, but very important, procedures that should be followed to assure that correct torque is applied:

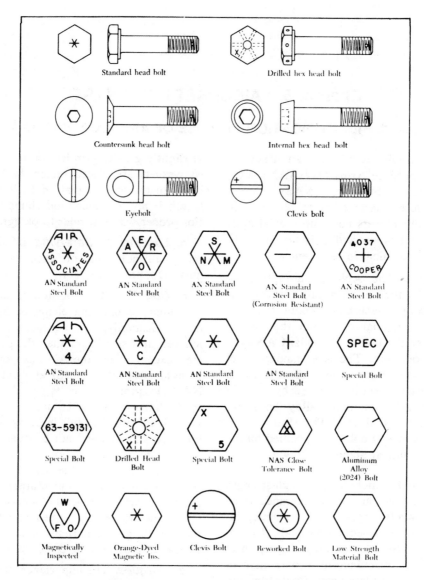

FIGURE 5.1.—Aircraft bolt identification.

(1) Calibrate the torque wrench periodically to assure accuracy; and re-check frequently.

(2) Be sure that bolt and nut threads are clean and dry (unless otherwise specified by the manufacturer).

(3) Run nut down to near contact with the washer or bearing surface and check "friction drag torque" required to turn the nut.

(4) Add the friction drag torque to the desired torque recommended by the manufacturer, or obtain desired torque as shown in figure 5.2. This is referred to as final torque which should register on the indicator or the setting for a snapover type wrench.

(5) Apply a smooth even pull when applying torque pressure. If chattering or a jerking motion occurs during final torque, back off and re-torque.

(6) When installing a castle nut, start alignment with the cotter pin hole at minimum recommended torque, plus friction drag. If the hole and nut castellation do not align, change washers and try again. Exceeding the maximum recommended torque is not recommended.

(7) If torque is applied to capscrews or boltheads, apply recommended torque plus friction drag torque as determined in step (3).

(8) If special adapters are used which will change the effective length of the torque wrench, the final torque indication or wrench setting must be adjusted accordingly. Determine the torque wrench indication or setting with adapter installed as shown in figure 5.3. Figure 5.2 is a composite chart of recommended torque to be used when specific torque is not recommended by the manufacturer. The chart includes standard nut and bolt combinations currently used in aviation maintenance.

f. *Hex-Head Bolts (AN–3 through AN–20).* The hex-head aircraft bolt is an all-purpose structural bolt used for general applications involving tension or shear loads. Alloy steel bolts smaller than No. 10–32 and aluminum alloy bolts smaller than 1/4-inch diameter are not to be used in primary structure. Do not use aluminum alloy bolts and nuts where they will be repeatedly removed for purposes of maintenance and inspection. Aluminum alloy nuts may be used with cadmiumplated steel bolts loaded in shear on land airplanes, but are not to be used on seaplanes due to the possibility of dissimilar metals corrosion.

g. *Close-Tolerance Bolts (AN–173 through AN–186 (Hex-Head), NAS–80 through NAS–86 (100° Countersunk)).* Close-tolerance bolts are used in high-performance aircraft in applications where the bolted joint is subject to severe load reversals and vibration. The standard AN hex-head bolts may be used for the same applications provided a light-drive fit is accomplished.

h. *Internal Wrenching Bolts (MS–20004 through MS–20024 or NAS–495).* These bolts are suitable for use both in tension and shear applications. In steel parts, countersink the bolthole to seat the large radius of the shank at the head or, as in aluminum alloys, use a special heat-treated washer (NAS–143C) that fits the head to provide adequate bearing area. A special heat-treated plain washer (NAS–143) is used under the nut. Use special high-strength nuts on

these bolts. (Refer to paragraph 230c(7).) Replace all internal wrenching bolts by another internal wrenching bolt. Standard AN hex-head bolts and washers cannot be substituted for them, as they do not have the required strength.

i. *Drilled-Head Bolts (AN–73).* The AN drilled-head bolt is similar to the standard hex-bolt, but has a deeper head which is drilled to receive wire for safetying. The AN–3 and the AN–73 series of bolts are interchangeable for all practical purposes from the standpoint of tension and shear strengths.

228. SCREWS. In general, screws differ from bolts by the following characteristics: Usually lower material strength, a looser thread fit (No. 2), head shapes formed to engage a screwdriver, and the shank threaded along its entire length without a clearly defined grip. However, several types of structural screws are available that differ from the standard structural bolts only in the type of head.

The material is equivalent and a definite grip is provided. The AN–525 washerhead screws, the AN 509–100° countersunk structural screws, and the NAS–204 through NAS–235 are such parts. The material markings are the same as those used on AN standard bolts.

a. *Structural Screws (NAS–204 through NAS–235, AN–509 and AN–525).* This type of screw, when made of alloy steel such as SAE–4130, NE–8630, or equivalent, and heat-treated from 125,000 p.s.i., may be used for structural assembly in shear applications similar to structural bolts.

b. *Self-Tapping Screws.* The AN–504 and AN–506 screws are used for attaching minor removable parts such as nameplates and the like. AN–530 and AN–531 are used in blind applications for the temporary attachment of sheet metal for riveting and the permanent assembly of nonstructural assemblies. AN–535 is a plain head self-tapping screw used in the attachment of nameplates or in sealing drainholes in corrosion-proofing tubular structures, and is not intended to be removed after installation. Never use self-tapping screws to replace standard

BOLTS Steel Tension	BOLTS Steel Tension	BOLTS Aluminum
AN 3 thru AN 20	MS 20004 thru MS 20024	AN 3DD thru AN 20DD
AN 42 thru AN 49	NAS 144 thru NAS 158	AN 173DD thru AN 186DD
AN 73 thru AN 81	NAS 333 thru NAS 340	AN 509DD
AN 173 thru AN 186	NAS 583 thru NAS 590	AN 525D
MS 20033 thru MS 20046	NAS 624 thru NAS 644	MS 27039D
MS 20073	NAS 1303 thru NAS 1320	MS 24694DD
MS 20074	NAS 172	
AN 509 NK9	NAS 174	
MS 24694	NAS 517	
AN 525 NK525	Steel shear bolt	
MS 27039	NAS 464	

NUTS		NUTS		NUTS	
Steel Tension	Steel Shear	Steel Tension	Steel Shear	Aluminum Tension	Aluminum Shear
AN 310	AN 320	AN 310	AN 320	AN 365D	AN 320D
AN 315	AN 364	AN 315	AN 364	AN 310D	AN 364D
AN 363	NAS 1022	AN 363	NAS 1022	NAS 1021D	NAS 1022D
AN 365	MS 17826	AN 365	MS 17826		
NAS 1021	MS 20364	MS 17825	MS 20364		
MS 17825		MS 20365			
MS 21045		MS 21045			
MS 20365		NAS 1021			
MS 20500		NAS 679			
NAS 679		NAS 1291			

FINE THREAD SERIES

Nut-bolt size	Torque Limits in.-lbs.		Torque Limits in.-lbs.		Torque Limits in.-lbs.		Torque Limits in.-lbs.		Torque Limits in.-lbs.		Torque Limits in.-lbs.	
	Min.	Max.	Min.	Max.	Min.	Max.	Min.	Max.	Min.	Max.	Min.	Max.
8 –36	12	15	7	9	--------	--------	--------	--------	5	10	3	6
10 –32	20	25	12	15	25	30	15	20	10	15	5	10
¼–28	50	70	30	40	80	100	50	60	30	45	15	30
5/16–24	100	140	60	85	120	145	70	90	40	65	25	40
⅜–24	160	190	95	110	200	250	120	150	75	110	45	70
7/16–20	450	500	270	300	520	630	300	400	180	280	110	170
½ –20	480	690	290	410	770	950	450	550	280	410	160	260
9/16–18	800	1,000	480	600	1,100	1,300	650	800	380	580	230	360
⅝ –18	1,100	1,300	660	780	1,250	1,550	750	950	550	670	270	420
¾ –16	2,300	2,500	1,300	1,500	2,650	3,200	1,600	1,900	950	1,250	560	880
⅞ –14	2,500	3,000	1,500	1,800	3,550	4,350	2,100	2,600	1,250	1,900	750	1,200
1 –14	3,700	4,500	2,200	2,300	4,500	5,500	2,700	3,300	1,600	2,400	950	1,500
1⅛ –12	5,000	7,000	3,000	4,200	6,000	7,300	3,600	4,400	2,100	3,200	1,250	2,000
1¼ –12	9,000	11,000	5,400	6,600	11,000	13,400	6,600	8,000	3,900	5,600	2,300	3,650

COARSE THREAD SERIES

Nut-bolt size	Min.	Max.	Min.	Max.	Min.	Max.	Min.	Max.	Min.	Max.	Min.	Max.
8 –32	12	15	7	9								
10 –24	20	25	12	15								
¼ –20	40	50	25	30								
5/16–18	80	90	48	55								
⅜ –16	160	185	95	110								
7/16–14	235	255	140	155								
½ –13	400	480	240	290								
9/16–12	500	700	300	420								
⅝ –11	700	900	420	540								
¾ –10	1,150	1,600	700	950								
⅞ – 9	2,200	3,000	1,300	1,800								
1 – 8	3,700	5,000	2,200	3,000								
1⅛ – 8	5,500	6,500	3,300	4,000								
1¼ – 8	6,500	8,000	4,000	5,000								

FIGURE 5.2.—Recommended torque values for nut-bolt combinations—
(without lubrication).

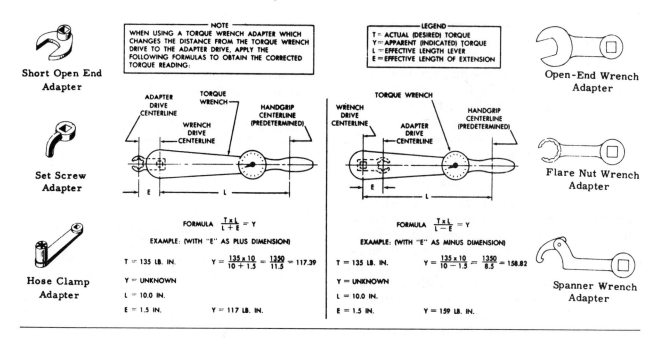

FIGURE 5.3.—Torque wrench with various adapters.

screws, nuts, bolts, or rivets in the original structure.

229. TAPER PINS (AN–385 AND AN–386). Plain and threaded taper pins are used in joints which carry shear loads and where absence of play is essential. The plain taper pin is drilled and usually safetied with wire. The threaded taper pin is used with a taper-pin washer (AN–975) and shear nut (safetied with cotter pin) or self-locking nut.

a. The Flathead Pin (MS–20392). Commonly called a clevis pin, the flathead pin is used in conjunction with tie rod terminals and in secondary controls which are not subject to continuous operation. The pin is customarily installed with the head up so that if the cotter pin fails or works out, the pin will remain in place.

b. The AN–380 Cotter Pin. This is used for safetying bolts, screws, nuts, other pins, and in various applications where such safetying is necessary. Use AN–381 cotter pins in locations where nonmagnetic material is required or in locations where resistance to corrosion is desired.

230. NUTS.

a. Self-Locking Nuts. Self-locking nuts are acceptable for use on certificated aircraft subject to the restrictions on the pertinent manufacturer's recommended practice sheets. Self-locking nuts are used on aircraft to provide tight connections which will not shake loose under severe vibration. Two types of self-locking nuts are currently in use, the all-metal type and the fiber or nylon lock type. Do not use self-locking nuts at joints which subject either the nut or bolt to rotation. They may be used with antifriction bearings and control pulleys, provided the inner race of the bearing is clamped to the supporting structure by the nut and bolt. Attach nuts to the structure in a positive manner to eliminate rotation or misalignment when tightening the bolts or screws.

(1) All-metal locknuts are constructed with either the threads in the locking insert out-of-phase with the load-carrying section, or with a saw-cut insert with a pinched-in thread in the locking section. The locking action of the all-metal nut depends upon the resiliency of the metal when the locking section and load-carrying section are engaged by screw threads.

(2) Fiber or nylon locknuts are constructed with an unthreaded fiber-locking insert held securely in place. The fiber or nylon has a smaller diameter than the nut, and when a bolt or screw is entered, it taps into the insert, producing a locking action. After the nut has been tightened, make sure the rounded or chamfered end bolts, studs, or screws extend at least the full round or chamfer through the nut. Flat end bolts, studs, or screws should extend at least 1/32 inch through the nut. When fiber-type self-locking nuts are reused, check the fiber carefully to make sure it has not lost its locking friction or become brittle. Do not reuse locknuts if they can be run up finger-tight. Bolts 5/16-inch diameter and over with cotter pinholes may be used with self-locking nuts but only if free from burrs around the holes. Bolts with damaged threads and rough ends are not acceptable. Do not tap the fiber-locking insert.

(3) Self-locking nut bases are made in a number of forms and materials for riveting and welding to aircraft structure or parts. Certain applications require the installation of self-locking nuts in channels, an arrangement which permits the attachment of many nuts with only a few rivets. These channels are track-like bases with regularly spaced nuts which are either removable or nonremovable. The removable type carries a floating nut, which can be snapped in or out of the channel, thus making possible the ready removal of damaged nuts. Nuts such as the clinch-type and spline-type which depend on friction for their anchorage are not acceptable for use in aircraft structures.

(4) Self-locking nuts may be used on aircraft engines and accessories when their use is specified by the engine manufacturer in his bulletins or manuals.

b. **Aircraft Castle Nut (AN–310).** The castle nut is used with drilled-shank AN hex-head bolts, clevis bolts, eye bolts, drilled-head bolts or studs, and is designed to accommodate a cotter pin or lockwire as a means of safetying.

c. **Miscellaneous Aircraft Nuts.**

(1) The plain nut (AN–315 and AN–335) has limited use on aircraft structures and re-

quires an auxiliary locking device such as a checknut or lockwasher.

(2) Light hex-nuts (AN–340 and AN–345) are used in miscellaneous applications and must be locked by an auxiliary device.

(3) The checknut (AN–316) is used as a locking device for plain nuts, screws, threaded rod ends, and other devices.

(4) The castellated shear nut (AN–320) is designed for use with clevis bolts and threaded taper pins, which are normally subjected to shearing stress only.

(5) Wing nuts (AN–350) are intended for use on hose clamps and battery connections, etc., where the desired tightness is ordinarily obtained by the use of the fingers or hand tools.

(6) Sheet spring nuts, such as speed nuts, are used with standard and sheet metal self-tapping screws in nonstructural locations. They find various uses in supporting line clamps, conduit clamps, electrical equipment, access doors, and the like, and are available in several types.

(7) Two commercial types of high-strength internal or external wrenching nuts are available, the internal and external wrenching elastic-stop nut and the Unbrako internal and external wrenching nut. Both are of the self-locking type, are heat-treated, and are capable of carrying the high-strength bolt-tension load.

231. **WASHERS.** The types of washers used in aircraft structure are: plain washers, lockwashers, and special washers.

a. **Plain washers (AN–960 and AN–970)** are widely used under hex nuts to provide a smoothbearing surface, to act as a shim and to adjust holes in bolts. Use plain washers under lockwashers to prevent damage to surfaces. Cadmiumplated steel washers are recommended for use under boltheads or nuts on aluminum alloy or magnesium structures where corrosion, if it occurs, will then be between the washer and the steel. The AN–970 steel washer provides a greater bearing area than the plain type, and is used in wooden structures under both boltheads and nuts to prevent local crushing of the surface.

b. Lock washers (AN–935 and AN–936) may be used with machine screws or bolts whenever the self-locking or castellated type of nut is not applicable. They are not to be used as fastenings to primary or secondary structures, or where subject to frequent removal or corrosive conditions.

c. Ball-socket and seat-washers (AN–950 and AN–955) are used in special applications where the bolt is installed at an angle to the surface, or when perfect alignment with the surface is required at all times. These washers are used together.

d. Taper-pin washers (AN–975) are used with the threaded taper pin.

e. NAS–143 washers are used with NAS internal wrenching bolts and internal wrenching nuts. Type "C" is countersunk to seat the bolthead shank radius and a plain-type washer is used under the nut. Both of these washers are heat treated from 125,000 to 145,000 p.s.i.

* **232. TYPES OF RIVETS. (See Figure 5.4.)** *

a. Standard solid-shank rivets and the universal head rivets (AN–470) are used in aircraft construction in both interior and exterior locations.

b. Roundhead rivets (AN–430) are used in the interior of aircraft except where clearance is required for adjacent members.

c. Flathead rivets (AN–442) are used in the interior of the aircraft where interference of adjacent members does not permit the use of roundhead rivets.

d. Brazierhead rivets (AN–455 and AN–456) are used on the exterior surfaces of aircraft where flush riveting is not essential.

e. All protruding head rivets may be replaced by MS–20470 (supersedes AN–470) rivets. This has been adopted as the standard for protruding head rivets in this country.

f. Countersunk head rivets MS–20426 (supersedes AN–426 100°) are used on the exterior surfaces of aircraft to provide a smooth aerodynamic surface, and in other applications where a smooth finish is desired. The 100° countersunk head has been adopted as the standard in this country.

233. MATERIAL APPLICATIONS.

* **a. 2117–T–4 is the most commonly** used rivet material utilized in aluminum alloy structures. Its * main advantage lies in the fact that it may be used in the condition received without further treatment.

* **b. The 2017–T3, 2017–T31, and 2024–T4 rivets** are used in aluminum alloy structures where strength higher than that of the 2117–T–4 rivet is needed. See Handbook MIL–HDBK–5 for differ- * ences between the two types of 17ST rivets specified here.

c. The 1100 rivets of pure aluminum are used for riveting nonstructural parts fabricated from the softer aluminum alloys, such as 1100, 3003, and 5052.

d. When riveting magnesium alloy structures, 5056 rivets are used exclusively due to their corrosion-resistant qualities in combination with the magnesium alloys.

e. Mild steel rivets are used primarily in riveting steel parts. Do not use galvanized rivets on steel parts subjected to high heat.

f. Corrosion-resistant steel rivets are used primarily in riveting corrosion-resistant steel parts such as firewalls, exhaust stack bracket attachments, and similar structures.

g. Monel rivets are used in special cases for riveting high-nickel steel alloys and nickel alloys. They may be used interchangeably with stainless steel rivets as they are more easily driven. However, it is preferable to use stainless steel rivets in stainless steel parts.

h. Copper rivets are used for riveting copper alloys, leather, and other nonmetallic materials. This rivet has only limited usage in aircraft.

i. Hi-shear rivets are sometimes used in connections where the shearing loads are the primary design consideration. Its use is restricted to such connections. It should be noted that hi-shear rivet patterns are not to be used for the installation of control surface hinges and hinge

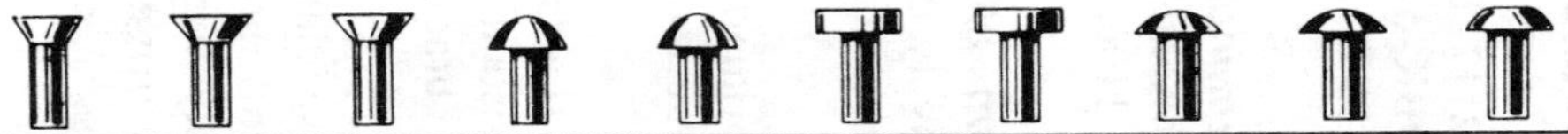

Material	Head Marking	AN Material Code	AN425 78° Counter-Sunk Head	AN426 100° Counter-Sunk Head MS20426*	AN427 100° Counter-Sunk Head MS20427*	AN430 Round Head MS20470*	AN435 Round Head MS20613*/MS20615*	AN441 Flat Head	AN442 Flat Head MS20470*	AN455 Brazier Head MS20470*	AN456 Brazier Head MS20470*	AN470 Universal Head MS20470*	Heat Treat Before Using	Shear Strength P.S.I.	Bearing Strength P.S.I.
1100	Plain	A	X	X		X			X	X	X	X	No	10000	25000
2117T	Recessed Dot	AD	X	X		X			X	X	X	X	No	30000	100000
2017T	Raised Dot	D	X	X		X			X	X	X	X	Yes	34000	113000
2017T-HD	Raised Dot	D	X	X		X			X	X	X	X	No	38000	126000
2024T	Raised Double Dash	DD	X	X		X			X	X	X	X	Yes	41000	136000
5056T	Raised Cross	B		X		X			X	X	X	X	No	27000	90000
7075-T73	Three Raised Dashes		X	X		X			X	X	X	X	No		
Carbon Steel	Recessed Triangle	F			X		X MS20613*	X					No	35000	90000
Corrosion Resistant Steel	Recessed Dash	F			X		X MS20613*	X					No	65000	90000
Copper	Plain	C			X		X	X					No	23000	
Monel	Plain	M			X			X					No	49000	
Monel Nickel-Copper Alloy	Recessed Double Dots	C					X MS20615*						No	49000	
Brass	Plain						X MS20615*						No		
Titanium	Recessed Large and Small Dot			Ms 20426				X					No	95000	

* New specifications are for Design purposes

FIGURE 5.4 Aircraft rivet identification.

This page intentionally left blank.

brackets. Do not paint the rivets prior to assembly, even where dissimilar metals are being joined. However, it is advisable to touch up each end of the driven rivet with zinc chromate primer to allow the later application of the general airplane finish.

j. *Blind rivets* in the MS–20600 through MS–20603 series rivets and the mechanically-locked stem NAS 1398, 1399, 1738, and 1739 rivets may be substituted for solid rivets in accordance with the blind rivet or aircraft manufacturer's recommendations. They should not be used where the looseness or failure of a few rivets will impair the airworthiness of the aircraft. Design allowables for blind rivets are specified in MIL–HDBK–5, "Metallic Materials and Elements for Flight Vehicle Structures." Specific structural applications are outlined in MS–33522. Nonstructural applications for such blind rivets as MS–20604 and MS–20605 are contained in MS–33557.

* k. *Identification of solid rivets.* AN-type aircraft solid rivets can be identified by code markings on the rivet heads. A rivet made of 1100 material is designated as an A rivet, and has no head marking. The 2217–T4 rivets are designated AD rivets, and have a dimple on the head. The 2017–T4 alloy rivets are designated as D rivets and have a raised teat on the head. Two dashes on a rivet head indicate a 2024–T4 alloy designated as DD. A B designation is given to a rivet of 5056–H–12 material and is marked with a raised cross on the rivet head. *

234. FASTENERS (COWL AND FAIRING). A number of patented fasteners are in use on aircraft. A variety of these fasteners are commercially available and the manufacturer's recommendations concerning the proper use of these types of fasteners should always be considered in other than replacement application.

***235. UNCONVENTIONAL ATTACHMENTS.** Do not use unconventional or new attachment devices in the primary structure unless approved by a manufacturer or a FAA representative. *

236.-246. RESERVED.

Chapter 6. CORROSION PROTECTION

247. TYPES OF CORROSION. Almost all metals used in aircraft are subject to corrosion. The attack may take place over an entire metal surface, or it may be penetrating in nature, forming deep pits. It may follow grain boundaries in its attack on metallic surfaces or it may penetrate a surface at random. It may be accentuated by stresses from external loads or existing in the metallic structure from lack of homogeneity or improper heat treatment. It is promoted by contact of the metals with materials that absorb water, such as wood, sponge rubber, felt, dirt, surface film, etc. Corrosion is referred to as the following types:

a. *Direct Surface Attack.* The most common type of general surface corrosion results from direct reaction of metal surface with oxygen in the air. Unless properly protected, steel will rust and aluminum and magnesium will form corrosion products. The attack may be accelerated by salt spray or salt-bearing air, by industrial gases, or by the aircraft engine exhaust gases.

b. *Dissimilar Metals Corrosion.* When two dissimilar metals are in contact and are connected by an electrolyte (continuous liquid or gas path—salt spray, exhaust gas, condensate) accelerated corrosion of one of the metals may occur. The most easily oxidized surface becomes the anode and corrodes. The less active member of the couple becomes the cathode of the galvanic cell. The degree of attack depends on the relative activity of the two surfaces; the greater the difference in activity, the more severe the attack. The materials listed in Group I are quite active and corrode easily. They require maximum protection. Group IV materials are the least active and therefore require minimum protection. Except as noted below, whenever metals from two different groups are in contact with each other, special protection is required to assure that dissimilar metal corrosion does not occur. Although aluminum alloys and tin are in different groups than magnesium, tin and the 5000 and 6000 series aluminum alloys may each be used in contact with magnesium without such protection. Tin may also be used with all aluminum alloys without special protection.

(1) **Group I.** Magnesium and its alloys.

(2) **Group II.** All aluminum alloys, cadmium, zinc.

(a) ***Subgroup A.*** 1100, 3003, 5052, 6061, 220, 355, 356. All clad alloys.

(b) ***Subgroup B.*** 2014, 2017, 2024, 7075, 195. Under severe corrosive conditions, the subgroups should be considered as dissimilar metals insofar as corrosion protection is concerned. This is particularly true when a large area of an alloy of Subgroup B is in contact with a small area of Subgroup A. Severe corrosion of the alloy from Subgroup A may be expected.

(3) **Group III.** Iron, lead, and tin and their alloys (except stainless steels).

(4) **Group IV.** Stainless steels, titanium, chromium, nickel, and copper and their alloys, graphite (including dry film lubricants containing graphite).

c. *Pitting.* While pitting may occur in any metal, it is particularly characteristic of passive materials such as the alloys of aluminum, nickel, and chromium. It is usually a localized breakdown of protection and may be due to a lack of homogeneity in the alloy surface, either from mechanical working or faulty heat treatment. It may also be due to an inclusion or rough spot in the metal surface or from localized contamination that breaks down the surface protection. Pitting takes place at random with no selective attack along grain boundaries. Isolated areas become anodic to the rest of the surface. Corrosion products formed accentuate the anodic characteristics in the pit area, and deep penetrating attack develops rather than a general surface attack.

d. Intergranular Corrosion. Selective attack along the grain boundaries of metal alloys is referred to as intergranular corrosion. It results from lack of uniformity in the alloy structure. It is particularly characteristic of precipitation hardened alloys of aluminum and some stainless steels. Aluminum alloys 2024 and 7075 which contain appreciable amounts of copper and zinc respectively are highly vulnerable to this type of attack if not quenched rapidly during heat treatment or given other special treatment such as the T73 temper condition for the 7075 alloys. Aluminum extrusions and forgings in general may contain non-uniform areas, which in turn may result in galvanic attack along the grain boundaries. This type of corrosion is difficult to detect in its original stage although ultrasonic and eddy current inspection methods are being used. When attack is well advanced, the metal may blister or delaminate. This is referred to as "exfoliation."

e. Stress Corrosion. This results from the combined effect of static tensile stresses applied to a surface over a period of time under corrosive conditions. In general, cracking susceptibility increases with stress, particularly at stresses approaching the yield point, and with increasing temperature, exposure time, and concentration of corrosive ingredients in the surrounding environment. Aluminum alloy bellcranks employing pressed-in taper pins, landing gear shock struts with pipe thread-type grease fittings, clevis joints, and shrink fits are examples of parts which are susceptible to stress corrosion cracking.

f. Corrosion Fatigue. Corrosion fatigue is a type of stress corrosion resulting from cyclic stresses on a metal in corrosive surroundings. Corrosion may start at the bottom of a shallow pit in the stressed area. Once attack begins, the continuous flexing prevents the repair of protective surface coating or oxide films and additional corrosion takes place in the area of stress. It is difficult to detect this type of attack in advance except as cracking develops.

g. Fretting. Fretting corrosion is a limited type of attack that develops when relative motion of small amplitude takes place between close fitting components. The rubbing contact destroys any protective film that may be present on the metallic surface and additionally removes small particles of virgin metal from the surface. These particles act as an abrasive and prevent the formation of any protective oxide film and exposes fresh active metal to the atmosphere. If the contact areas are small and sharp, deep grooves resembling brinnell markings or pressure indentations may be worn in the rubbing surface. As a result, this type of corrosion has also been called false brinnelling when developed on bearing surfaces.

248. CORROSION PROTECTION MEASURES FOR BASIC MATERIALS. In the repair or alteration of aircraft, apply corrosion proofing of the same type or equivalent to that originally applied unless the repair or alteration would result in increased susceptibility to corrosion, in which case use additional corrosion protection measures. Aluminum and magnesium alloys may be protected by a variety of surface treatments. Most aluminum alloy structural surfaces have been electrically anodized in chromic-sulfuric acid tanks before fabrication. Magnesium sheet has received cold nitric-chromic acid treatment; magnesium castings have usually received hot tank processing in fluoride dichromate mixtures. Steel surfaces may have been oxidized or plated during manufacture.

a. Anodizing and Related Processes. In anodizing, aluminum alloys are placed in an electrolytic bath causing a thin film of aluminum oxide to form on the surface of the aluminum. This is resistant to corrosion and affords a good paint base. Other processes which do not provide as good a corrosive protection as anodizing are, however, good paint bases. These processes are:

(1) Alkaline cleaning followed by chromic acid dip.

(2) Alcoholic phosphoric acid cleaner.

(3) Alkaline dichromate treatment.

b. Plating. Steels are commonly plated with other metals to prevent corrosion. Plating is accomplished by placing the article in an electrolytic bath and metal from the plating solution is deposited on it. Various metals used in plating vary in the corrosion protection they afford steel. For instance, cadmium and zinc corrode before the steel; hence, slight breaks or cracks through the plating of these metals will not result in rusting of the exposed steel, since the surface metal is corroded and protects the steel. Chromium does not protect steel by this method, as steel will corrode before the chromium and thus depends on the tightness of the plating for its protection. The process of postplate bake treatment to relieve hydrogen embrittlement is a necessary part of replating procedures for high-strength steel parts. High-strength nuts and bolts are highly susceptible to failure from hydrogen embrittlement, at the many stress risers and notches in their design, through normal usage of sustained and dynamic stresses. Because of the potential failures of embrittled parts, careful control over the heat treatment, grinding, preplate cleaning, plating, and postplate baking of high-strength parts is necessary.

c. Sherardizing. Steel parts may be sherardized by heating them in an atmosphere of zinc powder; however, this is not considered to be as effective against corrosion as zinc or cadmium plating.

d. Phosphate Rust-Proofing. This process is commercially known as Parkerizing, Bonderizing, Granodizing, etc. The coating placed on the part is used to protect steel parts after machining and before painting.

e. Chrome-Pickle Treatment. Magnesium parts which have been immersed or brushed with a solution of nitric acid and sodium dichromate will be protected for temporary storage. The coating also will serve as a bond for subsequent organic finishes. Sealed chrome-pickle treatment is used on magnesium parts for long term protection. Diluted chromic acid is a touch-up treatment. It is less critical to apply and can be applied over previously applied thin chromate films.

f. Dichromate Treatment. The dichromate treatment consists of boiling magnesium parts in a solution of sodium dichromate. This treatment provides good paint base and protective qualities on all standard wrought magnesium alloys except the magnesium-thorium alloys HK 31A, HM 21A, and HM 31A. No coating forms on these alloys. Acid pickling of the magnesium surface prior to application of the dichromate treatment is required if maximum corrosion resistance of the finish is expected.

g. Stannate Immersion Treatment. This treatment deposits a layer of tin. It is a protective paint base for magnesium alloy parts which contain inserts and fasteners of a dissimilar metal such as brass, copper, or steel. This treatment cannot be used with parts containing aluminum inserts or fasteners because the high alkalinity of the bath attacks the aluminum.

h. Galvanic Anodizing Treatment. This is an electrolytic process used to provide a paint base and corrosion preventive film on magnesium alloys containing manganese.

i. Cladding. Aluminum alloys which are susceptible to corrosion are frequently clad with pure aluminum. Slight pits, scratches, or other defects through the cladding material will not result in corrosion of the core, since the pure aluminum on the edges of the defect will be preferentially corroded, protecting the core.

j. Metal Spraying. Metal is melted and sprayed on the surface to be protected. The surface must be properly prepared and thoroughly cleaned to prevent peeling of the sprayed coat.

k. Shot-Peening. Shot-peening and other treatments by which the surface can be placed in compression are effective in preventing stress corrosion.

l. Organic Coatings. Zinc chromate primer, enamels, chlorinated rubber compounds, etc., are organic coatings commonly used to protect metals.

m. Dopeproofing. When doped fabrics are applied over an organic finished metal structure, the dope will have a tendency to loosen the finish on the metal. For this reason, organic coatings on the metal are usually covered with a dopeproof paint, with metal foil, or with cellulose tape to prevent the dope from striking through.

n. *Tube Interiors*. Protect the interiors of structural steel and aluminum tubing against corrosion. A small amount of water entrapped in a tube can corrode entirely through the tube thickness in a short period of time. Coat the tube interior by flushing with hot linseed oil, paralketone, or other corrosion inhibitor.

The flushing liquid is usually introduced through small holes drilled in the tubing. Allow the flushing liquid to drain and plug the holes with a screw or by other means to prevent entry of moisture. Air and watertight sealing of the tubing will also give adequate protection against corrosion if the tubing is internally dry before being sealed.

249. CONSTRUCTION OF CORROSION RESISTANT STRUCTURE.
During fabrication, the use of such practices as listed below will reduce the sources of corrosion initiation.

a. Use combinations of metals which are as close together as possible in the galvanic series —do not use small aluminum clips on large stainless steel webs; use stainless steel fasteners in stainless steel assemblies.

b. Insulate dissimilar metals but do not use materials which absorb moisture or conduct it in "wick" fashion.

c. Paint cut edges.

d. Seal edges of faying surfaces on butt joints.

e. Provide adequate drainholes.

250. CORROSION REMOVAL.
When corrosion is detected, remove it as quickly as possible and protect the surface from further corrosion. In those cases where the corrosion has progressed extensively, the strength of the part may be in jeopardy and the part may need to be replaced.

a. *For steel parts,* except for highly stressed steel or stainless steel surfaces, the use of abrasive papers, buffers, hand wire brushing, and steel wool are acceptable cleanup procedures. However, it should be recognized that it is practically impossible to remove all corrosion products from the bottom of small pits and crevices. As a result, a part once rusty usually corrodes again, more easily than it did the first time. Removing corrosion products from highly stressed steel parts requires careful handling.

b. *For aluminum parts,* treatment includes the mechanical removal of as much of the corrosion products as practicable, the inhibition of residual material by chemical means, followed by the restoration of permanent surface coatings. Do not use steel wool, emery cloth, steel (except stainless steel) wire brushes, or severe abrasive materials because particles of the steel wool or emery cloth will become embedded in the soft material and cause corrosion. Hand polishing corroded areas with household abrasives or with metal polish available under Specification MIL–P–6888 is acceptable for use on clad aluminum but must not be used on anodized aluminum since it is severe enough to actually remove the protective anodized film. If the surface is particularly difficult to clean. Type II material under Specification MIL–C–5410 mixed 50–50 percent with solvent or mineral spirits may be used. Treat any superficial corrosion with a 10 percent solution of sodium dichromate to which one percent of chromium trioxide has been added or with material available under Specification MIL–C–5541. Allow these solutions to remain on the corroded area for 5 to 20 minutes and then wipe the surface dry. A more severe cleaning procedure consists of using a 10 percent solution of chromic acid to which has been added approximately 20 drops of battery electrolyte per gallon. Thorough brushing with a stiff fiber brush should loosen or remove most existing corrosion and assure complete penetration of the inhibitor into crevices and pits. Allow the chromic acid to remain in place for at least 5 minutes, then remove the excess by flushing with water or wiping with a wet cloth. Apply a protective coating the same day that the corrosion treatment is accomplished.

c. *When an anodized surface coating is damaged,* it can only be partially restored by chemical surface treatment. Therefore, exercise care in any cleaning process to avoid unnecessary breaking of the protective film, particularly at the edges of the aluminum sheet. Chromic acid and other inhibitive treatments tend to restore the oxide film.

d. *More severe cleaning is necessary* with intergranular corrosion (attack along grain boundaries). The mechanical removal of all corrosion products and visible delaminated metal layers must be accomplished in order to determine the extent of the destruction and to evaluate the remaining structural strength of the component. Inspection with a 5- to 10-power magnifying glass or the use of dye penetrant will assist in determining if all unsound metal and corrosion products have been removed. Grinding to blend or fair out the edges of damaged areas can best be accomplished by using aluminum oxide-impregnated rubber-base wheels. Chemically inhibit the exposed surfaces and restore chemical surface films or paint in the same manner as for other aluminum surfaces.

e. *Magnesium is the most chemically active* of the metals used in aircraft construction and is therefore the most difficult to protect. The prompt and complete correction of the coating failure is imperative if serious structural damage is to be avoided. Treat the corroded area with 10 percent chromic acid solution to which has been added approximately 20 drops of battery electrolyte per gallon, in the same manner as for aluminum alloys.

251. CORROSION PROOFING OF LANDPLANES AND SEAPLANES. In the repair or alteration of aircraft, use corrosion proofing materials the same as, or equivalent to, that originally applied unless the repair or alteration would result in increased susceptibility to corrosion, in which case, employ additional corrosion protection measures.

252. CORROSION PROOFING OF LANDPLANES CONVERTED TO SEAPLANES. A special problem is encountered in the conversion of landplanes to seaplanes. In general, landplanes do not receive corrosion proofing to the same extent as do seaplanes manufactured as such. Corrosion-proofing standards for landplanes converted to seaplanes are divided into two classes: (1) Necessary minimum precautions; and (2) Recommended precautions. Regardless of such precautions, it is imperative that the exterior surfaces of seaplanes be washed with clear fresh water immediately following extended water operation, or at least once a day when operated in salty or brackish water. Wash interior surfaces of seaplanes exposed to spray, taking care to prevent damage to electrical circuits or other items subject to injury.

a. *Necessary Minimum Precautions.* The following procedures are considered the minimum to safeguard the airworthiness of the converted aircraft and are not in themselves intended to maintain airworthiness for an indefinite period.

(1) Unless already protected, treat exposed fittings or fittings which can be reached through inspection openings with two coats of zinc chromate primer, paralketone, nonwater-soluble heavy grease, or comparable materials. This applies to items such as wing-root fittings, wing-strut fittings, control-surface hinges, horns, mating edges of fittings, and attach bolts, etc.

(2) Coat nonstainless control cables with grease or paralketone or other comparable protective coating, if not replaced with corrosion-resistant cables.

(3) Inspect all accessible sections of aircraft structure. Clean structural parts showing corrosion and refinish if corrosion attack is superficial. If a part is severely corroded, replace with an adequately corrosion-proofed part.

b. *Recommended Precautions.* The recommended precautions are those which are suggested as a means of maintaining such aircraft in condition for safe operation over extended periods of time.

(1) Provide additional inspection openings to assist in detecting corrosion. Experience has shown openings to allow inspection of lower and rearward portion of the fuselage to be particularly desirable.

(2) Incorporate additional provisions for free drainage and ventilation of all interiors to

prevent collection of moisture (scoop-type drain grommets).

(3) Protect the interior of structural steel tubing. This may be done by air and watertight sealing or by flushing with hot linseed oil and plugging the openings. Inspect tubing for missing sealing screws, presence of entrapped water, local corrosion around sealing screws, welded clusters, and bolted fittings which may be indicative of entrapped moisture.

(4) Slit the fabric of fabric-covered aircraft longitudinally on the bottom of the fuselage and tail structure for access to these sections. Coat the lower structural members with zinc chromate primer (two coats); follow by a coat of dope-proof paint or wrap with cellophane tape and rejoin the fabric. This precaution is advisable within a few months after start of operation as a seaplane.

(5) Spray the interior of metal-covered wings and fuselages with an adherent corrosion inhibitor.

(6) Place bags of potassium or sodium dichromate in the bottom of floats and boat hulls to inhibit corrosion.

(7) Prevent the entry of water by sealing, as completely as possible, all openings in wings, fuselage, control-surface members, openings for control cables, tail-wheel wells, etc.

253. CLEANERS, POLISHES, BRIGHTENERS. It is important that aircraft be kept thoroughly clean of deposits containing contaminating substances such as oil, grease, dirt, and other foreign materials.

a. Materials. Avoid damage to aircraft by not using harmful cleaning, polishing, brightening, or paint-removing materials. Use only those compounds which conform to existing government or established industry specifications or products that have been specifically recommended by the aircraft manufacturer as being satisfactory for the intended application. Observe the product manufacturer's recommendations concerning use of his agent.

b. Chemical cleaners. Chemical cleaners must be used with great care in cleaning assembled aircraft. The danger of entrapping corrosive materials

in fraying surfaces and crevices counteracts any advantages in their speed and effectiveness. Use materials which are relatively neutral and easy to remove.

c. Removal of Spilled Battery Acid. In order to neutralize spilled battery acid, use sodium bicarbonate (baking soda), or sodium borate (borax) 20 percent by weight dissolved in water. After neutralization, remove alkali salt completely with large quantities of water to prevent corrosion. An application of acidproof paint to the structure surrounding the battery may be an effective control for this type of corrosion.

254. HANDLING AND CARE OF AIRCRAFT RECOVERED FROM WATER IMMERSION. Aircraft which were recovered from partial or total immersion in water, including flash floods, have been allowed to air dry, in certain instances, with no safety precautions other than a cursory inspection of the aircraft exterior. The lack of an adequate cleanup of water immersed areas may subsequently adversely affect the safety of the aircraft. That is, water immersion increases the probability of corrosive attack, the removal of lubrication, the deterioration of aircraft materials, and/or degradation of electrical and avionic equipment.

Sea water, because of salt content, is more corrosive than surface fresh water. However, fresh water may contain varying amounts of salt and, as drying occurs, the salt concentration is increased and corrosive attack accelerated.

The most important factor following recovery of an aircraft from sea or fresh water immersion is prompt action. Components of the aircraft which have been water immersed, such as the powerplant, accessories, airframe sections, actuating mechanisms, screws, bearings, working surfaces, fuel and oil systems, wiring, radio, and radar should be disassembled, to the extent considered necessary, so that the contaminants can be completely removed.

a. Initial Fresh Water/Detergent Wash. As soon as possible after the aircraft is recovered from water immersion, thoroughly wash contaminated internal and external areas of the aircraft using a water/detergent solution as follows:

(1) Mix liquid detergent (MIL–D–16791, Type I) and isopropyl alcohol (TT–I–735) in ratio of 8 parts detergent to 20 parts of alcohol. Add the detergent/alcohol mixture to 72 parts of tap water and mix thoroughly. For use, add one part of the foregoing concentrate to nine parts of tap water (warm water if available) and mix thoroughly.

* **(2)** If the above specified detergent/alcohol materials are not available, use water emulsion cleaning compound (MIL-C-43616). Add one part * compound to nine parts water. If the MIL cleaning compound is not available, use any available mild household detergent solution with fresh tap water.

b. Safety Precautions. The following safety precautions should be observed:

(1) Electrically ground the aircraft. Attach the ground lead to the aircraft at a point which is outside the area that could contain explosive vapors.

(2) If the landing gear of land planes is used as a supporting mechanism, install a spreader bar, jury strut, landing gear downlocks or other devices to insure that the gear will not collapse. If the landing gear is not serviceable, insure that the aircraft is solidly supported to prevent hazardous movement.

(3) Disconnect and remove wet- and/or dry-cell batteries and isolate aircraft from all sources of electricity or other spark-producing devices. Spark-producing static electricity is generated at compressed air hose outlets, so this method should not be used for ventilating or purging fuel vapors.

(4) Remove all fuel, oil, and hydraulic fluid.

(5) Flush all fuel and oil cells with clean fresh water.

(6) Deflate tires, especially on magnesium wheels. Depressurize landing gear struts, pneumatic systems, and hydraulic accumulators.

c. Reciprocating Engines and Propellers. The propeller should be removed from the engine and the engine from the aircraft. The exterior of the engine and propeller should be washed with steam, or hot or cold fresh water.

The major accessories, engine parts, etc., should be removed and all surfaces flushed with fresh water, preferably hot. If facilities are available, the removed parts, size permitting, should be immersed

in hot water or hot oil, 180° F., for a short period of time. Soft water is preferred and should be changed frequently. All parts must be completely dried by air blast or other means. If no heat drying facility is available, wipe the cleaned parts with suitable drying cloths.

The constant speed propeller mechanism should be disassembled, as required, to permit complete decontamination. Clean parts with steam or hot or cold fresh water. Dry the cleaned parts in an oven, but if a heat drying facility is not available, wipe the cleaned parts with suitable drying cloths.

d. Gas Turbine, Turboprop, and Turboshaft Engines. The engine exhaust shield, insulation blankets, separate exhaust collectors, compressor housing, pinion cowl and/or upper pinion housing should be removed. The engine accessories, outer housing exhaust shields, and other exposed parts should be steam cleaned. The steam-cleaned parts should be dried in an oven at approximately 200° F., or with hot air from a portable engine heater, or with clean wiping cloths.

Immerse remainder of engine in 10-20 percent water solution of sodium dichromate, or hot, fresh water and apply sufficient agitation to provide complete flushing.

If immersion cannot be accomplished, flood the lower section of the compressor housing and thoroughly flush rotor blades with sodium dichromate solution or warm fresh water. Seal off combustion chamber openings and alternately fill and drain the combustion chamber with fresh air from a portable engine heater or wipe with suitable drying cloths.

e. Airframe. The salvageable components of the fuselage, wings, empennage, seaplane and amphibian hulls and floats, and movable surfaces should be processed as follows:

(1) The fabric from fabric-covered surfaces should be removed and replaced.

(2) The aircraft interior and exterior should be cleaned using steam under pressure with steam-cleaning compound. The steam should be directed into all seams and crevices where corrosive water may have penetrated. Avoid steam *cleaning electrical equipment, such as terminal boards and relays.

(3) Areas that have been steam cleaned should be rinsed immediately with either hot or cold fresh water.

(4) Touch up all scratches and scars on painted surfaces using zinc chromate primer or preservative.

(5) Undrained hollow spaces or fluid entrapment areas should be provided temporary draining facilities by drilling out rivets at lowest point. Install new rivets after drainage.

(6) All leather, fabric upholstery, and insulation should be removed and replaced. Plastic or rubber foam which cannot be cleaned of all corrosive water should be replaced.

(7) All drain plugs or drive screws in tubular structures should be removed and the structure blown out with compressed air. If corrosive water has reached the tubular interiors, carefully flush with hot, fresh water and blow out water with compressed air. Roll the structure as necessary to remove water from pockets. Fill the tubes with hot linseed oil at approximately 180° F. Drain oil and replace drain plugs or drive screws.

(8) Clean sealed wood, metalite, and other nonmetallic areas, excluding acrylic plastics, with warm water. Wood, metalite, and other porous materials exposed to water immersion should be replaced, unless surfaces are adequately sealed to prevent penetration by corrosive water. Virtually all solvents and phenolic type cleaning agents are detrimental to acrylics and will either soften the plastic or cause crazing.

f. Helicopter Rotor Dynamic Components.

(1) All evidence of corrosive water should be removed from the exterior of transmissions and gear boxes by flushing with clean hot or cold fresh water.

(2) Where it is possible that corrosive water has reached the interior of the transmission or gear boxes, remove plugs and/or covers and drain completely. Flush interior of part with hot or cold fresh water. Drain residual water, replace plugs and/or covers, and reapply proper lubricant.

g. Helicopter Blades. Except for blades with wooden or other nonmetallic constructions, treat helicopter blades the same as propellers for reciprocating engines. Clean nonmetallic blades by hand, using warm water. Dry with wiping cloths or a warm air blast. When cleaning helicopter rotor blades, insure that nonsealed hollow members, such as the spars and blade pockets, are cleaned and dried.

h. Fuel and Oil Systems. Contaminated fuel and oil systems should be processed as follows:

(1) Flush oil system, including lines, using water-displacing preservative.

(2) Open fuel systems. Purge cells and fuel lines. Check effectiveness of the purging with combustible gas indicator. Remove bladder and self-sealing type fuel cells and all cavity liners or pads.

(3) Use clean, fresh water to wash fuel cells. After drying, spray interior walls with oil.

(4) Chemically treat bare metal surfaces of cleaned aluminum tanks with 10–20 percent water solution of sodium dichromate.

(5) Flush fuel lines with hot water (150° F. maximum). Dry, using clean, dry, compressed air.

i. Landing Gear. Process salvageable components of the landing gear, wheels, and brakes as follows:

(1) Remove tires and wheels.

(2) Steam clean wheels, rinse in fresh water, and dry.

(3) Remove wheel bearings and clean, using dry cleaning solvent.

(4) Immerse bearings in methyl alcohol and dry the cleaned bearings in air blast. Do not permit bearings to rotate during air blast drying. Reapply proper lubricant.

(5) Remove brakes, steam clean, and rinse with fresh water and dry.

j. Electrical Equipment.

(1) Wet cell batteries. The risk involved in using wet cell batteries that have been immersed in sea water may outweigh any economic advantage and should be replaced.

(2) Because of possible flight hazards and later defects caused by progressive corrosive attack, all electrical wiring immersed in corrosive water should be replaced. If wiring is*

merely splashed or sprayed with corrosive water, flush thoroughly with clean, fresh water and dry
* using compressed air. Following compressed air drying, coat with water dispensing preservative (MIL–C–81309, Type II).   *

k. *Miscellaneous Equipment.* The following equipment should be thoroughly washed to remove dirt, salt, and other contaminants. Dry with air blast or other means, and, if required, reapply proper lubricant:

(1) Wiring and fuselage hydraulic units.

(2) Electric landing gears.

(3) Actuators.

(4) Cables.

(5) Accumulators.

(6) Hydraulic reservoirs.

(7) Flight control.

(8) Torque tubes and bell cranks.

(9) Heating units, ducts, etc.

255.-264. RESERVED.

Chapter 7. IDENTIFICATION, TESTING, AND INSPECTION OF MATERIALS

Section 1. IDENTIFICATION OF METALS

265. IDENTIFICATION OF STEEL STOCK. The Society of Automotive Engineers (SAE) and the American Iron and Steel Institute (A.I.S.I.) use a numerical index system to identify the composition of various steels. The numbers assigned in the combined listing of standard steels issued by these groups represent the type of steel and make it possible to readily identify the principal elements in the material.

The first digit of the four number designation indicates the type to which the steel belongs. Thus "1" indicates a carbon steel, "2" a nickel steel, "3" a nickel chromium steel, etc. In the case of simple alloy steels, the second digit indicates the approximate percentage of the predominant alloying element. The last two digits usually indicate the mean of the range of carbon content. Thus the symbol "1020" indicates a plain carbon steel lacking a principal alloying element and containing an average of 0.20 percent (0.18 to 0.23) carbon. The symbol "2330" indicates a nickel steel of approximately 3 percent (3.25 to 3.75) nickel and an average of 0.30 percent, (0.28 to 0.33) carbon content. The symbol "4130" indicates a chromium-molybdenum steel of approximately 1 percent (0.80 to 1.10) chromium, 0.20 percent (0.15 to 0.25) molybdenum, and 0.30 percent (0.28 to 0.33) carbon. The basic numbers for the four digit series of the carbon and alloy steels may be found in figure 7.1.

266. INTERCHANGEABILITY OF STEEL TUBING.

a. *"1025" welded tubing* as per Specification MIL-T-5066 and "1025" seamless tubing conforming to Specification MIL-T-5066A are interchangeable.

b. *"4130" welded tubing* as per Specification MIL-T-6731, and "4130" seamless tubing conforming to Specification MIL-T-6736 are interchangeable.

FIGURE 7.1.—Numerical system for steel identification.

Type of steels	Numerals and digits
Carbon Steels	[1]xxx
Plain Carbon Steels	10xx
Free Cutting Steels	11xx
Manganese Steels (Manganese 1.60 to 1.90%)	13xx
Nickel Steels	2xxx
3.50% nickel	23xx
5.00% nickel	25xx
Nickel Chromium Steels	3xxx
9.70% nickel, 0.07% chromium	30xx
1.25% nickel, 0.60% chromium	31xx
1.75% nickel, 1.00% chromium	32xx
3.50% nickel, 1.50% chromium	33xx
Corrosion and heat resisting	30xxx
Molybdenum Steels	40xx
Chromium Molybdenum Steels	41xx
Nickel Chromium Molybdenum Steels	43xx
Nickel Molybdenum Steels	
1.75% nickel, 0.25% molybdenum	46xx
* 3.50% nickel, 0.25% molybdenum	48xx *
Chromium Steels	5xxx
Low chormium	51xx
Medium chromium	52xxx
Corrosion and heat resisting	51xxx
Chromium Vanadium Steels	6xxx
1.00% chromium	61xx
National Emergency Steels	8xxx
Silicon Manganese Steels	9xxx
2.00% silicon	92xx

c. *NE-8630 welded tubing* conforming to Specification MIL-T-6734, and NE-8630 seamless tubing conforming to Specification MIL-T-6732 are interchangeable.

267. IDENTIFICATION OF ALUMINUM. To provide a visual means for identifying the various grades of aluminum and aluminum alloys, such metals are usually marked with symbols such as Government Specification Number, the temper or condition furnished, or the commercial code marking. Plate and sheet are usually marked with specification numbers or code markings in rows approximately 5 inches apart. Tubes, bars, rods, and extruded shapes are marked with specification numbers or code markings at intervals of 3 to 5 feet along the length of each piece. The commercial code marking consists of a number which identifies the particular composition of the alloy. In addition, letter suffixes designate the following:

Nonheat-treatable Alloys		Heat-treatable Alloys	
Temper designation	Definition	Temper designation	Definition
–O	Annealed recrystallized (wrought products only) applies to softest temper of wrought products.	–O	Annealed recrystallized (wrought products only) applies to softest temper of wrought products.
–H12	Strain-hardened one-quarter-hard temper.	–T2	Annealed (castings only).
		–T3	Solution heat-treated and cold-worked by the flattening or straightening operation.
–H14	Strain-hardened half-hard temper.		
–H16	Strain-hardened three-quarters-hard temper.		
		–T36	Solution heat-treated and cold-worked by reduction of 6 percent.
–H18	Strain-hardened full-hard temper.		
–H22	Strain-hardened and partially annealed to one-quarter-hard temper.	–T4	Solution heat-treated.
		–T42	Solution heat-treated by the user regardless of prior temper (applicable only to 2014 and 2024 alloys).
–H24	Strain-hardened and partially annealed to half-hard temper.		
–H26	Strain-hardened and partially annealed to three-quarters-hard temper.	–T5	Artificially aged only (castings only).
		–T6	Solution heat-treated and artificially aged.
–H28	Strain-hardened and partially annealed to full-hard temper.		
		–T62	Solution heat-treated and aged by user regardless of prior temper (applicable only to 2014 and 2024 alloys).
–H32	Strain-hardened and then stabilized. Final temper is one-quarter hard.		
–H34	Strain-hardened and then stabilized. Final temper is one-half hard.	–T351, –T451, –T3510, –T3511, –T4510, –T4511.	Solution heat-treated and stress relieved by stretching to produce a permanent set of 1 to 3 percent, depending on the product.
–H36	Strain-hardened and then stabilized. Final temper is three-quarters hard.	–T651, –T851, –T6510, –T8510, –T6511, –T8511.	Solution heat-treated, stress relieved by stretching to produce a permanent set of 1 to 3 percent, and artificially aged.
–H38	Strain-hardened and then stabilized. Final temper is full-hard.		
–H112	As fabricated; with specified mechanical property limits.	–T652	Solution heat-treated, compressed to produce a permanent set and then artificially aged.
–F	For wrought alloys; as fabricated. No mechanical properties limits. For cast alloys; as cast.	–T81	Solution heat-treated, cold-worked by the flattening or straightening operation, and then artificially aged.
		–T86	Solution heat-treated, cold-worked by reduction of 6 percent, and then artificially aged.
		–F	For wrought alloys; as fabricated. No mechanical properties limits. For cast alloys; as cast.

FIGURE 7.2.—Basic temper designations and subdivisions for aluminum alloys.

a. *Clad aluminum alloys* have surface layers of pure aluminum or corrosion-resistant aluminum alloy bonded to the core material to inhibit corrosion. Presence of such a coating may be determined under a magnifying glass by examination of the edge surface which will show three distinct layers.

b. *Test for Distinguishing Heat-Treatable and Nonheat-Treatable Aluminum Alloys.* If for any reason the identification mark of the alloy is not on the material, it is possible to distinguish between some heat-treatable alloys and some nonheat-treatable alloys by immersing a sample of the material in a 10 percent solution of caustic soda (sodium hydroxide). Those heat-treated alloys containing several percent of copper (2014, 2017, and 2024) will turn black due to the copper content. High copper alloys when clad will not turn black on the surface, but the edges will turn black at the center of the sheet where the core is exposed. If the alloy does not turn black in the caustic soda solution it is not evidence that the alloy is not heat-treatable, as various high strength heat-treatable alloys are not based primarily on the use of copper as an alloying agent. These include among others 6053, 6061, and 7075 alloys. The composition and heat-treatability of alloys which do not turn black in a caustic soda solution can be established only by chemical or spectro-analysis.

268.–278. RESERVED.

Section 2. TESTING OF METALS

279. HARDNESS TESTING. Hardness testing provides a convenient means for determining, within reasonable limits, the tensile strength of steel. It has several limitations in that it is not suitable for very soft or very hard steels. In hardness testing, the thickness of the specimen being tested and the edge distance should be such that distortion of the metal due to these factors is eliminated. Several readings should be taken and the results averaged. In general, the higher the tensile strength, the greater is its hardness. Common methods of hardness testing are outlined in the following paragraphs. These tests are suitable for determining the tensile properties resulting from the heat treatment of steel. Care should be taken to have case hardened, corroded, pitted, decarburized, or otherwise nonuniform surfaces removed to a sufficient depth. Also, exercise caution not to cold-work and consequently harden the steel during removal of the surface. The relationship between tensile strength and hardness is indicated in figure 7.3.

280. BRINELL HARDNESS TEST. In this test a standard load is applied to a smooth surface of metal through a hardened steel ball, one centimeter in diameter. The numerical value of Brinell hardness is equal to the load divided by the surface area of the resulting spherical impression.

281. ROCKWELL HARDNESS TEST. In this test, a standard minor load is applied to seat a hardened steel ball or a diamond cone in the surface of the metal, followed by the application of a standard major load. The hardness is measured by depth of penetration. Rockwell superficial hardness tests are made using light minor and major loads and a more sensitive system for measuring depth of indentation. It is useful for thinner sections, very small parts, etc.

282. VICKERS HARDNESS TEST. In this test, a small pyramidal diamond is pressed into the metal. The hardness number is the ratio of the load to the surface area of indentation.

283. TESTING ALUMINUM. Hardness tests are useful for testing aluminum alloy chiefly as a means of distinguishing between annealed, cold-worked, heat-treated, and heat-treated and aged material. It is of little value in indicating the strength or quality of heat treatment. Typical hardness values for aluminum alloys are shown in figure 7.4.

FIGURE 7.4.—Hardness values for aluminum alloys.

Material commercial designation	Hardness temper	Brinell number 500 kg. load 10 mm. ball
1100	0	23
	H18	44
3003	0	28
	H16	47
2014	0	45
	T6	135
2017	0	45
	T6	105
2024	0	47
	T4	120
2025	T6	110
6151	T6	100
5052	0	47
	H36	73
6061	0	30
	T4	65
	T6	95
7075	T6	135
7079	T6	135
195	T6	75
220	T4	75
C355	T6	80
A356	T6	70

284.–294. RESERVED.

FIGURE 7.3.—Rockwell C scale steel hardness numbers comparison table.

Rockwell C-scale hardness number[a]	Diamond pyramid hardness number (Vickers)	Brinell hardness number 10-mm. ball, 3000-kg. load			Rockwell hardness number[a]			Rockwell, superficial hardness number, superficial brale penetrator			Shore scleroscope hardness number	Tensile strength[a] (approximate) in 1000 p. s. i.	Rockwell C-scale hardness number[a]
		Standard ball	Hultgren ball	Tungsten carbide ball	A-scale, 60-kg. load, brale penetrator	B-scale, 100-kg. load, 1/16-in. diam. ball	D-scale, 100-kg. load, brale penetrator	15-N scale, 15-kg. load	30-N scale, 30-kg. load	45-N scale, 45-kg. load			
Col. 1	Col. 2	Col. 3	Col. 4	Col. 5	Col. 6	Col. 7	Col. 8	Col. 9	Col. 10	Col. 11	Col. 12	Col. 13	Col. 14
68	940				85.6		76.9	93.2	84.4	75.4	97		68
67	900				85.0		76.1	92.9	83.6	74.2	95		67
66	865				84.5		75.4	92.5	82.8	73.3	92		66
65	832			739	83.9		74.5	92.2	81.9	72.0	91		65
64	800			722	83.4		73.8	91.8	81.1	71.0	88		64
63	772			705	82.8		73.0	91.4	80.1	69.9	87		63
62	746			688	82.3		72.2	91.1	79.3	68.8	85		62
61	720			670	81.8		71.5	90.7	78.4	67.7	83		61
60	697		613	654	81.2		70.7	90.2	77.5	66.6	81		60
59	674		599	634	80.7		69.9	89.8	76.6	65.5	80	326	59
58	653		587	615	80.1		69.2	89.3	75.7	64.3	78	315	58
57	633		575	595	79.6		68.5	88.9	74.8	63.2	76	305	57
56	613		561	577	79.0		67.7	88.3	73.9	62.0	75	295	56
55	595		546	560	78.5		66.9	87.9	73.0	60.9	74	287	55
54	577		534	543	78.0		66.1	87.4	72.0	59.8	72	278	54
53	560		519	525	77.4		65.4	86.9	71.2	58.6	71	269	53
52	544	500	508	512	76.8		64.6	86.4	70.2	57.4	69	262	52
51	528	487	494	496	76.3		63.8	85.9	69.4	56.1	68	253	51
50	513	475	481	481	75.9		63.1	85.5	68.5	55.0	67	245	50
49	498	464	469	469	75.2		62.1	85.0	67.6	53.8	66	239	49
48	484	451	455	455	74.7		61.4	84.5	66.7	52.5	64	232	48
47	471	442	443	443	74.1		60.8	83.9	65.8	51.4	63	225	47
46	458	432	432	432	73.6		60.0	83.5	64.8	50.3	62	219	46

See footnotes at end of table.

FIGURE 7.3.—Rockwell C scale steel hardness numbers comparison table—continued.

Rockwell C-scale hardness number[a]	Diamond pyramid hardness number (Vickers)	Brinell hardness number 10-mm. ball, 3000-kg. load			Rockwell hardness number[a]			Rockwell, superficial hardness number, superficial brale penetrator			Shore scleroscope hardness number	Tensile strength[a] (approximate) in 1000 p. s. l.	Rockwell C-scale hardness number[a]
		Standard ball	Hultgren ball	Tungsten-carbide ball	A-scale, 60-kg. load, brale penetrator	B-scale, 100-kg. load, 1/16-in. diam. ball	D-scale, 100-kg. load, brale penetrator	15-N scale, 15-kg. load	30-N scale, 30-kg. load	45-N scale, 45-kg. load			
Col. 1	Col. 2	Col. 3	Col. 4	Col. 5	Col. 6	Col. 7	Col. 8	Col. 9	Col. 10	Col. 11	Col. 12	Col. 13	Col. 14
------	446	421	421	421	73.1	------	59.2	83.0	64.0	49.0	60	212	45
------	434	409	409	409	72.5	------	58.5	82.5	63.1	47.8	58	206	44
------	423	400	400	400	72.0	------	57.7	82.0	62.2	46.7	57	201	43
------	412	390	390	390	71.5	------	56.9	81.5	61.3	45.5	56	196	42
------	402	381	381	381	70.9	------	56.2	80.9	60.4	44.3	55	191	41
------	392	371	371	371	70.4	------	55.4	80.4	59.5	43.1	54	186	40
------	382	362	362	362	69.9	------	54.6	79.9	58.6	41.9	52	181	39
------	372	353	353	353	69.4	------	53.8	79.4	57.7	40.8	51	176	38
------	363	344	344	344	68.9	------	53.1	78.8	56.8	39.6	50	172	37
------	354	336	336	336	68.4	(109.0)	52.3	78.3	55.9	38.4	49	168	36
------	345	327	327	327	67.9	(108.5)	51.5	77.7	55.0	37.2	48	163	35
------	336	319	319	319	67.4	(108.0)	50.8	77.2	54.2	36.1	47	159	34
------	327	311	311	311	66.8	(107.5)	50.0	76.6	53.3	34.9	46	154	33
------	318	301	301	301	66.3	(107.0)	49.2	76.1	52.1	33.7	44	150	32
------	310	294	294	294	65.8	(106.0)	48.4	75.6	51.3	32.5	43	146	31
------	302	286	286	286	65.3	(105.5)	47.7	75.0	50.4	31.3	42	142	30
------	294	279	279	279	64.7	(104.5)	47.0	74.5	49.5	30.1	41	138	29
------	286	271	271	271	64.3	(104.0)	46.1	73.9	48.6	28.9	41	134	28
------	279	264	264	264	63.8	(103.0)	45.2	73.3	47.7	27.8	40	131	27
------	272	258	258	258	63.3	(102.5)	44.6	72.8	46.8	26.7	38	127	26
------	266	253	253	253	62.8	(101.5)	43.8	72.2	45.9	25.5	38	124	25
------	260	247	247	247	62.4	(101.0)	43.1	71.6	45.0	24.3	37	121	24
------	254	243	243	243	62.0	100.0	42.1	71.0	44.0	23.1	36	118	23
------	248	237	237	237	61.5	99.0	41.6	70.5	43.2	22.0	35	115	22
------	243	231	231	231	61.0	98.5	40.9	69.9	42.3	20.7	35	113	21

FIGURE 7.3.—Rockwell C scale steel hardness numbers comparison table—continued.

					60.5		40.1	69.4	41.5	19.6			20
20	**238**	**226**	**226**	**226**	—	97.8	—	—	—	—	34	110	**20**
(18)	230	219	219	219	—	96.7	—	—	—	—	33	106	(18)
(16)	222	212	212	212	—	95.5	—	—	—	—	32	102	(16)
(14)	213	203	203	203	—	93.9	—	—	—	—	31	98	(14)
(12)	204	194	194	194	—	92.3	—	—	—	—	29	94	(12)
(10)	196	187	187	187	—	90.7	—	—	—	—	28	90	(10)
(8)	188	179	179	179	—	89.5	—	—	—	—	27	87	(8)
(6)	180	171	171	171	—	87.1	—	—	—	—	26	84	(6)
(4)	173	165	165	165	—	85.5	—	—	—	—	25	80	(4)
(2)	166	158	158	158	—	83.5	—	—	—	—	24	77	(2)
(0)	160	152	152	152	—	81.7	—	—	—	—	24	75	(0)

[1] The values in this table shown in bold-face type correspond to the values shown in the corresponding joint SAE–ASM–ASTM Committee on Hardness Conversions as printed in ASTM E48, table 2.

[2] Values in ( ) are beyond normal range and are given for information only.

[3] It is possible that steels of various compositions and processing histories will deviate in hardness-tensile strength relationship from the data presented in this table. Above the level of Rockwell C43, deviation increases with increasing hardness and the table shall not be used above Rc 48 except in the absence of other data specifically approved by the procuring agency.

Section 3. NONDESTRUCTIVE TESTING

295. GENERAL. The field of nondestructive testing (NDT) and inspection is to varied to be covered in detail in this handbook. This section provides a brief description of the various methods that are available for use in aircraft maintenance. The effectiveness of any particular method of NDT inspection depends upon the skill, experience, and training of the persons applying the process. Each process is limited in its usefulness as an inspection tool through its adaptability to the particular component to be inspected. Consult the aircraft or product manufacturer for specific instructions regarding NDT inspection of their product.

296. INSPECTION BY MAGNIFYING GLASS AFTER WELDING. Careful examination of all joints with a medium-power magnifying glass (at-least 10-power), after first removing all scale, is considered an acceptable method of inspection for repaired structures. The practice of filling steel tubular structures with hot linseed or petroleum base oils, under pressure, in order to coat the inside surface and inhibit corrosion, assists in the detection of weld cracks, as the hot oil will seep through cracks invisible to the eye. This practice, though not justifiable in all cases, is suggested where a very large portion of the structure has been rewelded.

* **297. MAGNETIC PARTICLE INSPECTION.** Magnetic particle inspection of Magnaflux can be used only on magnetic material; i.e., iron and steel. Most* stainless or high chromium nickel and manganese alloy steels, being nonmagnetic, cannot be inspected by this method. The method consists essentially of detection of discontinuities (cracks, voids, defects, pits, subsurface holes, etc.) by means of accumulation of magnetic particles on the discontinuities when the part has been magnetized. The magnetic particles are applied either dry as a powder or suspended in light oil. For complete magnetic inspection, both circular and longitudinal, magnetization should be employed.

Caution

Improper operation of Magnaflux equipment because of faulty equipment or by untrained persons, can jeopardize the airworthiness of parts being inspected. Minute electrical arc burns caused during inspection by improper operation of magnaflux equipment, can result in eventual failure of the part.

a. Circular magnetization is produced by transmitting an electric current directly through the article being tested, or through a central conductor placed through the part, in which case defects parallel to the flow of current may be detected. As an example, circular magnetization of a round steel bar would be produced by placing the ends of the steel bar between the heads of the magnetic inspection machine and passing a current through the bars. Magnetic particles applied either during or after passage of the current, or after passage of the current in magnetically retentive steels, would disclose discontinuities parallel to the axis of the bar.

b. Longitudinal magnetization is induced in a part by placing the part in a strong magnetic field, such as the center of a coil. Thus, longitudinal magnetization of a round steel bar would be produced by placing the ends of the bar between the heads of a magnetic-inspection machine and placing the D.C. solenoid around the bar. After application of the magnetic particles, either during or subsequent to magnetization, discontinuities perpendicular to the axis of the bar would be disclosed.

c. Red, black, and sometimes gray particles are used in the wet or dry methods. In the case of wet inspection, a fluorescent magnetic particle may also be used. This process is commercially known as Magnaglo. Articles inspected using the latter medium are illuminated by so-called black light, and the magnetic particles glow by fluorescence causing any defects or indications to be easily visible. The wet inspection procedure provides better control and standardization of the concentration of magnetic particles, easier application to complex shapes, and indications that are easier to interpret. This is due to the difficulty of obtaining efficient distribution of the dry powder during magnetization. The dry procedure is particularly suitable for detecting subsurface defects, such as, when inspecting heavy welds, forgings, castings, etc. The wet continuous process is recommended for most aircraft work.

d. *The presence of accumulations of magnetic particles* in magnetic inspection does not necessarily mean that a defect exists. Changes in section of the part, particularly where the change in section is very sharp, and also holes drilled through a part, will frequently cause indications. Surface defects are most easily detected, however, since a crack will cause a sharp line of magnetic particles to appear. Subsurface defects are less easily detected, since only a general collection of magnetic particles will be observed.

e. *After magnetic inspection* carefully demagnetize and clean the parts. Examine for possible evidence of electrical arc burns that may have occurred during inspection. All metal particles must be removed and the serviceable parts coated with a suitable preservative.

f. *Portable type magnetic particle inspection equipment* such as Sonoflux has been developed for use in the detection of surface or slightly subsurface discontinuities in ferromagnetic aircraft materials and parts. This type equipment usually gives better results when the wet suspension type of indicator, such as that conforming to Specification MIL–I–6868, is used with the powder supplied by the equipment manufacturer. As in other inspection methods, follow the manufacturers' recommendations concerning use of the procedure.

298. X-RAY OR RADIOGRAPHIC INSPECTION.
X-ray may be used on either magnetic or nonmagnetic materials for detecting subsurface

voids such as open cracks, blowholes, etc. When a photographic film or plate is used to record the X-ray (in a similar manner to exposing a photographic film), the process is known as radiography. When the X-rays are projected through the part onto a fluorescent screen, the process is known as fluoroscopy. The technique used for radiography should be capable of indicating the presence of defects having a dimension parallel to the X-ray beam of 3 percent of the thickness of the part being radiographed for magnesium alloys, and 2 percent for all other metals and alloys. Inspection using a fluoroscopic screen is much less sensitive. Consequently, the radiographic method is usually used for inspection and the fluoroscopic method is used for culling.

a. *Radiographic inspection* is extensively used in the aircraft industry for the inspection of all types of castings including sand castings, permanent-mold castings, die castings, etc. X-ray is particularly useful for this application, since it is capable of disclosing defects which exist below the surface, and also since the open types of defects which may occur in castings (shrinks, blowholes, dross inclusions, etc.) are readily disclosed by proper use of X-rays. In the inspection of forged or wrought metals, on the other hand, X-ray inspection is not used so extensively. This is due to the fact that the process of forging or working may cause defects which originally existed in the metal to become tightwalled cracks. Such defects are somewhat difficult to disclose by X-rays. If doubt exists as to the suitability of the X-ray examination, consult a laboratory familiar with the X-ray examination of aircraft parts.

b. *In radiography,* values of peak kilovoltage, radiographic density range and penetrometer characteristics are often selected that produce less than optimum radiological data. This selection of high kilovoltage is made in order to reduce the exposure time. The use of too high a kilovoltage reduces the resolvable detail recorded on the radiographic film. As the kilovoltage is increased, X-rays of shorter wave length and greater penetrating power are produced. This presents a sound argument for increased kilovoltages but does not take into account the effects of scatter both within the sample and the radiographic film, which in reality, reduces the resolvability of details recorded on the X-rays.

c. If for some reason a short exposure time is required, a faster film is normally used with a higher kilovoltage; however, this has the effect of increasing the granularity and reducing the resolution on the radiographic material.

d. The use of low voltages results in improved radiographic signal-to-noise ratio and improved resolution. The recommended kilovoltages are shown in figure 7.5.

FIGURE 7.5—Maximum recommended X-ray kilovolts.

Material	Atomic No.	Max. KV
Beryllium	4	25
Carbon	6	40
Magnesium	12	50
Alumium	13	75
Titanium	22	120
Steel	22-26	150
Steel	26-28	200
Silver	47	300
Lead	82	1-2 (megavolts)

299. FLUORESCENT PENETRANT. In this method of inspection the article, which may be of metal, plastic material, etc., is first carefully cleaned to permit the fluorescent material to penetrate cracks and defects. It should be noted that cleaning of aluminum may necessitate stripping of any anodizing, since the anodized film, if formed after the defect, could prevent penetration of the fluorescent material and an anodized film tends to hold penetrants which may obscure defect indications. After the article is cleaned, it is either sprayed, painted, or immersed in a bath of fluorescent penetrant. The penetrant is a light oil which has the property of fluorescing or emitting visible light when excited by invisible radiation in the near ultra-violet range (so-called black light). It is important that the penetrant be given sufficient time to penetrate cracks and defects, and for fatigue cracks a minimum of 30 minutes is stipulated by MIL–I–6866. Heat may also be applied to facilitate entry of the penetrant. After the penetrant has had sufficient time to enter any defects, the excess on

the surface of the article is washed off by water spray. This washing should be checked by inspection with black light, by which means any penetrant left on the surface may be detected. After washing, a developer is used to bring out the indication. This developer may be in a liquid form or may be a light powder that absorbs the penetrant as it oozes from cracks and defects in the part. The development may also be aided by application of heat to the part. After the indications have been developed, the part is inspected under black light. Any crevices into which the fluorescent material has penetrated will show as luminous areas.

Indications which appear are usually checked by close inspection with a magnifying glass, by etching with a suitable acid or caustic solution, or it may be necessary to cross-section the part, a procedure which, of course, destroys its usefulness. Usually a skilled operator can determine whether an indication actually shows a defect or whether it is a false indication. Also, the internal extent of the defect can sometimes be estimated with fair accuracy. It should be noted that this process of inspection, like all others, has its limitations. If the fluorescent material for any reason is not able to penetrate into a defect, such a defect cannot be detected.

300. DYE PENETRANTS. Several dye penetrant type inspection kits are now available which will reveal the presence of surface cracks or defects and subsurface flaws which extend to the surface of the part being inspected. These penetrant type inspection methods are considered acceptable, provided the part being inspected has been thoroughly cleaned, all areas are readily accessible for viewing, and the manufacturer's recommendations as to method of application are closely followed.

a. Cleaning. An inspection is initiated by first cleaning the surface to be inspected of dirt, loose scale, oil, and grease. Precleaning may usually be accomplished by vapor degreasing or with volatile cleaners. Use a volatile cleaner as it will evaporate from the defects before applying the penetrant dye. Sand blasting is not as desirable as a cleaning method, since surface indications may be obscured. It is not necessary to remove anodic films from parts to be inspected, since the dye readily penetrates such films. Special procedures for removing the excess dye should be followed.

b. *Application of Penetrant.* The penetrant is applied by brushing, spraying, or by dipping and allowing to stand for a minimum of 2 minutes. *Dwell time may be extended up to 15 minutes, depending upon the temperature of the part and fineness of the defect or surface condition. Parts being* inspected should be dry and heated to at least 70° F., but not over 130° F. Very small indications require increased penetration periods.

c. *Removal of Dye penetrant.* Surplus penetrant is usually removed by application of a special cleaner or remover, or by washing with plain water and the part allowed to dry. Water rinse may also be used in conjunction with the remover, subject to the manufacturer's recommendations.

d. *Application of developer.* A light and even coat of developer is applied by spraying, brushing, or dipping. When dipping, avoid excess accumulation. Penetrant which has penetrated into cracks or other openings in the surface of the material will be drawn out by the developer resulting in a bright red indication. Some idea of the size of the defect may be obtained after experience by watching the size and rate of growth of the indication.

301. ULTRASONIC FLAW DETECTION. Ultrasonic flaw detection equipment has made it possible to locate defects in all types of materials without damaging the material being inspected. Very small cracks, checks, and voids, too small to be seen by X-ray, are located by means of ultrasonic inspection. An ultrasonic test instrument requires access to only one surface of the material to be inspected, and can be used with either straight line or angle beam testing techniques. The instrument electronically generates ultrasonic vibrations and sends them in a pulsed beam through the part to be tested. Any discontinuity within the part, or the opposite end, will reflect the vibration back to the instrument, which measures the elapsed time between the initial pulse and the return of all reflections and indicates such time lapse on a cathode ray indicator or paper recorder. Ultrasonic inspection requires a skilled operator who is familiar with the equipment being used as well as the inspection method to be used for the many different parts being tested.

302.-312. RESERVED.

Section 4.   IDENTIFICATION OF FABRICS AND PLASTICS

313. IDENTIFICATION OF FABRIC. Cotton fabric is often used as covering for wing, fuselage, and control surfaces of aircraft. Acceptable grades of fabric for use on civil aircraft are listed in Chapter 3. In general, the fabric can be readily identified by a continuous marking to show the manufacturer's name or trademark and specification number. This marking may be found stamped along the selvage edge. The specification number for grade "A" fabric is AMS–3806, and for the intermediate grade AMS–3804. The corresponding FAA Technical Standard Order
✱ Numbers for these materials are TSO–C15 and TSO–C14, respectively. Increasing interest in ✱ the use of linen and certain synthetic fabrics in lieu of cotton has been noted. Identity of such materials should always be verified by the user.

314. IDENTIFICATION OF PLASTICS. Plastics cover a broad field of organic synthetic resins and may be divided into two main classifications—thermoplastic and thermosetting plastics.

a. Thermoplastics. Thermoplastics may be softened by heat and can be dissolved in various organic solvents. Two kinds of transparent thermoplastic materials are commonly employed in windows, canopies, etc. These materials are known as acrylic plastics and cellulose acetate plastics. These two plastics may be distinguished by the absence of color, the greater transparency, and the greater stiffness of the acrylic as compared to the slight yellow tint, lower transparency, and greater flexibility of cellulose acetate.

b. Thermosetting Plastics. Thermosetting plastics do not soften appreciably under heat but may char and blister at temperatures of 204° to 260° C. (400° to 500° F.). Most of the molded products of synthetic resin composition, such as phenolic, urea-formaldehyde, and melamine-formaldehyde resins, belong to the thermosetting group.

315.–320.   RESERVED.

Section 5.   CABIN INTERIOR MATERIALS, FIRE PROTECTION QUALITIES

321. REQUIREMENTS FOR FIRE PROTECTION. The cleaning, repairing, and/or replacement of cabin interior materials necessitates continuing compliance with the fire protection requirements of the FARs. A recent field survey on this matter revealed a wide variance in the procedures used for maintaining cabin interior materials with respect to the fire protection qualities of these materials.

a. Interior Materials. The methods, techniques, practices, and materials used in the cleaning, repair, and replacement of cabin materials must meet the requirements of Section 43.13 of the FARs.

b. Fire Protection. The requirements relative to fire protection qualities of cabin interior materials are specified in:

(1) Section 121.312, for aircraft operated under Parts 121, 123, and 135.

(2) Section 127.91, for helicopters used in passenger service under Part 127.

c. Source of Information. If information regarding the original or properly altered fire protection qualities of certain cabin interior materials is not available, requests for this information should be made to the aircraft manufacturers or the local FAA regional office, specifying the model aircraft, the aircraft manufacturer, the date the aircraft was manufactured or the serial number, and the FAR Part under which the aircraft is operated (i.e., Part 91, Part 121, etc.).   *

322.–325.   RESERVED.

Chapter 8. AIRCRAFT EQUIPMENT

Section 1. LANDING GEAR EQUIPMENT

326. GENERAL. Many factors affect the scope and frequency of landing gear system inspection and maintenance. The possibility of system malfunction increases with severe operating conditions, such as pilot training and agricultural operations. Cracks are the foremost area of concern, followed closely by worn, sheared, bent, or broken bolts, and elongated boltholes. Although these defects occur during normal aircraft usage, adverse operating conditions accelerate the problem.

Improper adjustment or lubrication can also cause malfunctioning, especially in landing gear retraction mechanisms. Excessive lubrication or the wrong type of lubricant can often be as bad or worse than none at all. With regard to lubrication, closely follow the manufacturer's service and maintenance instructions.

> **CAUTION**
>
> Inspect grease fittings after applying high pressure lubricant to determine that the spring-loaded ball has reseated. Failure of the ball to reseat is an indication of an internal failure of the fitting which can result in serious damage to the part being lubricated.

327. INSPECTION. Inspect the aircraft landing gear and all associated hardware closely for cracks, cleanliness, lubrication, leaks, deformation, excessive wear, and security of attachments. Before removing any accumulated dirt, closely observe the area being inspected while the wingtips are gently rocked up and down. Excessive motion between normally close fitting components may indicate wear, cracks, or improper adjustment. If a crack exists, it will generally be indicated by dirt or metallic particles which tend to outline the fault. Seepage of rust inhibiting oils, used to coat internal surfaces of steel tubes, also assists in the early detection of cracks. In addition, a sooty, oily residue around bolts, rivets, and pins is a good indication of looseness or wear.

Thoroughly clean and re-inspect the landing gear to determine the extent of any damage or wear. Some components may require removal and complete disassembly for detailed inspection. Others may require a specific check using an inspection process such as dye penetrant, magnetic particle, radiographic, ultrasonic, or eddy current (see Chapter 7). The frequency, degree of thoroughness, and selection of inspection methods are dependent upon the age, use, and general condition of the aircraft.

Inspect the aircraft structure surrounding any visible damage to insure that no secondary damage remains undetected. Forces can be transmitted along the affected member to remote areas where subsequent normal loads can cause failure at a later date.

a. Types of Malfunctions.

(1) Cracks. Prime locations for cracks on any landing gear are bolts, boltholes, pins, rivets, and welds. The following are typical locations where cracks may develop:

(a) Bolts. Most susceptible areas are at the radius between the head and the shank, and in the location where the threads join the shank, as shown in figure 8.1.

(b) Boltholes and Pinholes. Cracks primarily occur at the edge of boltholes or pinholes on

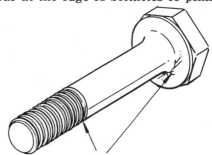

FIGURE 8.1.—Typical bolt cracks.

the surface and down inside the bore. (See figures 8.2 and 8.3.)

(c) **Riveted Joints or Seams.** The usual types of failure in this area are deformation of the rivet heads and skin cracks originating at the rivet holes.

(d) **Rod Ends.** Cracks and subsequent failures usually begin at the thread end near the bearing and adjacent to or under the jam nut. (See figure 8.4.)

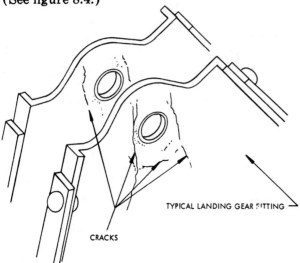

FIGURE 8.2.—Typical cracks near boltholes.

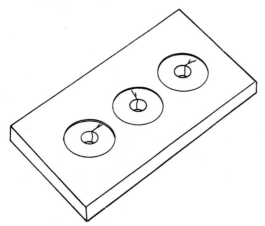

FIGURE 8.3.—Typical bolthole cracks.

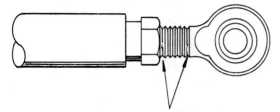

FIGURE 8.4.—Typical rod-end cracks.

(e) **Welds.** Cracks develop primarily along the edge of the weld adjacent to the base metal and along the centerline of the bead.

(2) **Elongated holes** are especially prevalent in taper-pin holes and boltholes or at the riveted joints of torque tubes and push-pull rods. (See figure 8.5.)

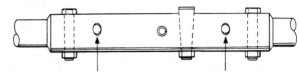

FIGURE 8.5.—Typical torque tube bolthole elongation.

(3) **Deformation** is common in rods and tubes and usually is noticable as stretched, bulged, or bent sections. As deformations of this type are difficult to see, the hands should be passed along the tube to feel for evidence of this discrepancy. Deformation of sheet metal web sections, at landing-gear component attachment points, usually can be seen when the area is highlighted with oblique lighting.

b. **Landing Gear Components.** The following items are susceptible to service difficulties and should be given attention.

(1) **Shock Absorbers.** Inspect the entire shock-strut for evidence of leaks, cracks, and possible bottoming of the piston, as this condition causes overloading of landing gear components and contributes to fatigue cracks. Check all bolts, boltholes, pins, and bushings for condition, lubrication and proper torque values. Grease fitting holes (pressure type) are especially vulnerable to cracks and cross-threading damage. Check all safety wire and other locking devices, especially at the main packing gland nuts.

When assembling shock-struts, use the correct type and number of "O"-rings, chevron seals, and backup rings. Use only the correct filler valve core assembly, and follow the manufacturer's instructions when servicing with fluid and air. Either too much or too little air or oil will affect aircraft handling characteristics during taxi, takeoff, and landing, and can cause structural overloads.

Shock cords and rubber discs deteriorate with age and exposure. When this type of shock absorber is used, inspect for general condition, i.e., cleanliness, stretching, fraying, and broken strands. These components must be kept free of petroleum products as they accelerate deterioration of the rubber.

(2) Nose Gear Assembly. Attention should be given to the steering mechanism and should include items such as: torque-links (scissors), torque-tubes, control rods and rod-end bearings, shimmy dampers, cables, and turning stops. In addition, check all nose landing gear components, including mud scrapers and slush deflectors, for damage from natural elements.

(a) Towing of some aircraft with the rudder locks installed may cause damage to the nose steering linkage and rudder control system. Exceeding the steering or towing stops should be followed by a close inspection of the entire nose steering assembly. A broken steering stop will allow turning beyond the design limit, transmitting excessive loads to structures and to the rudder control system. It is recommended that the nose steering arc limits be indicated on the steering collar or fuselage.

(b) Inspect shimmy dampers for leakage around the piston shaft and at fluid line connections, and for abnormal wear or looseness around the pivot points. Also check for proper rigging, "bottoming" of the piston in the cylinder, and the condition of the external stops on the steering collar.

(3) Tailwheels. Disassembly, cleaning, and rerigging of tailwheels are periodically necessary. Inspect for loose or broken bolts, broken springs, lack of lubrication, and general condition. Check steerable tailwheels for proper steering action, steering-horn wear, clearances, and for security and condition of steering springs and cables.

(4) Gear Doors. Inspect gear doors frequently for cracks, deformation, proper rigging, and general condition. Gear door hinges are especially susceptible to progressive cracking, which can ultimately result in complete failure, allowing the door to move and cause possible jamming of the gear. This condition could also result in the loss of the door in flight. In addition, check for proper safetying of the hinge pins and for distorted, sheared, loose, or cracked hinge rivets. Inspect the

wheelwells for improper location or routing of components and related tubing or wiring which could interfere with the travel of the gear door actuating mechanisms.

(5) Floats. In order to maintain floats in an airworthy condition, frequent inspections should be made because of the rapidity with which corrosion takes place on aluminum alloy metal parts, particularly when the aircraft is operated in salt water. Examine metal floats and all metal parts on wooden or fiberglas floats for corrosion and take corrective action in accordance with the procedures described in Chapter 6. Repair damage to metal floats in the general manner outlined in Chapter 2 pertaining to aluminum and aluminum alloy structures. In the case of wooden floats, make repairs in accordance with general procedure outlined in Chapter 1. Repair fiberglass floats in accordance with the manufacturer's instructions or other acceptable practices.

(6) Skis and Ski Installation. It is advisable to examine ski installations frequently to keep them maintained in airworthy condition. If shock cord is used to keep the ski runner in proper trim, periodically examine to assure that the cord has enough elasticity to keep the runner in its required attitude and the cord is not becoming loose or badly frayed. Replace old or weak shock cords. When other means of restraint are provided, examine for excessive wear and binding, and replace or repair when such conditions are found. Examine the points of cable attachment, both on the ski and the airplane structure, for bent lugs due to excessive loads having been imposed while taxiing over rugged terrain or by trying to break loose frozen skis. If skis which permit attachment to the wheels and tires are used, maintain proper tire pressure as underinflated tires may push off the wheels if appreciable side loads are developed in landing or taxiing.

(a) *Repair of Ski Runners.* Fractured wooden ski runners usually require replacement. If a split at the rear end of the runner does not exceed 10 percent of the ski length, it may be repaired by attaching one or more wooden crosspieces across the top of the runner using glue and bolts. Bent or torn metal runners may be straightened if minor bending has taken place and minor tears may be repaired in accordance with procedures recommended in Chapter 2 relative to repair of metal structures.

(b) Ski Pedestals.

1. Tubular pedestals. Damaged pedestals made of steel tubing may be repaired by using standard tube splices as shown in Chapter 2, figures 2.5 and 2.15.

2. Cast pedestals. Consult a Federal Aviation Administration (FAA) representative on the repair of cast pedestals.

3. Sheet metal pedestals. Repair damaged pedestals made of aluminum alloy sheet in the general manner outlined in Chapter 2.

(7) Wheels. Inspect wheels at periodic intervals for cracks, corrosion, dents, distortion, and faulty bearings in accordance with the manufacturer's service information. In split-type wheels, recondition boltholes which have become elongated due to some play in the through-bolt, by the use of inserts or other suitable means. Pay particular attention to the condition of the through-bolts and nuts. Carefully inspect wheels used with tubeless tires for damage to the wheel flange and for proper sealing of the valve. The sealing ring used between the wheel halves should be free of damage and deformation. In bolting wheel halves together, tighten the nuts to the proper torque value. Periodically accomplish an inspection to assure the nuts are tight and there is no movement between the two halves of the wheel. Maintain grease retaining felts in the wheel assembly in a soft, absorbent condition. If any have become hardened, wash them with a petroleum-base cleaning agent; if this fails to soften them, they should be replaced.

(a) Corrosion of Wheels. Thoroughly clean wheels if corroded and then examine for soundness. Smooth and repaint bare corroded spots with a protective coating such as zinc chromate primer and aluminum lacquer, or some other equally effective coating to prevent further corrosion. Replace wheels having severe corrosion which might affect their strength.

(b) Dented or Distorted Wheels. Replace wheels which wobble excessively due to deformation resulting from a severe side-load impact. In questionable cases, consult the local representative of the FAA concerning the airworthiness of the wheels. Dents of a minor nature do not affect the serviceability of a wheel.

(c) Wheel Bearings. Periodically inspect wheel bearings for condition. Replace damaged or * excessively worn parts. Maintain bearings and races as matched sets. Pack bearings with a high-melting-* point grease prior to their installation. Avoid preloading the wheel bearing when installing on aircraft by tightening the axle nut just enough to prevent wheel drag or sideplay.

(8) Brakes. Maintain the clearance between the moving and stationary parts of a brake in accordance with the manufacturer's instructions. Disassemble and inspect the brake periodically and examine the parts for wear, cracks, warpage, corro-* sion, elongated holes, etc. Discolored brake discs are an indication of overheated brakes and should be replaced. If any of these or other faults are indi-* cated, repair, recondition, or replace the affected parts in accordance with the manufacturer's recommendations. Surface cracks on the friction surfaces of the brake drums occur frequently due to high surface temperatures. These surface cracks may be disregarded as seriously affecting the airworthiness until they become cracks of approximately 1 inch in length.

(a) Hydraulic Brakes. For proper maintenance, periodically inspect the entire hydraulic system from the reservoir to the brakes. Maintain the fluid at the recommended level with proper brake fluid. When air is present in the brake system, bleed in accordance with the manufacturer's instructions. Replace flexible hydraulic hose which has deteriorated due to long periods of service and replace hydraulic piston seals when there is evidence of leakage. Service antiskid units according to the manufacturer's instructions.

* "327(8)(b). [Deleted] — Change 3"   *

(9) Micro-Switches. Inspect micro-switches for security of attachment, cleanliness, general condition, and proper operation. Check associated wiring for chafing, proper routing, and to determine that protective covers are installed on wiring terminals, if required. Check the condition of the rubber dust boots which protect the micro-switch plungers from dirt and corrosion.

328. CLEANING AND LUBRICATING. It is recommended that only easily removable neutral solutions be used when cleaning landing gear components. Any advantage, such as speed or effectiveness, gained by using cleaners containing corrosive materials, can be quickly counteracted if these materials become trapped in close-fitting surfaces and crevices. Wear points, such as landing gear up-and-down latches, jack-screws, door hinges, pulleys, cables, bell-cranks, and all pressure-type grease fittings should be relubricated after every cleaning operation. To obtain proper lubrication of the main support bushings, it may be necessary to jack the aircraft.

NOTE: Anytime the aircraft is on jacks, check the landing gear main support bushings for wear. Consult the aircraft manufacturer's overhaul manual for specific wear tolerances.

During winter operation, excess grease may congeal and cause increased loads on gear retraction system electric motors and hydraulic pumps. This condition can lead to component malfunctions; therefore, it is recommended that cleanliness be stressed during and after lubrication.

329. EMERGENCY SYSTEMS. Exercise emergency landing gear systems periodically to insure proper operation and to prevent inactivity, dirt, and corrosion from rendering the system inoperative when needed. Most emergency systems employ either mechanical, pressure-bottle, or free-fall extension capabilities. Check for proper safetying of triggering mechanisms, and for the presence

of required placards and necessary accessories such as cranks, levers, handles, etc.

330. SPECIAL INSPECTIONS. Any time an aircraft has experienced a hard or overweight landing, it is recommended that a special structural inspection, which includes the landing gear, be performed. Typical areas which required special attention are landing gear support trusses for cracked welds, sheared bolts and rivets, and buckled structures; wheels and tires for cracks and cuts; and upper and lower wing surfaces for wrinkles, deformation, and loose or sheared rivets. If any damage is found, a detailed inspection is recommended.

331. RETRACTION TESTS. Periodically, perform a complete operational check of the landing gear retraction system. Inspect the normal extension and retraction system, the emergency extension system, and the indicating and emergency warning system. Determine that the actuating cylinders, linkage, slide tubes, sprockets, chain or drive gears, gear doors, and the up-and-down locks are in good condition and properly adjusted and lubricated. In addition, an electrical continuity check of micro-switches and associated wiring is recommended. Only qualified personnel should attempt adjustments to the gear position and warning system micro-switches, and then only by closely following the manufacturer's recommendations.

332. TIRES. It is essential that tires be inspected frequently for cuts, worn spots, bulges on the sidewalls, foreign bodies in the treads, and tread condition. Defective or worn tires may be repaired or retreaded in accordance with the following paragraphs. The term, "retread," for the purpose of this advisory circular, refers to the several means of restoring a used tire, whether by applying a new tread alone or tread and sidewall material in varying amounts. It refers as well to the process of extending new sidewall material to cover the bead area of the tire. Repairs are included in the retreading of tires. Aircraft tires are identified by type and rating (figure 8.6).

Type	MFG under FAR 37.167 (TSO C62)	Design and rating
I	No	Smooth contour.[1]
II	No	High pressure.[1]
III	Yes	Low pressure.[2]
IV	No	Extra low pressure.[1]
V	No	N/A.
VI	No	Low profile.[1]
VII	Yes	Extra high pressure "low speed".[2]
VII	Yes	Extra high pressure "high speed." [3]
VIII	Yes	Extra high pressure—Low profile "low speed." [2]
VIII	Yes	Extra high pressure—low profile "high speed." [3]

[1] Inactive for new design.
[2] Low speed for ground speeds below 160 m.p.h.
[3] High speed for ground speeds above 160 m.p.h.

FIGURE 8.6.—Aircraft tire types and ratings.

Tires rated for groundspeeds in excess of 160 m.p.h. have the type and rating embossed on the sidewall.

a. *Repair and Retreading of Low-Speed Tires.* The following procedures are applicable to other than Type VII and Type VIII high-speed aircraft tires.

(1) **Tires having injuries of the following types** may be repaired:

(a) *Bead injuries* where only the chafe resistant material is damaged or loose, or where minor injuries do not penetrate into more than 25 percent of the tire plies, up to a maximum of three damaged plies.

(b) *Injuries in tread or sidewalls* may be repaired by the spot repair method. This includes cuts in the tread area that are smaller than 1/2 inch in length and do not penetrate more than the following number of plies into the cord body.

Ply rating:	Maximum cut depth
Less than 8	None.
8 through 16	2 plies.
More than 16	4 plies.

(2) **Nonrepairable Tires.** If any of the following conditions exist, repair of the tire is not recommended:

(a) Evidence of flex breaks.

(b) Bead injuries that exceed the limits outlined in paragraph (1) (a) or affect the seal of the bead on tubeless-type tires.

(c) Evidence of separation between plies or around bead wire.

(d) Injuries requiring reinforcement. This includes injuries larger than those outlined under paragraph (1) (b) and all injuries requiring sectional repair.

(e) Kinked or broken beads.

(f) Weathering or radial cracks extending into the cord body.

(g) Evidence of blisters or heat damage.

(h) Cracked, deteriorated, or damaged inner liners of tubeless tires.

(3) **Spot Repairs.** Use repair methods conforming to the best aviation industry practices. Skive injuries require spot repairs at an approximate 45° angle to remove damaged rubber and cords.

Buff away exposed cord (refer to paragraph (1) (b) for cord damage limits) leaving only the ends at the skive line and the rubber between the cord plies exposed. Clean the area thoroughly before applying the vulcanizing cement. As soon as the cement is completely dry, cover the skived area of the carcass with repair cushion gum. Fill the cavity in the carcass with repair cushion gum and roll to remove air. The tread cavity can then be filled with tread repair gum well-rolled, to provide a solid repair.

(4) **Bead or Chafe Repairs.** Use repair methods conforming to the best aviation industry practices. Trim the frayed fabric ends. Turn back the loose area, buff and clean the surface, and immediately cement. Secure the fabric back in position. Vulcanize repairs larger than 2 inches.

(5) **Retreadable Tires.** Tires which are sound or which can be repaired as listed above may be retreaded as set forth in Specification MIL–R–7726.

(6) **Marking of Retreaded Tires.** Permanently mark each retreaded tire. Whenever it is necessary to replace the area containing the original marking, such markings must be replaced. In addition, each retreaded tire will:

(a) Display the letter "R" followed by a

number "1", "2", etc., to signify the sequential number of retreads applied thereon.

(**b**) Display the speed category increase if the tire is qualified for the increased speed in accordance with the requirements specified in Federal Aviation Regulations (FAR) 37.167 (Technical Standard Order TSO-C62).

(**c**) Display the month and year of retread application.

(**d**) Display the name of the person retreading the tire.

(7) Balance. Each repaired or retreaded tire should not exceed the static unbalance limits as set forth in TSO-C62.

(8) Tire Installation. Install the tire on the wheel in such a manner that the tire-bead chafing area will not be torn or the tube pinched during the mounting process. When mounting tubeless tires, use procedures that assure a positive seal between the tire-bead and the wheel-rim area.

(9) Clearance. For retractable landing gears, maintain sufficient clearance between the tire and the surrounding structure during the retraction process. Carefully check clearances following installation of wheel assemblies equipped with retreaded tires because of the growth factor which may have increased the tire diameter and cross section.

b. *Retreading Types VII and VIII High-Speed Tires.* The following paragraphs describe ways of substantiating the acceptability of methods, techniques, and practices to be used in retreading of high-speed tires. Other methods may be used.

(1) Number of Retreads. The wide variation in tire operating environments which may affect total carcass life and serviceability makes it inadvisable to prescribe arbitrarily the maximum number of times a high-speed tire should be retreaded. This
* aspect is controlled by thorough inspection of the carcass, applying such methods as air needle injection or nondestructive testing.

(2) Condition of Tire to be Retreaded. Retread only those tire carcasses found serviceable by thorough inspection. During inspection, use equipment, techniques, and procedures which are recommended by the tire manufacturer or that are equivalent to those in general use by FAA certificated repair agencies rated for retreading of high-speed

aircraft tires. Determine the acceptability of damaged tires for retreading in accordance with established industry practices.

(3) Retreading Criteria.

(**a**) Processes, Methods, Techniques, Practices, and Equipment. The suitability of specific retread manufacturer's injury limitations, retreading processes, and equipment used is determined either by satisfactory service experience or substantiating tests.

(**b**) Materials. The acceptability of materials used in a retreading process may be determined by following the tire manufacturer's recommendations, or the materials may be substantiated by analysis and tests, such as dynamometer testing, or through satisfactory service experience.

(**c**) Unbalance. The moment of static unbalance in ounce-inches shall be no greater than the following moment values:

1. Tire diameters up to and including 28 inches: Moment $= .01D^2 + .38D$.

2. Tire diameters greater than 28 inches: Moment $= .034D^2 - .304D$.

D = Tire diameter (actual).

(**d**) Balance Marker. To indicate the light-weight point of the tire, remove old balance marker, and durably affix a new relocated balance marker, consisting of a single red dot of appropriate size to the sidewall of the tire immediately above the bead.

(**e**) Burst Pressure. Retreaded tires shall be capable of withstanding without failure, a burst pressure of at least 3 times the rated inflation pressure.

(**f**) Temperature. The airworthiness of retreaded tires shall not be adversely affected as a result of their being subjected to extreme ambient temperatures expected to be encountered during *
normal airplane operation.

(**g**) Tread Design. Substantiate decreases or increases in the number of tread ribs, grooves and changes in skid depth by dynamometer tests that are applicable to the tire groundspeed range.

(h) Underskid Thickness. The thickness of the rubber between the carcass and the bottom of the tread pattern (underskid) is not normally less than 30 percent of the mold skid depth. Requalify by dynamometer test, tire underskid/tread thickness which is greater than that previously qualified.

* (i) Venting. Substantiate changes in venting pattern by dynamometer test. Existing vent holes should be rebored if they do not vent during air needle test or if covered during the retreading process.

(j) Tire Weight. Tire weight will not be greater than 105 percent of the manufactured new tire weight or exceed the applicable aircraft type certificate limitations, whichever is more restrictive.

(k) Liner Leak/Separation Check. Tires will be checked for liner leaks, separations, and proper venting. This check is to be performed before and after the tire has been retreaded for those tires on which a liner repair has been made. Balance pads must be removed prior to the initial liner leak check.

(l) Cross Treading. Every effort should be made by the owner/operator to assure that no tire will be retreaded by other than the retreader of the original worn casing. Differences in materials, techniques, and procedures could cause noncompatability of the retread to the casing which may result in tire failure. *

(4) Marking and Identification. Do not obliterate the original manufacturer's marking and identifying data, unless it is necessary for proper retreading or repair. Permanently emboss the tire sidewall with retread information. If necessary, replace original identifying markings and include the following retread identification:

(a) Name of identifying letters of the retreading company.

(b) The letter "R" followed by a numeral "1", "2", etc., to signify first, second, etc., time the tire has been retreaded.

(c) Plant location of the retread manufacturer.

(d) Month and year of retread in numerical figures.

(e) If the dynamometer retread qualification speed is less than the previous (original) tire qualification speed, remove the previous speed marking and indicate the new (lower) rated speed. Identify tires that have been retreaded for use only on aircraft of a specific make/model and type design.

(5) Quality Control. The retreader's quality control system will be expected to maintain a satisfactory level of workmanship throughout the retreaded process including assurance that each retreaded tire is vented to prevent tread breakdown or separation.

(6) Records of Work Performed. Include at least the following information in the retreader's work record for each tire processed:

(a) Tire size.

(b) Ply rating.

(c) Speed rating.

(d) Serial number.

(e) Retread number.

(f) Type of tread applied.

(g) Month and year applied.

(7) Dynamometer tests. An acceptable means of determining that the methods, techniques, and practices utilized in the retread process will produce a tire that meets the requirements of FAR 43.13 is by subjecting a representative tire to the following dynamometer tests:

(a) General. Load-speed-time data compiled by the aircraft manufacturer is the basis for establishing representative dynamometer tests. To determine tire performance, simulate the most critical combination of takeoff weight, speed, and airplane center-of-gravity position. Also, consider increased speeds resulting from elevated airport operations and high ambient temperatures.

(b) Selection of Tires for Qualification Testing. Retread only tires that are worn at least 80 percent from actual aircraft usage or which have undergone simulated equivalent operation during dynamometer testing. The sample retreaded tire must be properly identified and bear the qualifying retreaders markings.

(c) Test Inflation Pressure. Inflate the sample tire to the pressure necessary to obtain the

* same deflection on the flywheel (under the rated static load) as the flat-plate deflection the tire would have at its rated static load and inflation.

(d) Test Speeds. The applicable dynamometer test speeds corresponding to the maximum operational groundspeeds (see page 149):   *

This page intentionally left blank.

*

Maximum operational ground speed of aircraft (m.p.h.)		Dynamometer test speed (m.p.h.)
Over	*Not over*	
160	180	180
180	200	200
200	225	225
225	250	250

(e) Test Landing Interval. Schedule minimum time between landings to assure carcass peak temperatures of not less than 160° F. or contained air peak temperatures of not less than 140° F. for each run. Measure the carcass temperatures within 1 inch of the rim flange and also in the shoulder or crown area. Record any unavoidable deviations in the substantiating test data.

(8) Dynamometer Test Procedures. The high-speed retreaded tire shall withstand 100 dynamometer landings and at least 3 taxi-test cycles. The dynamometer landings will consist of 50 Test A, load-speed-time cycles, and 50 Test B, energy cycles.

(a) Test A, Load-speed-time.

1. Speed cycle. Land the tire against a dynamometer flywheel rotating at a peripheral speed of S_1 m.p.h. Immediately thereafter, decrease the flywheel speed at an average deceleration rate of D ft./sec./sec. until a value of S_2 is attained. No specific rate of deceleration is required after the flywheel's peripheral speed reaches a value of S_2. Decrease the speed of the flywheel in the above manner until a roll distance of RD feet has been covered, at which time the tire is unlanded.

2. Load cycle. After landing, increase the load from zero to L_1 pounds within T_1 seconds. Linearly increase the load with time to a value of L_2 pounds within T_2 seconds after landing, or at the moment of unlanding, whichever occurs first. If it is necessary to continue the roll after T_2 seconds to complete the required roll distance (RD), maintain the load at L_2 pounds.

3. Symbol definitions. Determine the numerical values, which are used for the following symbols, from the applicable airplane load-speed-time data:

S_1 = Initial dynamometer test speed.

S_2 = Speed at which the average deceleration between S_1 and S_2 does not exceed the specified value.

D = Constant rate of deceleration between S_1 and S_2 speeds.

RD = Roll distance in feet.

L_2 = Maximum rated static load of the tire.

T_1 = Time for applying L_1 load. A T_1 tolerance of ± 1 second is acceptable.

$$T_2 = \frac{S_1 - \sqrt{S_1{}^2 - 2D\,(RD)}}{D}$$

T_2 is the elapsed time for applying the L_2 load. A T_2 tolerance of + 10 percent is acceptable. When T_2 is calculated by the aforementioned formulas, S_2 may be ignored and D is assumed constant throughout roll distance (RD).

4. Test load adjustment. If the test load curve results in loads at a given speed being less than those dictated by the applicable aircraft data, eliminate the condition by making adjustments in T_2, L_1, and/or T_1.

(b) Test B, Energy.

1. Kinetic energy. Calculate and adjust the kinetic energy of the flywheel for the rated maximum static load of the tire. In the event that the correct number of flywheel plates cannot be used to obtain the calculated kinetic energy value or proper flywheel width, select a greater number of plates and adjust the dynamometer speed to achieve the required kinetic energy.

2. Kinetic energy computation. Computer kinetic energy as follows:

$$KE = CWV^2$$

Where

KE = Kinetic energy, ft.-lb.
C = 0.011
W = tire load, pounds
V = 120 m.p.h.

3. Speed cycle. Land the test tire at 90 m.p.h. and unland at 0 m.p.h. Decrease the landing speed as necessary to assure that 56 percent of the calculated kinetic energy is absorbed by the tire.

4. Load cycle. Upon landing, and during the entire roll test, force the tire against the flywheel at its rated static load.

*

* **(c)** Taxi Test.

1. Test parameters. Conduct a minimum of three dynamometer taxi tests under the following conditions:

Speed = 35 m.p.h.
Tire Load = Maximum static rating.
Roll Distance = 35,000 feet.

2. Tire temperature. Heat the test tire to a temperature of not less than 120° F. at the start of each of the three taxi test cycles. Rolling the tire

on the dynamometer is acceptable in obtaining this minimum tire temperature. Make no adjustments in the tire inflation pressure to compensate for increases due to temperature rise.

(9) Alternate Dynamometer Tests.

(a) Variable Loading. An alternate dynamometer test which more realistically simulates actual airplane performance on the runway may be used in lieu of the deceleration load-speed-time schedule. An acceleration load-   *

This page intentionally left blank.

actual airplane performance on the runway may be used in lieu of the deceleration load-speed-time schedule. An acceleration load-speed-time schedule, wherein the dynamometer flywheel is accelerated to the applicable conditions, is acceptable.

(b) Alternate Procedure for Reinforced-tread Tires. Qualification of a high-speed tire with a given ply rating and reinforced tread will automatically qualify a lesser ply rating reinforced tread tire of the same size and skid depth, provided:

1. The test conditions S_1, RD, S_2, T_1, and T_2 are no less severe than those which are applicable to the lesser ply rating tire.

2. The ratio of the test loads, L_1 to L_2 is not less than that applicable to the lesser ply rating tire. Make any necessary adjustment in this ratio by increasing L_1.

(10) Optional Dynamometer Equipment. Dynamic tests may be conducted on any dynamometer test equipment which will provide the load, speed, time, and roll distance parameters of the tire.

c. Tubes. Punctured tubes may be repaired by the use of cemented or vulcanized patches.

(1) The procedure for making such repairs is substantially identical to that used in connection with repair of automobile tires:

(a) Keep the size of the patch to a minimum and avoid use of an excessive number of patches, particularly in one area, as the weight of the material may contribute to excessive wheel vibration due to the tube being out-of-balance.

(b) The use of vulcanized patches is recommended because they are considered more reliable.

(c) Reinstalled tires should be inflated, deflated, and again inflated to insure that the inner-tube is not pinched. A pinched tube will chafe against the walls of the carcass and a thin spot will result in the rubber. In time, the tube wall will leak at this point. The pinching generally is due to the sticking of the tube to the carcass wall during the first inflation and the failure of the carcass to properly seat against the flange.

(d) The tube is then confined to a smaller space and wrinkling (pinching) of the tube results. Complete deflation followed by inflation allows the tube to properly accommodate itself to the carcass which should now seat itself tightly against the flanges.

*333. TIRE SLIPPAGE.** To reduce the possibility of tire and tube failure due to slippage, and to provide a means of detecting tire slippage, tires should be marked and indexed with the wheel rim. Marking should be accomplished by painting a mark 1 inch in width and 2 inches in length across the tire sidewall and wheel rim. The paint used should be of a permanent type and contrasting color, such as white, red, or orange. Preflight inspection should include a check of slippage marks for alignment. If the slippage mark is not in alignment, the aircraft should not be operated until a detailed inspection is made, the reason determined, and if necessary the condition corrected.

334. TIRE MAINTENANCE. A program of tire maintenance can minimize tire failures and increase tire service life. Overinflation wears the center of the tread excessively, and reduces a tire's resistance to bruising, strains the tires beads, reduces traction and skid resistance. Underinflation increases deflection and may cause breakdown of the tire sidewalls. The manufacturer's recommendations should be followed to obtain maximum tire service life.

345.—349. RESERVED. *

Section 2. LIFE PRESERVERS AND LIFERAFTS

344. GENERAL. Inflatable life preservers and liferafts are subject to general deterioration due to aging. Experience has indicated that such equipment may be in need of replacement at the end of 5 years due to porosity of the rubber-coated material. Wear of such equipment is accelerated when stowed on board aircraft because of vibration which causes chaffing of the rubberized fabric. This ultimately results in localized leakage. Leakage is also likely to occur where the fabric is folded because sharp corners are formed. When these corners are in contact with the carrying cases, or with adjacent parts of the rubberized fabric, they tend to wear through due to vibration.

345. INSPECTION PROCEDURE FOR LIFE PRESERVERS. Life preservers should be inspected at 3-month intervals for cuts, tears, or other damage to the rubberized material. Check the mouth valves and tubing for leakage, corrosion, and deterioration. Remove the carbon dioxide cylinder and check the discharge mechanism by operating the lever to ascertain that the pin operates freely. Check the gaskets and valve cores of the cylinder container and the pull cord for deterioration. If no defects are found, inflate the preserver with air to a 2-pound pressure and allow to stand for 12 hours. If the preserver still has adequate rigidity at the end of that time, deflate and fit with CO_2 cylinders having weights not less than that indicated on them by the manufacturer. All cylinders made in accordance with joint Army/Navy Specification MIL–C–00601D are so stamped and have a minimum permissible weight stamped on them. The use of such CO_2 cylinders is recommended. These cylinders have the 5/32-inch end disc sealed by an electric welding process, which is intended to provide a superior seal compared to the older type, which have a similar disc surrounded by a thin rubber seal. Inasmuch as the rubber is subject to deterioration, its ability to maintain pressure will possibly be affected. Leaky electrically welded seals will probably be discovered upon final inspection at the manufacturer's plant. If such a cylinder is up to weight at the end of 3 months in all probability it will remain so until used; whereas, the old type with the rubber seal is apt to lose its pressure with age. Having fitted the preserver with an adequately charged cylinder, mark the preserver to indicate the date of inspection and pack into its container. It is recommended that the aforementioned procedure be repeated every 12-month period, utilizing the CO_2 cartridge for inflation. Carbon dioxide permeates the rubberized fabric at a faster rate than air and will indicate if the porosity of the material is excessive.

346. REPAIR OF LIFE PRESERVERS. Leaks may be disclosed by immersion in soapy water. Repair leaks by the use of patches in accordance with the recommendations of the manufacturer. Clean corroded metal parts and replace missing or weakened lanyards. Life preserves which do not retain sufficient rigidity after the 12-hour period, because of general deterioration and porosity of the fabric, are beyond economical repair and should be replaced.

347. INSPECTION PROCEDURE FOR LIFERAFTS. Liferafts should be inspected at 3-month intervals for cuts, tears, or other damage to the rubberized material. If the raft is found to be in good condition, remove the CO_2 bottle(s) and inflate the raft with air to a pressure of 2 pounds. The air should be introduced at the fitting normally connected to the CO_2 bottle(s). After at least 1 hour to allow for the air within the raft to adjust itself to the ambient temperature, check pressure and adjust, if necessary, to 2 pounds and allow the raft to stand for 24 hours. If, after 24 hours, the pressure is less than 1 pound, examine the raft for leakage by using soapy water. In order to eliminate pressure variations due to temperature differences at the time the initial and final reading are taken, test the raft in a room where the temperature is fairly constant. If the pressure drop is satisfactory, the raft should be considered as being in an airworthy condition and returned to service after being fitted with correctly charged CO_2 bottles as determined by weighing them. Rafts more than 5 years old are likely to be unairworthy due to deterioration. It is suggested that the rafts be marked to indicate the date of inspection and that soapstone be used when folding them preparatory to insertion into the carrying case. Take care to see that all of the raft's required equipment is on board and properly stowed. If the raft lanyard, used to prevent the raft from floating away from the airplane, is in need of replacement, use a lanyard not less than 20 feet long and having a breaking strength of about 75 pounds. It is recommended that the aforementioned procedure be repeated every 18-month period utilizing the CO_2 bottle(s) for inflation. If a single bottle is used for inflating both compartments, it should be noted whether the inflation is proceeding equally to both compartments. Occasionally the formation of "carbon-dioxide snow" may occur in one passage of the distribution manifold and divert a larger volume of gas to one compartment, which may burst if the mattress valve is not open to relieve the pressure. If the pressure is satisfactory, return the raft to service in accordance with the procedure outlined.

348. REPAIR OF LIFERAFTS. When leaks due to tears, abrasion, or punctures are found, make repairs in accordance with the recommendations of the manufacturer. Recement partially torn away supporting patches on the tube to restore the raft to its airworthy condition. Replace mildewed or weak lanyards, particularly those by which the CO_2 bottle is operated. This applies also to the line used to attach the raft to the airplane. Check all metal parts for corrosion, and clean or repair if found to be defective. If leaky mattress valves have been found, they must be replaced.

349.–359. RESERVED.

Section 3. MISCELLANEOUS EQUIPMENT

360. PARACHUTES. With reasonable care, parachutes normally last at least 5 years. They should not be carelessly tossed about, left in airplanes so that they may become wet, or left in open places where they may be tampered with. They should not be placed where they may fall on oily floors or be subject to acid fumes from adjacent battery chargers. When repacking is scheduled, a careful inspection of the parachute should be made by a qualified parachute technician (rigger). If repairs or replacements of parts are necessary to maintain the airworthiness of the parachute assembly, such work must be done by the original parachute manufacturer or by a qualified parachute rigger, certificated in accordance with FAR Part 65, or by an appropriately rated parachute loft certificated in accordance with FAR Part 149.

* **361. SAFETY BELTS.** The FARs require that when safety belts are to be replaced in aircraft manufactured after July 1, 1951, such belts must conform to standards established by the FAA.* These standards are contained in Technical Standard Order TSO–C22. Safety belts eligible for installation in aircraft may be identified by the marking TSO–C22 on the belt or by a military designation number since military belts comply with the
* strength requirements of the TSO. Each safety belt must be equipped with an approved metal to metal latching device. Airworthy type-certificated safety *
belts currently in aircraft may be removed for cleaning and reinstalled. However, when a type-certificated safety belt is found unairworthy, replacement with a TSO–C22 or a new belt is preferred.

* **a. The webbing of safety belts,** even when mildew-proofed, is subject to deterioration due to constant use, cleaning, and the effects of aging.

Fraying of belts is an indication of wear, and such belt are likely to be unairworthy because they can no longer hold the minimum required tensile load. *
Difference of opinion as to the airworthiness of a belt can be settled by testing a questionable belt to demonstrate that it will support the required load. Airworthy one-person type-certificated belts should be able to withstand a tensile load of 525 pounds, and TSO belts withstand the rated tensile load indicated on the belt label. Most one-person TSO belts are rated for 1,500 pounds. For two-person belts, double the loads. Since type-certificated belts will not afford the crash protection provided by a TSO or military belt, such type-certificated belts are not to be repaired nor should their buckles or end fittings be reused on safety belts. If replacement of webbing or hardware of TSO or military belt is attempted, use parts of identical design and material. Make the stitch pattern identical to the original and the number of stitches per inch equal to the number used in the original belt. There is no objection to having a greater total length of stitching, provided one line of stitches is not placed over another line. Space lines of stitching at least 3/16-inch apart. Keep a record, preferably in the logbook, stating the extent to which the belt was repaired and the date. Retain the original identification marking on the belt, conforming either to that required by TSO–C22 to a deviation from this marking, or to the military designation. Operators of a fleet of airplanes should follow the above suggestions, but keeping a record of renovations in a logbook is impractical, since the belts are never associated with any one particular aircraft for any length of time. Therefore, in addition to retaining the original identification label and attaching it to the renovated belt, use some additional simple marking to indicate

that the belt has been renovated and show the date of renovation. The use of letter "R" followed by the date would be acceptable. This marking could be in the form of an indelible ink stamping or cloth label stitched to the webbing.

362. FLARES. Parachute flares are made of materials which are subject to decomposition upon aging. Humidity affects the small igniting charge and also the materials of the candle (illuminant). Hence, the percentage of misfires in old flares is likely to be quite high. To assure unfailing performance of flares, periodically inspect the flare installation. Inspect the entire system, starting at the release mechanism in the cockpit and ending at the flare. Only a qualified person should attempt such inspection, since inadvertent discharge of such pyrotechnics may cause serious damage. Past experience has indicated that it is advisable to return all electrically or pistol-operated flares to the manufacturer for reconditioning within a maximum period of 3 years, and that for mechanically operated flares, a maximum period of 4 years is recommended.

363. OXYGEN SYSTEMS.

a. General. The following instructions are to serve as a guide for the inspection and maintenance of aircraft oxygen systems. The information is applicable to both portable and permanently installed equipment.

(1) Aircraft Gaseous Oxygen Systems. The oxygen in gaseous systems is supplied from one or more high- or low-pressure oxygen cylinders. Since the oxygen is compressed within the cylinder, the amount of pressure indicated on the system gauge bears a direct relationship to the amount of oxygen contained in the cylinder. The pressure-indicating line connection is normally located between the cylinder and a pressure-reducing valve.

NOTE: Some of the gaseous oxygen systems do not use pressure-reducing valves. The high pressure is reduced to a useable pressure by a regulator. This regulator is located between the high- and low-pressure system.

(2) Aircraft Liquid Oxygen Systems. Thus far it has not been a practice to use liquid oxygen in

civil aircraft due to its complexity. This however, may change at any time as technological advances are made.

(3) Portable Oxygen Systems. The three basic types of portable oxygen systems are: demand, pressure demand, and continuous flow. The component parts of these systems are identical to those of a permanent installation with the exception that some parts are miniaturized as necessary. This is done in order that they may be contained in a case or strapped around a person's shoulder. It is for this portability reason that it is essential special attention be given to assuring that any storage or security provision for portable oxygen equipment in the aircraft is adequate, in good condition, and accessible to the user.

NOTE: Check portable equipment including its security provisions frequently, as it is more susceptible to personnel abuse than a permanently installed system.

b. Inspection. Hands, clothing, and tools must be free of oil, grease, and dirt when working with oxygen equipment. Traces of these organic materials near compressed oxygen may result in spontaneous combustion, explosions, and/or fire.

(1) Oxygen Tanks and Cylinders. Inspect the entire exterior surface of the cylinder for indication of abuse, dents, bulges, and strap chafing.

(a) Examine the neck of cylinder for cracks, distortion, or damaged threads.

(b) Check the cylinder to determine if the markings are legible.

(c) Check date of last hydrostatic test. If the periodic retest date is past, do not return the cylinder to service until the test has been accomplished.

NOTE: This test period is established by the Department of Transportation in the Code of Federal Regulations, Title 49, Chapter I, Paragraph 173.34.

(d) Inspect the cylinder mounting bracket, bracket hold-down bolts and cylinder holding straps for cracks and deformation, cleanliness, and security of attachment.

(e) In the immediate area where the cylinder is stored or secured, check for evidence of any types of interference, chafing, deformation, or deterioration.

(2) Lines and Fittings.

(a) Inspect oxygen lines for chafing, corrosion, flat spots and irregularities, i.e., sharp bends, kinks, and inadequate security.

(b) Check fittings for corrosion around the threaded area where lines are joined together. Pressurize the system and check for leaks. (Ref. c(2) (b) 4.)

CAUTION

In pressurizing the system, actuate the valve slowly to avoid surging which could rupture the line.

(3) Regulators, Valves, and Gauges.

(a) Examine all parts for cracks, nicks, damaged threads or other apparent damage.

(b) Actuate regulator controls and valve to check for ease of operation.

(c) Determine if the gauge is functioning properly by observing the pressure build-up and the return to zero when the system oxygen is bled off.

(4) Masks and Hoses.

(a) Check the oxygen mask for fabric cracks and rough face seals. If the mask is a fullface model, inspect glass or plastic for cleanness and state of repair.

(b) When appropriate, with due regard to hygienic considerations, the sealing qualities of an oxygen mask may be tested by placing thumb over connection at end of mask tube and inhaling very lightly. Remove thumb from disconnect after each continuous inhalation. If there is no leakage, mask will adhere tightly to face during inhalation and definite resistance to inhalation will be noticeable.

(c) Flex the mask hose gently over its entirety and check for evidence of deterioration or dirt.

(d) Examine the mask and hose storage compartment of cleanliness and general condition.

(e) If the mask and hose storage compartment is provided with a cover or release mechanism, check its operation.

c. Maintenance.

(1) Oxygen Tanks, Cylinders, and Hold Down Brackets.

(a) Remove from service any cylinders that show signs of abuse, dents, bulges, cracks, distortion, damaged threads, or defects which might render the cylinder unsafe. Typical examples of oxygen cylinder damage are shown in figure 8.7.

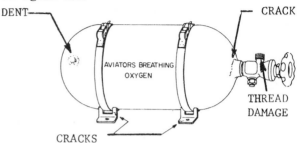

FIGURE 8.7.—Oxygen cylinder damage.

(b) When replacing an oxygen cylinder, be certain that the replacement cylinder is of the same size and weight as the one removed.

NOTE: Cylinders having greater weight or size will require strengthened cylinder mounting brackets, and a reevaluation to determine that the larger or heavier cylinder will not interfere with adjacent systems, components, or structural members, and that the strength of attaching structure is adequate.

(c) Replace or repair any cylinder mounting brackets that show sign of wear. Visible cracks may be welded in accordance with Chapter 2, Section 2 of this Advisory Circular. Replace cylinder straps or clamps that show wear or abuse. For typical mounting bracket crack and failure, see figure 8.8.

(2) Lines and Fittings.

(a) Replace any oxygen line that is chafed, rusted, corroded, dented, cracked, or kinked.

(b) Clean oxygen system fittings showing signs of rusting or corrosion in the threaded area. To accomplish this, use a cleaner recommended by manufacturers of oxygen equipment. Replace lines and fittings that cannot be cleaned.

1. The high-pressure lines which are located between the oxygen bottle, outside oxygen service filler, and the regulator are normally fabricated from stainless steel or thick-wall, seamless copper alloy tubing. The fittings on high-pressure lines are normally silver soldered.

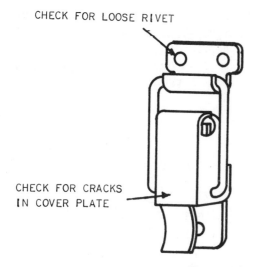

CHECK FOR LOOSE RIVET

CHECK FOR CRACKS
IN COVER PLATE

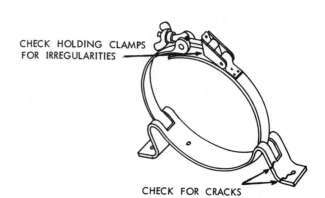

CHECK HOLDING CLAMPS
FOR IRREGULARITIES

CHECK FOR CRACKS

FIGURE 8.8.—Cylinder brackets and clamps.

NOTE: Use silver alloys free of cadmium when silver soldering. The use of silver solder which contains cadmium will emit a poisonous gas when heated to a molten state. This gas is extremely hazardous to health if inhaled.

2. The low-pressure lines extend from the pressure regulator to each passenger and crew oxygen outlet. These lines are fabricated from seamless aluminum alloy, copper, or flexible hose. Normally, flare- or flange-type connections are used. (Ref. Chapter 10, Section 1, para. 393b of this Advisory Circular.)

CAUTION

Do not allow oil, grease, flammable solvent, or other combustibles such as lint or dust to come in contact with threads or any parts that will be exposed to pressurized oxygen.

3. It is advisable to purge the oxygen system any time work has been accomplished on any of the lines and fittings. Use dry nitrogen or dry air for purging the system. All open lines should be capped immediately after purging.

4. When oxygen is being lost from a system through leakage, a sequence of steps may be necessary to locate the opening. Leakage may often be detected by listening for the distinct hissing sound of escaping gas. If this check proves negative, it will be necessary to soap-test all lines and connections with a castile soap and water solution or specially compounded leak-test material. Make the solution thick enough to adhere to the contours of the

fittings. At the completion of the leakage test, remove all traces of the soap and water.

CAUTION

Do not attempt to tighten any connections while the system is charged.

(3) Regulators, Valves, and Gauges. Line maintenance of oxygen regulators, valves, and gauges does not include major repair. These components are precision made and their repair usually requires the attention of a repair station or the manufacturer. Care must be taken when reinstalling these components to ascertain if the threaded area is free of nicks, burrs, and contaminants that would prevent the connections from sealing properly.

CAUTION

Do not use petroleum lubricants on these components.

(4) Masks and Hoses.

(a) Troubleshooting. If a mask assembly is defective (leaks, does not allow breathing, or contains a defective microphone), it is advisable to return the mask assembly to the manufacturer or a repair station.

(b) Maintenance Practice and Cleaning.

1. Clean and disinfect mask assemblies after use, as appropriate.

NOTE: Use care to avoid damaging microphone assembly while cleaning and sterilizing.

2. Wash mask with a mild soap solution and rinse it with clear water.

3. To sterilize, swab the mask thoroughly with a gauze or sponge soaked in a water merthiolate solution. This solution should contain 1/5 teaspoon of merthiolate per 1 quart of water. Wipe the mask with a clean cloth and air dry.

4. Replace the hose if it shows evidence of deterioration.

5. Hoses may be cleaned in the same manner as the mask.

6. Observe that each mask breathing tube end is free of nicks, and that the tube end will slip into the cabin oxygen receptacle with ease and not leak.

d. *Functional Testing After Repair.* Following repair, and before inspection plates, cover plates, or upholstering are replaced, test the entire system.

(1) Open cylinder valve slowly and observe the pressure gauge on a high-pressure system. A pressure of approximately 1,800 p.s.i. (at 70° F.) should be indicated on the gauge. (Cylinder pressure will vary considerably with radical temperature changes.)

(a) Check system by installing one of the mask hose fittings (minus the mask) in each of the cabin wall outlets to determine whether there is a flow. If a demand mask is used, check by breathing through the mask (if appropriate, clean mask according to Par. c(4) (b)) to see whether there is a flow of oxygen.

(b) Check the complete system for leaks in accordance with the procedure outlined in c(2) (b) 4.

(c) If leaks are found, close the cylinder valve; open an outlet to reduce the pressure in the system to zero.

(2) A pressure drop check of the system may be made as follows:

(a) Open the cylinder valve and pressurize the system. Observe the pressure gauge (a pressure of approximately 1,800 p.s.i. at 70° F. should be indicated). For the light weight ICC 3HT 1850 cylinders, pressurize the system to approximately 1,850 p.s.i. at 70° F.

(b) Close the cylinder valve and wait approximately 5 minutes for temperatures to stabilize.

(c) Record the pressure gauge reading and temperature and after 1 hour, record the pressure gauge reading and temperature again.

(d) A maximum pressure drop of 100 p.s.i. is permissible.

NOTE: Conduct the above tests in an area where changes of temperature will be less than 10° F. In the event that a change in temperature greater than approximately 10° F. occurs during the 1-hour period, suitable corrections would be required, or reconduct the test under conditions of unvarying temperatures.

e. *Service Requirements—Oxygen Cylinders.* Standard weight cylinders must be hydrostatic tested at the end of each 5-year period. This is a Department of Transportation requirement. These cylinders carry an ICC or DOT 3AA 1800 classification and are suitable for the use intended. The lightweight cylinders must be hydrostatic tested every 3 years, and must be retired from service after 15 years or 4,380 pressurizations, whichever occurs first. These cylinders carry an ICC or DOT 3HT 1850 classification.

CAUTION

Use only aviation breathing oxygen when having the oxygen bottle charged. MIL–O–27210C specifies that the moisture content of aviation breathing oxygen must not exceed 0.005 milligrams of water vapor per liter of gas at a temperature of 70° F. and a pressure of 760 millimeters of mercury.

(1) **Charging High-pressure Oxygen Cylinders.** The following are recommended procedures for charging high-pressure oxygen cylinders from a manifold system, either permanently installed or trailer mounted. *Never attempt to charge a low-pressure cylinder directly from a high-pressure manifold system or cylinder.*

(a) **Inspection.** Do not attempt to charge oxygen cylinders if any of the following discrepancies exist:

1. Contaminated fittings on the manifold, cylinder, or outside filler valve. If in doubt, wipe with stabilized trichloroethylene; however, do not permit solvent to enter any internal parts. Let air dry.

2. Cylinder out of hydrostatic test date. DOT regulations require ICC or DOT 3AA designation cylinders to be hydrostatic tested to 5/3 their working pressure, every 5 years. Cylinders bearing designation ICC or

DOT 3HT must be hydrostatic tested to 5/3 their working pressure every 3 years, and retired from service 15 years or 4,380 filling cycles after date of manufacture, whichever occurs first.

3. Cylinder is completely empty. Do not charge, as the cylinder must be removed, inspected, and cleaned.

(b) Charging.

1. Connect cylinder valve outlet or outside filler valve to manifold.

2. Slowly open valve of cylinder to be charged and observe pressure on gauge of manifold system.

3. Slowly open valve of cylinder on manifold system having the lowest pressure and allow pressure to equalize.

4. Close cylinder valve on manifold system and slowly open valve of cylinder having next highest pressure. Continue this procedure until the cylinder has been charged in accordance with e(1) (d), Table of Filling Pressures.

(c) Top-off.

After the cylinder has been filled in accordance with the filling table (shown under e(1) (d)):

1. Close all valves on manifold system.

2. Close valve on filled cylinder and remove the cylinder from the manifold.

3. Using leak detector, test for leakage around cylinder valve threaded connections. (If leakage is present, discharge oxygen and return cylinder to facility for repair.)

4. Let cylinder stabilize for period of at least 1 hour, and then recheck pressure.

5. Make any necessary adjustments in pressure.

(d) Table of Filling Pressures.

Initial Temp (°F.)	Filling Pressure (p.s.i.)
0	1,650
10	1,700
20	1,725
30	1,775
40	1,825
50	1,875
60	1,925
70	1,975
80	2,000
90	2,050
100	2,100
110	2,150
120	2,200
130	2,250

Initial Temperature—Refers to ambient temperature in filling room.

Filling Pressure—Refers to the pressure to which aircraft cylinders should be filled. This table gives approximations only, and assumes a rise in temperature of approximately 25° F. due to heat of compression. This table also assumes the aircraft cylinders will be filled as quickly as possible and that they will only be cooled by ambient air; no water bath or other means of cooling being used.

Example: If ambient temperature is 70° F., fill aircraft cylinders to approximately 1,975 p.s.i.—as close to this pressure as the gauge may be read. Upon cooling, cylinders should have approximately 1,850 p.s.i. pressure.

(2) Charging of Low-Pressure Oxygen Systems and Portables. For recharging a low-pressure aircraft oxygen system, or portable cylinders, it is essential that the oxygen trailer or cart have a pressure-reducing regulator. Military types E–2 or C–1 reducing regulators are satisfactory. These types of regulators reduce the large cylinder pressure from 2,000 p.s.i. to a line pressure of 450 p.s.i.g. (A welding pressure reducing regulator is not satisfactory.)

CAUTION

When refilling the low-pressure system or portable cylinders, open the oxygen filler tank valve slowly to allow the system or portable cylinders to be filled at a slow rate. After the refilling operation is completed, check for leaks with a leak detector. If a leak is detected, paragraph c(2)(b) 4 should be referred to for corrective action.

364.–374. RESERVED.

Chapter 9.   WINDSHIELDS, ENCLOSURES, AND EXITS

Section 1.   PLASTIC WINDSHIELDS AND ENCLOSURES

375. GENERAL. These repairs are applicable to plastic windshields, enclosures, and windows in nonpressurized airplanes. For pressurized airplanes replace or repair plastic elements in accordance with the manufacturer's recommendation.

a. *Types of Plastics.* Two types of plastics are commonly used in transparent enclosures of aircraft. These materials are known as acrylic plastics and polyester plastics.

376. REPLACEMENT PANELS. Use material equivalent to that originally used by the manufacturer of the aircraft for replacement panels. There are many types of transparent plastics on the ∗market. Their properties vary greatly, particularly in regard to expansion characteristics, brittleness under low temperatures, resistance to discoloration when exposed to sunlight, surface checking, etc. Information on these properties is in MIL-HDBK-17A, Plastics for Flight Vehicles, Part II — Transparent Glazing Materials, available from the Government Printing Office (GPO).∗ These properties have been considered by aircraft manufacturers in selecting materials to be used in their designs and the use of substitutes having different characteristics may result in subsequent difficulties.

377. INSTALLATION PROCEDURES. When installing a replacement panel, use the same mounting method employed by the manufacturer of the airplane. While the actual installation will vary from one type of aircraft to another, consider the following major principles when installing any replacement panel:

a. *Never force a plastic panel* out of shape to make it fit a frame. If a replacement panel does not fit easily into the mounting, obtain a new replacement or heat the whole panel and reform. When possible, cut and fit a new panel at ordinary room temperature.

b. *In clamping or bolting plastic panels* into their mountings, do not place the plastic under excessive compressive stress. It is easy to develop more than 1,000 pounds per square inch on the plastic by overtorquing a nut and bolt. Tighten each nut to a firm fit, then back off one full turn.

c. *In bolt installations,* use spacers, collars, shoulders, or stopnuts to prevent tightening the bolt excessively. Whenever such devices are used by the airplane manufacturer, retain them in the replacement installation. It is important that the original number of bolts, complete with washers, spacers, etc., be used. When rivets are used, provide adequate spacers or other satisfactory means to prevent excessive tightening of the frame to the plastic.

d. *Mount plastic panels* between rubbed, cork, or other gasket material to make the installation waterproof, to reduce vibration, and to help to distribute compressive stresses on the plastic.

e. *Plastics expand and contract* considerably more than the metal channels in which they are mounted. Mount windshield panels to a sufficient depth in the channel to prevent it from falling out when the panel contracts at low temperatures or deforms under load. When the manufacturer's original design permits, mount panels to a minimum depth of 1 1/8 inch and with a clearance of 1/8 inch between the plastic and the bottom of the channel.

f. *In installations involving bolts or rivets,* make the holes through the plastic oversize 1/8 inch diameter and center so that the plastic will not

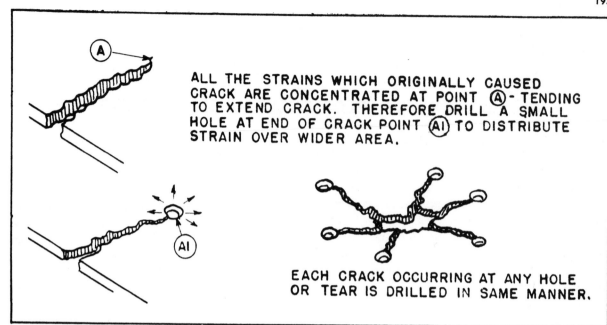

FIGURE 9.1.—Stop-drilling cracks.

bind or crack at the edge of the holes. The use of slotted holes is also recommended.

378. REPAIR OF PLASTICS. Replace extensively damaged transparent plastic rather than repair whenever possible since even a carefully patched part is not the equal of a new section either optically or structurally. At the first sign of crack development, drill a small hole at the extreme ends of the cracks as shown in figure 9.1. This serves to localize the cracks and to prevent further splitting by distributing the strain over a large area. If the cracks are small, stopping them with drilled holes will usually suffice until replacement or more permanent repair can be made. The following repairs are permissible; however, they are not to be located in the pilot's line of vision during landing or normal flight.

a. Surface Patch. If a surface patch is to be installed, trim away the damaged area and round all corners. Cut a piece of plastic of sufficient size to cover the damaged area and extend at least 3/4 inch on each side of the crack or hole. Bevel the edges as shown in figure 9.2. If the section to be repaired is curved, shape the patch to the same contour by heating it in an oil bath at a temperature of 248° to 302° F., or it may be heated on a hotplate until soft.

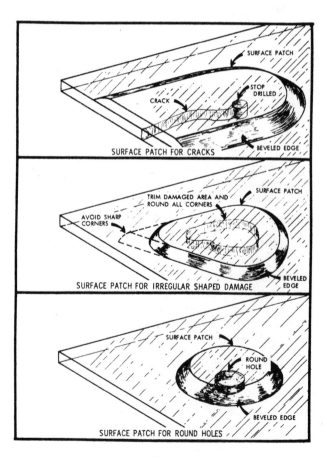

FIGURE 9.2.—Surface patches.

Boiling water should not be used for heating. Coat the patch evenly with plastic solvent adhesive and place immediately over the hole. Maintain a uniform pressure of from 5 to 10 pounds per square inch on the patch for a minimum of 3 hours. Allow the patch to dry 24 to 36 hours before sanding or polishing is attempted.

b. Plug Patch. In using inserted patches to repair holes in plastic structures, trim the holes to a perfect circle or oval and bevel the edges slightly. Make the patch slightly thicker than the material being repaired and similarly bevel the edges. Install patches in accordance with figure 9.3. Heat the plug until soft and press into the hole without cement and allow to cool to make a perfect fit. Remove the plug, coat the edges with adhesive, and then reinsert in the hole. Maintain a firm light pressure until the

PATCHES

PATCH SHOULD BE THICKER

PATCH AND HOLE SHOULD BE TRIMMED WITH TAPERED EDGES.

PATCH TAPERED ON SHARPER ANGLE THAN MATERIAL.

HEAT EDGES OF PATCH UNTIL SOFT AND FORCE IT IN HOLE. HOLD IT IN PLACE UNTIL COOL AND HARD TO ASSURE PERFECT FIT. THEN REMOVE PATCH FOR CEMENTING BATH.

DURING CEMENTING - PRESSURE NEED BE APPLIED ONLY ON TOP SURFACE. TAPER ASSURES EQUAL PRESSURE ON ALL SIDES.

AFTER CEMENT HAS HARDENED - SAND OR FILE EDGES LEVEL WITH SURFACE.

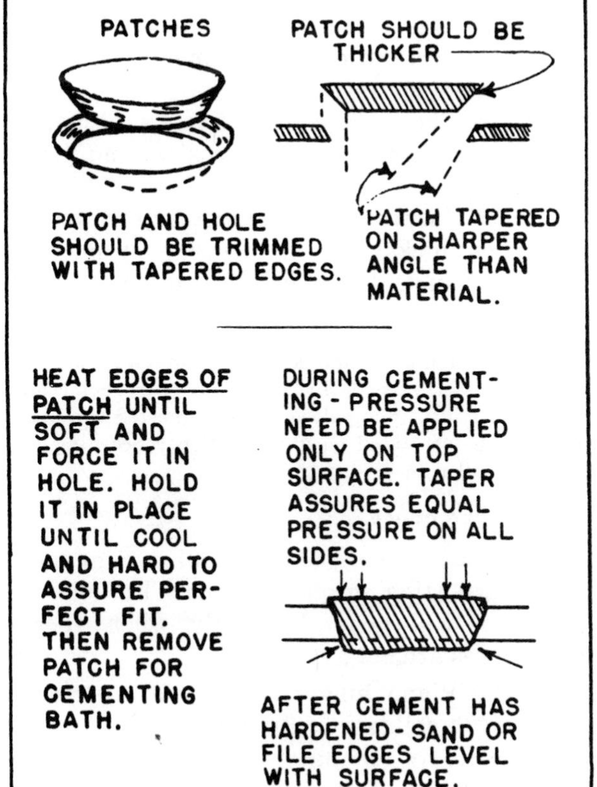

FIGURE 9.3.—Plug patch repair.

cement has set, then sand or file the edges level with the surface; buff and polish.

379. CLEANING AND POLISHING TRANSPARENT PLASTIC. Plastics have many advantages over glass for aircraft use, but they lack the surface hardness of glass, and care must be exercised while servicing the aircraft to avoid scratching or otherwise damaging the surface.

a. Cleaning. Clean the plastic by washing with plenty of water and mild soap, using a clean, soft, grit-free cloth, sponge, or bare hands. Do not use gasoline, alcohol, benzene, acetone, carbon tetracholoride, fire extinguisher or deicing fluids, lacquer thinners, or window cleaning sprays because they will soften the plastic and cause crazing.

b. Plastics should not be rubbed with a dry cloth since this is likely to cause scratches, and also build up an electrostatic charge which attracts dust particles to the surface. If after removing dirt and grease no great amount of scratching is visible, finish the plastic with a good grade of commercial wax. Apply the wax in a thin even coat and bring to a high polish by rubbing lightly with a soft cloth.

c. Polishing. Do not attempt hand polishing or buffing until the surface is clean. A soft, open-type cotton or flannel buffing wheel is suggested. Minor scratches may be removed by vigorously rubbing the affected area by hand, using a soft clean cloth dampened with a mixture of turpentine and chalk, or by applying automobile cleanser with a damp cloth. Remove the cleaner and polish with a soft, dry cloth. Acrylic and cellulose acetate plastics are thermoplastic. Friction created by buffing or polishing too long in one spot can generate sufficient heat to soften the surface. This will produce visual distortion and is to be guarded against.

380. EMERGENCY EXITS. The following material is intended as a guide for the inspection and maintenance of aircraft emergency exit provisions. Schedule inspections to coincide with all 100-hour/annual, progressive inspections or the maintenance procedures that have been approved by the Administrator. Before beginning inspection or maintenance activities of any type, consult the appropriate manufacturer's service manual for information specifying the type of exit release mechanism used.

a. Inspection. Examine the emergency exits and all associated hardware closely for deformation, excessive wear, security of attachment, lubrication, and cleanness.

(1) Doors.

(a) Inspect the door structure and skin for wrinkles, cracks, alignment with the fuselage, deep scratches, dents, loose rivets, corrosion, or any other indication of structural irregularity.

(b) Examine rubber seals for cuts, tears, excessive wear, proper contact with the entire door frame, and general deterioration.

(c) Inspect bearings, hinges, hinge fairings, latches, springs, pins, rods, handles, and related parts for wear and general condition.

(d) Examine the door jamb, frame, and supporting structure for cracks, loose fasteners, condition of stops, and corrosion or damage.

(e) Check the door for ease of operation and freedom of movement through its full range of travel.

(f) If a door warning light is provided, test it for proper operation and adjustment.

(g) Check the door locking mechanism for positive fit and at least the minimum lock pin engagement as specified in the applicable aircraft manual.

(2) Passenger Escape Hatches.

(a) Remove the escape hatch. Check for ease of removal and correct functioning of the release mechanism through all angles of pull likely to be encountered during emergency conditions.

CAUTION

If applicable, position one man outside the aircraft to catch the hatch, thereby preventing it from falling and damaging the wing and/or hatch.

(b) Examine the escape hatch structure for cracks, dents, deep scratches, alignment, loose rivets and/or bolts, corrosion, or any other indication of structural irregularity.

(c) Inspect the rubber seals for excessive wear, deterioration, cuts, tears, and proper contact with the fuselage.

(d) Check the operating mechanisms for wear, cracks, and general condition; springs for proper tension, alignment, and security.

(e) If applicable, inspect external release mechanisms for wear, cracks, and proper operation. Check for presence and legibility of external placards and exit location markings.

(f) Examine the escape hatch opening jamb, frame, stops, and skin for cracks and other evidence of damage or failure.

(g) If an emergency escape rope is provided, check it for accessibility, attachment, freedom of operation, rot, broken strands, and general condition. Inspect the storage container or tube for sharp edges or moisture.

(3) Crew Compartment Sliding Windows.

(a) Inspect the window frame for cracks, dents, questionable scratches, loose rivets, corrosion, or any other indication of structural irregularity.

(b) Examine the extrusion seal for wear, general deterioration, and proper contact with the fuselage canopy.

(c) Check the window teleflex mechanism for loose bearings, wear, corrosion, and proper operation.

(d) Inspect the windows for cracks, scratches, nicks, crazing, fogging or moisture between panes, delaminations, hot spots or discoloration.

NOTE: Fogging or delaminations of windows other than windshields are generally not cause for replacement unless visibility is impaired. It is suggested the manufacturer be consulted on any question concerning windows installed in pressurized aircraft.

b. Maintenance.

(1) Lubrication. Lubricate all moving parts of the exit latching mechanisms. The following practices will generally apply when specific procedures are not available.

(a) Piano hinges and operating mechanism pivot points—oil lightly and wipe off excess. Use only oil that is compatible with the type of seal used on that specific aircraft. Do not allow the oil to contact fabrics or finished surfaces.

(b) Latch bolts and sliding surfaces—

apply a light film from a graphite stick or latch lubricant (door ease).

(2) Seal Replacement. Information pertaining to special handling procedures for seals, gaskets, lubricants (dry or liquid), age limitations (shelf life), and types of adhesives may be found in the manufacturer's maintenance and overhaul manuals. Check the thickness of the seal or gasket for uniformity to prevent warping of the component, i.e., hatch or door. Exercise care when using adhesives to cement seals to the hatch frame or exit door as spillage or excessive amounts could cause the exit to bind.

NOTE: Replace seals and gaskets with materials recommended by the manufacturer. Many times these materials have been changed due to service experience, therefore a check of manufacturers' service information should be made to ascertain that any replacement parts, materials, etc., are those currently recommended.

(3) Hatch/Window Replacement. Check replacement hatches or windows for proper size and fit to preclude opening problems. Improper loading of the aircraft or an accident may cause binding of the hatch/window if inadequate clearance exists.

(4) Emergency Exit Service Difficulties. Emergency exits that fail to open unless extreme force is exerted are usually caused by one of the following:

(a) Paint or primers on the mating surfaces of the exit which are not allowed to dry completely. As a result, the surfaces will stick to each other.

(b) Latches that bind or fail to work unless pulled straight out.

(c) Failure to lubricate mating or rubbing surfaces.

(d) Failure to operate exits after final assembly. The exits may perform satisfactorily before the airplane is painted, but the finishing process results in the application of solvents, cleaners, primers, and paint finishes that may tend to make the exit inoperable. Check the exit for ease of release after painting and finishing of an aircraft.

c. Operational Considerations.

(1) Placards. Check to assure that all required placards and markings are installed (FAR 23.1557 (d) or 25.811). Make certain that curtains, drapes, clothes racks, etc. do not cover the placard or the exit operating handle.

When the normal exit identification signs are obstructed by compartmentation, galleys or other similar furnishings, use signs which contain the word "EXIT" and appropriate arrows to direct the attention of occupants to the exit locations.

(2) Precautions. Following any cabin interior modifications or configuration changes, check the accessability and operation of emergency exits by actual operation of the exit.

(a) Certain types of escape hatches have release handles which will not reinstall the lock pins into their locked position. If this type of release handle is pulled to any degree, either intentionally or inadvertently, it is necessary to ascertain that the locking pins are in position and safetied.

(b) Safety wire used to secure aircraft egress provisions should be of the type recommended by the manufacturer. Do not use stainless steel or other types of stiff wire. Acceptable substitutes would be either .011″ copper or .020″ aluminum soft safety wire.

(c) Some aircraft have inflatable door seals which assure a positive sealing capability during pressurization. Check these systems for proper operation in accordance with the manufacturer's maintenance instructions.

(d) Ascertain that seatbacks, tables, cabinets and other furnishings cannot interfere with the accessibility and opening of any exit either from inside or outside of the aircraft.

(3) Power Assist Devices. Some aircraft are presently equipped with powered systems to assist in door opening. It is imperative that the manufacturers' service instructions and manuals be reviewed before any maintenance is performed on such systems. These devices are usually hydraulically powered and, during an emergency condition, utilize a high-pressure bottle system as an alternate source (pneumatic or CO_2). Future designs will quite possibly involve various combinations of hydraulic, electrical, or pneumatic units. Strict attention to all servicing procedures will be essential to assure proper functioning of the power-assist device when needed in an emergency.

381.–391. RESERVED.

Chapter 10.   HYDRAULIC AND PNEUMATIC SYSTEMS

Section 1.   HYDRAULIC SYSTEMS

392. GENERAL. Maintain, service, and adjust airplane hydraulic systems in accordance with manufacturers' maintenance manuals and pertinent component maintenance manuals. Certain general principles of maintenance and repair which apply are outlined below.

393. HYDRAULIC LINES AND FITTINGS. Carefully inspect all lines and fittings at regular intervals to insure airworthiness. Investigate any evidence of fluid loss or leaks. Check metal lines for leaks, loose anchorages, scratches, kinks, or other damage. Inspect fittings and connections for leakage, looseness, cracks, burrs, or other damage. Replace or repair defective elements.

a. *Replacement of Metal Lines.* When inspection shows a line to be damaged or defective, replace the entire line or if the damaged section is localized, a repair section may be inserted. In replacing lines, always use tubing of the same size and material as the original line. Use the old tubing as a template in bending the new line, unless it is too greatly damaged, in which case a template can be made from soft iron wire. Soft aluminum tubing (1100, 3003, or 5052) under 1/4-inch outside diameter may be bent by hand. For all other tubing use an acceptable hand or power tube bending tool. Bend tubing carefully to avoid excessive flattening, kinking, or wrinkling. Minimum bend radii values are shown in figure 10.1. A small amount of flattening in bends is acceptable but do not exceed an amount such that the small diameter of the flattened portion is less than 75 percent of the orignial outside diameter. When installing the replacement tubing, line it up correctly with the mating part so that it is not forced into line by means of the coupling nuts.

* **b. *Tube Connections.*** Many tubing connections are made using flared tube ends, and standard connection fittings: AN-818 nut and AN-819 (MS 20819) sleeve. *

In forming flares, cut the tube ends square, file smooth, remove all burrs and sharp edges, and thoroughly clean. The tubing is then flared using the correct 37° aviation flare forming tool for the size of tubing and type of fitting. A double flare is used on soft aluminum tubing 3/8-inch outside diameter and under, and a single flare on all other tubing. In making the connections, use hydraulic fluid as a lubricant and then tighten. Overtightening will damage the tube or fitting, which may cause a failure; under-tightening may cause leakage which could result in a system failure.

Caution

Mistaken use of 45° automotive flare forming tools will result in improper tubing flare shape and angle causing misfit, stress and strain, and probable system failure.

*

FIGURE 10.1.—Tube data.

Dash Nos. Ref	Tubing OO inches	Wrench torque for tightening AN-818 Nut (pound inch)						Minimum bend radii measured to tubing centerline. Dimension in inches.	
		Aluminum-alloy tubing		Steel tubing		Aluminum-alloy tubing (Flare MS33583) for use on oxygen lines only			
		Minimum	Maximum	Minimum	Maximum	Minimum	Maximum	Alum. Alloy	Steel
-2	1/8	20	30	75	85	--	--	3/8	--
-3	3/16	25	35	95	105	--	--	7/16	2 1/32
-4	1/4	50	65	135	150	--	--	9/16	7/8
-5	5/16	70	90	170	200	100	125	3/4	1 1/8
-6	3/8	110	130	270	300	200	250	1 5/16	1 5/16
-8	1/2	230	260	450	500	300	400	1 1/4	1 3/4
-10	5/8	330	360	650	700	--	--	1 1/2	2 3/16
-12	3/4	460	500	900	1000	--	--	1 3/4	2 5/8
-16	1	500	700	1200	1400	--	--	3	3 1/2
-20	1 1/4	800	900	1520	1680	--	--	3 3/4	4 3/8
-24	1 1/2	800	900	1900	2100	--	--	5	5 1/4
-28	1 3/4	--	--	--	--	--	--	--	--
-32	2	1800	2000	2660	2940	--	--	8	7

*

This page intentionally left blank.

c. *Repair of Metal Tube Lines.* Minor dents and scratches in tubing may be repaired. Scratches or nicks no deeper than 10 percent of the wall thickness in aluminum alloy tubing, that are not in the heel of a bend, may be repaired by burnishing with hand tools. Replace lines with severe die marks, seams, or splits in the tube. Any crack or deformity in a flare is also unacceptable and cause for rejection. A dent less than 20 percent of the tube diameter is not objectionable unless it is in the heel of a bend. Dents may be removed by drawing a bullet of proper size through the tube by means of a length of cable. A severely damaged line should be replaced; however, it may be repaired by cutting out the damaged section and inserting a tube section of the same size and material. Flare both ends of the undamaged and replacement tube sections and make the connection by using standard unions, sleeves, and tube nuts. If the damaged portion is short enough, omit the insert tube and repair by using one union and two sets of connection fittings.

d. *Replacement of Flexible Lines.* When replacement of a flexible line is necessary, use the same type, size, and length of hose as the line to be replaced. If the replacement of a hose with swaged-end-type fittings is necessary, obtain a new hose assembly of the correct size and composition. Certain synthetic oils require a specially compounded synthetic rubber hose which is compatible. Refer to the aircraft manufacturer's service information for correct part number for replacement hose. If the fittings on each end are of the collet type or sleeve type, a replacement may be fabricated as shown in figure 10.2. Typical aircraft hose specifications and their uses are shown in figure 10.3. Install hose assemblies without twisting. (See figure 10.4.) Never stretch a hose tight between two fittings as this will result in overstressing and eventual failure. The length of hose should be sufficient to provide about 5 percent to 8 percent slack. Avoid tight bends in flex lines as they may result in failure. Never exceed the minimum bend radii as indicated in figure 10.5.

Teflon hose is used in many aircraft systems because of its superior qualities for certain applications. Teflon is compounded from tetrafluoroethylene resin which is unaffected by fluids normally used in aircraft. It has an operating range of $-65°$ F. to $450°$ F. For these reasons, Teflon is used in hydraulic and engine lubricating systems where temperatures and pressures preclude the use of rubber hose. Although Teflon hose has excellent performance qualities, it also has peculiar characteristics that require extra care in handling. It tends to assume a permanent set when exposed to high pressure or temperature. Do not attempt to straighten a hose that has been in service. Any excessive bending or twisting will cause kinking or weakening of the tubing wall. Replace any hose that shows signs of leakage, abrasion, or kinking. Any hose suspected of kinking may be checked with a steel ball of proper size. Figure 10.6 shows hose and ball sizes. The ball will not pass through if the hose is distorted beyond limits.

If the hose fittings are of the reusable type, a replacement hose may be fabricated as described in figure 10.2. When a hose assembly is removed the ends should be tied as shown in figure 10.7, so that its preformed shape will be maintained. Refer to figure 10.8 for minimum bend radii of Teflon hose.

All flexible hose installations should be supported at least every 24 inches. Closer supports are preferred. They should be carefully routed and securely clamped to avoid abrasion, kinking, or excessive flexing. Excessive flexing may cause weakening of the hose or loosening at the fittings.

e. *O-Ring Seals.* A thorough understanding of O-ring seal applications is necessary to determine when replacement must be made. The simplest application is where the O-ring merely serves as a gasket when it is compressed within a recessed area by applying pressure with a packing nut or screw cap. Leakage is not normally acceptable in this type of installation. In other installations the O-ring seals depend primarily upon their resiliency to accomplish their sealing action. When moving parts are involved, minor seepage may be normal and acceptable. A moist surface found on moving parts of hydraulic units is an indication the seal is being properly lubricated. In pneumatic systems, seal lubrication is provided by the installation of a grease-impreg-

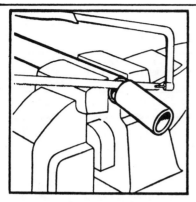

1. Place hose in vise and cut to desired length using fine tooth hacksaw or cut off wheel.

LOCATE AND SLIT COVER WITH KNIFE TO WIRE BRAID

TWIST OFF COVER WITH PLIERS

2. Locate length of hose to be cut off and slit cover with knife to wire braid. After slitting cover, twist off with pair of pliers. (see note below)

3. Place hose in vise and screw socket on hose counterclockwise.

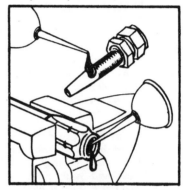

4. *Lubricate inside of hose and nipple threads liberally.

NOTE:
Hose assemblies fabricated per MIL–H–8790 must have exposed wire braid coated with a special sealant.

NOTE:
Step 2 applies to high pressure hose only.

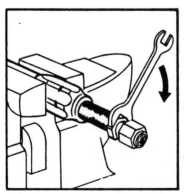

5. Screw nipple into socket using wrench on hex of nipple and leave .005 inches to .031 inches clearance between nipple hex and socket.

*CAUTION:
Do not use any petroleum product with hose designed for synthetic fluids "SKYDROL". For a lubricant during assembly use a vegetable soap liquid.

DISASSEMBLE IN REVERSE ORDER

FIGURE 10.2.—Hose assembly instructions.

SINGLE WIRE BRAID FABRIC COVERED

MIL. PART NO.	TUBE SIZE O.D.	HOSE SIZE I.D.	HOSE SIZE O.D.	RECOMM. OPER. PRESS.	MIN. BURST PRESS.	MAX. PROOF PRESS.	MIN. BEND RADIUS
MIL-H-8794- 3-L	3/16	1/8	.45	3,000	12,000	6,000	3.00
MIL-H-8794- 4-L	1/4	3/16	.52	3,000	12,000	6,000	3.00
MIL-H-8794- 5-L	5/16	1/4	.58	3,000	10,000	5,000	3.38
MIL-H-8794- 6-L	3/8	5/16	.67	2,000	9,000	4,500	4.00
MIL-H-8794- 8-L	1/2	13/32	.77	2,000	8,000	4,000	4.63
MIL-H-8794-10-L	5/8	1/2	.92	1,750	7,000	3,500	5.50
MIL-H-8794-12-L	3/4	5/8	1.08	1,500	6,000	3,000	6.50
MIL-H-8794-16-L	1	7/8	1.23	800	3,200	1,600	7.38
MIL-H-8794-20-L	1 1/4	1 1/8	1.50	600	2,500	1,250	9.00
MIL-H-8794-24-L	1 1/2	1 3/8	1.75	500	2,000	1,000	11.00
MIL-H-8794-32-L	2	1 13/16	2.22	350	1,400	700	13.25
MIL-H-8794-40-L	2 1/2	2 3/8	2.88	200	1,000	300	24.00
MIL-H-8794-48-L	3	3	3.56	200	800	300	33.00

Construction: Seamless synthetic rubber inner tube reinforced with one fiber braid, one braid of high tensile steel wire and covered with an oil resistant rubber impregnated fiber braid.

Identification: Hose is identified by specification number, size number, quarter year and year, hose manufacturer's identification.

Uses:
Hose is approved for use in aircraft hydraulic, pneumatic, coolant, fuel and oil systems.

Operating Temperatures:

Sizes -3 thru -12: Minus 65°F. to plus 250°F.

Sizes -16 thru -48: Minus 40°F. to plus 275°F.

NOTE: Maximum temperatures and pressures should not be used simultaneously.

MULTIPLE WIRE BRAID RUBBER COVERED

MIL PART NO.	TUBE SIZE O.D.	HOSE SIZE I.D.	HOSE SIZE O.D.	RECOMM. OPER. PRESS.	MIN. BURST PRESS.	MIN. PROOF PRESS.	MIN. BEND RADIUS
MIL-H-8788- 4-L	1/4	7/32	.63	3,000	16,000	8,000	3.00
MIL-H-8788- 5-L	5/16	9/32	.70	3,000	14,000	7,000	3.38
MIL-H-8788- 6-L	3/8	11/32	.77	3,000	14,000	7,000	5.00
MIL-H-8788- 8-L	1/2	7/16	.86	3,000	14,000	7,000	5.75
MIL-H-8788-10-L	5/8	9/16	1.03	3,000	12,000	6,000	6.50
MIL-H-8788-12-L	3/4	11/16	1.22	3,000	12,000	6,000	7.75
MIL-H-8788-16-L	1	7/8	1.50	3,000	10,000	5,000	9.63

Hose Construction: Seamless synthetic rubber inner tube reinforced with one fabric braid, two or more steel wire braids, and covered with a synthetic rubber cover (for gas applications request perforated cover).

Identification: Hose is identified by specification number, size number, quarter year and year, hose manufacturer's identification.

Uses: High pressure hydraulic, pneumatic, coolant, fuel and oil.

Operating Temperatures:
Minus 65°F. to plus 200°F.

FIGURE 10.3.—Aircraft hose specifications.

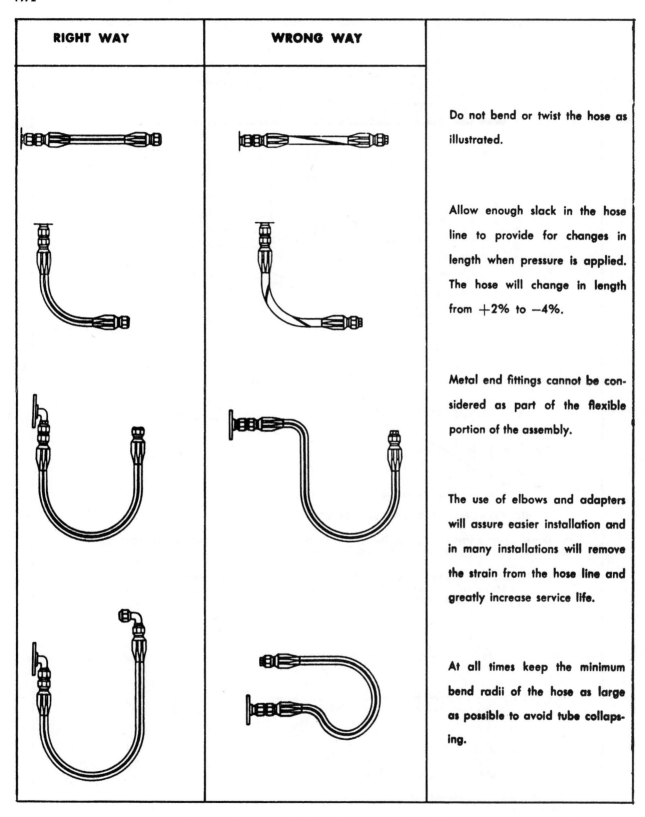

RIGHT WAY	WRONG WAY	
		Do not bend or twist the hose as illustrated.
		Allow enough slack in the hose line to provide for changes in length when pressure is applied. The hose will change in length from +2% to −4%.
		Metal end fittings cannot be considered as part of the flexible portion of the assembly.
		The use of elbows and adapters will assure easier installation and in many installations will remove the strain from the hose line and greatly increase service life.
		At all times keep the minimum bend radii of the hose as large as possible to avoid tube collapsing.

FIGURE 10.4.—Proper hose installations.

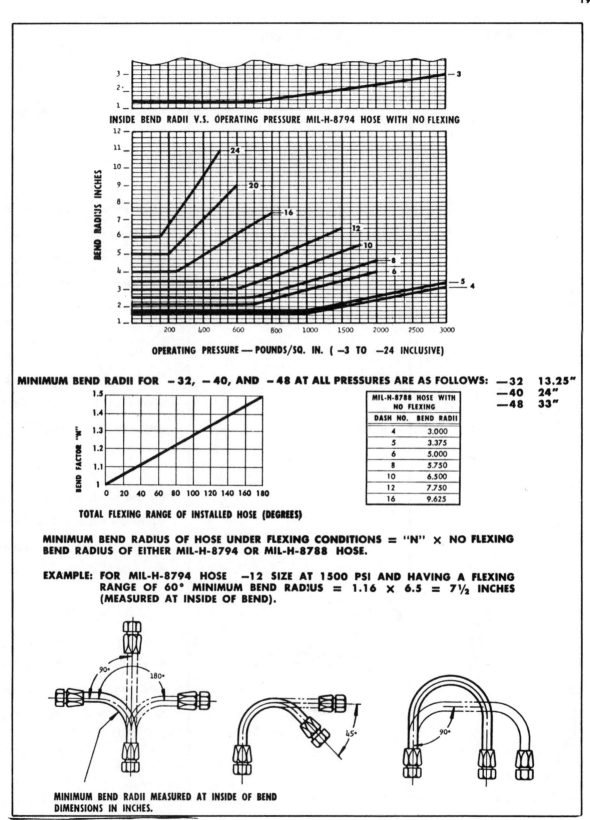

FIGURE 10.5.—Minimum bend radii.

nated felt wiper ring. When systems are static, seepage past the seals is not normally acceptable.

(1) Inspection. During inspection, consider the following to determine whether seal replacement is necessary:

(a) How much fluid or air is permitted to seep past the seals? In some installations minor seepage is normal. Refer to manufacturers' maintenance information.

HOSE SIZE	BALL SIZE
–4	5/64
–5	9/64
–6	13/64
–8	9/32
–10	3/8
–12	1/2
–16	47/64
–20	61/64

FIGURE 10.6.—Ball diameters for testing hose restrictions or kinking.

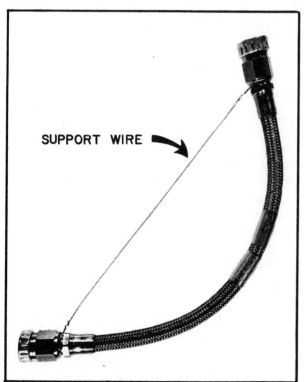

FIGURE 10.7.—Suggested handling of preformed hose.

(b) What effect does the leak have on the operation of the system? Know the system.

(c) Does the leak of fluid or air create a hazard or affect surrounding installations? A check of the system fluid and a knowledge of previous fluid replenishment is helpful.

(d) Will the system function safely until the next inspection?

(2) Do's and Don'ts That Apply to O-ring Seal Maintenance.

(a) Correct all leaks from static seal installations.

(b) Don't retighten packing gland nuts; retightening will, in most cases, increase rather than decrease the leak.

(c) Never reuse O-ring seals because they tend to swell from exposure to fluids, and become set from being under pressure. They may have minor cuts or abrasions that are not readily discernible by visual inspection.

(d) Avoid using tools that might damage the seal or the sealing surfaces.

(e) Do not depend upon color-coding. Coding may vary with manufacturer.

(f) Be sure that part number is correct.

(g) Retain replacement seals in their package until ready to use. This provides proper identification and protects the seal from damage and contamination.

(h) Assure that the sealing surfaces are clean and free of nicks or scratches before installing seal.

(i) Protect the seal from any sharp surfaces that it must pass over during installation. Use an installation bullet or cover the sharp surfaces with tape.

(j) Lubricate the seal so it will slide into place smoothly.

(k) Be sure the seal has not twisted during installation.

(l) Allow sufficient time for the seal to cold-flow to its original size before continuing with the installation.

(3) Storage of Replacement Seals.

(a) Store O-ring seals where temperatures do not exceed 120° F.

(b) Keep seals packaged to avoid exposure to ambient air and light, particularly sunlight.

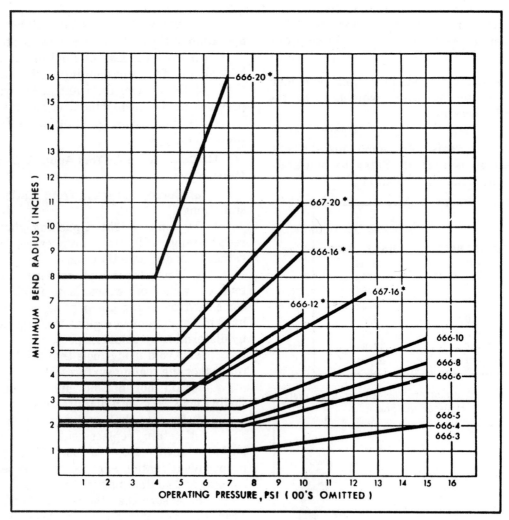

FIGURE 10.8.—Minimum bend radii—Teflon hose.

(c) Avoid storing O-ring seals on pegs or hooks, as in hardware stores. This practice leads to loss of identification, loss of cure dates, impairs cleanliness, and tends to cause the seals to become distorted and lose their resiliency from exposure to light and ambient air.

394. HYDRAULIC COMPONENTS. Hydraulic components such as pumps, actuating cylinders, selector valves, relief valves, etc., should be repaired or adjusted following the airplane and component manufacturer's instructions. Inspect hydraulic filter elements at frequent intervals and replace as necessary.

395.–405 RESERVED.

Chapter 11. ELECTRICAL SYSTEMS

Section 1. CARE OF ELECTRICAL SYSTEMS

406. GENERAL. The satisfactory performance of an aircraft is becoming more dependent upon the continued reliability of the electrical system. Reliability of the system is usually proportional to the amount of maintenance received and the knowledge of men who perform such maintenance. It is, therefore, important that maintenance be accomplished using the best techniques and practices to minimize the possibility of failure. This handbook is not intended to supersede or replace any government specification or specific manufacturer's instruction regarding electrical system maintenance.

The term "electrical system" as used in this circular means those parts of the aircraft which generate, distribute, and utilize electrical energy, including their support and attachments.

407. INSPECTION AND OPERATION CHECKS. Frequently, inspect equipment, electrical assemblies, and wiring installations for damage, general condition, and proper functioning to assure the continued satisfactory operation of the electrical system. Adjust, repair, overhaul, and test electrical equipment and systems in accordance with the recommendations and procedures set forth in aircraft and/or component maintenance instructions. Replace components of the electrical system that are damaged or defective with identical items or with equipment equivalent to the original in operating characteristics, mechanical strength, and the ability to withstand the environmental conditions encountered in the operation of the aircraft. A suggested list of items to look for and checks to be performed are:

a. Damaged or overheated equipment, connections, wiring, and installation.

b. Excessive resistance at high current carrying connections as determined by millivolt drop test.

c. Misalinement of electrically driven equipment.

d. Poor electrical bonding.

e. Dirty equipment and connections.

f. Improper support of wiring and conduit.

g. Loose connections, terminals, and ferrules.

h. Continuity of fuses.

i. Condition of electric lamps.

j. Insufficient clearance or poor insulation of exposed terminals.

k. Broken or missing safety wire, cotter pins, etc.

l. Operational check of electrically operated equipment such as motors, inverters, generators, batteries, lights, etc.

m. Voltage check of electrical system with portable precision voltmeter.

n. Miscellaneous irregularities such as poorly soldered or loose swaged terminals, loose quick disconnects, broken wire bundle lacing, broken or inadequate clamps, and insufficient clearance between exposed current-carrying parts and ground.

408. CLEANING AND PRESERVATION. Frequent cleaning of electrical equipment to remove dust, dirt, and grime is recommended. Fine emery cloth may be used to clean terminals and mating surfaces if they are corroded or dirty. Crocus cloth or very fine sandpaper may be used to polish commutators or slip rings. Do not use emery cloth on commutators since particles from the cloth may cause shorting and burning.

409. ADJUSTMENT. Accomplish adjustments to items of equipment such as regulators, generators, contactors, control devices, inverters, and relays outside the airplane on a test stand or test bench where all necessary instruments and test equipment are at hand. Follow the adjustment procedures outlined by the equipment manufacturer.

410. INSULATION OF ELECTRICAL EQUIPMENT. In some cases, a unit of electrical equipment is connected into a heavy current circuit, perhaps as a control device or relay. Such equipment is normally insulated from the mounting structure, since grounding the frame of the equipment may result in a serious ground fault in the event of equipment internal failure. If a ground connection for a control coil must be provided, use a separate small gauge wire.

411. BUS BAR MAINTENANCE. Periodically check bus bars used in aircraft electrical systems for general condition and cleanliness. Grease, oxide, or dirt on any electrical junction may cause the connectors to overheat and eventually fail. Clean bus bars by wiping with a clean soft cloth saturated with stoddard solvent and drying with a clean soft cloth.

412. JUNCTION BOXES.

a. Junction Box Construction. Fabricate replacement junction boxes using the same material as the original or from a fire-resistant, nonabsorbent material, such as aluminum alloy or an acceptable plastic material. Where fireproofing is necessary, a stainless steel junction box is recommended. Rigid construction will prevent "oil-canning" of the box sides, which could result in internal short circuits. In all cases, provide drainholes in the lowest portion of the box.

b. Internal Arrangement. The junction box arrangement should permit easy access to all installed items of equipment, terminals, and wires. Where marginal clearances are unavoidable, insert an insulating material between current-carrying parts and any grounded surface. It is not good practice to mount equipment on the covers or doors of junction boxes, since inspection for internal clearance is impossible when the door or cover is in the closed position.

c. Junction Box Installation. Securely mount junction boxes to the aircraft structure in such a manner that the contents are readily accessible for inspection. When possible, face the open side downward or at an angle so that loose metallic objects, such as washers or nuts, will tend to fall out of the junction box rather than wedge between terminals.

d. Junction Box Wiring. Junction box layouts must take into consideration the necessity for adequate wiring space and possible future additions. Lace or clamp electric wire bundles inside the box in a manner that terminals are not hidden, relay armatures are not fouled, and motion relative to any equipment is prevented. Protect cable at entrance openings against chafing using grommets or other suitable means.

413.–423. RESERVED.

Section 2. EQUIPMENT INSTALLATION

424. ELECTRICAL LOAD LIMITS. When installing additional equipment which consumes electrical power in an aircraft, determine that the total electrical load can be safely controlled or managed within the rated limits of the affected components of the aircraft's electrical power-supply system. Also determine that storage batteries forming a part of the affected system will be properly charged during flight.

a. Wires, Wire Bundles, and Circuit Protective Devices. Before any aircraft electrical load is increased, check the associated wires, wire bundles, and circuit protective devices (fuses or circuit breakers) to determine that the new total electrical load (previous maximum load plus added load) does not exceed the rated limits of the existing wires, wire bundles, or protective devices. Where necessary, add or replace with units having the correct rating.

425. GENERATORS. Compare the generator or alternator output ratings and limits prescribed by the manufacturer with the electrical loads which can be imposed on the affected generator or alternator by installed equipment. When the comparison shows that the probable total connected electrical load can exceed the output load limits of the generator(s) or alternator(s), reduce the load so that an overload cannot occur or provide means whereby the pilot or flight crew can readily and safely manage the electrical load so that it can be held within the prescribed limits. When a storage battery is part of the electrical power system, assure that the battery is continuously charged in flight, except when short intermittent loads are connected such as operation of radio transmitter, a landing gear motor, or other similar devices which may place short-time demand loads on the battery.

426. ACCEPTABLE MEANS OF CONTROLLING OR MONITORING THE ELECTRICAL LOAD.

a. The use of placards is recommended to inform the pilot and/or crewmembers the combination(s) of loads that may be connected to the power source.

b. Installations where the ammeter is in the battery lead, and the regulator system limits the maximum current that the generator or alternator can deliver, a voltmeter can be installed on the system bus. As long as the ammeter never reads "discharge" (except for short intermittent loads such as operating the gear and flaps) and the voltmeter remains at "system voltage," the generator or alternator will not be overloaded.

c. In installations where the ammeter is in the generator or alternator lead, and the regulator system does not limit the maximum current that the generator or alternator can deliver, the ammeter can be redlined at 100 percent of the generator or alternator rating. If the ammeter reading is never allowed to exceed the red line, except for short intermittent loads, the generator or alternator will not be overloaded.

d. Where the use of placards or monitoring devices is not practical or desired, and where assurance is needed that the battery in a typical small aircraft generator/battery power source will be charged in flight, the total continuous connected electrical load may be held to approximately 80 percent of the total rated generator output capacity. (When more than one generator is used in parallel, the total rated output is the combined output of the installed generators.)

e. When two or more generators are operated in parallel and the total connected system load can exceed the rated output of one generator, provide means for quickly coping with the sudden overloads which can be caused by generator or engine failure. Employ a quick load reduction system or procedure whereby the total load can be reduced to a quantity which is within the rated capacity of the remaining operable generator or generators.

f. Consider the total electrical load of devices that a pilot or flight crewmember would normally be expected to use as the probable continuous load. The use of placards or other load-monitoring devices or methods notwithstanding, the probable continuous load must not exceed the output capacity of the generator(s).

427. INVERTERS, ALTERNATORS, AND SIMILAR AIRCRAFT ELECTRICAL POWER SOURCES.

a. Connect the electrical load to inverters, alternators, and similar aircraft electrical power sources so that it cannot exceed the rated limits of the power source, unless effective monitoring means are provided whereby the pilot or flight crewmember can keep the load within the prescribed limits. Assure load circuit protective devices are time coordinated to trip prior to the inverter protective device or prior to electrical collapse of the inverter due to overload or fault in the load circuit. With the exception of the battery-charging provisions in the preceding paragraph, the same basic consideration with respect to load limits, inverters, alternators, and similar devices is applicable.

428. DETERMINATION OF ELECTRICAL LOAD.

a. The connected load of an aircraft electrical system may be determined by any one or a combination of several acceptable methods, techniques, or practices. However, regardless of the methods, techniques, or practice involved, any person who has need to know the status of a particular aircraft's electrical system should have available, current, and accurate data concerning the capacity of the installed electrical power source(s) and the load(s) imposed by installed electrical power consuming devices. Such data should provide a true picture of the status of the electrical system. Do not install new or additional electrical devices in an aircraft, nor change the capacity of any power source until the status of the electrical system in the aircraft has been determined accurately and found not to adversely affect the integrity of the electrical system.

429. CIRCUIT PROTECTION DEVICES.

a. *General.* Protect the wire with circuit breakers or fuses located as close as possible to the electrical power-source bus. Normally, the manufacturer of the electrical equipment specifies the fuse or breaker to be used when installing the respective equipment.

b. *Matching Protector to Wire.* The circuit breaker or fuse should open the circuit before the wire emits smoke. To accomplish this, the time-current characteristic of the protective device must fall below that of the associated wire. In order to obtain maximum utilization of the connected equipment, match the circuit protector characteristics.

c. *Circuit Protector Chart.* Figure 11.1 may be used as a guide for the selection of circuit breaker and fuse rating to protect copper conductor wire. This chart was prepared for the conditions specified by the notes which accompany the chart. If actual conditions deviate materially from those stated, ratings above or below the values recommended may be justified. For example, a wire run individually in the open air may possibly be protected by the circuit breaker of the next higher rating to that shown on the chart. In general, the chart is conservative for all ordinary aircraft electrical installations.

d. *Circuit Breaker Type.*

(1) All resettable type circuit breakers should open the circuit irrespective of the position of the operating control when an overload or circuit fault exists. Such circuit breakers are referred to as "trip free."

(2) Do not use automatic reset circuit breakers (which automatically reset themselves periodically) as circuit protective devices.

430. SWITCHES.

a. *General.* In all circuits where a switch

FIGURE 11.1.—Wire and circuit protector chart.

Wire AN gauge copper	Circuit breaker amp.	Fuse amp.
22	5	5
20	7.5	5
18	10	10
16	15	10
14	20	15
12	25 (30)	20
10	35 (40)	30
8	50	50
6	80	70
4	100	70
2	125	100
1		150
0		150

Figures in parentheses may be substituted where protectors of the indicated rating are not available.

Basis of chart:

(1) Wire bundles in 135° F. ambient and altitudes up to 30,000 feet.

(2) Wire bundles of 15 or more wires, with wires carrying no more than 20 percent of the total current-carrying capacity of the bundle as given in Specification MIL-W-5088 (ASG).

(3) Protectors in 75 to 85° F. ambient.

* (4) Copper wire Specification MIL-W-5088K or equivalent. *

(5) Circuit breakers to Specification MIL-C-5809 or equivalent.

(6) Fuses to Specification MIL-F-15160 or equivalent.

malfunction can be hazardous, use a switch specifically designed for aircraft service. These switches are of rugged construction and have sufficient contact capacity to break, make, and carry continuously the connected load current. Snap-action design is generally preferred to obtain rapid opening and closing of contacts irrespective of the speed of the operating toggle or plunger, thereby minimizing contact arcing.

b. Switch Ratings.

(1) Nominal Rating. The nominal current rating of the conventional aircraft switch is usually stamped on the switch housing and represents the continuous current rating with the contacts closed. Derate switches from their nominal current rating for the following types of circuits:

(a) High In-rush. Circuits containing incandescent lamps can draw an initial current which is 15 times greater than the continuous current. Contact burning or welding may occur when switch is closed.

(b) Inductive. Magnetic energy stored in solenoid coils or relays is released when the control switch is opened and may appear as an arc.

(c) Motors. Direct current motors will draw several times their rated current during starting, and magnetic energy stored in their armature and field coils is released when the control switch is opened.

(2) Switch Selection. Figure 11.2 provides an approximate method for selecting the proper nominal switch rating when the continuous load current is known. The procedure is essentially a derating to obtain reasonable switch efficiency and service life.

(3) Switch Installation. Hazardous errors in switch operation may be avoided by logical and consistent installation. Mount "on-off" two position switches so that the "on" position is reached by an upward or forward movement of the toggle. When the switch controls movable aircraft elements, such as landing gear or

FIGURE 11.2.—Switch derating factors.

Nominal system voltage	Type of load	Derating factor
24 V.D.C.	Lamp	8
24 V.D.C.	Inductive (Relay-Solenoid)	4
24 V.D.C.	Resistive (Heater)	2
24 V.D.C.	Motor	3
12 V.D.C.	Lamp	5
12 V.D.C.	Inductive (Relay-Solenoid)	2
12 V.D.C.	Resistive (Heater)	1
12 V.D.C.	Motor	2

NOTES:

1. To find the nominal rating of a switch to operate a given device, multiply the continuous load current required by the device by the derating factor corresponding to the voltage and type of load.

2. To find the continuous load current that a switch of a given nominal rating will handle efficiently, divide the switch nominal rating by the derating factor corresponding to the voltage and type of load.

flaps, the toggle should move in the same direction as the desired motion. Inadvertent operation of switches can be prevented by mounting suitable guards over the switches.

(4) **Relays.** Relays are used as a switching device where a weight reduction can be achieved, or to simplify electrical controls. It should be remembered that the relay is an electrically operated switch, and therefore subject to dropout under low system voltage conditions. Concerning contact ratings, the discussion of switch ratings in paragraph 430b(1) is generally applicable to relays.

431.–441. RESERVED.

Section 3. ELECTRIC WIRE

442. GENERAL. Aircraft service imposes severe environmental conditions on electric wire. To assure satisfactory service, inspect the wire at regular intervals for abrasions, defective insulation, condition of terminal posts, and buildup of corrosion
* under or around swaged terminals. *

a. *Voltage Drop in Wires.* The voltage drop in the main power wires from the generation source or the battery to the bus should not exceed 2 percent of the regulated voltage, when the generator is carrying rated current or the battery is being discharged at the 5–minute rate. The following tabulation shows the maximum acceptable voltage drop in the load circuits between the bus and the utilization equipment.

FIGURE 11.2a—Tabulation chart.

Nominal system voltage	Allowable voltage drop continuous operation	Intermittent operation
14	0.5	1
28	1	2
115	4	8
200	7	14

b. *Resistance.* The resistance of the current return path through the aircraft structure is always considered negligible. However, this is based on the assumption that adequate bonding of the structure or a special electric current return path has been provided which is capable of carrying the required electric current with a negligible voltage drop. A resistance measurement of .005 ohms from ground point of the generator or battery to ground terminal of any electrical device may be considered satisfactory. Another satisfactory method of determining circuit resistance is to check the voltage drop across the circuit. If the voltage drop does not exceed the limit established by the aircraft or product manufacturer, the resistance value for the circuit may be considered satisfactory. When utilizing the voltage drop method of checking a circuit,

maintain the input voltage at a constant value. Figures 11.3 and 11.4 show formulas that may be used to determine resistance in electrical wires.

FIGURE 11.3.—Examples determining voltage drop from electric wire chart (figure 11.7).

Voltage drop	Enter chart (feet)	Amperes	Wire size from chart	Check
1	100	20	No. 6	$VD = {}^2(.000436)(100)(20) = .872$
0.5	$\frac{100}{0.5} = 200$	20	No. 4	$VD = {}^2(.000274)(100)(20) = .548$
4	$\frac{100}{4} = 25$	20	No. 12	$VD = {}^2(.00188)(100)(20) = 3.76$
7	$\frac{100}{7} = 14$	20	No. 14	$VD = {}^2(.00299)(100)(20) = 5.98$

[1]It should be noted that the No. 14 wire should not be used if any portion of its 100-foot length is to be confined in conduit, large bundles, or locations of high ambient temperature, as the intersection of the wire size and current lines fall below curve 1.

[2]Resistance values from figure 11.5.

FIGURE 11.4—Examples determining voltage drop from electric wire chart (figure 11.7).

Voltage drop	Wire	Amperes	Max. length (ft.) from chart at voltage drop indicated	Check
1	No. 10	20	45	$VD = {}^1(.0011)(20)945) = .990$
0.5	- - - - -	- -	$(45)(.5) = 22.5$	$VD = {}^1(.0011)(20)(22.5) = .495$
4	- - - - -	- -	$(45)(4) = 180$	$VD = {}^1(.0011)(20)(180) = 3.96$
7	- - - - -	- -	$(45)(7) = 315$	$VD = {}^1(.0011)(20)(315) = 6.93$

[1]Resistance values from figure 11.5.

FIGURE 11.5.—Copper electric wire current carrying capacity.

Wire size	Single wire in free air—maximum amperes	Wire in conduit or bundled—maximum amperes	Maximum resistance—ohms/ 1,000 feet (20° C.)	Nominal conductor area—circular mills	Finished wire weight—pounds per 1,000 feet
AN–20	11	7.5	10.25	1,119	5.6
AN–18	16	10	6.44	1,779	8.4
AN–16	22	13	4.76	2,409	10.8
AN–14	32	17	2.99	3,830	17.1
AN–12	41	23	1.88	6,088	25.0
AN–10	55	33	1.10	10,433	42.7
AN–8	73	46	.70	16,864	69.2
AN–6	101	60	.436	26,813	102.7
AN–4	135	80	.274	42,613	162.5
AN–2	181	100	.179	66,832	247.6
AN–1	211	125	.146	81,807	....
AN–0	245	150	.114	104,118	382
AN–00	283	175	.090	133,665	482
AN–000	328	200	.072	167,332	620
AN–000	380	225	.057	211,954	770

FIGURE 11.6—Aluminum electric wire current carrying capacity.

Wire size	Single wire in free air—maximum amperes	Wire in conduit or bundled—maximum amperes	Maximum resistance—ohms/ 1,000 feet (20° C.)	Nominal conductor area—circular mills	Finished wire weight—pounds per 1,000 feet
AL–6	83	50	0.641	28,280	....
AL–4	108	66	.427	42,420	....
AL–2	152	90	.268	67,872	....
AL–0	202	123	.169	107,464	166
AL–00	235	145	.133	138,168	204
AL–000	266	162	.109	168,872	250
AL–0000	303	190	.085	214,928	303

443. AIRCRAFT ELECTRICAL WIRE. Use air-craft-quality wire. Correct wire selection is dependent upon knowledge of current requirements, operating temperatures, and environmental conditions involved in the particular installation.

a. *Conductors.* Copper conductors are coated to prevent oxidation and to facilitate soldering. Tinned copper or aluminum wire is generally used in installations where operating temperatures do not exceed 221° F. (105° C.). Aluminum wire shall be restricted to size 6 and larger. Aluminum wire shall neither be directly attached to engine-mounted accessories nor installed in other areas of severe vibration. It shall not be installed where frequent connections and disconnections are required. All installations of aluminum wire shall be relatively permanent. Aluminum wire shall not be used where the length of run is less than 3 feet, in areas where corrosive fumes exist. It is not recommended for use in communication or navigation systems.

Silver coated wire is used where temperatures do not exceed 392° F. (200° C.).

Caution

An inflammability hazard exists when silver or silver plated conductors impressed with direct current potential are saturated with water/glycol solutions. The positive (cathodic) may be of any conductive material. If the anode and cathode are in sufficient proximity to permit current (in the millampere range) to flow through a glycol solution which has contaminated the space between the two conductors, oxidation is rapid and an intensely hot flame appears. This phenomenon is not known to occur when the anode is other than

* silver or when the impressed voltage is alternating current. Nickel-coated copper wire is used for temperatures up to 500° F. (260° C.).

Nickel-coated wire is more difficult to solder than tinned or silver-coated wire, but with proper techniques, satisfactory connections can be made.

b. *Insulation.* Silicone rubber is rated at 392° F. (200° C.), is (continued on page 181) *

This page intentionally left blank.

highly flexible, and self-extinguishing except in vertical runs. Polytetrafluoroethylene (TFE Fluorocarbon) is widely used as high-temperature insulation. It will not burn, but will vaporize when exposed to flame. It is resistant to most fluids. Fluorinated ethylene propolene (FEP Fluorocarbon) is rated at 392° F. (200° C.), but will melt at higher temperatures. Other properties of FEP are similar to TFE.

c. *Thermal and Abrasion Resistant Materials.* Glass braid has good thermal and abrasion qualities but moisture absorption is high. Asbestos and other minerals provide high temperature and flame resistance, but are highly absorbent. Moisture absorption is reduced by use of silicone rubber, TFE, or other saturants. Nylon is widely used in low-temperature wires for abrasion and fluid resistance. Polyimide, a new material, has excellent thermal and abrasion resistant characteristics.

d. *Wire Selection.* When selecting wire, refer to structural and environmental characteristics. Wire normally used for chassis wiring, in enclosed areas, or in compact wire harnesses protected by molded or braided coverings, usually has low abrasion resistance. Wire used to interconnect units, or in long, open runs in the airframe, is designed to withstand normal aircraft environment without sleeving, jacketing, or other protection. Care must be taken in making all installations because no wire insulation or jacketing will withstand continuous scuffing or abrasion.

* 444. INSTRUCTIONS FOR USE OF ELECTRICAL WIRE CHART.

a. *To select the correct size* of electrical wire, two major requirements must be met:

(1) The size must be sufficient to prevent an excessive voltage drop while carrying the required current over the required distance. (See figure 11-2a, Tabulation Chart, for allowable voltage drops.)

(2) The size must be sufficient to prevent overheating of the wire carrying the required current.

b. *To meet the first requirement of 444a(1)* in selecting the correct wire size using figure 11-7 or 11-7a, the following must be known:

(1) The wire length in feet.

(2) The number of amperes of current to be carried.

(3) The amount of voltage drop permitted.

(4) Is the current to be carried continuous or intermittent?

c. *Example No. 1:* Find the wire size in figure 11-7 using the following known information:

(1) Fifty feet installation.

(2) Twenty ampere current load.

(3) Twenty-eight volt source from bus to equipment.

(4) Continuous current rating operation.

The scale on the left of the chart represents maximum wire length in feet to prevent an excessive voltage drop for a specified voltage source system (e.g., 14V, 28V, 115V, 200V).

The scale (slant lines) on top of the chart represents amperes. The scale at the bottom of the chart represents the size. From the left scale (wire length), find No. 50 under the 28V source column. Follow the horizontal line to the right until it intersects the slant 20 ampere line. At this point drop to the bottom of the chart. The value falls between No. 8 and No. 10 size wires. Select the larger wire size, No. 8. This is the smallest size wire that should be used to avoid an excessive voltage drop of one volt for a 28V system. This example is plotted on the wire chart, figure 11-7.

d. *The procedures in "c"* can be used to find the wire size for any continuous or intermittent operation (maximum 2 minutes) voltage (e.g., 14V, 28V, 115V, 200V) indicated on the scale left of the wire chart, figure 11-7 or 11-7a.

e. *To meet the second requirement of 444a(2)* in selecting the correct wire size using figure 11-7 or 11-7a, the following must be known:

(1) The number of amperes of current to be carried.

(2) Is the wire to be installed in conduit and/ or bundle on a continuous current rating (curve 1, figure 11-7)?

(3) Is the wire to be installed as a single wire in free air on a continuous current rating (curve 2, figure 11-7)?   *

*   **(4)** Is the wire used in an intermittent current rating of 2 minutes maximum (curve 3, figure 11–7a)?

f. *Example No. 2:* Find the wire size in figure 11–7 using the following known information.

(1) Fourteen feet installation.

(2) Twenty-eight volt source from bus to equipment.

(3) Continuous current through conduit or bundle.

Find the number 14 under 28 volts source column. Follow the horizontal line to the right until it intersects the slant 20-ampere line. At this point drop to the bottom of the chart. The value falls between No. 16 and No. 14, select the larger size, No. 14.

The wire will be placed in conduit, so curve 1 applies. The maximum continuous current for No. 14 wire is 17 amperes.

In this particular case, in order for the wire to carry 20 amperes, the intersection must lie above the rating curve or else the thermal limits of the wire will be exceeded. We must, therefore, increase the wire size to No. 12. This example is plotted on the wire chart figure 11–7.

g. *To find the wire size* for a wire installation run in a conduit and/or bundle (curve 1), use the same procedure and figure 11–7 as above.

h. *To find the wire size* for a wire installation run in an intermittent rating (curve 3), the same procedure applies (except you use the wire chart in figure 11–7a).   *

This page intentionally left blank.

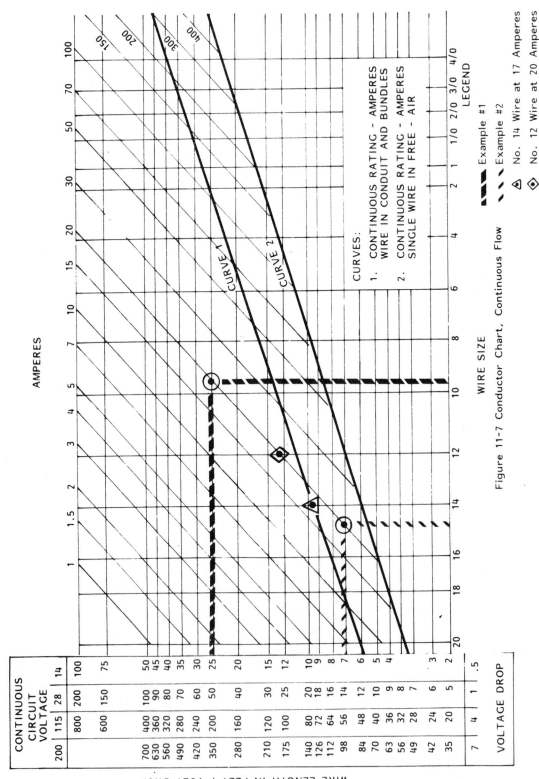

Figure 11-7 Conductor Chart, Continuous Flow

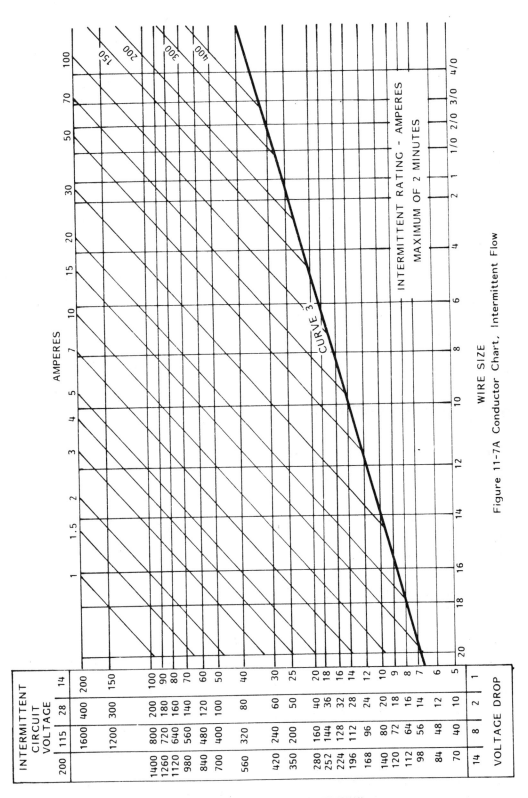

Figure 11-7A Conductor Chart, Intermittent Flow

This page intentionally left blank.

*

FIGURE 11.7b.—Wire used in aircraft installations.

Specification	Conductor	Insulation	Voltage rate	Conductor temp. rating	Remarks
MIL–W–8777	Silver-coated copper	Silicone rubber, glass braid, polyester braid	600 V.	200° C.	High temperature interconnection. Self-extinguishing. To 155° C. ambient.
MIL–W–8777 MS–27110	Silver-coated copper	Silicone rubber, glass braid, FEP fluorocarbon	600 V.	200° C. 392° F.	Same as MS–26477 but has smooth surface. To 155° C. ambient.
MIL–W–7139 Class 1	Silver-coated copper	TFE fluorocarbon and glass	600 V.	200° C. 392° F.	High temperature interconnection. Self-extinguishing. To 155° C. ambient.
MIL–W–7139 Class 2	Nickel-coated copper	TFE fluorocarbon and glass	600 V.	260° C. 500° F.	Same as Class 1. To 215° C. ambient.
MIL–W–22759/1	Silver-coated copper	TFE tapes/Glass braids	600 V.	200° C.	High temperature.
MIL–W–22759/2	Nickel-coated copper	TFE tapes/Glass braids	600 V.	260° C.	High temperature.
MIL–W–22759/3	Nickel-coated copper	TFE tapes/Glass braids	600 V.	260° C.	High temperature.
MIL–W–22759/4	Silver-coated copper	TFE tapes/Glass braids/FEP jacket	600 V.	200° C.	High temperature.
MIL–W–22759/5	Silver-coated copper	Mineral filled TFE	600 V.	200° C.	Abrasion resistant. Heavy wall.
MIL–W–22759/6	Nickel-coated copper	Mineral filled TFE	600 V.	260° C.	Abrasion resistant. Heavy wall.
MIL–W–22759/7	Silver-coated copper	Mineral filled TFE	600 V.	200° C.	Abrasion resistant. Medium wall.
MIL–W–22759/8	Nickel-coated copper	Mineral filled TFE	600 V.	260° C.	Abrasion resistant. Medium wall.
MIL–W–22759/9	Silver-coated copper	TFE		200° C.	
MIL–W–22759/10	Nickel-coated copper	TFE		260° C.	
MIL–W–22759/11	Silver-coated copper	TFE	600 V.	200° C.	
MIL–W–22759/12	Nickel-coated copper	TFE	600 V.	260° C.	

*

* FIGURE 11.7b.—Wire used in aircraft installations.

Specification	Conductor	Insulation	Voltage rate	Conductor temp. rating	Remarks
MIL–W–22759/ 13	Tin plated copper	FEP/PVF$_2$	600 V.	150° C.	Medium weight.
MIL–W–22759/ 14	Tin plated copper	FEP/PVF$_2$	600 V.	150° C.	Light weight.
MIL–W–22759/ 15	Silver coated high strength copper alloy	FEP/PVF$_2$	600 V.	200° C.	Light weight.
MIL–W–22759/ 16	Tin plated copper	ETFE	600 V.	150° C.	Medium weight. The maximum temperature for MIL–W–22759/16 should be limited to 110° C. conductor temperature and 65° C. ambient temperature. The insulation of MIL–W–22759/16, and other Tefzel insulations should have a nominal wall thickness of at least 10.5 mils.
MIL–W–22759/ 17	Silver coated high strength copper alloy	ETFE	600 V.	150° C.	Same as MIL–W–22759/16.
MIL–W–22759/ 18	Tin plated copper	ETFE	600 V.	150° C.	Light weight.
MIL–W–22759/ 19	Silver coated high strength copper alloy	ETFE	600 V.	150° C.	Light weight.
MIL–W–22759/ 22	Silver coated high strength copper alloy	TFE	600 V.	200° C.	Light weight.
MIL–W–22759/ 23	Nickel coated high strength copper alloy	TFE	600 V.	260° C.	Light weight.
MIL–W–25038/1	Nickel coated copper	Inorganic materials	600 V.	260° C.	Fire resistant circuits.
MIL–W–25038/2	Nickel coated copper	Inorganic materials	600 V.	260° C.	Fire resistant circuits.
MIL–W–16878 Type EE	Silver or nickel coated copper	Extruded TFE	1,000 V.	200° C. or 260° C.	Hook-up insulated. High temperature.

*

FIGURE 11.7b.—Wire used in aircraft installations.

Specification	Conductor	Insulation	Voltage rate	Conductor temp. rating	Remarks
MIL–W–81044/6	Tin coated copper	Crosslinked extruded polyalkene	600 V.	-65 to +135	Aerospace electric systems (General purpose aircraft wiring) normal weight.
MIL–W–81044/6B	Tin coated copper	Crosslinked extruded polyalkene	600 V.	-65 to +150	Aerospace electric systems (General purpose aircraft wiring) normal weight.
MIL–W–81044/7B	Silver plated high strength copper alloy	Crosslinked extruded polyalkene	600 V.	-65 to +150	Same as MIL-W–81044/6B.
MIL–W–81044/9B	Tin coated copper	Crosslinked extruded polyalkene	600 V.	-65 to +150	Aerospace electric systems (General purpose aircraft wiring) medium weight.
MIL–W–81044/10B	Silver plated high strength copper alloy	Crosslinked extruded polyalkene	600 V.	-65 to +150	Same as MIL-W–81044/9B.
MIL–W–81044/12B	Tin coated copper	Crosslinked extruded polyalkene	600 V.	-65 to +150	Aerospace electric systems (General electronic wiring) Internal wiring of meters, panels, and electrical and electronic equipment. Light weight.
MIL–W–81044/13B	Silver plated high strength copper alloy	Crosslinked extruded polyalkene	600 V.	-65 to +150	Same as MIL-W–81044/12B.
MIL–W–81381/7E	Silver coated copper	Polyimide/FEP film	600 V.	-65 to +200	Aerospace electric systems (General electronic wiring) Internal wiring of meters, panels, and electrical and electronic equipment. Light weight.
MIL–W–81381/8D	Nickel coated copper	Polyimide/FEP film	600 V.	-65 to +200	Same as MIL-W–81381/7E.

* FIGURE 11.7b.—Wire used in aircraft installations. (Continued)

Specification	Conductor	Insulation	Voltage rate	Conductor temp. rating	Remarks
MIL-W-81381/ 11	Silver coated copper	Polyimide/FEP film	600 V.	-65 to +200	Aerospace electric systems (General purpose aircraft wiring) medium weight. The insulation of MIL-W-81381/11, /12 and other Kapton insulations should have a nominal wall thickness of at least 10.0 mils with a minimum of 9.5 mils.
MIL-W-81381/ 12	Nickel coated copper	Polyimide/FEP film	600 V.	-65 to +200	Same as MIL-W-81381/11.

NOTES:

1. Wire part numbers that are asterisked (*) should not be used without additional mechanical protection, such as an overall shield and/or jacket, or installed within equipment or behind rigid covers.

2. It is recommended that all wire be typed identified along its entire length, specification number, or the aircraft manufacturer's wire part number.

3. Wire Stamping. Old wire stamping methods may not be suitable for wires with thin wall insulation. Wire manufacturer should provide stamping information.

4. Wires should have a 6-inch diameter loop near their connections to (electrical) components to accommodate any wire tensions that result from (aircraft) structural deformations during a crash.

5. Wire added should meet or exceed existing wire specs and should be as direct as possible.

6. All wire connections should be made on a component's least vulnerable side.

7. Electrical wires should be routed along the strongest (aircraft) structural members and should not, in general, traverse areas of anticipated severe structural deformation.

8. Wires that must pass through areas of anticipated structural deformation should be approximately 30% longer than necessary. The extra length should be accumulated in the form of loops or "S" shaped patterns and should be located at the ares of anticipated structural deformation.

9. When wires pass through (aircraft) structural openings or bulkhead holes, these openings/holes should be 8 to 12 times larger than the wire diameter, and appropriate grommets should be provided.

10. Wires should be attached to the aircraft structure with clamps or ties that will fail before breaking the wire.

11. Wire routing should not be near flammable fluid sources.   *

This page intentionally left blank.

* 445. SPLICES IN ELECTRIC WIRE. Splicing of electric wire should be kept to a minimum and avoided entirely in locations subject to extreme vibrations. Individual wires in a group or bundle may be spliced provided the completed splice is located so it can be periodically inspected. Stagger splices (see figure 11.8) so the bundle does not become excessively enlarged. Many types of aircraft splice connectors are available for use when splicing individual wires. Use of the self-insulated splice connector is preferred; however, a noninsulated splice connector may be used provided the splice is covered with plastic sleeving which is secured at both ends. Solder splices may be used; however, they are particularly brittle and not recommended. Splices are subject to the following:

a. *There shall be not more than one splice* in any one wire segment between any two connectors or other disconnect points, except as allowed by c and g below.

b. *Splices in bundles* shall be staggered and shall not increase the size of the bundle so as to prevent the bundle from fitting in its designated space or cause congestion which will adversely affect maintenance.

c. *Splices shall not be used* to salvage scrap lengths of wire.

d. *Splices shall not be used* within 12 inches of a termination device, except for e below.

e. *Splices may be used* within 12 inches of a termination device when attaching to the pigtail spare lead of a potted termination device, or to splice multiple wires to a single wire, or to adjust the wire sizes so that they are compatible with the contact crimp barrel sizes.

f. *The application* of splices shall be under design control and shall be authorized by engineering drawings.

g. *Splices may be used* to repair manufactured harnesses or installed wiring when approved by engineering.

446. OPEN WIRING. Electric wiring is often installed in aircraft without special enclosing means. This practice is known as open wiring and offers the advantages of ease of maintenance and reduced weight.

a. *Wire Bundles.* To simplify maintenance and to minimize the damage that may result from a single fault, limit the number of wires in the run. Shielded wire, ignition wire, and wires which are not protected by a circuit breaker or fuse are usually routed separately. Avoid bending radii less than 10 times the outer diameter of the bundle to prevent excessive stresses on the wire insulation.

b. *Insulating Tubing.* Soft insulating tubing (spaghetti) cannot be considered as mechanical protection against external abrasion of wire, since at best it provides only a delaying action. Use conduit or ducting when mechanical protection is needed.

c. *Clamping of Wire Bundles.* Use clamps lined with nonmetallic material to support the wire bundle along the run. Tying may be used between clamps, but should not be considered as a substitute for adequate clamping. Adhesive tapes are subject to age deterioration and, *

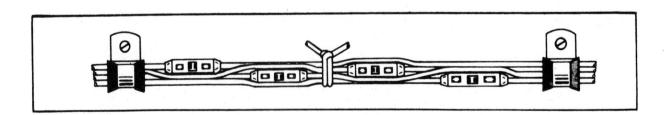

FIGURE 11.8.—Staggered splices in wire bundle.

therefore are not acceptable as a clamping means.

d. Separation from Flammable Fluid Lines. An arcing fault between an electric wire and a metallic flammable fluid line may puncture the line and result in a serious fire. Consequently, make every effort to avoid this hazard by physical separation of the wire from lines or equipment containing oil, fuel, hydraulic fluid, or alcohol. When separation is impractical, locate the electric wire above the flammable fluid line and securely clamp to the structure. In no case, should a wire be supported by a flammable fluid line.

447. HEAT PRECAUTIONS. Separate wires from high temperature equipment, such as resistors, exhaust stacks, heating ducts, etc., to prevent insulation breakdown. Insulate wires that must run through hot areas with a high temperature insulation material such as asbestos, fiberglas, or teflon. Avoid high temperature areas when using cables having soft plastic insulation such as polyethylene because these materials are subject to deterioration and deformation at elevated temperatures. Many coaxial cables have this type of insulation.

448. PROTECTION AGAINST CHAFING. Protect wire and wire groups against chafing or abrasion as damaged insulation may result in short circuits, malfunctions, or inoperative equipment. Support wire bundles using MS–21919 cable clamps as indicated in figure 11.9. When clamped in position, if there is less than 1/4-inch clearance between a bulkhead cutout and the wire bundle, install a suitable grommet as indicated in figure 11.10. The grommet may be cut at 45° angle to facilitate installation provided it is cemented in place and the slot is located at the top of the cutout.

449. STRIPPING INSULATION. Attachment of wire to connectors or terminals requires the removal of insulation to expose the conductors. This practice is commonly known as stripping. When performing the stripping operation, remove no more insulation than is necessary. Stripping may be accomplished in many ways;

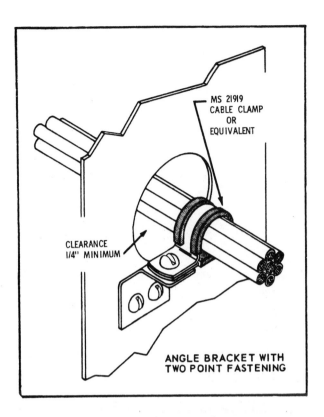

FIGURE 11.9—Cable clamp at bulkhead hole.

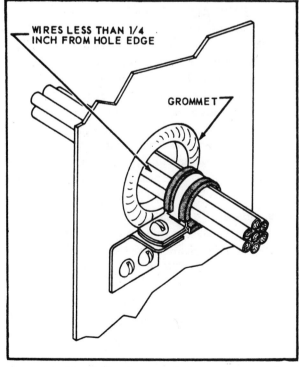

FIGURE 11.10—Cable clamp and grommet at bulkhead hole.

FIGURE 11.11.—Allowable nicked or broken strands.

Maximum allowable nicked and broken strands.

Wire Size #	Conductor material	Number of strands per conductor	Total allowable nicked and broken strands
24-14	Copper	19	2 nicked, none broken
12-10	or	37	4 nicked, none broken
8-4	Copper Alloy	133	6 nicked, none broken
2-1		665-817	6 nicked, 2 broken
0-00		1,045-1330	6 nicked, 3 broken
000		1,665-	6 nicked, 4 broken
0000		2,109-	6 nicked, 5 broken
6-000	Aluminum	All numbers of strands	None, None

however, the following basic principles should be practiced:

a. *Make sure all cutting tools* used for stripping are sharp.

b. *When using special wire stripping tools*, adjust the tool to avoid nicking, cutting, or otherwise damaging the strands.

c. *Damage to wires* should not exceed the limits specified in figure 11.11.

450. TERMINALS. Terminals are attached to the ends of electric wires to facilitate connection of the wires to terminal strips or items of equipment. The tensile strength of the wire to terminal joint should be at least equivalent to the tensile strength of the wire itself, and its resistance negligible relative to the normal resistance of the wire. Terminals specifically designed for use with the standard sizes of aircraft wire are available through normal supply channels. Haphazard choice of commercial terminals may lead to overheated joints, vibration failures, and corrosion difficulties.

a. *Solder Terminals.* For most applications, soldered terminals have been replaced by solderless terminals. The solder process has disadvantages that have been overcome by use of the solderless terminals. A few of these disadvantages are listed as follows:

(1) A more skilled operator is required.

(2) A corrosive flux may be used causing the joint to deteriorate.

(3) Maintenance is extremely difficult.

(4) The wire strands are stiffened by the solder and become more susceptible to breakage due to vibration.

(5) The wire insulation may be charred during the soldering process.

b. *Solderless Terminals.* The terminal manufacturer will normally provide a special crimping or swaging tool for joining the solderless terminal to the electric wire. Aluminum wire presents special difficulty in that each individual strand is insulated by an oxide coating. This oxide coating must be broken down in the crimping process and some method employed to prevent its reforming. In all cases, follow the terminal manufacturer's instructions when installing solderless terminals.

c. *Terminal Strips.* Wires are usually joined at terminal strips. Use a terminal strip fitted with barriers to prevent the terminals on adjacent studs from contacting each other. Studs must be anchored against rotation. When more than four terminals are to be connected together, use two or more adjacent studs and mount a small metal bus across the studs. In all cases, the current is to be carried by the terminal contact surfaces and not by the stud itself. Replace defective studs with studs of the same size and material as terminal strip studs of the smaller sizes may shear due to overtightening the nut. Assure that the replacement stud is securely mounted in the terminal strip and that the terminal securing nut is tight. Mount terminal strips in such a manner that loose metallic objects cannot fall across the terminals or studs. It is good practice to provide at least one spare stud for future circuit expansion, or in case a stud is broken.

*Inspect terminal strips which provide connection of radio and electronic systems to the aircraft electrical system for loose connections, metallic objects which may have fallen across the terminal strip, dirt and grease accumulation, etc. Such condition can cause arcing which may result in a fire.

d. Terminal lugs. Wire terminal lugs shall be used to connect wiring to terminal block studs or equipment terminal studs. No more than four terminal lugs or three terminal lugs and a bus shall be connected to any one stud (total number of terminal lugs per stud includes a common bus bar joining adjacent studs. Four terminal lugs plus a common bus bar thus are not permitted on one stud). When the terminal lugs attached to a stud vary in diameter, the greatest diameter shall be placed on the bottom and smallest diameter on top. Terminal lugs shall be selected with a stud hole diameter which matches the diameter of the stud. Tightening terminal connections shall not deform the terminal lugs of the studs. Terminal lugs shall be so positioned that bending of the terminal lug is not required to remove the fastening screw or nut, and movement of the terminal lugs will tend to tighten the connection.

e. Copper terminal lugs. Solderless crimp style copper wire terminal lugs shall be used. Terminal lugs shall conform to MIL–T–7928. Spacers or washers are not permitted between the tongues of terminal lugs.

f. Aluminum terminal lugs. Aluminum terminal lugs conforming to MIL–T–7099 (MS–25435, MS–25436, MS–25437 and MS–25438) shall be crimped to aluminum wire only. the tongue of the aluminum terminal lugs or the total number of tongues of aluminum terminal lugs when stacked, shall be sandwiched between two MS–25440 flat washers when terminated on terminal studs. Spacers or washers are not permitted between the tongues of terminal lugs. Special attention shall be given to aluminum wire and cable installation to guard against conditions that would result in excessive voltage drop and high resistance at junctions that may ultimately lead to failure of the junction.

Examples of such conditions are improper installation of terminals and washers, improper torsion ("torquing" of nuts, and inadequate terminal contact areas.

g. Class 2 terminal lugs. Class 2 terminal lugs conforming to MIL–T–7928 may be used for installation by contractors, provided that in such installations Class 1 terminal lugs are adequate for replacement without rework of installation or terminal lugs. Class 2 terminal lugs shall be the insulated type unless the conductor temperature exceeds 105 degrees C in which case uninsulated terminal lugs shall be used. Parts lists shall indicate the appropriate Class 1 terminal lugs to be used for service replacement of any Class 2 terminal lugs installed.

451. ATTACHMENT OF TERMINALS TO STUDS. Electrical equipment malfunction has frequently been traced to poor terminal connections at terminal boards. Loose, dirty, or corroded contact surfaces will produce localized heating which may ignite nearby combustible materials or overheat adjacent wire insulation to the smoking point.

452. BONDING JUMPER INSTALLATIONS. Make bonding jumpers as short as practicable, and install in such a manner that the resistance of each connection does not exceed .003 ohm. The jumper must not interfere with the operation of movable aircraft elements, such as surface controls, nor should normal movement of these elements result in damage to the bonding jumper.

a. Bonding Connections. To assure a low-resistance connection, remove nonconducting finishes; such as paint and anodizing films, from the attachment surface to be contacted by the bonding terminal. Do not ground electric wiring directly to magnesium parts.

b. Corrosion Prevention. Electrolytic action may rapidly corrode a bonding connection if suitable precautions are not taken. Aluminum alloy jumpers are recommended for most cases; however, use copper jumpers to bond together parts made of stainless steel, cadmium plated steel, copper, brass, or bronze. Where contact between dissimilar metals cannot be *

This page intentionally left blank.

FIGURE 11.12.—Stud bonding or grounding to flat surface.

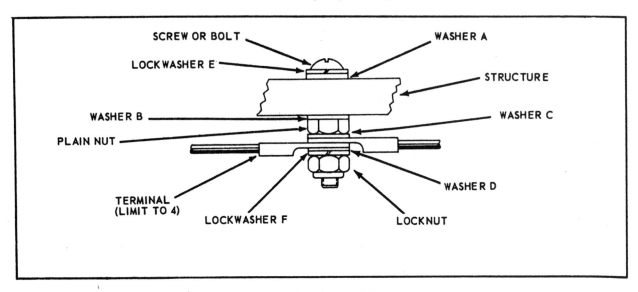

Aluminum Terminal and Jumper

Structure	Screw or Bolt and Lock nut	Plain nut	Washer A	Washer B	Washer C & D	Lock washer E	Lock washer F
Aluminum Alloys	Cad. Plated Steel	Cad. Plated Steel	Aluminum Alloy	Aluminum Alloy	Cad. Plated Steel or Aluminum	Cad. Plated Steel	Cad. Plated Steel
Magnesium Alloys	Cad. Plated Steel	Cad. Plated Steel	Magnesium Alloy	Magnesium Alloy	Cad. Plated Steel or Aluminum	Cad. Plated Steel	Cad. Plated Steel
Steel, Cadmium Plated	Cad. Plated Steel	Cad. Plated Steel	None	None	Cad. Plated Steel or Aluminum	Cad. Plated Steel	Cad. Plated Steel
Steel, Corrosion Resisting	Corrosion Resisting Steel	Cad. Plated Steel	None	None	Cad. Plated Steel or Aluminum	Cor. Resist Steel	Cad. Plated Steel

Tinned Copper Terminal and Jumper

Structure	Screw or Bolt and Lock nut	Plain nut	Washer A	Washer B	Washer C & D	Lock washer E	Lock washer F
Aluminum Alloys	Cad. Plated Steel	Cad. Plated Steel	Aluminum Alloy	Aluminum Alloy	Cad. Plated Steel	Cad. Plated Steel	Cad. Plated Steel or Aluminum
Magnesium Alloys[1]							
Steel, Cadmium Plated	Cad. Plated Steel	Cad. Plated Steel	None	None	Cad. Plated Steel	Cad. Plated Steel	Cad. Plated Steel
Steel, Corrosion Resisting	Corrosion Resisting Steel	Cor. Resist Steel	None	None	Cad. Plated Steel	Cor. Resist Steel	Cor. Resist Steel

[1] Avoid connecting copper to magnesium.

FIGURE 11.13.—Plate nut bonding or grounding to flat surface.

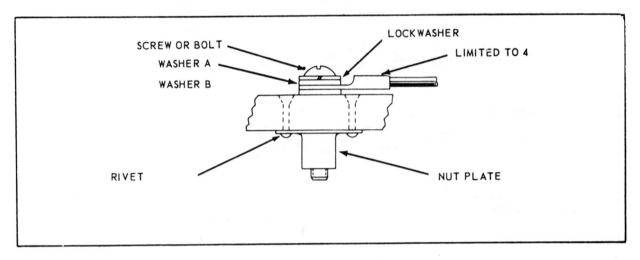

Aluminum Terminal and Jumper

Structure	Screw or Bolt and Nut plate	Rivet	Lockwasher	Washer A	Washer B
Aluminum Alloys	Cad. Plated Steel	Aluminum Alloy	Cadmium Plated Steel	Cad. plated steel or aluminum	None
Magnesium Alloys	Cad. Plated Steel	Aluminum Alloy	Cadmium Plated Steel	Cad. plated steel or aluminum	None or Magnesium alloy
Steel, Cadmium plated	Cad. Plated Steel	Cor. Resist. Steel	Cadmium Plated Steel	Cad. plated steel or aluminum	None
Steel, Corrosion Resisting	Corrosion Resist. Steel or Cad. Plated Steel	Cor. Resist. Steel	Cadmium Plated Steel	Cad. plated steel or aluminum	Cadmium plated steel

Tinned Copper Terminal and Jumper

Aluminum Alloys Magnesium Alloys[1]	Cad. Plated Steel	Aluminum Alloy	Cadmium Plated Steel	Cad. plated steel	Aluminum Alloy
Steel, Cadmium plated	Cad. Plated Steel	Cor. Resist. Steel	Cadmium Plated Steel	Cad. plated steel	None
Steel, Corrosion Resisting	Corrosion Resist. Steel	Cor. Resist. Steel	Cadmium Plated Steel	Cad. plated steel	None

[1] Avoid connecting copper to magnesium.

FIGURE 11.14.—Bolt and nut bonding or grounding to flat surface.

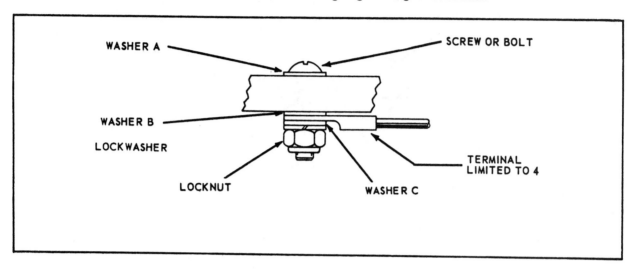

Aluminum Terminal and Jumper

Structure	Screw or Bolt and Nut plate	Lockwasher	Washer A	Washer B	Washer C
Aluminum Alloy	Cad. Plated Steel	Cad. Plated Steel	Cad. plated steel or aluminum	None	Cad. plated steel or aluminum
Magnesium Alloy	Cad. Plated Steel	Cad. Plated Steel	Magnesium Alloy	None or Magnesium Alloy	Cad. plated steel or aluminum
Steel, Cadmium plated	Cad. Plated Steel	Cad. Plated Steel	Cad. Plated Steel	Cadmium plated steel	Cad. plated steel or aluminum
Steel, Corrosion Resisting	Corrosion Resist. Steel or Cad. plated steel	Cad. Plated Steel	Corrosion Resisting Steel	Cadmium plated steel	Cad. plated steel or aluminum

Tinned Copper Terminal and Jumper

Structure	Screw or Bolt and Nut plate	Lockwasher	Washer A	Washer B	Washer C
Aluminum Alloy / Magnesium Alloy[1]	Cad. Plated Steel	Cad. Plated Steel	Cad. plated steel	Aluminum alloy	Cad. plated steel
Steel, Cadmium plated	Cad. Plated Steel	Cad. Plated Steel	Cad. plated steel	None	Cad. plated steel
Steel, Corrosion Resisting	Corrosion Resist. Steel or Cad. Plated Steel	Cad. Plated Steel	Corrosion Resisting Steel	None	Cad. plated steel

[1] Avoid connecting copper to magnesium.

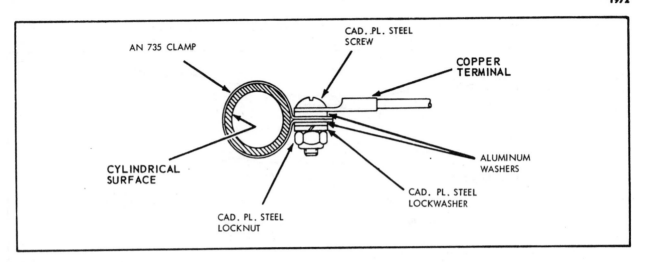

FIGURE 11.15—Copper jumper connecter to tubular structure.

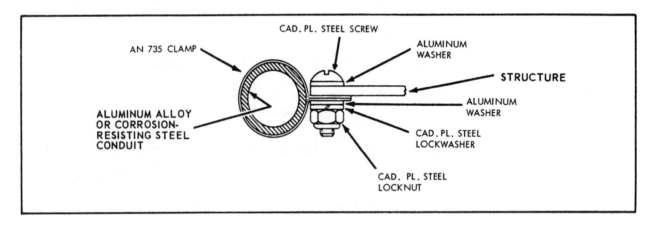

FIGURE 11.16.—Bonding conduit to structure.

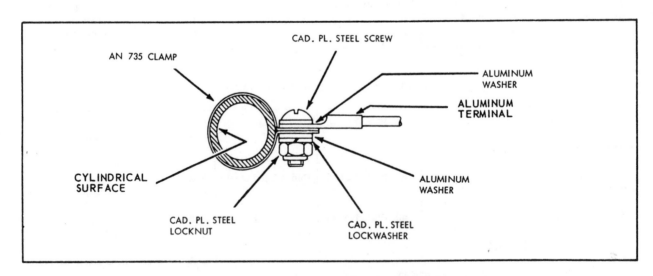

FIGURE 11.17.—Aluminum jumper connection to tubular structure.

avoided, the choice of jumper and hardware should be such that corrosion is minimized, and the part likely to corrode would be the jumper or associated hardware. Figures 11.12 through 11.17 show the proper hardware combinations for making a bond connection. At locations where finishes are removed, apply a protective finish to the completed connection to prevent subsequent corrosion.

c. *Bonding Jumper Attachment.* Avoid the use of solder to attach bonding jumpers. Bond tubular members by means of clamps to which the jumper is attached. Proper choice of clamp material will minimize the probability of corrosion.

d. *Ground Return Connection.* When bonding jumpers carry substantial ground return current, determine that the current rating of the jumper is adequate, and that a negligible voltage drop is produced.

453.–463. RESERVED.

Section 4. WIRE MARKING

464. WIRE IDENTIFICATION. To facilitate installation and maintenance, original wire-marking identification is to be retained. The wire identification marking should consist of a combination of letters and numbers which identify the wire, the circuit it belongs to, its gauge size, and any other information to relate the wire to a wiring diagram. The preferred method is to stamp the identification marking directly on the wire. Place identification markings at each end of the   wire and at 12- to 15–inch intervals along the length of the wire. Wires less than 3 inches long need not be stamped. Wire lengths 3 to 7 inches should be stamped at the center. If the outer covering or wire insulation will not stamp easily, insulating tubing may be stamped with the identification mark and installed on the wire. Identification sleeves are normally used for identifying the following types of wire or cable:

a. Unjacketed shielded wire.

b. Thermocouple wire.

c. Multiconductor cable.

d. High temperature wire with insulation difficult to mark (such as asbestos, teflon, and fiberglas).

(1) Thermocouple wire identification is normally accomplished by means of identification sleeves. As the thermocouple wire is usually of the duplex type (two insulated wires within the same casing), each wire at the termination point bears the full name of the conductor. Thermocouple conductors are alumel, chromel, iron, constantan, and copper.

Caution

Do not use metallic bands in place of insulating sleeves. Any method of marking is satisfactory, provided the identifying symbol is legible and contrasts with the wire insulation or sleeve; however, exercise care when machine marking coaxial cable, as flattening the cable may change its electrical characteristics.

465. SLEEVE SELECTION FOR IDENTIFICATION.

a. Flexible vinyl sleeving, either clear or opaque, is satisfactory for general use.

b. For sleeving exposed to high temperatures (over 400° F.), use materials such as silicone rubber or silicone fiberglas.

c. Use nylon sleeving in areas where resistance to solvent and synthetic hydraulic fluids is necessary. The size of identification sleeving for the various sizes of wire are shown in figure 11.18.

* **d. Plastic wire sleeving.** Inspect plastic wire sleeving for damage due to abrasion, solvents, or hydraulic fluids. *

FIGURE 11.18.—Sizes of identification sleeving.

Wire Size		Sleeving Size	
AN	AL	No.	Nominal I.D. (inches)
#24		12	.085
#22		11	.095
#20		10	.106
#18		9	.118
#16		8	.113
#14		7	.148
#12		6	.166
#10		4	.208
#8	#8	2	.263
#6	#6	0	.330
#4	#4	3/8 inch	.375
#2	#2	1/2 inch	.500
#1	#1	1/2 inch	.500
#0	#0	5/8 inch	.625
#00	#00	5/8 inch	.625
#000	#000	3/4 inch	.750
#0000	#0000	3/4 inch	.750

466. IDENTIFICATION OF WIRE BUNDLES AND HARNESSES. Due to complexity of modern aircraft electrical systems, the identification of wire bundles is becoming a common practice. Wire bundle identification may be accomplished by the use of a marked sleeve tied in place or by use of pressure-sensitive tape as indicated in figure 11.19.

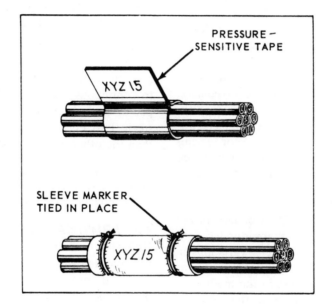

FIGURE 11.19.—Identification of wire bundles and harnesses.

467.–477. RESERVED.

Section 5. CONNECTORS

478. GENERAL PURPOSE CONNECTORS. Connectors (plugs and receptacles) are used to facilitate maintenance when frequent disconnection is required. Since the wires are soldered to the connector inserts, the joints should be individually installed and the wire bundle firmly supported to avoid damage by vibration. Connectors have been particularly vulnerable to corrosion in the past, due to condensation within the shell. Special connectors with waterproof features have been developed and may be used to replace nonwaterproof type plugs in areas where moisture causes a connector problem. Use a replacement connector of the same basic type and design as the connector it replaces. Connectors that are susceptible to corrosion difficulties may be treated with a chemically inert waterproof jelly. When replacing connector assemblies, use the socket-type insert on that half which is live or "hot" after the connector is disconnected to prevent unintentional grounding.

479. TYPES OF CONNECTORS. Connectors are identified by AN numbers and are divided into types and classes with manufacturer's variations in each type and class. The manufacturer's variations are differences in appearance and in the method of meeting the specification; however, they do not preclude mating plugs and receptacles of different manufacturers. There are six basic types of AN connectors used in aircraft which are further broken down into five classes as indicated in figures 11.20 and 11.21. Each class of connector has slightly different construction characteristics which are noted as follows: Classes A, B, C, and D are made of aluminum; Class K is made of steel.

Class A—Solid one-piece back shell general purpose connector.

Class B—Connector back shell separates into two parts lengthwise. Use primarily where it is important that the soldered connectors are readily accessible. The back shell is held together by a threaded ring or by screws.

Class C—A pressurized connector with inserts that are not removable. Looks like a Class A connector but the inside sealing arrangement is sometimes different and is used on walls of bulkheads of pressurized equipment.

Class D—Moisture and vibration resisting connector which has a sealing grommet in the back shell. Wires are threaded through tight fitting holes in the grommet, thereby sealing against moisture.

Class K—A fireproof connector used in areas where it is vital that the electric current is not interrupted, even though connector may be exposed to continuous open flame. Wires are crimped to the pin or socket contacts and the shells are made of steel. This class of connectors is normally longer than the other classes of connectors.

* NOTE: Inspect connectors for loose soldered connections, proper insulation of metallic parts, and fraying of wires in the plug and receptacle inserts.   *

480. ARMY/NAVY (AN) CONNECTOR IDENTIFICATION. Code letters and numbers are marked on the coupling ring or shell to identify the connector. This code provides all the information necessary to obtain the correct replacement for a defective or damaged part. To facilitate ready identification the code found on a typical connector (as shown in figure 11.22) is explained as follows:

a. *The letters AN* indicate the connector was made to a government standard.

b. *Type 3106* indicates this is a straight plug.

c. *Letter A* indicates this is a general purpose connector with a solid back shell.

d. *Number 18* indicates the size of the coupling. This size is determined in 1/16-inch increments. Therefore, the size of the plug in the example is 1 1/8 inch.

FIGURE 11.20.—AN connectors.

FIGURE 11.21.—Classes of AN connectors.

AN Class	Application	Shell	Availability					
			3100	3101	3102	3106	3107	3108
A	General Purpose	Solid Aluminum Alloy	Yes	Yes	Yes	Yes	Yes	Yes
B	General Purpose	Split Aluminum Alloy	Yes	Yes	No	Yes	Yes	Yes
C	Pressurized	Solid Aluminum Alloy	Yes	Yes	Yes	Yes	No	Yes
D	Environmental Resistant	Solid Aluminum Alloy	Yes	Yes	Yes	Yes	No	Yes
K	Fire & Flame Proof	Solid Steel	Yes	No	Yes	Yes	No	Yes

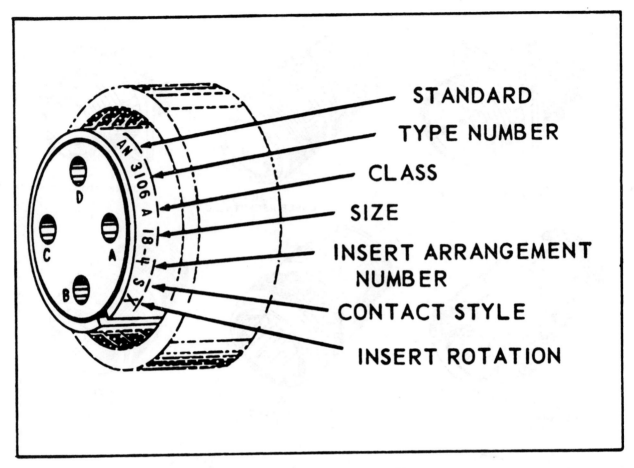

FIGURE 11.22.—AN connector marking.

e. Number 4 indicates a certain arrangement of contacts; however, this number does not indicate the number of contacts. Manufacturers of connectors provide charts giving diagrams of the various contact arrangements.

f. Letter(s) indicates contact style. This letter may be either a (P) or (S) which indicates whether the contacts are pins or sockets.

g. A letter may or may not follow the contact style identification symbol. This letter is used to indicate one of several alternate positions to which the insert can be turned. If a letter does not appear, the insert position is standard as shown on the contact arrangement chart.

481. SPECIAL PURPOSE CONNECTOR. Many special purpose connectors have been designed for use in aircraft applications such as subminia-ture connector, rectangular shell connector, connectors with short body shells or of split shell construction used in applications where potting is required.

482. POTTING COMPOUNDS. Potting compounds meeting Specification MIL–S–8516 are prepared in ready-to-use tube-type dispensers, or in the unmixed state consisting of the base compound and accelerator packed in paired containers. To obtain the proper results, it is important that the manufacturer's instructions be closely followed. Potting compounds normally cure at temperatures of 70° to 75° F. If the mixed compound is not used at once, the working life (normally 90 minutes) can be prolonged by storing in a deep freeze at −20° F. for a maximum of 36 hours. The time factor starts from the instant the accelerator is added to the base compound and includes the time expended during the mixing and application processes. Mixed compounds that are not to be used immediately must be cooled and thawed quickly to avoid wasting the short working life. Chilled compounds should be thawed by blowing compressed air over the outside of the container. Normally the compound will be ready for use in 5 to 10 minutes.

CAUTION

Do not use heat or blow compressed air into the container when restoring to working temperature.

483. POTTING CONNECTORS. Connectors that have been potted primarily offer protection against concentration of moisture in the connectors. A secondary benefit of potting is the reduced possibility of breakage between the contact and wire due to vibration.

Solder wires to all contacts of the connector prior to the application of the potting compound. Wires that are not to be used should be long enough to permit splicing at a later date. Identify the wires not used as shown in figure 11.23 and cap the cut ends with potting compound prior to securing to the wire bundle. After the soldering operation, scrape off the resin and wash the connector with clean stoddard solvent, brushing vigorously. Rinse the areas to be potted with methylene chloride and complete the potting operation within 2 hours after this cleaning. Allow the potting com-

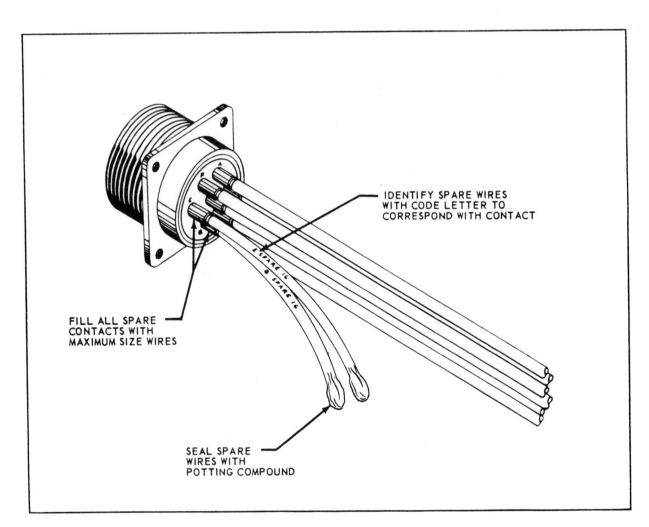

IDENTIFY SPARE WIRES WITH CODE LETTER TO CORRESPOND WITH CONTACT

FILL ALL SPARE CONTACTS WITH MAXIMUM SIZE WIRES

SEAL SPARE WIRES WITH POTTING COMPOUND

FIGURE 11.23.—Spare wires for potting connector.

pound to cure for 24 hours at a room temperature of 70 to 75° F. or carefully place in a drying oven at 100° F. for 3 to 4 hours.

484. THROUGH BOLTS. Through bolts are sometimes used to make feeder connections through bulkheads, fuselage skin, or firewalls. Mount through bolts in such a manner that they are mechanically secure and independent of the terminal nuts. Provide sufficient cross section to insure adequate conductivity against overheating and enough contact area to minimize voltage drop. Mechanically secure such bolts independent of the terminal mounting nuts, taking particular care to avoid dissimilar metals among the terminal hardware. During inspection, pay particular attention to the condition of the insulator plate or spacer and the insulating boot that covers the completed terminal assembly.

* "485. [Transferred to paragraph 450c.] — Change 3" *

486.—496. RESERVED.

Section 6. CONDUITS

497. GENERAL. Conduit is manufactured in metallic and nonmetallic materials and in both rigid and flexible forms. Primarily its purpose is for mechanical protection of the cable within. Inspect conduit for proper end fittings, absence of abrasion at the end fittings, and proper clamping. Inspect for distortion, adequate drain points which are free of dirt, grease, or other obstructions, and freedom from abrasion or damage due to moving objects such as aircraft control cables or shifting cargo. *

498. SIZE OF CONDUIT. When selecting conduit size for a specific wire bundle application, it is common practice to allow for ease in maintenance and possible future circuit expansion by specifying the conduit inner diameter about 25 percent larger than the maximum diameter of the wire bundle. The nominal diameter of rigid metallic conduit is the O.D. Therefore, to obtain the I.D., subtract twice the tube wall thickness.

499. CONDUIT FITTINGS. From the abrasion standpoint, conduit is vulnerable at its ends. Affix suitable fittings to conduit ends in such a manner that a smooth surface comes in contact with wire within. When fittings are not used, flare the end of the conduit to prevent wire insulation damage. Support the conduit using clamps along the conduit run.

500. CONDUIT INSTALLATION. Many of the past troubles with conduit can be avoided by proper attention to the following details:

   a. *Do not locate conduit* where passengers or maintenance personnel might use it as a handhold or footstep.

   b. *Provide drainholes* at the lowest point in a conduit run. Drilling burrs should be carefully removed.

   c. *Support conduit* to prevent chafing against structure and to avoid stressing its end fittings.

501. RIGID CONDUIT. Repair conduit sections that have been damaged to preclude injury to the wires or wire bundle which may consume as much as 80 percent of the tube area. Minimum acceptable tube bend radii for rigid conduit is shown in figure 11.24. Kinked or wrinkled bends in rigid conduits are not considered acceptable. Tubing bends that have been flattened into an ellipse and the minor diameter is less than 75 percent of the nominal tubing diameter is not considered satisfactory because the tube area will have been reduced at least 10 percent. Carefully deburr tubing that has been formed and cut to final length to prevent wire insulation damage. When installing replacement tube sections with fittings at both ends, exercise care to eliminate mechanical strain.

502. FLEXIBLE CONDUIT. Flexible aluminum conduit conforming to Specification MIL–C–6136 is available in two types; Type I, Bare Flexible Conduit, and Type II, Rubber Covered Flexible Conduit. Flexible brass conduit conforming to Specification MIL–C–7931 is available and normally used instead of flexible aluminum where necessary to minimize radio interference. Flexible conduit may be used where it is impractical to use rigid conduit such as areas that have

FIGURE 11.24.—Bend radii for rigid conduit.

Nominal tube O.D.	Minimum bend radii (inches)
$\frac{1}{8}$	$\frac{3}{8}$
$\frac{3}{16}$	$\frac{7}{16}$
$\frac{1}{4}$	$\frac{9}{16}$
$\frac{3}{8}$	$\frac{15}{16}$
$\frac{1}{2}$	$1\frac{1}{4}$
$\frac{5}{8}$	$1\frac{1}{2}$
$\frac{3}{4}$	$1\frac{3}{4}$
1	3
$1\frac{1}{4}$	$3\frac{3}{4}$
$1\frac{1}{2}$	5
$1\frac{3}{4}$	7
2	8

motion between conduit ends or where complex bends are necessary. The use of transparent adhesive tape is recommended when cutting flexible tubing with a hacksaw to minimize fraying of the braid. Center the tape over the cut reference mark and saw through the tape.

After cutting the flexible conduit, remove the transparent tape, trim the frayed ends of the braid, remove burrs from inside the conduit, and install coupling nut and ferrule. Minimum acceptable bending radii for flexible conduit is shown in figure 11.25.

FIGURE 11.25.—Minimum bending radii for flexible aluminum or brass conduit.

Nominal I.D. of conduit (inches)	Minimum bending radius inside (inches)
$\frac{3}{16}$	$2\frac{1}{4}$
$\frac{1}{4}$	$2\frac{3}{4}$
$\frac{3}{8}$	$3\frac{3}{4}$
$\frac{1}{2}$	$3\frac{3}{4}$
$\frac{5}{8}$	$3\frac{3}{4}$
$\frac{3}{4}$	$4\frac{1}{4}$
1	$5\frac{3}{4}$
$1\frac{1}{4}$	8
$1\frac{1}{2}$	$8\frac{1}{4}$
$1\frac{3}{4}$	9
2	$9\frac{3}{4}$
$2\frac{1}{2}$	10

503.–513. RESERVED.

Section 7. ROUTING, TYING, LACING, AND CLAMPING

514. GENERAL. Route and support aircraft wiring and conduits to prevent relative movement within the aircraft and provide protection against chafing between wires or other objects. Provide extra protection where wires or wire bundles may be subjected to rough handling. Soft insulation tubing is not regarded as satisfactory mechanical protection against abrasion or considered a substitute for proper clamping or tying. Secure all wiring so it is electrically and mechanically sound and neat in appearance.

515. WIRE BEND RADII. A wire bundle consists of a quantity of wires fastened or secured together—all traveling in the same direction. Wire bundles may consist of two or more groups of wires. It is often advantageous to have a number of wire groups individually tied within the wire bundle for ease of identity at a later date, as shown in figure 11.26. To improve the appearance and to minimize the possibility of insulation abrasion, comb wire groups and bundles so the wires lie parallel to each other. A combing tool similar to that shown in figure 11.27 may be made from any suitable insulating material, taking care to assure all edges are rounded to protect the wire insulation. Bends in wire groups or bundles should not be less than 10 times the outside diameter of the wire group or bundle. However, a bend 3 times the diameter is acceptable to facilitate connections to terminal strips,

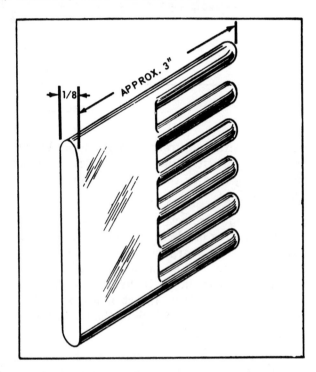

FIGURE 11.27.—Comb for straightening wires in bundles.

provided the wire group or bundle is supported at each end of the bend.

516. SLACK. Normally, wire groups or bundles should not exceed 1/2 inch deflection between support points, as shown in figure 11.28. This measurement may be exceeded provided there is no possibility of the wire group or bundle touching a surface which may cause abrasion.

a. Provide sufficient slack at each end to:

(1) Permit replacement of terminals;

(2) Prevent mechanical strain on wires;

(3) Permit shifting of equipment for maintenance purposes.

517. ROUTING WIRES. In the process of accomplishing an aircraft repair, it is often neces-

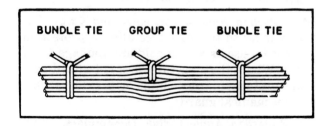

FIGURE 11.26.—Group and bundle ties.

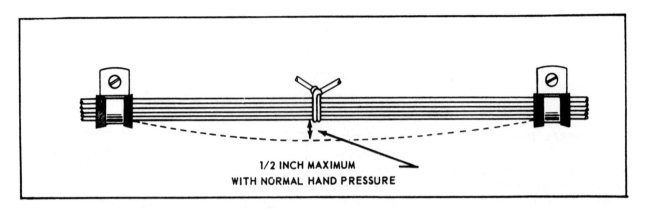

FIGURE 11.28.—Slack between supports.

sary or desirable to reroute a group or bundle of wire. When it is necessary to deviate from the routing used by the manufacturer, consider the following:

a. Chafing. Protect wires or wire groups against chafing or abrasion where contact with other wires or sharp surfaces would damage the insulation. When a wire bundle passes through a hole in a bulkhead, support as shown in figure 11.9. Insert a grommet if a wire passes within 1/4 inch of the hole edge, as shown in figure 11.10.

b. Protection Against Battery Acids, Solvents, and Fluids. It is not advisable to route wires below a battery or closer than 6 inches from the bilge of the fuselage. Protect wires that will be exposed to damage from fluids by an outer sleeving of plastic tubing, as shown in figure 11.29. Extend the plastic tubing well beyond the area of exposure and provide a 1/8-inch drainhole at the lowest point. Assure the wire insulation is not damaged when cutting the hole in the plastic. Frequently inspect wires exposed to battery acid or fluids and replace when the insulation jacket shows signs of discoloration or saturation by fluids.

c. Protection in Wheel Wells and Landing Gear Areas. Wires located on landing gear and in the wheel well area can be exposed to many hazardous conditions if not suitably protected. Encase all wiring attached to a landing gear or located in the wheel well areas in conduit or protect by sleeves of flexible tubing and secure to prevent relative movement. Where wire bun-

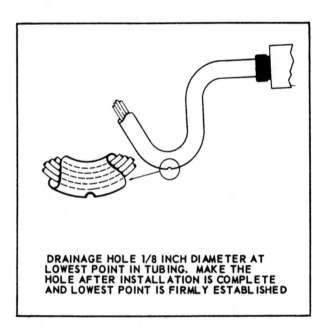

DRAINAGE HOLE 1/8 INCH DIAMETER AT LOWEST POINT IN TUBING. MAKE THE HOLE AFTER INSTALLATION IS COMPLETE AND LOWEST POINT IS FIRMLY ESTABLISHED

FIGURE 11.29.—Drainage hole in low point of tubing.

dles pass flex points, there should be no strain on attachments or excessive slack when parts are fully extended or retracted. Inspect the wiring and protective tubing frequently and replace at the first sign of wear.

d. Protection Against Personnel and Cargo. Install wiring so the structure affords protection against its use as a handhold and damage from cargo. Where the structure does not afford adequate protection, use conduit or provide a suitable mechanical guard.

e. Protection Against High Temperature. Wire insulation deteriorates rapidly when subjected to high temperatures. Insulate wires that must be run through hot areas with a material such as asbestos, fiberglass, or an equivalent high temperature-resistant product. Wherever possible, keep wires separated from high-temperature equipment; and when replacing wires, do not use low-temperature insulated wires to replace high-temperature insulated wires.

f. *Wiring Precautions.* Maintain a minimum clearance of 3 inches from any control cable. When this clearance cannot be maintained, install a mechanical guard. When wiring is run parallel to combustible fluid or oxygen lines, maintain as much separation as possible. Locate wires above or on a level with the fluid lines and, wherever possible, maintain a minimum separation of 6 inches. Where the separation is 1/2 inch to 2 inches, install clamps as shown in figure 11.30 to maintain separation. These clamps are not to be used as a means of supporting the wire bundle. Install additional clamps to support the wire bundle and fasten the clamps to the same structure used to support the fluid line to prevent relative motion. Maintain a minimum separation of at least 1/2 inch between plumbing lines and any wire.

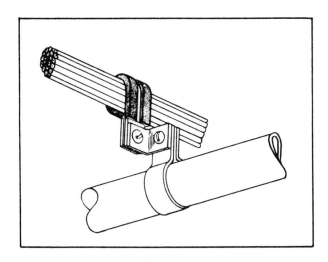

FIGURE 11.30.—Separation of wires from plumbing lines.

518. CLAMPING. Support wires and wire bundles using clamps meeting Specification MS-21919. Exercise care to assure the wire is not pinched when installing clamps to support electrical wiring as shown in figures 11.31 through 11.34. Whenever

practical, rest the back of the clamp against a structural member. Install clamps in such manner that the electrical wires do not come in contact with other parts of the aircraft when subjected to vibration. Leave sufficient slack between the last clamp and the electrical equipment to prevent strain at the terminal and to minimize adverse effects on shockmounted equipment. Where wires or wire bundles pass through bulkheads or other structural members, provide a grommet or suitable clamp to prevent abrasion.

*518-1. WIRE AND CABLE CLAMPS. Inspect wire and cable clamps for proper tightness. Where cables pass through structure or bulkheads, inspect for·proper clamping or grommets. Inspect for sufficient slack between the last clamp and the electronic equipment to prevent strain at the cable terminals and minimize adverse effects on shock mounted equipment.   *

519. TIES AND LACING. Ties, lacing, and straps are used to secure wire groups or bundles, to provide ease of maintenance, inspection, and installation. Cord meeting Specification MIL-C-5649 and twine meeting Specification JAN-T-713 are suitable for lacing or tying wires. In lieu of applying ties, straps meeting Specification MS-17821 or MS-17822 may be used in areas where the temperature does not exceed 120° C. or where the wiring can be damaged by operating units if the strap fails.

a. *Lacing.* Lace wire groups or bundles inside junction boxes or other enclosures. Single cord-lacing method shown in figure 11.35 may be used for wire groups of bundles 1 inch in diameter or less. The recommended knot for starting the single cord-lacing method is a clove hitch secured by a double-looped overhand knot as shown in step a of figure 11.35. Used the double cord-lacing method on wire bundles 1 inch in diameter or larger as shown in figure 11.36. When using the double cord-lacing method, employ a bowline on a bight as the starting knot. Reference step a of figure 11.36.

b. *Tying.* Use wire group or bundle ties where the supports for the wire are more than 12 inches apart. A tie consists of a clove hitch around the wire group or bundle secured by a square knot as shown in figure 11.37.

* **520. INSULATION TAPE.** Insulation tape shall be of a type suitable for the application, or as called out for the specific use. Insulation tape shall be used primarily as a filler under clamps and as secondary support. Nonadhesive tape may be used as a wraparound wiring for additional protection, such as in wheel wells. All tape shall have the ends tied or otherwise suitably secured to prevent unwinding. Tape used for protection shall be applied so that overlapping layers shed liquids, and shall be provided with drainage holes at all trap points, and at each low point between clamps. Plastic tapes which absorb moisture, or which have volatile plasticizers that produce chemical reactions with other wiring shall not be used. (Reference: MIL-W-5088K).   *

521.-530. RESERVED.

This page intentionally left blank.

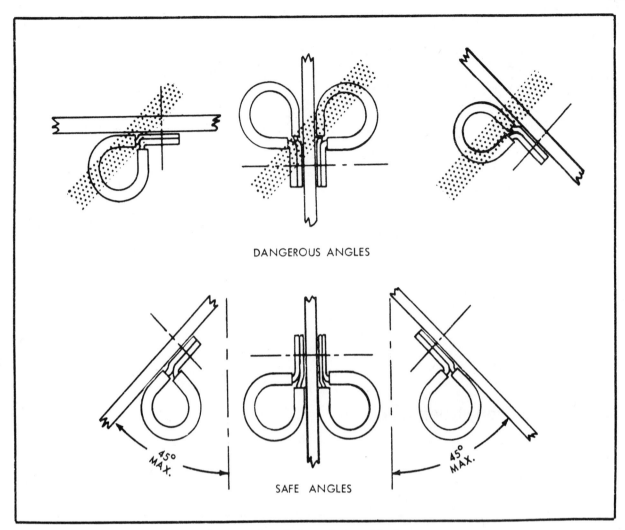

FIGURE 11.31.—Safe angle for cable clamps.

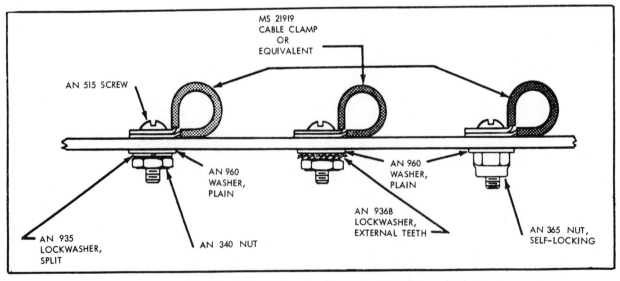

FIGURE 11.32.—Typical mounting hardware for MS–2919 cable clamps.

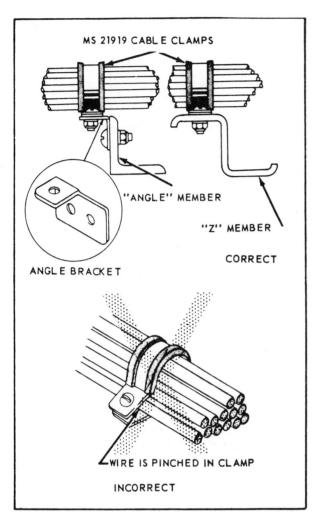

FIGURE 11.33.—Installing cable clamp to structure.

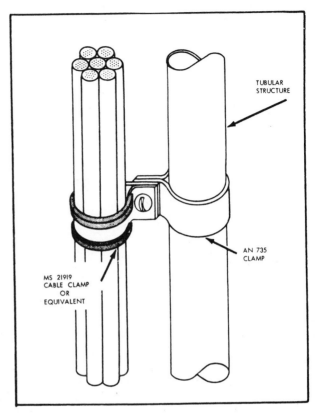

FIGURE 11.34.—Installing cable clamps to tubular structure.

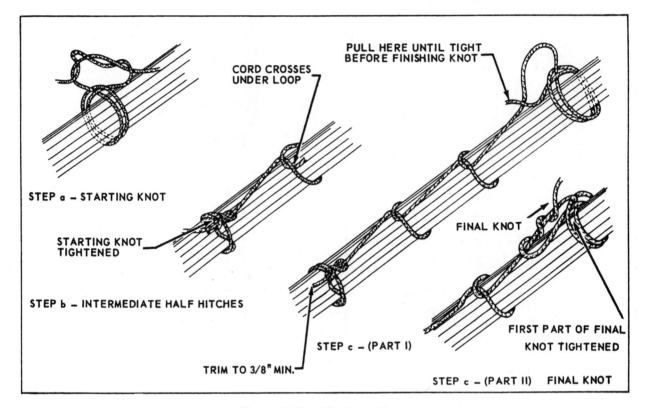

STEP a – STARTING KNOT

STARTING KNOT
TIGHTENED

STEP b – INTERMEDIATE HALF HITCHES

CORD CROSSES
UNDER LOOP

PULL HERE UNTIL TIGHT
BEFORE FINISHING KNOT

TRIM TO 3/8" MIN.

STEP c – (PART I)

FINAL KNOT

FIRST PART OF FINAL
KNOT TIGHTENED

STEP c – (PART II)   FINAL KNOT

FIGURE 11.35.—Single cord lacing.

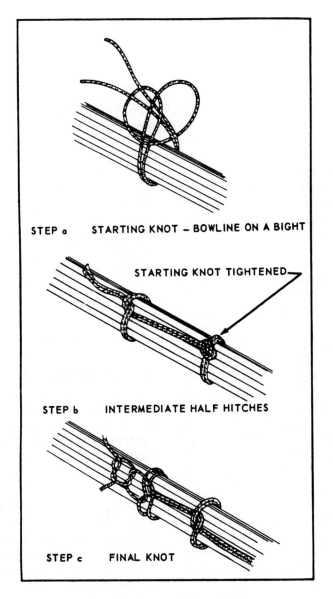

FIGURE 11.36.—Double cord lacing.

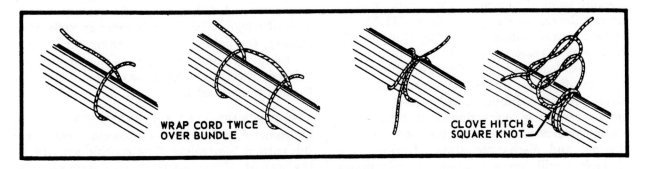

FIGURE 11.37.—Making ties.

Section 8. STORAGE BATTERIES

531. GENERAL. Lead-acid and nickel-cadmium batteries are the two most common types used in aircraft. These batteries possess different characteristics and, therefore, should be maintained in accordance with the manufacturer's recommendations. Storage batteries are usually identified by the material used for the plates.

532. BATTERY OVERHEAT FAILURE. Operation of storage batteries beyond their ambient temperature or charging voltage limits will result in excessive cell temperatures leading to electrolyte boiling, rapid deterioration of the cell, and finally battery failure. The relationship between maximum charging voltage and the number of cells in the battery is also significant, since this will determine (for a given ambient temperature and state of charge) the rate at which energy is absorbed as heat within the battery. For lead-acid batteries, the voltage per cell should not exceed 2.35 volts. In the case of nickel-cadmium batteries, the charging voltage limit varies with design and construction with values of 1.4 and 1.5 volts per cell found satisfactory. In all cases, follow the recommendations of the battery manufacturer as to the proper charging voltage limits.

533. BATTERY FREEZING. Lead-acid batteries exposed to cold temperatures are subject to plate damage due to freezing of the electrolyte. The freezing point of electrolyte for various specific gravity levels is shown in figure 11.38. To prevent freeze damage, maintain the specific gravity at a reasonably high level, bearing in mind that lead-acid batteries are subject to a constant discharge due to the internal chemical action. Nickel-cadmium battery electrolyte is not as susceptible to freezing because no appreciable chemical change takes place between the charged and discharged state. However, the electrolyte will freeze at approximately minus 75° F.

FIGURE 11.38.—Lead-acid battery electrolyte freezing points.

Specific gravity	Freeze point	
	C.	F.
1.300	−70	−95
1.275	−62	−80
1.250	−52	−62
1.225	−37	−35
1.200	−26	−16
1.175	−20	− 4
1.150	−15	+ 5
1.125	−10	+13
1.100	− 8	+19

534. TEMPERATURE CORRECTION. U.S. manufactured lead-acid batteries are considered fully charged when the specific gravity reading is between 1.275 and 1.300. A 1/3 discharged battery reads about 1.240 and a 2/3 discharged battery will show a specific gravity reading of about 1.200 when tested by a hydrometer. However, to determine precise specific gravity readings, a temperature correction should be applied to the hydrometer indication as shown in figure 11.39. As an example, the hydrometer reading is 1.260; the temperature of the electrolyte is 40° F. or 16 points below the norm established for battery electrolyte. Therefore, the corrected specific gravity reading of the electrolyte is 1.244. Take care to assure the electrolyte is returned to the cell from which it was extracted. When a specific gravity difference of 0.050 or more eixsts between cells of a battery, the battery is approaching the end of its useful life and replacement should be considered. Electrolyte level may be adjusted by the addition of distilled water.

535. CHECKING LEAD-ACID BATTERIES. Use a hydrometer to determine the specific gravity of the battery electrolyte. The specific gravity is the weight of the electrolyte as compared to the weight of pure water.

FIGURE 11.39.—Sulfuric acid temperature correction.

Electrolyte temperature		Points to be subtracted or added to specific gravity readings
°C.	°F.	
60	140	+24
55	130	+20
49	120	+16
43	110	+12
38	100	+ 8
33	90	+ 4
27	80	0
23	70	− 4
15	60	− 8
10	50	−12
5	40	−16
− 2	30	−20
− 7	20	−24
−13	10	−28
−18	0	−32
−23	−10	−36
−28	−20	−40
−35	−30	−44

536. CHECKING NICKEL-CADMIUM BATTERIES.
The state of charge of a nickel-cadmium battery cannot be determined by measuring the specific gravity of the electrolyte with a hydrometer as the electrolyte specific gravity does not change with the state of charge. The only accurate way to determine the state of charge of a nickel-cadmium battery is by a measured discharge. After the battery has been fully charged and allowed to stand for at least 2 hours, the fluid level may be adjusted, if necessary, using distilled or demineralized water. Because the fluid level varies with the state of charge, water should never be added while the battery is installed in the aircraft. Overfilling the battery will result in electrolyte spewage during charging. This will cause corrosive effects on the cell links, self discharge of the battery, dilution of the electrolyte density, and possible blockage of the cell vents and eventual cell rupture.

CAUTION
Servicing equipment used for lead-acid batteries is not to be used for servicing nickel-cadmium batteries as acid is detrimental to the proper functioning of a nickel-cadmium battery.

537. ELECTROLYTE CORROSION.
Electrolyte spillage or leakage may result in serious corrosion of the nearby structure or control elements as both sulfuric acid and potassium hydroxide are actively corrosive. Electrolyte may be spilled during ground servicing, leaked when cell case rupture occurs, or sprayed from cell vents due to excessive charging rates. If the battery is not case enclosed, properly treat structural parts near the battery which may be affected by acid fumes. Treat all case and drain surfaces which have been affected by electrolyte with a solution of sodium bicarbonate (for acid electrolyte) or boric acid, vinegar, or a 3 percent solution of acetic acid for potassium hydroxide electrolyte.

CAUTION
Serious burns will result if the electrolyte comes in contact with any part of the body. Use rubber gloves, rubber apron, and protective goggles when handling electrolyte. If sulphuric acid is splashed on the body neutralize with a solution of baking soda and water, and shower or flush the affected area with water. For the eyes, use an eye fountain and flush with an abundance of water.

If potassium hydroxide contacts the skin, neutralize with 3 percent acetic acid, vinegar, or lemon juice, and wash with water.

For the eyes, wash with a weak solution of boric acid or a weak solution of vinegar and flush with water.

538. NOXIOUS FUMES.
When charging rates are excessive, the electrolyte may boil to the extent that fumes containing droplets of the electrolyte are emitted through the cell vents. These fumes from lead-acid batteries may become noxious to the crewmembers and passengers; therefore, thoroughly check the venting system. Nickel-cadmium batteries will emit gas near the end of the charging process and during overcharge. The battery vent system in the aircraft should have sufficient air flow to prevent this explosive mixture from accumulating. It is often advantageous to install a jar in the battery vent discharge system serviced with an agent to neutralize the corrosive effect of battery vapors.

539. INSTALLATION PRACTICES.
a. Clean the external surface of the battery prior to installation in the aircraft.

b. *When replacing lead-acid batteries* with nickel-cadmium batteries, neutralize the battery box or compartment and thoroughly flush with clear water and dry. Acid residue can be detrimental to the proper functioning of a nickel-cadmium battery.

c. *Check the condition* of the vent system.

d. *When installing batteries* in an aircraft, exercise care to prevent inadvertent shorting of the battery terminals. Serious damage to the aircraft structure can be sustained by the resultant high discharge of electrical energy. This condition may normally be avoided by insulating the terminal posts during the installation process.

e. *Assure the battery holddown devices* are secure but not so tight as to exert excessive pressure which may cause the battery to buckle causing internal shorting of the battery.

f. *If a quick disconnect type* of battery connector which prohibits crossing the battery lead is not employed, assure that the aircraft wiring is connected to the proper battery terminal. Reverse polarity in an electrical system can seriously damage a battery. Assure battery cable connections are tight to prevent arcing or a high resistance connection.

* **540. AIRCRAFT BATTERY INSPECTION.**

a. *Inspect battery sump jar* and lines for condition and security.

b. *Inspect battery terminals* and quick-disconnect plugs and pins for evidence of corrosion and pitting, arcing, and burns. Clean as required.

c. *Inspect battery drain* and vent lines for restriction, deterioration, and security.   *

541.-552. RESERVED.

Chapter 12. PROPELLERS, ROTORS, AND ASSOCIATED EQUIPMENT

Section 1. INSPECTION OF PROPELLERS

553. WOOD OR COMPOSITION PROPELLERS AND BLADES. Due to the nature of the wood itself, it is necessary that wood propellers and blades be inspected frequently to assure continued airworthiness. Inspect for such defects as cracks, bruises, scars, warpage, evidence of glue failure and separated laminations, sections broken off, and defects in the finish. Composition blades must be handled with the same consideration as wood blades.

a. *The fixed-pitch propellers* are normally removed from the engine at engine overhaul periods. Whenever the propeller is removed, visually inspect the rear surface for any indication of cracks. When any indications are found, disassemble the metal hub from the propeller. Inspect the bolts for wear and cracks at the head and threads and, if cracked or worn, replace with new AN bolts. Inspect for elongated boltholes, enlarged hub bore, and check for cracks inside of bore or anywhere on the propeller. Repair propellers found with any of these defects. If no defects are found, the propeller may be reinstalled on the engine. Prior to installation, touch up with varnish all places where the finish is worn thin, scratched, or nicked. Track and balance the propeller, and coat the hub bore and boltholes with some moisture preventive such as asphalt varnish. In case the hub flange is integral with the crankshaft of the engine, final track the propeller after it is installed on the engine. In all cases where a separate metal hub is used, accomplish final balance and track with the hub installed in the propeller.

b. *On new fixed-pitch propeller* installations, inspect bolts for tightness after first flight and after the first 25 hours of flying. Thereafter, inspect and check the bolts for tightness at least every 50 hours. No definite time interval can be specified, since bolt tightness is affected by changes in the wood caused by the moisture content in the air where the airplane is flown and stored. During wet weather, some moisture is apt to enter the propeller wood through the drilled holes in the hub. The wood swells, but since expansion is limited by the bolts extending between the two flanges, some of the wood fibers become crushed. Later, when the propeller dries out during dry weather or due to heat from the engine, a certain amount of propeller hub shrinkage takes place, and the wood no longer completely fills the space between the two hub flanges. Accordingly, the hub bolts become loose.

c. *In-flight tip failures* may be avoided by frequent inspections of the metal cap and leading edge strip, and the surrounding areas. Inspect for such defects as looseness or slipping, separation of soldered joints, loose screws, loose rivets, breaks, cracks, eroded sections, and corrosion. Inspect for separation between metal leading edge and cap, which would indicate the cap is moving outward in the direction of centrifugal force. This condition is often accompanied by discoloration and loose rivets. Inspect tip for cracks by grasping with hand and slightly twisting about the longitudinal blade centerline and by slightly bending the tip backward and forward. If leading edge and cap have separated, carefully inspect for cracks at this point. Cracks usually start at the leading edge of the blade. A fine line appearing in the fabric or plastic may indicate a crack in the wood.

d. *Examine the wood close to the metal sleeve* of wood blades for cracks extending outward on the blade. These cracks sometimes occur at the threaded ends of the lag screws, and may be an indication of internal cracking of the wood. Check tightness of the lag screws, which attach the metal sleeve to the wood blade, in accordance with the manufacturer's instructions. Inspect and protect the shank areas of composition blades next to the metal sleeve in the same manner as for wood blades.

554. METAL PROPELLERS AND BLADES. Metal propellers and blades are generally susceptible to fatigue failure resulting from concentration of stresses at the bottoms of sharp nicks, cuts, and scratches. It is especially necessary, therefore, to frequently and carefully inspect them

for such injuries. Propeller manufacturers have published service bulletins and instructions which prescribe the manner in which these inspections are to be accomplished.

555. LUBRICATION. Inspect controllable pitch propellers frequently to determine that all parts are lubricated properly. It is especially recommended that all lubrication be accomplished at the periods and in the manner specified by the propeller manufacturer.

556.–566. RESERVED.

Section 2. REPAIR OF WOOD AND COMPOSITION PROPELLERS

567. GENERAL. Repair propellers in accordance with the best accepted practices and the latest techniques. Manufacturer's recommendations should in all cases be followed. It is necessary to mark the name of the manufacturer and model designation on the repaired propeller in the event original markings were removed during the repair or refinishing operations.

568. REPAIR OF WOOD PROPELLERS. Carefully examine wood propellers and blades requiring repair to be sure that they can be restored to their original airworthy condition. Refer doubtful cases to the manufacturer. Carefully evaluate propellers damaged to the following extent prior to attempting a repair:

A crack or deep cut across the grain of the wood.

Split blades.

Separated laminations, except the outside laminations of fixed-pitch propellers.

More screw or rivet holes, including holes filled with dowels, than used to attach the metal leading edge strip and tip.

An appreciable warp.

An appreciable portion of wood missing.

A crack, cut, or damage to the metal shank or sleeve of blades.

Broken lag screws which attach the metal sleeve to the blade.

Oversize shaft hole in fixed-pitch propellers.

Cracks between the shaft hole and bolt-holes.

Cracked internal laminations.

Excessively elongated boltholes.

a. *Fill small cracks* parallel to the grain with glue, thoroughly worked into all portions of the cracks, dried, and then sanded smooth and flush with the surface of the propeller. This also applies to small cuts. Dents or scars which have rough surfaces, or shapes that will hold a filler and will not induce failure, may be filled with a mixture of glue and clean fine sawdust thoroughly worked and packed into the defect, dried, and then sanded smooth and flush with the surface of the propeller. It is very important that all loose or foreign matter be removed from the place to be filled so that a good bond of the glue to the wood is obtained.

b. *Blade Inlays.* Inlays shown in figure 12.1 may be used. Make inlays of the same wood as the propeller blade; i.e., inlay a yellow birch propeller with yellow birch, not with white birch, and as near the same specific gravity as possible. Make repair joints to conform with figure 12.1 for taper of 10:1 from deepest point to feather edge or end of inlay. Measurements are taken along a straight line parallel to the grain or general slope of the surface on thrust and camber face. This rule applies also to the edge repairs. Extend grain of inlays in the same direction as the grain of the propeller laminations. Make inlays using a fishmouth, scarf, or butt joint. The permanency of the joint is in the order named, the fishmouth being preferable. Dovetail-type inlays should not be used. Do not exceed 1 large, 2 medium, or 4 small widely separated inlays per blade. Do not overlap a trailing and a leading edge inlay more than 25 percent, as shown in figure 12.1A. Propeller blades of a thickness ratio of .12 or more may be repaired, provided the cross-grained cut does not exceed 20 percent of the chord in length and the depth of cuts does not exceed 1/8 the blade thickness at the deepest point of damage. Blades with airfoil sections less than .12 thickness ratio may be repaired if the maximum depth of damage does not exceed 1/20 of the blade section thickness at the deepest point of damage. To determine the thickness ratio for a propeller blade, divide the maximum thickness of the airfoil section by the blade chord at the 3/4 radius station.

Example 1.

Given
6″ Chord
.72 Maximum thickness of airfoil section

Computation
.72 ÷ 6 = .12 thickness ratio

Example shows the blade thickness ratio to be .12; therefore, an inlay ⅛ of blade thickness at the point of damage may be inserted.

Example 2.

Given
4″ Chord
.36″ Maximum thickness of airfoil section

Computation
.36 ÷ 4 = .09 thickness ratio

Example shows blade thickness ratio to be less than .12; therefore, an inlay 1/20 the blade thickness at the point of damage may be inserted.

c. *Hub Inlays.* Inlays in the sides of hubs of fixed-pitched propellers which would exceed in depth a value greater than 5 percent of the difference between the hub and bore diameters are not acceptable. In the portion of the blade where it fairs into the hub, allowable depths for inlays are dependent upon the general proportions. Where the width and thickness are both very large in proportion to the hub and blade, maximum inlay depths of 7 1/2 percent of the section thickness at the inlay are permissible. Where the width and thickness are excessively small, maximum inlay depths of 2 1/2 percent of the section thickness at the center of the inlay are permissible; for propellers over 50 horsepower, cuts 2 1/2 percent deep may be filled with glue and sawdust, while for propellers under 50 horsepower, cuts 5 percent deep may be filled with glue and sawdust.

d. *Blade Profiling.* Narrow slivers up to 1/8 inch wide broken from the trailing edge at the wider portions of the blade may be repaired by sandpapering a new trailing edge, removing the least material possible, and fairing in a new trailing edge of smooth contour. Narrow both blades by the same amount. Near the hub or tip, use an inlay which does not exceed, at its greatest depth, 5 percent of the chord.

e. *Propeller Tip Repairs.* In order to replace the wood worn away at the end of the metal tipping, remove enough of the metal to make the minimum repair taper 10:1 each way from the deepest point. Due to the convex leading edge of the average propeller, this taper usually works out 8:1. Repairs under the metal tipping must not exceed 7 1/2 percent of the chord for butt or scarf joints, and 10 percent for fishmouth joints, with 3/4 inch maximum depth for any repair. Methods of repairing or replacing propeller blade metal caps or leading edge strips are contained in paragraph 569.

The scarfing of wood tips onto a propeller blade to replace a damaged tip is not considered an acceptable repair. The success of this type of repair is fully dependent upon the strength and quality of the glue joint. Since it is difficult to apply pressure evenly over the glue area, and since no satisfactory means are available for testing the strength of such joints, it is quite possible for defective glue joints to exist and remain undected until failure occurs.

f. *Lamination Repairs.* Whenever the glue joint of an outside lamination of fixed-pitch propellers is open, repair the propeller by removing the loose lamination and gluing on a new lamination of kiln dried wood of the same kind as the original lamination. It is not usually economical to attempt to repair separations between other laminations. Repair outside laminations, which have been crushed at the hub due to excessive drawing up of hub bolts, by planing and sanding one hub face smooth, removing a lamination on the other hub face and replacing it with a new lamination, thus building the hub thickness up to the original thickness. It is permissible to replace both outer laminations if necessary and feasible.

g. *Repair of Elongated Boltholes.* It is permissible to repair elongated boltholes by the insertion of a steel bushing around each bolt, as illustrated in figure 12.7. Machine the inside diameter of the bushing to fit the bolt snugly, and the outside diameter approximately 1/4 inch larger than the bolt size. Make the bushing approximately 1/2 inch long. Drill the face of the hub with a hole concentric with the bolt-

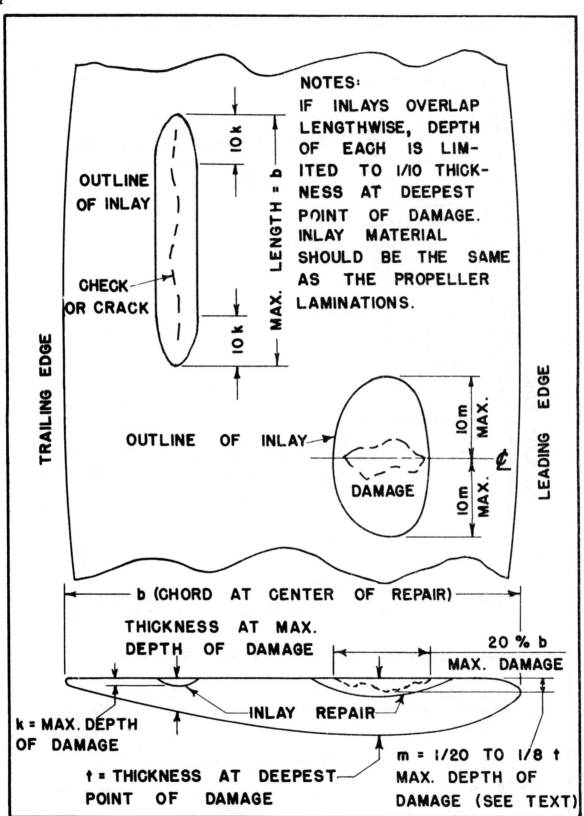

FIGURE 12.1.—Propeller repair by addition of small inlay. (See continuation.)

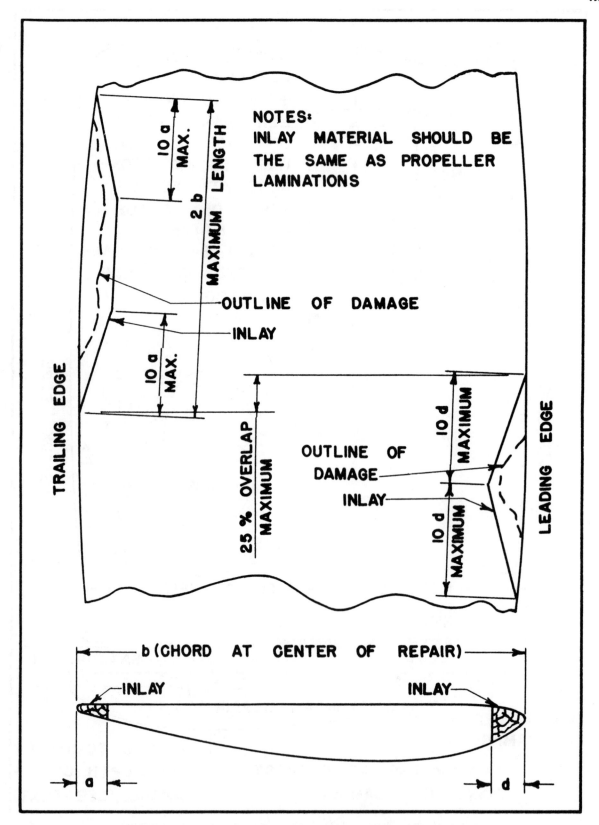

NOTES:
INLAY MATERIAL SHOULD BE
THE SAME AS PROPELLER
LAMINATIONS

FIGURE 12.1A.—Propeller repair by addition of small inlay—continued.

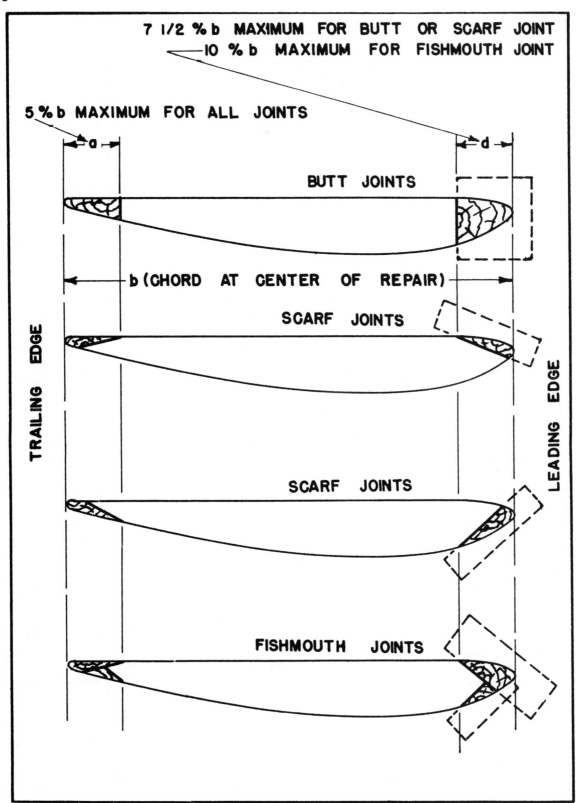

FIGURE 12.1B—Propeller repair by addition of small inlay—continued.

hole and only to a sufficient depth to accommodate the bushing so that it does not protrude above the surface of the wood hub. Do not drive the bushing into the hub. Fit the bushing into the hole in the hub with a clearance not exceeding .005 inch after moistureproofing. Protect the bushing hole from moisture by two coats of aluminum paint, varnish, glue, or other moisture-resistant coating.

h. *Repair of Plastic Covered Propellers and Blades.* Repair small cracks, dents, scratches, and cuts in the plastic of plastic-covered wood propellers and blades by using special repair cement supplied by the manufacturer. Instructions accompany the cements. Polishes and cleaners are available for preserving the gloss finish of varnished or plastic-covered propellers and blades.

569. REPAIR OF COMPOSITION BLADE. Repair composition blades in accordance with the manufacturer's instructions. For repairs to the metal cap and leading edge strip, the methods and procedures discussed in the following paragraphs may be followed:

a. *Replace fabric used to strengthen* the tips of wood blades when it becomes loose or worn through. Launder the fabric (mercerized cotton airplane cloth) to remove all sizing. Cut a piece of fabric to approximate size required to cover both faces of outer portion of blade. Recover the same portion that the original fabric covered. Apply glue to the wood where the fabric is to be put, using a rather thick solution of the glue. Use resorcinol glue when the temperature of the workroom can be kept above 21° C. (70° F.). Put the fabric on glued surface, starting at the leading edge of the thrust face, and work toward the trailing edge. Fold the fabric around the trailing edge over the camber face and toward the leading edge. Make a joint on the leading edge where it will be covered by the metal tipping. As the fabric is put on, smooth it out over the wood to prevent air bubbles or uneven gluing. Fabric must be perfectly flat on the blade. Trim excess fabric off with small scissors. Under no circumstances cut or score fabric with a knife. Allow the glue under the fabric to dry about 6 hours, then

brush two coats of nitrate dope on the fabric, allowing one-half hour for drying time. Then sand the fabric lightly and brush a coat of pigment dope over it. Lightly sand the uncovered portion of the wood and apply two coats of a good grade of moisture-resistant varnish, allowing 12 to 16 hours drying time between coats.

b. *Metal Tip Replacement.* Replace tipping when it cannot be properly repaired. Cracks in the narrow necks of metal between pairs of lobes of the tipping are to be expected and are not defects. All other cracks are defects that require repair or elimination by new tipping. If the propeller does not require fabric, apply two coats of varnish to the wood to be covered by the metal tipping. If new fabric has been applied, puncture it with a pointed tool at each screw and rivet hole. Apply varnish, white lead, aluminum paint, etc., to all holes, allowing the wood to absorb as much as it can. With a soft lead pencil, draw guide centerlines on the propeller extending about 4 inches from the centers of old screw and rivet holes. This procedure is followed to insure use of the original screw and rivet holes in the propeller. New holes are not to be drilled. A number of wood propeller tip failures have occurred which have been attributed to the practice of drilling new rivet and/or screw holes in the wood tips when replacing the metal tipping. To avoid continued occurrence of these failures, it is strongly recommended that the manufacturer's procedure be closely adhered to, and any procedure which involves drilling new holes in the wood tip and plugging old holes with dowels is to be discontinued immediately.

(1) Obtain new tips and leading-edge strips, cut to size and formed to the approximate shape of the leading edge of the propeller. These pieces are usually supplied without holes so that the holes can be drilled in them to line up with the old screw and rivet holes in the propeller as stated below. If such material cut to shape is not available, the old tipping can be hammered flat and used as a pattern to lay off a new tip. For this purpose, use a piece of sheet metal of the same material and thickness as the old tip, and remove the burr from the cut edges of this piece.

(2) Lay the cutout flat metal strip over the leading edge, and proceed to bend this metal down over the leading edge of the propeller, being careful that the metal extends an equal width on thrust and camber faces. This can be done by following the impressions of the old tipping lines. Numerous waves will occur in the metal, but these will be eliminated as the work progresses. Obtain several pieces of strong rubber tape, 4 feet long, 1/2 inch wide, and 1/16 inch thick. While forming the metal, hold it in place on the propeller by wrapping the rubber tape around the blade. Start at the tip and work inboard, being careful not to cover the pencil lines placed on the propeller which show the location of the rivet holes. While metal is held in place, tap the leading edge with a rawhide or rubber mallet, using moderate force to make sure the metal is seated against the wood along the nose of the leading edge. Smooth the metal by hammering it with the mallet, backing up the opposite side of the blade with a laminated hardwood bucking block having an iron weight built in the center and a piece of leather fastened to the end on which the propeller bears. The block should measure about 2 by 4 inches. Start at the end of the blade and work toward the hub, moving bucking block so that it is always under the section being hammered. Continue to do this until the metal is well shaped to the profile of the propeller. Check to see that the metal has not moved from its original position. If this happens, remove the rubber tape, reset the metal, and rewrap the rubber tape, thus forming the metal to the leading edge.

(3) With a centerpunch and a hammer, proceed to locate the old screw and rivet holes, using the pencil marks on the blade as a guide. Punch the metal approximately 1/4 inch from the edge. After all holes have been located, remove the metal from the propeller. Drill screw and rivet holes in the metal with a 1/8-inch drill. File off burrs on the inside of the metal. Run the drill through the original rivet holes in the propeller in order to clean them. Cut or saw slots in the metal at the original positions. (Refer to old tipping metal for location of the slots.) Place the metal leading edges on the blades they were formed to fit, and hold them in place with rubber tape. With a centerpunch as large as or slightly larger than the diameter of the screw and rivet heads, proceed to punch metal into the original countersunk holes in the wood so that the screw and rivet heads may be entered to the correct depth (not more than 1/32 inch below the surface of the metal). Use screws and rivets of the appropriate material. Use screws one size larger than were originally in the propeller, and rivets of the solid flat countersunk-head type. Insert screws and rivets in their respective holes, and install rivets with their heads on the thrust face of the propeller. After rivets are tapped in place, cut off the excess length of the rivet, leaving 1/8 inch for heading. End cutters built up with solder to accurately measure this distance are very useful. When an assistant backs up the rivets with a steel bar 18 inches long and pointed to fit the rivet head, hammer the rivets either by hand or with a pneumatic hammer. Screws may be driven either by hand or with an electric screwdriver.

(4) Cut the metal of the cap tip on the camber face of the propeller to the shape of the propeller tip. Bevel the edge by hand-filing and trim off flat side of metal cap so that it extends about 3/16 inch all around the tip of the propeller. Form a hardwood block to the shape of the propeller tip thrust face. Put metal tipping in place and clamp this block to the underside of the tip with a C-clamp; turn this 3/16 inch of metal up and over the camber face of the tip. Tighten and complete the lap joint. Mount the propeller blade solidly, with the thrust face up, on a stand supporting the blade at several points along its radius. With a hammer and a flat-faced tool, proceed to smooth the metal, starting at the nose of the leading edge and working toward the edge of the metal until all wrinkles and high spots are removed. At the edge, use a caulking tool and, in the same manner, press the metal edge tightly against the wood. Turn the propeller over and repeat this operation on the camber face. Make sure that the thin tip is supported at all times when hammering. Apply solder over rivet and screwheads and over the metal seam of the tip of the propeller. Use 50–50 solder in wire form. Use muriatic acid as flux when soldering

brass. Use stainless steel soldering flux when soldering stainless steel tipping. File excess solder off and check the propeller balance while doing so. Polish the metal with a fine emery cloth or an abrasive drum driven by a flexible shaft. Vent the tipping by drilling three holes, No. 60 drill (.040), 3/16 inch deep in the tip end. Drill ventholes parallel to the longitudinal axis of the blade.

570. REFINISHING. After repairing a blade, it is usually necessary to refinish it. In some cases it may be necessary to completely remove the old finish. Apply the finish, where necessary, in accordance wih the recommendations of the propeller manufacturer, or with a material which has satisfactory adhesion and high moisture-resistant properties. Refinishing of plastic-covered blades requires special techniques. Some manufacturers make this information available through service bulletins. Refinish or repaint wood blades carefully so that the balance of the entire propeller is not disturbed. Coating one blade heavier than the other will produce unbalance and cause a noticeable vibration during flight.

571. PROPELLER BALANCING. It is always necessary to check the balance of the propeller after any repairs or refinishing. Accomplish final balance on a rigid knife-edge balancing stand or on a suspension-type balancer in a room free from air currents. There must not be any persistent tendency to rotate from any position on the balance stand, or to tilt on the suspension balancer. Horizontal unbalance may be cor-

rected by the the application of finish or solder to the light blade. The light blade may be coated with a high grade of primer allowing for a finishing coat. After allowing each coat to dry 48 hours, recheck the balance. Then, as may be necessary, either the required amount of finish must be removed by carefully sandpapering or applying an additional finishing coat. Recheck the balance and sandpaper or apply additional finish as may be required to effect final balancing. Correct vertical unbalance in fixed-pitch propellers by applying putty to the light side of the wood hub at a point on the circumference approximately 90° from the longitudinal centerline of the blades. Weigh the putty and prepare a brass plate weighing slightly more than the putty. The thickness of the plate should be from 1/16 inch to 1/8 inch, depending on the final area, and be of sufficient size to accommodate the required number of flathead attaching screws. The plate may be made to fit on the hub face or to fit the shape of the light side of the wood hub, and drilled and countersunk for the required number of screws. Attach the plate and tighten all of the screws. After the plate is finally attached to the propeller, secure the screws to the plate by soldering the screwheads and recheck the propeller balance. All edges of the plate may be beveled to reduce its weight as necessary. The drilling of holes in the propeller and the insertion of lead or other material to assist in balancing will not be permitted.

572.–582. RESERVED.

Section 3. REPAIR OF METAL PROPELLERS

583. GENERAL. Reject damaged blades with model numbers which are on the manufacturer's list of blades that cannot be repaired. Follow manufacturer's recommendations in all cases, and make repairs in accordance with latest techniques and best industry practices.

584. STEEL BLADES. Due to the critical effects of surface injuries and their repair on the fatigue life of steel blades, all repairs must be made in accordance with the manufacturer's instructions.

585. ALUMINUM PROPELLER REPAIRS. Aluminum-alloy propellers and blades with dents, cuts, scars, scratches, nicks, leading-edge pitting, etc., may be repaired, provided the removal or treatment does not materially affect the strength, weight, or performance of the blade. Remove these damages or otherwise treat as explained below unless contrary to manufacturer's instructions or recommendations. More than one injury is not sufficient cause alone for rejection of a blade. A reasonable number of repairs per blade may be made and not necessarily result in a dangerous condition, unless their location with respect to each other is such to form a continuous line of repairs that would materially weaken the blade. Suitable sandpaper or fine-cut files may be used for removing the necessary amount of metal. In each case, the area involved will be smoothly finished with No. 00 sandpaper or crocus cloth, and each blade from which any appreciable amount of metal has been removed will be properly balanced before it is used. Etch suspected cracks and all repairs as discussed in paragraph 605. To avoid removal of an excessive amount of metal, local etching should be accomplished at intervals during the process of removing suspected cracks. Upon completion of the repair, carefully inspect the entire blade by etching or anodizing. Remove all effects of the etching process with fine emery paper. Blades identified by the manufacturer as being cold-worked (shot-blasted or cold-rolled) may require peening after repair. Accomplish repair and peening operations on this type of blade in accordance with the manufacturer's instructions. However, it is not permissible in any case to peen down the edges of any injury wherein the operation will lap metal over the injury.

a. Round out nicks, scars, cuts, etc., occurring on the leading edge of aluminum alloy blades as shown in figure 12.2 (view B). Blades that have the leading edges pitted from normal wear in service may be reworked by removing sufficient material to eliminate the pitting. In this case, remove the metal by starting well back from the edge, as shown in figure 12.3, and working forward over the edge in such a way that the contour will reman substantially the same, avoiding abrupt changes in contour or blunt edges. Trailing edges of blades may be treated in substantially the same manner. On the thrust and camber face of blades, remove the metal around any dents, cuts, scars, scratches, nicks, longitudinal surface cracks, and pits to form shallow saucer-shaped depressions as shown in figure 12.2 (view C). Exercise care to remove the deepest point of the injury and also remove any raised metal around the edges of the injury as shown in figure 12.2 (view A). For repaired blades, the permissible reduction in width and thickness for minimum original dimensions, allowed by the blade drawing and blade manufacturing specifications are shown in figure 12.4 for locations on the blade from the shank to 90 percent of the blade
* radius. Beyond the 90 percent blade radius point, the blade width and thickness may be modified as per manufacturer's instructions. *

b. Shortening blades. When the removal or treatment of defects on the tip necessitates shortening a blade, shorten each blade used

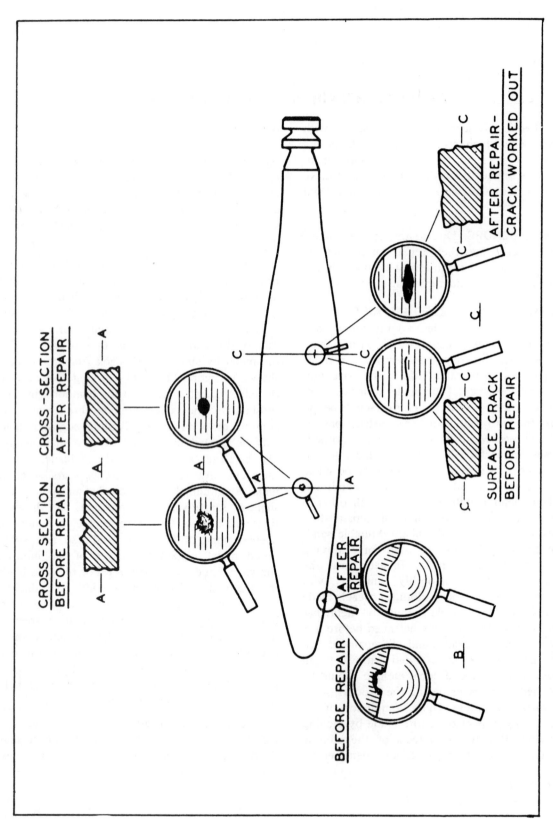

FIGURE 12.2.—Method of repairing surface cracks, nicks, etc., on aluminum alloy propellers.

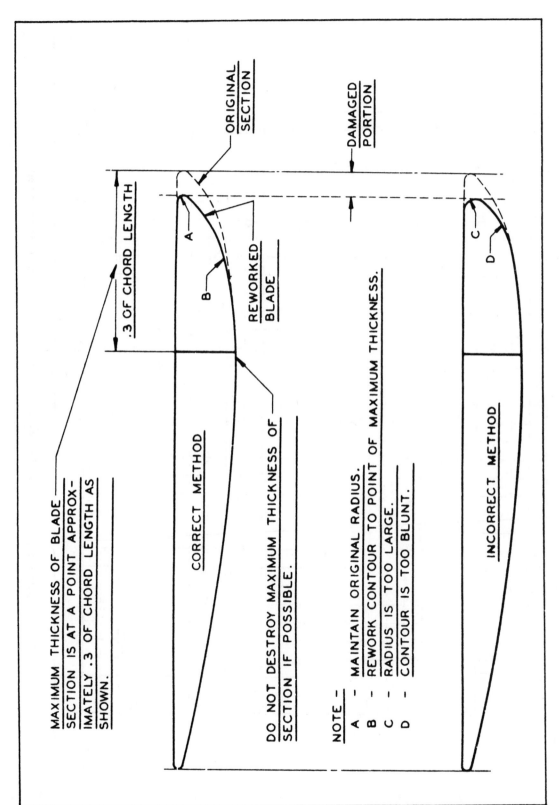

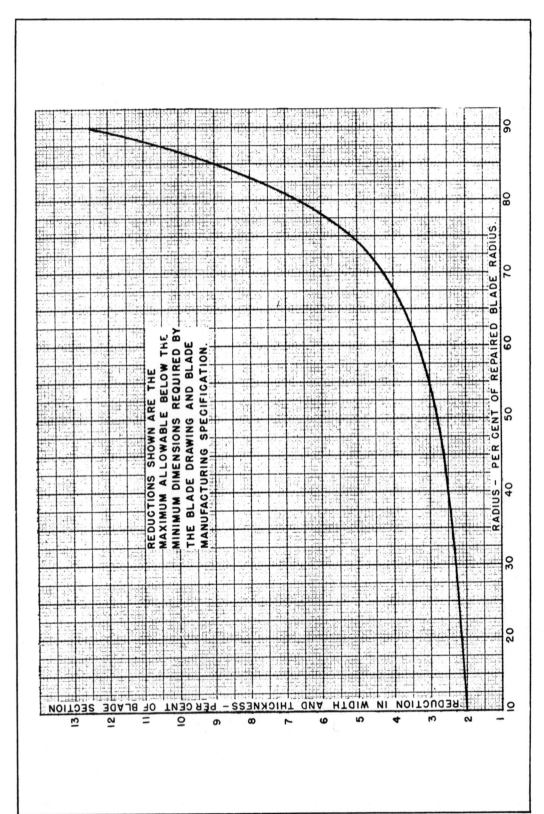

FIGURE 12.4.—Repair limits to blade section width and thickness for aluminum alloy propellers.

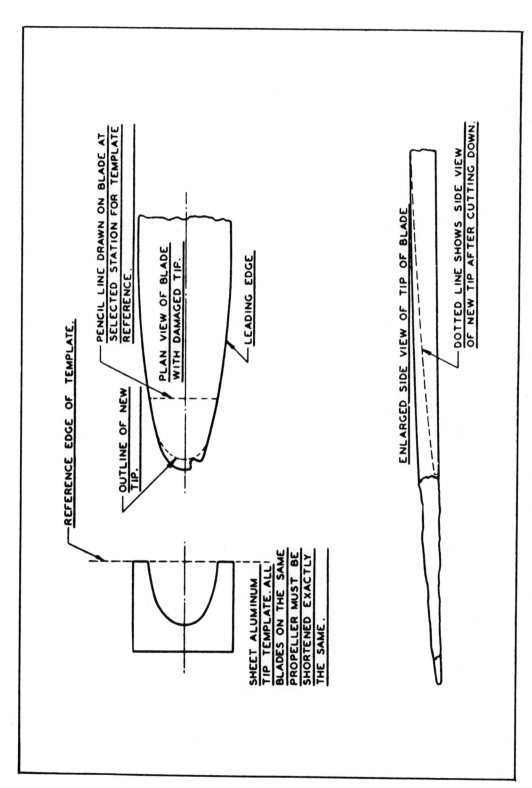

FIGURE 12.5.—Method of repairing damaged tip of aluminum alloy propellers.

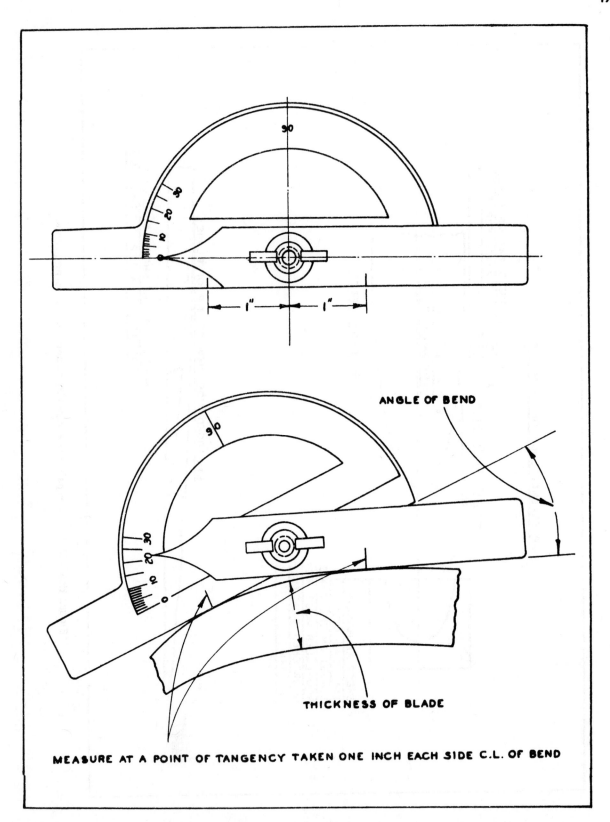

FIGURE 12.6.—Protractor and method of measuring angle of bend in aluminum alloy propellers.

with it and keep such sets of blades together (see figure 12.5 for acceptable methods). Mark the shortened blades to correspond with the manufacturer's system of model designation to indicate propeller diameter. In making the repair, it is not permissible to reduce the propeller diameter below the minimum diameter limit shown on the pertinent airplane specification.

c. *Straightening Propeller Blades.* Repair bent blades in accordance with the manufacturer's instructions. Carefully check the extent of a bend in face alinement by means of a protractor similar to the one illustrated in figure 12.6. Only bends not exceeding 20° at 0.15-inch blade thickness to 0 degrees at 1.1-inch blade thickness may be cold straightened. Straighten blades with bends exceeding these values only upon recommendation of the manufacturer, and only at facilities having proper heat-treatment equipment. In all cases, inspect the blades (as discussed in paragraph 605) for cracks and other injuries both before and after straightening.

586. REPAIR TOLERANCES. The following tolerances are those listed in the blade manufacturing specification for aluminum alloy blades and govern the width and thickness of new blades. These tolerances are to be used with the pertinent blade drawing to determine the minimum original blade dimensions to which the reduction of figure 12.4 may be applied. When repairs reduce the width or thickness of the blade below these limits, reject the blade. The face alignment or track of the propeller should fall within the limits recommended by the manufacturer for new propellers.

Basic diameter less than 10 feet 6 inches:
  Blade width—from shank to 24-inch
         station _____ ± 3/64
        from 24-inch station
          to tip _____ ± 1/32
  Blade thickness _____ ± 0.025

Basic diameter 10 feet 6 inches to less than 14 feet 0 inches:
  Blade width—from shank to 24-inch
         station _____ ± 1/16

        from 30-inch station
         to tip _____ ± 1/32
  Blade thickness—from shank to 24-inch
         station _____ ± 0.030
        from 30-inch station
         to tip _____ ± 0.025

Basic diameter 14 feet 0 inches and over:
  Blade width—from shank to 30-inch
         station _____ ± 3/32
        from 36-inch station
         to tip _____ ± 1/16
  Blade thickness—from shank to 30-inch
         station _____ ± 0.040
        from 36-inch station
         to tip _____ ± 0.035

a. No repairs are permitted to the shanks (roots or hub ends) of aluminum alloy adjustable pitch blades. The shanks must be within manufacturer's tolerances.

587. PROPELLER BALANCE. Upon completion of repairs, check horizontal and vertical balance and correct any unbalance as recommended by the manufacturer. A coaxial hole is drilled in the butt end of certain aluminum alloy detachable blades for the application of lead to obtain static horizontal balance. The size of this hole must not be increased by the repair agency.

To effect vertical balance, follow the manufacturer's specific instructions. The outside of an eccentric hole must not be closer than 1/4 inch to the nearest external blade surface. As an alternate to drilling the two holes mentioned above, the manufacturer may have drilled a single eccentric hole having a diameter and depth conforming to the eccentric hole dimensions given in the table for application of lead. The outer edge of the hole must not be closer than 1 inch to the nearest external blade surface. Finish the ends of all balancing holes with a full sized drill having a spherical end to eliminate sharp corners. Remove the sharp edges of all holes by a 1/32-inch chamfer. The following table is included for inspection information only:

Size and depth of balancing holes.

Shank size	Max. concentric hole diameter (inch)	Max. concentric hole depth (inches)	Max. eccentric hole depth (⅜-inch max. dia.) (inches)
00	7/16	2½	2¼
0–V2	19/32	3⅜	3
½	⅝	3⅝	3½
1	¾	4¼	4
1½	13/16	4⅞	4½
2	⅞	5½	5
3	31/32	6⅛	6

588. STEEL HUBS AND HUB PARTS. Repairs to steel hubs and parts must be accomplished only in accordance with the manufacturer's recommendations. Welding and remachining is permissible only when covered by manufacturer's service bulletins.

589. PROPELLER HUB AND FLANGE REPAIR. When the propeller boltholes in a hub or crankshaft flange for fixed-pitch propellers become damaged or oversized, it is permissible to make repairs by methods (A) or (B) in figure 12.7, or by use of aircraft standard bolts 1/16 inch larger than the original bolts. Make the repairs in accordance with the recommendations of the propeller metal hub manufacturer or the engine manufacturer as applicable. Obtain from the engine or propeller hub manufacturer suitable flange bushings with threaded or smooth bores, as illustrated in methods (A) or (B) of figure 12.7. Drill the flange and insert the bushings as recommended by the engine manufacturer. Drill the rear face of the propeller to accommodate the bushings, and protect the holes with 2 coats of aluminum paint or other high moisture-resistant coating. Use bolts of the same size as those originally used. Any of the following combinations may

be used: (1) safety bolt and castellated nut, (2) safety bolt (drilled head) and threaded bushing, or (3) undrilled bolt and self-locking nut. Where it is desirable to use oversized bolts, obtain suitable aircraft standard bolts 1/16 inch larger than the original bolts. Enlarge the crankshaft propeller flange holes and the propeller hub holes sufficiently to accomodate the new bolts without more than 0.005-inch clearance. Such reboring will be permitted only once. Further repairs of boltholes may be in accordance with the methods (A) or (B) of figure 12.7.

NOTE: Methods (A) or (B) are preferred over the oversized bolt method, because a propeller hub flange redrilled in accordance with this latter method will always require the redrilling of all new propellers subsequently used with the redrilled flange.

590. CONTROL SYSTEMS. Components used to control the operation of certificated propellers should be inspected, repaired, assembled, and/or tested in accordance with the manufacturer's recommendations. Only those repairs which are covered by the manufacturer's recommendations should be made, and only those replacement parts which are approved under FAR Part 21 should be used.

591. DEICING SYSTEMS. Components used in propeller deicing systems should be inspected, repaired, assembled, and/or tested in accordance with the manufacturer's recommendations. Only those repairs which are covered by the manufacturer's recommendations should be made, and only those replacement parts which are approved under FAR Part 21 should be used.

592.–602. RESERVED.

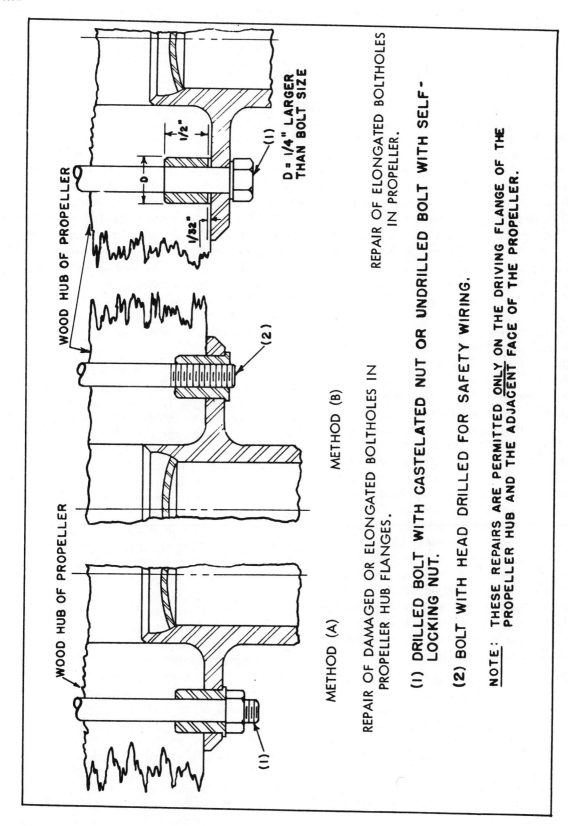

WOOD HUB OF PROPELLER

D = 1/4" LARGER THAN BOLT SIZE

1/2"

D

1/32"

(1)

REPAIR OF ELONGATED BOLTHOLES IN PROPELLER.

WOOD HUB OF PROPELLER

(2)

METHOD (B)

WOOD HUB OF PROPELLER

(1)

METHOD (A)

REPAIR OF DAMAGED OR ELONGATED BOLTHOLES IN PROPELLER HUB FLANGES.

(1) DRILLED BOLT WITH CASTELATED NUT OR UNDRILLED BOLT WITH SELF-LOCKING NUT.

(2) BOLT WITH HEAD DRILLED FOR SAFETY WIRING.

NOTE: THESE REPAIRS ARE PERMITTED ONLY ON THE DRIVING FLANGE OF THE PROPELLER HUB AND THE ADJACENT FACE OF THE PROPELLER.

FIGURE 12.7.—Repair of fixed-pitch hub and propeller with elongated or damaged boltholes.

Section 4.   OVERHAUL OF PROPELLERS

603. HUB AND HUB PARTS. Disassemble propellers submitted for overhaul and clean all hub parts in accordance with the manufacturer's recommendations. Make an inspection of the parts to determine that the critical dimensions are within the manufacturer's specified tolerances. Take particular care to check the 90° relation between shaft bore and blade socket centerline and track of the blade sockets, as these are the dimensions which are most likely to be affected by accidents. Reject and replace any hub which is sprung, worn, or damaged. Stress risers such as cuts, nicks, or tool marks must be carefully stoned or the part rejected. Carefully inspect splines and cone seats for signs of wear, and check splines with a single key "no-go" gauge made to plus 0.002 inch of the base drawing dimensions for spline land width. If the gauge enters more than 20 percent of the spline area, reject the hub. Cones and cone seats may show discoloration, pitting, and corrosion. Generally, corrosion and discolored spots may be removed by light lapping. Pitting is not grounds for rejection, if 75 percent of the bearing area is not affected and the pitted areas are well dispersed about the cone bearing area. After cleaning, minutely inspect steel hubs and parts for cracks by the wet or dry magnetic particle method at every major overhaul period. It is not necessary to remove the plating or special external finish for this inspection unless so specified in the manufacturer's recommended practice.

Steel hubs which adapt fixed-pitch propellers to all taper crankshafts are susceptible to cracks along the keyway which often extend into the flange lightening holes. Carefully inspect these hubs by the magnetic particle method at engine overhaul periods. Any crack is cause for rejection.

604. PLATING FOR HUBS AND PARTS. Replate hubs and parts from which the plating has been removed after they have been satisfactorily inspected. All replating must be of the same material as the original plating and be done in accordance with the manufacturer's recommendations. Chrome or nickel plating is not an acceptable substitute for cadmium or zinc plating. The use of zinc chromate primer on the external surfaces followed by a coating of aluminum lacquer in lieu of cadmium plating is considered acceptable where recommended by the manufacturer. However, this type of finish will require replacement more frequently than cadmium plating.

605. INSPECTION OF ALUMINUM PROPELLERS AND BLADES. Carefully inspect aluminum propellers and blades for cracks and other injuries. A transverse (chordwise) crack or flaw of any size is cause for rejection. Refer any unusual condition or appearance revealed by these inspections to the manufacturer. Acceptable inspection methods are the acid-etching process, the anodizing process, the fluorescent penetrant process, or the dye penetrant process. Where applicable, supplement one process with another. Etching is accomplished by immersing the blade in a warm 20 percent caustic soda solution and cleaning with a warm 20 percent nitric acid solution, with a warm water rinse between the caustic bath and the acid bath, and also a warm water rinse following the acid bath. Remove all effects of the etching by polishing. Maintain the caustic and acid solution at a temperature of from 160° F. to 180° F. Some blades incorporate parts made of steel and other materials, and the caustic soda and the nitric acid must not be allowed to come in contact with these parts. The blade surfaces are then examined with a magnifying glass of at least three-power. A crack will appear as a distinct black line. The fluorescent penetrant method is recommended as a supplement to the caustic etch for the inspection of the shanks (roots or hub ends) of adjustable pitch blades.

a. *Suspected cracks or defects* should be repeatedly local etched until their nature is determined. With a No. 00 sandpaper, or fine crocus cloth, clean and smooth the area containing the apparent crack. Apply a small quantity of caustic solution to the suspected area with a swab or brush. After the area is well darkened, thoroughly wipe it with a clean (dampened) cloth. Too much water may entirely remove the solution from a crack and spoil the test. If a crack extending into the metal exists, it will appear as a dark line or mark, and by using a magnifying glass, small bubbles may be seen forming in the line or mark. Immediately upon completion of the final checks, remove all traces of the caustic solution by use of the nitric acid solution. Wash the blade thoroughly with clean (fresh) water.

b. *The chromic acid anodizing process* is superior to caustic etching for the detection of cracks and flaws and should therefore be used, whenever it is available, for general inspection of blades, for material defects, and for final checking of repairs performed during overhaul. Immerse the blades in the anodizing bath as far as possible, but all parts not made of aluminum alloy must be kept out of the chromic acid bath or be separated from the blade by nonconductive wedges or hooks. Follow the anodizing treatment by a rinse in clear, cold, running water from 3 to 5 minutes, and dry the blades as quickly as possible, preferably with an air blast. Allow the dried blades to stand for at least 15 minutes before examination. Flaws (cold shuts or inclusions) will appear as fine black lines. Cracks will appear as brown stains caused by chromic acid bleeding out onto the surface. The blades may be sealed for improved corrosion resistance by immersing them in hot water (180° F. to 212° F.) for one-half hour. In no case, immerse the blades in hot water before the examination for cracks, since heat expands cracks and allows the chromic acid to be washed away.

606. ASSEMBLY. Accomplish the assembly of the propeller hub and blade in accordance with the manufacturer's recommendations. Replace clevis pins, bolts, and nuts which show wear or distortion. Never use cotter pins and safety wire a second time. The use of self-locking nuts is permissible only where originally used or approved by the manufacturer.

607.–617. RESERVED.

Section 5. ASSEMBLY OF PROPELLER TO ENGINE

618. FIXED-PITCH PROPELLERS. Loose hub bolts and bolts installed through the lightening holes in the integral hub flange of certain engine crankshafts cause the majority of the serious difficulties experienced with fixed-pitch propellers. Either of the conditions, if not corrected, will ultimately cause the loss of the propeller.

a. *Loose hub bolts* cause elongated boltholes and damage to the hub bolts. When not corrected, the bolts break off, or friction causes enough heat to affect the glue and chars the wood. After successive running, cracks start at the boltholes. These cracks are caused, or at least accentuated, by shrinkage of the wood due to the excessive heat generated. If allowed to progress, the propeller usually flies apart or catches on fire.

b. *On some engines* equipped with a crankshaft having an integral propeller hub flange, the outer edge of the lightening holes are at the same radius as the corresponding edge of the propeller hub boltholes. When inserting the bolts through the propeller, care must be exercised so that the bolts are inserted through the proper holes in the flange. Cases have been reported where the bolts were inserted through the larger lightening holes and, accordingly, the bolt nuts bore only on the outer edges of the lightening holes. In such cases, continuous running of the propeller may cause the boltheads or nuts to slip off the flange and through the large openings in the flange, resulting in the subsequent loss of the propeller.

c. *Both the conditions discussed* above are very easy to detect, and must be corrected immediately. In case the hub flange is integral with the crankshaft, first ascertain the bolts are properly installed, then make the inspection for bolt tightness in the same manner as for any other propeller hub. Use an open-end wrench to determine hub bolt tightness; and, if the nuts can be turned, remove the cotter keys and retorque the nuts to the desired setting. Tighten hub bolts, preferably with a torque wrench, to the recommended values which usually range from 15 to 24 foot-pounds. If no torque wrench is available, an ordinary socket wrench may be used. This socket wrench should have a 1-foot extension lever and the wrench pulled up with the recommended force 12 inches away from the center of the bolt which is being tightened. The tightening is best accomplished by tightening each bolt a little at a time, being sure to tighten alternate bolts which are diametrically opposite. Exercise care not to overtighten the hub bolts, thereby damaging the wood underneath the hub flanges. Avoid the practice of overtightening bolts to draw a propeller into track. Safety the nuts by means of cotter keys of proper size or heavy safety wire twisted between each nut. A continuous length of single safety wire is not acceptable, as wire failure will result in all nuts becoming unsafetied.

619.-629. RESERVED.

Section 6. PRECAUTIONS

630. BLADE-TIP IDENTIFICATION. Many persons have been fatally injured walking into whirling propellers. Painting a warning strip on the propeller serves to reduce chances of such injuries. Cover approximately 4 inches of the propeller tips on both sides with an orange-yellow nonreflecting paint or lacquer. Open the drain holes in the metal tipping of wood blades after the tips have been painted.

631. GROUND-HANDLING PRACTICES. Wood propellers are especially susceptible to damage from improper handling. When moving an airplane, avoid bumping the propeller. The practice of pushing or pulling on a propeller blade to move an airplane should be avoided; it is extremely easy to impose forces on a blade in excess of those for which the blade is designed. It is continually necessary to ascertain that the glue joints are in good condition, and that the finish on the entire propeller will protect the propeller from absorbing moisture. Place two-bladed wood propellers, whether on or off an airplane, in a horizontal position to prevent unbalance from moisture absorption. A good precaution is to cover the propeller with a well-fitted waterproof cover when not in use. It is very important to protect the shank section of wood blades from moisture changes to prevent swelling and subsequent loosening in the metal sleeve. In the case of varnished blades, it is advisable to occasionally apply varnish around the shank at the junction of wood and metal. In the case of the plastic-covered blade, repair cement may be applied around the same joint.

632. COMPOSITION PROPELLER SERVICE LIMITS. In certain cases where the blade has been manufactured from laminated planks of composition material, longitudinal cracks or splitting between laminations have been observed after several hundred hours of operation. Do not permit these cracks to progress beyond the limits established by the manufacturer.

633.–643. RESERVED.

Section 7. MAINTENANCE OF ROTOR BLADES

644. GENERAL. The design, materials, construction, and performance requirements for rotorcraft main and tail rotor blades vary considerably from those used in the manufacture and operation of airplane propellers. Major dissimilarities also exist among the blades fabricated for the various makes and models of rotorcraft currently in operation. For these reasons, it is of utmost importance that the specific maintenance requirements of each rotorcraft manufacturer be consulted prior to performing any maintenance. In all instances, the restoration of blades will be determined by the repair limitations provided in the blade manufacturer's current service and maintenance manual data. The information in this section may serve as a general guide for maintaining the airworthiness of rotorcraft blades.

a. *Leading Edge Strip.* Examine leading edge abrasion strips (A in figures 12.8, 12.9 and 12.10) for nicks, cuts, gouges, or worn spots resulting from abrasion. Damage of this type can usually be considered minor provided the injuries are not concentrated in one area, do not penetrate the strip, or do not affect the aerodynamic performance of the blade.

The limits for leading edge strip bond separations or edge voids (B in Figure 12.8) are established by the blade manufacturer. When a separation is suspected, carefully examine the blade assembly and determine whether it is within the manufacturer's tolerances for continued operation. If it is permissible for the blade to remain in service, recheck that blade area at frequent intervals thereafter to assure that the separation is not progressing beyond allowable limits.

Inspect the rotor blade for evidence of paint deterioration in the area where the aft edge of the leading edge metal strip terminates. If the surface of the paint in this area is cracked, blistered, or missing, carefully examine the metal surface of the blade for evidence of elec-trolytic corrosion or pitting (C in Figure 12.8). Treat minor cases of localized corrosion promptly by cleaning and coating the area with a preservative that will arrest further surface deterioration until the blade can be completely refinished. When the area of corrosion appears to be extensive or pitting is deep, remove the blade for complete evaluation of the damage.

b. *Blade Surface.* Examine the blade upper and lower surfaces between the leading edge strip and the trailing edge for evidence of cracks (B in figures 12.9 and 12.10). Cracks of any magnitude in this area are cause for blade removal if allowable crack limitations are not prescribed by the blade manufacturer. Trailing edge cracks in blades having bonded trailing edges are also cause for removing the blade for service. Blades incorporating rivets along the trailing edge that have cracks at the edge (C in figures 12.9 and 12.10) which terminate at a rivet hole or cracks that extend between two adjacent rivets (D in figures 12.9 and 12.10) are not permissible and the blade should be removed from further service until repairs are made.

Inspect the adhesive bonding at the blade root end doublers (E in figures 12.9 and 12.10), skin to spar joint (A in figure 12.11), and the trailing edge (C in figure 12.11) for evidence of bond separation. This may initially appear as a hairline crack and any indication of a separation is cause for removing the blade from service to thoroughly examine and evaluate the condition prior to attempting repair.

Check the entire bonded (honeycomb core) area of the blade for evidence of bond separations or voids (B in figure 12.11). In many instances these can be detected by a difference in sound heard while the surface of the blade is being tapped with a light object such as a coin. A dull or dead sound is indicative of a void or separation. The acceptability of voids or sepa-

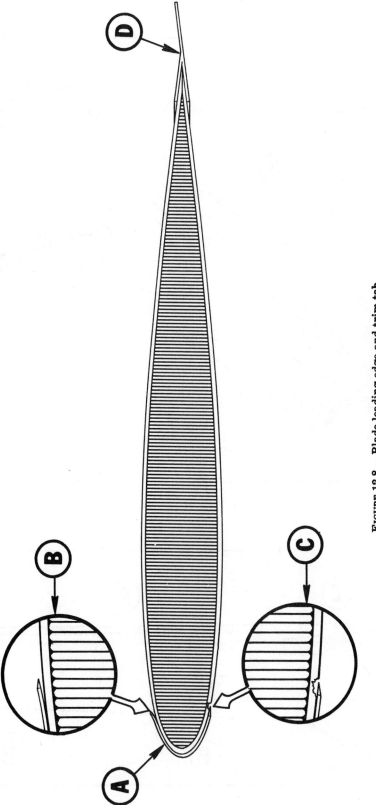

FIGURE 12.8.—Blade leading edge and trim tab.

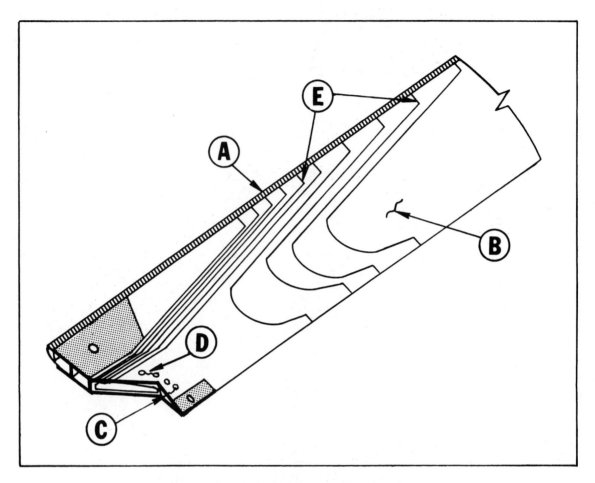

FIGURE 12.9.—Blade bonding and crack location.

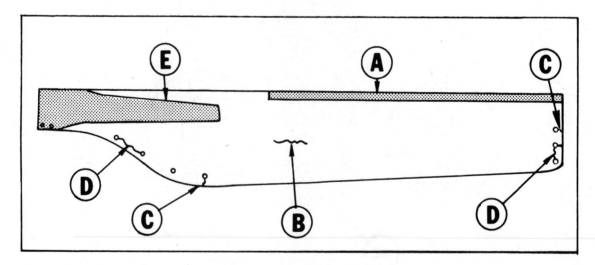

FIGURE 12.10.—Blade damage location.

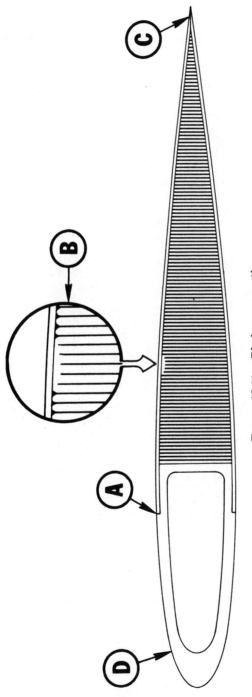

FIGURE 12.11.—Blade cross-section.

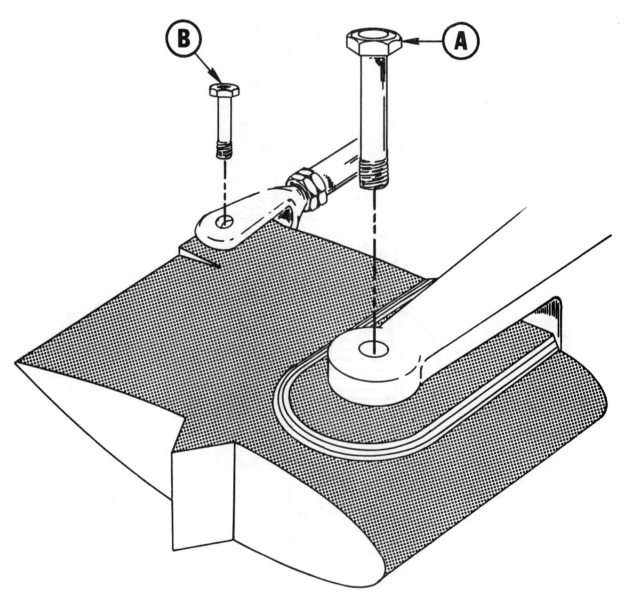

FIGURE 12.12.—Blade retention and link attach points.

rations depends upon their location and the size of the area involved. Consult the applicable blade manufacturer's service manual for the allowable limits.

NOTE: The presence of water in the honeycomb core of a blade is cause for retiring a blade from service.

Examine the blade trim tabs for security of attachment and evidence of cracks in the area where they are bent (D in figure 12.8). When either of these conditions exists, take appropriate corrective action prior to approving the blade for return to service.

c. *Main Spar or Beam*. Inspect all of the exposed surfaces of blade spars for such damage as cuts, nicks, scratches, or erosion. When the blade leading edge is an integral part of an extruded spar or beam (D in figure 12.11), carefully examine the blade edge for wear resulting from abrasives. Use a penetrant method of inspection when checking the exposed surfaces of the metal spar or beam for cracks. If the spar is not exposed, an X-ray or comparable type of inspection is recommended. Any spar or beam crack is cause for removing a blade from service. Other types of spar damage must be evaluated, and if permissible, repaired in accordance with data provided in the applicable manufacturer's service manual.

d. *Blade Retention*. Examine the blade main retention components and drag (lead/lag) link attach points (A and B in figure 12.12) for evidence of looseness. If there are any indications of excessive play, remove the main retention and drag link attaching bolts or pins and check them for wear or stretch. Use a dye penetrant or magnetic particle method to inspect the bolts or pins for cracks. Check the threads for evidence of necking or distortion. Examine the main and drag link bushings for wear or elongation. Carefully inspect the area around the bushing holes for evidence of cracks or delamination. Consult the manufacturer's overhaul or service manual to determine what main retention and drag link attachment wear tolerances are acceptable.

e. *Blade Tip Assembly*. Inspect the tip area of the blade for evidence of abrasive erosion. If this condition is readily visible and appears to be deep or covers an appreciable area, the blade should be removed from service in order to fully evaluate the degree of wear. Accomplish repairs in accordance with the manufacturer's recommendations if the wear limits for continued operation are exceeded.

Check the blade tip for loose rivets or bond separation. If either condition is evident, remove the blade from service and perform the necessary repairs. Any deformation of the blade tip must be corrected in the manner specified by the manufacturer of the blade.

If a blade tip cap is installed, remove it and carefully examine the blade balance weights for security of attachment. Check the condition of the tip cap screws and anchor nuts prior to replacing the cap.

f. *Blade Life*. Most rotor blade manufacturers prescribe permissible limits for wear, repairs, and hours of operation for specific blade models. Close adherence to these limitations is recommended, to assure continued airworthiness and reliability of the blades.

645.–655. RESERVED.

Chapter 13. WEIGHT AND BALANCE

656. GENERAL. The removal or addition of equipment results in changes to the center of gravity and empty weight of the aircraft, and the permissible useful load is affected accordingly. Investigate the effects of these changes, otherwise the aircraft flight characteristics may be adversely affected. Information on which to base the record of weight and balance changes to the aircraft may be obtained from the pertinent aircraft specification, the prescribed aircraft operating limitations, airplane flight manual, and the aircraft weight and balance report.

Removal or addition of minor items of equipment such as nuts, bolts, rivets, washers, and similar standard parts of negligible weight on fixed-wing aircraft do not require a weight and balance check. Since rotorcraft are in general more critical with respect to control with changes in c.g. positions, the procedures and instructions in the particular model maintenance or flight manual should be followed.

657. TERMINOLOGY. The following terminology is used in the practical application of weight and balance control.

a. Maximum Weight. The maximum weight is the maximum authorized weight of the aircraft and its contents as listed in the specifications.

b. Empty Weight. The empty weight of an aircraft includes all operating equipment that has a fixed location and is actually installed in the aircraft. It includes the weight of the airframe, powerplant, required equipment, optional and special equipment, fixed ballast, full engine coolant, hydraulic fluid, and the fuel and oil as explained in paragraph 658 f and g. Additional information regarding fluids which may be contained in the aircraft systems and which must be included in the empty weight will be indicated in the pertinent aircraft specifications whenever deemed necessary.

c. Useful Load. The useful load is the empty weight subtracted from the maximum weight of the aircraft. This load consists of the pilot, crew if applicable, maximum oil, fuel, passengers, and baggage, unless otherwise noted.

d. Weight Check. A weight check consists of checking the sum of the weights of all items of useful load against the authorized useful load (maximum weight less empty weight) of the aircraft.

e. Datum. The datum is an imaginary vertical plane from which all horizontal measurements are taken for balance purposes with the aircraft in level flight attitude. The datum is indicated on most FAA Aircraft Specifications. On some of the older aircraft, where the datum is not indicated, any convenient datum may be selected. However, once the datum is selected, all moment arms and the location of the permissible c.g. range must be taken with reference to it. Examples of typical locations of the datum are shown in figure 13.1.

f. Arm (or Moment Arm). The arm is the horizontal distance in inches from the datum to the center of gravity of an item. The algebraic sign is plus (+), if measured aft of the datum, and minus (–) if measured forward of the datum. Examples of plus and minus arms are shown in figure 13.2.

g. Moment. Moment is the product of a weight multiplied by its arm. The moment of an item about the datum is obtained by multiplying the weight of the item by its horizontal distance from the datum. A typical moment calculation is given in figure 13.3.

h. Center of Gravity. The center of gravity is a point about which the nose-heavy and tail-heavy moments are exactly equal in magnitude. If the aircraft were suspended from there, it would have no tendency to pitch in either di-

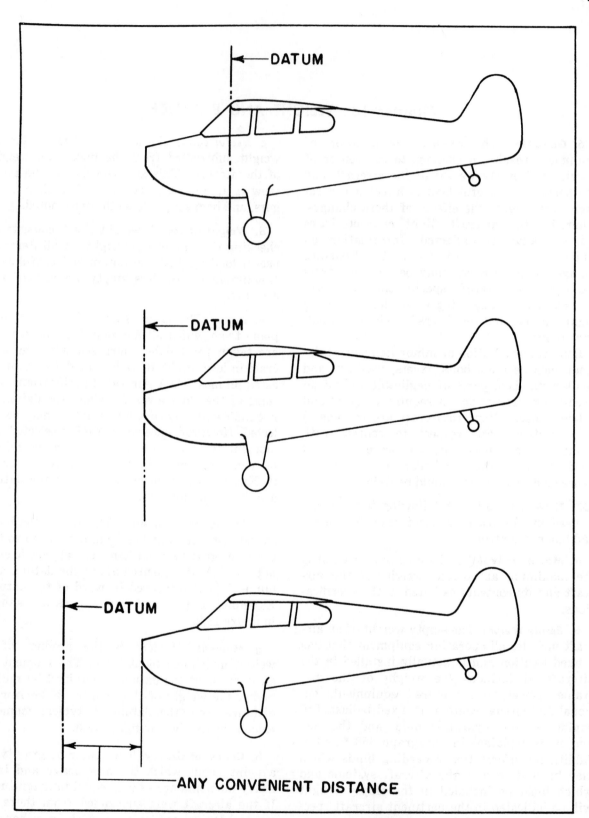

FIGURE 13.1.—Typical datum locations.

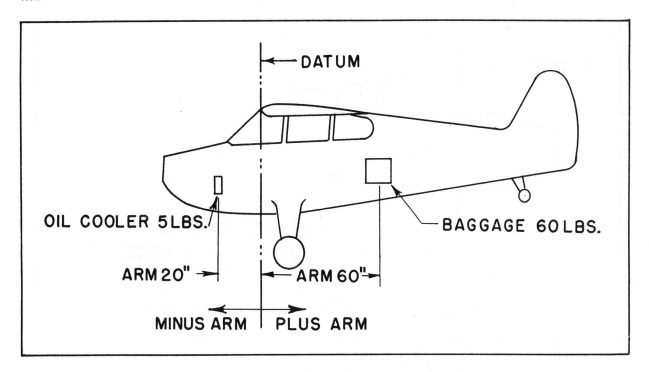

FIGURE 13.2.—Illustration of arm (or moment arm).

rection (nose up or down). The weight of the aircraft (or any object) may be assumed to be concentrated at its center of gravity. (See figure 13.3.)

i. Empty Weight Center of Gravity. The empty weight c.g. is the center of gravity of an aircraft in its empty weight condition, and is an essential part of the weight-and-balance record. Formulas for determining the center of gravity for tail and nosewheel type aircraft are given in figure 13.4. Typical examples of computing the empty weight and empty weight c.g. for aircraft are shown in figures 13.5 and 13.6.

j. Empty Weight Center-of-Gravity Range. The empty weight center-of-gravity range is determined so that the empty weight c.g. limits will not be exceeded under standard specification loading arrangements. In cases where it is possible to load an aircraft in a manner not covered in the Aircraft Specification (i.e., extra tanks, extra seats, etc.), complete calculations as outlined in paragraph 661. The empty weight c.g. range, when applicable, is listed on the Aircraft Specifications. Calculation of

empty weight c.g. is shown in figures 13.5 and 13.6.

k. Operating Center-of-Gravity Range. The operating c.g. range is the distance between the forward and rearward center of gravity limits indicated on the pertinent aircraft specification. These limits were determined as to the most forward and most rearward loaded c.g. positions at which the aircraft meets the requirements of the Federal Aviation Regulations. The limits are indicated on the specification in either percent of mean aerodynamic chord or inches from the datum. The c.g. of the loaded aircraft must be within these limits at all times as illustrated in figure 13.7.

l. Mean Aerodynamic Chord (MAC). For weight and balance purposes it is used to locate the c.g. range of the aircraft. The location and dimensions of the MAC will be found in the Aircraft Specifications, Aircraft Flight Manual, or the Aircraft Weight and Balance Report.

m. Weighing Point. If the c.g. location is determined by weighing, it is necessary to obtain horizontal measurements between the points on the scale at which the aircraft's weight is

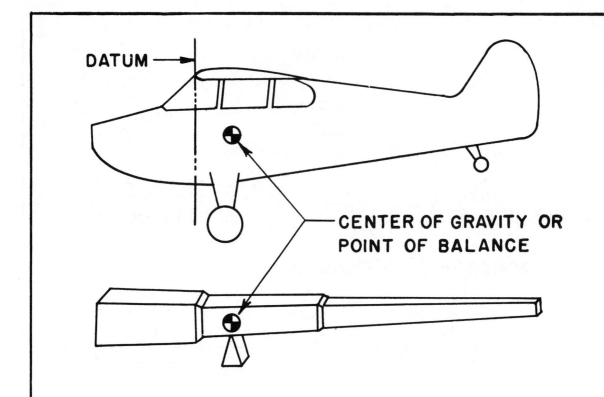

DATUM

CENTER OF GRAVITY OR
POINT OF BALANCE

The entire aircraft weight may be considered to be concentrated at the center of gravity. Therefore, the moment
of the aircraft about the datum is the weight of the aircraft times the horizontal distance between the C.G. and
the datum.

Example: If the weight of this airplane is 2000 lbs. and
the arm from the datum to the center of gravity is 16
inches, the moment of the aircraft about the datum is
2000 x 16 or 32,000 in. lbs.

FIGURE 13.3.—Example of moment computation.

concentrated. If weighed, using scales under the landing gear tires, a vertical line passing through the centerline of the axle will locate the point on the scale at which the weight is concentrated. This point is called the "weigh-ing point." Other structural locations capable of supporting the aircraft, such as jack pads on the main spar, may also be used if the air-craft weight is resting on the jack pads. Indi-cate these points clearly in the weight and bal-

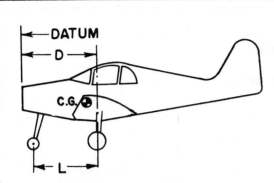

NOSE WHEEL TYPE AIRCRAFT

DATUM LOCATED FORWARD OF THE MAIN WHEELS

$$C.G. = D - \left(\frac{F \times L}{W}\right)$$

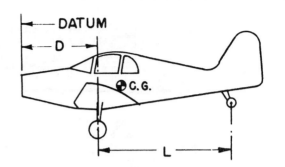

TAIL WHEEL TYPE AIRCRAFT

DATUM LOCATED FORWARD OF THE MAIN WHEELS

$$C.G. = D + \left(\frac{R \times L}{W}\right)$$

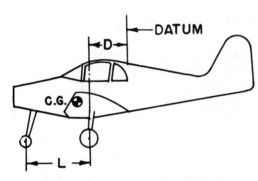

NOSE WHEEL TYPE AIRCRAFT

DATUM LOCATED AFT OF THE MAIN WHEELS

$$C.G. = -\left(D + \frac{F \times L}{W}\right)$$

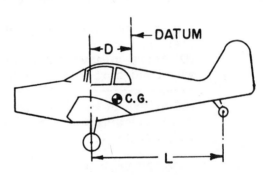

TAIL WHEEL TYPE AIRCRAFT

DATUM LOCATED AFT OF THE MAIN WHEELS

$$C.G. = -D + \left(\frac{R \times L}{W}\right)$$

CG = Distance from datum to center of gravity of the aircraft.
W = The weight of the aircraft at the time of weighing.
D = The horizontal distance measured from the datum to the main wheel weighing point.
L = The horizontal distance measured from the main wheel weighing point to the nose or tail weighing point.
F = The weight at the nose weighing point.
R = The weight at the tail weighing point.

FIGURE 13.4.—Empty weight center-of-gravity formulas.

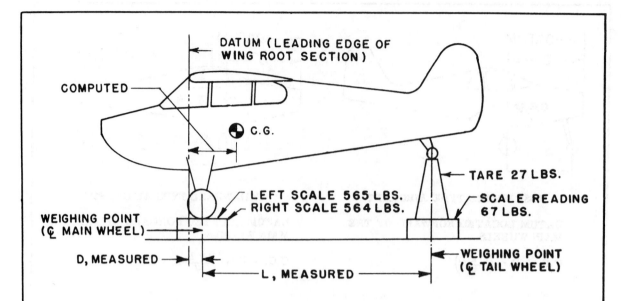

TO FIND: EMPTY WEIGHT AND EMPTY WEIGHT CENTER OF GRAVITY

Datum is the leading edge of the wing (from aircraft specification)

(D) Actual measured horizontal distance from the main wheel weighing point ℄ main wheel) to the Datum--3"

(L) Actual measured horizontal distance from the rear wheel weighing point (℄ rear wheel) to the main wheel weighing point--222"

SOLVING: EMPTY WEIGHT

Weighing Point	Scale Reading #	Tare #	Net Weight #
Right	564	0	564
Left	565	0	565
Rear	67	27	40
Empty Weight (W)			1169

SOLVING: EMPTY WEIGHT CENTER OF GRAVITY

Formula: $C.G. = D + \dfrac{R \times L}{W} = 3" + \dfrac{40 \times 222}{1169} = 3" + 7.6" = 10.6"$

Reference for formula, Figure 13.4

This case is shown properly entered on a sample weight and balance report form, Figure 13.17

FIGURE 13.5.—Empty weight and empty weight center of gravity—tail-wheel type aircraft.

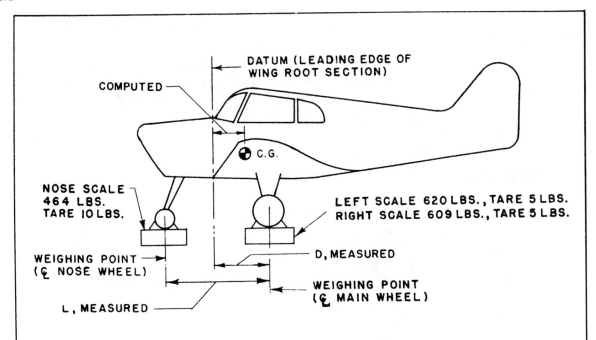

TO FIND: EMPTY WEIGHT AND EMPTY WEIGHT CENTER OF GRAVITY

Datum is the leading edge of the wing (from aircraft specification)

(D) Actual measured horizontal distance from the main wheel weight point (₵ main wheel) to the Datum-- 34.0''

(L) Actual measured horizontal distance from the front wheel weighing point (₵ front wheel) to the main wheel weighing point-- 67.8''

SOLVING: EMPTY WEIGHT

Weighing Point	Scale Reading #	Tare #	Net Weight
Right	609	5	604
Left	620	5	615
Front	4 64	10	454
Empty Weight (W)			1673

SOLVING: EMPTY WEIGHT CENTER OF GRAVITY

Formula: $C.G. = D - \dfrac{F \times L}{W} = 34'' - \dfrac{454 \times 67.8}{1673} = 34'' - 18.3'' = 15.7''$

Reference for formula, Figure 13.4.

FIGURE 13.6.—Empty weight and empty weight center-of-gravity—nose-wheel type aircraft.

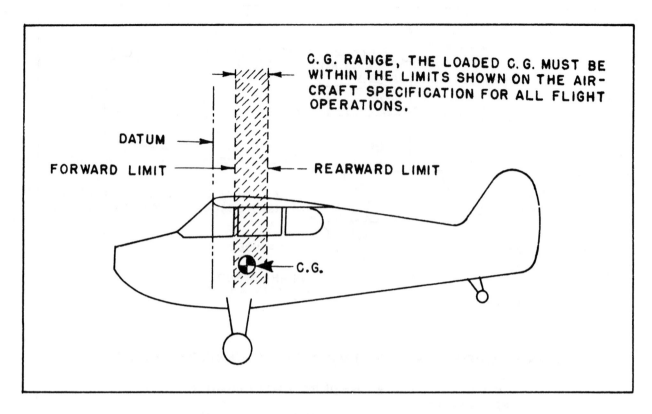

FIGURE 13.7.—Operating center-of-gravity range.

ance report when used in lieu of the landing gear. Typical locations of the weighing points are shown in figure 13.8.

n. Zero fuel weight is the maximum permissible weight of a loaded aircraft (passengers, crew, cargo, etc.) less its fuel. All weights in excess of maximum zero fuel weight must consist of usable fuel.

* **o. Minimum fuel.** Minimum fuel for balance purposes is 1/12 gallon per maximum-except-take-off horsepower (METO), and is the maximum amount of fuel which could be used in weight and balance computations when low fuel might adversely affect the most critical balance conditions. To determine the weight of fuel in pounds divide the METO horsepower by two.   *

p. Full Oil. Full oil is the quantity of oil shown in the aircraft specifications as oil capacity. Use full oil as the quantity of oil when making the loaded weight and balance computations.

q. Tare. Tare is the weight of chocks, blocks, stands, etc., used when weighing aircraft, and is included in the scale readings. Tare is deducted from the scale reading at each respective weighing point where tare is involved to obtain the actual aircraft weight.

*658. WEIGHING PROCEDURE. Weighing procedures may vary with the aircraft and the type of weighing equipment employed. The weighing procedures contained in the manufacturing manual should be followed for each particular aircraft. Accepted procedures when weighing an aircraft are: *

a. Remove excessive dirt, grease, moisture, etc., from the aircraft before weighing.

b. Weigh the aircraft inside a closed building to prevent error in scale reading due to wind.

c. To determine the c.g., place the aircraft in a level flight attitude.

d. Have all items of equipment included in the certificated empty weight installed in the aircraft when weighing. These items of equipment are

* a part of the current weight and balance report. (See paragraph 662.)

e. *Properly calibrate,* zero, and use the scales in accordance with the scale manufacturer's instructions. The scales and suitable support for the aircraft, if necessary, are usually placed *

This page intentionally left blank.

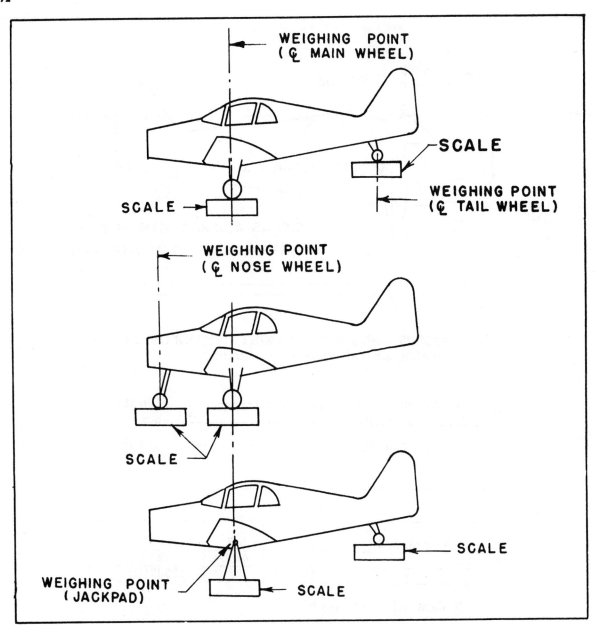

FIGURE 13.8.—Weighing point centerline.

under the wheels of a landplane, the keel of a seaplane float, or the skis of a skiplane. Other structural locations capable of supporting the aircraft, such as jack pads, may be used. Clearly indicate these points in the weight and balance report.

f. Unless otherwise noted in the aircraft specification, drain the fuel system until the quantity indicator reads "zero" or empty with the aircraft in level flight attitude. The amount of fuel remaining in the tank, lines, and engine is termed "residual fuel" and it is to be included in the empty weight. In special cases, the aircraft may be weighed with full fuel in tanks provided a definite means of determining the exact weight of the fuel is available.

g. Unless otherwise noted in the aircraft specification, the oil system should be completely

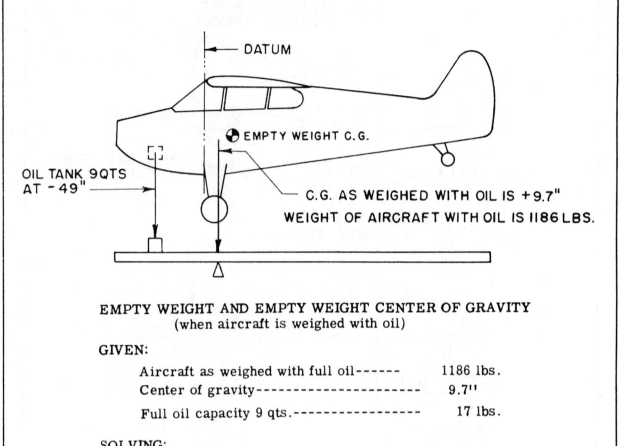

EMPTY WEIGHT AND EMPTY WEIGHT CENTER OF GRAVITY
(when aircraft is weighed with oil)

GIVEN:

Aircraft as weighed with full oil------	1186 lbs.
Center of gravity---------------------	9.7''
Full oil capacity 9 qts.----------------	17 lbs.

SOLVING:

	Weight # x	Arm'' =	Moment ''#
Aircraft as weighed	+ 1186	+ 9.7	+ 11504
Less oil	- 17	- 49.0	+ 833
Total	+ 1169(A)		+ 12337(B)

Empty Weight (A) = 1169 pounds.

Empty Weight Center of Gravity $\quad \dfrac{B}{A} = \dfrac{12337}{1169} = +10.6''$

FIGURE 13.9.—Empty weight and empty weight center-of-gravity when aircraft is weighed with oil.

drained with all drain cocks open. Under these conditions, the amount of oil remaining in the oil tank, lines and engine is termed "residual oil," and it will be included in the empty weight. When weighed with full oil, actual empty weight equals the actual recorded weight less the weight of the oil in the oil tank (oil weight = oil capacity in gallons × 7.5 pounds). Indicate in all weight and balance reports whether weights include full oil or oil drained (see figure 13.9).

h. Do not set brakes while taking scale reading.

i. *Note tare* when the aircraft is removed from the scales.

659. WEIGHT AND BALANCE COMPUTATIONS.

It is often necessary, after completing an extensive alteration, to establish by computation that the authorized weight or c.g. limits as shown on the Type Certificate Data Sheets and Specifications (TCDS) are not exceeded. Paragraph b. explains the significance of algebraic signs used in balance computations.

The Aircraft Specifications contain the following information relating to the subject:

- Center of gravity range.

- Empty weight c.g. range when applicable.

- Leveling means.

- Datum.

- Maximum weights.

- Number of seats and arm.

- Maximum baggage and arm.

- Fuel capacity and arm.

- Oil capacity and arm.

- Equipment items and arm.

The FAA TCDS do not list the basic required equipment prescribed by the applicable airworthiness regulations for certification. Refer to the manufacturer's equipment list for such information.

a. *Unit Weight for Weight and Balance Purposes.*

Gasoline ------------------ 6 pounds per U.S. gal.

Turbine Fuel ------------ 6.7 pounds per U.S. gal.

Lubricating oil ------ 7.5 pounds per U.S. gal.

Crew and

passengers ---------------- 170 pounds per person.

b. *Algebraic Signs.* It is important to retain the proper algebraic sign (+ or –) through all balance computations. For the sake of uniformity in these computations, visualize the aircraft with the nose to the left. In this position any arm to the left (forward) of the datum is "minus" and any arm to the right (rearward) of the datum is "plus." Any item of weight added to the aircraft either side of the datum is plus weight. Any weight item removed is a minus weight. When multiplying weights by arms, the answer is plus if the signs are alike, and minus if the signs are unlike.

The following combinations are possible:

Items added forward of the datum—

(+) weight x (–) arm = (–) moment.

Items added to the rear of the datum—

(+) weight x (+) arm = (+) moment.

Items removed forward of the datum—

(–) weight x (–) arm = (+) moment.

Items removed rear of the datum—

(–) weight x (+) arm = (–) moment.

The total weight of the airplane is equal to the weight of the empty aircraft plus the weight of the items added, minus the weight of the items removed.

The total moment of the aircraft is the algebraic sum of the empty weight moment of the aircraft and all of the individual moments of the items added and/or removed.

660. WEIGHT AND BALANCE EXTREME CONDITIONS. The weight and balance extreme conditions represent the maximum forward and rearward c.g. position for the aircraft. Include the weight and balance data information showing that the c.g. of the aircraft (usually in the fully loaded condition) falls between the extreme conditions.

a. *Forward Weight and Balance Check.* When a forward weight and balance check is made, establish that neither the maximum weight nor the forward c.g. limit listed in the Aircraft Specifications is exceeded. To make this check, the following information is needed:

(1) The weights, arms, and moment of the empty aircraft.

(2) The maximum weights, arms, and moments of the items of useful load which are located ahead of the forward c.g. limit; and

(3) The minimum weights, arms, and moments of the items of useful load which are located aft of the forward c.g. limit.

*A typical example of the computation necessary to make this check, using the above data, is shown in figure 13.10.

b. *Rearward Weight and Balance Check.* When a rearward weight and balance check is made, establish that neither the maximum weight nor the rearward c.g. limit listed in the*

This page intentionally left blank.

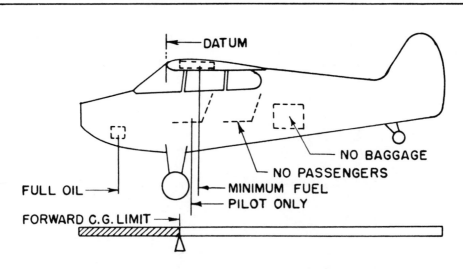

TO CHECK: MOST FORWARD WEIGHT AND BALANCE EXTREME.

GIVEN: Actual empty weight of the airplane -------------- 1169#
Empty weight center of gravity ----------------- +10.6''
*Maximum weight --------------------------- 2100#
*Forward C.G. limit -------------------------- + 8.5''
*Oil, capacity 9 qts. ------------------------- 17# at - 49
*Pilot in farthest forward seat equipped with
controls (unless otherwise placarded) ----------- 170# at + 16''
*Since the fuel tank is located to the rear of
the forward C.G. limit, minimum fuel should be
included. $\dfrac{\text{METO HP}}{12} = \dfrac{165}{12} = 13.75$ gal. x 6# ------- 83# at + 22''

*Information should be obtained from the aircraft specification.

Note: Any items or passengers must be used if they are located
ahead of the forward C.G. limit.
Full fuel must be used if the tank is located ahead of the
forward C.G. limit.

CHECK OF FORWARD WEIGHT AND BALANCE EXTREME

	Weight (#)	x Arm ('')	= Moment (''#)
Aircraft Empty	+ 1169	+ 10.6	+ 12391
Oil	+ 17	- 49	- 833
Pilot	+ 170	+ 16	+ 2720
Fuel	+ 83	+ 22	+ 1826
Total	+ 1439 (TW)		+ 16104 (TM)

Divide the TM (Total Moment) by the TW (Total Weight) to obtain
the forward weight and balance extreme.
$$\frac{TM}{TW} = \frac{16104}{1439} = + 11.2''$$

Since the forward C.G. limit and the maximum weight are not
exceeded, the forward weight and balance extreme condition is
satisfactory.

FIGURE 13.10.—Example of check of most forward weight and balance extreme.

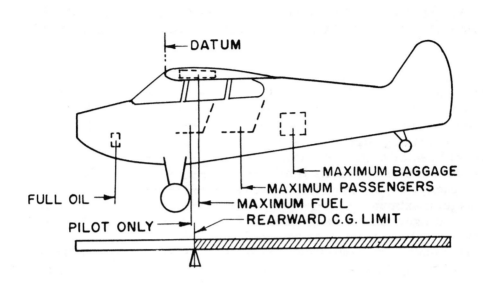

TO CHECK: MOST REARWARD WEIGHT AND BALANCE EXTREME.

GIVEN: Actual empty weight of the airplane --------- 1169#
        Empty weight center of gravity ------------- 10.6''
        *Maximum weight ------------------------ 2100#
        *Rearward C.G. limit --------------------- 21.9''
        *Oil capacity 9 qts. ---------------------- 17# at - 49''
        *Baggage, placarded do not exceed 100 lbs. --- 100# at + 75.5''
        *Two passengers in rear seats, 170 x 2 ------ 340# at + 48''
        *Pilot in most rearward seat equipped with
         controls (unless otherwise placarded) ------- 170# at + 16''
        *Since the fuel tank is located aft of the
         rearward C.G. limit full fuel must be used --- 240# at + 22''

        * Information should be obtained from the aircraft specification.

        Note: If fuel tanks are located ahead of the rearward C.G. limit
               minimum fuel should be used.

CHECK OF REARWARD WEIGHT AND BALANCE EXTREME

	Weight (#)	x Arm ('')	= Moment (''#)
Aircraft empty	+ 1169	+ 10.6	+ 12391
Oil	+ 17	- 49	- 833
Pilot (1)	+ 170	+ 16	+ 2720
Passengers (2)	+ 340	+ 48	+ 16320
Fuel (40 gals.)	+ 240	+ 22	+ 5280
Baggage	+ 100	+ 75.5	+ 7550
Total	+ 2036 (TW)		+ 43428 (TM)

Divide the TM (Total Moment) by the TW (Total Weight) to obtain the
rearward weight and balance extreme.

$$\frac{TM}{TW} = \frac{43428}{2036} = + 21.3''$$

Since the rearward C.G. limit and the maximum weight are not exceeded,
the rearward weight and balance extreme condition is satisfactory.

FIGURE 13.11.—Example of check of most rearward weight and balance extreme.

EXAMPLE OF THE DETERMINATION OF THE NUMBER OF
PASSENGERS AND BAGGAGE PERMISSIBLE WITH FULL FUEL

GIVEN:

Actual empty weight of the aircraft ------------------ 1169#
Empty weight center of gravity ---------------------- 10.6"
Maximum weight ------------------------------------- 2100#
Datum is leading edge of the wing
  Forward center of gravity limit --------------------- 8.5"
  Rearward center of gravity limit -------------------- 21.9"
Oil capacity, 9 qts.; show full capacity --------------- 17# at –49"
Baggage, maximum ---------------------------------- 100# at +75.5"
Two passengers in rear seat, 170# x 2 -------------- 340# at +48"
Pilot in most rearward seat equipped with
controls (unless otherwise placarded) -------------- 170# at +16"
Full fuel, 40 gals. x 6# ---------------------------- 240# at +22"

	Weight(#)	x Arm(")	= Moment("#)
Aircraft empty	+ 1169	+ 10.6	+ 12391
Oil	+ 17	– 49	– 833
Full fuel	+ 240	+ 22	+ 5280
Passengers, 2 rear	+ 340 *	+ 48	+ 16320
Pilot	+ 170	+ 16	+ 2720
Baggage	+ 100	+ 75.5	+ 7550
Total	+ 2036 (TW)		+ 43428 (TM)

Divide the TM (total moment) by the TW (total weight) to obtain the
loaded center of gravity.

$$\frac{TM}{TW} = \frac{43428}{2036} = +21.3"$$

The above computations show that with full fuel, 100 pounds of baggage
and two passengers in the rear seat may be carried in this aircraft
without exceeding either the maximum weight or the approved C.G. range.

This condition may be entered in the loading schedule as follows:

GALLONS OF FUEL	NUMBER OF PASSENGERS	POUNDS OF BAGGAGE
Full	2 Rear	100

* Only two passengers are listed to prevent the maximum weight
  of 2100 lbs. from being exceeded.

FIGURE 13.12.—Loading conditions: determination of the number of passengers and baggage permissible with full fuel.

Par 660

Chap 13

aircraft specification is exceeded. To make this check, the following information is needed:

(1) The weight, arms, and moments of empty aircraft;

(2) The maximum weights, arms, and moments of the items of useful load which are located aft of the rearward c.g. limit; and

(3) The minimum weights, arms, and moments of the items of useful load which are located ahead of the rearward c.g. limit.

A typical example of the computation necessary to make this check, using the above data, is shown in figure 13.11.

661. LOADING CONDITIONS AND/OR PLACARDS. If the following items have not been covered in the weight and balance extreme condition checks, or are not covered by suitable placards in the aircraft, additional computations are necessary.

These computations should indicate the permissible distribution of fuel, passengers, and baggage which may be carried in the aircraft at any one time without exceeding either the maximum weight or c.g. range. The conditions to check are:

a. With full fuel, determine the number of passengers and baggage permissible.

b. With maximum passengers, determine the fuel and baggage permissible.

(1) Examples of the computations for the above items are given in figures 13.12, 13.13, and 13.14 respectively. The above cases are mainly applicable to the lighter type personal aircraft. In the case of the larger type transport aircraft, a variety of loading conditions is possible and it is necessary to have a loading schedule.

662. EQUIPMENT LIST. A list of the equipment included in the certificated empty weight may be found in either the approved Airplane Flight Manual or the weight and balance report. Enter in the weight and balance report all required, optional and special equipment installed in the aircraft at time of weighing and/or subsequent equipment changes.

a. Required equipment items are items so listed in the pertinent aircraft specification.

b. Optional equipment items are so listed in the pertinent aircraft specification and may be installed in the aircraft at the option of the owner.

c. Special equipment is any item not corresponding exactly to the descriptive information in the aircraft specification. This includes such items as flares, instruments, ashtrays, radios, navigation lights, carpets, etc.

d. Required and optional equipment may be shown on the equipment list making reference to the pertinent item number listed in the applicable specification only when they are identical to that number item with reference to description, weight, and arm given in the specification. Show all special equipment items by making reference to the item by name, make, model, weight, and arm. When the arm for such an item is not available, determine by actual measurement.

(1) **Equipment Changes.** The person making an equipment change is obligated to make an entry on the equipment list indicating items added, removed, or relocated with the date accomplished, and identify himself by name and certificate number in the aircraft records. Examples of items so affected are the installation of extra fuel tanks, seats, or baggage compartments. Figure 13.15 illustrates the effect on balance when equipment items are added within the acceptable c.g. limits and fore and aft of the established c.g. limits. Moment computations for typical equipment changes are given in figure 13.16 and are also included in the sample weight and balance sheet in figure 13.18.

663. SAMPLE WEIGHT AND BALANCE REPORT. Suggested methods of tabulating the various data and computations for determining the c.g., both in the empty weight condition and fully loaded condition, are given in figures 13.17 and 13.18, respectively, and represent a suggested means of recording this information. The data presented in figure 13.17 have previously been computed in figures 13.10 and

EXAMPLE OF THE DETERMINATION OF THE POUNDS OF FUEL AND BAGGAGE PERMISSIBLE WITH MAXIMUM PASSENGERS

	Weight (#)	x Arm (")	= Moment ("#)
Aircraft empty	+ 1169	+ 10.6	+ 12391
Oil	+ 17	– 49	– 833
Pilot	+ 170	+ 16	+ 2720
Passenger, 1 front	+ 170	+ 16	+ 2720
Passengers, 2 rear	+ 340	+ 48	+ 16320
Fuel (39 gals.)	+ 234	+ 22	+ 5148
Baggage	---	---	---
Total	+ 2100		+ 38466

Divide the TM (total moment) by the TW (total weight) to obtain the loaded center of gravity.

$$\frac{TM}{TW} = \frac{38466}{2100} = + 18.3''$$

The above computations show that with the maximum number of passengers, 39 gallons of fuel and zero pounds of baggage may be carried in this aircraft without exceeding either the maximum weight or the approved C.G. range.

This condition may be entered in the loading schedule as follows:

GALLONS OF FUEL	NUMBER OF PASSENGERS	POUNDS OF BAGGAGE
* FULL	*2 rear	* 100
39	1(F) 2(R)	None

* Conditions as entered from Figure 13.12
(F) Front seat
(R) Rear seat

FIGURE 13.13.—Loading conditions: determination of the fuel and baggage permissible with maximum passengers.

13.11 for the extreme load conditions, and figure 13.16 for equipment change and represent suggested means of recording this information.

664. INSTALLATION OF BALLAST. Ballast is sometimes permanently installed for c.g. balance purposes as a result of installation or removal of equipment items and is not used to correct a nose-up or nose-down tendency of an aircraft. It is usually located as far aft or as far forward as possible in order to bring the c.g. position within acceptable limits with a minimum of weight increase. Permanent ballast is often

EXAMPLE OF THE DETERMINATION OF THE FUEL AND THE NUMBER AND LOCATION OF PASSENGERS PERMISSIBLE WITH MAXIMUM BAGGAGE

	Weight (#)	x Arm ('')	= Moment (''#)
Aircraft empty	+ 1169	+ 10.6	+ 12391
Oil	+ 17	- 49	- 833
Pilot	+ 170	+ 16	+ 2720
Passenger (1) rear	+ 170	+ 48	+ 8160
Passenger (1) front	+ 170	+ 16	+ 2720
Fuel (40 gals.)	+ 240	+ 22	+ 5280
Baggage	+ 100	+ 75.5	+ 7550
Total	+ 2036		+ 37988

Divide the TM (total moment) by the TW (total weight) to obtain the loaded center of gravity.

$$\frac{TM}{TW} = \frac{37988}{2036} = + 18.7$$

The above computations show that with maximum baggage, full fuel and 2 passengers (1 in the front seat and 1 in the rear seat) may be carried in this aircraft without exceeding either the maximum weight or the approved C.G. range.

This condition may be entered in the loading schedule as follows:

GALLONS OF FUEL	NUMBER OF PASSENGERS	POUNDS OF BAGGAGE
* Full	* 2 Rear	*100
** 39	*1(F) 2(R)	**None
Full	1(F) 1(R)	Full

```
 *  Conditions as entered from Figure 13.12
**  Conditions as entered from Figure 13.13
   (F)  Front seat
   (R)  Rear seat
```

FIGURE 13.14.—Loading conditions: determination of the fuel and the number and location of passengers permissible with maximum baggage.

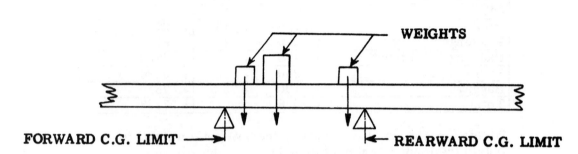

Weights added anywhere between the C.G. limits
will not upset the balance of the aircraft.

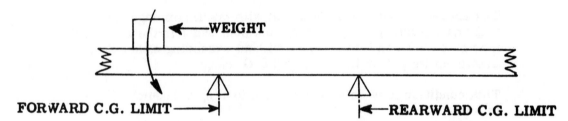

Any weights added ahead of the forward C.G. limit would tend to
upset the balance around the forward balance limit.

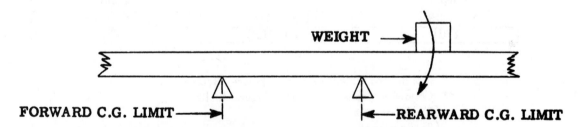

Any weights added aft of the rearward C.G. limit would tend to
upset the balance around the rearward balance limit.

FIGURE 13.15.—Effects of the addition of equipment items on balance.

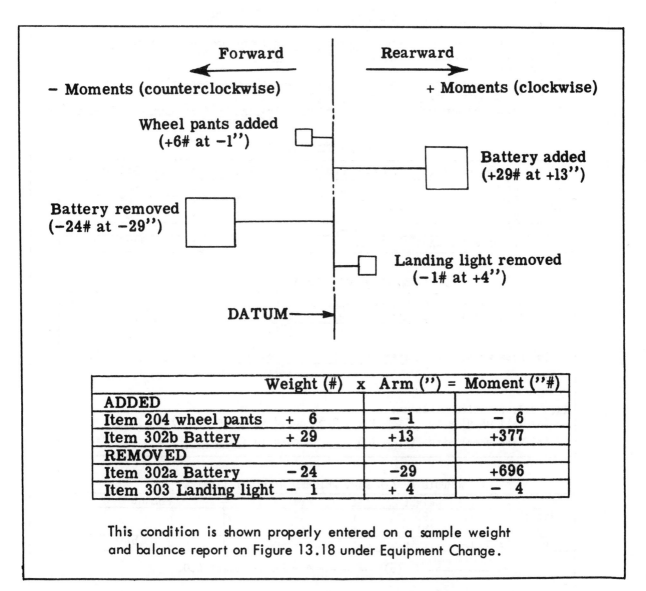

FIGURE 13.16.—Example of moment and weight changes resulting from equipment changes.

MAKE __MA-700__ MODEL ___A___ SERIAL # __0000__ REGISTRATION # __N1234__
DATUM IS ____leading edge of wing.____

COMPUTE AS FOLLOWS IF AIRCRAFT WEIGHED

1. Leveling means: level top longeron between front and rear seats.
2. Main wheel weighing point is located (_____"FORWARD)(+__3__" AFT) of datum.
3. Actual measured distance from the main weight point centerline to the tail (or nose) point centerline_222_".
4. Oil over and above "ZERO" tank reading = (a.__–__ Gals.)(b.__–__ Lbs.)(c.__–__ In.)

ACTUAL EMPTY WEIGHT

	Weight Point	Scale Reading	– Tare	= Net Weight
5.	Right	564	0	564
6.	Left	565	0	565
7.	Tail	67	27	40
8.	Nose	——	——	——
9.	Total Net Weight			1169

CENTER OF GRAVITY AS WEIGHED

10. C.G. relative to main wheel weighing point:
    (a) Tail wheel airc. (item 3, 222) X (Item 7, 40) = + _7.6_ = C.G.
    (Item 9, 1169)

    (b) Nose wheel airc. (Item 3 ——) X (Item 8 ——) = _____ = C.G.
    (Item 9 ——)

11. C.G. relative to datum:
    (a) Tail wheel airc. (Item 10a, + 7.6) added to (Item 2, + 3) = + 10.6" = C.G.
    (b) Nose wheel airc. (Item 10b, _____) added to (Item 2, ___) = _____ = C.G.

COMPUTE IF AIRCRAFT WEIGHED WITH OIL (Item 4)

	Weight X	Arm =	Moment
Aircraft	(9)	(11)	
Less Oil	(4b)	(4c)	
Empty Totals	(a)		(b)

(b)———————— = (c)————————" = Empty weight C.G.

12.   (a)

REPAIR AGENCY_____ _____ DATE_____
                          Name   Number

FIGURE 13.17.—Sample weight and balance report to determine empty weight center-of-gravity.

EQUIPMENT LIST

*Required or Optional Item Numbers as Shown in Aircraft Specification

1	2	101	102	103	104	105
106	201	202	203	301	302(a)	303
401(a)	402	----	----	----	---	----

Special Equipment

Item	Make	Model	Weight	Arm
3 Flares 1½ Min.	XYZ	03	25#	150"

Enter above those items included in the empty weight.

WEIGHT AND BALANCE EXTREME CONDITIONS

Approved fwd limit 8.5"   Approved max.weight 2100#   Approved aft limit 21.9"

Item	FORWARD CHECK			REARWARD CHECK		
	Weight X	Arm =	Moment	Weight X	Arm =	Moment
Airc.Empty	+ 1169 (9 or 12a)	+ 10.6 (11 or 12c)	+ 12391	+ 1169 (9 or 12a)	+ 10.6 (11 or 12c)	+ 12391
Oil	+ 17	- 49	- 833	+ 17	- 49	- 833
Pilot	+ 170	+ 16	+ 2720	+ 170	+ 16	+ 2720
Fuel	+ 83	+ 22	+ 1826	+ 240	+ 22	+ 5280
Passenger(s)				+ 340	+ 48	+ 16320
Baggage				+ 100	+ 75.5	+ 7550
TOTAL	+ 1439= TW		+ 16104= TM	+ 2036=TW		+ 43428=TM

$$\frac{TM}{TW} = \frac{16104}{1439} = +11.2" = \qquad \frac{TM}{TW} = \frac{43428}{2036} = +21.3" =$$

Most Forward C.G. location   Most rearward C.G. location

LOADING SCHEDULE

Gallons of Fuel	Number of Passengers	Pounds of Baggage
40	2(R)	100

The above includes pilot and capacity oil.

EQUIPMENT CHANGE

Computing New C.G.

Item, Make, and Model*	Weight	X	Arm	=	Moment
Airc. Empty	+ 1169 (9 or 12a)		+ 10.6 (11 or 12c)		+ 12391
204 added	+ 6		- 1		- 6
302(b) added	+ 29		+ 13		+ 377
302(a) removed	- 24		- 29		+ 696
303 removed	- 1		+ 4		- 4
NET TOTALS	- 1179 = NW				+ 13454 = NM

$$\frac{NM}{NW} = \frac{13454}{1179} = + 11.4" = \text{New C.G.}$$

*ITEM NUMBERS WHEN LISTED IN PERTINENT AIRCRAFT SPECIFICATION MAY BE USED IN LIEU OF "ITEM, MAKE, AND MODEL".

PREPARED BY _____   DATE_____

FIGURE 13.18.—Sample weight and balance report including an equipment change for aircraft fully loaded.

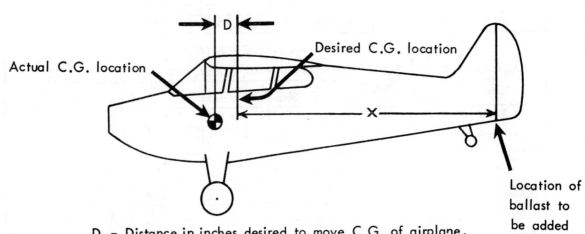

D – Distance in inches desired to move C.G. of airplane.

W – Weight of airplane as loaded.

X – Distance in inches from point where ballast is to be installed, to the desired location of the new C.G.

B – Weight of ballast required in pounds.

$$B = \frac{D \times W}{X}$$

Compute the new C.G. of the aircraft with ballast installed.

NOTE: If greater accuracy is desired, repeat the entire formula using the NEW aircraft weight and the NEW C.G. in the second operation.

FIGURE 13.19.—Permanent ballast computation formula.

in the form of lead plate wrapped around and/or bolted to the fuselage primary structure (tail-post, longerons, or bulkhead members). Permanent ballast invariably constitutes a concentrated load; therefore, the strength of the local structure and the attachment of the ballast thereto should be investigated for the design loading conditions pertinent to the particular aircraft. Placard permanent ballast "Permanent ballast—do not remove." It is not desirable to install permanent ballast by pouring melted lead into the tail-post or longerons, due to difficulties that may be encountered in subsequent welding repair operations. It should be noted that the installation of permanent ballast results in an increase of aircraft empty weight. See figure 13.19 for ballast computation. When disposable ballast is carried, the local strength of the compartment in which the ballast is carried and the effect of the ballast on aircraft balance and weight should be investigated.

665. LOADING SCHEDULE. The loading schedule should be kept with the aircraft and usually forms a part of the airplane flight manual. It includes instructions on the proper load distribution, such as filling of fuel and oil tanks, passenger seating, restrictions of passenger movement; distribution of cargo, etc.

a. Other means of determining safe loading conditions, such as the use of a graphical index, load adjuster, etc., are acceptable and may be used in lieu of the information in paragraph 661.

b. Compute a separate loading condition when the aircraft is to be loaded in other than the specified conditions shown in the loading schedule.

666.–676. RESERVED.

Chapter 14.   ENGINES AND FUEL SYSTEMS

Section 1.   ENGINES

677. GENERAL. Persons should avail themselves of the manufacturer's manuals, service bulletins, and instruction books regarding the repair and overhaul, inspection, installation, and maintenance of aircraft engines. The repair and overhaul of engines are too many and varied for the different types and models of engines to be mentioned here in specific detail.

678. INSPECTION. All moving and/or highly-stressed parts and those subjected to high temperature should have a critical visual inspection at the time of overhaul. It is often necessary to supplement the visual inspection by employing one of the following procedures:

   a. *Wet or dry magnetic dust inspection* of magnetic materials;

   b. *wet or dry penetrant inspection* of non-magnetic materials;

   c. *x-ray or sonic inspection* of any material; or

   d. *hydrostatic inspection* testing of fluid lines and internal passages and assemblies such as cylinder heads.

*679. POWERPLANT SUDDEN STOPPAGE. Sudden stoppage is a very rapid and complete stoppage of the engine. It can be caused by engine seizure or by one or more of the propeller blades striking an object in such a way that r.p.m. goes to zero in less than one complete revolution of the propeller. Sudden stoppage may occur under such conditions as complete and rapid collapse of the landing gear, nosing over the aircraft, or crash landing. Sudden stoppage can cause internal damage, such as cracked propeller gear teeth, gear train damage in the rear section, crankshaft misalignment, or damaged propeller bearings. When sudden stoppage occurs, the engine is usually replaced. Any aircraft powerplant that has been sub- * jected to sudden stoppage should be inspected to the extent necessary to assure continued safe operation. These procedures will serve as a guide for locating damage that may occur whenever an aircraft powerplant has been subjected to sudden deceleration or stoppage.

To fully evaluate any unsatisfactory findings resulting from this type of inspection, it will be necessary to refer to the applicable manufacturer's service and overhaul data. In addition, many of the prime aeronautical engine manufacturers now have specific recommendations on the subject of sudden stoppage involving their products. To assure continued airworthiness and reliability, it is essential that such data be used. In the event the manufacturer has not specified an instruction to follow, the following may be used as a guideline.

   a. *Reciprocating Engine (Direct Drive).*

   (1) Powerplant Exterior Inspection. Remove the engine cowling and examine the engine for visible external damage and audible internal damage.

   (a) Rotate the propeller shaft to determine any evidence of abnormal grinding or sounds.

   (b) With the propeller removed, inspect the crankshaft flange or splines for signs of twisting, cracks, or other deformation. Remove the thrust-bearing nut and seal and thoroughly inspect the threaded area of the shaft for evidence of cracks.

   (c) Rotate the shaft slowly in 90° increments while using a dial indicator or an equivalent instrument to check the concentricity of the shaft.

*   **(d)** Remove the oil sump drain plug and check for metal chips and foreign material.

      (e) Remove and inspect the oil screens for metal particles and contamination.

      (f) Visually inspect engine case exterior for signs of oil leakage and cracks. Give particular attention to the propeller thrust-bearing area of the nose case section.   *

This page intentionally left blank.

(g) Inspect cylinders and cylinder hold-down area for cracks and oil leaks. Thoroughly investigate any indication of cracks, oil leaks or other damage.

(2) Powerplant Internal Inspection.

(a) On engines equipped with crankshaft vibration dampers, remove the cylinders necessary to inspect the dampers and inspect in accordance with the engine manufacturer's inspection and overhaul manual. When engine design permits, remove the damper pins, and examine the pins and damper liners for signs of nicks or brinelling.

(b) After removing the engine-driven accessories remove the accessory drive case and examine the accessory and supercharger drive gear train, couplings, and drive case for evidence of damage.

1. Check for cracks in the case in the area of accessory mount pads and gear shaft bosses.

2. Check the gear train for signs of cracked, broken, or brinelled teeth.

3. Check the accessory drive shaft couplings for twisted splines, misalignment and runout.

(3) Accessory and Drive Inspection. Check the drive shaft of each accessory, i.e., magnetos, generators, external supercharger, and pumps for evidence of damage.

(4) Engine Mount Inspection.

(a) Examine the engine flex mounts when applicable for looseness, distortion, or signs of tear.

(b) Inspect the engine mount structure for bent, cracked, or buckled tubes.

(c) Check the adjacent airframe structure for cracks, distortion, or wrinkles.

(d) Remove engine mount bolts and mount holddown bolts and inspect for shear, cracks, or distortion.

(5) Exhaust-driven Supercharger (Turbo) Inspection. Sudden stoppage of the powerplant can cause the heat in turbine parts to heat soak the turbine seals and bearings. This excessive heat causes carbon to develop in the seal area and varnish to form on the turbine bearings and journals.

(a) Inspect all air ducts and connections for air leaks, warpage, or cracks.

(b) Remove compressor housing and check the turbine wheel for rubbing or binding.

(6) Propeller Inspection Repair. Any propeller that has struck a foreign object during service should be promptly inspected in accordance with the propeller manufacturer's prescribed procedures for possible damage resulting from this contact with the foreign object and, if necessary, repaired according to the manufacturer's instructions. If the propeller is damaged beyond the repair limits established by the propeller manufacturer and a replacement is necessary, install the same make/model or alternate approved for this installation. Refer to the aircraft manufacturer's optional equipment list, applicable FAA Aircraft Specification, Data Sheet, or Supplemental Type Certificate Data.

b. Reciprocating Engine (Geared Drive). Inspect the engine, propeller and components as in preceding paragraphs.

(1) Remove the propeller reduction gear housing and inspect for:

(a) Loose, sheared, or spalled cap screws or bolts.

(b) Cracks in the case.

(2) Disassemble the gear train and inspect the propeller shaft, reduction gears and accessory drive gears for nicks, cracks, or spalling.

c. Turbine, Engine, Ingestion Inspection. When the components of the compressor assembly or turbine section are subjected to ingestion damage, refer to the engine manufacturer's inspection and overhaul manual for specific inspection procedures and allowable tolerances. In general, an inspection after ingestion of foreign materials consists of the following areas:

(1) Inspect the external areas of the engine cases, attached parts and engine mounts for cracks, distortion, or other damage.

(2) Inspect the turbine disc for warpage or distortion.

(3) Inspect turbine disc seal for damage from rubbing or improper clearance.

(4) Inspect compressor rotor blades and stators for nicks, cracks, or distortion.

(5) Check rotor and main shaft for misalignment.

(6) Inspect shaft bearing area for oil leaks.

(7) Inspect the hot section for cracks or hot spots.

(8) Inspect the accessory drives as prescribed under paragraph a(2)(b).

NOTE: Turbine disc seal rubbing is not unusual and may be a normal condition. Consult the engine manufacturer's inspection procedures and table of limits.

d. *Turboprop Engine Inspection.*

(1) When sudden stoppage is the result of compressor ingestion of foreign material, inspect the engine as follows:

(a) Inspect the powerplant as described in paragraph c, "Turbine Engine, Ingestion Inspection."

(b) Inspect the reduction gear section as described in paragraph b(1) and b(2) where reduction gear damage is suspected.

(2) When sudden stoppage is the result of the propeller striking foreign objects, inspect the engine as follow:

(a) Inspect the reduction gear section as described in paragraph b(1) and b(2).

(b) Inspect mainline shafts and coupling shafts for runout and spiral cracks.

(c) Inspect bearings for brinelling.

(d) Inspect engine compressor and turbine blades for tip clearance.

e. *Approval for Returning Engine to Service.*

(1) Correct all discrepancies found in the foregoing inspection in accordance with the engine manufacturer's service instructions.

(2) Test run the engine to determine that the engine, propeller, and accessories are functioning properly.

(3) After shutdown, check the engine for oil leak and check oil screens for signs of contaminants.

(4) If everything is normal the engine is ready for preflight runup and test flight.

680. CRANKSHAFTS. Carefully inspect for misalignment and replace if bent beyond the manufacturer's permissible service limit. Make no attempt to straighten crankshafts damaged in service without consulting the engine manufacturer for appropriate instructions. Worn journals may be repaired by regrinding in accordance with manufacturers' instructions. It is recommended that grinding operations be performed by appropriately rated repair stations or the original engine manufacturer to assure adherence to aeronautical standards. Common errors that occur in crankshaft grinding are the removal of nitrided journal surface, improper journal radii, unsatisfactory surfaces, and grinding tool marks on the journals. If the fillets are altered, do not reduce their radii. Polish the reworked surfaces to assure removal of all tool marks. Most opposed engines have nitrided crankshafts and manufacturers specify that these crankshafts must be nitrided after grinding.

681. REPLACEMENT PARTS IN CERTIFICATED ENGINES. Only those parts which are approved under FAR Part 21 should be used. Serviceable parts obtained from the engine manufacturer, his authorized service facility, and those which are FAA/PMA approved meet the requirements of FAR Part 21 and are acceptable for use as replacement parts. It is suggested that the latest type parts as reflected on the current parts list be obtained. Parts from military surplus stocks, which are applicable to the specific engine may be used provided they were originally accepted under the military procurement agency's standards, are found to be serviceable, and are not prohibited from use by the Administrator.

a. *Parts for obsolete engines* for which new parts are no longer obtainable from the original manufacturer or his successor are sometimes fabricated locally. When it becomes necessary to do this, physical tests and careful measurements of the old part may provide adequate technical information. This procedure is usually regarded as a major change which requires engine testing and is not recommended except as a last alternative.

b. *Parts from certain military surplus* tank or ground power unit engines are used on engines used in restricted aircraft and amateur-built aircraft. Users of such parts are cautioned to determine that they do not exceed the design limits of the engine. For example, a particular tank engine utilized a piston design that developed a compression ratio well in excess of the crankshaft absorption rate of the aircraft engine counterpart—result, crankshaft failure.

682. CYLINDER HOLDDOWN NUTS AND CAPSCREWS. Great care is required in tightening cylinder holddown nuts and capscrews. They must be tightened to recommended torque limits to prevent improper stressing and to insure even loading on the cylinder flange. The installation of baffles, brackets, clips, and other extraneous parts under nuts and capscrews is not considered good practice and should be discouraged. If these baffles, brackets, etc., are not properly fabricated or made of suitable material, they may cause loosening of the nuts or capscrews even though the nuts or capscrews were properly tightened and locked at installation. Either improper prestressing or loosening of any one of these nuts or capscrews will introduce the danger of progressive stud failure with the possible loss of the engine cylinder in flight. Do not install parts made from aluminum alloy or other soft metals under cylinder holddown nuts or capscrews.

683. REUSE OF SAFETYING DEVICES. Do not use cotter pins and safety wire a second time. Flat steel-type wristpin retainers and thin lockwashers likewise should be replaced at overhaul unless the manufacturer's recommendations permit their reuse.

684. SELF-LOCKING NUTS FOR AIRCRAFT ENGINES AND ACCESSORIES. Self-locking nuts may be used on aircraft engines provided the following criteria are met:

a. Where their use is specified by the engine manufacturer in his assembly drawing, parts list, and bills of material,

b. When the nuts will not fall inside the engine should they loosen and come off,

c. When there is at least one full thread protruding beyond the nut,

d. When the edges of cotter pin or lockwire holes are well rounded to preclude damage to the locknut,

e. Prior to reuse, the effectiveness of the self-locking feature is found to be satisfactory,

f. Where the temperature will not exceed the maximum limits established for the self-locking material used in the nut. On many engines the cylinder baffles, rocker box covers, drive covers and pads, and accessory and supercharger housings are fastened with fiber insert locknuts which are limited to a maximum temperature of 250° F. Above this temperature the fiber insert will usually char and consequently lose its locking characteristic. For locations such as the exhaust pipe attachment to the cylinder, a locknut which has good locking features at elevated temperatures will give invaluable service. In a few instances, fiber insert locknuts have been approved for use on cylinder holddown studs. This practice is not generally recommended, since especially tight stud fits to the crankcase must be provided, and extremely good cooling must prevail so that low temperatures exist at this location on the specific engine for which such use is approved.

g. All proposed applications of new types of locknuts or new applications of currently used self-locking nuts must be investigated since many engines require specifically designed nuts. Such specifically designed nuts are usually required for one or more of the following reasons to provide:

(1) Heat resistance,

(2) Adequate clearance for installation and removal,

(3) For the required degree of tightening or locking ability which sometimes requires a stronger, specifically heat-treated material, a heavier cross-section, or a special locking means,

(4) Ample bearing area under the nut to reduce unit loading on softer metals, and

(5) To prevent loosening of studs when nuts are removed.

h. Information concerning approved self-locking nuts and their use on specific engines is usually found in engine manufacturer's manuals or bulletins. If the desired information is not available, it is suggested that the engine manufacturer be contacted.

685. WELDING OF HIGHLY STRESSED ENGINE PARTS.

In general, welding of highly-stressed engine parts is not recommended for parts that were not originally welded. However, under the conditions given below, welding may be accomplished if it can be reasonably expected that the welded repair will not adversely affect the airworthiness of the engine when:

a. *The weld* is externally situated and can be inspected easily;

b. *the part* has been cracked or broken as the result of unusual loads not encountered in normal operation;

c. *a new replacement part* of obsolete type engine is not available; or

d. *the welder's experience and equipment employed* will insure a first-quality weld in the type of material to be repaired and will insure restoration of the original heat treat in heat-treated parts. Refer to Chapter 2 for information on process details.

686. WELDING OF MINOR ENGINE PARTS.

Many minor parts not subjected to high stresses may be safely repaired by welding. Mounting lugs, cowl lugs, cylinder fins, covers, and many parts originally fabricated by welding are in this category. The welded part should be suitably stress-relieved after welding.

687. METALLIZING.

Metallizing internal parts of aircraft engines is not acceptable unless it is proved to the FAA that the metallized part will not adversely affect the airworthiness of the engine. Metallizing the finned surfaces of steel cylinder barrels with aluminum is acceptable, since many engines are originally manufactured in this manner.

688. PLATING.

Restore plating on engine parts in accordance with the manufacturer's instructions. In general, chromium plating should not be applied to highly stressed engine parts. Certain applications of this nature have been found to be satisfactory; however, engineering evaluation of the details for the processes used should be obtained.

a. *Dense chromium plating* of the crankpin and main journals of some small engine crankshafts has been found satisfactory, except where the crankshaft is already marginal in strength. Plating to restore worn low-stress engine parts such as accessory driven shafts and splines, propeller shaft ends, and seating surfaces of roller- and ball-type bearing races is acceptable.

b. *Porous chromium plated walls* of cylinder barrels have been found to be satisfactory for practically all types of engines. Dense or smooth chromium plating without roughened surfaces, on the other hand, has not been found to be generally satisfactory.

(1) Cylinder barrel pregrinding and chromium plating techniques used by the military are considered acceptable for all engines, and military approved facilities engaged in doing this work in accordance with military specifications are eligible for approval by the FAA.

(2) Chromium plated cylinder barrels have been required for some time to be identified in such a manner that the markings are visible with the cylinder installed. Military processed cylinders are banded with orange enamel above the mounting flange. It has been the practice to etch on either the flange edge or on the barrel skirt the processor's initials and cylinder oversize. Most plating facilities use the orange band as well as the permanent identification marks.

(3) A current list of engine and maximum permissible cylinder barrel oversize follows:

Engine manufacturer	Engine series	Maximum oversize (in.)
Air Cooled Motors (Franklin)	No oversize for sleeved cylinders..	
	Solid cylinders	0.017
Continental Motors	R–670, W–670, R9A	0.010 to 0.020
	All others	0.015
Jacobs	All	0.015
Kinner	All	0.015
Pigman, LeBlond, Rearwin, Ken Royce	All	0.025
Lycoming	All	0.010 to 0.020
Menasco	All	0.010

(Table continues on next page.)

Engine manufacturer	Engine series	Maximum oversize (in.)
Pratt & Whitney	R–2800B, C, CA, CB	0.025
	*R–959 and R–1830..........	0.030
	All others	0.020
Ranger	6–410 early cyls. 6–390	0.010
	6–410 late cyls. 6–440 (L–440) series..	0.020
Warner	All...............................	0.015
Wright	All..................................	0.020

*(The above oversize limits correspond to the manufacturer's requirements, except for P&W R–985 and R–1830 series engines.)

* NOTE: Check for latest manufacturer specifications.

"688b(4). [Deleted]—Change 3"   *

(5) Cylinder barrels which have been plated by an agency whose process is approved by the FAA and which have not been preground beyond maximum permissible limits will be considred acceptable for installation on certificated engines. It will be the reponsibility of the owner or the repairing agency to provide this proof. In some cases, it may be necessary to remove cylinders to determine the amount of oversize since this information may be etched on the mating surface of the cylinder base flange.

689. ENGINE ACCESSORIES. Overhaul and repair of engine accessories in accord with the engine and the accessory manufacturers' instructions are recommended.

690. CORROSION. Accomplish corrosion preventive measures for temporary and dead storage in accord with the instructions issued by the pertinent engine manufacturer. Avoid the use of strong solutions which contain strong caustic compounds and all solutions, polishes, cleaners, abrasives, etc., which might possibly promote corrosive action. (Refer to Chapter 6.)

691. ENGINE RUN-IN. After an aircraft engine has been overhauled, it is recommended that the pertinent aircraft engine manufacturer's run-in instructions be followed. Observe the manufacturer's recommondations concerning engine termperatures and other criteria.

Repair processes employed during overhaul often necessitate amending the manufacturer's run-in procedures. Follow the approved amended run-in procedures in such instances.

692. COMPRESSION TESTING OF AIRCRAFT ENGINE CYLINDERS. The purpose of testing cylinder compression is to determine the internal condition of the combustion chamber by ascertaining if any appreciable leakage is occurring.

a. *Types of Compression Testers.* The two basic types of compression testers currently in use are the direct compression and the differential pressure type testers. The optimum procedure would be to utilize both types of testers when checking the compression of aircraft cylinders. In this respect, it is suggested that the direct compression method be used first and the findings substantiated with the differential pressure method. This provides a cross-reference to validate the readings obtained by each method and tends to assure that the cylinder is defective before it is removed. Before beginning a compresssion test, consider the following points:

(1) When the spark plugs are removed, identify them to coincide with the cylinder. Close examination of the plugs will reveal the actual operating conditions and aid in diagnosing problems within the cylinder. Paragraph 693d. of this section contains more information on this subject.

(2) The operating and maintenance records of the engine should be reviewed. Records of previous compression tests are of assistance in determining progressive wear conditions and help to establish the necessary maintenance actions.

(3) Before beginning a compression check, precautions should be taken to prevent the accidental starting of the engine.

(b) *Direct Compression Check.* This type of compression test indicates the actual pressures within the cylinder. Although the particular defective component within the cylinder is difficult to determine with this method, the consistency of the readings for all cylinders is an indication of the condition of the engine as a whole. The following are suggested guidelines for performing a direct compression test.

(1) Thoroughly warm up the engine to operating temperatures and perform the test as soon as possible after shutdown.

(2) Remove the most accessible spark plug from each cylinder.

(3) Rotate the engine with the starter to expel any excess oil or loose carbon in the cylinders.

(4) If a complete set of compression testers is available, install one tester in each cylinder; however, if only one tester is being used, check each cylinder in turn.

(5) Rotate the engine at least three complete revolutions using the engine starter and record the compression reading.

NOTE: It is recommended that an external power source be used, if possible, as a low battery will result in a slow engine-turning rate and lower readings. This will noticeably affect the validity of the second engine test on a twin-engine aircraft.

(6) Recheck any cylinder which shows an abnormal reading when compared with the others. Any cylinder having a reading approximately 15 p.s.i. lower than the others should be suspected of being defective.

(7) If a compression tester is suspected of being defective, replace it with one known to be accurate, and recheck the compression of the affected cylinders.

c. *Differential Pressure Compression Check.* The differential pressure tester is designed to check the compression of aircraft engines by measuring the leakage through the cylinders caused by worn or damaged components. The operation of the compression tester is based on the principle that, for any given airflow through a fixed orifice, a constant pressure drop across that orifice will result. The restrictor orifice dimensions in the differential pressure tester should be sized for the particular engine as follows:

1. Engines up to 1,000 cubic inch displace-

ment .040 orifice diameter, .250 inch long, 60° approach angle.

2. Engines in excess of 1,000 cubic inch displacement .060 orifice diameter, .250 inch long, 60° approach angle.

A typical schematic diagram of the differential pressure tester is shown in figure 14.1.

As the regulated air pressure is applied to one side of the restrictor orifice with the air valve closed, there will be no leakage on the other side of the orifice and both pressure gauges will read the same. However, when the air valve is opened and leakage through the cylinder increases, the cylinder pressure gauge will record a proportionally lower reading.

(1) **Performing the Check.** The following procedures are listed to outline the principles in-

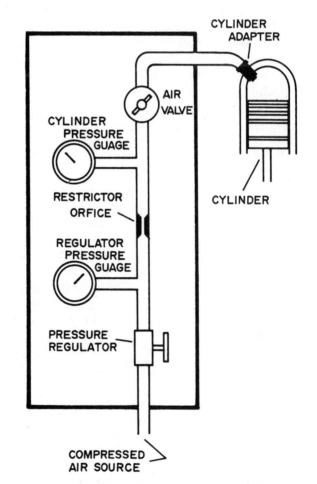

FIGURE 14.1.—Schematic of typical differential pressure compression tester.

volved, and are intended to supplement the manufacturer's instructions for the particular tester being utilized.

(a) Perform the compression test as soon as possible after the engine is shut down to ensure that the piston rings, cylinder walls, and other engine parts are well lubricated.

(b) Remove the most accessible spark plug from each cylinder.

(c) With the air valve closed, apply an external source of clean air (approximately 100 to 120 p.s.i.) to the tester.

(d) Install an adapter in the spark plug bushing and connect the compression tester to the cylinder.

(e) Adjust the pressure regulator to obtain a reading of 80 p.s.i. on the regulator pressure gauge. At this time, the cylinder pressure gauge should also register 80 p.s.i.

(f) Turn the crankshaft by hand in the direction of rotation until the piston (in the cylinder being checked) is coming up on its compression stroke. Slowly open the air valve and pressurize the cylinder to approximately 20 p.s.i.

CAUTION

Care must be exercised in opening the air valve since sufficient air pressure will have built up in the cylinder to cause it to rotate the crankshaft if the piston is not at TDC.

Continue rotating the engine against this pressure until the piston reaches top dead center (TDC). Reaching TDC is indicated by a flat spot or sudden decrease in force required to turn the crankshaft. If the crankshaft is rotated too far, back up at least one-half revolution and start over again to eliminate the effect of backlash in the valve operating mechanism and to keep piston rings seated on the lower ring lands.

(g) Open the air valve completely. Check the regulated pressure and adjust, if necessary, to 80 p.s.i.

(h) Observe the pressure indication on the cylinder pressure gauge. The difference between this pressure and the pressure shown by the regulator pressure gauge is the amount of leakage through the cylinder. A loss in excess of 25 percent of the input air pressure is cause to suspect the cylinder of being defective; how-

ever, recheck the readings after operating the engine for at least 3 minutes to allow for sealing of the rings with oil.

(i) If leakage is still occurring after a recheck, it may be possible to correct a low reading. This is accomplished by placing a fiber drift on the rocker arm directly over the valve stem and tapping the drift several times with a hammer to dislodge any foreign material between the valve face and seat.

NOTE: When correcting a low reading in this manner, rotate the propeller so the piston will not be at TDC. This is necessary to prevent the valve from striking the top of the piston in some engines. Rotate the engine before rechecking compression to reseat the valves in the normal manner.

693. SPARK PLUGS. The spark plug provides the high voltage electrical spark to ignite the fuel/air mixture in the cylinder. The types of spark plugs used in different engines will vary in regard to heat range, reach, thread size and other characteristics required by the particular installation.

a. Heat Range. The heat range of a spark plug is a measure of its ability to transfer heat to the cylinder head. The plug must operate hot enough to burn off the residue deposits which can cause fouling, yet remain cool enough to prevent a preignition condition from occurring. The length of the nose core is the principal factor in establishing the plug's heat range. "Hot" plugs have a long insulator nose thereby creating a long heat transfer path, whereas "cold" plugs have a relatively short insulator to provide a rapid transfer of heat to the cylinder head. (See figure 14.2.)

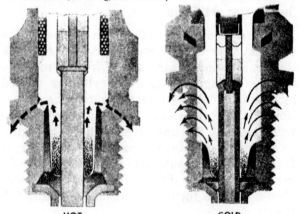

HOT   COLD

FIGURE 14.2.—Spark plug heat ranges.

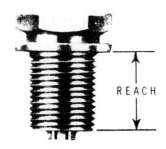

FIGURE 14.3.—Spark plug reach.

b. *Reach.* The spark plug reach (figure 14.3) is the threaded portion which is inserted into the spark plug bushing of the cylinder. A plug with the proper reach will insure that the electrode end inside the cylinder is in the best position to achieve ignition. Spark plug seizure or improper combustion within the cylinder will probably occur if a plug with the wrong reach is used.

c. *Installation Procedures.* When installing spark plugs, observe the following procedure:

(1) Visually inspect the plug for cleanliness and condition of the threads, ceramic, and electrodes.

NOTE: Never install a spark plug which has been dropped.

(2) Check the plug for the proper gap setting using a round wire feeler gauge as shown in figure 14.4. In the case of used plugs, procedures for cleaning and regapping are usually contained in the various manufacturers' manuals.

(3) Check the plug and cylinder bushing to ascertain that only one gasket is used per spark plug. When a thermocouple-type gasket is used, no other gasket is required.

(4) Apply antiseize compound sparingly to the shell threads, but do not allow the compound to contact the electrodes as the material is conductive and will short out the plug. If desired, the use of antiseize compound may be eliminated on engines equipped with stainless steel spark plug bushings or inserts.

(5) Screw the plug into the cylinder head as far as possible by hand. If the plug will not turn easily to within 2 or 3 threads of the gasket, it may be necessary to clean the threads.

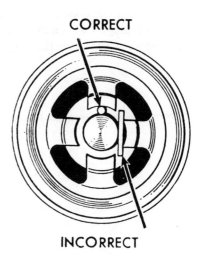

FIGURE 14.4—Method of checking spark plug gap.

NOTE: Cleaning inserts with a tap is not recommended as permanent damage to the insert may result.

(6) Seat the proper socket securely on the spark plug and tighten to the torque limit specified by the engine manufacturer before proceeding to the next plug.

Caution

A loose spark plug will not transfer heat properly and, during engine operation, may overheat to the point where the nose ceramic will become a "hot spot" and cause preignition. However, avoid overtightening as damage to the plug and bushing may result.

(7) Connect the ignition lead after wiping clean with methylethylketone (MEK), acetone, or similar material. Insert the terminal assembly into the spark plug in a straight line. (Care should be taken as improper techniques can damage the terminal sleeves.) Screw the connector nut into place until finger tight; then tighten an additional one-quarter turn while holding the elbow in the proper position.

Caution

MEK is highly toxic, read label before using. *

(8) Perform an engine runup after installing a new set of spark plugs. When the engine has reached normal operating temperatures, check the magnetos and spark plugs in accordance with the manufacturer's instructions.

d. *Operational Problems.* Whenever problems develop during engine operation which appear to

* be caused by the ignition system, it is recommended that the spark plugs and ignition harnesses be checked first before working on the magnetos. The following are the most common spark plug malfunctions and are relatively easy to identify: *

This page intentionally left blank.

(1) Fouling.

(a) *Carbon fouling* (figure 14.5a) is identified by the dull black, sooty deposits on the electrode end of the plug. Although the primary causes are excessive ground idling and rich idle mixtures, plugs with a cold heat range may also be a contributing factor.

(b) *Lead fouling* is characterized by hard, dark, cinderlike globules which gradually fill up the electrode cavity and short out the plug. (See figure 14.5b). The primary cause for this condition is poor fuel vaporization combined with a high tetraethyl-lead content fuel. Plugs with a cold heat range may also contribute to this condition.

(c) *Oil fouling* is identified by a wet, black carbon deposit over the entire firing end of the plug as shown in figure 14.5c. This condition is fairly common on the lower plugs in horizontally opposed engines, and both plugs in the lower cylinders of radial engines. Oil fouling is normally caused by oil drainage past the piston rings after shutdown. However, when both spark plugs removed from the same cylinder are badly fouled with oil and carbon, some form of engine damage should be suspected, and the cylinder more closely inspected. Mild forms of oil fouling can usually be cleared up by slowly increasing power while running the engine until the deposits are burned off and the misfiring stops.

(2) Fused Electrodes. There are many different types of malfunctions which result in

FIGURE 14.5b.—Typical lead fouled spark plug.

FIGURE 14.5c.—Typical oil fouled spark plug.

fused spark plug electrodes; however, most are associated with preignition either as the cause or the effect. For this reason, any time a spark plug is found with the following defects, further investigation of the cylinder and piston should be conducted.

(a) *Cracked Nose Ceramics.* Occasionally, the ceramic nose core will crack, break away, and remain trapped behind the ground electrode. This piece of insulation material will then build up heat to the point where it will ignite the fuel/air mixture prematurely. The high temperatures and pressures encountered during this condition can cause damage to the cylinder and piston and ultimately lead to fusing and shorting out of the plug.

FIGURE 14.5a.—Typical carbon fouled spark plug.

(b) Copper Runout. Some erosion or "cupping" of the exposed center electrode copper core is normal and will gradually decrease with the service life of the plug until it practically ceases. This condition, depicted in figure 14.6a, is not a cause for rejection until the erosion has progressed to a point more than 3/32 inch below the tip of the center electrode.

The high temperatures and pressures associated with preignition can cause the condition shown in figure 14.6b. In this instance, the copper center electrode melted and flowed out, bridged the electrodes, and caused a shorted condition.

(3) Bridged Electrodes. Occasionally, free combustion chamber particles will settle on the electrodes of a spark plug and gradually bridge the electrode gap, resulting in a shorted plug. Small particles may be dislodged by slowly cycling the engine as described for the oil-fouled condition; however, the only remedy for more advanced cases is removal and re-

FIGURE 14.7.—Typical spark plug with bridged electrodes.

placement of the spark plug. This condition is shown in figure 14.7.

(4) Metal Deposits. Whenever metal spray is found on the electrodes of a spark plug, it is an indication that a failure of some part of the engine is in progress. The location of the cylinder in which the spray is found is important in diagnosing the problem, as various types of failures will cause the metal spray to appear differently. For example, if the metal spray is located evenly in every cylinder, the problem will be in the induction system, such as an impeller failure. If the metal spray is only found on the spark plugs in one cylinder, the problem is isolated to that cylinder and will generally be a piston failure. In view of the secondary damage which occurs whenever an engine part fails, any preliminary indication such as metal spray should be thoroughly investigated to establish the cause and correct it.

(5) Flashover. It is important that spark plug terminal contact springs and moisture seals be checked regularly for condition and cleanness to prevent "flashover" in the connector well. Foreign matter or moisture in the terminal connector well can reduce the insulation value of the connector to the point where ignition system voltages at higher power settings may flash over the connector well surface to ground and cause the plug to misfire. If moisture is the cause, hard starting can also result. The cutaway spark plug shown in figure 14.8

FIGURE 14.6a.—Typical eroded spark plug.

FIGURE 14.6b.—Typical spark plug with copper runout.

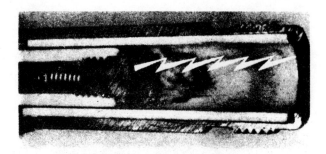

FIGURE 14.8.—Spark plug well flashover.

illustrates this malfunction. Any spark plug found with a dirty connector well may have this condition, and should be reconditioned before reuse.

e. Pre-reconditioning Inspection. All spark plugs should be inspected visually prior to reconditioning to eliminate any plug with obvious defects. A partial checklist of common defects includes:

(1) Ceramic chipped or cracked either at the nose core or in the connector well.

(2) Damaged or badly worn electrodes.

(3) Badly nicked, damaged, or corroded threads on shell or shielding barrel.

(4) Shielding barrel dented, bent, or cracked.

(5) Connector seat at the top of the shielding barrel badly nicked or corroded.

694. IGNITION HARNESSES. Aircraft quality ignition harness is usually made of either medium or high temperature wire. The type used will depend upon the manufacturing specification for the particular engine. In addition to the applicable manufacturer's maintenance and repair procedures, the following is a quick-reference checklist for isolating some of the malfunctions inherent to ignition harnesses.

a. Carefully inspect the lead conduit or shielding. A few broken strands will not affect serviceability, but if the insulation in general looks worn, replace the lead.

b. When replacing a lead, if the dressing procedure is not accomplished properly, strands of shielding may be forced through the conductor insulation. If this occurs, a short

will exist in the conductor; therefore, it is essential this task be performed properly.

c. The high temperature coating used on some lightweight harnesses is provided for vibration abrasion resistance and moisture protection. Slight flaking or peeling of this coating is not serious, and a harness assembly need not be removed from service because of this condition.

d. Check the spark plug contact springs for breaks, corrosion, or deformation. If possible, check the lead continuity from the distributor block to the contact spring.

e. Check the insulators at the spark plug end of the lead for cracks, breaks, or evidence of old age. Make sure they are clean.

f. Check to see that the leads are positioned as far away from the exhaust manifold as possible and are supported to prevent any whipping action.

g. When lightweight harnesses are used and the conduit enters the spark plug at a severe angle, use clamps as shown in figure 14.9 to prevent overstressing the lead.

695. MAGNETO INSPECTION. Whenever ignition problems develop and it is determined that the magneto is the cause of the difficulty, the following are a few simple inspection procedures which may locate the malfunction quickly. However, conduct any internal inspection or repair of a magneto in accordance with the manufacturer's maintenance and overhaul manuals.

a. Inspect the distributor block contact springs. If broken or corroded, replace.

b. Inspect the felt oil washer if applicable. It should be saturated with oil. If it is dry, check for a worn bushing.

c. Inspect the distributor block for cracks or a burned area. The wax coating on the block should not be removed. Do not use any solvents for cleaning.

d. Look for excess oil in the breaker compartment. If oil is present, it may mean a bad oil seal or bushing at the drive end. This condi-

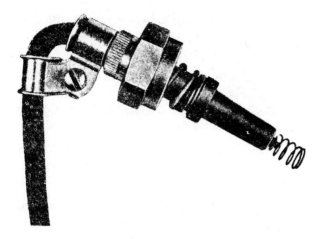

FIGURE 14.9.—Typical method of clamping leads.

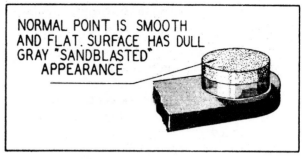

NORMAL POINT IS SMOOTH AND FLAT. SURFACE HAS DULL GRAY "SANDBLASTED" APPEARANCE

FIGURE 14.10.—Normal contact point.

tion could require complete overhaul, as too much oil may foul and cause excessive burning of the contact points.

e. Look for frayed insulation on the leads in the breaker compartment of the magneto. See that all terminals are secure. Be sure that wires are properly positioned.

f. Inspect the capacitor visually for general condition, and check the mounting bracket for cracks or looseness. If possible, check the capacitor for leakage, capacity, and series resistance.

g. Examine the points for excessive wear or burning. Discard points which have deep pits or excessively burned areas. Desired contact surfaces have a dull gray, sandblasted (almost rough) or frosted appearance over the area where electrical contact is made. Figure 14.10 shows how the normal contact point will look when surfaces are separated for inspection. Minor irregularities or roughness of point surfaces are not harmful (see figure 14.11); neither are small pits or mounds, if not too pronounced. If there is a possibility of the pit becoming deep enough to penetrate the pad (figure 14.12), reject the contact assembly.

Generally, no attempt should be made to dress or stone contact point assemblies; however, if provided, procedures and limits contained in the manufacturer's manuals may be followed.

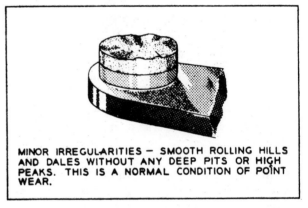

MINOR IRREGULARITIES – SMOOTH ROLLING HILLS AND DALES WITHOUT ANY DEEP PITS OR HIGH PEAKS. THIS IS A NORMAL CONDITION OF POINT WEAR.

FIGURE 14.11.—Point with minor irregularities.

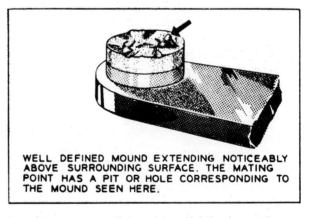

WELL DEFINED MOUND EXTENDING NOTICEABLY ABOVE SURROUNDING SURFACE. THE MATING POINT HAS A PIT OR HOLE CORRESPONDING TO THE MOUND SEEN HERE.

FIGURE 14.12.—Point with well-defined mound.

CAUTION

When inspecting the contact points for condition, do not open further than absolutely necessary. Excess tension on the spring will weaken it and adversely affect the performance of the magneto.

h. Adjustment of magneto point gap must be correct for proper internal timing of magneto. (See applicable manufacturer's publications for internal timing procedures.)

i. Check breaker cam to assure cleanness and smoothness. Check cam screw for tightness. If new points have been installed, blot a little oil on the cam. In addition, check contact point assembly to ascertain that the cam follower is securely fastened.

j. If the impulse coupling is accessible, inspect for excessive wear on the contact edges of the body and flyweights. In addition, check the flyweights for looseness on the axles.

k. Further examination of the impulse coupling body may disclose cracks caused by exceedingly tight flyweight axle rivets.

l. Check the magneto ventilators for proper functioning and obstructions. If drilled plugs are used, they should be in the lowest vent hole of the magneto to serve as a drain for condensation and oil.

696. MAGNETO-TO-ENGINE TIMING. While the actual process of timing magnetos to an engine is covered in the engine manufacturer's technical manuals, the following general procedures may be applied:

a. Before installing a new magneto, the correct "E" gap setting specified by the magneto manufacturer should be verified.

b. When setting or checking the magneto-to-engine timing, always turn the crankshaft steadily in the normal direction of rotation to eliminate any error caused by gear backlash.

c. Recheck magneto-to-engine timing after any point gap adjustment, or after replacement of the breaker points.

d. Never advance the magneto timing beyond the engine timing specification recommended by the engine manufacturer.

e. The possibility of a timing error exists if a timing indicator which attaches to the propeller shaft or spinner of geared engines is used. Engine timing specifications are always given in degrees of crankshaft travel, and cannot be applied directly to geared propeller shafts because of the gear ratio. Therefore, the correct position of the propeller shaft, if used for timing, must be determined by multiplying the crankshaft timing angle in degrees before top center (BTC) by the propeller gear ratio.

697.–707. RESERVED.

Section 2. FUEL SYSTEMS

708. GENERAL. Maintain, service, and adjust aircraft fuel systems and fuel system components in accordance with the applicable manufacturer's maintenance instructions. Certain general fuel system maintenance principles are outlined below.

709. FUEL LINES AND FITTINGS. When fuel system lines are to be replaced or repaired, consider the following fundamentals in addition to the applicable airworthiness requirements. Additional inspection and repair practices for aircraft tubing systems may be found in paragraph 393.

a. Compatibility of Fittings. All fittings are to be compatible with their mating parts. Although various types of fittings appear to be interchangeable in many cases they have different thread pitch or minor design differences which prevent proper mating and may cause the joint to leak or fail.

b. Routing. Make sure that the line does not chafe against control cables, airframe structure, etc., or come in contact with electrical wiring or conduit. Where physical separation of the fuel lines from electrical wiring or conduit is impracticable, locate the fuel line below the wiring and clamp it securely to the airframe structure. In no case may wiring be supported by the fuel line.

c. Alignment. Locate bends accurately so that the tubing is aligned with all support clamps and end fittings and is not drawn, pulled, or otherwise forced into place by them. Never install a straight length of tubing between two rigidly mounted fittings. Always incorporate at least one bend between such fittings to absorb strain caused by vibration and temperature changes.

d. Bonding. Bond metallic fuel lines at each point where they are clamped to the structure.

Integrally bonded and cushioned line support clamps are preferred to other clamping and bonding methods.

e. Support of Line Units. To prevent possible failure, all fittings heavy enough to cause the line to sag should be supported by means other than the tubing.

f. Support Clamps.

(1) Place support clamps or brackets for metallic lines as follows:

Tube O.D.		Approximate distance between supports
⅛"–³⁄₁₆"	- - - - - - - - - - - - - - - - - - - -	9"
¼"–⁵⁄₁₆"	- - - - - - - - - - - - - - - - - - - -	12"
⅜"–½"	- - - - - - - - - - - - - - - - - - - -	16"
⅝"–¾"	- - - - - - - - - - - - - - - - - - - -	22"
1"–1¼"	- - - - - - - - - - - - - - - - - - - -	30"
1½"–2"	- - - - - - - - - - - - - - - - - - - -	40"

(2) Locate clamps or brackets as close to bends as possible to reduce overhang (see figure 14.13).

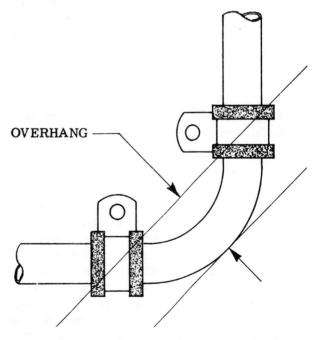

OVERHANG

FIGURE 14.13.—Location of clamps at tube bends.

710. FUEL TANKS AND CELLS. Welded or riveted fuel tanks that are made of commercially pure aluminum, 3003, 5052, or similar alloys, may be repaired by welding. Tanks made from heat-treatable aluminum alloys are generally assembled by riveting. In case it is necessary to rivet a new piece in a tank, use the same material as used in the tank undergoing repair, and seal the seams with a compound that is insoluble in gasoline. Special sealing compounds are available and should be used in the repair of tanks. Inspect fuel tanks and cells for general condition, security of attachment, and evidence of leakage. Examine fuel tank or cell vent line, fuel line, and sump drain attachment fittings closely.

CAUTION

Purge defueled tanks of explosive fuel/air mixtures in accordance with the manufacturers' service instructions. In the absence of such instructions, utilize an inert gas such as CO_2 as a purgative to assure the total deletion of fuel/air mixtures.

a. Integral Tanks. Examine the interior surfaces and seams for sealant deterioration and corrosion (especially in the sump area). Follow the manufacturer's instructions for repair and cleaning procedures.

b. Internal Metal Tanks. Check the exterior for corrosion and chafing. Dents or other distortion, such as a partially collapsed tank caused by an obstructed fuel tank vent, can adversely affect fuel quantity gauge accuracy and tank capacity. Check the interior surfaces for corrosion. Pay particular attention to the sump area, especially those which are made of cast material. Repairs to the tank may be accomplished in accordance with the practices outlined in Chapter 2 of this handbook.

c. Removal of Flux After Welding. It is especially important, after repair by welding, to completely remove all flux in order to avoid possible corrosion. Promptly upon completion of welding, wash the inside and outside of the tank with liberal quantities of hot water and then drain. Next, immerse the tank in either a 5 percent nitric or 5 percent sulfuric acid solution. If the tank cannot be immersed, fill the tank with either solution, and wash the outside with the same solution. Permit the acid to re-main in contact with the weld about one hour and then rinse thoroughly with clean water. Test the efficiency of the cleaning operation by applying some acidified 5 percent silver nitrate solution to a small quantity of the rinse water used last to wash the tank. If a heavy white precipitate is formed, the cleaning is insufficient and the washing should be repeated.

d. Flexible Fuel Cells. Inspect the interior for checking, cracking, porosity, or other signs of deterioration. Make sure the cell retaining fasteners are properly positioned. If repair or further inspection is required, follow the manufacturer's instructions for cell removal, repair, and installation. Do not allow flexible fuel cells to dry out. Preserve them in accordance with the manufacturer's instructions.

711. FUEL TANK CAPS, VENTS, AND OVERFLOW LINES. Inspect the fuel tank caps to determine that they are the correct type and size for the installation.

a. Vented caps, substituted for unvented caps, may cause loss of fuel or fuel starvation. Similarly, an improperly installed cap that has a special venting arrangement can also cause malfunctions.

b. Unvented caps, substituted for vented caps, will cause fuel starvation and possible collapse of the fuel tank or cell. Malfunctioning of this type occurs when the pressure within the tank decreases as the fuel is withdrawn. Eventually, a point is reached where the fuel will no longer flow, and/or the outside atmospheric pressure collapses the tank. Thus, the effects will occur sooner with a full fuel tank than with one partially filled.

c. Check tank vents and overflow lines thoroughly for condition, obstructions, correct installation, and proper operation of any check valves and ice protection units. Pay particular attention to the location of the tank vents when such information is provided in the manufacturer's service instructions. Inspect for cracked or deteriorated filler opening recess drains, which may allow spilled fuel to accumulate within the wing or fuselage. One method of inspection is to plug the fuel line at the outlet and observe fuel placed in the filler opening recess. If drainage takes place, investigate condition of the line and purge any excess fuel from the wing.

d. *Assure that filler opening markings* are stated according to the applicable airworthiness requirements and are complete and legible.

712. FUEL CROSSFEED, FIREWALL SHUTOFF, AND TANK SELECTOR VALVES. Inspect these valves for leakage and proper operation as follows:

a. *Internal leakage* can be checked by placing the appropriate valve in the "off" position, draining the fuel strainer bowl, and observing if fuel continues to flow into it. Check all valves located downstream of boost pumps with the pump(s) operating. Do not operate the pump(s) longer than necessary.

b. *External leakage* from these units can be a severe fire hazard, especially if the unit is located under the cabin floor or within a similarly confined area. Correct the cause of any fuel stains associated with fuel leakage.

c. *Selector Handles.* Check the operation of each handle or control to see that it indicates the actual position of the selector valve. Assure that stops and detents have positive action and feel. Worn or missing detents and stops can cause unreliable positioning of the fuel selector valve.

d. *Worn Linkage.* Inaccurate positioning of fuel selector valves can also be caused by worn mechanical linkage between the selector handle and the valve unit. An improper fuel valve position setting can seriously reduce engine power by restricting the available fuel flow. Check universal joints, pins, gears, splines, cams, levers, etc., for wear and excessive clearance, which prevent the valve from positioning accurately or from obtaining fully "off" and "on" positions.

e. *Assure that required placards* are complete and legible. Replace those that are missing or cannot be read easily.

713. FUEL PUMPS. Inspect, repair, and overhaul boost pumps, emergency pumps, auxiliary pumps, and engine-driven pumps in accordance with the appropriate manufacturer's instructions.

714. FUEL FILTERS, STRAINERS, AND DRAINS. Check each strainer and filter element for contamination. Determine and correct the source of any contaminants found. Replace throwaway filter elements with the recommended type. Examine fuel strainer bowls to see that they are properly installed according to direction of fuel flow. Check the operation of all drain devices to see that they operate properly and have positive shutoff action.

715. INDICATOR SYSTEMS. Inspect, service, and adjust the fuel indicator systems according to the manufacturer's instructions. Determine that the required placards and instrument markings are complete and legible.

716. TURBINE FUEL SYSTEMS. The use of turbine fuels in aircraft has resulted in two problem areas not normally associated with aviation gasolines: (1) Entrained water (microscopic particles of free water suspended in the fuel) and (2) microbial contaminants.

a. *Entrained water* will remain suspended in aviation turbine fuels for a considerable length of time. Unless suitable measures are taken, the fine filters used in turbine fuel systems will clog with ice crystals when the temperature of the fuel drops below the freezing temperature of the entrained water. Some fuel systems employ heated fuel filters or fuel heaters to eliminate this problem. Others rely upon anti-icing fuel additives.

b. *Microbial contamination* is a relatively recent problem associated with the operation and maintenance of turbine engine fuel systems. The effects of these micro-organisms are far reaching. They can cause powerplant failure due to clogging of filters, lines, fuel controls, etc., and the corrosive acids which they produce can lead to structural failure of integral tanks. Microbial contamination is generally associated with fuel containing free water introduced by condensation or other extraneous sources.

c. *Maintain* turbine engine fuel systems and use anti-icing and antibacterial additives in accordance with the manufacturer's recommendations.

717.–727. RESERVED.

Section 3.   EXHAUST SYSTEMS

728. GENERAL. Any exhaust system failure should be regarded as a severe hazard. Depending upon the location and type of failure, it can result in carbon monoxide (CO) poisoning of crew and passengers, partial or complete engine power loss, or fire. Exhaust system failures generally reach a maximum rate of occurrence at 100 to 200 hours' operating time, and over 50 percent of the failures occur within 400 hours.

729. MUFFLER/HEAT EXCHANGER FAILURES. Approximately one-half of all exhaust system failures are traced to cracks or ruptures in the heat exchanger surfaces used for cabin and carburetor air heat sources. Failures in the heat exchanger's surface (usually the muffler's outer wall) allow exhaust gases to escape directly into the cabin heat system. The failures are, for the most part, attributed to thermal and vibration fatigue cracking in areas of stress concentration; e.g., tailpipe and stack inlet attachment areas (figures 14.14 thru 14.17).

Failures of the spot welds which attach heat transfer pins, as shown in figure 14.15A, can result in exhaust gas leakage. In addition to the carbon monoxide hazard, failure of heat exchanger surfaces can permit exhaust gases to be drawn into the engine induction system and cause engine overheating and power loss.

730. MANIFOLD/STACK FAILURES. Exhaust manifold and stack failures are also usually fatigue-type failures which occur at welded or clamped joints; e.g., stack-to-flange, stack-to-manifold, muffler connections, or crossover pipe connections. Although these failures are primarily a fire hazard, they also present a carbon monoxide problem. Exhaust gases can enter the cabin via defective or inadequate seals at firewall openings, wing strut fittings, doors, and wing root openings. Manifold/stack

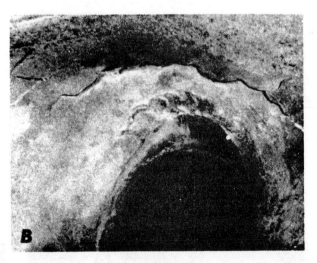

FIGURE 14.14.—Typical muffler wall fatigue failure at exhaust outlet. (A. Complete muffler assembly with heat shroud removed; B. Detail view of failure.)

failures, which account for approximately 20 percent of all exhaust system failures, reach a maximum rate of occurrence at about 100 hours' operating time. Over 50 percent of the failures occur within 300 hours.

731. INTERNAL MUFFLER FAILURES. Internal failures (baffles, diffusers, etc.) can cause partial or complete engine power loss by restricting

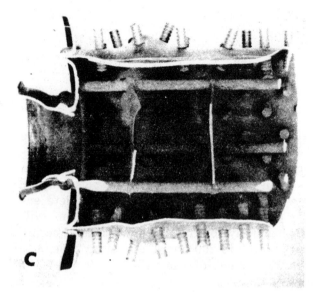

FIGURE 14.15.—Typical muffler wall failure. (A. Complete muffler assembly with heat shroud removed; B. Detail view of failure; C. Cross section of failed muffler.)

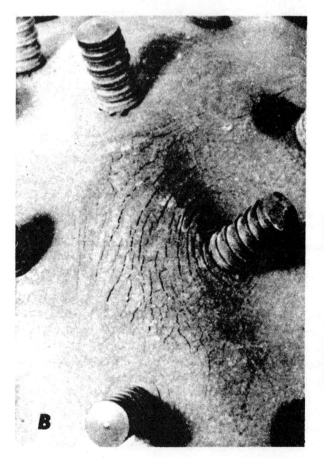

FIGURE 14.16—Typical muffler wall fatigue failure. (A. Complete muffler assembly with heat shroud partially removed; B. Detail view of failure.)

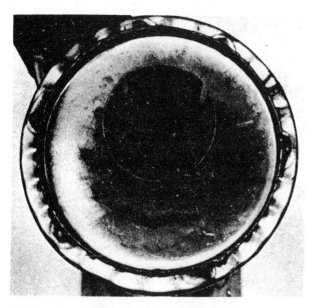

FIGURE 14.17.—Typical fatigue failure of muffler end plate at stack inlet.

FIGURE 14.18.—Section of muffler showing typical internal baffle failure.

the flow of the exhaust gases (figures 14.18 thru 14.21). As opposed to other failures, erosion and carbonizing caused by the extreme thermal conditions are the primary causes of internal failures. Engine backfiring and combustion of unburned fuel within the exhaust system are probable contributing factors. In addition, local hot spot areas caused by uneven exhaust gas flow results in burning, bulging, and rupture of the outer muffler wall (figure 14.15). As might be expected, the time required for these failures to develop is longer than that for fatigue failures. Internal muffler failures account for nearly 20 percent of the total number of exhaust system failures. The highest rate of internal failures occur between 500 and 750 hours of operating time. Engine power loss and excessive backpressure caused by exhaust outlet blockage may be averted by the installation of an exhaust outlet guard as shown in figures 14.22a, and 14.22b. The outlet guard may be fabricated from 3/16″ stainless steel welding rod. Form the rod into two "U" shaped segments, approximately 3 inches long and weld into the exhaust tail pipe as shown in figure 14.22a so that the guard will extend 2 inches inside the exhaust muffler outlet port. Installation of an exhaust outlet guard does

FIGURE 14.19.—Loose pieces of failed internal baffle.

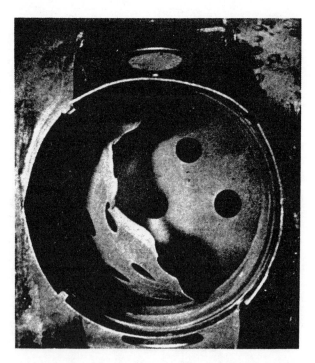

FIGURE 14.20.—Failed internal baffle partially obstructing muffler outlet.

FIGURE 14.21.—Failed internal baffle completely obstructing muffler outlet.

not negate the importance of thorough inspection of the internal parts of the muffler or the necessity of replacing defective mufflers.

732. INSPECTION. Inspect exhaust systems frequently to ascertain complete system integrity.

CAUTION

Marking of exhaust system parts—NEVER USE LEAD PENCILS, GREASE PENCILS, ETC., TO MARK EXHAUST SYSTEM PARTS. Carbon deposited by those tools will cause cracks from heat concentration and carbonization of the metal. If you must mark on exhaust system parts, USE CHALK, PRUSSIAN BLUE OR INDIA INK that is carbon free.

a. Prior to any cleaning operation, remove cowling as required to expose the complete exhaust system. Examine cowling and nacelle areas adjacent to exhaust system components for telltale signs of exhaust gas soot indicating possible leakage points. Check to make sure that no portion of the exhaust system is being chafed by cowling, engine control cables, or other components. The exhaust system often operates at red-hot temperatures of 1000 degrees F. or more; therefore, parts such as igni-

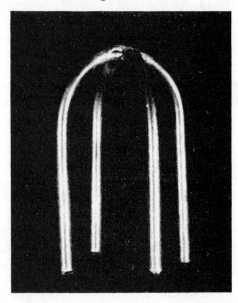

FIGURE 14.22a.—Example of exhaust outlet guard.

tion leads, hoses, fuel lines, and flexible air ducts, should be protected from radiation and convection heating by heat shields or adequate clearance.

b. Remove or loosen all exhaust shields, car-

FIGURE 14.22b.—Example of exhaust outlet guard installed.

FIGURE 14.23.—Effect of improperly positioned exhaust pipe/muffler clamp.

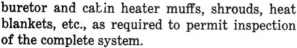

buretor and cabin heater muffs, shrouds, heat blankets, etc., as required to permit inspection of the complete system.

c. Perform necessary cleaning operations and inspect all external surfaces of the exhaust system for cracks, dents, and missing parts. Pay particular attention to welds, clamps, supports, and support attachment lugs, bracing, slip joints, stack flanges, gaskets, flexible couplings, etc. (See figures 14.23 and 14.24.) Examine the heel of each bend, areas adjacent to welds, any dented areas, and low spots in the system for thinning and pitting due to internal erosion by combustion products or accumulated moisture. An ice pick or similar pointed instrument is useful in probing suspected areas. Disassemble the system as necessary to inspect internal baffles or diffusers.

d. Should a component be inaccessible for a thorough visual inspection or hidden by nonremovable parts, remove it and check for possible leaks by plugging its openings, applying approximately 2 p.s.i. internal pressure, and submerging it in water. Any leaks will cause bubbles that can be readily detected. Dry thoroughly before reinstallation.

733. REPAIRS. It is generally recommended that exhaust stacks, mufflers, tailpipes, etc., be replaced with new or reconditioned components rather than repaired. Welded repairs to exhaust systems are complicated by the difficulty of accurately identifying the base metal so that the proper repair materials can be selected. Changes in composition and grain structure of the original base metal further complicate the repair. However, when welded repairs are necessary, follow the general procedures outlined in paragraph 68 of this handbook. Retain the original contours and make sure that the completed repair has not warped or otherwise affected the alignment of the exhaust system. Repairs or sloppy weld beads which protrude internally are not acceptable since they cause local hot spots and may restrict exhaust gas flow. When repairing or replacing exhaust system components, be sure that the proper hardware and clamps are used. Do not substitute steel or low temperature self-locking nuts for brass or special high temperature locknuts used by the manufacturer. Never reuse old gaskets. When disassembly is necessary, replace gaskets with new ones of the same type provided by the manufacturer.

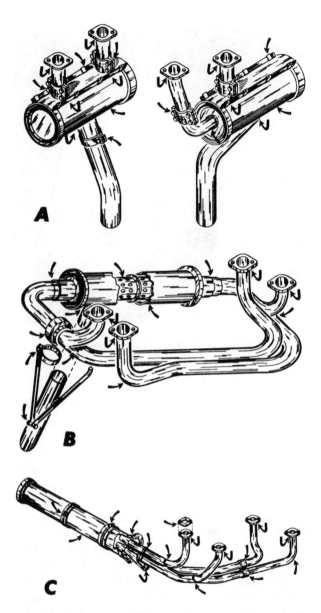

FIGURE 14.24.—Primary inspection areas (A. Separate system; B. Crossover type system; C. Exhaust/augmentor system.)

734. TURBOSUPERCHARGER. When a turbosupercharger is included, the exhaust system operates under greatly increased pressure and temperature conditions. Extra precautions should be taken in the exhaust system's care and maintenance. During high altitude operation, the exhaust system pressure is maintained at or near sea level values. Due to the pressure differential, any leaks in the system will allow the exhaust gases to escape with torchlike intensity that can severely damage adjacent structures. A common cause of turbosupercharger malfunction is coke deposits (carbon buildup) in the waste gate unit causing erratic system operation. Excessive deposit buildups may cause the waste gate valve to stick in the closed position, causing an overboost condition. Coke deposit buildup in the turbosupercharger itself will cause a gradual loss of power in flight and low deck pressure reading prior to takeoff. Experience has shown that periodic decoking, or removal of carbon deposits, is necessary to maintain peak efficiency. Clean, repair, overhaul, and adjust turbosupercharger system components and controls in accordance with the applicable manufacturer's instructions.

735. AUGMENTOR SYSTEMS. Inspect augmentor tubes periodically for proper alignment, security of attachment, and general overall condition. Regardless of whether or not the augmentor tubes contain heat exchanger surfaces, they should be inspected for cracks along with the remainder of the exhaust system. Cracks can present a fire or carbon monoxide hazard by allowing exhaust gases to enter nacelle, wing or cabin areas.

736.–746. RESERVED.

Chapter 15. RADIO AND ELECTRONIC SYSTEMS

Section 1. MAINTENANCE OF RADIO AND ELECTRONIC SYSTEMS

747. GENERAL. The safety of aircraft operated in the National Airspace System is dependent in a large degree upon the satisfactory performance of the airborne radio and electronic systems. Reliability and performance of the system(s) is proportional to the quality of maintenance received and the knowledge of those who perform such maintenance. It is, therefore, important that maintenance be accomplished using the best techniques and practices to assure optimum performance.

The term "system" as used in this chapter means those units of antenna, power source, sensors, receivers, transmitters, and indicators which together perform a function of communications or navigation.

This chapter is not intended to supersede or replace any Federal Aviation Administration regulation or specific manufacturer's instructions pertaining to radio and electronic equipment maintenance. Chapter 11 supplements the information provided in this chapter.

748. MAINTENANCE OF EQUIPMENT. Inspect units or radio/electronic equipment, assemblies, wiring and control systems for damage, general condition, and proper functioning to assure the continuous satisfactory operation of the system. Test, adjust, and repair radio and electronic equipment and systems in accordance with the manufacturer's maintenance instructions, manuals, and applicable Federal Aviation Regulations.

749. REPLACEMENT OF COMPONENTS. Replace damaged or defective components of radio or electronic units with identical items or items equivalent to the original in electrical and mechanical characteristics, operating tolerances, and the ability to function in the physical environmental conditions encountered in the operation of the aircraft.

750. INSPECTION OF INSTALLATIONS. Some items to look for and checks to be made during the inspection are:

a. Damaged or overheated equipment, connections, or wiring.

b. Poor electrical bonding.

c. Improper support of wiring and conduit.

d. Dirty equipment and connections.

e. Loose connections, terminals, plugs, and receptacles.

f. Condition of fuses, circuit breakers, and electric lamps.

g. Insufficient clearance of equipment from mounting rack, insecure or improper mountings.

h. Broken or missing antenna insulators, lead-through insulators, springs, safety wires, etc.

i. Miscellaneous irregularities such as loose quick-disconnects, metal objects in terminal strips or junction boxes, tightness of connections in plugs and receptacles, broken wire bundle lacing, pinched or dented conduit, broken or inadequate cable clamps, etc.

751. CLEANING. Frequent cleaning of radio and electronics equipment is recommended. Dust, dirt, and lint contribute to overheating of equipment, poor ventilation, and malfunctioning. Equipment chassis may be cleaned with a blast of dry air and a small brush. Special attention should be given that ventilation openings in equipment housings are open and free from obstructing lint and dust.

752. CONTACT CLEANERS. When cleaning radio equipment internally, spray cleaners can be used effectively, especially on switching assemblies. There are many contact cleaners on the market which, while they work well on micarta wafer switches, can cause irreparable damage to plastic wafer switches. Do not use contact cleaners on plastic wafer switches unless recommended or known to be harmless to the plastic.

753. OPERATIONAL CHECKS. An operational check is recommended during 100–hour or periodic inspections of radio and electronic systems. Although individual units of equipment may receive bench checks at various times, the proper functioning of a system can best be determined by an operational check in the aircraft. The various units of communications, navigation, weather radar, distance measuring equipment (DME), and transponder systems are interdependent upon each other for proper operational performance.

* **754. RADIO EQUIPMENT OPERATION.** Determine that the radio and electronic equipment operates satisfactorily throughout the voltage range of the aircraft electrical system under taxi, takeoff, slow cruise, normal cruise, and landing operating conditions. *

755.-765. RESERVED.

Section 1. MAINTENANCE OF WIRING AND CABLES

766. WIRING AND CABLE INTEGRITY. Inspect interconnecting wiring, cables, and conduit between various pieces of electronic equipment to determine that they do not rub against the airframe or each other under vibration conditions encountered in flight. Inspect open wiring and cabling for fraying, damage or distortion resulting from heavy objects being placed on it, being stepped on, or being used as handholds.

767. PROTECTION FROM FLUIDS. Separate wiring or cables from flammable fluids lines or those which carry fluids which have a deteriorating effect on wire insulation. Wiring or cables should be routed above such lines and securely clamped to the aircraft structure. An arcing fault between an electric cable and a fluid line may puncture the line and result in a fire.

768. WIRE AND CABLE CLAMPS. Inspect wire and cable clamps for proper tightness. Where cables pass through structure or bulkheads, inspect for proper clamping or grommets. Inspect for sufficient slack between the last clamp and the electronic equipment to prevent strain at the cable terminals and minimize adverse effects on shock mounted equipment.

769. CONDUIT. Conduit is manufactured in metallic and nonmetallic materials and in both rigid and flexible forms. Primarily its purpose is for mechanical protection of the cable within. Inspect conduit for proper end fittings, absence of abrasion at the end fittings, and proper clamping. Inspect for distortion, adequate drain points which are free of dirt, grease, or other obstructions, and freedom from abrasion or damage due to moving objects such as aircraft control cables or shifting cargo.

770. PLASTIC WIRE SLEEVING. Inspect plastic wire sleeving for damage due to abrasion, solvents, or hydraulic fluids.

* "771. [Deleted] — Change 3"   *

772.-782. RESERVED.

Section 3.   JUNCTION BOXES AND TERMINAL STRIPS

783. JUNCTION BOXES. Inspect junction boxes for "oil canning" of the cover and sides, internal shorts due to distortion of the box, internal cleanliness, absence of stray metallic objects, proper grommeting where wires or cables enter the box, and freedom of drain holes from foreign objects or material.

784. INTERNAL ARRANGEMENT. Electric cable inside the box should be laced or clamped in such a manner that terminals are not hidden, relay armatures are not fouled, and motion relative to any equipment is prevented. Where marginal clearances are unavoidable, an insulating material should be interposed between current-carrying parts and any grounded surface.

785. TERMINAL STRIPS. Inspect terminal strips which provide connection of radio and electronic systems to the aircraft electrical system for loose connections, metallic objects which may have fallen across the terminal strip, dirt and grease accumulation, etc. Such conditions can cause arcing which may result in a fire.

786. PLUGS AND RECEPTACLES. Inspect this type of power connector for loose soldered connections, proper insulation of metallic parts, and fraying of wires in the plug and receptacle inserts.

787.–797. RESERVED.

Section 4. POWER SOURCES AND DISTRIBUTION SYSTEMS

798. BATTERY ELECTROLYTE CORROSION. Electrolyte spilled during ground servicing should be neutralized at once with solutions of sodium bicarbonate (for acid electrolyte) or boric acid, vinegar, or a 3 percent solution of acetic acid (for alkaline electrolyte). Residue should be washed off with clean water and the area thoroughly dried.

799. GENERATORS AND ALTERNATORS. Inspect generators and alternators and their associated wiring and distribution systems for wear, damage, general condition, and proper functioning to assure the continued satisfactory operation of the electrical system. Frequent visual inspections, operating checks of all electrical circuits and equipment, and replacement or repair when deficiencies are found are effective in minimizing electrical troubles and hazards in aircraft.

800. ALTERNATOR DIODES. Alternators employ diodes for the purpose of converting the alternating current to direct current. These diodes are electronic devices and are particularly susceptible to damage if abused. A diode will allow passage of current in one direction with little resistance, but will allow passage of current in the opposite direction only if the voltage applied exceeds that value for which the device was designed. A voltage surge in the line, if it exceeds the design value, will destroy the diode very quickly.

801. DIODE PROTECTION. The best protection against diode destruction by voltage surges is to make certain that the battery is never disconnected for the aircraft electrical system when the alternator is in operation. The battery acts as a large capacitor and tends to damp out voltage surges. Make certain that the battery is never connected with reversed polarity. This will subject the diodes to a direct short circuit and will generally destroy them instantly.

802. ALTERNATOR/BATTERY CONNECTIONS. Some alternators require that the battery be connected in the circuit initially before it will produce any output.

803. STATIC ELECTRICAL POWER CONVERTERS. Static power converters employ solid state devices to convert the aircraft primary electrical source voltage to higher values for the operation of radio and electronic equipment. They contain no moving parts and are relatively maintenance free. Various types are available for AC to DC or DC to AC conversion. Exercise care in locating and mounting static converters to insure adequate ventilation for cooling purposes. Heat radiating fins should be kept clean of dirt and other foreign matter which may impair their cooling properties.

804. CLEANING AND PRESERVATION. Frequent cleaning of electrical and electronic equipment to remove dust, dirt, and grime is recommended. Fine emery cloth may be used to clean terminals and mating surfaces if they appear corroded or dirty. Crocus cloth or very fine sandpaper should be used to polish commutators or slip rings. Use of emery cloth on commutators is not acceptable because metallic particles from the cloth may cause shorting and burning.

805. MISCELLANEOUS CHECK ITEMS. Make frequent checks for miscellaneous irregularities such as loose terminal connections, poorly soldered or loosely swaged terminals, missing safety wire, loose quick-disconnects, broken wire bundle lacing, broken or inadequate wire clamps, and insufficient clearance between exposed current-carrying parts and ground. Replacement or repair should be accomplished as a part of routine maintenance.

806. ADJUSTMENT AND REPAIR. Accomplish all adjustment, repair, overhaul, and testing of electrical equipment and systems in accordance with the recommendations and procedures set forth in maintenance instructions or manuals published by the aircraft and equipment manufacturers.

807. ELECTRICAL SWITCH INSPECTION. Special attention should be given to electrical circuit switches, especially the spring-loaded type, during the course of normal airworthiness inspection. An internal failure in this type of switch may allow the switch to remain closed even though the toggle or button returns to the "off" position. During inspection, attention should also be given to the possibility that improper switch substitution may have been made.

* "808. [Transferred to paragraph 754.] — Change 3" *

809.-819. RESERVED.

Section 5. NOISE SUPPRESSION

820. GENERAL. Elimination or suppression of sources of radio interference within the aircraft is necessary in order to obtain the optimum performance of airborne radio equipment. This is done by bonding, shielding, and the use of static dischargers.

821. BONDING. Radio equipment should be bonded to the aircraft in order to provide a low impedance ground and to minimize radio interference from static electricity charges. Bonding jumpers should be as short as practicable and be installed in such a manner that the resistance of each connection does not exceed 0.003 ohm. Where a jumper is for radio-noise prevention only and not for current-carrying purposes, a resistance of 0.01 ohm is satisfactory.

822. SHIELDING. The most effective method of minimizing engine ignition radio interference is to shield the ignition system. Use a metallic braid covering and special end connectors for ignition wires between the magneto and spark plugs. The primary leads to the magneto and the magneto switch itself should be shielded. Provide shielded type spark plugs and a shielded metal cover for the magneto if it is not so equipped. All connections in the shielding should be tight metal-to-metal contact.

823. SPARK PLUGS. The engine ignition noise may be suppressed by replacing the spark plugs with resistor spark plugs of a type approved for the engine if it is not feasible to shield the engine ignition system.

824. FILTERS. If an intolerable radio noise level is present despite shielding of the ignition wiring and plugs, it may be necessary to provide a filter between the magneto and magneto switch to reduce the noise. This may consist of a single by-pass capacitor or a combination of capacitors and choke coils. When this is done, the shielding between the filter and magneto switch can usually be eliminated and the special shielded magneto switch need not be used.

Inspect supporting brackets and wiring details for magneto filters for conformance with standard aircraft electrical practice. The reliability of the magneto filter installation should be at least equivalent to that of the remainder of the magneto ground lead installation.

825. PRECIPITATION STATIC. Precipitation static is a general term applied to noise in radio receiving systems caused by precipitation. It is not always caused by true precipitation, such as ice, snow, or rain. Dust, sand, or other airborne particles may cause it. It may be the result of ionization in the exhaust of jet engines. As a result of precipitation static charging, the electrical potential of the aircraft rises until it reaches the corona threshold. Corona is the discharge of electric current from an object into the surrounding air and occurs as short pulses of current and produces a noise spectrum which contains appreciable energy at radio frequencies. The noise produced is coupled into the aircraft antennas.

826. STATIC DISCHARGERS. Static dischargers are installed on aircraft to bleed off precipitation static before the potential reaches the corona threshold. These dischargers are normally mounted on the control surfaces and other extremities of the aircraft. The three major types in use are: (1) flexible, vinyl-covered, carbon-impregnated braid, (2) semiflexible metallic braid, and (3) null-field.

827. MAINTENANCE OF STATIC DISCHARGERS. Inspect flexible and semiflexible dischargers for physical security of mounting attachments, wear or abrasion of wicks, missing wicks, etc. Inspect flexible, vinyl-covered wicks to assure that one inch of the inner braid extends beyond the vinyl covering. Null-field discharges are epoxy bonded to the aircraft structure. Measure the resistance of the bond to determine compliance with the manufacturer's recommended tolerances, and inspect for physical damage.

828.–838. RESERVED.

Section 6.   ANTENNAS

839. FIXED AND TRAILING WIRE ANTENNAS. Inspect fixed and trailing wire antennas for cracked or broken insulators, broken tension springs, and missing end thimbles. Inspect feed-through and strain insulators for damage due to arcing or corona discharge. Replace damaged insulators. If insulated wire is used for the fixed antenna, inspect the insulating covering for pinholes resulting from corona discharge or lightning. Inspect fixed antenna masts for security of mounting and absence of skin cracks in the mounting area.

840. WHIP AND BLADE ANTENNAS. Inspect security of mounting, condition of sealant around antenna base, and physical damage resulting in bending or deformation of the antenna itself.

841. FLUSH MOUNTED ANTENNAS. Many high performance aircraft use flush mounted antennas where the antenna itself is recessed in the fuselage or other portions of the aircraft structure. The recesses in which such antennas are mounted are covered with fiberglass or other material which allows the passage of radio frequency energy. Inspect such covers frequently for integrity of seals and cracks in the covering. If the covers are painted, they should be painted with a type of paint which will not interfere with the passage of radio frequency energy.

842. COAXIAL CABLES AND FITTINGS. Inspect coaxial cable antenna connectors for proper fastening. Certain types of connectors depend on the positioning of the center pin by its physical connection to the center conductor of the cable. Frequent connecting and disconnecting of the connector causes this pin to position so that it does not make contact with the female connector. If the connectors become physically separated from each other or the unit, equipment failure will result. Cable connectors may be clamped or safetied so that they do not become separated.

843. RADOMES. A radome is a covering whose primary purpose is to protect a radar antenna from the elements. It is a part of the airframe, but must have certain electrical as well as physical properties. Electrically, a radome must permit the passage of the radar transmitted signals and return echoes with minimum distortion and absorption. In order to do this it must have a certain electrical thickness. A variation in electrical thickness can make the difference between an efficient radome and one that can reduce radar range, distort displays, and cause inaccurate directions and false targets. Hence, a radome must be properly maintained and repaired to deliver optimum performance.

844. RADOME INSPECTION. Inspection of aircraft having weather radar installations should include a visual check of the radome surface for signs of surface damage, holes, cracks, chipping, and peeling of paint, etc. Attach fittings and fastenings, neoprene erosion caps, and lightning strips, when installed, should also be inspected.

   a. Scuff marks on the radome are usually an indication of impact damage from birds, foreign objects, or hangar/ramp equipment. Further detailed inspection is required to determine whether physical damage has occurred.

   b. Surface cracks on the radome paint do not always indicate structural damage, but may be due to paint shrinking or becoming brittle. If accompanied by impact marks, static discharge or lightning burn marks, or evidence of oil canning, a more detailed inspection is required to determine whether physical damage has occurred.

   c. Paint chipping usually results from inflight encounter with hail, surface static discharges, or lightning. A detailed external and internal inspection of the radome should be made for fractures or delamination of the radome structure.

d. Paint peeling on the radome is usually caused by flight in heavy precipitation or by improperly applied paint coatings. If detected in its early stages, usually no damage results. Corrective action should be taken to prevent further erosion and water absorption. A rapid breakdown of the structure will occur when trapped moisture freezes resulting in greatly reduced efficiency of radar operation.

e. Neoprene erosion caps provide protection from rain erosion; however, they do conceal the radome surface and make impact damage difficult to detect. When in doubt about impact damage, remove the radome and inspect the inside surface. Other erosion cap inspection items are air bubbles, surface fraying, and loose edges around the cap.

f. Lightning diverter strips are intended to protect the radome from lightning damage, and prevent radio interference from static charge build-up on the radome. Proper grounding of these strips to the aircraft structure should be assured each time a radome is inspected or repaired. Damaged or burned-out strips should be replaced.

845. RADOME MAINTENANCE AND REPAIR. Any repair to a weather radome should be accomplished according to manufacturer's recommended procedures by qualified personnel using the equipment and materials recommended by the manufacturer. The use of improper materials and repair techniques may result in reduced performance and accuracy of the weather radar system.

a. Plastic nose caps should not be installed over a radome unless the manufacturer recommends such installation. Such caps may cause radar beam distortion, weak signal returns, poor definition, and radar display clutter. Moisture leaks or condensation between the plastic cap and radome can block or distort the signal without the cause for such condition being apparent.

b. Radome protective coating should be a type, and contain only materials, recommended by the radome manufacturer. Metallic paints or undercoating can set up reflections in the radar system which may damage the equipment.

c. Solvents should not be used to wash the radome. They may weaken the bond between the radome and the neoprene erosion cap.

d. Chemical type paint strippers should not be used. They will attack the resins used in the radome construction, and may weaken its structural integrity.

e. The testing of a radome after maintenance or repair is a determination that must be made by the person approving it for return to service since he is responsible for its airworthiness. All repairs to radomes are not necessarily major repairs, and minor repairs may not require testing. The decision to test should be based upon the nature and complexity of the repair.

846. LOOP ANTENNAS. Loop antennas are designed for use with a particular receiver. Connecting wires between the loops and receivers are also designed for the specific equipment. Use only components meeting the specification characteristics of the receiver manufacturer. The outstanding characteristic of a loop antenna is its directional sensitivity which makes it useful as an accurate navigational device.

847. LOOP QUADRANTAL ERROR. Compensation of a loop for quadrantal error requires technical knowledge of the equipment and its operational use and should be accomplished only by a qualified technician. Quadrantal error is that error caused by the metal in the fuselage, wings, etc., distorting the electromagnetic field of a received signal and resulting in azimuth reading inaccuracies which are greatest between the four cardinal points with respect to the centerline of the aircraft.

848. COMPENSATION FOR QUADRANTAL ERROR. It will be necessary to check the direction of the radio bearings every 45 degrees from the fore-and-aft axis of the aircraft (preferably every 15 degrees) after installation of the loop in order to determine and compensate for the deviations caused by distortion of the radio field pattern due to the wing, engine nacelle(s), antennas, and other parts of the aircraft. If the loop is of the type which includes compensating means, it is important that no compensation be present in the loop at the time this calibration is made. If the loop has no provision for adjustment of quadrantal error, the calibration data should be used for the preparation of a correction card to be mounted in the cockpit near the indicator to provide the pilot with corrected bearing information.

849. GROUND CALIBRATION. The calibration may be made on the ground for installations in which the loop is on top of the aircraft, but the accuracy of the calibration should be checked in the air. However, for installations in which the loop is beneath the fuselage, the use of the flight method is necessary if accuracy is to be obtained.

850. AIR CALIBRATION. Air calibration of loops are best made on a day when the wind is less than 8 miles per hour and the air is smooth, using a medium or high-powered radio station between 25 and 100 miles distant. The station should normally provide good bearings with little or no fluctuation of the indicator pointer. Do not make the calibration within two hours of sunrise or sunset or when wide fluctuations of bearings are noted.

851. CALIBRATION POINTS. Select a landmark or series of landmarks such as a road, railroad tracks, section lines, etc., which will provide a direct line toward the radio station. Powerlines and railroads on or adjacent to the landmarks can distort the radio path, so make a check to determine whether or not distortion is present. This can be done by crossing the reference line at various angles while maintaining fixed courses by means of the directional gyro. If the bearing changes rapidly as the line is approached, distortion is present and should be eliminated by flying at a higher altitude, or by selecting a new reference landmark.

852. CALIBRATION PROCEDURE. Fly directly toward the station along the reference line with the aircraft in level flight at an altitude low enough to avoid parallax error. When passing over some predetermined point or intersecting line to the reference, record simultaneously the indicator bearing and the directional gyro reading. Repeat the above procedure until sufficient readings have been taken at all required bearings. Since the radiocompass deviation changes to some extent with frequency, take calibration data at several frequencies to ensure greater accuracy in use.

853. CALIBRATION DATA. Calibration data obtained for a particular type of airplane is usable without modification for all aircraft of that type if the location of the loop and other antennas are the same. Since all aircraft of the same type may not have the same radio installations, an accurate diagram with antenna dimensions and exact loop location will add to the usefulness of the recorded data.

854.–863. RESERVED.

Chapter 16. INSTRUMENTS

Section 1. MAINTENANCE OF INSTRUMENTS

864. GENERAL. The complexity of modern instruments, integrated flight systems, auto-pilots, air data computers, and inertial guidance systems necessitates complex maintenance procedures, sophisticated test equipment, and qualified personnel. The safety of aircraft operated in the National Airspace System is dependent in a large degree upon the satisfactory performance of airborne instrument systems. It is, therefore, important that maintenance be accomplished using the best techniques and practices to assure optimum performance.

The term "system" as used in this chapter means those units of power source, sensors, transmitters, indicator, and controllers which together perform a function of display, interpretation, or control of the functions of an aircraft, its systems, or the environment in which it operates.

* 865. DEFINITION. The definition of an instrument means a device using an internal mechanism to show visually or aurally the attitude, altitude, or operation of an aircraft or aircraft part. It includes electronic devices for automatically controlling an aircraft in flight. *

866. MAINTENANCE OF INSTRUMENTS. Repairs and overhaul of aircraft instruments should be made only by a Federal Aviation Administration (FAA) approved facility having proper test equipment, adequate manufacturer's maintenance manuals and service bulletins, and qualified personnel. Details concerning the repair and overhaul of various instruments differ considerably. Test, repair, and adjust instruments and instrument systems in accordance with the manufacturer's maintenance instructions, manuals, and applicable Federal Aviation Regulations (FAR). Consult the airframe manufacturer for specific maintenance instructions involving instruments that are installed or supplied by them.

867. TEST/ADJUSTMENT OF INSTRUMENTS. Certain instruments, such as altimeters and vertical speed (rate of climb) indicators, are equipped with simple adjusting means. The barometric correlation adjustment should not be adjusted in the field; changing this adjustment may nullify the correspondence between the basic test equipment calibration standards and the altimeter. Additionally, correspondence between the encoding altimeter and its encoding digitizer or the associated blind encoder may be nullified. These adjustments should be accomplished by qualified personnel, using proper test equipment and adequate reference to the manufacturer's maintenance manuals.

*867-1. LIQUID QUANTITY INDICATING SYSTEM. Any time a component is changed in a liquid quantity indication system, the system shall be calibrated. This applies to all aircraft liquid systems such as fuel, oil, alcohol, etc. Refer to applicable aircraft maintenance manual for procedures. *

868. REPLACEMENT OF COMPONENTS. Replace damaged or defective instruments with identical serviceable components or components equivalent to the original in electrical and mechanical characteristics, operating tolerances, and the ability to function in the physical environmental conditions encountered in the operation of the aircraft. The replacement of instruments with other than identical or optional approved instruments may require FAA approval. Consult type certificate data sheet or parts manual. Be sure all shipping plugs and gyro caging devices that may have been installed for shipping purposes are removed before installing an instrument. Check new installations carefully prior to applying electrical power or connecting test equipment to avoid damaging sensitive mechanisms. Test the new instrument after installation for proper functioning (where applicable).

869.-879. RESERVED.

INTENTIONALLY LEFT BLANK

Section 2.   INSPECTION AND CHECKS

880. GENERAL. Proper operation of aircraft instruments is important to safe flight. Inspection is an important part of instrument maintenance. Inspection of instruments and instrument systems should include at least the following items (where applicable):

a. *Inspect* external pitot-static equipment for poor condition, cleanliness and deformation.

b. *Inspect instruments* for poor condition, mounting, marking, broken or loose knobs, bent or missing pointers, and (where applicable) improper operation.

c. *Check power-off indications* of instrument pointers, tape scales, and warning flags for proper indications.

d. *Apply power and check* for excessive mechanical noise, erratic or intermittent operation, failure to indicate, sluggishness or indication of excessive friction.

e. *Check that erection or warmup time* is not excessive, caging functions are normal, and warning flags and indicating lights and test circuits are operable.

f. *Note the operation* of instruments during engine runup (where applicable). Check for intermittent or improper operation of any instrument.

g. *Inspect all systems* for improper installation, poor general condition, apparent and obvious defects, and insecurity of attachment.

881. PERIODIC INSPECTION. Periodic inspections should be performed in accordance with ap-

plicable parts of the Federal Aviation Regulations.

882. ADDITIONAL INSPECTIONS. Periodic inspections may be supplemented by additional inspections based on the intended function of the aircraft and frequency of use. These additional inspections may be performed at any time to help maintain an airworthy aircraft. A suggested list of additional items is:

a. *Check tubing connections* and airframe mounts for security and condition.

b. *Check pneumatic tubing* for leaks, corrosion, erosion, cracks, bends and pinching, and evidence of chafing.

c. *Check the instrument lighting system* for range of illumination, burned out bulbs, and defective controls.

d. *Check electrical connections,* fuses, fuse clips and circuit breakers for proper size, security and condition.

e. *Check wiring* for excessive bends, chafing, excessive tension, improper support or broken lacing and ties.

f. *Check for evidence of overheating or contamination* of equipment by foreign matter or water. Dust, dirt, and lint contribute to overheating of equipment, poor ventilation, and malfunctioning. Special attention should be given that ventilation openings in equipment housings are open and free from obstructing lint and dust.

883.–893. RESERVED.

Section 3. INSTRUMENT POWER SOURCES

894. ELECTRICAL COMPATIBILITY. When replacing an instrument with one which provides additional functions or when adding new instruments, check the following electrical parameters (where applicable) for compatibility:

a. Voltage (AC/DC).

b. Voltage polarity (DC).

c. Voltage phase(s) (AC).

d. Frequency (AC).

e. Grounding (AC/DC).

f. System impedance matching.

g. Compatibility with system to which connected.

895. VACUUM SYSTEMS. The differential pressure to operate vacuum instruments is supplied by an engine driven vacuum pump or on a turbine engine by a pressure bleed operated venturi tube. Variation in pressure may be achieved by a pressure regulator valve according to the design requirements of the instruments; e.g., 4 1/2 inches mercury differential pressure for horizon gyro and 2 inches mercury differential pressure for a turn-and-bank indicator.

a. *Filters*. Inspect the air filters in the vacuum system and clean or change them at any time that the vacuum system differential pressure reaches established limits. Clean or change all system filters at the same time and make any necessary pressure adjustment.

b. *Tubing*. A noncollapsible, flexible tubing should be used in vacuum systems when vibration isolation is required or desired.

896.–906. RESERVED.

Section 4. PITOT-STATIC SYSTEMS

907. SYSTEM COMPONENTS. Conventional design of the pitot-static system consists of pitot-static tubes or pitot tubes with static pressure ports or vents and their related heaters, if any, and includes lines, tubing, water drains and traps, and selector valves. Pressure actuated indicators such as the altimeter, airspeed, and rate-of-climb indicators, and control units such as air data transducers, and automatic pilots may be connected to the system.

908. PITOT-STATIC TUBES AND LINES. The pitot tube is installed with the axis parallel to the longitudinal axis of the aircraft unless otherwise specified by the manufacturer. When lines are attached or removed from a bulkhead feed-through fitting or at a union, precautions must be taken to assure that the line attached to the opposite end is not loosened, twisted, or damaged by rotation of the fitting. Such fittings normally are provided with a hex flange for holding.

909. PRESSURE PORTS OR VENTS. Static pressure ports or vents should be mounted flush with the fuselage skin. Inspect for elevation or depression of the port or vent fitting. Such elevation or depression may cause airflow disturbances at high speeds and result in erroneous airspeed indications.

910. CLEANING OF SYSTEM. Inspect air passages in the systems for water, paint, dirt, or other foreign matter. Probe the drains in the pitot tube to remove dirt or other obstructions. Tubing diameter should be checked when a problem is experienced with drainage of the pitot-static system or freezing at altitude. If this diameter is less than 3/8 inch, it should be replaced with larger tubing. Water may not drain freely from smaller diameter lines. Water or obstructions may be removed from the lines by disconnecting them near the instrument and blowing clean, dry air through them. No instruments should be connected to the system during this process.

911. HEATER ELEMENTS. Some pitot-static tubes have replaced heater elements, while others do not have replaceable elements. Check replacement of the heater element or the entire tube for proper operation by noting either ammeter current or that the tube or port gets hot to the touch.

912. SYSTEM LEAK TESTING. Pitot-static leak tests should be made with all instruments connected to assure that no leaks occur at instrument connections. Such tests should be made whenever a connection has been loosened or an instrument replaced.

*913. STATIC SYSTEM TEST. Advisory Circular AC 43-203B describes an acceptable means of complying with static system tests required by FAR Part 91, Section 91.171 and 91.172, for airplanes operated in controlled airspace under the instrument flight rule (IFR). (This circular also provides information concerning the test equipment used, and precautions to be taken when performing such tests.) Aircraft not operated in controlled airspace under IFR should be tested in accordance with the aircraft manufacturer's instructions.

If the manufacturer has not issued instructions for testing static systems, the following may be used:

a. Connect the test equipment directly to the static ports, if practicable. Otherwise, connect to a static system drain or tee connection and seal off the static ports. If the test equipment is connected to the static system at any point other than the static port, it should be made at a point where the connection may be readily inspected for system integrity. Observe testing precautions given in paragraph 915.

b. *Apply a vacuum* equivalent to 1,000 feet altitude, (differential pressure of approximately 1.07 inches of mercury or 14.5 inches of water) and hold.

c. *After one minute, check* to see that the leakage has not exceeded the equivalent of 100 feet of altitude (decrease in differential pressure of approximately 0.105 inches of mercury or 1.43 inches of water).

914. PITOT SYSTEM TEST. Pitot systems should be tested in accordance with the aircraft manufacturer's instructions. If the manufacturer has not issued instructions for testing pitot systems, the following may be used:

a. *Test the pitot system* by sealing the drain holes and connecting the pitot pressure openings to a tee to which a source of pressure and a manometer or reliable airspeed indicator is connected.

b. *Apply pressure* to cause the airspeed indicator to indicate 150 knots (differential pressure 1.1 inches of mercury or 14.9 inches of water), hold at this point and clamp off source of pressure. After 1 minute, the leakage should not exceed 10 knots (decrease in differential pressure of approximately 0.15 inches of mercury or 2.04 inches of water). **Warning: Do not apply suction to pitot lines.**

915. PRECAUTIONS IN TESTING. Observe the following precautions in all pitot-static system leak testing:

a. *Perform all other work* and inspections before leak testing.

b. *Use a system diagram.* It will prevent applying reverse pressure to any instrument, and help determine the location of a leak while observing instrument indications.

c. *Be certain that no leaks exist in the test equipment.*

d. *Run full range tests only if you are thoroughly familiar* with the aircraft instrument system and the test equipment.

e. *Pressure in the pitot system* must always be equal to or greater than that in the static system. A negative differential pressure across an airspeed indicator can damage it.

f. *The rate of change or the pressure applied* should not exceed the design limits of any pitot or static instruments connected to the systems.

g. *After the conclusion of the leak test,* be certain that the system is returned to its normal flying configuration, such as removing tape from static ports and pitot tube drain holes and replacing the drain plugs, etc.

916.–926. RESERVED.

Section 5. MECHANICAL ADJUSTMENT OF MAGNETIC DIRECTION INDICATORS

927. CORRECTION FOR ERRORS. When a magnetic direction indicator does not provide satisfactory directional indications, it can be adjusted by the "ground swinging" technique to compensate for errors.

928. GROUND SWINGING. The ground swinging technique is as follows:

a. Move aircraft to a location free from influence of steel structures, underground pipes and cables, reinforced concrete, or other aircraft.

b. Place the aircraft in level flying position.

c. Check indicator for fluid level and cleanliness. If fluid is required, the compass is defective.

d. Remove compensating magnets from chambers or reset the fixed compensating magnets to neutral positions, whichever is applicable, before swinging.

e. Check the pivot friction of the indicator by deflecting the card with a small magnet. The card should rotate freely in a horizontal plane.

f. Align the aircraft with the North magnetic heading and compensate with compensating magnets. Repeat for the East magnetic heading. Then place on South and West magnetic headings and remove half of the indicated error by adjusting the compensators. Engine(s) should be running.

g. Turn the aircraft on successive 30° headings through 360°. Prepare a placard to show the correction to be applied at each of these headings. When significant errors are introduced by operation of electrical/electronic equipment or systems, the placard should also be marked at each 30° heading showing the correction to be applied when such equipment or systems are turned on or energized.

929. REMOTE GYRO COMPASS SYSTEMS. Adjustment and compensation of remote indicating gyro compasses, polar path compasses, and other systems of this type may also be accomplished using the "ground swinging" technique. Reference should be made to the manufacturer's manual for special tools, instructions, and procedures.

930.–940. RESERVED.

Section 6.   PRESERVATION AND PACKAGING

941. PRESERVATION. Preserve all instruments, serviceable or unserviceable, in accordance with the manufacturer's recommendations or other acceptable standards. Protect the unit against humidity, extreme temperatures, dust, rough handling or other damage until it is repaired or installed in an aircraft. The method used should be pickling, wrapping, sealing in plastic covering, rigid boxes with plastic or foam padding, or other methods appropriate to the instrument or subassembly.

942. STORAGE. Instruments should be stored in a location and a manner which provides maximum protection from physical damage. Serviceable instruments should remain packaged until installed in an aircraft. If a drying agent is used, the package should be dated so that the drying agent may be inspected for condition. Inspect units that remain in storage for extended periods of time for general condition and integrity of packaging and preserving materials.

943. SHIPPING. Protect the instrument from damage during shipment by sealing it in a moisture proof covering and protecting it with a drying agent. Use plastic foam, rubberized hair, or foam rubber molded to the configuration of the instrument case to support it inside a rigid shipping container. Large units may be shock-mounted on fitted pallets or racks and protected with covers.

944.–954. RESERVED.

AC NO: 43.13–2A

DATE: Revised 1977

ADVISORY CIRCULAR

DEPARTMENT OF TRANSPORTATION
FEDERAL AVIATION ADMINISTRATION

SUBJECT: ACCEPTABLE METHODS, TECHNIQUES, AND PRACTICES— AIRCRAFT ALTERATIONS

---

1. PURPOSE.

This advisory circular contains methods, techniques, and practices acceptable to the Administrator for use in altering civil aircraft.

2. CANCELLATION.

Advisory Circular 43.13–2 dated 1965 is cancelled.

3. REFERENCE.

Part 43 of the Federal Aviation Regulations requires that methods, techniques, and practices acceptable to the Administrator must be used when altering civil aircraft. Methods, techniques, and practices other than those prescribed in this advisory circular may be used provided they are acceptable to the Administrator. FAA Inspectors are prepared to answer questions that may arise in this regard. Persons engaged in alteration of civil aircraft should be familiar with FAR Part 43, and subparts A, D, and E of FAR Part 65, and the applicable airworthiness requirements under which the aircraft was type certificated.

J. A. FERRARESE
Acting Director, Flight Standards Service

Initiated by: AFS–580/AFS–830

CONTENTS

Chapter 1. STRUCTURAL DATA

Chapter 2. RADIO INSTALLATIONS

Chapter 3. ANTENNA INSTALLATIONS

Chapter 4. ANTICOLLISION AND SUPPLEMENTARY LIGHT INSTALLATIONS

CONTENTS—Continued

Chapter 5. SKI INSTALLATIONS

Chapter 6. OXYGEN SYSTEM INSTALLATIONS IN NONPRESSURIZED AIRCRAFT

Chapter 7. ROTORCRAFT EXTERNAL-LOAD DEVICE INSTALLATIONS

Section 1. CARGO SLINGS

Section 2. CARGO RACKS

CONTENTS—*Continued*

Chapter 8.   GLIDER AND BANNER TOW-HITCH INSTALLATIONS

Chapter 9.   SHOULDER HARNESS INSTALLATIONS

Chapter 10.   BATTERY INSTALLATIONS

CONTENTS—Continued

LIST OF ILLUSTRATIONS

CONTENTS—Continued

LIST OF ILLUSTRATIONS—Continued

v

CONTENTS—*Continued*

LIST OF ILLUSTRATIONS—*Continued*

IAP, Inc.–June, 1988　　384

CONTENTS—Continued

LIST OF ILLUSTRATIONS—Continued

LIST OF TABLES

Chapter 1. STRUCTURAL DATA

1. GENERAL. The minimum airworthiness requirements are those under which the aircraft was type certificated. Addition or removal of equipment involving changes in weight could affect the structural integrity, weight, balance, flight characteristics, or performance of an aircraft.

2. STATIC LOADS. Utilize equipment supporting structure and attachments that are capable of withstanding the additional inertia forces ("g." load factors) imposed by weight of equipment installed. Load factors are defined as follows:

a. Limit Load Factors are the maximum load factors which may be expected during service (the maneuvering, gust, or ground load factors established by the manufacturer for type certification).

b. Ultimate Load Factors are the limit load factors multiplied by a prescribed factor of safety. Certain loads, such as the minimum ultimate inertia forces prescribed for emergency landing conditions, are given directly in terms of ultimate loads.

c. Static Test Load Factors are the ultimate load factors multiplied by prescribed casting, fitting, bearing, and/or other special factors. Where no special factors apply, the static test load factors are equal to the ultimate load factors.

d. Critical Static Test Load Factors are the greater of the maneuvering, gust, ground, and inertia load static test load factors for each direction (up, down, side, fore, and aft).

Static tests using the following load factors are acceptable for equipment installations:

Direction of Force Applied	Normal-Utility FAR 23 (CAR 3)	Acrobatic FAR 23 (CAR 3)	Transport FAR 25 (CAR 4b)	Rotorcraft FAR 27, 29 (CAR 6, 7)
Sideward	1.5g	1.5g	1.5g	2.0g
Upward	3.0g	4.5g	**	1.5g
Forward*	9.0g	9.0g	9.0g	4.0g
Downward	6.6g	9.0g	**	4.0g

* When equipment mounting is located externally to one side, or forward of occupants, a forward load factor of 2.0g is sufficient.

** Due to differences among various aircraft designs in flight and ground load factors, contact the aircraft manufacturer for the load factors required for a given model and location. In lieu of specific information, the factors used for FAR 23 utility category are acceptable for aircraft with never exceed speed of 250 knots or less and the factors used for FAR 23 acrobatic category for all other transport aircraft.

The following is an example of determining the static test loads for a 7-pound piece of equipment to be installed in a utility category aircraft (FAR Part 23).

Load Factors (From the above table)		Static Test Loads (Load factor × 7 pounds)
Sideward	1.5g	10.5 pounds
Upward	3.0g	21.0 pounds
Downward	6.6g	46.2 pounds
Forward	9.0g	63.0 pounds

When an additional load is to be added to structure already supporting previously installed equipment, determine the capability of the structure to support the total load (previous load plus added load).

3. STATIC TESTS.

Caution: The aircraft and/or equipment can be damaged in applying static loads, particularly if careless or improper procedure is used.

It is recommended, whenever practicable, that static testing be conducted on a duplicate installation in a jig or mockup which simulates the related aircraft structure. Static test loads may exceed the yield limits of the assemblies being substantiated and can result in partially sheared fasteners, elongated holes, or other damage which may not be visible unless the structure is disassembled. If the structure is materially weakened during testing, it may fail at a later date. Riveted sheet metal and composite laminate construction methods especially do not lend themselves to easy detection of such damage. To conduct static tests:

a. Determine the weight and center of gravity position of the equipment item.

b. Make actual or simulated installation of attachment in the aircraft or preferably on a jig using the applicable static test load factors.

c. Determine the critical ultimate load factors for the up, down, side, fore, and aft directions. A hypothetical example which follows steps (1) through (4) below is shown in figure 1.1.

(1) Convert the gust, maneuvering, and ground load factors obtained from the manufacturer or FAA engineering to ultimate load factors. Unless otherwise specified in the airworthiness standards applicable to the aircraft, ultimate load factors are limit load factors multiplied by a 1.5 safety factor. (See columns 1, 2, and 3 for items A, B, and C of fig. 1.1.)

(2) Determine the ultimate inertia load forces for the emergency landing conditions as prescribed in the applicable airworthiness standards. (See items D and E, column 3, of fig. 1.1.)

(3) Determine what additional load factors are applicable to the specific seat, litter, berth, or cargo tiedown device installation. The ultimate load factors are then multiplied by these factors to obtain the static test factors. (To simplify this example, only the seat, litter, berth, and safety belt attachment factor of 1.33 was assumed to be applicable. See Item E, column 4, of fig. 1.1.)

(4) Select the highest static test load factors obtained in Steps 1, 2, and/or 3 for each direction (up, down, side, fore, and aft). These factors are the *critical static test load factors* used to compute the static test load. (See column 6 of fig. 1.1.)

d. Apply load at center of gravity position (of equipment item or dummy) by any suitable means that will demonstrate that the attachment and structure are capable of supporting the required loads.

When no damage or permanent deformation occurs after 3 seconds of applied static load, the structure and attachments are acceptable. Should permanent deformation occur after 3 seconds, repair or replace the deformed structure to return it to its normal configuration and strength. Additional load testing is not necessary.

4. MATERIALS. Use materials conforming to an accepted standard such as AN, NAS, TSO, or MIL–SPEC.

5. FABRICATION. When a fabrication process which requires close control is used, employ methods which produce consistently sound structure that is compatible with the aircraft structure.

6. FASTENERS. Use hardware conforming to an accepted standard such as AN, NAS, TSO, or MIL–SPEC. Attach equipment so as to prevent loosening in service due to vibration.

7. PROTECTION AGAINST DETERIORATION. Provide protection against deterioration or loss of strength due to corrosion, abrasion, electrolytic action, or other causes.

8. PROVISIONS FOR INSPECTION. Provide adequate provisions to permit close examination of equipment or adjacent parts of the aircraft that regularly require inspection, adjustment, lubrication, etc.

9. EFFECTS ON WEIGHT AND BALANCE. Assure that the altered aircraft can be operated within the weight and center of gravity ranges listed in the FAA Type Certificate (T.C.) Data Sheet or Aircraft Listing. Determine that the altered aircraft will not exceed maximum gross weight. (If applicable, correct the loading schedule to reflect the current loading procedure.) Consult Advisory Circular 43.13–1A, "Acceptable Methods, Techniques, and Practices—Aircraft Inspection and Repair" for Weight and Balance Computation Procedures.

10. EFFECTS ON SAFE OPERATION. Install equipment in a manner that will not interfere with or adversely affect the safe operation of the aircraft (controls, navigation equipment operation, etc.).

11. CONTROLS AND INDICATORS. Locate and identify equipment controls and indicators so they can be operated and read from the appropriate crewmember position.

12. PLACARDING. Label equipment requiring identification and, if necessary, placard operational instructions. Amend weight and balance information as required.

13.–20. [RESERVED]

Utility Category Aircraft (FAR 23)

TYPE OF LOAD	Direction	LOAD FACTORS					
		1 Limit	2 X Safety	3 = Ultimate	4 X Special	5 Static = Test	6 Critical Static Test
A. Maneuvering	Fwd	(None)					
	Down	6.2g	1.5	9.30g		9.3g	9.3g
	Side	(None)					
	Up	−3.8g	1.5	−5.7g		−5.7g	5.7g
	Aft	1.0g	1.5	1.5g		1.5g	
B. Gust (= 30 FPS @ KVc) *For locations aft of fuselage Sta. 73.85.	Fwd	(None)					
	Down	6.0g	1.5	9.0g		9.0g	
	Down*	6.4g	1.5	9.6g		9.6g	*9.6g
	Side	1.6g	1.5	2.4g		2.4g	2.4g
	Up	−2.8g	1.5	−4.2g		−4.2g	
	Aft	(None)					
C. Ground	Fwd	6.6g	1.5	9.9g		9.9g	9.9g
	Down	4.0g	1.5	6.0g		6.0g	
D. Ultimate Inertia Forces for Emergency Landing Condition (FAR 23.561). **For Separate cargo compartments.	Fwd	Already Prescribed as Ultimate	"	9.0g			
	Fwd**	"	"	4.5g			**4.5g
	Down	"	"	(None)			
	Side	"	"	1.5g		1.5g	
	Up	"	"	−3.0g		−3.0g	
	Aft	"	"	(None)			
E. Ultimate Inertia Forces for Emergency Landing Condition For Seat, Litter, & Berth Attachment to Aircraft Structure (FAR 23.785).	Fwd	"	"	9.0g	1.33	12.0g	12.0g
	Down	"	"	(None)			
	Side	"	"	1.5g	1.33	2.0g	
	Up	"	"	−3.0g	1.33	−4.0g	
	Aft	"	"	(None)			

*Asterisks denote special load conditions for the situation shown.

FIGURE 1.1—Hypothetical example of determining static test loads.

Chapter 2. RADIO INSTALLATIONS

21. INSTALLATION. When installing radio equipment, first consider areas or locations designated by the airframe manufacturer and use factory supplied brackets or racks. Follow the aircraft manufacturer's installation instructions. When this information is not available, use locations in the aircraft of known load carrying capabilities. Baggage compartments and cabins or cockpit floors are good mounting platforms providing the floor attachments meet the strength requirements. Another method is to fabricate support racks, brackets, or shelves, and attach them to the aircraft structure to provide a mounting that will withstand the inertia forces stipulated in chapter 1 of this handbook.

a. Determine that the location and installation of radio equipment provides:

(1) Sufficient air circulation to avoid overheating.

(2) Sufficient clearance between high temperature areas of equipment and readily flammable materials.

(3) Protection from potentially hazardous fluids and/or fumes; e.g., water (condensation), fuel, hydraulic fluid, or oxygen units.

(4) Protection against damage from baggage or by seat deflection.

(5) Sufficient clearance to avoid equipment striking adjacent parts of the aircraft or other equipment.

(6) Minimum interference to other installed navigational equipment from the emission of radar/pulse frequencies or from electromagnetic induction.

22. EQUIPMENT MANUFACTURER'S INSTRUCTIONS. Installation instructions provided by the aircraft radio manufacturer are acceptable guidelines when adapted to the aircraft in accordance with data contained in this chapter.

23. INSTRUMENT PANEL MOUNTING. Data in this paragraph is supplemented by chapter 2 of AC 43.13–1A, "Acceptable Methods, Techniques, and Practices—Aircraft Inspection and Repair"

and is applicable to the installation of radio units in instrument panels.

a. Stationary Instrument Panels—Nonstructural and Structural. The stationary instrument panel in some aircraft is primary structure. Prior to making any additional "cutouts" or enlargement of an existing "cutout" determine if the panel is primary structure. If the panel is structural, make additional "cutouts" or the enlargement of existing "cutouts" in accordance with the aircraft manufacturer's instructions, or substantiate the structural integrity of the altered panel in a manner acceptable to the Administrator. Radius all corners and remove all burrs from "cutout" and drilled holes.

b. Added Equipment — Stationary Instrument Panel. When radio equipment is to be installed in a stationary panel already supporting instruments, glove compartments, etc., determine the capability of the panel to support the total load.

c. Case Support. To minimize the load on a stationary instrument panel, whenever practicable, install a support between the rear (or side) surface of the radio case and a nearby structural member of the aircraft.

d. Added Equipment—Shockmounted Panels. When installing radio equipment designed for use in shockmounted panels, total accumulated weight of equipment installed must not exceed the weight carrying capabilities of the shockmounts. Determine that the structure to which the shockmounts are connected is satisfactory for the added weight.

e. Existing Factory Fasteners. When possible, utilize existing plate nuts and machine screws provided by the aircraft manufacturer for attachment of the radio case or rack. If additional fastening is required, use machine screws and elastic stop nuts (preferably plate nuts).

f. Magnetic Direction Indicator. As a function of the radio installation, determine if it is necessary to compensate the compass. Install a suitable placard which indicates the compass error with the radio(s) on and off. The receiver(s) should be tuned through the low, middle and higher frequencies to cover all contingencies involving the operation of relays which would cause electromagnetic induction to the magnetic compass. When inverters are installed, determine what effect their operation has on the magnetic compass. Maximum acceptable deviation in level flight is 10° on any heading. The following is an example of a typical compass calibration card.

24. OTHER MOUNTING AREAS. The following are acceptable methods for installing radio equipment at other than instrument panel locations.

a. Shockmounted Units.

(1) Wood or Composition Flooring. Secure the shockmounted base assembly (suitable to radio unit) directly to the floor using machine screws. Add a doubler to the bottom of the floor thereby sandwiching the composition floor between each shockmount foot and the doubler. Subsequent removal and reinstallation of the shockmount foot will be facilitated if plate nuts are secured to the doubler. Where practicable, use small retaining screws to keep the doubler in position. Install a ground strap between the radio rack and metal structure of the aircraft.

Typical Compass Calibration Card

FOR	N	30	60	E	120	150
Radio **On.** Steer	4°	35°	63°	93°	123°	154°
Radio **Off.** Steer	358°	27°	58°	88°	118°	148°
FOR	S	210	240	W	300	330
Radio **On.** Steer	183°	214°	224°	274°	304°	337°
Radio **Off.** Steer	178°	208°	238°	268°	293°	327°

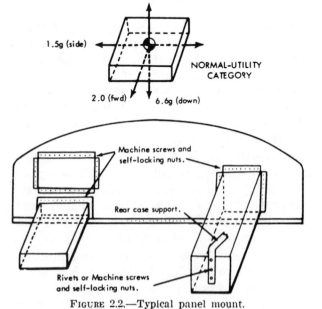

FIGURE 2.1.—Typical radio installations in stationary instrument panels.

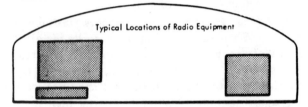

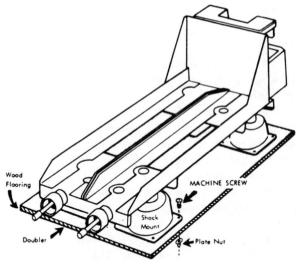

FIGURE 2.3.—Typical shockmounted base.

(2) Metal Flooring. Secure the shockmounted base assembly directly to the floor using machine screws, washers, and self-locking nuts. Floor area under and around the radio mounting bases may require installation of doublers or other reinforcement to prevent flexing and cracking. Installation of plate nuts on the floor or doubler will facilitate removal and installation of the shockmounts. Install a ground strap between the shockmount foot and the radio rack.

FIGURE 2.2.—Typical panel mount.

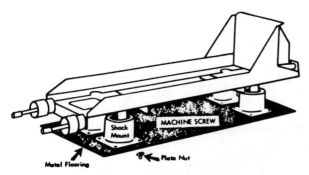

FIGURE 2.4.—Typical shockmounted base.

b. *Rigid-Mounted Unit Base.* Secure radio mounting base plate(s) to floor (wood, composite, or metal) using machine screws as shown in figure 2.5. Use a reinforcing plate or large area washers or equivalent under wood or composite flooring. When mounting base is secured to wood or composite material, install a ground strap between the base and aircraft metal structure.

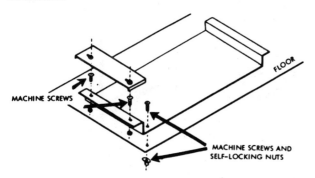

FIGURE 2.5.—Typical rigid baseplate mount.

25. FABRICATION OF SUPPORTING BRACKETS FOR ATTACHMENT TO STRUCTURE OTHER THAN FLOORING.

a. *Typical supporting brackets* usually consist of a shelf or platform upon which the radio unit mounting base assembly can be installed in the same manner as described in applicable paragraph 24.

b. *Fabricate bracket* in accordance with good aircraft design, layout, assembly practices, and workmanship to obtain results compatible with the airframe structure. Generally the thickness of bracket material will depend on the size or area of the platform and load it must sustain in accordance with provisions set forth in chapter 1 of this handbook.

c. *Use a rivet size* and pattern compatible with the aircraft structure to provide the strength needed to assure support of the loads imposed under all flight and landing conditions.

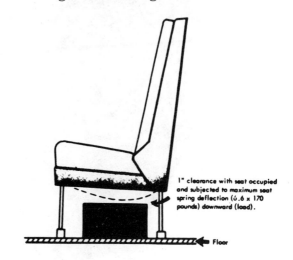

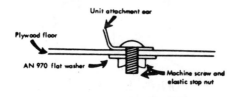

FIGURE 2.6.—Typical underseat installation.

26. SUPPORTING STRUCTURE REINFORCEMENT.

a. *Attach equipment* supporting structure to the aircraft so that its supported load will be transmitted to aircraft structural members. If direct attachment to existing structure (bulkheads, horizontal stringers, etc.) is not feasible, add the necessary stringers, doublers, bulkhead flange reinforcements, etc., to provide adequate support and assure load transfer to primary structure.

b. *Placard.* Fasten on the shelf or bracket a permanent placard (as the example below) stating the design load which the installed structure has been determined to be capable of supporting.

Shelf load not to exceed

_____ lbs.

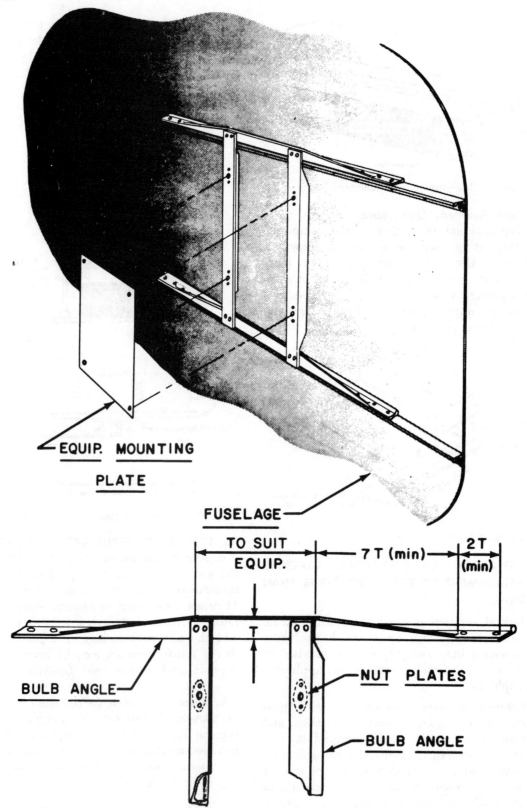

EQUIP. MOUNTING
PLATE

FUSELAGE

TO SUIT
EQUIP.

7 T (min)

2 T
(min)

T

BULB ANGLE

NUT PLATES

BULB ANGLE

FIGURE 2.7.—Typical remote unit mounting base—vertical or horizontal.

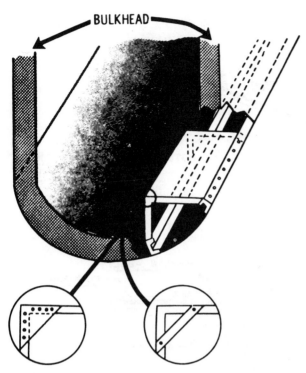

Use standard aircraft practices and procedures for fabrication and attachment of shelf. Reinforce fore and aft corners with gussets or bulb angle.

FIGURE 2.8.—Typical shelf installation.

Fabricate platform using 2017T4(17ST) or equivalent. Apply standard aircraft practices for fabrication and installation.

The equipment manufacturer mounting bases that meet load requirements and can be utilized are acceptable.

27. ELECTRICAL SYSTEMS. The following data in addition to that shown in chapter 11 in AC 43.13–1A is applicable to radio installations.

a. Installation of Wiring.

(1) Use a type and design satisfactory for the purpose intended.

(2) Install in a manner to be suitably protected from fuel, oil, water, other detrimental substances and abrasion damages.

b. Power Sources.

(1) Connect radio electrical systems to the aircraft electrical system at a terminal strip, or use a plug and receptacle connection.

(2) Radio electrical systems must function properly whether connected in combination or independently.

c. Protective Devices.

(1) Incorporate a "trip free" resettable type circuit breaker or a fuse in the power supply from the bus. Mount in a manner accessible to a crewmember during flight for circuit breaker resetting or fuse replacement.

(2) Select circuit breakers or fuses that will provide adequate protection against overloading of the radio system circuits.

(3) Connect all leads in such a manner that the master switch of the aircraft will interrupt the circuit when the master switch is opened.

(4) Radio system controls are to provide independent operation of each system installed and are to be clearly placarded to identify their function relative to the unit of equipment they operate.

d. Available Power Supply. To preclude overloading the electric power system of the aircraft when additional equipment is added, make an

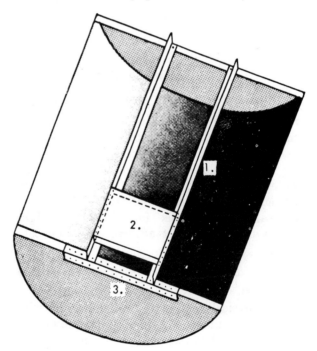

1. BULB ANGLE

2. STIFFENING FLANGE OR ANGLE AT ENDS OF PLATFORM

3. REINFORCEMENT ANGLE FOR BULKHEAD

FIGURE 2.9.—Typical rail platform installation— aluminum alloy structure.

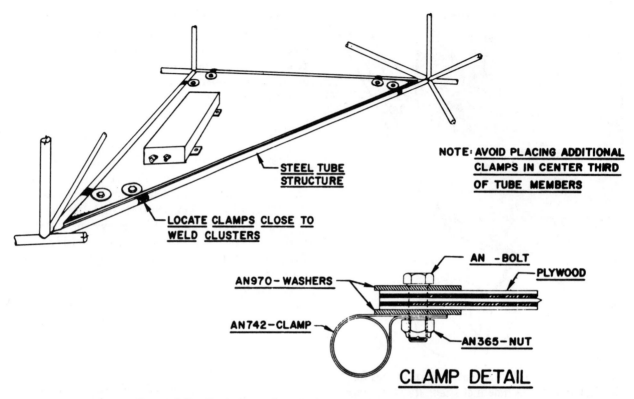

STEEL TUBE
STRUCTURE

NOTE: AVOID PLACING ADDITIONAL
CLAMPS IN CENTER THIRD
OF TUBE MEMBERS

LOCATE CLAMPS CLOSE TO
WELD CLUSTERS

AN -BOLT
PLYWOOD
AN970-WASHERS
AN742-CLAMP
AN365-NUT

CLAMP DETAIL

FIGURE 2.10.—Typical attachment of support structure to tubular frame.

electrical load analysis to determine whether the available power is adequate. Radio equipment must operate satisfactorily throughout the voltage range of the aircraft electrical system under taxi, takeoff, slow cruise, normal cruise, and landing operating conditions. If night and instrument flight is contemplated, compute the electrical load analysis for the above flight regimes under the most adverse operating conditions.

e. Wire Bundle Separation from Flammable Fluid Lines.

(1) Physically separate radio electric wire bundles from lines or equipment containing oil, fuel, hydraulic fluid, alcohol, or oxygen.

(2) Mount radio electrical wire bundles above flammable fluid lines and securely clamp to structure. (In no case must radio electrical wire bundles be clamped to lines containing flammable fluids.)

f. Cable Attachment to Shockmounted Units.

(1) Route and support electrical wire bundles and mechanical cables in a manner that will allow normal motion of equipment without strain or damage to the wire bundles or mechanical cables.

g. Radio Bonding. It is advisable to bond radio equipment to the aircraft in order to provide a low impedance ground and to minimize radio interference from static electrical charges. When bonding is used, observe the following:

(1) Keep bonding jumpers as short as possible.

(2) Prepare bonded surfaces for best contact (resistance of connections should not exceed .003 ohm).

(3) Avoid use of solder to attach bonding jumpers. Clamps and screws are preferred.

(4) For bonding aluminum alloy, use aluminum alloy or tinned or cadmium-plated copper jumpers. Use brass or bronze jumpers on steel parts.

(5) When contact between dissimilar metals cannot be avoided, put a protective coating over the finished connection to minimize corrosion.

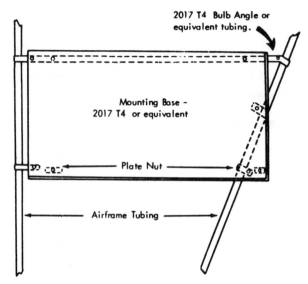

Secure mounting base to airframe tubing with loop-type clamp (AN 742 or equivalent), machine screws, and self-locking nuts.

FIGURE 2.11.—Typical mounting plates for remote location of radio units.

h. **Radio Interference.** Radio interference generated by aircraft components can be eliminated or reduced by exercising proper precautions. The following paragraphs contain two major sources of interference which affect audio reception.

(1) *Ignition system interference* can be minimized with shielding. To be effective, all parts of the ignition system should be shielded in metal in order to eliminate noise resulting from RF radiation.

(a) A metallic braid covering and special end connectors are effective between the magneto and shielded type spark plugs.

(b) Shield the primary lead to the magneto.

(c) Provide a shielded metal cover for the magneto if it is not of a shielded type.

(d) Provide a tight metal-to-metal contact of all connections in the shielding system.

(e) If it is not feasible to shield the engine ignition system, the engine ignition noise may be suppressed by replacing the spark plugs with resistor spark plugs of a type approved for the engine.

(f) If it is found that despite shielding of the ignition wiring and plugs an intolerable noise level is present in the radio system, it may be necessary to provide a filter between the magneto and magneto switch to reduce the noise. This may consist of a single bypass capacitor or a combination of capacitors and choke coils. When this is done, the shielding between the filter and magneto switch can usually be eliminated and the special shielded magneto switch need not be used.

(g) Supporting brackets and wiring details for magneto filters should be in conformance with standard aircraft electrical practice. The reliability of the magneto filter installations should be at least equivalent to that of the remainder of the magneto ground lead installation.

(2) *Inverter interference* is noticeable by a constant noise or hash induced and amplified by the audio circuits of the communication or navigation systems. This noise level can reach such a magnitude that all intelligence of audio reception is lost. Inverter interference can be effectively minimized or eliminated by observing the following precautions during installation:

(a) Locate the inverters in an area separated from other electronic equipment.

(b) Assure that the inverter input and output wires are separated.

(c) Shield the inverter output wires and ground the shields at the inverter end only.

(d) Make sure the inverter case is adequately bonded to the airframe.

i. **Mutual Radio Frequency Interference in DME/ ATC Radar Beacon Systems.** Distance measuring equipment (DME) and ATC radar beacon (transponder) systems operate within the same frequency range. Therefore, simultaneous operation of two or more of these systems may result in mutual RF interference. Certain makes of DME and transponder equipment have intersystem suppressor circuitry designed to eliminate mutual interference. When such connections are provided, follow the manufacturer's recommendations for use and wire bundle installation.

28. EMERGENCY LOCATOR TRANSMITTER (ELT) INSTALLATIONS. The ELT unit should be attached to the airframe or other solid structures. Airframe preparation for either vertical or shelf-type mountings is displayed in figures 2.7 and 2.8. The equipment manufacturer mounting bases that meet load requirements and can be utilized are acceptable.

The installation of the ELT antenna should be located as far as practicable from other installed antennas. Methods for securing whip-type antennas to the structure are shown in figures 3.1 and 3.3. Follow the manufacturer's installation procedures when available.

29.–35. [RESERVED]

Chapter 3. ANTENNA INSTALLATIONS

36. PERFORMANCE. For proper performance, it is important that the radio equipment manufacturer's instructions be carefully followed in matching and coupling the antenna to the radio equipment.

a. *The location of the antenna is of primary importance.* When selecting a mounting position, consideration should be given but not limited to the following:

(1) Obstruction to signal reception by aircraft or aircraft components.

(2) Ignition noise (RF radiation pickup).

(3) Vibration.

(4) Flutter.

(5) Instrument static source interference.

b. *Attach antenna mounting* (masts, base receptacles, and/or supporting brackets) so that the loads imposed (e.g., air, ice, etc.) are transmitted to the aircraft structure.

37. VHF ANTENNA—WHIP.

a. Locate this type antenna so that there is a minimum of structure between it and the ground radio stations. The antenna may be mounted on the top or bottom of the fuselage. It is not advisable to mount the antenna on the cowl forward of the windshield because a lightning strike might possibly blind the pilot.

b. Methods of securing whip antennas to the structure are shown in figures 3.1 and 3.3.

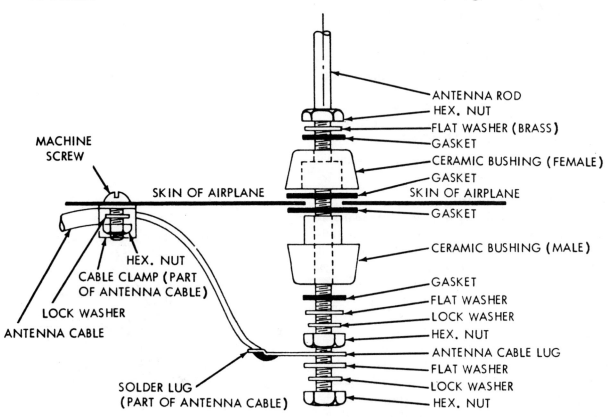

FIGURE 3.1.—Typical whip antenna installation.

c. On fabric-covered aircraft or aircraft with other types of nonmetallic skin, the manufacturer's recommendations should be followed in order to provide the necessary ground plane. An acceptable method of accomplishing this is by providing a number of metal foil strips in a radial position from the antenna base and secured under the fabric or wood skin of the aircraft. (See fig. 3.2.)

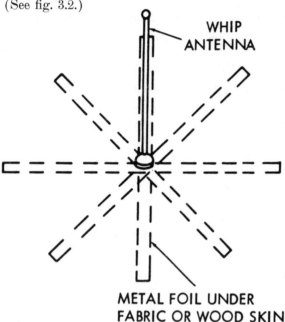

WHIP ANTENNA

METAL FOIL UNDER FABRIC OR WOOD SKIN

NOTE: THE LENGTH OF EACH FOIL RADIAL SHOULD BE AT LEAST EQUAL TO THE ANTENNA LENGTH.

FIGURE 3.2.—Antenna ground plane for nonmetallic aircraft.

38. VHF ANTENNA—RIGID.

a. *When it is necessary to cover a broader frequency range* than can be covered by a whip antenna, a blade type should be used because it is resonant over a much broader frequency range. However, a broadband antenna is not as efficient as a small diameter whip antenna and, accordingly, should not be used with relatively low output transmitters (under 5 watts).

(1) The antennas shown in figure 3.4 are normally installed at a point on the fuselage directly above the cabin or baggage compartment.

When a rigid antenna is installed on the vertical stabilizer, evaluate the flutter and vibration characteristics of the installation.

(2) The approximate drag load an antenna is required to withstand can be determined by the following formula:

$$D = .000327 \, AV^2$$

(The formula includes a 90 percent reduction factor for streamline shape of antenna.)

Where D is the drag load on the antenna in lbs.,

A is the frontal area of the antenna in sq. ft., and

V is the V_{ne} of the aircraft in m.p.h.

The frontal area of typical antennas are approximately as follows:

Antenna (*Fig. 3.4*)	Area (*sq. ft.*)
a	.073
b	.135
c	.135
d	.025
e	.045

Example: Antenna "b" at 250 m.p.h.

$$D = .000327 \times .135 \times (250)^2$$
$$= .000327 \times .135 \times 62,500$$
$$= 2.75 \text{ lbs.}$$

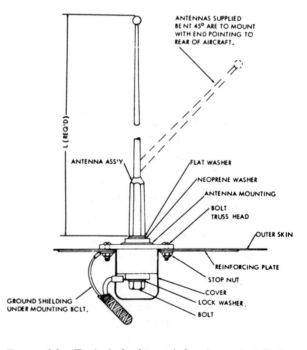

ANTENNAS SUPPLIED BENT 45° ARE TO MOUNT WITH END POINTING TO REAR OF AIRCRAFT.

L (REQ'D)

ANTENNA ASS'Y

FLAT WASHER

NEOPRENE WASHER

ANTENNA MOUNTING

BOLT TRUSS HEAD

OUTER SKIN

REINFORCING PLATE

STOP NUT

COVER

LOCK WASHER

BOLT

GROUND SHIELDING UNDER MOUNTING BOLT.

FIGURE 3.3.—Typical shockmounted antenna installation.

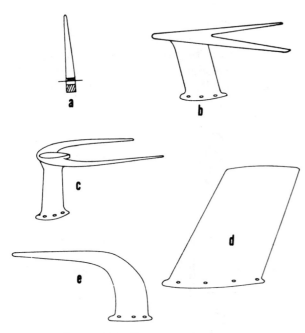

FIGURE 3.4.—Typical rigid antennas.

(4) Route transmission line cable to the receiver, secure the cable firmly along its entire length at intervals of approximately 2 feet, and take care to prevent fouling of control cables.

39. VHF NAVIGATION RECEIVING ANTENNAS. Locate antennas for omnirange (VOR), and instrument landing system (ILS) localizer receivers at a position on the aircraft where they will have the greatest sensitivity for the desired signals and minimum response to undesired signals such as electrical energy radiated by the engine ignition system. A good location for the VOR localizer receiving antenna on many small

b. *Installation of Rigid Antennas.*

(1) Place a template similar to figure 3.5 on the fore-and-aft centerline at the desired location. Drill the mounting holes and the correct diameter hole for the transmission line cable in the fuselage skin.

(2) Install a reinforcing doubler of sufficient thickness to reinforce the aircraft skin. The length and width of the plate should approximate that illustrated in figures 3.6 or 3.8.

(3) Install antenna on fuselage, making sure that the mounting bolts are tightened firmly against the reinforcing doubler, and that the mast is drawn tight against the gasket.

When a gasket is not used, seal the crack between the mast and fuselage with a sealer, such as zinc chromate paste or equivalent.

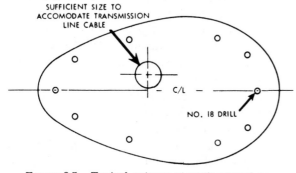

FIGURE 3.5.—Typical antenna mounting template.

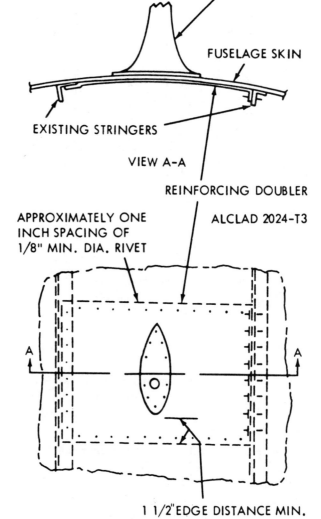

FIGURE 3.6.—Typical antenna installation on a skin panel.

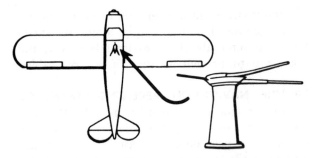

FIGURE 3.7.—Preferred VOR antenna location for maximum signal pickup with minimum ignition interference.

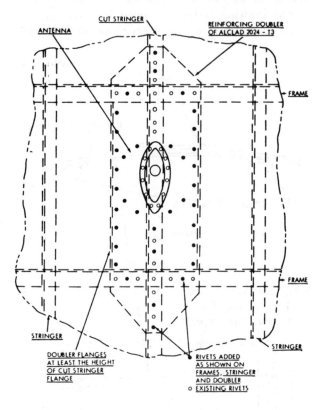

FIGURE 3.8.—Typical antenna installation involving a cut stringer.

airplanes is over the forward part of the cabin. Mount the rigid V-type antenna so that the apex of the "V" points forward and the plane of the "V" is level in normal flight.

a. VOR Antenna Balun and Transmission Lines. A dual element or balanced antenna system requires a balun or an impedence matching device for maximum signal transfer into an unbalanced coaxial cable. Rigid antennas, as displayed in figure 3.4, incorporate a balun as an integral component of the antenna assembly. Follow the

manufacturer's installation procedures and assure that the balun is properly grounded to the airframe. Refer to AC 43.13–1A "Acceptable Methods, Techniques, and Practices—Aircraft Inspection and Repair" chapter 11, for acceptable bonding practices.

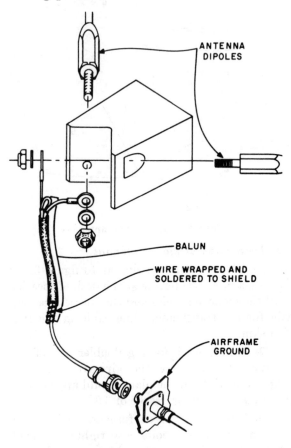

FIGURE 3.9 Typical dipole antenna assembly.

(2) Figure 3.10 is an illustration of a typical VOR antenna balun. A balun made from a section of the transmission line functions as a tuned circuit or transformer which produces a standing-wave ratio to provide the desired matching impedence. When the antenna is matched to the line, the line measurement in multiples of wave lengths is not critical.

(2) Radio wave velocity is less in a cable than in air; therefore, the wave length in cable will be shorter than in air. Appropriate test equipment must be used for transmission line measurements because the physical and electrical lengths of lines are not always equal.

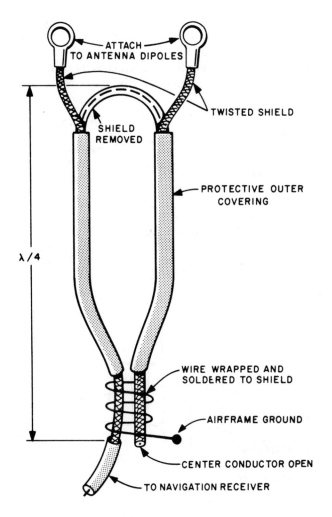

FIGURE 3.10 Typical VOR antenna balun.

(3) The transmission line should be kept as short as possible. Any bends in the cable should have at least a 3-inch radius. Follow the equipment manufacturer's recommendations regarding transmission lines and lengths.

b. Assembly of Coaxial Cable Connectors. Optimum performance of a radio system is dependent upon the coaxial cable connector assembly. Follow the manufacturer's assembly instructions. Assure that the cable is not distorted or flattened when cutting. The electrical characteristics of the cable change when flattened or bent sharply.

(1) To remove the outer jacket, cut with a sharp knife around the circumference, then make a lengthwise slit and peel off the outer jacket. Do not nick, cut or damage the shield.

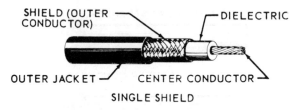

FIGURE 3.11 Coaxial cable preparation.

(2) Comb out the braid and bend back to expose the dielectric. Use a sharp knife to cut the dielectric around the circumference, not quite through to the center conductor. Do not nick or cut the conductor. Remove the dielectric by twisting and pulling.

(3) Solder the contact to the center conductor. Use a clean, well-tinned soldering iron.

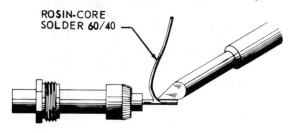

FIGURE 3.12 Coaxial cable tinning center lead.

(4) Do not apply heat too long as this will swell the dielectric and make it difficult to insert into the body of the connector.

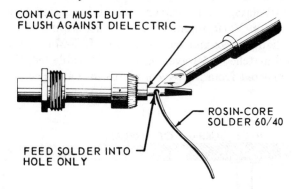

FIGURE 3.13 Coaxial cable soldering center lead.

(5) Install connector body and tighten until secure. Do not overtighten as this will distort the cable.

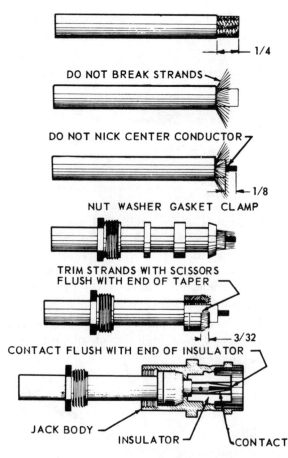

DO NOT BREAK STRANDS

DO NOT NICK CENTER CONDUCTOR

NUT WASHER GASKET CLAMP

TRIM STRANDS WITH SCISSORS
FLUSH WITH END OF TAPER

CONTACT FLUSH WITH END OF INSULATOR

JACK BODY   INSULATOR   CONTACT

FIGURE 3.14 Coaxial cable install connector body.

(6) Use only the crimping tool recommended by the manufacturer, or an equivalent tool when installing connectors which utilize a crimp-type contact.

c. *Dual VOR/NAV Receiver Installations.* Two VOR navigation receivers can be connected to a common VOR antenna. This is accomplished by utilizing a coaxial tee connecter (UG–274 A/U) and matched 0.5 wavelength coaxial cable lengths connected from the tee connector to the respective

VOR receivers. Typical cable lengths are from 22 to 35 inches and multiples of these lengths. Another method of coupling two VOR navigation receivers to a common antenna is by utilizing a device called a coupler or diplexer. This de-

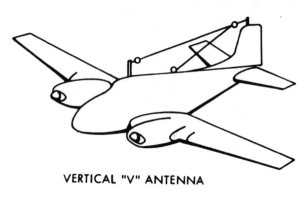

VERTICAL "V" ANTENNA

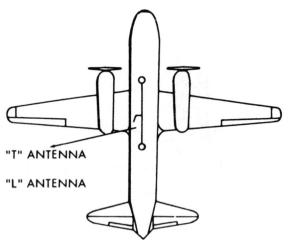

"T" ANTENNA

"L" ANTENNA

NOTE: AN "L" TYPE ANTENNA IS SIMILAR TO A "T" ANTENNA EXCEPT THAT THE LEAD-IN WIRE IS CONNECTED TO THE END OF THE ANTENNA INSTEAD OF THE CENTER.

FIGURE 3.15.—Typical wire antenna locations.

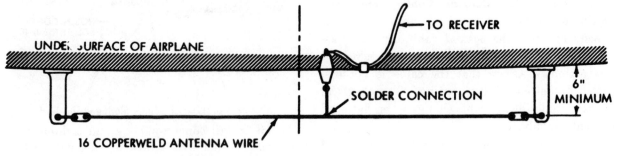

FIGURE 3.16.—Typical marker beacon receiving antenna.

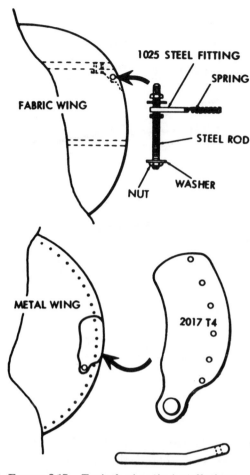

FIGURE 3.17.—Typical wing tip installations.

tion without interference. A whip or other vertical type of antenna should not be used for marker reception since the ground facility transmits from a horizontally polarized antenna.

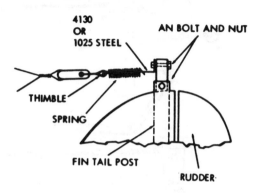

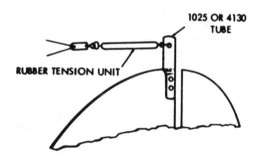

FIGURE 3.18.—Typical fin tip installations.

vice, in addition to impedance matching, also provides isolation between VOR navigation receivers while keeping line insertion losses at a minimum.

40. RANGE RECEIVING ANTENNAS. Mount "T", "L", or "V" antennas on top or bottom of the aircraft with approximately 1-foot clearance from the fuselage and wings. Typical wire antenna installations are shown in figures 3.15 through 3.19.

41. MARKER RECEIVING ANTENNA. The marker receiver operates at a frequency of 75 MHz. In order to keep to a minimum the number of antennas on the aircraft, the marker receiver may utilize the same antenna as the range receiver if that antenna is mounted on the underside of the aircraft. However, both receivers should include provisions to permit simultaneous opera-

42. ATC RADAR BEACON (TRANSPONDER) AND DISTANCE MEASURING EQUIPMENT (DME) ANTENNAS. Locate these antennas at an unobstructed location on the underside of the fuselage, preferably at the lowest point of the aircraft when in level flight. To the extent practicable, mount the antenna so that the base is horizontal when the aircraft is in cruise attitude.

a. Installation. Mount the antennas at least 36 inches away from obstructions and as far as possible from other antennas. Tests have shown that the location of the antenna with respect to obstructions is of greater importance than having the antenna installed in a vertical position. However, signal strength and pattern become noticeably affected as the angle of the antenna approaches 45° from the desired vertical position. On fabric-covered aircraft or aircraft with other types of nonmetallic skin, it will be necessary to provide a flat metallic surface or "ground plane" extending at least 12 inches in all direc-

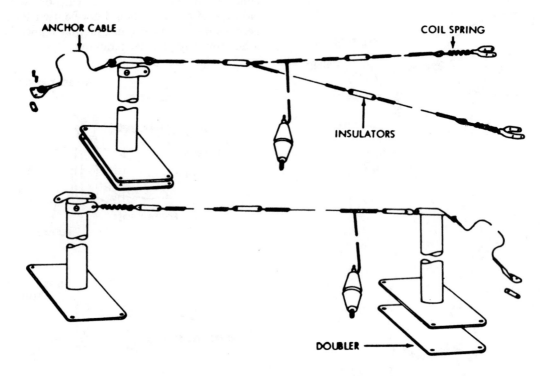

FIGURE 3.19.—Typical wire antenna installations.

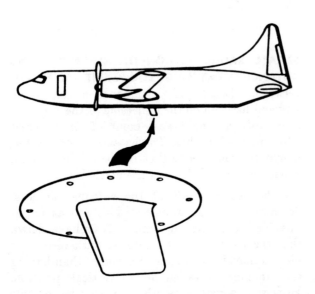

FIGURE 3.20.—Preferred position for distance measuring and/or ATC radar beacon antennas.

tions from the center of the antenna. Be sure the antenna makes a good, direct electrical connection with the ground plane. Install gaskets, pressurization seals, and/or sealant as required.

b. Dual System Installations. When dual ATC radar systems, dual DME systems, or combinations of these systems are installed, determine that the separation between their respective antennas is within the manufacturer's prescribed limits. (See paragraph 27i for mutual interference in DME and ATC radar beacon systems.)

c. Antenna Cable. Route the antenna cable in the most direct path practicable. Since losses can be relatively high at these frequencies, follow the equipment manufacturer's recommendations regarding transmission lines and lengths.

43. DIRECTION FINDING ANTENNAS (100 to 1750 KHz). Manual or automatic loop-type antennas are used with direction-finding receivers. The loops are designed for use with a particular receiver. Connecting wires between the loops and receivers are also designed for the specific equipment. Accordingly, only components meeting the specification characteristics of the receiver manufacturer should be used.

a. Loops enclosed in streamlined housings or exposed loops are satisfactory for external mounting on an aircraft. Loops may also be flush mounted on the aircraft when proper attention is given to avoid interference from metallic structure and skin of the aircraft.

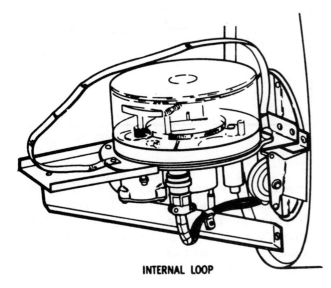

INTERNAL LOOP

ENCLOSED LOOP

FIGURE 3.21.—Typical ADF antenna installations.

b. Sense antennas are used to resolve radio bearing ambiguity in direction finding systems. The sense and its lead-in must be matched to the input capacitance of the ADF receiver. The sense antenna capacitance is a function of length, spacing between antenna and fuselage, and lead-in capacitance. To achieve this antenna/receiver capacitance match, it is important that the sense antenna be installed in accordance with the ADF manufacturer's recommendations for the particular make and model of aircraft.

c. Installation kits are designed for either top or bottom fuselage mounting of loop and sense antennas, or a combination of these two locations. Particular attention should be paid to the manufacturer's installation instructions for antenna location (top or bottom) and loop output connections, in order to prevent 180° errors in bearing indications.

d. Optimum ADF performance is achieved when the "T", rather than the "L", type of sense antenna is used, (see fig. 3.15). The "T" type has a noise cancelling effect due to the antenna cable being connected in the center of the antenna. The "L" type antenna has directional characteristics and may not produce a definite station passage indication as the "T" type does. A whip antenna of a type and dimension recommended by the equipment manufacturer may be used in place of the "T" or "L" types. Methods of installing a whip antenna are shown in figures 3.1, 3.2, and 3.3.

e. Because the ADF receiver is susceptible to aircraft radiated noise, antenna lead-ins should be routed so that they are kept away from electric power cables, alternators, solid state power supplies, anti-collision lights, pulse transmitting equipment, etc. They may be rounted against airframe members for extra shielding.

f. Loop-ins should be of the recommended type and length. The length of lead-in specified by the manufacturer for a particular installation may be excessive for the physical dimensions between the antenna and receiver. Excessive lead-in should not be trimmed, but should be coiled to take up the extra length. Do not coil excess cable in any area subject to electrical noise.

g. After completing the installation, it is essential that the loop be calibrated. One acceptable means of compliance is contained in AC 43.13–1A, chapter 15, section 6, paragraphs 848 through 853.

44. ANTENNA INSTALLATION ON PRESSURIZED AIRCRAFT. The use of doublers, to reinforce the aircraft skin to support antennas, is previously described in this chapter. The material contained in this paragraph concerns the methods of applying sealant to guard against the passage of air, liquids, and vapors from pressurized structures.

a. Typical Antenna Installation Procedure. When the attaching parts and the antenna are ready for installation, clean all faying surfaces with a cleaning solvent. Clean a larger area than that to which sealant is to be applied. Remove the solvent from the faying surfaces by blasting with dry air and wiping with a clean soft cloth.

(1) Coat the affected area with the primer specified by the sealant manufacturer.

(2) Apply the sealant to one surface, using a spatula or brush, and spread it over the entire faying surface until a uniform thickness of approximately 1/32-inch is obtained. (See fig. 3.22 and 3.23.)

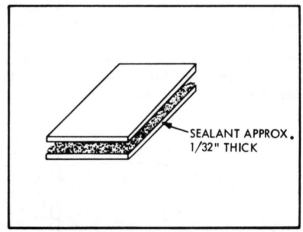

FIGURE 3.23.—Faying surface sealing.

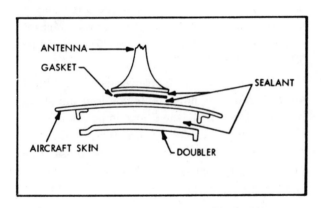

FIGURE 3.22.—Typical antenna installation.

(3) Place the component parts together and install the required fasteners. If permanent fasteners cannot be installed, use temporary fasteners to hold the component parts together until the sealant has cured. Install permanent fasteners with fresh sealant by dipping the fastener in sealant or by filling the fastener hole with sealant. (See fig. 3.24.)

(4) Fill holes and joggles by injecting the sealant into the voids and/or cavities. This method is used where the sealant cannot be applied with a spatula or brush. Figure 3.25.

(5) Allow the sealant to cure, then remove excess sealant from the periphery of the antenna using a nonmetallic scraper.

Warning

Sealants may contain toxic and/or flammable components. Avoid inhalation of vapors. Supply adequate ventilation and provide a suitable exhaust system. Wear approved respiratory protection while using these materials in confined areas. Do not allow the sealant to come in contact with the skin or eyes. Insure that no source of ignition is present in the working area.

b. High Speed Aircraft. The sealant methods described should be used to prevent moisture or water from entering the aircraft and the expulsion of air and vapors when the aircraft structure is pressurized.

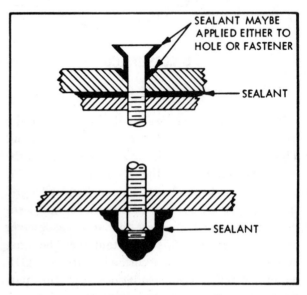

FIGURE 3.24.—Fastener sealing.

FIGURE 3.25.—Injection sealing.

(1) Figure 3.26 displays a blade type antenna mounted on a flat surface using a sealing gasket. This type of installation does not require the application of a sealant.

(2) Figures 3.27 and 3.28 display two types of flush mounted antennas. The antenna unit and fiberglass cover are manufactured as one integral assembly.

(3) Flush mounted antennas installed on a vertical fin are normally part of the primary structure. The radiating elements of the antenna and the fiberglass cover are individual units.

(a) Clean all metal surfaces necessary to insure good electrical bonding contact between the antenna mounting surface and the aircraft structure.

(b) After the fiberglass cover is installed, sealer may be applied to fill the space between the fiberglass cover and skin of the vertical fin. Figure 3.29 displays one-half of a vertical fin antenna installation. An identical installation is required on each side.

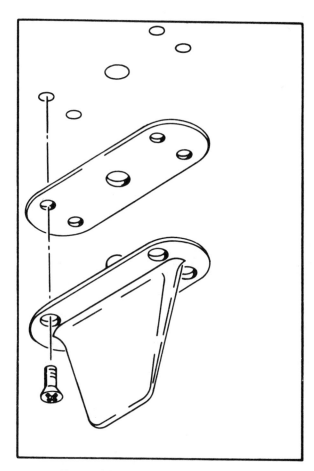

FIGURE 3.26.—Blade antenna installation.

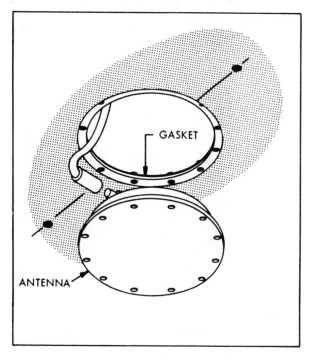

FIGURE 3.27.—ATC flush mounted antenna.

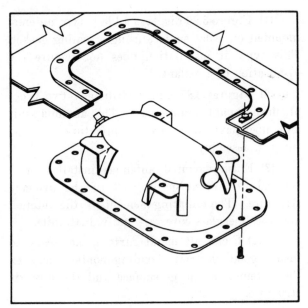

FIGURE 3.28.—Marker beacon flush mounted antenna.

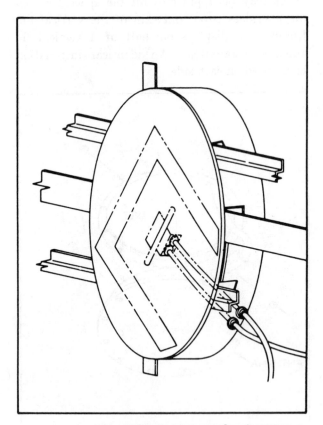

FIGURE 3.29.—VOR flush mounted antenna.

45.–50. [RESERVED]

Chapter 4. ANTICOLLISION AND SUPPLEMENTARY LIGHT INSTALLATIONS

51. ANTICOLLISION AND SUPPLEMENTARY LIGHT SYSTEMS.

a. Anticollision Lights. The requirements for anticollision lights are included in Federal Aviation Regulations, Parts 23, 25, 27, and 29. Aircraft for which an application for type certificate was made before April 1, 1957, may conform either to the above regulations or to the following standards:

(1) Anticollision lights (when installed) should be installed on top of the fuselage or tail in such a location that the light will not be detrimental to the flight crew's vision and will not detract from the conspicuity of the position lights. If there is no acceptable location on top of the fuselage or tail, a bottom fuselage installation may be used.

(2) The color of the anticollision light shall be aviation red or white in accordance with the specifications of FAR Part 23.

(3) The arrangement of the anticollision light (i.e., number of light sources, beam width, speed of rotation, etc.) should be such as to give an effective flash frequency of not less than 40 and not more than 100 cycles per minute.

b. Supplementary lights may be installed in addition to position and anticollision lights required by applicable regulations, provided that the required position and anticollision lights are continuously visible and unmistakably recognizable and their conspicuity is not degraded by such supplementary lights.

52. INTERFERENCE.

a. Crew Vision. Partial masking of the light may be necessary to prevent direct or reflected light rays from any anticollision or supplementary light from interfering with crew vision. Determine that the field of coverage requirements are met. An acceptable method of preventing light reflection from propeller disc, nacelle, or wing surface is an application of nonreflective paint on surfaces which present a reflection problem. Perform a night flight-check to assure that any objectionable light reflection has been eliminated. Enter a notation to that effect in the aircraft records.

b. Communication and Navigation. Assure that the installation and operation of any anticollision/supplementary light does not interfere with the performance of installed communication or navigation equipment. Capacitor discharge light (strobe) systems may generate radio frequency interference (RFI). This radiated interference can be induced into the audio circuits of communication or navigation systems and is noticeable by audible clicks in the speaker or headphones. The magnitude of the RFI disturbance does not usually disrupt the intelligence of audio reception.

c. Precautions. RFI can be reduced or eliminated by observing the following precautions during installation of capacitor discharge light systems:

(1) Locate the power supply at least three (3) feet from any antenna, especially antennas for radio systems that operate in the lower frequency bands.

(2) Assure that the lamp unit (flash tube) wires are separated from other aircraft wiring placing particular emphasis on coaxial cables and radio equipment input power wires.

(3) Make sure that the power supply case is adequately bonded to the airframe.

(4) Ground the shield around the interconnecting wires between the lamp unit and power supply at the power supply end only.

53. MARKINGS AND PLACARDS. Identify each switch for an anticollision/supplementary light and indicate its operation. The aircraft should be flight tested under haze, overcast, and visible moisture conditions to ascertain that no interference to pilot vision is produced by operation of these lights. If found unsatisfactory by test, or in the absence of such testing, a placard should be provided to the pilot stating that the appropriate lights be turned off while operating in these conditions.

54. ELECTRICAL INSTALLATION. Install an individual switch for the anticollision light or supplementary light system that is independent of the position light system switch. Data for the installation of wiring, protection device, and generator limitations is contained in chapter 11 of Advisory Circular 43.13–1A, "Acceptable Methods, Techniques, and Practices—Aircraft Inspection and Repair." Assure that the terminal voltage at each light is within the limits as prescribed by the manufacturer.

55. ALTERATION OF STRUCTURE.

a. *The simplest light installation* is to secure the light to a reinforced fuselage skin panel. The reinforcement doubler shall be of equivalent thickness, material, and strength as the existing skin. (Install as shown in fig. 4.1.)

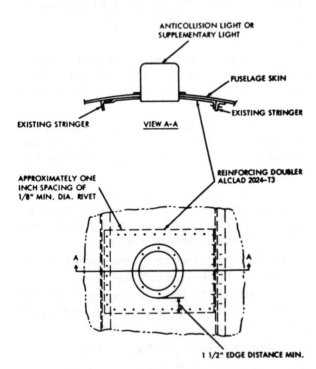

FIGURE 4.1.—Typical anticollision or supplementary light installation in a skin panel (unpressurized).

b. *When a formed angle stringer is cut and partially removed,* position the reinforcement doubler between the skin and the frame. Doubler to be equivalent to the stringer in thickness and extend lengthwise beyond the adjacent fuselage frames. The distance between the light and the edge of the doubler is twice the height of the doubler flange. (See fig. 4.2 for typical installation.)

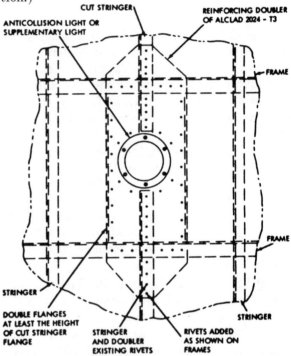

FIGURE 4.2.—Typical anticollision or supplementary light installation involving a cut stringer (unpressurized).

c. *Engineering evaluation* is required for installations involving the cutting of complex formed or extruded stiffeners, fuselage frames, or pressurized skin of pressurized aircraft.

d. *Vertical stabilizer installations* may be made on aircraft if the stabilizer is large enough in cross section to accommodate the light installation, and aircraft flutter and vibration characteristics are not adversely affected. Locate such an installation near a spar, and add formers as required to stiffen the structure near the light. (A typical installation is shown in fig. 4.3.)

e. *Rudder installations* are not recommended because of the possible structural difficulties. However, if such installations are considered, make an engineering evaluation to determine whether the added mass of the light installation

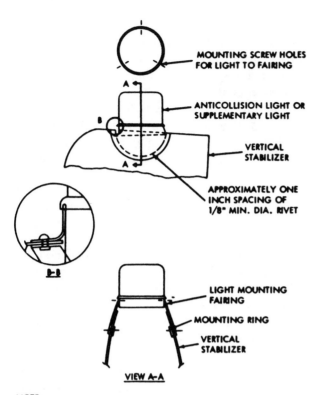

NOTE:
SKIN THICKNESS OF MOUNTING RING AND
FAIRING ARE AT LEAST EQUIVALENT

FIGURE 4.3.—Typical anticollision or supplementary light installation in a fin tip.

will adversely affect the flutter and vibration characteristics of the tail surfaces.

f. Pressurized Aircraft Installation. Doubler installation to reinforce the aircraft skin previously described in this chapter is adaptable to pressurized structure with the application of sealant. Sealant is used to prevent moisture or water from entering the aircraft and the expulsion of air when the aircraft structure is pressurized.

(1) Sealant procedures for aircraft skin reinforcing doubler and doubler fasteners are contained in paragraph 44, chapter 3 of this manual. The aircraft manufacturer's data may recommend the specific sealant to be used and provide instructions for the application.

(2) Figures 4.4 and 4.5 illustrate two different designs of anticollision light assemblies. The application of sealant is required when either type of light assemblies is installed. Sealant procedures would be identical for installation of a capacitor discharge (strobe) light system.

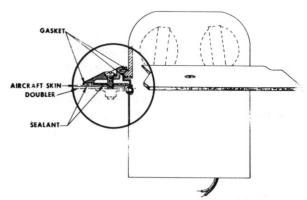

FIGURE 4.4.—Typical rotating type anticollision light installation for pressurized aircraft.

Caution: Sealant and solvents may contain toxic and/or flammable components. Avoid inhalation of vapors and supply adequate ventilation. Wear appropriate respiratory protection while using these materials in confined areas. Avoid contact with the skin and eyes.

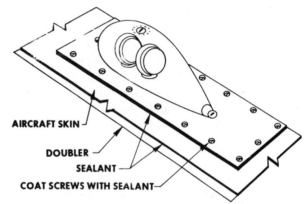

FIGURE 4.5.—Typical oscillating type anticollision light installation for pressurized aircraft.

56. GUIDELINES FOR INSTALLATIONS.

a. Prior Approval. Due to the complexity of measurements for intensity, field of coverage, and color, evidence of FAA approval should be obtained from the light manufacturer before installation.

b. System Performance.

(1) **Field of Coverage.** Evidence of FAA approval for "field of coverage" should be obtained from the light manufacturer before installation. To insure that the manufacturer's approved field of coverage is applicable to an installation, his mounting tolerance should not be exceeded.

(2) Obstructed Visibility. Measure all solid angles of obstruction within the required field of coverage. For multiple light installations, coverage between the mounting levels is not necessary. When a multiple light installation is being evaluated, shadows for each light should be measured independently, and only shadow areas repeated in each independent measurement (overlap) should be counted. Methods for determining the amount of obstructed visibility are given below; however, other methods can give acceptable results.

(a) Wall Shadows. This procedure is applicable to installations where shadows from light obstructions appear on a vertical surface such as a hangar wall. Validity is based on two facts: (1) that a vertical surface can approximate a sphere surface if the distance from the light is considerable, and the shadow is reasonably small, and (2) that sphere surface area can be converted to steradians by dividing by the radius squared.

1 Position the aircraft in a darkened hangar so that longitudinal axis is perpendicular to a hangar wall. Level as for weight and balance. To keep measure errors low, the distance from light to wall should be as great as practicable considering hangar size. The distance should not be less than 20 feet.

2 Turn on the lights and measure the area of wall shadows. Sufficient points should be marked and identified so that the shadow pattern can be transferred to graph paper for accurate evaluation. Area can be found by counting squares on the graph or by using a planimeter. Measurements should include areas of transition from shadowed to lighted areas. For top light measurements on multiple light installations, only shadows above the level of the top light should be considered.

3 Compute the solid angle obstruction in steradians, by dividing each shadow area by the square of the distance from the center of the area to the light.

4 Evaluate the results to determine if the system consists of enough lights to illuminate the vital areas around the aircraft, considering the physical configuration and flight characteristics of the aircraft. The field of coverage must extend in each direction within at least 30° above and 30° below the horizontal plane of the aircraft, except that there may be solid angles of obstructed visibility totalling not more than the requirements of paragraph .1401(b) of the applicable airworthiness regulations.

5 For installations where shadows are restricted to directly aft and centered about the longitudinal axis, the following procedures apply:

a Establish a point on the wall which corresponds to a line parallel to the longitudinal axis and through the light associated with the shadow.

b Measure the distance from the light to the point and determine the area representing 0.15 steradians ($A = 0.15d^2$). The distance (d) should be at least 20 feet.

c Draw a circle, with the established point as the center, having an area equal to that found in *b* above.

d If the shadow falls within this circle, its position is acceptable. For multiple light installations, consider only the shadow above light level.

e If the shadow is partially out of the circle, the shape of the 0.15 steradian area may be varied, but the established point should remain at the center of the area (centroid).

(b) Ramp Shadows. This procedure is applicable to shadows which appear on a horizontal plane such as a flat level ramp and will be associated with a top mounted light and a 0.5 steradian limit. Area measurements as described in the wall shadow method should not be used. Some error is inherent, because horizontal angles are measured on a plane displaced from the light source. To compensate for these measurement errors, a table (fig. 4.8) is furnished to convert from measured solid angles to true solid angles. A term "square degrees" is used to aid in the discussions of solid angle measurements.

1 If no masking is required, remove the red cover and attach its clamp ring to the light base. If masking is used, obtain a clear cover and install it with a duplicate mask.

2 Center the aircraft on the largest available dark ramp. A minimum of 50 feet radius of clear ramp space will usually be needed. If the installation is symmetrical, clear ramp space will be needed on one side only. Level the aircraft as for weight and balance check. Trim the flaps, rudder, elevator and ailerons. With jacks in place, raise the gear if the measurement results would otherwise be affected.

3 Chalk the following marks on the ramp:

a A reference point directly below the light.

b A circle centered on this reference point having a radius equal to 1.732 times the height of the light above the point. (The circle represents area beyond the minus 30° vertical limit and does not require lighting.)

c A line parallel to the aircraft longitudinal centerline which passes through the reference point.

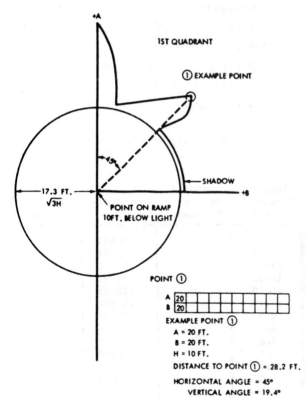

FIGURE 4.6.—Ramp shadow pattern.

d A line perpendicular to the above line, which also passes through the reference point.

4 At night, turn on the anticollision light and chalk all shadow patterns (except jack shadows) which appear outside the circle. If the light rotates so as to cause the shadows to oscillate, lay twine along the outermost edge of the shadow, and chalk along the line.

5 Move the aircraft to facilitate area measurements. Measure, sketch, and chart the ramp marks and other information as shown in Figure 4.6. Measure enough points along the shadow patterns to accurately describe them. Make enough sketches to include all shadows.

6 Convert the above measurements to a graph showing vertical degrees vs. horizontal degrees as shown in Figure 4.7 (first quadrant). The second quadrant will have to be measured also to obtain the total shadow area for one side. If the shadow pattern is symmetrical, no other measurements will be necessary. Use 1 degree for each space on the graph paper and count the square degrees of shadow. A total of 1,642 or less is within limits. A total of 1,872 or more is out of limits, and if possible, should be reduced by adding or moving a light, or by trimming a mask. If the count is between 1,642 and 1,872, proceed as follows: For each 1 degree segment of vertical (pitch), convert the counted square degrees to true square degrees by use of the table of Figure 4.8. If the sum of the true square degrees from all segments exceeds 1,642 (0.5 steradian), the installation is out of limits.

(c) Scale Drawings. Accurate scale drawings can be used to measure solid angles of obstruction. Such drawings should have sufficient size and accuracy to give dependable results. In some cases, actual measurements can be combined with small drawings as shown in Figure 4.9. For the 6 points established on the left wing, a string can be used to connect the light successively to each. A protractor can then be used to measure the vertical angle from level. The horizontal angle for each point can be measured on the top view (center). When both horizontal and vertical angles for each point have been determined, they can be plotted on a graph as shown in Figure 4.10. If a symmetrical condition exists, only the first and second quadrants need be measured.

The first quadrant contains approximately 450 square degrees of obstruction. The other wing quadrant will double this to 900 square degrees.

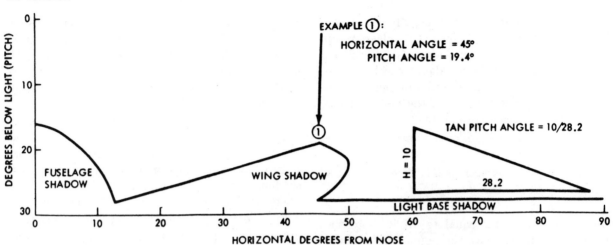

FIGURE 4.7.—Conversion to vertical vs. horizontal degrees.

A measurement of the fin and rudder shadows adds approximately 100 for a total of 1,000 square degrees. Since a maximum of 1,642 square degrees is allowed (0.5 steradians), this installation is well within limits. Due to limitations of the method, results within 10% (0.05 steradians) of the limit are questionable. Many times a mask is required to prevent reflections into the cockpit. In the example of figures 4.9 and 4.10, the installed mask blocks the light for ±10 horizontal degrees and from −10 to −30 vertical degrees. These 400 square degrees were measured at the light.

When larger drawings are used and no actual aircraft measures are made, vertical angles should not be taken directly from the drawing, but should be computed as follows:

1 On the aircraft side view, measure the vertical distance from a point to the light level.

2 On the top view, measure the distance from the point to the light.

3 Compute:

$$\text{Tangent of vertical angle} = \frac{\text{vertical distance}}{\text{horizontal distance}}$$

Pitch Segment (Degrees)	Measured Square Degrees	Correction Factor	True Square Degrees	Pitch Segment (Degrees)	Measured Square Degrees	Correction Factor	True Square Degrees
30-29	90	.87036	78.33	15-14		.96815	
29-28	90	.87882	79.09	14-13		.97237	
28-27	44	.88701	39.03	13-12		.97630	
27-26		.89493		12-11		.97992	
26-25		.90259		11-10		.98325	
25-24		.90996		10-9		.98629	
24-23		.91706		9-8		.98902	
23-22		.92388		8-7		.99144	
22-21		.93042		7-6		.99357	
21-20		.93667		6-5		.99540	
20-19		.94264		5-4		.99692	
19-18		.94832		4-3		.99813	
18-17		.95372		3-2		.99905	
17-16		.95882		2-1		.99966	
16-15		.96363		1-0		.99996	
						TOTAL	

FIGURE 4.8.—Conversion to true square degrees—1st quadrant.

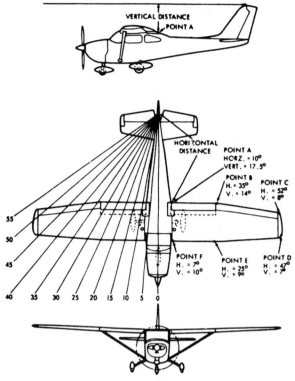

FIGURE 4.9.—Scale drawings.

(d) *Flashing Characteristic.* Turn off any flashing supplementary lighting. Observe the flashing of the anticollision light system at a point where each light can be observed independently, and determine that each flashing rate is between 40 and 100 flashes per minute. For multiple light systems, observe at a point where overlap occurs, and determine that the combined flashing rate does not exceed 180 flashes per minute. Flashing outside the required field of coverage is not necessary.

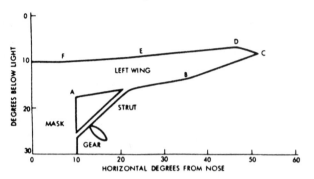

FIGURE 4.10.—Solid angle blockage—1st quadrant.

57.–60.　[RESERVED]

Chapter 5. SKI INSTALLATIONS

Section 1. SELECTION OF SKIS

61. DETERMINING ELIGIBILITY OF AIRCRAFT. Only aircraft approved for operation on skis are eligible for ski installations in accordance with this chapter. Eligibility can be determined by referring to the Aircraft Specifications, Type Certificate Data Sheets, Aircraft Listing, Summary of Supplemental Type Certificates, or by contacting the manufacturer. Also determine the need for the nature of any required alterations to the aircraft to make it eligible for ski operation.

62. IDENTIFICATION OF APPROVED MODEL SKIS. Determining that the skis are an approved model can be done by referring to the identification plate or placard displayed on the skis. A Technical Standard Order (TSO) number; Type Certificate (TC) number; or an aircraft part number, if the skis have been approved as a part of the aircraft, will be shown thereon if the skis are approved models.

63. MAXIMUM LIMIT LOAD RATING. In order for an approved ski to be installed on any given

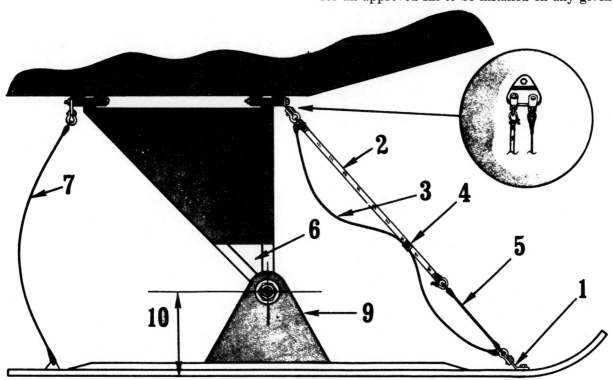

1. Fitting	6. Fabric removed to facilitate inspection
2. Shock Cord	7. Check Cable
3. Safety Cable	8. Clevis
4. Tape	9. Ski Pedestal
5. Crust-cutter Cable	10. Pedestal Height

FIGURE 5.1.—Typical ski installation.

aircraft, determine that the maximum limit load rating (L) as specified on the ski identification plate or placard is at least equal to the maximum static load (S) times the limit landing load factor (η) previously determined from static drop tests of the airplane by the aircraft manufacturer.

$$L = S \times \eta$$

In lieu of a value η determined from such drop tests, a value of η determined from the following formula may be used:

$$\eta = 2.80 + \frac{9000}{W + 4000}$$ where "W" is the certificated

gross weight of the airplane.

Skis approved for airplanes of greater gross weight than the airplane on which they are to be installed may be used provided the geometry of the ski is similar to that of a ski previously approved for the airplane (not more than 10 percent difference in width or length of contact surface). This limitation is to assure that the performance of the airplane will not be adversely affected by oversize skis.

64. LANDING GEAR MOMENT REACTIONS. In order to avoid excessive moment reactions on the landing gear and attachment structure, the ski pedestal height must not exceed 130 percent of the axle centerline height with the wheel and tire installed.

65. [RESERVED]

Section 2. CONVERSION AND INSTALLATION

66. HUB-AXLE CLEARANCE. The pedestal hub should fit the axle to provide a clearance of .005″ minimum to .020″ maximum. Hubs may be bushed to adjust for axle size, using any ferrous or nonferrous metal, hard rubber, or fiber. If rubber or fiber bushings are used, use retaining washers of sufficient size on each side to retain the hub if the bushing should slip or fail. (See fig. 5.2.)

67. CRUST-CUTTER CABLES. Crust-cutter cables are optional. However, when operating in severe crust conditions, it is advisable to have this cable installed to prevent the shock cord from being cut if the nose of the ski breaks through the crust while taxiing.

68. CABLE AND SHOCK CORD ATTACHMENT AND ATTACHMENT FITTINGS. Service reports indicate that failure of the ski itself is not a predominant factor in ski failures. Rigging (improper tension and terminal attachments) and cast-type pedestal material failures are predominant. Usually, failures of the safety cable and shock cord attachment fittings occur at the ski end and not at the fuselage end.

Do not attach tension cords and safety cables at the same point on the fuselage fittings. Provide separate means of attaching cables and shock cords at the forward and aft ends of the skis. Usually, approved skis are supplied with cables, shock cord, and fittings; however, the following specifications may be used for their fabrication and installations:

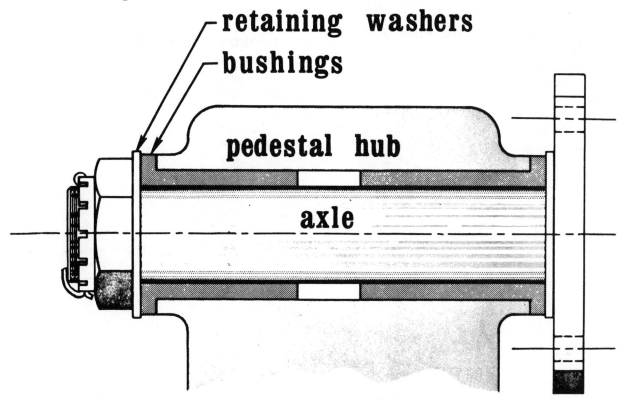

FIGURE 5.2.—Typical hub installation.

Minimum Cable and Shock Cord Sizes

Ski Limit Load Rating	Single Safety Cable	Double Safety Cable	Single Crust-Cutting Cable	Double Crust-Cutting Cable	Single Shock Cord	Double Shock Cord
1500–3000	1/8''	1/8''	1/8''	1/8''	1/2''	1/2''
3000–5000	____	1/8''	____	1/8''	____	1/2''
5000–7000	____	5/32''	5/32''	5/32''	3/4''	3/4''
7000–9000	____	3/16''	____	5/32''	____	3/4''

a. Cables. Make the check cable, safety cable, and crust-cutting cable ends by the splice, swage, or nicopress methods; or if adjustable lengths are desired, use cable clamps. Use standard aircraft hardware only. (Hardware used to attach cables must be compatible with cable size.)

b. Shock cord ends may be fabricated by any of the following methods:

(1) Make a wrapped splice using a proper size rope thimble and No. 9 cotton cord or .035'' (minimum) safety wire. Attach with clevis or spring steel snap fastener. (*Do not* use cast iron snaps.)

(2) Use approved spring-type shock cord end fasteners.

c. Fitting Specifications (see figure 5.3) and Installation:

(1) Fittings fabricated for 1/8-inch cable or 1/2-inch shock cord shall be at least .065'' 1025 steel or its equivalent.

(2) Fittings fabricated for 5/32-inch cable or 3/4-inch shock cord shall be at least .080'' 1025 steel or its equivalent.

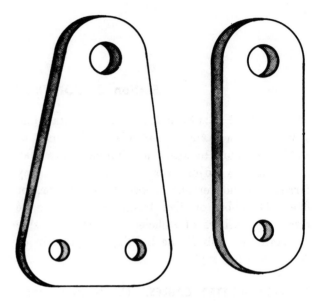

FIGURE 5.3.—Typical fuselage fitting.

(3) An improperly installed fitting may impose excessive eccentric loads on the fitting and attach bolts and result in failure of the fitting or bolts.

69. PROVISIONS FOR INSPECTION. Aircraft using fabric-covered landing gear may have the lower 4 inches of fabric removed to facilitate inspection of the axle attachment area. (See fig. 5.1.)

70. [RESERVED]

Section 3. RIGGING OF SKIS

71. LOCATION OF ATTACH FITTINGS ON FUSE-LAGE OR LANDING GEAR. Locate fittings so the shock cord and cable angles are not less than 20° when measured in the vertical plane with the shock absorber in the fully extended position (see angle B, figs. 5.4 and 5.5).

NOTE: Do not attach fittings to wing-brace struts, except by special approval (manufacturer or FAA).

72. MAIN SKI INCIDENCE ANGLES. (Aircraft leveled and shock absorbers fully extended.)

a. Adjust length of check cable to provide a zero to 5-degree ski incidence angle (reference figs. 5.4 and 5.6).

b. Adjust length of safety cable to provide −20 to −35-degree ski incidence angle (reference figs. 5.5 and 5.6).

73. TENSION REQUIRED IN MAIN SKI SHOCK CORDS. Apply sufficient shock cord tension to fore end of the skis to prevent flutter at various airspeeds and attitudes. Because of the various angles used in attaching shock cord to the skis, shock cord tension cannot be specified. In most installations the downward force applied at the fore end of the ski, sufficient to cause the check

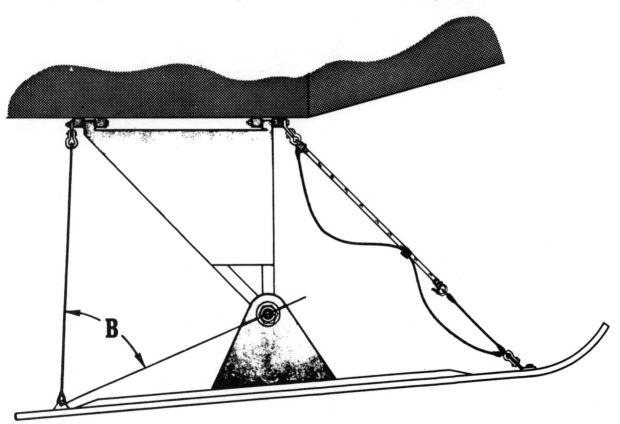

FIGURE 5.4.—Main ski at maximum positive incidence (check cable tight).

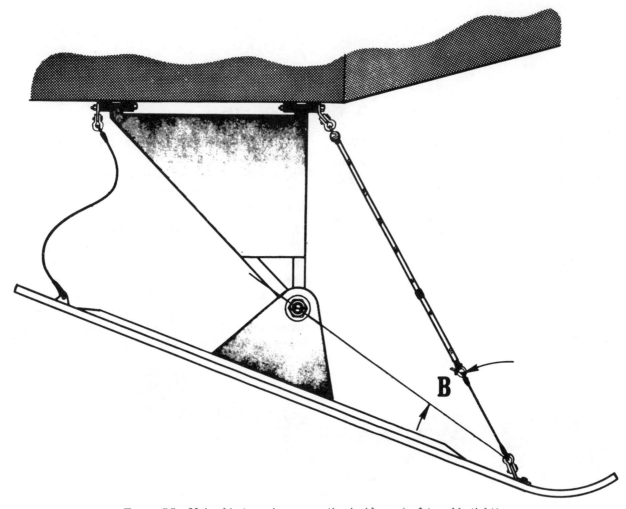

FIGURE 5.5.—Main ski at maximum negative incidence (safety cable tight).

cable to slacken, should be approximately as listed below:

Ski Limit Load Rating	Downward Force (pounds)
1500–3000	20–40
3000–5000	40–60
5000–7000	60–120
7000–9000	120–200

74. NOSE SKI INSTALLATION. The nose ski is installed in the same manner as the main skis (see fig. 5.7) except:

a. Adjust length of safety cable to provide −5- to −15-degree ski incidence.

b. Where it is possible for the nose ski rigging to contact the propeller tips due to vibration, install a ¼-inch shock cord to hold the rigging out of the propeller arc.

75. TAIL SKI INSTALLATION.

a. Use tail skis that have been approved on airplanes of approximately the same weight (within 10 percent) or select as outlined in sec-

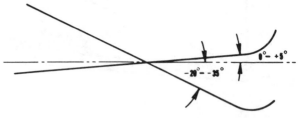

FIGURE 5.6.—Main ski incidence angles.

tion 1. Depending upon the type of ski selected, the tail wheel may or may not have to be removed.

b. Adjust the length of the limiting cable (ref. fig. 5.8) to allow the ski to turn approximately 35 degrees either side of the straight-

forward position with the weight of the airplane resting on the ski.

c. The shock cord (ref. fig. 5.8) must be of a length that will hold the ski in the straight-forward position during flight.

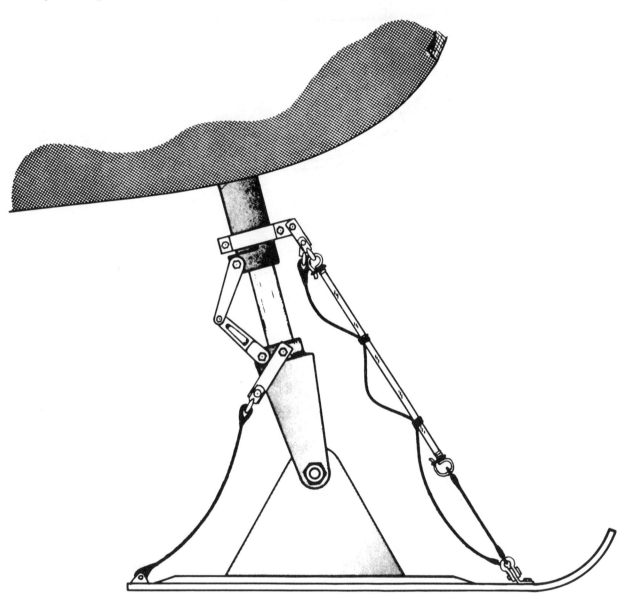

FIGURE 5.7.—Typical nose ski installation.

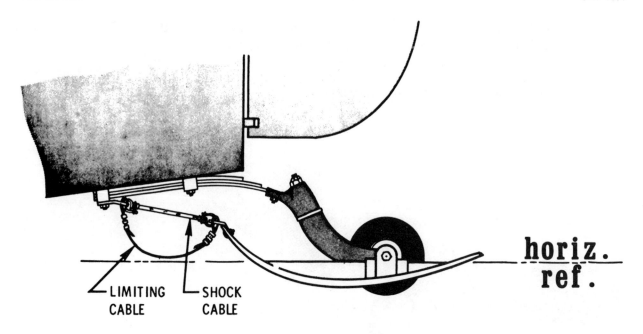

FIGURE 5.8—Typical tail ski installation.

76.–78. [RESERVED]

Section 4. OPERATION

79. PERFORMANCE INFORMATION. The following FAA policies concern performance data and operational check flights for ski installations.

a. For aircraft over 6,000 pounds maximum certificated weight, state the following or similar information in the performance information section of the Airplane Flight Manual and obtain FAA approval.

(1) Takeoff. Under the most favorable conditions of smooth packed snow at temperatures approximating 32° F, the skiplane takeoff distance is approximately 10 percent greater than that shown for the landplane.

NOTE: In estimating takeoff distances for other conditions, caution should be exercised as lower temperatures or other snow conditions will usually increase these distances.

(2) Landing. Under the most favorable conditions of smooth packed snow at temperatures approximating 32° F, the skiplane landing distance is approximately 20 percent greater than that shown for the landplane.

NOTE: In estimating landing distances for other conditions, caution should be exercised as other temperatures or other snow conditions may either decrease or increase these distances.

(3) Climb Performance. In cases where the landing gear is fixed (both landplane and skiplane), where climb requirements are not critical, and the climb reduction is small (30 to 50 feet per minute), the FAA will accept a statement of the approximate reduction in climb performance placed in the performance information section of the Airplane Flight Manual. For larger variations in climb performance, or where the minimum requirements are critical, or where the landing gear of the landplane was retractable, appropriate climb data should be obtained to determine the changes, and new curves, tables, or a note should be incorporated in the Airplane Flight Manual.

b. For aircraft of 6,000 pounds or less maximum certificated weight, make the information in 79a available to the pilot in the form of placards, markings, manuals, or any combination thereof.

80. FLIGHT AND HANDLING OPERATIONAL CHECKS. Accomplish an operational check which includes more than one landing to determine the ground-handling characteristics as well as takeoff and landing characteristics. Take note of ski angles during tail high and tail low landings to avoid having the ski dig in or fail from localized stress. Determine there is sufficient ground control to satisfactorily complete a landing run with a turnoff at slow speed in cases where brakes are not provided. In flight, the ski should ride steady with no unusual drag and produce no unsatisfactory flight characteristics. Enter a notation of these checks in the aircraft records.

81. INTERCHANGING OF SKIS AND WHEELS After the initial installation, removing the skis and reinstalling the wheels or vice versa may be considered a preventive maintenance operation when no weight-and-balance computation is involved.

82.–85. [RESERVED]

Chapter 6. OXYGEN SYSTEM INSTALLATIONS IN NONPRESSURIZED AIRCRAFT

86. SYSTEM REQUIREMENTS. Install oxygen cylinders conforming to Interstate Commerce Commission requirements for gas cylinders which carry the ICC 3A, 3AA, or 3HT designation followed by the service pressure metal-stamped on the cylinder. The 3HT designated cylinders must not be used for portable oxygen equipment.

a. Tubing.

(1) In systems having low pressure (400 p.s.i.), use seamless aluminum alloy or equivalent having an outside diameter of 5/16 inch and a wall thickness of .035″. Double flare the ends to attach to fittings.

(2) In high-pressure systems (1800 p.s.i.), use 3/16 inch O.D., .035″ wall thickness, seamless copper alloy tubing meeting Specification WW–T–779a type N, or stainless steel between the filler valve and the pressure-reducing valve. Silver-solder cone nipples to the ends of the tubing to attach the fittings in accordance with Specification MIL–B–7883.

(3) Use 5/16-inch O.D. aluminum alloy tubing after the pressure-reducer (low-pressure side).

(4) Use flexible connections specifically designed for oxygen between all points having relative or differential motion.

b. Valves. A slow opening valve is used as a cylinder shutoff valve, or system shutoff valve. Rapid opening and the subsequent sudden and fast discharge of oxygen into the system can cause dangerous heating which could result in fire or explosion of combustibles within the system.

c. Regulators. The cylinder or system pressure is reduced to the individual cabin outlets by means of a pressure-reducing regulator which can be manually or automatically controlled.

d. Types of Regulators. The four basic types of oxygen systems, classified according to the type of regulator employed, are:

(1) Demand type.

(2) Diluter-demand type.

(3) Pressure-demand type.

(4) Continuous-flow type.

e. Flow Indicators.

(1) A pith-ball flow indicator, vane, wheel anemometer, or lateral pressure indicator which fluctuates with changes in flow or any other satisfactory flow indicator may be used in a continuous flow-type system.

(2) An Air Force-Navy flow indicator or equivalent may be used in a diluter-demand type system. Each flow indicator should give positive indication when oxygen flow is occurring.

f. Relief Valve.

(1) A relief valve is installed in low-pressure oxygen systems to safely relieve excessive pressure, such as caused by overcharging.

(2) A relief valve is installed in high-pressure oxygen systems to safely relieve excessive pressure, such as caused by heating.

g. Gauge. Provide a pressure gauge to show the amount of oxygen in the cylinder.

h. Masks. Only masks designed for the particular system should be used.

87. INSTALLATION.

Oxygen systems present a hazard. Therefore, follow the precautions and practices listed below:

a. Remove oil, grease (including lip salves, hair oil, etc.), and dirt from hands, clothing, and tools before working with oxygen equipment.

b. Prior to cutting the upholstery, check the intended route of the system.

Make sure that all system components are kept completely free of oil or grease during installation and locate components so they will not contact or become contaminated by oil or hydraulic lines.

c. Keep open ends of cleaned and dried tubing capped or plugged at all times, except during attachment or detachment of parts. Do *not* use tape, rags, or paper.

d. Clean all lines and fittings which have not been cleaned and sealed by one of the following methods:

(1) A vapor-degreasing method with stabilized trichlorethylene conforming to Specification MIL–T–7003 or carbon tetrachloride. Blow tubing clean and dry with a stream of clean, dried, water-pumped air, or dry nitrogen (water-vapor content of less than 0.005 milligrams per liter of gas at 70° F and 760 millimeters of mercury pressure).

(2) Flush with naptha conforming to Specification TT–N–95; blow clean and dry of all solvent with water-pumped air; flush with anti-icing fluid conforming to Specification MIL–F5566 or anhydrous ethyl alcohol; rinse thoroughly with fresh water; and dry thoroughly with a stream of clean, dried, water-pumped air, or by heating at a temperature of 250° to 300° F for one-half hour.

(3) Flush with hot inhibited alkaline cleaner until free from oil and grease; rinse thoroughly with fresh water; and dry thoroughly with a stream of clean, dried, water-pumped air, or by heating at a temperature of 250° to 300° F for one-half hour.

e. Install lines, fittings, and equipment above and at least 6 inches away from fuel, oil, and hydraulic systems. Use deflector plates where necessary to keep hydraulic fluids away from the lines, fittings, and equipment.

f. Allow at least a 2-inch clearance between the plumbing and any flexible control cable or other flexible moving parts of the aircraft. Provide at least ½-inch clearance between the plumbing and any rigid control tubes or other rigid moving parts of the aircraft.

g. Allow a 6-inch separation between the plumbing and the flight and engine control cables, and electrical lines. When electrical conduit is used, this separation between the plumbing and conduit may be reduced to 2 inches.

h. Route the oxygen system tubing, fittings, and equipment away from hot ducts and equipment. Insulate or provide space between these items to prevent heating the oxygen system.

i. Mount all plumbing in a manner which prevents vibration and chafing. Support 3/16-inch O.D. copper line each 24 inches and 3/16-inch O.D. aluminum each 36 inches with cushioned loop-type line support clamps (AN–742) or equivalent.

j. Locate the oxygen supply valve (control valve) so as to allow its operation by the pilot during flight. The cylinder shutoff valve may be used as the supply control valve, if it is operable from the pilot's seat. Manifold plug-in type outlets, which are incorporated in automatic systems, may be considered as oxygen supply valves since the pilot can control the flow of oxygen by engaging and disengaging the plug-in type oxygen mask.

NOTE: Locate the oxygen shutoff valve on or as close as practicable to the cylinder to prevent loss of oxygen due to leakage in the system.

88. LOCATION AND MOUNTING. Determine the weight factor and c.g. limits for the installation prior to commencing the installation.

a. Mount the cylinder in the baggage compartment or other suitable location in such a position that the shutoff valve is readily accessible. If possible, provide access to this valve from inside the cabin so that it may be turned on in flight in the event that it was not opened prior to takeoff.

b. Fasten the cylinder brackets securely to the aircraft, preferably to a frame member or floorboard using AN bolts with fiber or similar locking nuts. Add sufficient plates, gussets, stringers, cross-bracing, or other reinforcements, where necessary, to provide a mounting that will withstand the inertia forces stipulated in chapter 1 of this handbook.

c. When cylinders are located where they may be damaged by baggage or stored materials, protect them by a suitable guard or covering.

d. Provide at least ½ inch of clear airspace between any cylinder and a firewall or shroud isolating a designated fire zone.

e. Mount the regulator close to the cylinder to avoid long high-pressure lines.

f. Store the masks in such a way that there will be a minimum delay in removing and putting them into use.

89. THREAD COMPOUND. Use antiseize or thread-sealing compound conforming to Specification MIL–T–5542–B, or equivalent.

a. Do not use compound on aluminum alloy flared tube fittings having straight threads. Proper flaring and tightening should be sufficient to make a flared tube connection leakproof.

b. Treat all male-tapered pipe threads with antiseize and sealing compound (MIL–T–5542–B, or tetrafluroethylene tape MIL–T–27730), or equivalent.

c. Apply the compound in accordance with the manufacturer's recommendation. Make sure that the compounds are carefully and sparingly applied only to male threads, coating the first three threads from the end of the fitting. Do not use compound on the coupling sleeves or on the outside of the tube flares.

90. FUNCTIONAL TEST.

Before inspection plates, cover plates, or upholstering are replaced, make a system check including at least the following:

a. Open cylinder valve slowly and observe the pressure gauge.

b. Open supply valve and remove one of the mask tubes and bayonet fittings from one of the masks in the kit. Plug the bayonet into each of the oxygen outlets. A small flow should be noted from each of the outlets. This can be detected by holding the tube to the lips while the bayonet is plugged into an outlet.

c. Check the complete system for leaks. This can be done with a soap solution made only from a mild (castile) soap or by leak-detector solution supplied by the oxygen equipment manufacturer.

d. If leaks are found, close the cylinder shutoff valve and reduce the pressure in the system by plugging a mask tube into one of the outlets or by carefully loosening one of the connections in the system. When the pressure has been reduced to zero, make the necessary repairs. Repeat the procedure in 90c until no leaks are found in the system.

Caution: Never tighten oxygen system fittings with oxygen pressure applied.

e. Test each outlet for leaks at the point where the mask tube plugs in. This can be done by drawing a soap bubble over each of the outlets. Use the solution sparingly to prevent clogging the outlet by soap. Remove all residue to prevent accumulation of dirt.

f. Examine the system to determine that the flow of oxygen through each outlet is at least equal to the minimum required by the pertinent requirements at all altitudes at which the aircraft is to be operated. This can be accomplished by one of the following methods:

(1) In a continuous flow system when the calibration (inlet pressure vs. flow) of the orifices used at the plug-in outlets is known, the pressure in the low-pressure distribution line can be measured at the point which is subject to the greatest pressure drop. Do this with oxygen flowing from all outlets. The pressure thus measured should indicate a flow equal to or greater than the minimum flow required.

(2) In lieu of the above procedure, the flow of oxygen, through the outlet which is subject to the greatest pressure drop, may be measured with all other outlets open. Gas meters, rotometers, or other suitable means may be used to measure flows.

(3) The measurement of oxygen flow in a continuous flow system which uses a manually adjusted regulator can be accomplished at sea level. However, in a continuous flow system which uses an automatic-type regulator, it may be necessary to check the flow at maximum altitude which will be encountered during the normal operation of the aircraft. The manufacturer of the particular continuous-flow regulator used should be able to furnish data on the operating characteristics of the regulator from which it can be determined whether a flight check is necessary.

(4) The checking of the amount of flow through the various outlets in a diluter-demand or straight-demand system is not necessary since the flow characteristics of the particular regulator being used may be obtained from the manufacturer of the regulator. However, in such systems the availability of oxygen to each regulator should be checked by turning the lever of the diluter-demand regulator to the "100 percent oxygen" position and inhaling through the tube via the mask to determine whether the regulator valve and the flow indicator are operating.

g. Provide one of the following acceptable means or equivalent to indicate oxygen flow to each user by:

(1) Listening for audible indication of oxygen flow.

(2) Watching for inflation of the rebreather or reservoir bag.

(3) Installation of a flow indicator.

91. OPERATING INSTRUCTIONS. Provide instructions appropriate to the type of system and masks installed for the pilot on placards. Include in these instructions a graph or a table which will show the duration of the oxygen supply for the various cylinder pressures and pressure altitudes.

ACTUAL DURATION IN HOURS AT VARIOUS ALTITUDES					
Number of Persons	*8000 Ft.*	*10,000 Ft.*	*12,000 Ft.*	*15,000 Ft.*	*20,000 Ft.*
Pilot only _____	7.6 hr.	7.1 hr.	6.7 hr.	6.35 hr.	5.83 hr.
Pilot and 1 Passenger _____	5.07 hr.	4.74 hr.	4.47 hr.	4.24 hr.	3.88 hr.
Pilot and 2 Passengers _____	3.8 hr.	3.55 hr.	3.36 hr.	3.18 hr.	2.92 hr.
Pilot and 3 Passengers _____	3.04 hr.	2.84 hr.	2.68 hr.	2.54 hr.	2.34 hr.
Pilot and 4 Passengers _____	2.53 hr.	2.37 hr.	2.24 hr.	2.12 hr.	1.94 hr.

NOTE: The above duration time is based on a fully charged 48 cubic-foot cylinder. For duration using 63 cubic-foot cylinder, multiply any duration by 1.3.

FIGURE 6.1—Typical oxygen duration table.

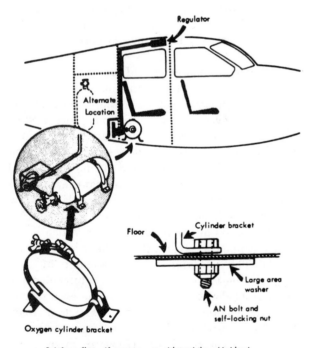

Reinforce floor, if necessary, to withstand the added load. Use aluminum or plywood of suficient thickness.

FIGURE 6.2.—Typical floor mounting.

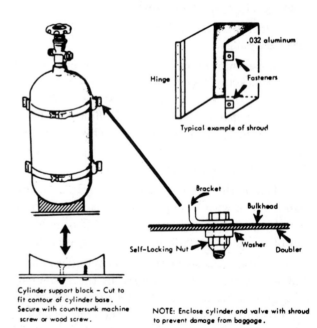

NOTE: Enclose cylinder and valve with shroud to prevent damage from baggage.

FIGURE 6.3.—Typical baggage compartment mounting.

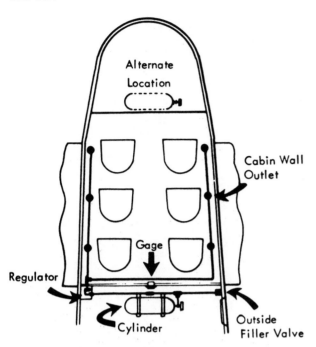

FIGURE 6.4.—Typical oxygen installation in light twin aircraft.

92.–95. [RESERVED]

Chapter 7. ROTORCRAFT EXTERNAL-LOAD DEVICE INSTALLATIONS
Section 1.   CARGO SLINGS

96. GENERAL. This section contains structural and design information for the fabrication and installation of a cargo sling used as an external-load attaching means for a Class B rotorcraft-load combination operation under FAR Part 133. As an external-load attaching means, a "cargo sling" includes a quick-release device and the associated cables, fittings, etc., used for the attachment of the cargo sling to the rotorcraft.

97. QUICK-RELEASE DEVICE. Section 133.43(d) of the FARs specifies the requirements for the

quick-release device. In addition to commercially manufactured helicopter cargo hooks, some surplus military bomb releases meet the requirements of that section.

98. LOCATION OF CARGO RELEASE IN RELATION TO THE ROTORCRAFT'S C.G. LIMITS.

   a. *An ideal location of the cargo release* would be one that allows the line of action to pass through the rotorcraft's center of gravity at all times. (See fig. 7.1, illus. A.) However, with

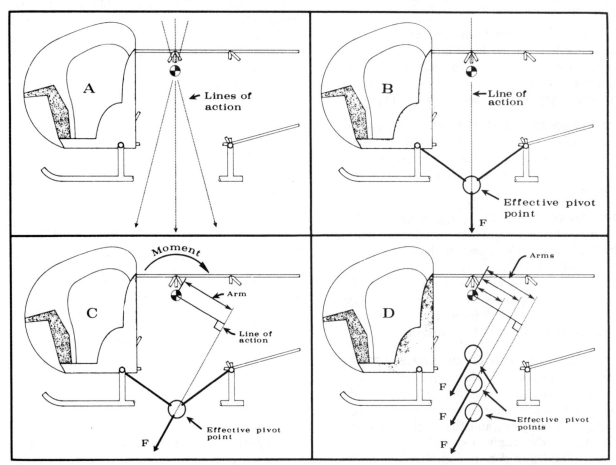

FIGURE 7.1.—Location of cargo release in relation to the rotorcraft's center of gravity.

most cargo sling installations, this ideal situation is realized only when the line of action is vertical or near vertical and through the rotorcraft's c.g. (See fig. 7.1, illus. B.)

b. *Whenever the line of action* does not pass through the rotorcraft's c.g. due to the attachment method used, acceleration forces, or aerodynamic forces, the rotorcraft-load combined center of gravity will shift from the rotorcraft's c.g. position. Depending upon the factors involved, the shift may occur along either or both the longitudinal or lateral axes. The amount of shift is dependent upon the force applied (F) and the length of the arm of the line of action. Their product (F x Arm) yields a moment which can be used to determine the rotorcraft-load combined center of gravity. (See fig. 7. 1, illus. C.) If the rotorcraft-load center of gravity is allowed to shift beyond the rotorcraft's approved center of gravity limits, the rotorcraft may become violently uncontrollable.

c. *Thus, any attachment method or location* which will decrease the length of the arm will reduce the distance that the combined center of gravity will shift for a given load (F) and line of action angle. (See fig. 7.1, illus. D.)

99. MAXIMUM EXTERNAL LOAD.
The maximum external load (including the weight of the cargo sling) for which authorization is requested may not exceed the rated capacity of the quick-release device.

100. STATIC TEST.
The cargo sling installation must be able to withstand the static load required by FAR 133.43(a). Conduct the test as outlined in Chapter 1 of this advisory circular. If required during the test, supports may be placed at the landing gear to airframe attach fittings to prevent detrimental deformation of the landing gear due to the weight of the aircraft.

101. SLING-LEG ANGLES OF CABLE-SUPPORTED SLINGS.
The optimum sling-leg angle (measured from the horizontal) is 45 to 60 degrees. Minimum tension in a sling leg occurs with a sling-leg angle of 90 degrees, and the tension approaches infinity as the angle approaches zero. Thus, larger sling-leg angles are desirable from a standpoint of cable strength requirements. Slings

should not be attached in such a manner as to provide sling-leg angles of less than 30 degrees.

102. MINIMUM SLING-LEG CABLE STRENGTH.
An analysis which considered the effects of 30-degree sling angles showed that the minimum cable strength design factor required would be 2.5 times the maximum external load for each leg regardless of the number of legs. Although this is the minimum strength required by Part 133, it may be desirable to double this value to allow for deterioration of the sling-leg cables in service. This will result in a cable strength equal to 5 times the maximum external load.

> Example: Maximum external load 850 pounds
> Minimum required sling-leg cable strength 850 x 2.5 = 2125
> Minimum desired sling-leg cable strength 850 x 2.5 x 2 = 4250

A 3/16-inch, nonflexible 19-wire cable (MIL–W–6940) provides a satisfactory cable strength. See figure 4.1, chapter 4, of AC 43.13–1A for a table of breaking strength of steel cable. For convenience, the cable sizes desired for various loads have been calculated and are tabulated in figure 7.2 based on a factor of 5:

Maximum External Load (pounds)	Aircraft Cable Size For Each Cargo Sling Leg		
	MIL–C–5693 and MIL–W–6940	MIL–W–1511	MIL–C–5424
100	1/16	3/32	3/32
200	3/32	1/8	1/8
300	7/64	1/8	1/8
400	1/8	1/8	5/32
500	5/32	5/32	3/16
600	5/32	3/16	3/16
700	3/16	3/16	3/16
800	3/16	3/16	7/32
900	3/16	7/32	7/32
1,000	7/32	7/32	7/32
1,200	7/32	1/4	1/4
1,400	1/4	1/4	9/32
1,600	1/4	9/32	5/16
1,800	5/16	5/16	5/16
2,000	5/16	11/32	3/8

FIGURE 7.2.—Cable Load Table.

103. SLING INSTALLATION.
Attach the cargo sling to landing gear members or other structure capable of supporting the loads to be carried. Install

the quick-release device in a level attitude with the throat opening facing the direction as indicated on the quick-release device. When cables are used to support the quick-release device, make sure the cables are not twisted or allowed to twist in the direction to unlay the cable.

Some cargo release devices are provided with a fitting to permit installation of a guideline to assist in fully automatic engagement of the load target ring or load bridle. Secure the guideline to the quick-release device with a shear pin of a definite known value which will shear if a load becomes entangled on or over the guideline. Provision should also be made for cable-supported slings to be drawn up against the fuselage into a stowage position to prevent striking or dragging the release on the ground when not in use.

104. INSTALLATION OF RELEASE CONTROLS. See figure 7.3 for typical wiring diagram of the electrical controls.

a. Install a cargo release master switch, readily accessible to the pilot, to provide a means of deactivating the release circuit. The power for the electrical release circuit should originate at the primary bus. The "auto" position of the release master switch on some cargo release units provides for automatic release when the load contacts the ground and the load on the release is reduced to a preset value.

b. Install the cargo release switch on one of the pilot's primary controls. It is usually installed on the cyclic stick to allow the pilot to release the load with minimum distraction after maneuvering the load into the release position.

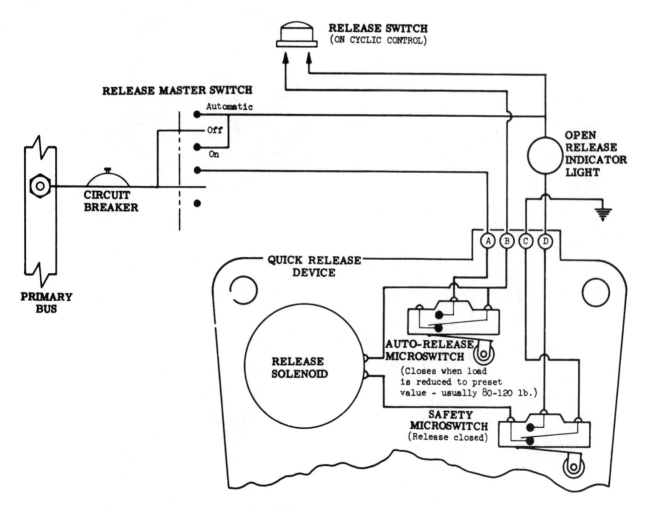

FIGURE 7.3.—Typical cargo sling wiring diagram.

c. *Install the emergency manual release control* in a suitable position that is readily accessible to the pilot or other crewmember. Allow sufficient slack in the control cable to permit complete cargo movement without tripping the cargo release.

d. *The manual ground release handle,* a feature of some cargo release units, permits opening of the cargo release by ground personnel.

e. *Label or placard* all release controls as to function and operation.

105. FUNCTIONAL TEST. Test the release action of each release control of the quick-release device with various loads up to and including the maximum external load. This may be done in a test fixture or while installed on the rotorcraft, if the necessary load can be applied.

If the quick-release device incorporates an automatic release, the unit should not release the load when the master switch is placed in the "automatic" position until the load on the device is reduced to the preset value, usually 80 to 120 pounds.

106. SUPPLEMENTAL FLIGHT INFORMATION. The aircraft may not be used in Part 133 external-load operations until a Rotorcraft-Load Combination Flight Manual is prepared in accordance with section 133.47 of that Part.

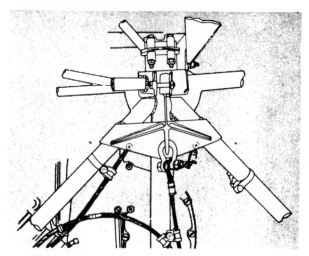

FIGURE 7.5.—Typical cargo sling installation No. 1 (showing fuselage attachment fitting).

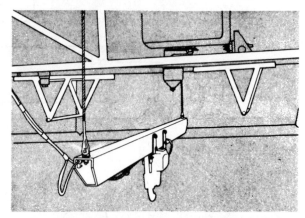

FIGURE 7.6—Typical cargo sling installation No. 1 (showing fore and aft limiting stops).

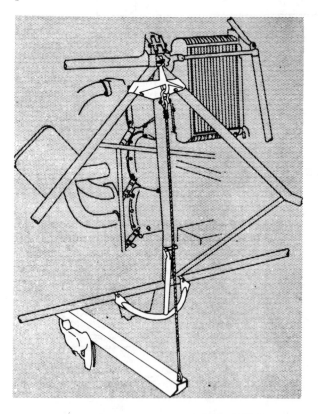

FIGURE 7.4.—Typical cargo sling installation No. 1.

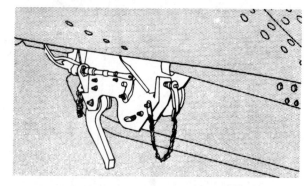

FIGURE 7.7.—Typical cargo sling installation No. 2 (cargo hook attached directly to underside of fuselage).

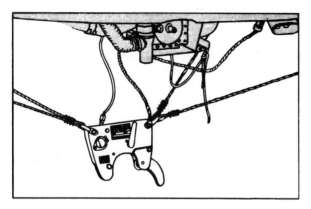

FIGURE 7.8.—Typical cargo sling installation No. 3
(4-leg, cable suspended).

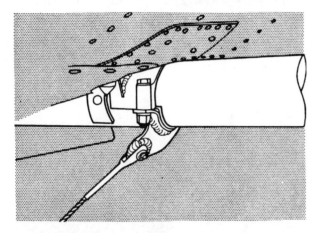

FIGURE 7.9.—Typical cargo sling installation No. 3 (showing cable sling leg attachment to landing gear cross-
tube fitting).

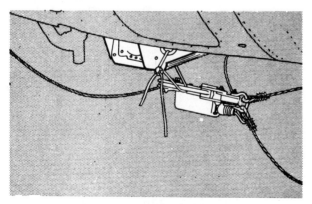

FIGURE 7.10.—Typical cargo sling installation No. 3
(showing cargo sling in stowed position).

107.–110.   [RESERVED]

Section 2. CARGO RACKS

111. GENERAL. This section contains structural and design information for the fabrication and installation of a cargo rack used as an external-load attaching means for a Class A rotorcraft-load combination operation under FAR Part 133.

112. FABRICATION OF CARGO RACKS. The type of construction and method of attachment depend upon the material to be used and the configuration of the rotorcraft involved. Illustrations of typical construction and installation methods are shown in fiigures 7.11–7.15.

113. STATIC TEST. The cargo rack installation must be able to withstand the static test load required by FAR 133.43(a). Conduct the test as outlined in chapter 1 of this handbook.

114. SUPPLEMENTAL FLIGHT INFORMATION. The aircraft may not be used in Part 133 external-load operations until a rotorcraft-load combination flight manual is prepared in accordance with section 133.47 of that Part.

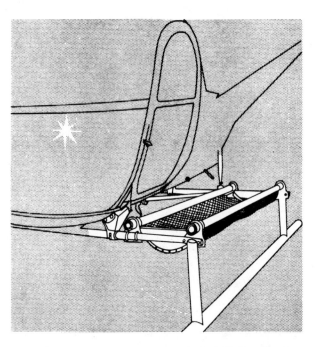

FIGURE 7.11.—Typical cargo rack installation No. 1.

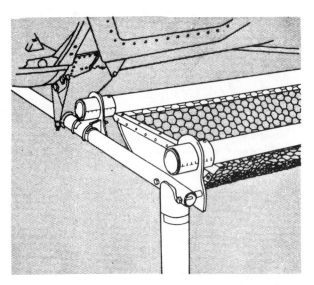

FIGURE 7.12.—Typical cargo rack installation No. 1 (showing attachment detail).

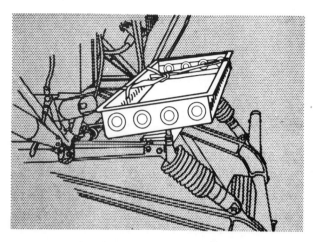

FIGURE 7.13.—Typical cargo rack installation No. 2.

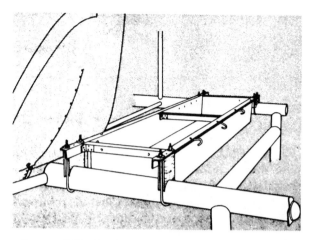

FIGURE 7.15.—Typical cargo rack installation No. 3.

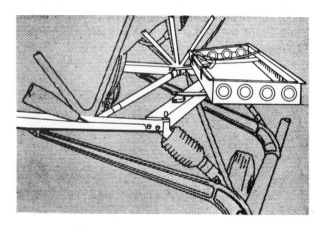

FIGURE 7.14.—Typical cargo rack installation No. 2 (showing rack partially installed).

115.–120. [RESERVED]

Chapter 8. GLIDER AND BANNER TOW-HITCH INSTALLATIONS

Section 1. TOWPLANE CONSIDERATIONS

[Deleted] Change 1

Section 2. TOW-HITCH INSTALLATIONS

126. STRUCTURAL REQUIREMENTS. The structural integrity of a tow-hitch installation on an aircraft is dependent upon its intended usage. Hitches which meet the glider tow criteria of this chapter are acceptable for banner tow usage. However, because the direction and magnitude of maximum dynamic banner towline loads occur within a more limited rearward cone of displacement than do glider towline loads, hitches which meet the banner tow criteria of this chapter may not be satisfactory for glider towing. Due to the basic aerodynamic difference between the two objects being towed, glider and banner tow-hitch installations are treated separately with regard to loading angles.

* **a. *Glider tow hitches.*** Protection for the towplane is provided by requiring use of a towline assembly which will break prior to structural damage occurring to the towplane. The normal tow load of a glider rarely exceeds 80 percent of the weight of the glider. Therefore, the towline assembly design load for a 1,000-pound glider could be estimated at 800 pounds. By multiplying the estimated design load by 1.5 (to provide a safety margin), we arrive at a limit load value of 1,200 pounds. The 1,200-pound limit load value is used in static testing or analysis procedures per paragraph 127 of this handbook to prove the strength of the tow hook installation. When the hook and structure have been proven to withstand *

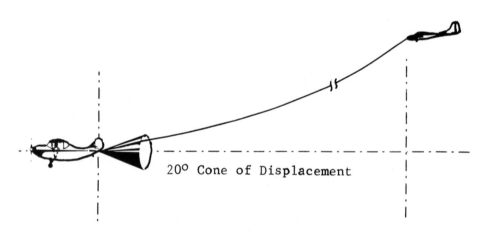

20° Cone of Displacement

FIGURE 8.1.—Glider tow angle.

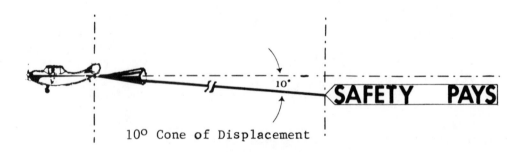

10° Cone of Displacement

FIGURE 8.2.—Banner tow angle.

*the limit load, then the *maximum* breaking strength of the towline assembly is established at the design load of 800 pounds. Thus, the towline will break well before structural damage will occur to the towplane.

Another approach can be applied if the limit load carrying capabilities of a tow hook and fuselage are known. In this case, the known load value can be divided by 1.5 to arrive at the design load capabilities if the tow hook and fuselage limit loads are known to be 1,800 pounds. By dividing by 1.5 (1800 ÷ 1.5 = 1,200) we arrive at a design load value of 1,200 pounds. Thus, the maximum breaking strength of the towline assembly is established at 1,200 pounds and provides protection for the towplane.

Thus, in considering tow hook installations, one may establish maximum towline breaking strength by:

(1) Dividing the known limit load capabilities of the fuselage and two hook installation by 1.5; or

(2) Knowing the design load needs of the towline assembly and multiplying by 1.5 to arrive at a limit load. Then by analysis or static testing, determine that the hook and fuselage are capable of withstanding that limit load.

b. Banner tow hitches. Install the hitch to support a limit load equal to at least two times the operating weight of the banner.

127. STRUCTURAL TESTING. Adequacy of the aircraft structure to withstand the required loads can be determined by either static test or structural analysis.

a. Static testing. When using static tests to verify structural strength, subject the tow hitch to the limit load (per paragraph 126 a or b) in a rearward direction within the appropriate cone of displacement per figure 8.2. Testing to be done in accordance with the procedures of Chapter 1, paragraph 3, of this handbook.

b. Structural analysis. If the local fuselage structure is not substantiated by static test for the proposed tow load, using a method that experience has shown to be reliable, subject the fuselage to engineering analysis to determine that the local structure is adequate. Use a fitting factor of 1.15 or greater in the loads for this analysis.

128. ATTACHMENT POINTS. Tow-hitch mechanisms are characteristically attached to, or at, tiedown points or tailwheel brackets on the air-

frame where the inherent load-bearing qualities can be adapted to towing loads. Keep the length of the hitch-assembly arm from the airframe attachment point to the tow hook to a minimum as the loads on the attachment bolts are multiplied by increases in the moment arm.

129. ANGLES OF TOW. Tests should be conducted on the system at various tow angles to insure that:

a. There is no interference with the tailwheel or adjacent structure.

b. The towline clears all fixed and movable surfaces at the maximum cone of displacement and full surface travel.

c. The mechanism does not significantly decrease the clearance from the tailwheel to the rudder.

d. The tow hitch does not swivel. Experience has shown swiveling could result in fouling both the release line and towline during operations by the towplane.

e. The opened jaw of the hitch does not strike any portion of the aircraft.

130. PLACARDS. A placard should be installed in a conspicuous place in the cockpit to notify the pilot of the structural design limits of the tow system.
The following are examples of placards to be installed:

a. For glider tow—"Glider towline assembly breaking strength not to exceed _____*_____ pounds."

b. For banner tow—"Tow hitch limited to banner maximum weight of _____**_____ pounds."

* Value established per paragraph 126 a (1) pr (2).
** Banner hitch limitations are one-half the load applied per paragraph 126 b.

131. WEIGHT AND BALANCE. In most cases, the weight of the tow-hitch assembly will affect the fully loaded aft c.g. location. To assure that the possibility of an adverse effect caused by the installation has not been ignored, enter all pertinent computations in the aircraft weight & balance records. (In accordance with the provisions contained in FAR 43.5(a) (4).)

132. TOW RELEASE MECHANISM.

a. Release lever. A placard indicating the direction of operation should be installed to allay the possibility of confusion or inadvertant opera-*

* tion, and the design of the release lever should provide the following:

(1) Convenience in operation.

(2) Smooth and positive release operation.

(3) Positioned so as to permit the pilot to exert a straight pull on the release handle.

(4) Sufficient handle travel to allow for normal slack and stretch of the release cable.

(5) A sufficient handle/lever ration to assure adequate release force when the towline is under high loads. (See fig. 8.3)

(6) Protection of cables from hazards such as:

(a) Wear and abrasion during normal operation.

(b) Binding where cables pass through fairleads, pulleys, etc.

(c) Accidental release.

(d) Interference by other aircraft components.

(e) Freezing and moisture accumulation when fixed or flexible tubing guides are used.

b. *Test of the release.* A test of the release and hook for proper operation through all angles of critical loading should be made using the design load for the glider or banner.

c. *Release cable.* Representative size and strength characteristics of steel release cable are as shown in figure 8.4; however, it is recommended that all internally installed release cables be 1/16-inch or larger.

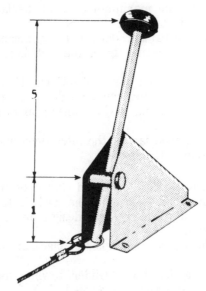

FIGURE 8.3—Typical tow-hitch release handle.

Diameter inches	Nonflexible Carbon Steel 1 x 7 and 1 x 19 (MIL-W-6904B)		Flexible Carbon Steel 7 x 7 and 7 x 19 (MIL-W-1511A and MIL-C-5424A)	
	Breaking strength (lbs.)	Pounds 100 ft.	Breaking strength (lbs.)	Pounds 100 ft.
1/32	185	.25	—	—
3/64	375	.55	—	—
1/16	500	.85	480	.75
5/64	800	1.40	—	—
3/32	1,200	2.00	920	1.60

FIGURE 8.4.—Representative steel cable qualities.

133. 〖Deleted〗 Change 1.

FIGURE 8.5.— 〖Deleted〗 Change 1. *

IAP, Inc.–June, 1988   446

operating weight of the glider, install two weak links as follows:

(1) At the glider end with a strength of not less than 80% and not more than twice the glider operating weight.

(2) At the towplane end with a strength greater but not more than 25% greater than the link at the glider end and not more than twice the glider operating weight (ref. paragraph 126a).

b. *Service life*. The practical life of a manila towline is usually limited to 1 year. After this period of service the line cannot be relied upon, even though it may still look good. Conversely, nylon, polypropylene or polyethylene towlines do not have an age limit, provided the fibers are not broken or frayed.

c. *Construction*. A steel tow ring should be used at each end of the towline. A welded ring having an approximate outside diameter of 2″ and made from ¼″ round 4130 steel stock is satisfactory, if properly fabricated. Inspect completed rings in accordance with the procedures contained in chapter 7 of AC 43.13–1A, "Acceptable Methods, Techniques, and Practices—Aircraft Inspection and Repair." Use a thimble to prevent the towline from wearing against the ring. Splices, when necessary or desirable, will preserve approximately 90% of the line strength. On manila ropes use five "tucks" in an eye splice, for nylon ropes use six "tucks" because the fibers are slippery. Splices may be made more secure, and the rope around the thimble can be made to last longer if the splice is wrapped with plastic tape.

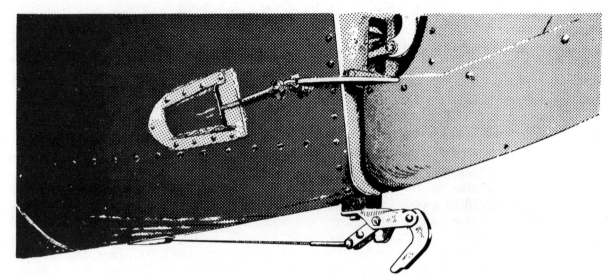

FIGURE 8.6.—Tricycle gear aircraft.

FIGURE 8.7.—Conventional gear aircraft—leaf spring type tailwheel.

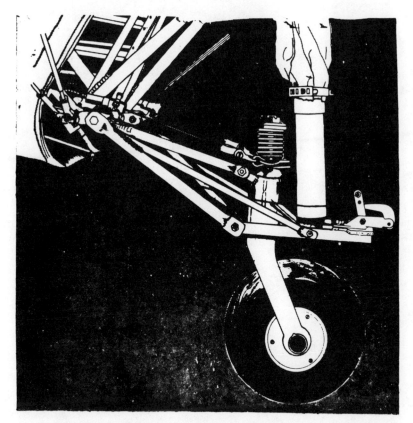

FIGURE 8.8.—Conventional gear aircraft—shock strut type tailwheel.

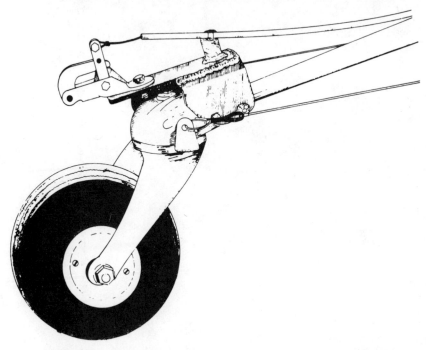

FIGURE 8.9.—Conventional gear aircraft—tubular spring type tailwheel.

134.–145. **[RESERVED]**

Chapter 9. SHOULDER HARNESS INSTALLATIONS
Section 1. RESTRAINT SYSTEMS

146. GENERAL. The primary objective in shoulder harness design is to prevent incapacitating and/or fatal injuries to personnel involved in a survivable crash condition in which the aircraft cabin structure remained reasonably intact. Any harness configuration which achieves this objective is satisfactory from a safety viewpoint, regardless of the type of harness and mounting position used.

Basic requirements of the aircraft airworthiness rules are designed to provide an aircraft structure to give each occupant a reasonable chance of escaping serious injury in a crash landing. These requirements adequately provide for conditions that can be expected to occur in various types of survivable accidents.

The human body has the inherent capability of withstanding decelerations of 20g's for time periods of up to 200 milliseconds (.2 second) without injury. Experience with aircraft used in agricultural and military operations shows that even in such unusual operations a high rate of survival in crashes is achieved when a restraint system is designed on the order of 20g to 25g deceleration loads.

In view of the foregoing, persons installing a shoulder harness may wish to use a restraint system designed to withstand 20g to 25g loads. In addition, seat belts and seat belt anchorages designed to these load limits may be used.

147. TYPES OF RESTRAINT SYSTEMS. There are two generalized types of shoulder harnesses currently in use. They are the single diagonal type harness and the double over-the-shoulder type harness. The over-the-shoulder harness may utilize either two independent attach points, or join in a "Y" configuration and attach at a single point. (See figs. 9.1 and 9.2) In all cases, however, the original safety belt or a combination harness utilizing a lap belt must be used in the installation.

148. ADVANTAGES OF DIFFERENT HARNESS TYPES. The single diagonal chest strap in combination with a lap belt is the simplest harness system and works effectively for longitudinal decelerations. However, during side decelerations, an occupant in this type harness has a tendency to slip out and away from the chest strap even when it fits snugly. The double over-the-shoulder type harness works well for both longitudinal and side decelerations.

149. MOUNTING CONFIGURATIONS. The type of shoulder restraint configuration acceptable for installation is dependent upon the attachments available in each individual aircraft. Basic harness mounting configurations are:

  a. Seat mounted.
  b. Airframe mounted.
    (1) Side
    (2) Ceiling
    (3) Floor
    (4) Directly rearward

150. STANDARDS. At the present time, there is a lack of standards for materials acceptable for use in shoulder harnesses. Until such time as a TSO is developed for shoulder harnesses, standards established in TSO–C22f pertaining to the materials and testing of safety belts may be accepted for this purpose.

151. MATERIALS.
  a. *Webbing.* Synthetic materials, such as nylon and dacron, may be used for shoulder harness webbing. It is recommended that the webbing of the shoulder harness be the same as that of the lap belt to avoid problems in cleaning, staggered replacement of harness components due to wear or age, etc.

b. *Fittings.* Use hardware that:

(1) Conforms to an acceptable standard such as AN, NAS, TSO, or MIL-SPEC.

(2) Meets the strength required by FAR 23.1413 or 25.1413, as appropriate.

(3) Will not loosen in service due to vibration or rotational loads.

C. *Inertia Reels.* The function of the inertia reel is to lock and restrain the occupant in a crash yet provide the ability for normal movement without restrictions. In addition, automatic rewinding of any slack assures that the harness is always snug, which results in a more comfortable restraint system.

Self-contained inertia reel units may be mounted at readily accessible locations and will generally operate effectively in any attitude. Their use in a body restraint system is satisfactory if mounted in accordance with acceptable methods, techniques, and practices, and will meet static strength requirements equal to those outlined in FAR 23.1413.

Check the reel itself for the following operational hazards:

(1) *Inadvertent Lockup.* If the inertia mechanism is set at a low "g" setting, unwanted lockup, or binding, of the system may occur. A reel lockup range between .9 and 2.5 "g" is acceptable.

(2) *Improper Webbing Length.* Install adequate webbing on the takeup reel to allow the occupant to reach all necessary switches and controls in the cockpit. Any additional webbing will result in decreasing the reel spring "takeup" tension exerted on the shoulder.

(3) *Incorrect Belt Opening Alignment.* Position the reel so that the belt opening is aligned in the direction of loading. This will prevent the belt from rubbing and fraying due to normal usage.

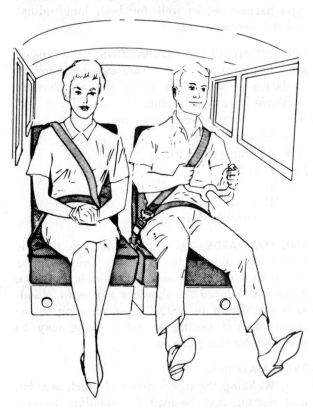

FIGURE 9.1.—Single diagonal type harness.

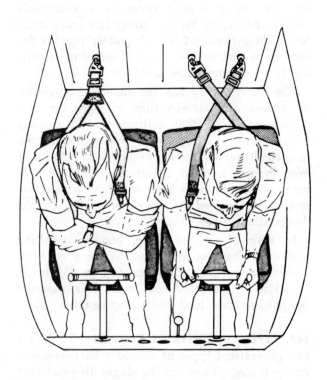

FIGURE 9.2.—Double over-the-shoulder type harness.

152.–155. [RESERVED]

Section 2. EFFECTIVE RESTRAINT ANGLES

156. RELATIONSHIP OF THE HARNESS ASSEMBLY TO THE OCCUPANT. Most restraint systems are designed so that each belt section maintains a certain relationship to the body. The attachment end of a restraint belt must maintain a relative angle and spacing to the head and neck surfaces as it passes over the shoulder and away from the body. This angle must provide sufficient freedom to assure normal body movements of the seated occupant without neck contact or interfering with vision.

157. ATTACHMENT AREAS FOR SHOULDER HARNESS. Effective attachment areas for the various types of shoulder harnesses are defined as angles formed by the attachment ends. Assure that when installing a harness for one seat that in a crash, a passenger to the rear would not sustain head impact injuries on the harness or its attach point.

a. Single Diagonal Type Harness. The optimum rearward attachment area for this type of harness is within an angle of 30 degrees above the horizontal measured from the midpoint on the occupant's shoulder as shown in figures 9.3 and 9.4.

Belt attachments should be located to the rear and outboard of the shoulder. This mounting area is shown in figure 9.5.

(1) Attachment points inboard of this area would permit the harness to impinge on the neck and could result in neck injury during crash impact. In addition, the constant rubbing of the strap on the neck would be uncomfortable and, as a result, act as a distraction to the safe operation of the aircraft. Attachment points forward of this area would reduce the effectiveness of the harness, due to a lack of contact between the harness and the upper torso of the occupant. In addition, a shoulder strap attached forward of

FIGURE 9.3.—Side mounted—single diagonal type harness.

FIGURE 9.4.—Ceiling mounted inertia reel—single diagonal type harness.

the shoulder midpoint could obstruct vision and create a potential safety hazard.

(2) The harness should be kept snug as any decrease in the distance between the occupant's head and the forward cabin structure increases the opportunities for head impact injuries. Also, the chances for twisting out of the harness are significantly increased.

b. *Double Over-the-Shoulder Type Harness.* If this type of harness is intended to be mounted either directly rearward or to the ceiling, mount it within the 30-degree vertical angle as shown in figure 9.6.

Because of the limited number of rearward shoulder harness attachment points in many aircraft, a 5-degree angle below the horizontal is also considered acceptable.

Shoulder harness attach areas as viewed from above are shown in figure 9.7. These mounting areas may be used for either the independent or the "Y" type belts. The outboard limit is established to prevent the belt section from slipping off the shoulder, and the maximum inboard angle is limited to a point which will prevent impingement on the neck surface.

158. AREA AND ANGLE DEVIATIONS. While the areas and angles given in the above paragraphs are intended to assist in the selection of attachment points, they should be considered as the optimum and not be interpreted as being mandatory. Area and/or angle deviations could result in a decrease in the overall efficiency of the restraint system; however, they may be necessary in order to permit a harness installation in an aircraft which otherwise could not be accomplished. It is probable that other compromises may be necessary when adapting a specific restraint system to an aircraft in order to fit a body of average dimensions. These compromises, however, should be permitted only when they are compatible with proper restraint functions.

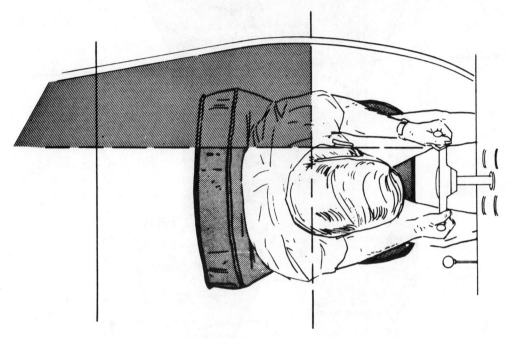

FIGURE 9.5.—Acceptable mounting area—single diagonal type harness.

FIGURE 9.6.—Ceiling mounted inertia reel—double over-the-shoulder type harness.

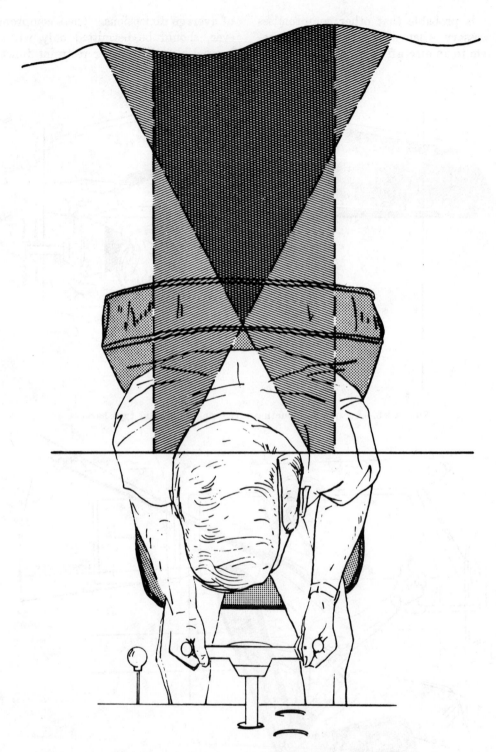

FIGURE 9.7.—Acceptable mounting areas—double over-the-shoulder type harness.

159.–160. [RESERVED]

Section 3. ATTACHMENT METHODS

161. STRUCTURAL ATTACHMENTS. For best results, the restraint system should be anchored to the primary aircraft structure. Design the structural attachment to spread the suddenly applied impact loads over as large an area of the structure as possible. The shoulder harness may be attached to selected secondary members which will deform slowly or collapse at a limited rate. This will assist in dissipating the high impact "g" loads to a level tolerable to the human body. However, the possibility of secondary members collapsing and making it difficult for an occupant to extract himself from the harness should not be overlooked.

162. FLOOR AND SEAT ATTACHMENTS. The double over-the-shoulder type harness shown in figure 9.8 may be used with either floor or seat

mounting points, and typical installation methods are illustrated in figures 9.9 and 9.10. Two prerequisites necessary to ensure an effective restraint system are:

a. The seat structure and its anchorages should be capable of withstanding the additional "g" loads imposed by the restrained occupant during an abrupt deceleration. This capability may be determined by static testing in accordance with FAR 23.785, 25.785, 27.785, or 29.785, as appropriate; or, by securing a statement attesting this adequacy from the airframe manufacturer's engineering department.

b. The level of the seat back should at least be equal to the shoulder height of the seated occupant. This will reduce the inherent downward impact loads which would otherwise impart compressive forces on the occupant's torso.

FIGURE 9.8.—Floor mounted inertia reel—double over-the-shoulder type harness.

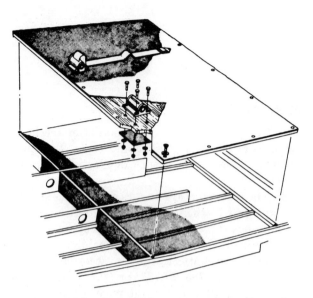

FIGURE 9.9.—Typical floor mounted inertia reel installation.

FIGURE 9.10.—Typical seat mounted inertia reel installation.

Seats which utilize a fold-over type of seat back must have some type of locking mechanism so that the seat can support the loads without allowing the occupant to move forward. The lock should be of a type which has a quick release

to allow rear seat occupants to rapidly evacuate the aircraft. This type of installation should only be considered if other means of attachment are not available since making a folding seat rigid greatly reduces the protection afforded a passenger to the rear. When a folding seat is provided with a lock, the passenger to the rear should also be provided a shoulder restraint system, or, the back of the forward seat should be provided with sufficient absorptive material to adequately compensate for the added rigidity. Also, the change in load distribution due to the loads being applied to the seat back may require reinforcing the seat and/or belt anchorages to meet airworthiness requirements.

163. AIRFRAME ATTACHMENTS. The method used for the attachment of shoulder harness anchorages is dependent upon the construction features of the aircraft involved.

a. *Monocoque/Semimonocoque Type Constructions.* Illustrations of typical aircraft members and installation methods are shown in figures 9.11 through 9.15.

b. *Tube Type Construction.* Various typical methods of attaching shoulder harness anchorages are shown in figure 9.16. When aircraft cable is used as a component in a shoulder harness anchorages, swage the cable terminals in accordance with the procedures contained in chapter 4 of AC 43.13–1A, "Acceptable Methods, Techniques, and Practices—Aircraft Inspection and Repairs."

164. STRUCTURAL REPAIR KITS. In many instances, structural repair kits are available from the aircraft manufacturer. While these kits are primarily intended for use in repairing defective or damaged structure, they may also be used as a reinforcement for shoulder harness attach fittings.

165. FLEXIBLE ATTACHMENTS. Various aircraft are designed so that fuselage members and/or skin will flex or "work." This type of structure should not be heavily reinforced for the purpose of attaching shoulder harnesses as this would defeat the design purpose. In cases such as these, use a localized reinforcement, such as shown in figure 9.15, at the attachment point. This will allow the fuselage to flex while still maintaining a collapsible structure to absorb the loads encountered in a crash.

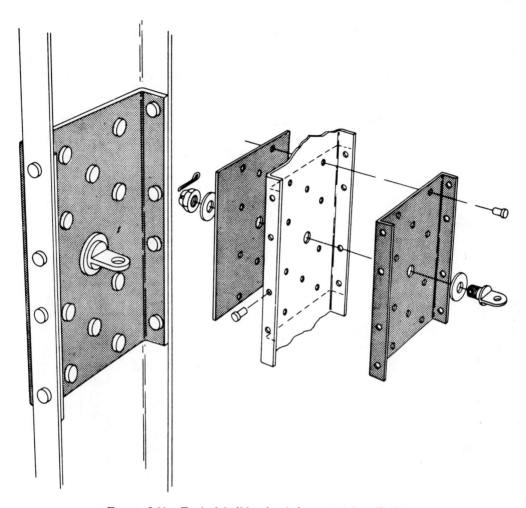

FIGURE 9.11.—Typical bulkhead reinforcement installation.

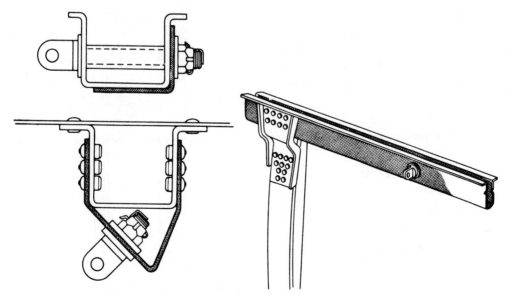

FIGURE 9.12.—Typical wing carry-through member installation.

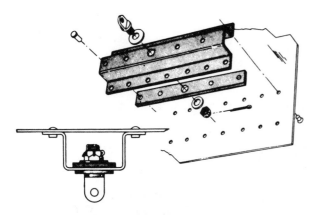

FIGURE 9.13.—Typical hat section reinforcement installation.

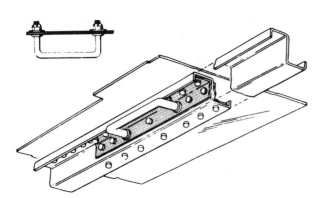

FIGURE 9.14.—Typical stringer section reinforcement installation.

166. SIMPLIFIED INSTALLATION CRITERIA. To encourage the addition of shoulder restraints to existing aircraft with a minimum of testing and engineering necessary, yet provide a satisfactory restraint, the following general conditions will be acceptable.

a. *Utilize the original seat belt attachments* and either the original or a new belt provided with shoulder harness fittings.

b. *Use webbing approved* for standard seat belts (TSO–C22f).

c. *Use hardware approved* for use on seat belts per TSO–C22f.

d. *Secure the lower end of the shoulder strap* to one side of the original seat belt or belt anchorage.

e. *Use a mount* for the shoulder restraint in-

dependent of the seat such as the aft or ceiling mounts per paragraph 128.

f. *Test the added mount* by applying a test load of at least 500 pounds forward at the shoulder point.

167. ENGINEERING APPROVAL. Installations which involve cutting or drilling of critical fuselage members or skin of pressurized aircraft will usually require engineering evaluation. For this reason it may be desirable to contact the airframe manufacturer to obtain his recommendations.

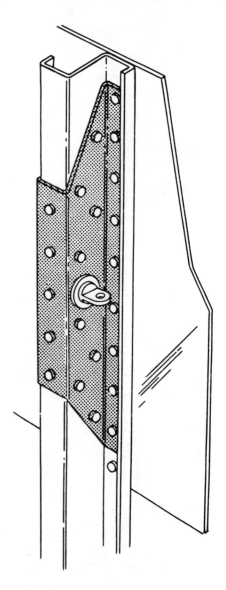

FIGURE 9.15.—Typical stringer section reinforcement installation.

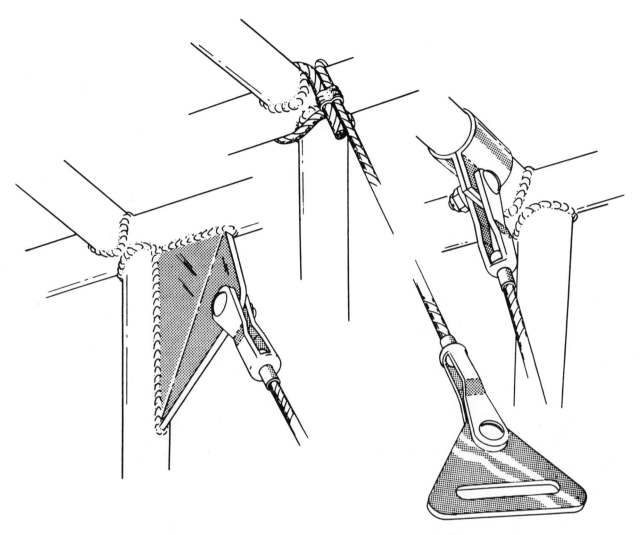

FIGURE 9.16.—Typical attachment to tubular members (adequate chafing protection for tube should be provided. Detail omitted for clarity.)

168.–175.   [RESERVED]

Chapter 10.   BATTERY INSTALLATIONS

Section 1.   GENERAL

176. GENERAL. This section contains structural and design considerations for the fabrication of aircraft battery installations.

177. LOCATION REQUIREMENTS. The battery location and/or its installation should provide:

a. Accessibility for Battery Maintenance and Removal. The electrolyte level of the battery needs frequent checking; therefore, install the battery so that it is readily accessible for this service without the removal of cowling, seats, fairings, etc. Inaccessibility is often the source of neglect of this important piece of equipment. Certain types of batteries cannot be conveniently serviced while installed. Therefore, install and/or locate the battery so that it can be readily removed and reinstalled.

b. Protection from Engine Heat. The installation should protect the battery from extreme engine heat, which would be detrimental to the battery's service life and reliability. Such pro-

tection should provide for the temperatures encountered after engine shutdown as well as during engine operation. When locating the battery within the engine compartment, choose a location that will not interfere with the flow of engine-cooling air.

c. Protection from Mechanical Damage. Vibration and other shock loads are a major cause of short battery life. Whenever possible, install the battery in a manner or location that will minimize damage from airframe vibration and prevent accidental damage by passengers or cargo.

d. Passenger Protection. Enclose the battery in a box or other suitable structure to protect

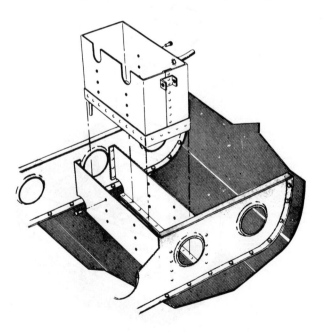

FIGURE 10.2.—Typical battery box installation in **aft** fuselage area, below cabin floorboards, or **may also** be adapted for within wing locations (shaded portions indicate original structure).

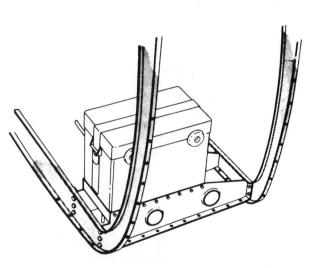

FIGURE 10.1.—Typical battery box installation in aft fuselage area.

passengers from any fumes or electrolyte that may be spilled as a result of battery overheating, minor crash, inverted flight, and/or rapid decompression if the battery is located within the aircraft's pressure vessel.

e. *Airframe Protection.* Protect the airframe structure and fluid lines by applying asphaltic- or rubber-base paint to the areas adjacent to and below the battery or battery box. Apply paralketone, heavy grease, or other comparable protective coating to control cables in the vicinity of the battery or battery box. Damage to adjacent fabric covering and electrical equipment can be minimized by providing a battery sump jar containing a neutralizing agent, properly locating battery drains and vent discharge lines, and adequately venting the battery compartment.

178. DUPLICATION OF THE MANUFACTURER'S INSTALLATION. The availability of readymade parts and attachment fittings may make it desirable to consider the location and type of installation selected and designed by the airframe manufacturer. Appreciable savings in time and work may be realized if previously approved data and/or parts are used.

179. OTHER INSTALLATIONS. If the battery installation has not been previously approved, or if the battery is to be installed or relocated in a manner or location other than provided in previously approved data, perform static tests on the completed installation as outlined in chapter 1 of this handbook. Because of the concentrated mass of the battery, the support structure should also be rigid enough to prevent undue vibration which would lead to early structural failure. Typical illustrations of battery support structure are shown in figures 10.1 thru 10.4.

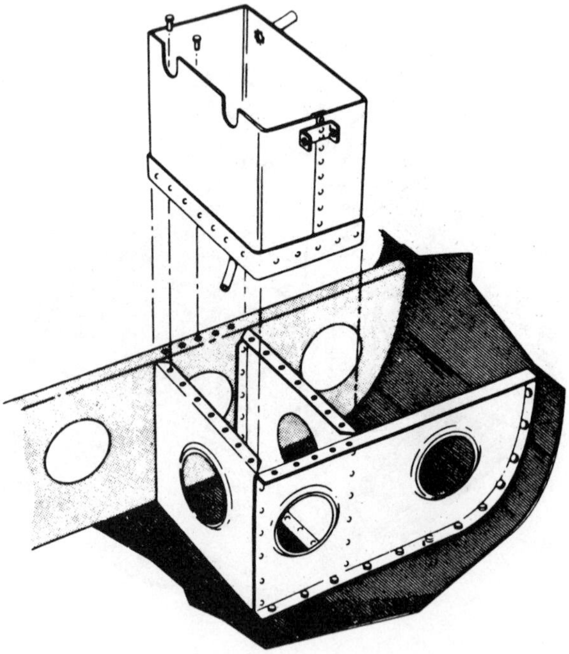

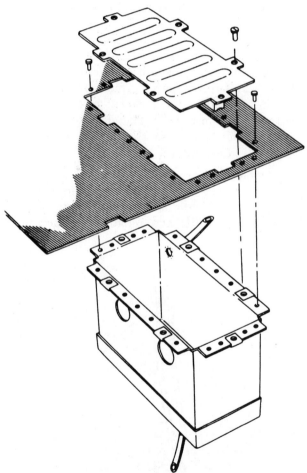

FIGURE 10.4.Typical battery box installation suspended from cabin floorboard section.

FIGURE 10.3.—Typical battery box installation in aft fuselage area (shaded portions indicate original structure).

180.—185. [RESERVED]

Section 2. INSTALLATION

186. SECURING THE BATTERY. Install the battery box or holddowns in such a manner as to hold the battery securely in place without subjecting it to excessive localized pressure which may distort or crack the battery case. Use rubber or wooden blocks protected with parafin or asphaltic paint as spacers within the battery box, as necessary, to prevent shifting of the battery and possible shorting of the battery terminals or cables. Also, provide adequate clearance between the battery and any bolts and/or rivets which may protrude into the battery box or compartment.

187. VENTING. Provide suitable venting to the battery compartment to prevent the accumulation of the hydrogen gas evolved during operation. For most aircraft batteries, an airflow of 5 cu. ft. per minute is sufficient to purge the battery compartment of explosive concentrations of hydrogen.

a. Manifold Type. In this type of venting, one or more batteries are connected, via battery or battery box vent nipples, to a hose or tube manifold system as shown in figure 10.5. Fasten such hoses securely to prevent shifting and maintain adequate bend radii to prevent kinking.

(1) The upstream side of the system is connected to a positive pressure point on the aircraft, and the downstream side is usually discharged overboard to a negative pressure area. It is advisable to install a battery sump jar in the downstream side to neutralize any corrosive vapors that may be discharged.

(2) When selecting these pressure points, select points that will always provide the proper direction of airflow through the manifold system during all normal operating attitudes. Reversals of flow within the vent system should not be permitted when a battery sump jar is installed, as the neutralizing agent in the jar may contaminate the electrolyte within the battery.

b. Free Airflow Type. Battery cases or boxes that contain louvers may be installed without an individual vent system, provided:

(1) The compartment in which the battery is installed has sufficient airflow to prevent the accumulation of explosive mixtures of hydrogen;

(2) Noxious fumes are directed away from occupants; and

(3) Suitable precautions are taken to prevent corrosive battery fluids or vapors from damaging surrounding structure, covering, equipment, control cables, wiring, etc.

188. DRAINS. Position battery compartment drains so that they do not allow spillage to come in contact with the aircraft during either ground or flight attitudes. Route the drains so that they have a positive slope without traps. Drains should be at least ½" in diameter to prevent clogging.

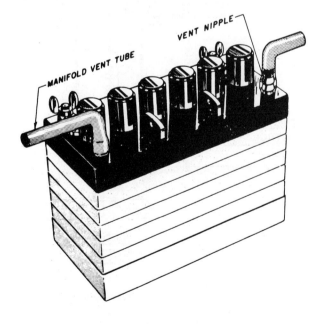

FIGURE 10.5.—Battery with integral vent nipples.

189. ELECTRICAL INSTALLATION.

a. Cables/Connectors. Use cables and/or connectors that are adequately rated for the current demand and are properly installed (See AC 43.13–1A, "Acceptable Methods, Techniques, and Practices—Aircraft Inspection and Repair," chapter 11). It may be necessary to contact the battery manufacturer to determine current value of the battery at the 5-minute discharge rate. Cable size can also be selected by using the same gage as used on a previously approved production aircraft with the same battery.

(1) The cables should be of sufficient length to prevent undue strain on the battery connector or terminals.

(2) Clamp and protect cables, including the bus, in a very secure manner. Since these units are not fused, any fault could cause loss of the entire electrical system in addition to a possible fire hazard.

(3) Route cables so that cable or terminals cannot short to the battery case or hold-down frame.

(4) Route cables outside the battery box whenever practicable to prevent corrosion by acid fumes. When internal routing is unavoidable, protect the cable inside the box with acid-proof tubing. Assure that cables will not be inadvertently reversed on the battery terminals either by proper cable lengths and clamps or, if this is not practicable, use conspicuous color coding.

b. Battery Cutoff. Install a battery cutoff relay to provide a means of isolating the battery from the aircraft's electrical system. An acceptable battery cutoff circuit is shown in figure 10.6. Mount the relay so that the cable connecting the relay to the battery is as short as feasible, in any case not to exceed two feet, to reduce the possibility of a fire occurring because of a short within this section of cable.

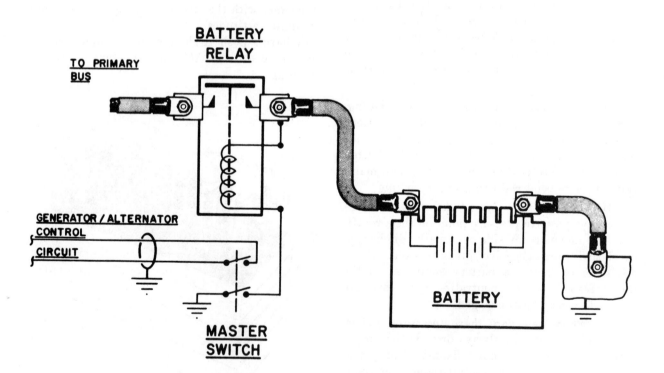

FIGURE 10.6.—Typical battery cutoff and generator alternator control circuit.

190.–195.   [RESERVED]

Section 3. REPLACEMENT OF LEAD-ACID BATTERIES WITH NICKEL-CADMIUM BATTERIES

196. GENERAL. Nickel-cadmium batteries fulfill a need for a power source that will provide large amounts of current, fast recharge capability, and a high degree of reliability. The exchange of lead-acid for nickel-cadmium batteries requires careful evaluation of certain areas.

197. ELECTRICAL ANALYSIS. The ampere hour capacity of a nickel-cadmium battery is selected to accommodate the aircraft load requirements. When making this selection, the following items should be considered.

a. *The low internal resistance* permits it to recharge very quickly. This high recharge rate can exceed the generator rated capacity and deprive essential circuits of necessary operating current. Total system load (battery recharging plus system loads) must not exceed the pre-established electrical capacity.

b. *Compare the discharge characteristics curves* of the batteries to make sure a reduced capacity nickel-cadmium battery is adequate regarding the following:

(1) Ability to provide engine starting or cranking requirements. Turbine engines require an initial surge of approximately 1200 amperes which tapers off within 10 seconds to approximately 800 amperes cranking current. Reciprocating engines require approximately 100 amperes cranking current.

(2) Ability to provide sufficient capacity for low temperature starting. Nickel-cadmium batteries deliver their rated capacity when the ambient temperature range is 70° to 90° F. Increased battery capacity will offset the effects of low-temperature starting.

198. MAINTENANCE CONSIDERATIONS. To provide for ease of inspection and because nickel-cadmium batteries are generally not serviced in the aircraft, it is important that the battery be located where it can easily be inspected, removed, and installed. Some battery cases are designed with viewports on each side of the case for visual monitoring of the cell electrolyte level. If this type of case is to be utilized, consideration should be given to the location of the battery compartment to accommodate this feature.

199. STRUCTURAL REQUIREMENTS. Most lead-acid battery compartments provide adequate structure attachment for the installation of nickel-cadmium batteries. However, cantiliver supported battery boxes/compartments may not be suitable for nickel-cadmium battery installations unless modified to compensate for an increased overhang moment. This may be caused by a change in battery shape and c.g. location even though the replacement battery weighs less than the original lead-acid battery. (See fig. 10.7.) When ever the total installation weight and/or the overhang moment exceed those of the original installation, perform a static test as outlined in chapter 1 of the handbook. If the battery compartment is to be relocated, follow the procedures outlined in Sections 1 and 2 of this chapter.

200. ISOLATION OF BATTERY CASE. Because of the material from which nickel-cadmium battery cases are generally made (stainless or epoxy coated steel), it is desirable to electrically isolate the case from aircraft structure. This will eliminate the potential discharge current produced when spillage or spewage of the electrolyte provides a current path between the cell terminal or connector and exposed metal of the battery case. This isolation is also desirable in that it could prevent a fault within the battery or faulting the generator output to the stucture.

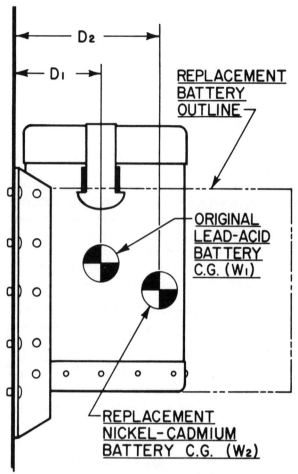

FIGURE 10.7.—Change in cantilever support battery overhang moment.

Example:

Original Overhang Moment with Lead-Acid Battery

W_1 = 25 lb.,

D_1 = 4 inches

4 inches X 25 lb., = 100 in.—lb.

New Overhang Moment with Replacement Nickel-Cadmium Battery

W_2 = 19.5 lb.,

D_2 = 6 inches

6 inches X 19.5 lb. = 117 in.—lb.

201. VENTILATION. During the charging process, nickel-cadmium batteries produce hydrogen and oxygen gases. This occurs near the end of the charging cycle when the battery reaches what is called the gassing potential. To avoid a buildup of these gases, and possible accidental ignition, ventilation should be provided to evacuate this gas from the aircraft. There are two types of nickel-cadmium battery cases, one with vent nozzles and the type with viewports.

a. *The vent nozzle type* utilizes vent hoses to evacuate the gas overboard by use of forced air or by venturi effect.

b. *Battery cases with viewports* or louvers must have an air flow sufficient to keep the mixture of air and hydrogen below 4 percent. The gases from this type of case are evacuated into the battery compartment. Regardless of the ventilation system used, the air flow should be a minimum of 5 cubic feet per minute.

202. PREINSTALLATION REQUIREMENTS. Inspect the replacement battery for possible damage incurred during shipment or storage. Give particular attention to signs of spilled liquid within the shipping container, as it may indicate a damaged cell. Follow procedures outlined in Section 2 for battery venting and electrical connections.

a. *Preinstallation battery servicing.* Check at least the following in accordance with the battery manufacturer's instruction:

(1) Remove the shipping plugs (if used) and clean and install the filler cap vent plugs.

(2) Check the tightness of terminal hardware including each cell connector strap to the proper torque values.

(3) Check the polarity of each cell to be sure they are connected in the proper series or sequence.

(4) Charge and check battery voltage and electrolyte level.

b. *Compartments or battery boxes* which have previously housed lead-acid batteries must be washed out, neutralized with ammonia or a baking soda solution, allowed to dry thoroughly, and painted with alkaline-resistant paint. Remove all traces of sulfuric acid and its corrosion products from the battery vent system to prevent contamination of the potassium hydroxide electrolyte and/or possible damage to the cell case material. Replace those parts of the vent system which cannot be thoroughly cleansed (hoses, etc.). When sump jars are incorporated into the vent system, replace the old pad with a new one that has been saturated in a three-percent solution (by weight) of boric acid and water.

203. SECURING THE BATTERY. Follow the procedures outlined in Section 2 of this chapter. Make certain that the holddown bolts are not drawn up so tightly that the battery case/cover becomes distorted. Should the cover become distorted, there is a possibility that the cell terminal hardware may eventually puncture the neoprene cover liner used in many batteries, and short circuit.

Caution: In installations where care has been taken to isolate the battery cases, inadvertent grounding may occur through improper or careless use of safety wire. Use no wood in nickel-cadmium battery boxes as it becomes conductive with time causing a current flow from the battery case to ground. Use only fiberglass or other acceptable material as liners and spacers in the battery box.

204. VOLTAGE AND CURRENT REGULATION. It is essential that the charging voltage and current be checked and, if necessary, the voltage regulator reset to meet the requirements of the nickel-cadmium battery being installed. IMPORTANT——improper charging current or voltage can destroy a battery in a short period of time.

205. WEIGHT AND BALANCE. After installation of the nickel-cadmium battery the weight and balance of the aircraft should be recomputed if:

a. *The weight* of the nickel-cadmium battery is different from that of the original lead-acid battery.

b. *The location* of the nickel-cadmium battery is different from that of the original lead-acid battery.

Weight and balance procedures for aircraft are contained in chapter 13 of AC 43.13–1A.

206. RESTORATION OF LEAD-ACID BATTERIES.

When lead-acid batteries are restored in lieu of nickel-cadmium batteries the procedures contained in sections 1, 2, and 3 of this chapter should be used. Structural requirements are referenced in paragraph 199 and figure 10.7.

Airframe protection is specified in paragraph 177. Follow the procedures outlined in section 2 of this chapter for battery security, battery venting, and battery drains. Assure that all electrical requirements have been accomplished. Place emphasis on aircraft weight and balance. Refer to chapter 13 of AC 43.13–1A.

207.–210. [RESERVED]

Chapter 11. ADDING OR RELOCATING INSTRUMENTS

211. GENERAL. This chapter contains structural and design information to be considered when aircraft alterations involving the addition and relocation of instruments are being made.

212. PREPARATION. First determine what regulation, (CAR 3, 4b, FAR 23, 25, etc.) is the basis for the aircraft type certificate. That regulation establishes the structural and performance requirements to be considered when instruments are to be added or relocated.

a. Structure. Chapter 1 of this handbook provides information by which structural integrity may be determined. Chapter 2, paragraph 23a through f provides information pertinent to instrument panel installation.

b. Location. Consult the applicable regulation for the specific requirements for instrument location and arrangement.

(1) In the absence of specific requirements, installation of IFR flight instruments in a "T" arrangement is recommended. Locate the aircraft attitude indicator at top center, airspeed indicator to the left, altimeter to the right and directional indicator directly below, thus forming the letter "T." When a radio altimeter is used, the indicator may be placed on the immediate right of the attitude indicator with the pressure altimeter to the right of the radio altimeter indicator.

213. INSTALLATION. Mount all instruments so they are visible to the crewmember primarily responsible for their use. Mount self-contained gyroscopic instruments so that the sensitive axis is parallel to the aircraft longitudinal axis.

a. Structure. When making structural changes such as adding holes in the instrument panel to mount instruments, refer to chapter 2, paragraph 23a through f of this handbook. Refer to the aircraft manufacturer's instructions and Advisory Circular 43.13–1A, "Acceptable Methods, Tech-

niques, and Practices—Aircraft Inspection and Repair," chapter 2, section 3, for methods and techniques of retaining structural integrity.

b. Plumbing. Refer to the manufacturer's instructions for fabrication, routing and installation of instrument system lines. Advisory Circular 43.13–1A provides information regarding the installation and fabrication of aircraft plumbing.

c. Vacuum Source. Minimum requirements for installation and performance of instrument vacuum systems are covered in the applicable FAR Airworthiness Standards under "Instruments: Installation."

(1) In the absence of specific requirements for vacuum pump installation, refer to FAR Part 25, section 25.1433 for guidance. It is desirable to install a "T" fitting between the pump and relief valve to facilitate ground checking and adjustment of the system.

(2) When a venturi tube power source is used, it should not be taken for granted that a venturi will produce sufficient vacuum to properly operate one or more instruments. Many of the venturi tubes available for aircraft have a flow rate of approximately 2.3 cubic feet per minute at 3.75 inches of mercury (in. Hg) vacuum. Therefore, it is essential that the vacuum load requirements be carefully evaluated.

(3) Vacuum loads may be calculated as follows:

(a) Gyroscopic instruments require optimum value of airflow to produce their rated rotor speed. For instance, a bank and pitch indicator requires approximately 2.30 cubic feet per minute for its operation and a resistance or pressure drop of 4.00 in. Hg. Therefore, operating an instrument requiring 4.00 in. Hg from one venturi would be marginal. Similarly, the directional gyro indicator consumes approximately 1.30 cubic feet per minute and a pressure drop of 4.00 in. Hg. The turn and bank indicator has a flow requirement of 0.50 cubic feet per minute and reaches this flow at a pressure drop of 2.00 in. Hg. The above instruments are listed in Tables 11.1 and 11.3. Optimum values are shown in Table 11.3. It should be noted that the negative pressure air source must not only deliver the optimum value of vacuum to the instruments, but must

Table 11.1.—Instrument air consumption.

Instrument	Air consumption at sea level	
	Differential drop in. Hg suction (Optimum)	Cubic feet/per minute
AUTOMATIC PILOT SYSTEM (Types A–2, A–3, & A–3A)		
Directional gyro control unit across mount assembly	5.00	2.15*
Bank & climb gyro control unit across mount assembly	5.00	3.85*
Total	——	6.00*
AUTOMATIC PILOT SYSTEM (Type A–4)		
Directional gyro control unit	5.00	3.50*
Bank & climb gyro control unit	5.00	5.00*
Total	——	8.50*
Bank & pitch indicator	4.00	2.30
Directional gyro indicator	4.00	1.30
Turn & bank indicator	2.00	.50

(*) NOTE.—Includes air required for operation of pneumatic relays.

also have sufficient volume capacity to accommodate the total flow requirements of the various instruments which it serves.

(b) To calculate the flow requirements of a simple vacuum system, assume four right-angle elbows and 20 feet of line (½ O.D. x .042) tubing.

1 Assume the flow requirements for:

Turn & bank indicator	.50 CFM
Directional gyro indicator	1.30 CFM
Bank & pitch indicator	2.30 CFM
Total flow required	4.10 CFM

2 The pressure drop for one 90° ½-inch O.D. x .042 elbow is equivalent to 0.62 feet of straight tubing, figure 11.1. Therefore, the pressure drop of four 90° elbows is equivalent to 2.48 feet of tubing.

Table 11.2.—Equivalent straight tube line drops for 90° elbows.

Tubing size		Pressure drop in a 90° elbow in terms of length of straight tube equivalent to a 90° elbow
O.D inch	Wall thickness inch	Feet
¼ ×	.035	0.28
⅜ ×	.035	0.46
½ ×	.042	0.62
⅝ ×	.042	0.81
¾ ×	.049	0.98
1 ×	.049	1.35

3 Determine the pressure drop through 22.48 feet (20 feet + 2.48 equivalent feet) of ½ O.D. × .042 tubing at 4.10 CFM flow. From figure 11.1, pressure drop per each 10-foot length = 0.68 in. Hg. Divide 22.48 feet of tubing by 10 to obtain the number of 10-foot sections, i.e., 22.48 ÷ 10 = 2.248. Multiply the number of sections by 0.68 in. Hg to obtain the pressure drop through the system. (0.68 × 2.248 = 1.53 in. Hg)

4 The pump must therefore be capable of producing a minimum pressure differential of

Table 11.3.—Differential pressure across instrument inlet and outlet.

Instrument	Suction in inches of mercury		
	Minimum	Optimum	Maximum
AUTOMATIC PILOT SYSTEM (Types A–2, A–3, & A–3A)			
Directional gyro control unit across mount assembly	4.75	5.00	5.25
Bank & climb gyro control unit across mount assembly	4.75	5.00	5.25
Gauge reading (differential gauge in B & C control unit)	3.75	4.00	4.25
AUTOMATIC PILOT SYSTEM (Type A–4)			
Directional gyro control unit	3.75	5.00	5.00
Bank & climb gyro control unit	3.75	5.00	5.00
Bank & pitch indicator	3.75	4.00	5.00
Directional gyro indicator	3.75	4.00	5.00
Turn & bank indicator	1.80	2.00	2.20

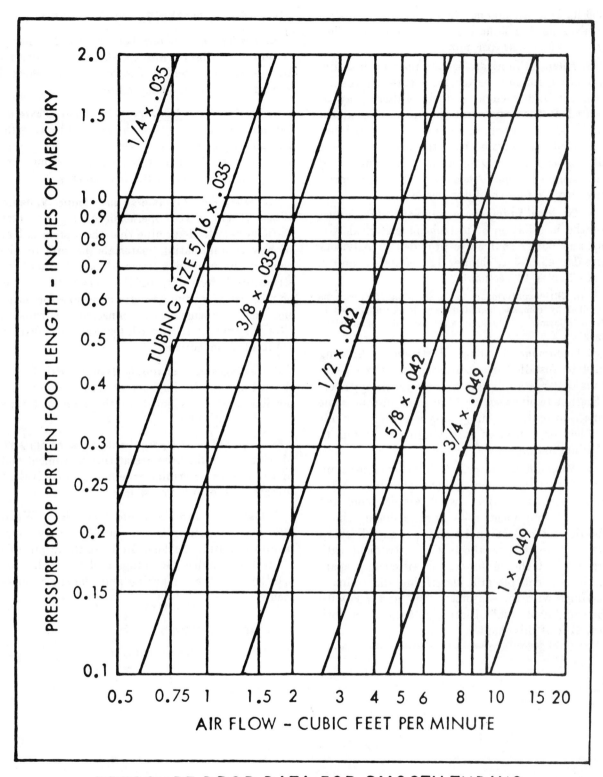

PRESSURE DROP DATA FOR SMOOTH TUBING

FIGURE 11.1

5.53 in. Hg, i.e., 4.00 in. Hg for maximum instrument usage + 1.53 in. Hg (determined) at a flow of 4.10 cubic feet per minute.

d. Filter. Filters are used to prevent dust, lint and other foreign matter from entering the instrument and vacuum system. Filters may be located at the instrument intake port or at the manifold intake port when instruments are interconnected. Determine that the capacity of the filter is as great or greater than the capacity of the vacuum system. Assure that there is no pressure drop across the filter media.

e. Electrical Supply for Instruments. Guidelines for the installation of instrument electrical wiring and power source are provided in Advisory Circular 43.13–1A, chapter 11, sections 2 and 3, and Chapter 16, section 3.

NOTE: Strict conformance to the shielding specifications supplied by compass manufacturers is recommended in all installations to eliminate any possibility of spurious signals.

f. Instrument Lighting. Instrument lighting must be installed in accordance with the regulations that are applicable to the aircraft type certification requirements. If in some instances the reflection of the lights is unsatisfactory, provide a shield or a means for controlling the intensity of illumination.

g. Magnetic Headings. Calibrate magnetic instruments with the powerplants operating. After this initial calibration, switch all nav/com and electrical equipment, such as windshield wipers and defrosters, "on" to determine if any electrical system interference affects the instrument calibration. If the calibration is affected, prepare an instrument placard identifying the compass headings with the equipment "on" and also with the equipment "off." Placard in accordance with par. 214f of this chapter.

214. TESTING, MARKING, AND PLACARDING.

a. Testing the Venturi Tube-Powered Systems. At normal inflight cruise speed, check the venturi tube-powered system to assure that the required vacuum pressure is being supplied.

b. Testing the Vacuum Air Pump Powered System. When the system is powered by vacuum air pumps, check the system while the pumps are operating at their rated r.p.m. and measure the vacuum available to the instruments.

c. Testing of Altimeters and Static Systems. When checking the operation of an altimeter static system to determine that the system is free of any contaminating materials, be sure to disconnect the plumbing from all air operated instruments before purging the lines with dry air or nitrogen since the pressure necessary for purging may damage any connected instrument. Static system test procedures are provided in FAR 43, Appendix E.

d. Testing electrical supply (instruments). Check the voltage at the instrument terminals and determine that it is equal to the manufacturer's recommended values.

e. Fuel, Oil, and Hydraulic (Instrument Supply). Measure the fluid pressure at the instrument end of the line to determine whether it is equivalent to that at the pressure source.

f. Instrument Markings and Placards. When additional instruments are installed they must be appropriately marked. Refer to the applicable CAR/FAR under "Markings and Placards" for specific instrument marking and placard requirements.

215.–240. [RESERVED]

Chapter 12. LITTER, BERTH, AND CARGO TIEDOWN DEVICE INSTALLATIONS

241. GENERAL. This chapter provides data for making acceptable litter, berth, and cargo tiedown device installations in airplanes and rotorcraft. Prior to proceeding with the alteration, determine the airworthiness standards applicable to the contemplated alteration. Refer to the proper volume of the FAA publication "Type Certificate Data Sheets and Specification" for the certification basis of the aircraft involved. When airworthiness standards pertinent to the airplane involved are not available, current airworthiness standards may be used. For example, FAR 23, 25, 27, or 29, as applicable, may be used in place of CAR 4a, 4b, 6, or 7 or Bulletin 7a.

242. INSTALLATION CONSIDERATIONS.

a. Assure that the altered aircraft can be operated within the weight and center of gravity ranges. Refer to chapter 1, paragraph 9 of this handbook.

b. Determine that there will be free access to all equipment and controls essential to the proper operation of the aircraft, required emergency exits, and emergency equipment.

c. Use only materials that are at least flame-resistant for covering of floors, litters, or berths. Refer to the applicable airworthiness standards for the aircraft involved to determine the required flame-resistant qualities. For aircraft in air taxi or other commercial operations, refer to the applicable operating rule for special requirements regarding fire protection, cargo bins, location of cargo with respect to passengers, cargo compartment, or aisle width.

243. FABRICATION AND INSTALLATION.

a. Litters and berths may be fabricated from tubing, sheet metal, extrusions, canvas, webbing, or other suitable material, using acceptable methods, techniques, and practices. (Ref. Advisory Circular 43.13–1A "Acceptable Methods, Techniques, and Practices—Aircraft Inspection and Repair") Commercially available litters or stretchers may be utilized provided they meet installation and load criteria.

Provide a padded end board, canvas diaphragm, or other means at the forward end of each litter or berth that will withstand the total forward static test load. Safety belts used for litters and berths installed parallel to the aircraft's longitudinal axis are not required to withstand forward loads as these loads are to be taken up by the padded end boards.

Design litters or berths intended for adults for occupants weighing at least 170 lbs. In those instances where litters or berths are for children, design the installation for the maximum intended weight. See paragraph 247 for placarding.

Provide approved seats for any cabin attendants or other passengers that will be carried when litters are installed.

b. Cargo tiedown devices may be assembled from webbing, nets, rope, cables, fittings, or other material which conforms to NAS, TSO, AN, MIL–SPEC, or other acceptable standards. Use snaps, hooks, clamps, buckles, or other acceptable fasteners rather than relying upon knots for securing cargo. Install tensioning devices or other means to provide a method of tightening and adjusting the restraint system to fit the cargoes to be carried.

Provide covers or guards where necessary to prevent damage to or jamming of the aircraft's equipment, structure, or control cables.

244. STRUCTURAL ATTACHMENT. Commercially available seat tracks, rails, or other types of anchor plates may be used for structural attachment, provided they conform to an accepted standard (see chapter 1, paragraph 6). This type of hardware permits a ready means of mounting a wide variety of quick-disconnect fittings for litters, berths, and cargo tiedown. Typical examples of such fittings and their attachment are shown in figures 12.1 through 12.5.

EXTRUDED TRACK

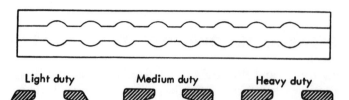

Light duty   Medium duty   Heavy duty

ANCHOR PLATE

Extruded track and anchor plates are available in several different styles and load capacities and will accommodate a wide variety of quick attachment fittings.

SINGLE PIN TYPE HOLD DOWN FITTINGS

These types of fittings are suitable for litter or berth attachment to the extruded track and anchor plate styles shown above.

SINGLE PIN TYPE CARGO TIE DOWN FITTINGS

Adjustable

These types of fittings are suitable for cargo tie down attachment to the extruded track and anchor plate styles shown above.

DUAL PIN TYPE CARGO TIE FITTINGS

360° Rotation

Low profile

 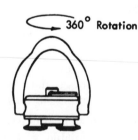 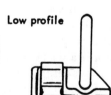

These types of cargo tie down fittings are of greater capacity than the single pin types and are suitable for use with the extruded track style shown above.

FIGURE 12.1. Extruded track, anchor plates, and associated fittings.

PAN FITTINGS

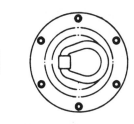 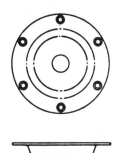

Stud & Cargo ring   Cargo ring only   Stud only

SINGLE STUD FITTINGS

Round head   Hex head

SINGLE STUD CARGO TIE DOWN FITTING

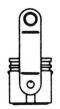 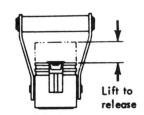

Lift to release

These types of fittings are suitable for cargo tie down attachment to the single stud fittings or stud equipped pan fittings shown above.

SINGLE STUD HOLD DOWN FITTINGS

These types of fittings are suitable for litter or berth attachment to the single stud fittings or stud equipped pan fittings shown above.

STUD/RING

EYE BOLT

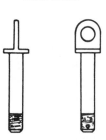

These types of fittings are suitable for litter, berth, and/or cargo tie down attachment directly to the aircraft structure.

FIGURE 12.2. Miscellaneous litter, berth, and cargo tiedown fittings.

A.   Attachment method utilizing a honeycomb doubler.

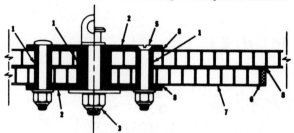

Single Studs or Eye Bolts.

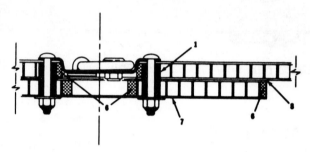

Pan Fittings.

B.   Attachment methods utilizing reinforcing plates.

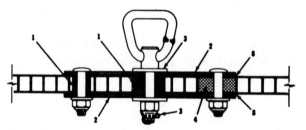

Stud/Rings.

1. Bed all inserts and spacers in a suitable potting compound.
2. Reinforcing plate.
3. Where fitting is subject to rotation, place washers on both sides and use a positive safety means.
4. (Alternate method in lieu of spacers) Undercut honeycomb, inject potting compound, and drill through when set.
5. Countersink if required for clearance or if desired for appearance.
6. Undercut all open edges of honeycomb 1/16″ and seal with potting compound.
7. Honeycomb doubler.
8. Use epoxy or other suitable adhesive to attach doubler and reinforcing plates.

FIGURE 12.3.   Typical attachment of fittings to honeycomb structures.

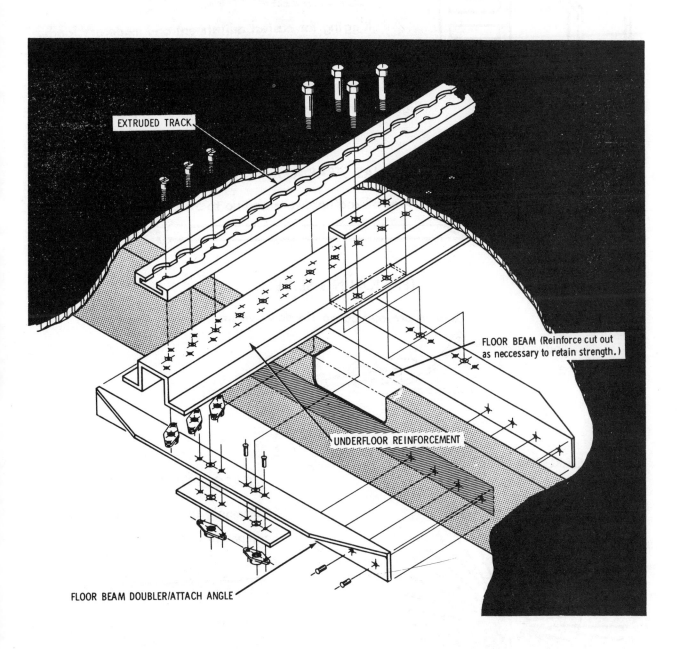

FIGURE 12.4.   Installation of underfloor support for extruded track.

THREE BAR TYPE SLIDE

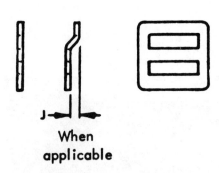

When applicable

Rigging for easiest adjustment and moderate loads.

Rigging for maximum load whether slide is joggled or not.

TYPICAL NAS STRAP ASSEMBLY

Available with various types of end hardware and up to 5000# capacity.

TENSIONING SLIDE

Used to preload cargo tie down straps.

Handhold →

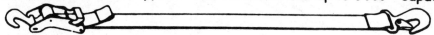

CARGO BARRIER NET

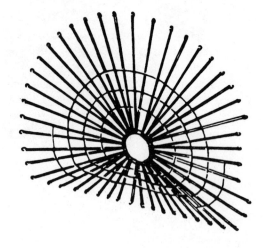

CARGO TIE DOWN NET

Commonly used to restrain bulky or composite cargo.

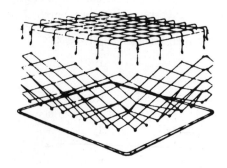

FIGURE 12.5. Typical cargo tiedown straps and cargo nets.

When installing these fittings, reinforce the existing floorboards and/or other adjacent structure to obtain the necessary load carrying capacity. Seat tracks installed longitudinally across lateral floor beams generally require full length support for adequate strength and rigidity between beam attach points (see fig. 12.4).

Consider the inherent flexibility of the aircraft structure and install any reinforcement in a manner that will avoid localized stress concentrations in the structural members/areas. Give specific attention to the size, shape, and thickness of the reinforcement, fastener size and pattern, and the effects of any adhesives used.

Fittings used for litter, berth, safety belt, and/or cargo tiedown attachment need not be substantiated by static tests if it can be shown that the fitting's rated minimum breaking strength would not be exceeded by the applicable static test loads. Existing racks, rails, or other points used for attachment may be verified by static tests, analysis, or a written statement by the aircraft manufacturer attesting to its adequacy to withstand the necessary loads.

For litters which are to be readily installed and removed, it may be desirable to utilize existing seat structure, safety belt attach fittings, seat tracks, or other seat attach fittings. When using such attach points, assure by static tests or manufacturer's written statement that they will not be stressed beyond the loads for which they were originally intended.

245. LOAD FACTORS. Use the load factor established by the aircraft manufacturer for type certification as the basis for substantiating the litter or berth and its attachment to the aircraft structure. Cargo tiedown devices installed within passenger compartments are subject to the same load factors as litter or berth installations. Refer to the applicable operating rules for any additional load factor requirements if the aircraft is to be used for air taxi or other commercial operations.

The critical load factors to which the installation is to be substantiated are generally available from the person currently holding the aircraft's Type Certificate (T.C.). When the T.C. holder is no longer active, such data may be obtained from the controlling FAA regional engineering office. The addresses of T.C. holders and FAA controlling regions are given in the FAA publication "Type Certificate Data Sheets and Specifications."

246. STATIC TESTS. It is recommended that static testing be conducted on a duplicate installation in a jig or mockup which simulates the related aircraft structure. Refer to chapter 1, paragraph 3 for static test information.

If the actual installation is used for static testing, inspect both the aircraft and the litter, berth, or cargo tiedown device installation thoroughly before releasing to service. Check all members and fittings for cracks, distortion, wrinkles, or elongated holes. Replace all bolts and threaded fittings that are not inspected by magnetic particle or other acceptable N.D.T. inspection process. Inspect riveted joints for tipped rivet heads and other indications of partially sheared rivets or elongated holes.

a. For litter and berth installations, compute the up, down, side, fore, and aft static test loads required for substantiation by multiplying the standard passenger weight, 170 lb., by each of the *critical static test load factors.* Refer to chapter 1 of this handbook for computation procedures. (For utility category aircraft use 190 lb., and for litters or berths intended for children use the placarded weight.) Perform tests as necessary to substantiate the complete litter or berth installation for each intended position (forward, aft, or side-facing). When testing for a particular load, install or adjust the litter or berth to the most critical position for that load.

When the safety belt or harness and/or the padded end board is attached to the litter or berth structure, all loads are to be borne by the litter or berth structure and its attachment fittings. Where these are not attached to the litter or berth structure, substantiate the total litter or berth installation for the loads which would be imposed for that safety belt attachment/end board configuration.

b. Cargo Tiedown Installations. All cargo tiedown installations must be tested to the critical ultimate load factor. Refer to chapter 1 of this handbook for computation and testing procedures.

When the cargo compartment is separated from the cockpit by a bulkhead that is capable of withstanding the inertia forces of emergency conditions a forward load factor of 4.5g. may be used. All other applications require the use of a 9g. forward load factor.

Each cargo tiedown fitting installation must be static tested under forward, side, and up load conditions. Individual fittings may be tested by applying a single pull of 12.6g. forward load at an angle of 18.5° up and 9.5° to the left or right, as applicable, of the aircraft longitudinal axis. For example, assuming a 5,000 pound static pull (rating of a typical tiedown fitting) is applied as described and divided by the g. load factor we find the fitting installation will be capable of restraining a 397 pound load under emergency conditions.

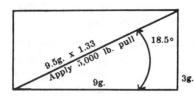

$$9.5g. \times 1.33 = 12.6g.$$

$$\frac{5,000 \text{ lb.}}{12.6g.} = 397 \text{ lb.}$$

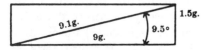

When a cargo-restraining net or cargo container with multiple attachments is used the static load requirements for each tiedown fitting may be divided equally between the fittings. For example, assume that the maximum cargo load to be carried is 1,800 pounds and 10 tiedown fittings are to be used, the static load requirement for each fitting is approximately 2,155 lbs.

$$\frac{9g. \times 1.33 \times 1,800 \text{ lbs.}}{10 \text{ fittings}} = 2154.6 \text{ lbs.}$$

Placard individual tiedowns for the maximum weight to be secured.

247. OPERATING LIMITATIONS, LOADING INSTRUCTIONS, AND PLACARDS. Prepare revisions or supplements to the aircraft's Flight Manual or operating limitations, weight and balance records, and equipment list changes as necessitated by the installation of the litter, berth, or cargo tiedown systems.

NOTE.—Revisions or supplements to the approved portions of the aircraft's Flight Manual markings, placards, or other operating limitations require FAA engineering approval. Submit the requested changes and supporting data to the local FAA Flight Standards Office for review and processing.

Provide instructions covering the installation and use of the litter or cargo restraint systems. For aircraft which require a Flight Manual, incorporate these instructions as a supplement. On other aircraft, provide a placard which references the appropriate instruction. In the instructions, cover such items as removal and reinstallation of seats or other equipment exchanged for litters or cargo restraint systems, use of cargo nets, barrier nets, number and positioning of tiedown straps, maximum load for each compartment or tiedown area, permissible load per square foot, number of tiedown points allowable per foot of track, and maximum height of the load's center of gravity above the floor.

a. Cargo Area Placards. Install placards or other permanent markings to indicate the maximum allowable cargo load and weight per square foot limitation for each cargo area. Placard seat tracks as to number of tiedown points permissible per foot of track. Attach a permanent lable or other marking on each cargo net, barrier net, and at cargo tiedowns to indicate the maximum cargo weight that the net or attachment will restrain when installed according to the loading instructions.

b. Litter and Berth Placards. Install a placard or other permanent marking on each litter or berth indicating its permissible direction of installation (forward, aft, or side-facing), passenger weight limitation (if less than 170 lbs.), and whether or not the litter or berth may be occupied during takeoffs and landings.

248.–260. [RESERVED]

Chapter. 13.   PENETRATION THROUGH PRESSURIZED STRUCTURE

Section 1.   ELECTRICAL WIRE BUNDLES AND COAXIAL CABLE FEED THROUGH PRESSURIZED STRUCTURE

261. GENERAL. This section describes typical methods for sealing openings where wires and coaxial cable are installed through pressurized structure.

a. Assure that the strength of the structure is maintained when installations require additional opening.

b. The aircraft manufacturer's data may specify the size and location where additional openings are permitted and the reinforcement required to maintain the design strength of the affected area.

c. The manufacturer's data may also recommend the specific sealant to be used and provide instructions for the application.

> **Caution:** Sealant and solvents may contain toxic and/or flammable components. Avoid inhalation of vapors and supply adequate ventilation. Wear appropriate respiratory protection while using these materials in confined areas. Avoid contact with the skin and eye.

262. CLEANING. Use a cleaning solvent and clean a larger area than required for the fair-lead or connector. Remove solvent by blasting with dry air and wiping with a clean soft cloth.

263. APPLICATION OF SEALANT. Seal electrical wire bundles and connectors where they pass through the opening in the pressurized structure.

a. Separate and coat each wire with sealant over the length which is to pass through the fair-lead, fig. 13.1A. After coating each wire with sealant, pull the wire bundle into position in the fair-lead, fig. 13.1B. Assure that the fair-lead is located on the pressure side of the structure.

b. Apply sealant to the surface of the fair-lead which comes in contact with the pressurized structure. Use a spatula or brush and spread sealant on the entire surface approximately $\frac{1}{32}$-inch in thickness. Attach the fair-lead to the pressurized structure, sealant, sealant should extrude around the mounting flange (see fig. 13.1C).

c. Wrap the fair-lead with at least three turns of masking tape as shown in fig. 13.1D. Puncture the masking tape over the injection hole in the fair-lead assembly and inject sealant with a sealing gun. Apply sealant over each fair-lead fastener as shown in fig. 13.1E.

d. Complete all of the aforementioned steps during the application time of the sealant. Allow sealant to cure, remove masking tape and excess sealant which extruded from the fair-lead mounting flange.

e. Figures 13.2 and 13.3 illustrate a different type fair-lead and wire bundle connector. The procedure for sealant application is the same as previously described.

f. Figure 13.4 illustrates various coaxial connectors frequently used for installation through structure. Fair-leads are not recommended for installation of coaxial cable. Sealant application is the same as previously described.

264.–290.   [RESERVED]

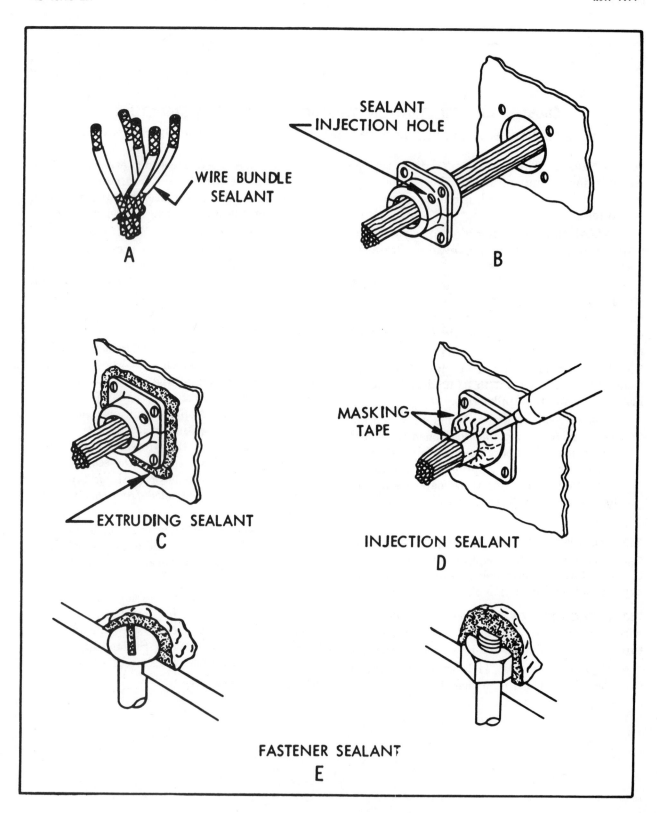

FIGURE 13.1 Sealant application.

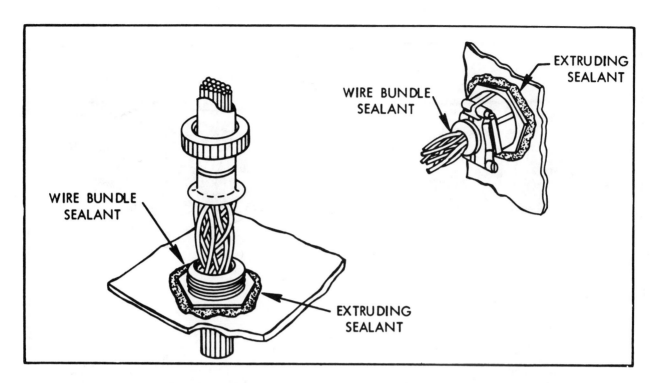

FIGURE 13.2   Fair-lead feed through.

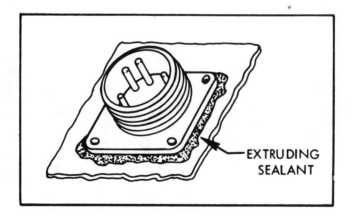

FIGURE 13.3   Typical connector.

AC 43.13—2A

Rev. 1977

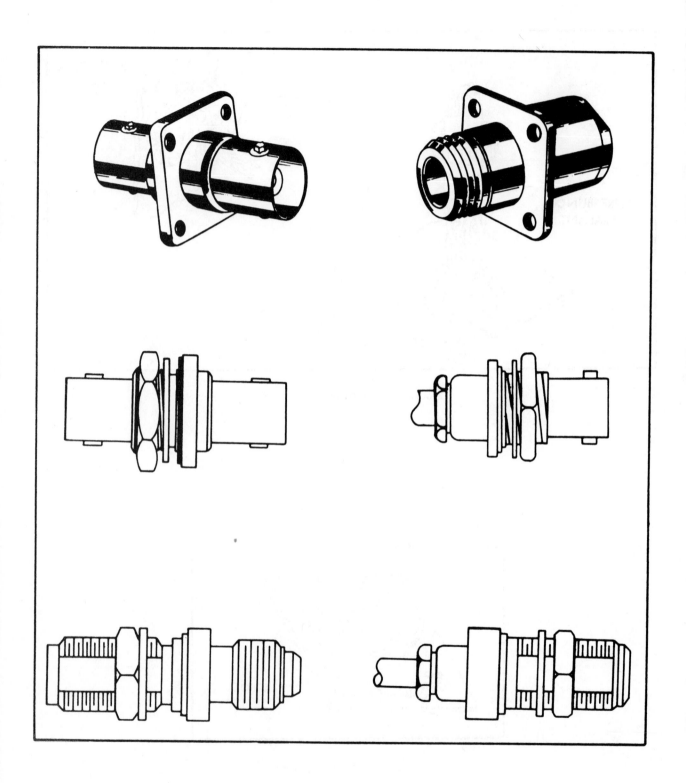

FIGURE 13.4 Coaxial connectors.

100

Chap 13

IAP, Inc.–June, 1988   486